THE VOICE OF ENGLAND

THE
VOICE OF ENGLAND

A History of English Literature

SECOND EDITION

By Charles Grosvenor Osgood

With a chapter in postscript on English Literature since 1910
By Thomas Riggs, Jr., *Princeton University*

HARPER & BROTHERS PUBLISHERS

New York

To

ISABELLA OWEN OSGOOD

—for every reason

CONTENTS

CONTENTS

PREFACE

I HAVE small excuse, I know, for rehearsing the old tale herein set down, except that it *is* an old story, and a good one, and many are the ways of telling it.

Our modern habit of viewing all things with a scientific eye, tracing their evolution, discerning their kinds and classes, pondering the influences that formed them and which they in turn put forth, a habit most fruitful in our modern scholarship, has paid for its splendid achievement with a price. While our talk is all of sources, analogues, congeners, periods, and "schools," of texts and the history of ideas, of classicism, neo-classicism, semiclassicism, realism, romanticism, idealism, of tragical-comical-historical-pastoral, we are prone to forget that, after all, literature was created by men and women. We have labelled them and accounted for them till they are reduced pretty much to disanimated exhibits. Or they are torn and mutilated athwart those rigid classifications of Prose, Poetry, Drama, Novel, Lyric, and the many increasing isms so dear to our pedagogic hearts; and their scattered members have lost all semblance of the living soul.

I have tried therefore to humanize the greater figures in English Literature, at whatever cost to orthodox categories; and to portray them against the background of their times. I have, with the distinguished encouragement of Dr. Johnson, inclined to "the biographical part of literature," a leaning confirmed by many years' experience in the teaching of literature.

Literature, both song and prose, has, it would seem, been growing less audible with every year of the printing-press. Yet far the most of it, certainly the greatest of it, was first conceived in the ear, and only through the ear can impart its fullest effect. I have therefore tried in what ways I could to make the reader aware of this fact, and more attentive to the

Sphere-born harmonious Sisters, Voice and Verse,

without whose aid neither literature nor the just appreciation of literature is possible.

So brief a review, thus conceived, perforce involves itself in certain embarrassing encounters. Some may be disturbed, as I was myself, to find Wither appearing among the Cavaliers; or to come upon Jane Austen consorting with the Romantics. Let us comfort ourselves by re-reading Mr. Kipling's *Janeites* and his poem on Jane in Heaven; or noting the ecstatic alteration of voice and eye in her worshippers whenever her name is mentioned. In any event Jane herself is more important than her label.

Whoever takes the trouble to read this book is sure to exclaim: "Here are A and B. Where, then, are M and N?" I can only reply that within a compass so limited the writer is continuously forced to restrict the number of distinguishable portraits, or else drift into a dull and dead catalogue of names and titles. In this respect, as in others, probably no history of literature can be wholly satisfactory, even to the writer.

A historian of literature nowadays grows increasingly diffident of "facts." Let a fact call itself well-known or established, and at once it is under suspicion. Quite likely it will turn out to be alleged, untenable, or disguised, or be exploded in your very fingers. Every day brings new evidence, new dates, new theories, until the chronicler commits errors in sheer bewilderment. I know that there must be a good many mistakes in this book, and I shall be most grateful for corrections.

From many errors I have been saved by willing friends who have been so kind as to read the portions of the manuscript dealing with matters on which they are authority, or in which they have special interest. I am thus deeply and gratefully indebted to my colleagues, Professors Robert H. Ball, Joseph E. Brown, Robert R. Cawley, Morris W. Croll, Albert R. Elsasser, Gordon H. Gerould, Asher E. Hinds, Hoyt H. Hudson, Dean Robert K. Root, Professors Henry L. Savage, Donald A. Stauffer, Willard Thorp, Mr. Franklin H. Gary, and Mr. Walter B. C. Watkins; to Professor Kemp Malone, Dr. Ray Heffner, Dr. Stephen A. Larrabee, Dr. Samuel Shellabarger, Mr. Edward B. Sheldon, and Mr. Owen E. Holloway. I am obliged to Professor Richard L. Greene for most helpful suggestions in shaping the plan of the book. Dean Frederick M. Padelford generously read the entire manuscript, and to him I would express my warmest thanks for countless improvements. Grateful as I am for all this help, I retain full responsibility for whatever the book contains.

It is vain for me to try to weigh my debt to my wife, who has not only done most of the routine work in typing and preparing the manuscript and making the index, but with comment, criticism, encouragement, and discussion has helped me immeasurably in both the matter and expression of what I have written.

CHARLES GROSVENOR OSGOOD

Princeton, March 14, 1935

Prefatory Note to the
Second Edition

Since this book was written, English Literature has assumed characteristics sufficiently marked to define a new "period." And though it is difficult at so close range to discern and describe these characteristics, some attempt to chart a way through this new country may save readers from being hopelessly lost in the modern wilderness. I am indeed fortunate to have persuaded my friend and one-time pupil, Thomas Riggs, Jr., to write a chapter on English Literature since 1910. This he has done with his competent hand in the spirit of the rest of the book, but with complete independence of observation and judgment. For his help I am deeply grateful.

C. G. O.

THE VOICE OF ENGLAND

PART ONE
HERO AND SAINT

CHAPTER 1

Northumbria

CÆDMON; EARLY COMPONENTS *first English lit 8th century*

IT IS now some twelve hundred and fifty years since one of the first recorded bits of English Literature was composed. The poet was an untutored man; it seems, an hostler, whose song, like Burns's, was spontaneous and inspired, not manufactured— an excellent omen for the great literature of the centuries to follow.

He was well on in his humble life, and for years had suffered social chagrin because at gay gatherings he could not sing and play like everyone else. Often he had slunk home in shame. One night he took refuge in the familiar stable, seeking perhaps the dumb sympathy of the horses he loved. There among them he fell asleep, when there appeared to him a stranger, saying:

"Cædmon, sing me something." *first English poet*

"I don't know how," answered Cædmon; "and that is just why I left the table and came out here—because I *couldn't* sing."

1

Quick the answer: "Nay, but for *me* you have a song."
"What am I to sing?"
"Sing the beginning of all creatures."

And upon the word Cædmon all of himself "began to sing
verses in praise of God the Creator which he had never heard
before, whose sense was: 'Now should we praise the Founder
of the Kingdom of Heaven. . . .' " Thus Bede, not many years
later, tells the story, and observes that Cædmon, admitted a
brother in the great local monastery of Whitby, excelled all
others in the sweetness and humility of his English poems on
scriptural subjects.

All this happened before 680; but, as the story implies, English song was much older, deep-rooted in the composite origins
of the English nation.

English Literature is first of all a spontaneous expression in
well-wrought song or prose of passions, observations, imaginings, and thoughts of great English men and women. A great-
souled human being is always present in a masterpiece of literature. But literature is also national, and expresses, as we say,
the "genius of the race."

English genius in the making has been a complex and remote
matter. It has been fertilized, strengthened, and matured by
inundation after inundation of invading peoples and cultures,
often seemingly bent on destroying all remnant of it; yet by a
strange fate, giving it in the end new vigor, direction,
intelligence.

The story goes back a thousand or more years before Cædmon, when successive waves of fair-skinned Celts swept across
the island from the east, and subjugated and absorbed the dark-
haired, blue-eyed Iberians, a type we often recognize among
British-born today. The Celtic-Iberian life was tribal and turbulent until, in the first century after Christ, the wave of
Roman occupation, with its great highroads and fortress-cities,
its baths and country-houses, brought four centuries of comparative quiet, order, and culture. Such at any rate was the case
south of the Cheviot hills, and east of the Welsh and Cumberland mountains—in most of what is England today. Towards
the end of this Roman period Christianity, with its new and

lively ideas, took its first root in Britain, especially among the Celts.

But after four centuries of occupation the Romans weakened, and had to withdraw their legions, and the Celts had lost their earlier skill and talents in war. Then rose the most important inundation of all. Nordic tribes in and about the Danish peninsula, known as Angles and Saxons and Jutes, increased, grew bold and enterprising, and in their long boats overflowed westward in raid after raid up the British rivers and along the Roman roads, ruining towns and buildings, stealing and enslaving the helpless Celts. At length, however, they brought their own womenfolk, and by degrees cut farms out of the timber, and developed a new agricultural civilization in place of the old Roman life of cities. They were like our Puritan forebears at least in their ultimate quest for a homestead in the new land. They first appeared as pirates as early as 300 A.D. But from about 450 the newcomers were fully occupied for some two hundred years in destroying the old civilization and driving the Picts and Scots back into Scotland and Ireland; in fishing and seafaring, cutting timber, making their farms, and setting up their own rule. Two centuries these were of hard work, violence, and disorder, of bloodfeud between families, of wars with the Welsh and between their own petty kingdoms. Of these kingdoms three emerged as the most conspicuous— Northumbria from the river Humber to the Forth; Mercia (chiefly the midlands); and Wessex (of the West Saxons) in the South.

Through all the struggles and turmoil of the last thousand years, in spite of hatred and antipathies, cruelties and violence, it was inevitable that each wave of invasion should absorb something from the preceding race. And the Anglo-Saxon of the year 600 surely embodied, through contact and inter-breeding, modifications of thought and imagination which he had not brought overseas, but which had filtered down from his predecessors on English soil—Iberian, Celt, and Roman. He was a countryman, no maker or lover of towns, no trader, but a farmer, forester, cattle-raiser, fisherman, soldier.

He was used to war—the little English kingdoms were ever

at it, among themselves or against the unconquered Celts, north and west—but he delighted in it less than had his ancestors. He retained something of their old heathen belief in Odin and Thor and other Nordic gods, but it had mostly degenerated to superstitions and charms against the ordinary ills of man and beast and crop, or to forms of nature-worship, or a natural regard for "Wyrd", the fate which determines all. He retained in song and tale many a strange legend of old Nordic heroes, with a faded shred of historic truth left in them. And we can fancy the songs which were poor Cædmon's despair at the feast to have been riddles and charms, such as have survived, but also snatches of old pagan legend familiar to all. Clearly the art of English song was highly developed by Cædmon's time.

IRISH CHRISTIANITY

Over such an England, before and after the year 600, swept one of the greatest cultural revivals in her history. By degrees it transformed men's mode of thinking, their political ideals, their behavior; and with Cædmon it opened upon two centuries or more of poetry which mark one of the high periods of English Literature. Indeed English culture during these two centuries was the richest of all Europe.

This time the invasion was peaceful. It was the revival in Britain of Christianity, and its first advent to the Anglo-Saxons.

The new religion came to the English from two directions— from Ireland and the North; from Rome and the South.

It is easy to forget that in the sixth century the Christian culture of Ireland was the most vigorous in Christendom. St. Patrick, a Welshman, had, in the early fifth century, first brought Christianity and Latin literature to Ireland. There they had fertilized in the lively Irish mind to produce in the following centuries world-wide achievement, both religious and secular.

Like Irish tribal society, the Irish church was not highly organized. There were no cathedrals, no clergy of many ranks, no elaborate monastic system, none of the Roman imperial discipline which shaped the Roman church. In wild secluded spots good men gathered into a community for study, prayer, and good works, each with his separate hut, amid a cluster of small churches. But they turned this freedom to noble account. Each monastery was a school. The brothers studied, compiled, composed songs and prose, both in Irish and Latin, taught, carved sacred story in great stone crosses, wrought with their hands in various useful arts, and developed to an extraordinary height the art of illuminating manuscripts. The Book of Kells at Trinity College, Dublin, with its exquisite, involved, but vigorous tracery, still unfaded after 1250 years, is one of many examples of beautiful design that the Irish taught all Western Christendom. For the energy of these great Irishmen, fortified by Christian faith and reinforced by Latin culture, could not brook the bounds of an Irish hut, but thrust boldly out into a disordered and decadent world, carrying Irish lore, art, and vision, and flooding the dark places of Europe with its high concentration of zeal, learning, and Celtic warmth.

The movement began with the heroic St. Columba or Colum-kill, but continued through generations of his disciples. One learned and dauntless evangel, by name Columban, raised new monasteries in the Vosges mountains in France, and even in Italy. At St. Gall, in Switzerland, the Irish Gall founded a monastery whose library of manuscripts still survives as one of the richest of Europe. Over one hundred such Irish founda-tions are on record—in Germany, Alsace, France, Brittany, England, Scotland—besides some three hundred churches reaching as far as Iceland, many of them sanctified by the martyred blood of these Irish pioneers.

Columba (521-597) himself was of royal stock. He was withal a genius, poet, scholar, statesman, ruler, and saint. Tall and handsome, he spoke with a voice at once sweet and sonorous, so that it was at times heard more than a mile off chanting the Psalms above the voices of the brethren. Fiery, intrepid, winsome, affectionate, we cannot wonder that his birth, life, and death are as involved with legendary miracle as a holy text on parchment with the countless many-colored folds of Irish tracery. Before he was forty-two he had founded over thirty monasteries in various parts of his beloved Ireland. Then came a crisis. His passion for truth and justice was consuming. It led to a bloody tribal battle for which his temper and will were chiefly responsible. In bitter contrition he entered into voluntary exile for the rest of his life in the bleak island of Iona, close to the coast of Scotland, whence his great spirit ruled, and propagated Irish Christianity everywhere. Thither came many a penitent and scholar and guest, among them Englishmen, attracted by his charm and his extraordinary insight in human affairs. Many a journey he took in all directions, even among dangerous Druids and heathen peoples. But his courage never failed, and man and beast became submissive, often not knowing why. Deep tenderness he felt for all who were oppressed or weak or helpless. He loved pets, and his biographer and kinsman tells of a crane which fell exhausted near his hut, and which he nourished back to life till it could fly home to Ireland. In bitter homesickness he sang of the gulls on Lough Foyle below the oaks of his beloved Derry. For with all his great public enterprise, he enjoyed quieter occupations, composing song and verse, and copying many volumes of Gospel and Psalter. Such was the type and model of Irish missionaries in the sixth century, and such the culture that they brought to Northumbrian soil.

Oswald, saintly king of Northumbria, during an exile in Iona had been converted. From Iona in 635 he brought Aidan, trained in Columba's school, to found a similar school at Lindisfarne, a half island off the east coast of Northumbria. And like Iona it was to be in the seventh century a fountain of Irish culture and mother of churches throughout the north of England. Many an illuminated manuscript and stone cross, many a flash of poetic color or phrase, give proof of this Celtic inspiration today; and the great English literary revival from Cædmon's time owed much of its quality and power to this accession of Irish genius. Indeed throughout the seventh century many Englishmen, noble and humble, went to Ireland to complete their education. The Irish monks welcomed them with food, books, and free tuition.

ROMAN CHRISTIANITY

But nearly forty years before Aidan's arrival, Christian civilization had entered England from Rome and the South. It was Augustine, a missionary of Pope Gregory the Great, who landed with his comrades in Kent in 597, and sang his first services in an ancient little church of pre-Saxon days, now embodied in the tiny church of St. Martin, which today overlooks the great cathedral from the east hill at Canterbury. From this spot during the next sixty or seventy years the new faith made its brave way against many a crushing reverse, but with many sudden successes, from kingdom to kingdom. In spite of wholesale baptisms, more than once the old worship of Thor and Odin reasserted itself, and the fortunes of the old faith and the new swung back and forth with the battles and alliances, wars and marriages, between the kingdoms. The world has seen no finer examples of practical bravery and discipline, as well as of higher virtues, than the men, missionary bishops and English kings, who carried Roman Christianity to the English.

An incident of about 627 illustrates the impact of the new upon the old. Paulinus, a missionary, came to present his case at the council of the king of Northumbria's advisers. A hard-headed pagan priest spoke out, and said that as far as he could see the old religion "had no virtue in it." Here was he who had been most diligent in it, and what had it got him in wealth or king's favor? Let us at least see what the new doctrines can do. But one of graver mind said: "The present life of man, O king, seems to me, in comparison of that time which is unknown to us, like to the swift flight of a sparrow through the room wherein you sit at supper in winter, with your commanders and ministers, and a good fire in the midst, whilst the storms of rain and snow prevail abroad. The sparrow, I say, flying in at one door, and immediately out at another, whilst he is within, is safe from the wintry storm; but after a short space of fair weather, he immediately vanishes out of your sight into the dark winter from which he had emerged. So this life of man appears for a short space; but of what went before, or what is to follow, we are utterly ignorant. If, therefore, this new doctrine contains something more certain, it seems justly to deserve to be followed." And the calculating old priest aforesaid rushed out to smash the idols and burn the temples.

For some seventy years from its beginning in 597 the work of evangelization went on—the Irish from the north, with their free, ardent, individual spirit, the movement from Rome and the south, more ordered and disciplined, both bent on the like task of founding outposts of faith and enlightenment, churches and monasteries and monastic schools. For all their common aim, the two movements came into repeated conflict, usually and ostensibly over the question of which Sunday should be Easter. Really it was the question whether the Irish Church, long so independent, should submit to the usage and discipline of Rome. Inevitably it did—in 664 at the famous Council of Whitby. But many an Englishman could never lose his Irish training, and Irish arts and enlightenment and spirit had well become, and continued henceforward to be, a part of the English genius.

In the year 669 arrived at Canterbury from Rome two men who were to begin a most important revival of learning in England. One of these was Theodore, of St. Paul's city, Tarsus, a monk; elderly but vigorous, "well-instructed," says Bede, "in worldly and divine literature, as also in Greek and Latin." The other was Hadrian, an African, from a Neapolitan monastery, "excellently skilled both in the Greek and Latin tongues." Theodore, as the first archbishop "whom all the English church obeyed," and Hadrian, as abbot of the great school in Canterbury, travelled over the whole of England. "And forasmuch as both were, as has been said before, well-read both in sacred and secular literature, they gathered a crowd of disciples, and there daily flowed from them rivers of knowledge to water the hearts of their hearers; and together with the books of Holy Writ, they also taught them the arts of ecclesiastical poetry, astronomy, and arithmetic. A testimony of which is, that there are still living at this day [forty or fifty years later] some of their scholars who are as well versed in the Greek and Latin tongues as in their own in which they were born."

If the Greek tradition did not survive Bede's time, yet Latin learning, already implanted by both Irish and Roman teachers, and much strengthened by Theodore and Hadrian, flourished throughout the prolific period of Old English poetry.

One more means of refinement doubtless had its part in the literary revival, and that is church music. Pope Gregory had reformed the music of the services, and the church in England had cultivated music with such leisure as it could. But the eminent master, John, brought from Rome by Benedict about 680, gave English church music new life. Its close relation to popular English song is suggested by the famous story of the great Aldhelm, in his more obscure days at Malmesbury. People would sneak out of church before sermon. Very well; he would see to that. Taking his stand on the bridge where they must pass by from church, he struck up a popular English song of his student days; and as the charmed crowd increased, he slipped over into a sacred burden, and so won them by his arts that insensibly they became interested in things spiritual, even in sermons. Aldhelm himself not only wrote Virgilian Latin verse, and sang the church canticles in Gregorians, but composed songs in the vernacular. His case was doubtless that of the great English poets of the period—an ear attuned both to the grand melody of the Latin psalms and canticles, and to the traditional English song. It was inevitable that the finer Gregorian song should attemper and vary the cadences of Old English verse.

The great poetry of the seventh and eighth centuries came, and could come, only from the monastery. The world outside was still in disorder—kingdom clashing with kingdom, nation with nation. Within the monastery's bounds alone were not only physical security, but books, and intellectual companionship, and education, and the peace and leisure of mind necessary for sustained composition.

But the nation had been pretty suddenly converted after all, and naturally retained many reminiscent habits, beliefs, and practices of the old religion. The Christian pioneers, both Irish

and Roman, had been wise in suffering such survivals to continue and in adapting them to the new life, where a more
intolerant policy would have ruined their cause.

With all the rest, the people, both religious and secular,
beguiled many a dreary hour with heathen tales treasured out
of their past, old heroic exploits of the race, some with a basis
of original fact, but all of them growing more and more
sublimated with wonders and romance as they descended orally
from generation to generation. Hence it comes that some Old
English poetry is full of apparently baffling anachronisms, as
it mingles with Christian ideas the cherished legend, tale, social
relations, and usage of English life from centuries back, even
from the rude pagan day when the tribes still dwelt in Denmark and thereabouts. But to the higher civilization of the
monasteries from the seventh century on we owe it that these
ancient literary relics, whether religious or secular, were set
down in permanent and final form.

Thus English genius had been, for a millennium or more,
nurtured for the century of high achievement, let us say
roughly from 675 to 800, when English Literature and culture
rose above that of all the rest of Europe. Successive invasions
and widely different nationalities had cross-fertilized. A great
and dominant Anglo-Saxon stock, full of crude and latent
vigors, had resumed much that was needful from its predecessors in the island. Then came the finer and even more powerful influence of the Mediterranean—Hebrew, and Latin, and
Greek—blended and borne thither by Christianity, and mingled
on one side with Roman discipline and regularity, and on the
other with the magic, fire, and beauty of Irish imagination.
Politically, the warring kingdoms began to approach greater
unity. At first Northumbria under certain enlightened kings
surpassed the others. Here the great monasteries were founded
—at Lindisfarne, York, Whitby, and elsewhere—and, naturally,
here in the North, the great poetry was produced.

BEOWULF

Some brother, it would seem, educated in one of these
monasteries, and here protected from the disorders of the

time, had in rich measure the rare gift of poetic genius. And cherishing as he did the fine old tales inherited from pagan days, he wrought them into the grand masterpiece known as *Beowulf.* This great poem is by no means the crude and primitive work that some have wished to think; it bears many a mark of sophisticated skill, and exhibits virtues and vigors premonitory of *King Lear* and *Paradise Lost.*

The poet, in his zeal to begin at the beginning, sings of the fame and death of Scyld, mythical ancestor of King Hrothgar of the poem. He had been picked up a helpless foundling; but he grew to be a terror to his enemies, a comfort to his people, a generous friend to his thanes. At his death his devoted followers sadly bore their leader to the beach, laid him tenderly on a ship, heaped treasure upon him, and with a great golden banner floating aloft, sent him seaward on his last lonely journey.

> No man knoweth,
> None can say—courtier, counsellor,
> Warrior in all the world—who at last that burden found.

Such the prelude or overture. For of such breed came King Hrothgar of the Danes. He of a time resolved to build a great feasting hall—named Heorot—greatest in the world. All his warrior-thanes and tribes labored together till the high timber walls and roof were done. There they feasted, and drank mead, there he gave generous gifts, and there rose the voice of the bard or scop in the song of Creation. But their joy was short. An evil spirit named Grendel, spawn of Cain, was lurking in moor and fen. One night he sneaked into Heorot, killed and carried off thirty sleeping warriors. The next night he came again. And for twelve long years no one knew when his own turn would come. King and people in helpless despair sacrificed to their devilish idol gods. Alas, poor heathen, what knew they of the true God!

Now the news of Grendel came to the ears of a mighty young thane of King Hygelac, King of the Geats, named Beowulf. With perhaps mixed motives, selfish and unselfish, he gathered fourteen fellows, pushed quickly off, and on the

second day came to land. Galloping down the sands came a
sentinel of the Danes. "Are you enemies, spies, or friends?
I never saw a finer man in face or figure, than your leader."
"We are Geats; I am old Ecgtheow's son, and I have come
to help Hrothgar in his trouble." "Come then, I will guide
you."

Inland, over the headlands, they go till Heorot, the wonder,
towers before them. At the door they lay their clanking arms,
and Beowulf is led in before Hrothgar, sad, old, and snow-
white, amid his thanes. Yes, the old king remembered him as
a little boy. "I have come," says Beowulf, "to fight Grendel.
Not with weapons, but with bare hands. Many a warrior,
many a sea-monster have I slain. And if I am killed, it is the
Lord's will—or Wyrd's."

Then Hrothgar spread a feast of welcome to Beowulf and
his men. But Unferth, jealous and hasty, made a scene. "Oh,
you are the Beowulf that had that seven-days' swimming match
with Breca. I believe Breca beat you; and I will give Grendel
less than one night to do it again, and for good." "You
are drunk, friend Unferth, and voluble. I *did* swim with Breca
on a youthful dare, swords in hand to ward off the sea-beasts.
One dragged me down at night, but I killed him in the depths;
and at dawn I rose and gained the windy headlands. Wyrd
saves a man of courage. But you I know for a slayer of your
own kin, damned to hell, worse even than this Grendel; whom
you fear, and leave me to meet!" The thanes roared with
laughter, but Hrothgar's heart was comforted; and his gracious
queen bore the cup about. Then twilight fell and Beowulf and
his men were left alone.

In the night came Grendel. Quickly he broke down the door,
devoured Beowulf's follower, Hondscioh, and attacked
Beowulf. But the strong warrior leapt upon him, and caught
his arm in that famous grip. Back and forth they reeled and
struggled and crashed till the great hall roared and swayed.
At last Beowulf wrenched the arm from its socket, and Grendel
slunk away to die in his fen.

In the morning came Danes from far and near in joy, racing
their stallions and calling on a singer for a lay of old heroes,

and old Hrothgar received Beowulf as if he were his son. He proclaims a feast in Heorot, the bloody arm is hung as a trophy, and the king's bard strikes up the old song of Finn. Again comes the queen, giving Beowulf gifts and bespeaking his strong protection for her two stripling sons there. So they feasted till night fell, and lay down in peace, all unaware of a new danger.

For Grendel's mother, a witch monster, in an agony of grief for her son, plotted revenge. In the night she stole upon Heorot, seized the king's chief thane, and made off amid cries of dismay. Beowulf, asleep elsewhere, is summoned. At the king's appeal he rides forth on her track with the king and a crowd of warriors. Over moor and cliff and desert she leads them till they come on a deep and rocky tarn in the woods, where they find the head of her victim. They find, too, strange serpents and beasts. But Beowulf, undaunted and in full armor, bearing a sword which his taunter Unferth had lent him, plunges in and disappears. The old witch-dragon seizes him and drags him down to her hall. There a gleaming flame lights the place so that he can strike at her with his sword. It cleaves her helmet, but makes no wound, and he casts it away. Nought remains but his terrible hug. So he springs upon her, stumbles, and falls. In a flash she is upon him with her dagger, but his armor saves him. Then his eye catches the gleam of a giant sword hanging by. Up he starts, seizes it, and desperate and raging he strikes:

> The blow caught her neck, hard biting,
> Broke the bone rings; deep the blade cleft
> Her doomed body; down she crumpled.
> The sword sweat blood; the hero exulted.

But the watchers above, when they saw the water clouded red with blood, lost hope and went sadly away, all but Beowulf's men. At length, from the depths he rose, laden with spoil, and they bore him off in triumphant joy. To Hrothgar he presented the hilt of the ancient sword, for the blade had melted in the monster's blood.

At last he bade Hrothgar farewell. The old king loaded

him with gifts, and sped him on his way with hot tears and a bursting heart; for he had loved this young savior of his kingdom as his son.

Back in his own land, after many battles, Beowulf one day became king and ruled for fifty years. It seems that an old hoard of treasure in a mound had been usurped by a fire dragon, but he was left undisturbed until a poor slave who knew the secret was forced by his fellows to steal a precious goblet from the store. In a rage the dragon attacked and burned Beowulf's hall. And Beowulf, now old but unbowed, once more donned his familiar arms and went out to his last fight. At the cave's mouth he stood and shouted. First came forth a hot blast of the dragon's breath, then the beast himself in a rage. Beowulf struck, but the blow failed, and the place was filled with intolerable flame. All the king's thanes fled but one, young Wiglaf, who remembered his lord's gifts and kindness, and sprang to his side. Thrice the beast advanced, burning away Wiglaf's shield and hand. Beowulf's mighty arm had not weakened; his brand gave way under his heavy stroke. Then the dragon seized him and bit deep into his neck. But Wiglaf plunged his sword into the monster's belly, and Beowulf, in one last heroic effort, clove the serpent asunder with his short sword.

But the grizzled old hero sank down and knew that death was at hand. "Would that I had a son to come after me! Yet, Wiglaf, let me see this treasure while I can." So Wiglaf, hurrying in and out, built a glittering heap of treasures before the dying king, who thanked the eternal God for them and for victory. "But Wyrd hath carried away all my kin. Now must I follow."

So they built a great pyre on the headland, and tenderly laid on it the body of their beloved king; with the roar of the flames mingled the sobs and cries of many. But the voice of one among them, an aged woman, rose above the rest, lamenting the evil days now come upon her, the fear of war and bondage, since the strong protector was gone. Who was she?

So they mourned—the Geat people—
His hearth comrades, bewailing their lord;
Declared that he was of all kings on earth
The mildest of men, and aye the gentlest,
Kind to his people, craving most a good name.

Such in brief is the story of *Beowulf*. A poem of 3182 lines, it seems to be the work of one English poet, sheltered and trained in a Northumbrian or Mercian monastery. It was composed perhaps as early as 700, or as late as 750. The scenery is that of the Northumbrian coast, not of Denmark. The poem is touched with the qualities, teaching, and ideals of Irish and Roman missionaries. It exhibits traces of acquaintance with the *Aeneid* of Virgil, perhaps with the story of the *Odyssey*, not only in details, but especially in the treatment of the banquet scenes, where Beowulf, like Aeneas and Odysseus, tells of his exploits, where Unferth reminds one of the taunting Euryalus, Hrothgar of Alcinous, or Wealhtheow of Dido or Queen Arete. Which is the more likely, as one recalls the Latin and Greek learning imported and naturalized by Theodore and Hadrian and cultivated in the monasteries.

Yet with all its literary art, *Beowulf* is clearly an accumulation of preceding centuries, layer upon layer. A stratum of history is embedded in the poem. Certain historical characters are mentioned, such as Hygelac, Beowulf's king; and the poet alludes to Hygelac's historical raid on the Frisians in which he was killed. Certain Danish history seems to be included also, but how much cannot be ascertained. Such as they are, the events all occurred just before and just after the year 500.

All three stories—the fight with Grendel, with Grendel's dam, and with the dragon—have strong kinship with early Scandinavian fable, and bear points of striking resemblance to more than one old folk legend. Some scholars indeed have been sure of a Celtic or Irish origin for the first two tales, noting especially the Celtic brilliancy of detail in the hall where Beowulf killed the witch.

Along with all this freight of legend from the old continental home, generation after generation had handed down

the antique details—archaic burial by sea, or burning on the
pyre, old pagan sacrifice and superstition, the doom of Wyrd,
shreds of various Germanic legends—until they came into the
Christian poet's hand; and he touches the old materials with
the cherishing tenderness and animation of one who loves that
which his fathers have loved.

As for Beowulf himself, who knows what actual primitive
strong man with terrible hug, nicknamed Bee-wolf or Bear,
may have been his original? But we may thank the English
poet for the art with which he has conceived and fashioned
the noble figure in the poem. For amid all its fabulous marvels
rises the real and human Beowulf. As a child of seven, we
learn, his father brought him to be reared in the household of
his kinsman the king, and he became as dear to the old man
as his own sons. But he overgrew into a hulking, sluggish
youth, tormented by the taunts and contempt of his mates for
his lack of spirit. Then, as his vast strength matured, he one
day surprised and distinguished himself by a great swimming
exploit. Thereafter his old tormentors, as they saw him in
battle, changed their minds. But higher virtues than mere
valor were his; amid wars and forays he stood trustworthy
and loyal. Then came the news of Grendel, stirring his egoism,
his young lust for new worlds and adventure and fame and
wealth, but also his generous desire to help men in trouble.
Years after, in the hour of death, it is the one episode of all
his crowded and useful life upon which he most loves to dwell.
He has always talked freely of his successes; but he never
swaggers: he would not admire our sophisticated modesty. The
figure of the old king, dying in victory, lonely and childless
amid the host of his adoring people, deserted by all his men
except one loyal, heart-broken thane—it expresses the gentle
grandeur of old age in a manner never surpassed in our literature, neither by Colonel Newcome, nor the Vicar of Auburn,
nor old Jolyon Forsyte.

From beginning to end Beowulf lives as a rare instance of
greatness and manners and charm without priggishness, which
it is most difficult to portray. One wonders whether the vigor of

the portrait may not owe something to an admired original in the flesh, possibly in still living memory, such as the heroic King Oswald of Northumbria.

CONVENTIONS OF OLD ENGLISH POETRY

We cannot hope to feel the full power of this early poetry. Much evaporates in the best translation. No study of grammar, lexicon, and metre can ever recall the sound of the original recital by scop or gleeman, as it fell on the ears of young thanes in the banquet hall. The varieties, cadences, energies, tenderness, exultant joys, and sorrows of that song are well-nigh mute. Like all the best poetry it was song.

To us the metre seems rigid. The line contains four stresses, with a pause between the second and third, dividing the line into two parts, though some would read these parts as single lines. Usually the first three stresses, or often two, of which one is always the third—are alliterative, that is, beginning with the same consonant, or with different vowels. The few patterns are pretty strict. But there is also room for wide variety, especially in the shifting number of unstressed syllables allowed before, between, and after the stresses.

> Swa féla fýrena   féond máncynnes,
> Átol ángengea,   óft gefrémede.

But if it seems to us artificial and inflexible, as well it may without the old singer's voice, nevertheless the spirit and cadence of it, indigenous in the language, persist through the centuries, and are audible in later verse, long after Old English poetry is forgotten. Its reverberation often interrupts and suspends Milton's stately measure, and we have many four-stress and, indeed, alliterative lines in *Paradise Lost* like

> On the fírm brímstone   and fíll all the pláins . . .
> Wár wéaried   hath perform'd what Wár can dó. . . .
> Both of lóst háppiness   and lásting páin;

which to the experienced ear are but early rhythms of the language instinctively reasserting themselves. It was a metre which more easily fitted the language in its earlier stage, when verb.

noun, and adjective were highly inflected, and unstressed syllables were more numerous than today.

It suited also the development of the Old English poet's
thought, and "clothed his fancy in fit sound." He deals little
in abstract ideas and words, delights in an ingenuity which can
expand a single term into a variety of appositive terms or
phrases or "kennings," as they were called. Again it is like
the word in an illuminated manuscript of the time, widening
in an involved Irish design into bright concentric circles of
intricate filigree. Thus, the plain statement, "King Athelstan
and Edmund, Edward's sons, won a victory near Brunanburh
with their swords," becomes:

> Now Athelstan King, lord of earls,
> Giver of gifts and his brother with him,
> Edmund the Prince—perennial fame
> They gained in the fight, with sword's edge,
> By Brunanburh; split the board buckler,
> Shattered the linden shields, with hammer-born arms—
> Heirs of Edward.

The sea is variously the whale's path, swan-road, gannet's
bath; a ship is an ocean-stallion, ocean-house, foamy-necked
floater; the sun is the gem of heaven, candle of joy.

This technique of poetry was already highly developed when
the earliest recorded literature in English was composed. It
shows not only the kinship of Old English verse with other
Nordic verse, but that the art of poetry had been practised and
slowly improved by ancestors of the English for centuries before. We shall be in error if we think of Old English poetry,
even of the *Beowulf*, as primitive, "natural," unconscious. So
many strains of culture, so many centuries, had united to produce the Old English poet, so exquisite and so strict were the
rules of his art, that he could not help being a conscious and
sophisticated craftsman.

Like all poets he naturally loved old times and traditions.
Hence he instinctively turned to ancient lays and legends such
as those he wrought into the *Beowulf*. How many other poems
of the sort were composed no one knows. Digressions in the

Beowulf glance at other stories, perhaps embodied in other English poems now lost. Indeed one of these digressions, in a lay sung by a gleeman at the feast after Grendel's death, reviews part of a famous fight at Finnsburg between Danes and Frisians; and another detached fragment of 48 verses proves to be from an English poem on the same subject. Another fragment called the *Waldere* contains passages ostensibly from a longer poetic or "epic" narrative of the story of Walter of Aquitaine.

Many "kennings," or synonymous phrases, and many turns of expression, became common poetic property, traditional for centuries. Mere resemblance of detail does not necessarily prove that one poem influenced another. For example, again and again in battle-scenes spears and swords clash on the lindenwood bucklers, or break through the shield-barrier, while wolves and the "dewy-feathered" ravens gather to gorge on the dead heroes, stripped of their gear. This is the conventional way of describing a battle. Sometimes it includes preliminary speeches of defiance, sometimes the ceremonial burning of the dead. But it is none the less spirited and vigorous for being conventional.

The favorite theme of the Old English poet is the loyalty of thane to king or lord. Tacitus, centuries before, had noted among the Nordics the simple polity inherent in this relation, and called it *comitatus*. Throughout the three centuries of Old English poetry it recurs in wide variety. The thanes live in close personal relation to their lord, bound by affection and admiration, but also by his rich gifts of bracelets, rings, armor, and horses. He leads and protects them among unneighborly neighbors, and they feast in his hall, fight, and die for him at last. Disloyalty, treachery, conspiracy are the blackest of sins, but they are committed constantly both in the history and in the poetry of the times; which is perhaps the very reason that the poet so insists upon loyalty, so condemns defection, and so powerfully depicts the blood feud which ever threatens the social order. Quite naturally, then, his events swing forward and back from the bright feast in the timber hall, often swaggering and drunken, but graced too with voice of scop or gleeman in a lay of loyalties and feuds in other days, to the elegiac lament for glories and better days now gone.

The scop, or singer at the feast, was a thane of dignity equal to the rest, who both composed and sang; not distinct in a professional sense, it would seem, but a thane with exceptional gift as a poet, highly honored and in great demand.

ELEGIAC POETRY

Widsith, "Far Journey," a late seventh century poem of 143 lines, purports to be the reminiscence of such a scop, who visited an impossible number of pagan and Christian peoples and kings of divers times and places, and was honored of them all. The autobiographical figment is a clever device to enliven an epitome of historical and geographical folklore. But the vibrant music of remote and magical proper names must have produced an effect not unlike similar splendors in Milton and Whitman.

A far greater poem—one of the loveliest, ancient or modern—is called *The Wanderer*. A homesick bard, friendless and far away, grieves alone in the gray dawn for his lost comrades and lord. For a man of high breeding will tell his troubles only to himself. In his sleep he has dreamed happily of the old days when his lord embraced him and gave him rich gifts, and all was merry in the hall. Then he awakes by the lonely winter sea to the incessant hovering cry of gulls in this alien land. Gone for ever the hall, sunk in frosty ruin; gone his friends, by war, shipwreck, sudden lonely death.

> Where now the charger? Where the young chief? Where the
>   lord bountiful?
> Where too the banquet-halls—their song and revelry?
> For O the bright beaker! And O the mailed warrior!
> And O the king's splendor! How spent is their course,
> Sunk neath the cope of night as they had never been!

Of similar tone is a fragment called *The Seafarer*, in which the singer, impersonating a frost-bitten, battered old mariner, recounts without illusion the hard realities of sea life. But

among these he thrusts a foil—the lure and challenge of the
sea, the stir of the blood in the spring, the mystery of strange
lands, the instinct to leave home and travel; wherefore some
have read in this poem, so careful to present both sides of this
perennial question, a dialogue between an old and a young
sailor. Be that as it may, the poet's answer is that only in the
happy fear of God is there any insurance against the ebb and
flow of time.

The elegiac mood is a favorite in Old English poetry, and,
for that matter, throughout English Literature from Beowulf's
dying speeches even to Housman.

Another fine instance is a fragment called *The Ruin*. The
singer is deeply moved as he wanders among the crumbling,
frost-bound remains of an old towered city, whose halls were
once radiant with jewels and feast and revelry, while within
were hot baths welling from the ground. But alas! war came
and swept it all away. Naturally we guess that the poet is at
Bath amid the ruins of the great Roman baths, which his own
barbaric fathers had ignorantly destroyed, whose skilful arches
and walls, though in ruin, were eloquent of a lost and lamented art. Doubtless many an Englishman of the more enlightened Christian times thus regarded Roman remains which
he could not understand; hence in the poetry an occasional
glimpse of old mysterious stone-work, or of "gray army-roads,
ancient foundations."[1]

BIBLICAL THEMES

It is clear that English poetry and culture, as they rose in the
monasteries of Northumbria, treasured the old traditions. But
they embodied with these traditions also the richer material, Hebrew, Greek, and Christian, which the new culture had brought
to England. Bible story, and myth, and saint's life abounded in
matter which fitted Old English poetic tradition, and stirred
the poet's energies much as did old pagan themes. He is keen
to discern in the new matter the old sharp issue of loyalty and
disloyalty, the conflict of heroic right with skulking or truculent
wrong, the revelings in hall, of Balthasar, Holofernes,

[1] *Exodus*, 284-5

Pharaoh, the heroic sufferings of the righteous, the transience of worldly glory. God is a good king, giver of gifts; his faithful thanes are angels, saints, good men. Satan is a disloyal, treacherous thane, who alienates angels and men from their King, and is for ever exiled in hell. The saints are heroes, steadfast, brave, resourceful, like Beowulf, in their conflict with the oppressor. Heaven is a triumphant reunion in the hall of the King.

In Bede's story of Cædmon he tells us that, after Cædmon received the gift of song and became a monk, he composed poetic versions of Genesis, of the Israelites' flight from Egypt and other stories in the Bible, of the birth, passion, resurrection, and ascension of Christ, of Pentecost and the Last Judgment. The so-called Junius manuscript, written in the tenth century, now at Oxford, contains a series of poems on various of these subjects, notably on Genesis, Exodus, and the story of Daniel; whence it was easily assumed that these were the very poems of Cædmon. Closer examination, however, proves that probably none of them was from Cædmon's hand. Yet a large part of this poetry is very early, from shortly after 700, perhaps older than the *Beowulf*, which it appears to have influenced. It may, therefore, seem a bit confusing that the *Beowulf*, dealing, as it does, with primitive and pagan matter, should be younger than these poems containing foreign stories more recently acquired. This, however, is only another illustration of how persistently old pagan memories and usage survived late into Christian times.

The first of these poems is called the *Genesis*. It is chiefly a rendering, in nearly 3000 lines, of the first half of the book of Genesis. But one section of some 600 lines, setting forth the fall of Satan and Paradise lost, has been identified as a separate and superior poem at least two centuries later than the rest. We shall return to it again. It is usually called *Genesis B*, and the rest *Genesis A*. The *Genesis A* is of stout, durable poetic fibre, with moments of marked power when the poet refers to the sea, as in the creation, and especially in the weltering rise of the Flood, or when God bids Abraham

See the heavens! Count the jewels,
The stars of the sky, as far and wide
They spread their radiant beauty
And blaze out over the vast deep.

And when the "Northmen" overcome Sodom, and Abraham marches with his "earls" to avenge the defeat, there is the same hard handplay, clash of sword, shield, and spear, the cloud of scavenger birds, that invariably enliven an Old English poetic picture of battle.

But a far greater poem than the *Genesis A* is the *Exodus*. In its compass of nearly 600 lines it attempts no paraphrase of the Book of Exodus, but only a highly concentrated recast of two chapters recounting the escape from Egypt, omitting, rearranging, adding, inventing, with a final effect of intense power. The poet first leads forth the heroic figure of Moses, the folk-lord. Swiftly at midnight God smote the first-born of the Egyptians. Far and wide rose their cry, and clenched were the hands of those that had made laughter. In serried ranks, by tribes and cohorts, the Israelites moved forth. In front rose the beacon of flame, and arms and bucklers gleamed and glanced under it as they marched along. By day God spread over them a vast tent or sail of cloud, whose mysterious guy-ropes no man understood. Four days they marched and camped. Then came word that the Egyptians were pursuing—those faithless men, who quarreled and broke covenant with Moses, men of treachery and sudden anger. On they came, a forest of spears led by the trumpet song. Wolves and ravens, hopeful of prey, hung about. All night in fear the Hebrews prepared for battle. The fittest men were mustered and armed, and were awaiting the onset by the sea, when the sunrise lit their linden shields.

Then a herald lifts his shield and Moses addresses his people: "Fear not. God is with you, and lo! by His help I have divided the sea before you!" When the speech of their dear lord is done, they advance by tribes, and the sea-vikings bear their shields over the salt sea-marsh unafraid.

Up to this point the poet has employed all the traditional

resources of his art in preparing for a battle. At the instant of highest suspense he suddenly interrupts the poem's headlong momentum with a curious reversion to the story of Noah, and of Abraham's sacrifice of Isaac. As suddenly the theme is resumed: the Egyptians are struggling in the water; waves and rocks are blood-stained; the sea spouts gore; confusion is worse confounded of war gear, shouts, roaring water; and over all rises the death-mist of battle.

> Doomed were the sands,
> Awaiting their wyrd, as streaming waves
> And the ice-cold sea in briny billows
> Came weltering back to its old abode—
> A naked bringer of ill, a foe new come,
> Who o'erwhelms his enemy.

Not a man returned to tell of the march or report to their wives how the heroes had died.

At this point Moses, alert to the occasion, preached a brief sermon to his people. There by the sea he appropriately enough showed, after the Anglo-Saxon manner, the vanity of life over against the eternal justice of God, who (in a fine peroration) will keep his word to our fathers, that we shall triumph at last and in victory hold the beer-halls of the brave by the two seas!

And the poem ends with rejoicing, as glad African maidens in gold array distribute the spoil. But the vast army of their foes lay in the place of death.

This spirited poem, it appears, is from the gifted hand of some ecclesiast or monk. His treatment of the theme shows close association with the ceremonies of baptism on Holy Saturday, when Noah's flood and the Red Sea were recalled as appropriate symbols. The interpolated sermon also reflects the skill and resourcefulness of a good preacher. But over and above his special gifts or function, the man was an artist and a poet, who was pleased no doubt to invent a means of grace, but delighted also in fashioning his matter into a coherent whole, and imbuing it with new poetic life and vigor.

Less in merit than the *Exodus* are the remaining poems of this group—the episodic version of the first five chapters of

Daniel, and a so-called *Christ and Satan*, including Satan's lament in Hell, the Harrowing of Hell, and the Temptation of Christ—all of them subjects which no doubt engaged the poet's imagination by the acute and critical struggle involved in each.

BEDE (673-735)

Old English poetry exhibits our forefathers' quality and ideals, but rarely a distinct personality of the times. It is therefore pleasant to discern one very vivid and actual literary man of the great period—the Venerable Bede. He was born in 673, about the time Cædmon first sang, and died in 735, perhaps after *Beowulf* and other of these poems which we have reviewed had been written.

Off in the north, now almost submerged in the grimy industrialism of Newcastle and Sunderland, stand two ancient churches. They are all that is left of the twin monasteries of St. Paul at Jarrow, and St. Peter at Monkwearmouth, some four miles to the south. These were the work of Benedict Biscop, a zealous and enlightened monk of royal blood, who, in the primitive seventh century, spent his wealth and life in many arduous journeys to and from Rome, and always arrived home with a freight of manuscripts and pictures, or glass for his churches. He it was who brought over with him John, the great church musician, to the vast improvement of English church music.

In the neighborhood of Jarrow a little boy of seven was left without father or mother. His name was Bede. He was put to be reared in the monastery under the great Benedict, and it proved to be just the life for him. He says himself: "Amidst the observance of regular discipline, and the daily care of singing in the church, I always took delight in learning, teaching, and writing." On one occasion when all the brothers were ill, only the abbot appeared for service in the church, with the little boy Bede to sing the responses. Disciples of the humanists Theodore and Hadrian were still in the land, learned in Latin and Greek, and, as Bede's works show, it was possible for him without leaving his monastery home to possess himself of extraordinary learning and culture. For situated where he was in the North, he caught the spirit and enthusiasm of Irish Christianity as well as that from Rome. In the struggle between the two he sided with Rome, but his long associations make him speak always with gentle affection of the great Irishmen in Britain. He must have been an indefatigable worker, for he lists nearly forty of his works—Biblical commentaries, Saints' Lives, hymns and other verse, books on chronology and rhetoric and history. A pupil of his tells how even in his latest hour he made all haste to dictate the end of his last work; and how, sinking then on the floor of his cell, he raised his voice as he had loved to do since he was a lad, singing, "Glory be to the Father," and thus breathed his last.

It is Bede's great _Ecclesiastical History of the English People_, written in Latin, which tells us more about early English times than any other work. It reviews the first conquests and settlements, the struggles of the little kingdoms, pagan and Christian, the coming of Irish missionaries, and of Roman, the founding of the monasteries and the new culture. One wonders at the care Bede took with his work—the number of men all over England whom he interviewed, the conscience with which he verified his documents and statements, his high maturity for his times in the technique of writing history. It abounds in pious miracles, to be sure, but even in these Bede is always careful, and never extravagant or fabulous. Through his stories glow the lines of many a distinct portrait—Cædmon, Wilfred, Chad, Aidan, King Oswald—it is these and the charm with which he tells an anecdote that make his history good reading at any time. But above all is the winsome quality of the man himself unconsciously revealed. Modest and simple for all his eminent learning, warm, loyal, and affectionate, it is small wonder that his beloved pupils adored him, as many a reader of his work has been won to do now these twelve centuries.

ALCUIN

Throughout the latter eighth century the North still maintained the cultural supremacy of England, and continued to produce literature. Among all the schools, the school at York, the archbishop's city, rose to be the most active in England, and, indeed, in all Europe. Two great bishop-teachers, in the generations just after Bede, Egbert and Albert Æthelbert, built up a rich library, including Virgil, Cicero, and Aristotle, revived music, rebuilt the cathedral, and travelled to Rome and elsewhere in quest of every means of culture. One illustrious pupil of the school was Alcuin (735-804), who has left us a pleasant picture in Latin verse of Egbert, reclining on his couch of a forenoon, and refreshing the thirsty minds of his pupils gathered about with instruction in various of the liberal arts—poetry, rhetoric, and science. Alcuin could tell good teaching when he saw it, as we know from the skilful examples of the Socratic method in one of his numerous writings. An enthusiastic student of Virgil, and of theology, yet he was, as his many letters show, a man among men. Less original than Bede, he became a successful propagator of culture, far beyond England: so that the great Charlemagne, recognizing his talents and equipment, made him chief adviser in his educational reforms, and Alcuin's enthusiasm for learning was everywhere infectious.

CYNEWULF AND HIS KIND

Out of this same Northern revival emerges another figure, more shadowy than that of Alcuin, but greater. It is the one Old English poet to any extent identified by his English works. A poem called *Elene*, of 1300 lines, was found in an Old English manuscript which had strangely made its way to Vercelli in Italy. Into this poem were curiously wrought old forms of letters called runes, which when deciphered in order revealed the name of the poet—Cynewulf. A fragment called *Fates of the Apostles* is signed in like manner. In the other chief manuscript of Old English poetry, the "Exeter Book" at Exeter Cathedral, are two other poems, the *Christ*, of some 1700 lines, and *Juliana* of 700. In these occurs the same hidden signature; so that we here have three long poems and one short of whose authorship we are sure. Cynewulf has given us more than his signature. In the *Elene* he has interwoven with it a few personal notes, which, taken together

with less direct evidence, and the qualities of his poetry, project for us a substantial idea of the man. He was born an
Anglian of the North, and lived his life approximately between 750 and 825. In some way he acquired the best education of the times, either at York or in a monastic school. In
his youth he seems to have been a lively thane in a noble or
royal household, receiving gifts of gold, and a horse on which
he dashed exultantly over the "mile-paths." He had at some
time mingled in battle, and had come to know the sea with
poet's eye.

Then change overtook him—sorrow, disillusionment, conversion—and he became dedicated to the religious life, especially, it
would seem, to the praise and adoration of the Cross. Whatever the experience, it enlisted for the rest of a long life all
his wide-reaching and ingathering powers in poetry of high
ardor and intensity.

Elene tells the tale of St. Helen's recovery of the Cross. It
opens with the battle scene in which Constantine saw his famous vision, followed by an equally lively account of his
mother's voyage to Judea in search of the Cross. Then takes
place a highly dramatized encounter with the wary wise men of
the land, which gives ample play to eloquence and the parry
of debate. At last one poor Jew, who has craftily guarded the
secret of the hiding-place until he is overwhelmed by conversion to the new faith, on Calvary itself proclaims the recovered
Cross in ecstatic outpouring of soul. Appended is the autobiographic signature already described.

Like *Elene*, *Juliana* seizes upon critical moments in a saint's
life. It tells a cruder tale of conflict between this beleaguered
but loquacious maiden saint and her father, her lover, and
Satan in person, and ends in a martyrdom gruesome enough.
But the Fiend slinks away to Hell: "he knew better, that sower
of sin, than to tell his fellows, thanes of torment, how he
fared on that trip."

Towering far above these poems in grandeur and elaborate
proportions is the *Christ*. It is like a great triptych, for it exhibits in its three parts the Birth, Ascension, and Last Judgment
of Christ. But into each part the poet, like an old painter, has

wrought miniatures of various scenes in sacred history which reinforce his main themes; or like a composer has interspersed these themes with high rhapsodies drawn from old canticles of the church. Thus, in Part I, between lyric prelude and postlude out of an ancient Christmas service, is set an idyll of Mary explaining to the troubled Joseph the coming of the mysterious child. Part II follows a different scheme. It opens with the grand scene of the Ascension amid throngs of angels and the sudden burst of heavenly music. This wakens reminiscences of other sacred events, back and forwards, from Advent to the Second Coming, with a thanksgiving for God's varied gifts to men—to one, eloquence; to another, wisdom; to another, skill in song before warriors; to others, prowess in battle, or good seamanship, or physical strength, or knowledge of stars or topography or sword-forging. For in life we are as if on our sea-steeds headed far over the cold, perilous, heaving, trackless sea, until God's Spirit-Son brings our ocean-stallions into a safe haven.

Part III reaches heights not overpassed by any other English religious poetry. The dominant theme of Doomsday, beginning furtively, rises in sudden crescendo—of trumpets, the last sunrise, confusion of men, devils, and angels, rush of wind and flame—to the coming of Christ in glory to judgment. In grand lyric volume the terrible theme reverberates and crashes forward and back, touching again events in sacred history, and surging about the Cross which towers fixed and unmoved above the tumult. The Cross streams red and sends its blaze far down into the dark places. Again both righteous and wicked stare at the Crucified, dumb with a new sense of the sacrifice. Then follows Christ's terrible indictment of the doomed, who at the sweep of his sword sink into the pit. But the righteous enter into their new life, a glad multitude. No more cold, nor heat, nor darkness, nor hunger or thirst, nor bodily suffering, nor old age; no more quarrels, no separation, no weariness of heart; but, for ever shining, the dear face of the Lord.

These old severities seem distasteful to us, in our comfortable, subtle, modern life, yet they reveal the sharp values of

Cynewulf's eighth-century world, its hardships, its crudities and cruelties, its insecurity, its fears, the blackness of its treacheries and violence, and, by contrast, the shining whiteness of its virtues.

Other poems, unsigned, have been regarded as Cynewulfian, though his authorship cannot be proved, and in the case of the *Andreas* is now rejected. One of these, close in theme to *Elene* and Part III of the *Christ*, is *The Dream of the Rood*, wherein to the poet appeared the Cross transfigured in shifting color, now gold, now blood-red, now glancing with varied jewels. Then the Cross spoke and told how

A young hero stripped—it was God Almighty—
Stout and steadfast, climbed the high cross,
Bold in sight of all, when he would free mankind.
I trembled as the hero embraced me yet dared I not bend to earth,
Fall flat to the ground, but had to stand fast.
As the Rood I was reared; I lifted the great King,
Lord of the Heavens—I could not bow down.

Another poem of the group sings the life and death of a young English saint, Guthlac, of Bede's generation, who re-nounced the pride of life and retreated to the most desolate spot in the fen country, where he, good thane of God, wrestled day and night with shrieking fiends, amid torture of body and soul. At length his protector, St. Bartholomew, brought him news of his release, and he emerged into fifteen years of calm. Fiends still shrieked helpless in the offing, but many a heart-sick man sought comfort from the saint, and even the birds fluttered about him for food. When he was ill unto death, he sent loving messages to a devoted sister, gave thanks for the good angel-thane whom God had daily sent to succor him, and in the arms of a comrade yielded up his spirit. Both in the story and the figure of Guthlac the type of the Irish hermit saint, passionate, stormy, winsome, exalted, as foreshadowed by Co-lumba and his kind, seems still to persist.

One more work which some scholars still assign to Cynewulf is the *Phoenix*. It recounts the well-known myth of the Arabian bird rejuvenated at long intervals by fire. The poet follows a

Latin poem, *De Phoenice,* by Lactantius, but elaborates the
instance rather obviously as a symbol of Christian regeneration
and immortality. With a hint from his original he has painted
in detail the other-world land of the phoenix, but with unde-
niable qualities of English country in its woods and streams
and meadows blossoming under a cloudy sky. The gorgeous
description of the bird is a bit unusual in Old English poetry,
and has perhaps surprised critics into overpraising the work. In
any event, the warm breath of the Mediterranean blows most
gratefully through this poem into the cool shadows of English
poetry, and it is in this respect one of the first of a countless
number—reaching down to this very moment.

The *Andreas* is another matter. Who wrote it? Cynewulf,
or Bishop Acca of Hexham, or some poet for ever unnamed?
The question is too complex and unsettled to detain us now.
But a great poet he was without dispute. The poem has been
called a "Christian *Beowulf,*" and with some reason; for while
it ostensibly sets forth with pious intention to recount the perseverance of St. Andrew in his mission to the cannibal Mermedonians, the poet takes the delight in adventure and battles
and hairbreadth escape for their own sake that pervades any
great epic or romance. Indeed, he was clearly a devoted reader
of *Beowulf* and of the *Aeneid* of Virgil.

Andrew, the Apostle, was called by God to go to the rescue
of Matthew, whom the Mermedonians had imprisoned and
threatened to devour. He makes difficulties. There is no ship.
Yet he is no coward. At dawn, where the billows thunder on
the beach, is riding a wide-bosomed ship outbound to Mermedonia. Three are the crew, of whom one is no less than Christ
himself in guise of the captain. The ensuing dialogue between
him and Andrew, leading to a fine recognition at the end of
the voyage, shows in this early poet no little dramatic power.
Would the captain take Andrew to Mermedonia? Alas, it is
no place for an alien. Yet if he is bent on it, he must pay first.
"But I have no money." "No money, and travelling? Then
food and drink perhaps." "We are God's thanes, on his business." "Then come." "God reward you, Sir, for your kindness."

A fine ship with that heroic company, she put out only to

run into a terrific storm, the fiercest in Old English poetry. Yet Andrew ate a hearty meal, with grace after meat, though his "thanes" were so terrified that the Captain offered to put back. "Not we. What! to be lordless, loathed, and ashamed when in council the warriors ask which with hand and brand best succored his lord in the battle-game?" But Andrew comforted them with recollection of Christ on Galilee, the storm subsided, and they sank into deep slumber.

Then Andrew admired the Captain's skill: "This is my seventeenth voyage, but I never saw your equal. In a rough sea this boat keeps her speed, flies foamy-necked, most like a bird. And yet you are very young. Would you teach me?" And the Captain replies in effect: "We sailors, exposed to storm and mishap, naturally believe in God. *I* can see that you are a thane of God, and the waves saw it too, and subsided." Then Andrew thanks God that he has given this youth not only skill, but wit. The Captain asks him about this Christ, and Andrew reviews the whole story until he falls asleep, and he and his thanes are borne by angels to Mermedonia. There the young seafarer reappears, now the manifest Christ, and Andrew sinks down in humiliation that he had not known him before.

But he rises to new strength, and through a rapid succession of miracle, menacing mob, torture, libels by Satan and the thanes of Hell, exhaustion, despair, he at last comes forth to invoke a terrible flood and fire upon these savages, which overwhelms maný and frightens the rest into conversion.

The nameless poet of the *Andreas* has taken the simple marvels of the old legend, and by his energy and insight transformed them to poetry which is at times very noble. In such moments as the storm at sea, or Andrew's recognition of his Lord, or the bitter winter's night in prison as he awaited his doom, or when exhausted and bleeding he cried out, mindful of his Master's word: "Why hast thou forsaken me?" or when the floods came streaming into the streets, bearing down warriors and cup-bearers, driving crowds to the hills, whence they were thrust back by unseen hands, and a confused wail rose above the din—in such moments the poet reveals not only his schooling in poetic tradition both English and Roman, but the power of genius which dominates its schooling to great artistic ends.

Amid all this exaltation, one wonders what every-day poetic fare people had. Abundant it was, no doubt. Everyone was expected to sing at the parties which so embarrassed Cædmon. But scanty fragments remain. Of these are some ninety odd riddles, once ascribed to Cynewulf, but now thought to be chiefly by some anonymous northern poet. Some are from Latin originals of Symphosius and Aldhelm, and most, if not all, belong to the body of riddle-stuff common to many ages and peoples. They have come to us without answers and the solution is sometimes difficult. Often coarse, racy, homespun, they describe objects of household and farm, birds, and things seasonal; sometimes with humor, as of mead and ale, sometimes with high dignity and seriousness, as of the storm, and the shield:

> I am alone—wounded with iron,
> Scored with the brand, sick of the battle work,
> Weary of war. Many the fight I've seen.
> Desperate struggle—no hope in sight. . . .
> No leech in the land could ever I find
> To heal my wounds with wort or simple:
> But wound after wound the sword-edge scores,
> Dealing its death-blow by night or by day.

And a bit of light playfulness unusual in these relics of Old English poetry is the swallow:

> Up in the air over the hillside
> Float this tiny folk—black or dun-feathered,
> Dark is their hue. They gather in flocks,
> And lift a loud, clear song as they fly
> Skimming the wooded cliff—or sometimes the village
> Where menfolk dwell. Tell their right name.

Nearly one hundred and fifty old charms and exorcisms have been recorded, some of them in verse, some mere gibberish like counting-out rhymes, and most of them a queer mingling of old heathen practice with masses, paternosters, and other Christian prayers. They save you from dwarfs, from warts, headache, and various other ailments, danger by flood or field, loss of cattle, barrenness of land and what not. One, the ploughman's charm, is far beyond the rest, beginning:

Erce, Erce, Erce, Earthen Mother,
Pray God Almighty, Lord Eternal,
Grant thee fields that wax and fatten,
Increasing, flourishing
With good stand of hemp, with shining harvest,
With broad stretch of barley-crop,
With white spread of wheat-crop,
With full crops of all the earth yields. . . .

CHAPTER 2

Wessex

DURING Cynewulf's lifetime the political supremacy in England was no longer Northumbrian. Mercia, the middle kingdom, gained it under her strong king Offa; only to relinquish it in 825, after two generations or less, to the southern kingdom Wessex. Two centuries of able West Saxons followed—the ablest no less than Alfred the Great. Their courage and counsel it was that saved and united a moribund England, and to them we no doubt owe the rescue of the few important relics of Old English literature which we now cherish. For *Beowulf* and all the other great poetry of the North have come to us in Wessex copies.

It is again the old story of a new invasion, of renewed strength and union against a new enemy. Even while Cynewulf was still a young man, the terrible dragon-prowed, black longboats, loaded with Danish pirates, had begun to swoop like hawks on the helpless English coast. It was all part of a great Scandinavian Viking migration—north to Iceland, east to Constantinople, west to Ireland and even America, south to France and the Mediterranean. In England the first easy mark was the rich monasteries—Lindisfarne, Jarrow, and many another which after the Irish tradition stood near the sea. Then the invaders pushed inland up rivers and creeks, among inland farms, ruining, killing, plundering, sometimes trading, but eventually arriving, wives and all, to stay and farm the land, and finally to rebuild Roman cities and establish new ones; for the English were rather a village people. For a hundred years the Danish tide rolled over north and central England, but dashed in vain against the resistance of Wessex, and particularly the abilities of Alfred the Great, who reigned from 871 to 901. The old homes of culture, which had produced Cæd-mon, the *Beowulf*, Bede, Cynewulf, were gone, and a hopeless intellectual decline grew deeper and deeper. It was Alfred's work to restore English enlightenment, first by thrusting back the Danes and gaining peace, then by providing for his people the means and impulse to new civilization.

ALFRED *the Great*

Bishop Asser (d. 909?), for a time the king's confidential secretary, has written a brief Latin *Life of Alfred*, which, whatever its faults, has given us intimate acquaintance with the actual man. The king was the sort whom men obey without question; yet his authority was graced and enhanced by devoted affection on both sides. He clearly exercised great charm both of person and manner. From adolescent years his health was wretched; yet his open mind was always on the stretch—whether finding new ways to beat the Danes, or hunting wild game, or seeking out scholars and counsellors abroad and at home, or setting the right persons at work, jewel-making, building, copying, translating, teaching, reading aloud—whatever made for better things. From boyhood he loved the old English poems, probably such as *Beowulf* and many a lost heroic tale; and Asser tells how he once snatched from his older brothers the prize of a beautifully illuminated old poem which his good mother had offered to the one who would first learn it by heart. In later years he also made his subjects learn the old poems—perhaps the best propaganda of patriotism, and the best way of teaching literature. In him the passionate scholar was united with the man of affairs. "This is his peculiar and most confirmed habit," says Asser, "both night and day, amid all his other occupations of mind and body, either himself to read books, or to listen to the reading of others." The books which he himself wrote, or got written for his people, were carefully chosen as the most effective means of education.

He says in his preface to the *Pastoral Care*: "Therefore I think it better, if you agree, that we also translate certain

books which all men most need to know into the language we
can all understand; and so bring it to pass—as well we may
with God's help in a time of peace—that all the free youth in
England who are rich enough to afford it be set to study as
long as they are yet unfit for other duties, until they well know
how to read English. Then on to Latin let him go who seems
suited for higher training and rank."

So he prepared English versions of Bede's great *Ecclesiastical
History*, that his people might know their own past. To the
same end he revived and set going the so-called *Anglo-Saxon
Chronicle* or memorandum year by year of English events, from
the beginnings in England to 1154. He chose also a history of
the world by a fifth-century Spaniard, Orosius, to which he
added two interesting accounts which Alfred had at first-hand
from Ohthere and Wulfstan, of their voyages beyond the
North Cape and in the Baltic. To these he added Boethius's *On
the Consolation of Philosophy,* a book often useful to Alfred
himself, as one can well believe, and to many another Englishman in the next seven hundred years or more; the *Solilo-
quies* of St. Augustine, a book for the doubter; and, not least
interesting, Gregory the Great's *Pastoral Care*, a practical handbook for teachers and pastors containing the best of suggestions
for both. It is in his prefaces to these various works that Alfred
expressed his great intentions, in English which still puts forth
the man's compelling power. And here, in these works of
Alfred, we mark the beginning of English prose literature.

GENESIS B

The intellectual and spiritual revival for which Alfred
yearned and strove was not apparent till after his time. But
his efforts were united with Benedictine influences from new
French abbeys; and as the Danes became Christian, intermarried, and behaved themselves, the revival grew. Thus arose the
great Dunstan, with a touch of the old Irish quality. And thus,
here and there an English voice again broke into song.

Somewhere in this tenth century was made the poem on
the Fall of Man, already mentioned as *Genesis B*. The theme
had been a favorite long before, and is often touched by earlier

poets; but here is a finished poem in 602 lines, embodying no doubt a tradition of treatment which had been accumulating for two hundred years. As a matter of fact *Genesis B* is a translation, or at times an adaptation, of an Old Saxon poem from the Continent of about 840, but it moves with the vigor and spirit of an original, in a series of sharply defined dramatic scenes and metrical variations which mark a proficiency in literary technique beyond earlier poetry.

With a parting warning God left Adam and Eve amid his new creation, and returned to Heaven. Of all his angel-thanes he loved one most, and gave him beauty like the stars, and power. But power and gifts only made him proud; "Why toil for another—me with stout hands and fair body, with devoted friends and followers? I will build a throne higher than God's. I will rule this realm." But God knew his conspiring, and hurled him headlong three days down into Hell, flaming all night;

> Then comes at dawn on eastern wind
> Frost, bitter cold, like fire or spear-point.

Here, helpless, in chains, Satan blames God and meditates revenge. "Look! There is that new-created Adam with his Eve. If we could corrupt them, I could rest easier. Who will go? The one who succeeds shall sit next to me." Then sprang up a thane, donned his helmet-mask, and burst upward through the doors of Hell.

In the garden he found Adam and Eve near two trees, which are altered from the Biblical account, possibly by an old secular legend, into the tree of life and the tree of death. Round the tree of death coils the fiend in serpent form, and without pre-amble offers Adam the fruit, "for God had so bidden me do as I sat at his side." But Adam is not deceived. This is no mes-senger from God—"not like any of his angels I ever saw."

Then the fiend turned aside to Eve, first frightened her with God's wrath at the rebuff of his messenger, then promised her a sight of God and power over Adam, and—confidentially—not to tell God how abusive Adam had been to him—if only she would heed him. And with ironic mixture of truth and lie: "I know well the high vaults of Heaven. It has been a long time that I have joyfully served God. I am no devil sort."

So Eve succumbed, and gained the vision, which was only the fiend's contriving, while he begged her to share it with Adam, "though he deserves nought for his hard words against me."

Eve's plea with Adam is a breathless insistence that the fruit is good, the messenger genuine. "I know it by his gear. Let us not offend him. We need his good-will in our case with God. I can see God now, enthroned in the south and east mid his angels in their feather-robes. I hear them singing. Such is the power of this fruit." All day she plied him close, with the fiend at her elbow, till she won him to her will.

> Then laughed and capered
> That ill-boding scout—uttered thanks for the twain,
> Blessing his master. "Now mine is thy favor,
> Made fast and sure; for I have done thy will."

Exulting in revenge and his success, he plunges again down into the broad-sloping flames to claim his reward. The poet omits, to our regret, the scene of the thane's return to his fettered lord. But he concludes with a very touching presentation of Adam and Eve disillusioned. One thinks inevitably of the corresponding scene in Milton, more subtle, more sophisticated, grander, more generalized, of more heroic proportions, but surely without the simplicity that moves to pity for these two poor helpless victimized children.

Genesis B, though a free translation, perhaps as late as 970, shows that the vigor of Old English poetry still outlives the raids of the Danes, and the decline of English energies. Three other poems of the tenth century give like proof. One is called *Judith*, a highly skilful, but simple, straightforward, vivid and rapid presentation of Judith beheading the drunken Holofernes, returning to her people with the head, of the defeat, pursuit, and spoiling of the Assyrians, and the joyous triumph of the Hebrews. The poem follows the story in the Apocrypha closely, but with an enthusiastic realization which, as in *Genesis B,* creates an original poem.

ÆLFRIC, WULFSTAN, THE OLD ENGLISH BIBLE

King Alfred's glorious endeavors to repel the brigands and to revive culture in his realm brought benefits which lasted for two or three generations after his time, well through the tenth century. It was a richer, and in its livelier intercourse with France, a more sophisticated England. Old monasteries were reorganized and new ones founded under the high and noble purpose of such men as Dunstan, Æthelwold, and Oswald. But it was also a weaker England than it had been, more corruptible, more luxurious, and less resistant to its enemies.

The monasteries, which, as before, were the only sources of light and learning to their times, were put under the Benedictine rule, that rule which made learning and humane regularity of life characteristic of its devotion. They produced no great original poet as in earlier days, but did bring forth one eminent teacher and writer of prose, Ælfric, who was trained at Winchester, taught there and at Cerne, and was during his last twenty years Abbot of Eynsham, on the river a little above Oxford.

Ælfric (d. about 1020), though not a man of genius and great ideas, had the eminent virtues of his own prose writings. He was a practical and sympathetic teacher who, like Milton, would save England by educating her best young men. To that end he translated and adapted into English many little sermons out of the Fathers for the different days of the church year, many lives of English and foreign saints, and certain parts of the Old Testament with explanations; he also wrote a grammar for boys, and his most interesting *Colloquium*, a Latin dialogue between a master and his boys, full of Ælfric's own wise and genial practice as a teacher.

It was his aim to reach and educate not only the clergy but the laity as well. His English prose is admirable for the purpose—simple, easy, and concrete. But in his later sermons and saints' lives, which were designed for oral delivery, he sometimes launches forth into a prose so ornate with alliteration, balance, rhyme, and cadence that it has even been taken for verse; whereas it is only attempting in English prose certain fancy tricks long known to writers of church Latin with which the good Ælfric was perfectly familiar. If he is obscure when he attempts to philosophize, it is not so much Ælfric's fault as a lack of philosophical and abstract terms in the English of his time. These our language had yet to find and adopt in its greater and fuller centuries to come.

Yet a certain flexibility of the language appears as one passes from the sweet reasonableness of Ælfric's manner to the flaming prophecies of Wulfstan (d. 1023), a younger friend of Ælfric, who rose to be Archbishop of York. For he knows how to awaken the thunders of the English speech of his day and send them reverberating over the land as he warns his countrymen in his preaching of the judgment of God soon to overtake them for their sins, at the hands of the Danes.

Old English literature, one need hardly say, owed its heaviest literary debt to the Bible. Poetical paraphrase abounds from Cædmon to *Genesis B*, and prose renderings of passages from Bede to Ælfric. But no extended Old English version of the Bible survives except that of the Four Gospels in West Saxon dialect, which was made by an unknown hand during Ælfric's lifetime, about the year 1000. One who is curious to know what our language was like a millennium ago cannot do better than run over familiar passages in this Old English version. He may be a bit baffled by the language in its more highly inflected state. But he cannot miss even in this early stage the simple and concrete qualities of the tongue which have made it in every age an almost perfect receptacle for the treasured meaning of Holy Writ.

BATTLE OF BRUNANBURH

King Alfred had revived the *Anglo-Saxon Chronicle*. Its recital of events year by year is prosaic enough, but occasionally during this tenth century it bursts into an interlude of song. One instance, made deservedly famous by Tennyson's rendering, celebrates the Battle of Brunanburh in 937, an important victory somewhere in the northwest, where King Alfred's grandson, Athelstan, routed a combination of Danes,

Scots, Britons, and Irish Norsemen, and saved Wessex once more. The poem is not a narrative, but an exultant lyric recollection of the events of the long day's fight; and though it is almost a mosaic of phrases from earlier poems, particularly *Judith*, it is vibrant with its own feeling and goes forward under its own momentum.[1]

> Five still lay
> On the field of the fight—young kings all,
> Lulled by the sword; seven more such,
> Earls of Anlaf—and an endless horde,
> Pirates and Scots.

Two fairly peaceful generations follow. Then in 991 the storm breaks again, this time raging at intervals till Canute the Dane becomes king of all England.

BATTLE OF MALDON

One episode in the new invasion was a victory of the Danes at Maldon on the east coast in 991, during the reign of the incompetent Æthelred. The *Battle of Maldon* is a circumstantial, but poetic account of the fight in 325 lines. Apparently the clash took place at a causeway between Northey Island and the mainland southeast of the modern town of Maldon. The Danes held the island. Byrhtnoth led the English, a white-haired thane of the king.

Between the two armies flows the tidal river Panta. Byrhtnoth arrays his men, while the tide is rising. Then speaks a viking: "Pay us tribute, buy us off, and we will go away." It was the old story. "Our tribute," retorts the gray fighter, "is spears, poisoned arrows, swords. Grim battle-play comes before tribute."

As the tide falls the battle begins; a few English on the causeway hold the Danes at bay, and do valiant damage. Then the vikings ask leave to march over, and Byrhtnoth, more in confidence than wisdom, and perhaps with some heart for a full-length affair, bids them come on.

[1] See p. 18

> The slaughter wolves wade over, the water they scorn,
> The viking horde. West over Panta
> Through the clear water, bearing their bucklers
> Land the sea rovers, linden shields in hand.

And full-length it becomes. All goes well till Byrhtnoth falls and dies, still fighting and commending his soul to the Lord of Angels. Some flee, among them Godric, on the dead Earl's horse, forsaking his dear lord, who had given him many a steed. But the young Ælfwine rallies the rest, reminding them of their boasts in hall on the mead-bench. A half dozen hurl defiance at the pirates and plunge forward to revenge their fallen lord. Near the end speaks an old comrade of Byrhtnoth:

> Sterner the will shall be, keener the heart,
> Higher the courage, as our strength fails.
> Here lies our leader, all torn and bloody,
> A good man laid low. Woe worth the man
> Who now has a mind to flee from this war-play!
> I have seen many years, yet hence will I not;
> For here with my lord I purpose to fall,
> And close by his dear side will I lie.

Clearly the day is lost. The very end of the poem is gone, yet little remained to be told. And with these last lines the noble strains of Old English poetry die away for ever.

As one reads the *Battle of Maldon*, composed perhaps three centuries after the *Beowulf*, he notices above all the persistence of habits and motives in Old English poetry—the old Germanic alliterative line, the *comitatus*, the kennings, the epic tags, the battle pieces, the elegiac mood. Old Byrhtnoth dies like old Beowulf, deserted by all his followers but the best, who like Wiglaf stand by with a noble speech. One wonders at the tenacity with which the English clung to their poetic inheritance as late as King Alfred, and Dunstan, who "loved the vain songs of ancient heathendom," and even the singer of Maldon.

Yet there are differences. The late poet is recounting new matter. events which he witnessed or learned at first-hand. His characters look actual. His style too has changed. It is more flexible and mellow. It has lost much of its wealth of exuberant synonyms, kennings, and compounds. The metre is less strict; rhymes are not infrequent; the melodic movement seems freer. Indeed, the poet may well have heard much Danish verse at this time which modulated his own strain.

The simple old *comitatus* is gone. Thanes are still loyal or disloyal to the person of their lord, and he still gives rich gifts; but with the rest he now gives lands and holdings, as did Alfred to Asser. The realm is broader, social gradations increase, and the English world is already growing feudal towards a new age.

OLD ENGLISH POETRY

Summation

Such was Old English poetry—at least such are the small remnants, for doubtless far more has been lost than saved. One cannot too often recall that it was oral, not read, that to the very end scops sang or declaimed to noble audiences in hall, that even the religious poetry must have been recited in appropriate places, and that among the commoner people song and recital were a universal entertainment. With oral transmission few copies were made, and many poems were not set down. Everything happens to a book in the course of a thousand disordered and careless years. What we have left, then, is a fragment of the whole.

The full glory of this early poetry of ours we cannot measure, not only because it is fragmentary, but because we cannot hear it. The sound of Old English metre in its day is still largely a mystery. Yet in our poor way we may catch afar off its massive measured rhythms, reverberating, rising, falling, now constricted, now relaxed, now exultant, now even plaintive and tender.

If we miss matters of more modern interest—romantic love, life of common folk, children—it may be that the sun of Christian idealism had not yet risen quite high enough to touch these nearer and more intimate points with poetic light. Yet the grander aspects of life are ever in full view—loyal courage, intrinsic worth, joy in conflict, reliability, tender affection, sadness for what is passing, striving for a happier and more stable world. And into what he handles the old poet breathes the energy of life. He animates even the inanimate— swords, ships, the chip of bark that bears a message, the plough, the Cross. How much more his men and women—Beowulf, Hrothgar, Guthlac, Andrew, Judith, Satan's thane, Byrhtnoth? These poetic energies are not to be lost. Once familiar with them, the reader recognizes them everywhere surviving through later literature, mingled with other virtues, transformed, adapted, but still essentially the same enduring energies that made Old English poetry.

tion, sadness for what is passing, striving for a happier and more stable world. And into what he handles the old poet breathes the energy of life. He animates even the inanimate—swords, ships, the ship of bark that bears a message, the plough, the Cross. How much more his men and women—Beowulf, Heathosar, Guthlac, Andrew, Judith, Satan's fiends, Byrhtnoth! These poetic energies are not to be lost. Once familiar with them, the reader recognizes them everywhere surviving through later literature, mingled with other virtues, transformed, adapted, but still essentially the same enduring energies that made Old English poetry.

PART TWO

KNIGHT AND CLERIC

CHAPTER 3

Reconstruction

THE *Battle of Maldon* (991) is our latest remnant of Old English poetry. It comes three hundred years after Cædmon; it is the last protruding peak of the high but half-submerged range which rose even to *Exodus, Beowulf,* and the *Christ* of Cynewulf. Nearly four hundred years more must pass before English poetry can rise again to equal or surpassing heights in the work of Chaucer and his contemporaries.

We may do well to realize that Chaucer is in time nearer to us than he is to Cædmon—that fertilization of literature is continuous, if not always manifest, and that the deep stirrings and building of the soil, the invasions, setbacks, reforms, interbreeding of peoples, take a long time and absorb enormous creative energy. So it was especially during these almost dumb centuries from the *Battle of Maldon* to Chaucer.

Old English poetry died away with the final triumph of the Danes under Canute. Fifty years later a more overwhelming triumph long postponed any hope of literary revival. This was the Norman Conquest.

These Normans who subdued England were Norsemen and

Danes who had invaded northern France two or three cen
turies earlier. Like their kinsmen who had overrun Anglo-
Saxon England in the ninth and tenth centuries they were
men of fierce native energies and a high talent for war. But
they excelled the earlier Danes in political genius. With
all these innate powers they assumed easily the French language and feudal institutions, and quickly shaped the duke-
dom of Normandy into the most powerful political agent in
Europe. This new energetic civilization, a union of Nordic
with Latin, is what the "Conquest" brought to England.

It seems almost as if the curtain were lowered or the lights
dimmed on the story of English Literature for the three centuries that followed the Conquest. The first hundred years or
more produced little. The next century and a half yielded
a few works which have perhaps been remembered more than
they deserved because there was nothing better. Not till the
time is ripe, and Chaucer and his contemporaries enter, will
literature revive and flourish again, as it had flourished in the
time of Bede more than six centuries earlier.

In *Gawain and the Green Knight*, a poem written in
Chaucer's time (1360-1380), Gawain arrives at the castle of
Bercilak de Hautdesert. In the late afternoon it rises before him
out of its moat, a square mass of cut stone, breaking, above its
corbels, into countless battlements, towers, loop-holes, chimneys,
and pinnacles. At the bridge he is greeted courteously by knights
and squires, and brought into the great hall, where a fire blazes
on the hearth; and then to his "bower." His bed is hung and
covered with pure silk, hemmed with gold, and bordered with
fur. French and Turkish carpets adorn the walls and cover
the floor. Wrapped snugly in an ermine-lined mantle he sinks
into a richly cushioned chair before the fire, until his bath is
ready. Then he sits down to a supper of many courses and
highly spiced sauces, graced with white linen, silver
service, and courteous badinage. After evensong in the chancel
he meets the lady of the castle, lovelier than Guinevere; salutes
her with a well-bred kiss, and speaks with knightly courtesy,
asking that he may be her servant; and so to a long evening
of games, and spiced wine, and pleasantries in hall.

One wonders what Beowulf, or King Alfred, or even rough William the Conqueror would say to all this. Yet the scene reflects or implies in one detail or other the profound transformation of England following the Norman occupation. Though the literary revival was long delayed, in other respects these were great progressive centuries—in politics, trade, architecture, education. They were the time of St. Francis, of St. Thomas Aquinas, of Simon de Montfort, Adelard of Bath, Dante. Up to the terrible plague in Chaucer's day, the population in England almost trebled.

The "Conquest" had really begun twenty years before the coming of William, under Edward the Confessor, who, with his Norman mother and education, had set many Normans in high places, especially in the Church. But William the Conqueror pushed ruthlessly from Hastings far into the North, shattering the loose old earldoms, confirming in their places the Saxon counties, and imposing everywhere the feudal system of king, baron, knight, and villein, headed by Normans and highly organized for political, social, and military purposes. Under such a rigid system all England became an obedient unit as never before. But rigid as it seems, the system contained the means of enormous progress.

With a feudal state, William brought also a highly organized and disciplined Church, quickened by the great revivals at Bec and Cluny, and to be distinguished by such men as Lanfranc, the sainted Anselm and Becket, and, in time, Bishop Grossetête of Lincoln.

As always, there were episodes and even generations of gross brutality, injustice, dishonesty, bigotry, misrule. But enlightened rulers appeared in each century, such as William, Henry II, and Edward I; and if there were shadows, there were also high lights of idea and achievement. Bad rulers like Rufus, Stephen, John could damage but not undo the work of their predecessors. England emerged from the age with a Parliament, a Magna Charta, a young House of Commons, newly defined laws, reformed courts, two universities, and a growing middle class. Through primogeniture, the youngei sons of barons were thrown upon their own resources in the

world. At the other end of society, through various developing handcrafts, and the raising of raw wool for French and
Flemish looms, serf rose to villein, and villein to freeman, as
wealth increased. The process was much favored by the comparative peace at home during these centuries. No petty kingdoms were for ever tearing each other asunder as of yore,
no barbaric hordes blackening the land. The Crusades took
many Englishmen across Europe to the East. Home with them
came luxuries, spices, tapestries, jewels, legends, science, and
learning; and the paths they had broken became routes of
growing trade and pilgrim travel.

The buildings of the time are eloquent witnesses of its
progress. First the rude mound-fortress, then the grim square
stone Norman keep, fit only for defence or confinement, then
the spacious hall, with high timber roof and mullioned windows and fireplace—a place of habitation and genial comfort.
Within a century a grand and sturdy new architecture will be
seen at Durham and Ely and Winchester, superseding the
flimsier Saxon building, an architecture capable also of exquisite refinement of feeling as in Anselm's tower at Canterbury, or the church at Iffley. In two centuries the heavy, cumbersome Norman arches and piers, adorned, if at all, with
rough-cut, vigorous, barbaric figures, will have turned to what
seem easy stone miracles of Gothic, like Canterbury, Lincoln,
and Wells, animated with subtle line and symbol, and abounding with spiritual suggestion.

By a "migration" of English students from Paris in the
latter twelfth century, began Oxford; and troubles at Oxford
about 1209 sent a similar migration to settle at Cambridge. In
France the revival of education had begun with a revival of
interest in the Latin and even the Greek classics. Perhaps the
finest product of it was an Englishman, John of Salisbury,
private secretary to Thomas à Becket, a man of high but irre-
proachable activity in the politics of all Christendom, who
died in 1180 as bishop of Chartres. His Latin writings on
politics and education are those of a man by any standards
highly cultivated, a true humanist who cites Latin poets freely,

not for "the awkward ostentation of useless learning," but from a deep sense of their authority in all things human. Such culture as John's might have been common, had not the schools become preoccupied with the logic of Aristotle as a means of settling the dogma of the Church. But, though the Renaissance was thus postponed for two or three centuries, the medieval discipline in logic, called "scholasticism," was a powerful agent in refining mental processes, and teaching men the art of using their minds in more secular things.

CHIVALRY

Historians point out that the Normans won at Hastings by their skill in cavalry charge, whereas the English, by perverse custom, as at Maldon, left their horses in the rear and fought on foot. With the Normans arrived the man on the horse (*cheval*), and with him the code and usage of Chivalry. In Shakespeare's *Henry IV* five hundred years later Hotspur cries out to his lady: "When I am o' horseback, I will swear I love thee infinitely."

His light jest contains the three basic elements of the most lasting cult of the Middle Ages—the knight, the horse, and the lady. The lady-worship of Chivalry springs from the warm shores of Italy and Provence. Transmitted through the French feudal court, it breathes once more the refining influences of the Mediterranean into the ruder Northern natures of the men on horseback. Perhaps nothing else did so much to check the brutal instincts of men as this unwritten code of behavior to others, especially to women. To be sure its graces often disguised much sensuality and misconduct. But its ideals persisted, heightened no doubt by medieval worship of Mary, blessed Maid and Mother; and, however ineffectual in many an instance, it subtly continued—and still continues—to elevate and refine manners, instincts, and action, and to fertilize and spur the poetic imagination to the highest creative efforts. Out of this imagination thus fertilized springs all the vast romance of chivalry through eight centuries from Geoffrey of Monmouth to Spenser and Tennyson.

THE LANGUAGE

It may seem strange that in this great age, when learning and architecture sprang to sudden life, literature lagged long behind. But it was clearly the lack of a language that caused the delay. For three hundred years England used three languages, but was without one tongue for everyone. It was French for the classes, Latin for churchmen, English for the obscure. In such anarchy of speech great English literature was long impossible.

The wonder is that English survived. The social and political odds against it were heavy, especially after the advent of the Angevin Kings in 1154, and "rising" persons were ashamed of it. For some time few French words were taken over. Nearly a century after the Conquest John of Salisbury tells of snobs who clumsily introduce French words to pretend their French breeding, and get laughed at by gentlemen. After 1200, however, French and Latin words flow into English apace, but the gulf between French and English still yawns. About 1300 Robert of Gloucester writes that the Normans had continued to speak French just as they did at home, "and had their children taught in the same manner, so that people of rank in this country who came of their blood all stick to the same language that they received of them; for if a man knows no French people will think little of him. But the lower classes still stick to English and their own language. I imagine there are in all the world no countries that do not keep their own language except England alone."

But English had not only to compete with French; it had to contend with divisions within itself. Three distinct dialects, Northern, Midland, and Southern, corresponding roughly to dialectal differences between Northumbria, Mercia, and Wessex in Old English days, so differed that even in Chaucer's time people of one section had utmost difficulty in conversing with people of another.

Furthermore, from the Danish invasions the North had accepted a far greater number of Scandinavian words and sounds than the South, many of which, like the form "they are," have eventually become a part of the enduring bone and sinew of English everywhere.

Yet in spite of everything, by a strange vitality English overcame in the end. It was, throughout the struggle, the speech of common people, not often subject to the fixing process of writing. By such common wear and tear it changed rapidly— became easier, freer, and more flexible. In this simpler form it was more receptive to increasing importation of new words, especially in the sophisticated south about London and the Court. But the bone and joints of the language, the frame and structure, remained English; the importations gave and have given it fullness, diversity, and the means of grace—new sweetness and new power.

Nor is it strange that the sophisticated dialect, the East Midland dialect of London, should have risen with that most progressive part of England to be the dominant literary dialect in Chaucer's time, and the parent of English as it has come to be spoken round the world.

The triumph of English over French was no doubt gradual, though in the end it looks sudden. As early as 1200 there was a demand for translation of poetical histories and religious books into English, which implies the increasing social importance of people whose only language was English. And though English writings multiplied rapidly, in 1348 French was still the mark of the gentleman. In a generation, however, came the reversal, and Trevisa writes in 1385 that "in all the grammar-schools of England children are forsaking French, and construing and learning in English," with the advantage that they can learn their grammar in less time than they used to do. At the same time English was crowding back French in Parliament and even in the courts, where quaint shreds of old law French still linger today. This apparently sudden triumph had been long on the way. Somehow English, simplified and limbered by long oral use in practical life, enriched by addition of such French and Latin as it needed, had prevailed by its very usefulness and convenience.

NEW METRES

Nowhere else is the amazing change in the language so evident as in the metres. Old English verse, as we said, was normally an alliterative four-stress line, divided in the middle, with varying numbers of unstressed syllables interspersed. It was a measure which easily fitted a tongue still retaining many unstressed inflectional endings, and the subject English population doubtless cherished it orally among themselves as a comfort in their affliction. But as the unstressed endings wore away, it became readily subject to the new alien influences.

There was an even four-stress, eight-syllable metre common among Latin hymns:

> Dies irae, dies illa
> Solvet saeclum in favilla. . . .

This eight-syllable rhymed couplet was also the common metre of Old French poetry, familiar in thousands of lines to the Norman ear. What so natural as that English verse, like English speech, should affect and adopt the new metrical fashions? Rhyme was already increasing in Old English verse, though still incidental. Now in the new four-stress couplet it becomes regular. Alliteration, on the other hand, ceases to be regular and becomes incidental. This new metre enjoyed great medieval popularity in England, especially in the romances, and lived to be known to all in examples like Milton's *L'Allegro* and Scott's *Lady of the Lake*.

Another breaking down of the old line results in one of our commonest folk-measures. In certain poems like the *Brut* of Layamon, the *Moral Ode,* and *Ormulum.* about or before 1200, we have long lines which now and again still retain the cadence and alliteration of Old English verse. But most of the lines are breaking down—sometimes into a familiar jingle.

The *Brut* of Layamon halts curiously between lines that ring with Old English alliterative cadence, and something like a four-stress, eight-syllable couplet, with varying jingles between. But old alliteration and new rhyme are casual, following no

apparent rule of recurrence. In the rhymed *Moral Ode* occur
such lines as

> Ich aem elder then ich wes, a winter and a lorè;
> Ic woelde morè thanne ic dude; mi wit ah to ben morè.

Which the modern ear warps into

> I am older than I was,
> In years and eke in learning;
> I have more strength than once I did;—
> But am I more discerning?

And here we have essentially the metre of most of the ballads, of *John Gilpin*, nay, of *Yankee Doodle* and many another popular song.

But the Old English line also survived, or *r*evived, in something like its original form, and reappears in some of the
greatest works of Chaucer's time. They are mostly produced
in northern and western parts, more remote from French fashion. Hence in dialect as well as metre they are more difficult
and seem more primitive. But whether the old line had continued meanwhile in oral and obscure tradition, only to emerge
at last, somewhat altered with the language, or whether this
is a conscious patriotic revival, or both, no one can tell.

In any case it is different from the old metre, because the
language has changed. New tongues, new tunes, one might
say. So the new English is too rapid, lively, supple for the
old massive measure, which, as we have seen, keeps breaking
down into lighter, more regular metre.

This fitting of the language to its tune was gradual. The
earlier attempts, like *King Horn*, seem hopeless. They are the
first faint wavering snatches of a songbird rehearsing in February. But in the fullness of time, every shred and phrase of the
common language seems lyric music ready made, and sings
itself. How much sweeter this new language, with its new cadence, melody, and timbre, when the voice of a great master
gave it utterance.

Nothing will repay the reader more than to hear the best
poetry of this great period recited by an accurate and skilful

reader, who can give right value to vowels and consonants, and to the final *e*. He will be charmed with a melody, and with a cadence, sweeter than any other which the language has contained, whether before or since. If he will take the small trouble necessary to practise this reading himself, he will gain an inexhaustible source of poetic pleasure. For Middle English poetry, like all true poetry, is heard, not seen, is music more than matter, and cannot be finally considered or discussed as poetry in other terms. No commentary nor criticism nor analysis can realize its true quality as can the ear.

LATIN AND FRENCH LITERATURE

During that two hundred years of all but silence—the long *entr'acte* from Maldon to 1204—the forces that shaped literature in English were in full action. The two peoples, Norman and English, at first distinct, intermingled and intermarried and wore down the partitions between them.

Meanwhile the twelfth century brought a great Renaissance not only to England and France, but to all Europe, and this revival of culture was of highest importance to subsequent English Literature. It is a singular instance of a great literature lined and reinforced by two other literatures on the same soil.

Of these the first was in Latin, largely by churchmen, and therefore unconfined by national bounds, whether produced on English soil or on the Continent. The intellectual revival of the times called forth in England alone more than a dozen writers of history—that is, of chronicles beginning with Adam, rehearsing secular "history" as well as Biblical, but speaking with authority of their own times. Among such were William of Malmesbury, Gerald the Welshman, and the all-important Geoffrey of Monmouth. He it was who collected and saved in his *Historia Regum Brittaniae*, beginning with the arrival of the Trojans in England, the early legends of Arthur, Merlin, and many another who awaited later fame in English poetry— Lear, Cymbeline, Sabrina. No book of the period was so popular; it was read, translated, and plundered on every side. This was the century too of the great John of Salisbury, and many another Englishman distinguished in learning on the Continent. It produced Walter Map, and started the scalding satire of "goliardic" verse against unfit monks and churchmen; it yielded Wireker's *Speculum Stultorum*; it assembled such collections of "scientific" curiosities as Neckam's *De Naturis Rerum*; such libraries of fiction as *The Seven Sages of Rome* and *The Gesta Romanorum*. It produced a vast body of fine Latin hymns and saints' lives and other works for religious edification. Embedded here and there in this mass was many a tale and anecdote to be taken out and reworked in English in after times in other connections or for its own sake.

On the same English ground, and during the same great twelfth century, grew up another rich literature in polite Norman-French, usually called Anglo-Norman. It bore a close relation to the contemporary Old French literature on the Continent, but is distinct in many ways. In particular these Anglo-Norman poets made excellent use of legendary material local in Britain, especially of the legends of Arthur. Geoffrey had led off about 1140 with his popular account in his Latin *Historia*. This was translated into French verse by Gaimar in his *History of the English* (1147-1151) and more ably by Wace in his *Brut* (1155), whence sprang the vigorous literary traffic in history and legend indiscriminate that went on for centuries. Into Norman-French, and so into continental French verse, went not only stories of Arthur, Tristram, the Grail, but of legendary English or Danish heroes—Horn, Havelok, Guy of Warwick, Bevis of Hampton—of Alexander the Great, of Thebes, of adventures on crusades, of oriental yarns brought home by Crusaders and tradesmen, of old Breton lays and tales. But the Arthurian story was especially rich—so rich that the great continental French poet, Chrétien de Troyes, confesses his debt to it. Vigorous these romances of adventure often were, yet numerous and prolix and diffuse. Poets, minstrels, listeners, and readers thought nothing at all of a poem of 15,000 verses.

Let us recall that Henry II was an Angevin as well as a Norman; that at the height of this great twelfth century he ruled a realm which reached from the Cheviot Hills to the Pyrenees. His queen, Eleanor of Aquitaine, was a patroness

of poets, and welcomed them from the far south of Provence.
Thus the alliance between the feudal energy of the north and
the new love-cult of the south was strengthened into an institution and code of supreme importance to all subsequent literature. This was the code and institution of Chivalry.

Not only "romance" but other literary sorts flourished in
Norman French—shorter tales, some pious, some very otherwise called *fabliaux,* history deep-dyed with fiction, religious
allegory and secular allegory, saints' lives, bestiaries and lapi-
daries, songs, sermons, "debates," and works of religious edification. All of these produced lusty offspring in medieval
English Literature.

Such was the glory of Old French poetry on both sides of
the Channel that it became, from the twelfth century on, the
purveyor of poetic material and forms for all Europe. "Romances" about Arthur, Tristram, Alexander, Charlemagne and
his peers, and all the other worthies of chivalry were composed in Spain, Italy, Norway, Germany, and elsewhere, more
or less naturalized to the audiences of those countries.

ANCREN RIWLE (ABOUT 1140) ;
MORAL ODE (AFTER 1150)

Hardly more than two generations after the Conquest a
work was written in English prose called the *Ancren Riwle* or
Rule of Nuns. Though once taken for a translation from
French, it is now recognized as an English original. A wise
and gentle churchman is advising three dear sisters on the
right manner of life for a good anchoress, both as to inward
and outward conduct. Explicit are his details on the daily order
of prayer and work, on the seven deadly sins, on management
of the five senses and the heart, on confession and penance.
These monitions are strewn throughout with legends, historical bits, chivalric matter, beast-lore, symbol, homely figure,
and many another curiosity. But the external life of the times
which the book discloses is most vivid. Each nun lives apart
in a little house against the church wall, with only her maid
and her cat. A window opens into the church; another from
her parlor into the world; and the management of this latter

window naturally gives the author deep and long concern. About it hover many dangers—gazing, wantonness, gossip. A good nun is silent like Our Lady, not a hen like cackling Eve. No, the window is best closed and curtained with black. Yet amid the warnings we catch many a glimpse through that window of the busy medieval street and market outside.

" 'The upright love thee,' saith the bride to the bridegroom." So begins the treatise, and the figure of the mystic marriage of the soul to Christ is interwoven throughout the book. Snatches from the love-song of Solomon or allusions to it are frequent. The finest passage is a sustained allegory of the soul as a disdainful lady, long besieged in her castle by devils, but delivered at length by "her noble wooer," Christ, who shed his blood in tournament to prove his love for her. No wonder this skilful piece of instruction was popular for centuries.

Not long after the *Ancren Riwle* follows the *Moral Ode* or *Poema Morale* so-called, already quoted. It is a vivid warning from one who considers himself old enough to know, that men had better behave if they hope for Heaven and would flee the pains of Hell. Judging by the number of surviving copies, this simple and dignified monition found many listeners.

ANIMALS AND BIRDS

In spite of these first spirited endeavors, English Literature produced little that remains during the first two hundred years after the Conquest. One specimen called the *Bestiary*, is worth a moment's attention, less for its merit than its tradition. Like earlier poems in other tongues, notably Latin, Old English, and French, and even Greek, it sets forth the nature of various beasts and birds—lion, panther, eagle, and the like—with an explanation of the meaning of each as a symbol of points in religion. The device still survives in the secular use of animal alphabets or skits in humorous periodicals. The *Bestiary* itself well exhibits the lively medieval traffic in animal symbolism, which we observe not in literature alone, but everywhere in carving and illuminations.

Medieval interest in animal lore enlivens another early poem

—in some respects the greatest performance until Chaucer's time. It is an anonymous poem in about 1800 four-stress couplets called *The Owl and the Nightingale* (about 1195). Deep withdrawn into a "summerdale" at twilight, the poet overhears a wrangle between the two birds—violent, personal, abusive—the owl perched on an ivy-grown stump; the nightingale on a spray of blossoms in a tangled hedge. But mere jangling is vain, so they agree each to plead his case in order, and to refer the decision of the debate to Nicholas of Guilford at Portisham; for Nicholas will be a just judge since, as the owl observes, he had known some wildish nightingale days in his youth, but has latterly grown steady, cool, and discreet. The argument proceeds, by formal charge, countercharge, and refutation mixed, after the medieval custom, with plenty of epithet and abuse. The owl, urges the nightingale, is a bird of darkness, blind, a witch, with raucous song, "like a hen in the snow," fouling its own nest; but she, the nightingale, sings sweetly, usefully, and is beloved of men. The owl retorts that the nightingale is wanton, useless, chattering like an Irish priest, local and provincial, while she, the owl, sings cheerfully and in order, in the winter, in every country, prophesying, advising, and edifying mankind, and ridding of mice the houses of men and God. Even after death she is useful as a scarecrow. All night they debate. The nightingale claims the victory just as the dawn breaks, and all about little songbirds burst into chorus in the nightingale's favor. But the wise wren calls for the verdict, and they all fly off to find good Nicholas.

> But how they sped, and what the doom,
> When they to Portisham had come,
> I know not, so I cannot tell;
> Here ends the tale. And so—farewell.

The general question is an old one—youth vs. age, pleasure vs. sobriety, and the like. In particular, however, it may present the respective claims of the traditional secular love-poetry of the Provençal type and the equally traditional religious poetry of the times. But it has clearly another purpose—to recommend the neglected talents of the worthy clerk Nicholas to

recognition by the church dignitaries. Some think Nicholas, ?
whose literary gifts the poem recounts, wrote the poem himself. Whoever did—perhaps a friend of Nicholas who was a
canon lawyer—knew the process and technique of legal debate
and much else besides. The poem is an epitome or sample
case of many motives in medieval literature, and deserves study
as such.

First there is the debate, a popular theme at times ever since
shepherds debated in the pastoral poems of Theocritus and
Virgil. But in these thirteenth century days, when scholastic
debate at the universities waxed high and skilful, the theme
was a favorite from Provence to England—debates between
Spring and Winter, wine and water, soldier and scholar, heart
and eye, violet and rose, and what not, abound in Latin and
French.

Then, the poem is an allegory, in this case using animal symbol and animal story. Both contestants also cite illustrations
or *exempla* from beast lore, of fox, and cat, and falcon. They
stiffen their arguments with old proverbs out of a collection
popularly ascribed to King Alfred, with natural history, geography, church lore of seven deadly sins and such, and folk-
song on the jealous husband. But learned as the poet is, never
is he the pedant. Out of his many devices he has shaped a
charming and lively thing, satiric, racy, tuneful, exquisite, delicate—all of these by turns, yet serious beneath the surface,
and rounded into a perfect whole.

LAYAMON (ABOUT 1200); ORM

Of the rare new literary stirrings in the transformed English tongue is the work of Layamon, called the *Brut* or *History
of the Brutons* (for were not Britons Brutons, descended from
Brutus of Troy?). Layamon was a secular priest of a village
parish of Areley Kings, tucked away in the upper Severn Valley. Doubtless he was a good and dutiful shepherd of his
flock; but, like many of his kind to this day, he had a passionate talent for literature and antiquities, read old books, perhaps
Bede, and certainly some version of Wace's *Brut*.

Layamon laid before him these books and turned the leaves.
In them he found a light—God have mercy on him.
Quills then he seized quickly and wrote on bookskins.

In his earlier wanderings he had busily collected and stored
up legendary stuff for his great poem. And great it is, not in
compass only—it runs over 15,000 long lines—but in quality.
With steady, unflagging progress, the story moves on its event-
ful course, unimpeded by ornament, quickened by many lively
scenes and by the loves and hates and patriotism of the poet.
It begins with Brutus's ancestors, and ends with the final expulsion of the Welsh into Wales in 689. But the focal point of
the poem is the figure and story of Arthur to whom Layamon
devotes a third of his work. Nor does he make him a centre of
the love-cult and intrigue of later romance, but a warlike, generous king with some unconscious remnant in him of Beowulf
and his kind. Thus the poem both in matter and in metre, as
we saw, links the old with the new. And who can say what
patriotic purpose burned in this high-minded poet's heart to
stir and keep alive in his fellow Englishmen, through uncertain
days, their sense of national tradition already venerable—the
very purpose that later moved Spenser, and Tennyson, and
tempted Milton, to the same use of the same material?

While Layamon collected and composed, a monk named
Orm, off in the northeast, wrote a poem which he named
Ormulum—"little Orm." It sets forth the Gospel, with commentaries, for the days of the year, doubtless for the use of
monks who knew English better than Latin or French, and
especially for Walter, his brother both after the flesh and the
spirit.

KING HORN

About 1225 was written down in English the popular legend
of King Horn, which bears traces of Danish origin. It is the
earliest of the "romances" in our tongue, though, as usual, a
French version is earlier.

Horn was a young prince of "Suddene," in all respects a paragon. But a band of Saracens one day devastated his land and

set him adrift with two mates, one of them, Fikenhild, a villain. They first land in "Westerness" where the king is greatly taken with this likely young fellow until his daughter Rimenhild, a young woman with a mind of her own, makes it up.

> "Horn," she said, "no use of strife;
> I am going to be your wife."

Fikenhild, the dastard, betrays him to the king, and he wanders on to Ireland where his graces involve him awkwardly with another princess. But his heart is true to Rimenhild. Meanwhile she, threatened with a forced marriage, sends for Horn. He arrives in disguise on her wedding-day. He announces his death. She lays in her marriage-bed a dagger for her hated husband and herself. Horn throws a magic betrothal ring which she had once given him into her wineglass, and snatches off his disguise. "I am Horn. Do you know me?" She does.

Such, in 1500 short lines, is the crowded tale. Sudden love, exile and return, nick-of-time recognition, happy ending—the well-worn devices; but here is a fresh and primitive importation into the language, spirited, rapid, dramatic, if at times naïve. Evidently it was composed for the common English ear, to be sung or recited at fairs and merrymakings. A clumsy trace here and there of chivalric high life only heightens the authentic verve with which the poet touches familiar things—beggars, shipping, and horses. No subtleties, no refined mental processes; it is all things and events. Horn does not mind slaying a hundred "heathen hounds" at any moment's notice. The metre, rough, halting between old and new, shows how stubborn a medium the language yet is. Again it is like an attempt of a strong, unpractised hand to cut in granite a miniature of a legend from high life.

HAVELOK (ABOUT 1290)

Another piece of equal literary merit does not occur for more than fifty years. Then, near the end of the thirteenth century a hearty English version of the story of Havelok was made. French versions, as usual, preceded it; yet this romance has the fresh vigor of an original devised for popular use at inns and fairs. Like *King Horn* it shows traces of Danish origin.

The dying king of Denmark entrusted his son Havelok to the bad Earl Godard, who turned him over to an old fisherman, Grim, to drown. But a strange flame leaping from the mouth of the lad in his sleep shows that he is the prince. So Grim sells everything, and with his family and Havelok flees to England and settles Grimsby in Lincolnshire. There young Havelok becomes famous for his strength and graces. Fair Goldborough, an English princess, what with a dead father and a bad earl, is in like sad case with Havelok. Meanwhile Havelok has risen to be cook's assistant in the earl's household. To insult Goldborough, the earl shamefully marries her to the scullion Havelok; but lo, at night the flame shows his royal birth. Back to Denmark they go with Grim's family. Here Havelok beats and hangs the bad Danish earl, returns to burn the bad English earl, and rules both countries happily with his dear queen.

Throughout the 3,000 lines of rhymed couplet there is not a dull moment. The story is told over a "cup of ful god ale" to common folk by someone of religious associations and high native talent, who knew well enough that his simple listeners would of all the tale best understand Grim's humble way of life. His hard fare, his lowly cottage and hearth, his live-stock, his seacraft, the fish of his catching with net and hook, his marketing them in panniers at Lincoln, are all as vivid as a Dutch painting. Then, Havelok in an old sailcloth smock jostling with his mighty shoulders among the porters and fish and hubbub at the bridge in Lincoln, or wrestling and putting the stone at the fair, makes a scene so alive as to annihilate the seven hundred years since. Not less vivid is the story of the fight where Havelok with the door-bar finally beat a gang of thieves that broke into the house where he and his wife were guests at supper. High life is viewed amusingly from below, and the great behave like villagers dressed up.

ROMANCES

About 1300 some gifted northern churchman compiled in 25,000 lines a poem which he called *Cursor Mundi,* because "almast it overrennes al." That is, all of sacred history. But his prologue pays interesting respect to romances. Folk love, he says, both to hear and to read divers "romans," concerning Alexander, Greece and Troy; Arthur and his knights, King Charles (Charlemagne) and Roland, Tristram and "Ysote," and such; in fact "paramours" are, alas, all the fashion these days.

King Horn and *Havelok* were early instances of the so-called "romance" of chivalry in English. We know of not more than a half dozen others composed before 1300. Yet altogether more than one hundred romances in English have survived which were written down before 1500. The material for these romances was commonly imported, already highly finished, from French, whether Anglo-Norman or continental, either by translation, or recollection, or adapted transformation. The transformation into English shows interesting and quite natural changes: the English romances are on the whole shorter, less sophisticated in both art and manners, more moral, more given to derring-do, less prone to sentiment. The difference is not merely national but social. In France, and in English high life, the romance was typically courtly and aristocratic, and minstrels wandered from castle to castle, purveying to baron, knight, and lady, their old or new wares, in recital or song. In England romances were commonly diffused by humbler artists on lower levels, with resourceful changes of costume, custom, and setting to fit the new audience. A few notable examples, however, in time sprang from this stock, and rose to higher levels. *Gawain and the Green Knight* is a masterpiece, a first-rank specimen not of romance only, but of all medieval literature.

English romances move rapidly. Most of them tell their tale in 3,000 lines or less, often much less; and if they rarely climb to the neighborhood of 10,000 or above, as in two Troy romances, and two Arthurian, they are not successful. The eight-syllable, four-stress couplet is the commonest metre, but a very common half-lyric measure from the French called tail-rhyme, originally used in Latin hymns, increased in fashion in shorter poems. In tail-rhyme or *rime couée* Chaucer cast his burlesque on romance called *Sir Thopas*; Scott loved its swing—

> Wild through their red or sable hair
> Look'd out their eyes with savage stare,
>   On Marmion as he pass'd;
> Their legs above the knee were bare;
> Their frame was sinewy, short, and spare,
>   And harden'd to the blast;

and Tennyson, by skilful variations, has made exquisite use of it in *The Lady of Shalott*. There is, besides, the revived—or surviving—alliterative long line, especially in the north and west. As adapted to the new language and matter, it often attains to a dignity and breadth of stroke somewhat as in its Old English days which is quite beyond reach of the shorter metres. Passages in the *Gest Historiale of the Destruction of Troy*, especially describing a storm on the sea, are noteworthy. Its besetting sins are artificiality and the surrender of sense to mere sound.

It is customary to classify the romances according as their "matter" deals with Arthur and his knights, with Charlemagne and his peers, with the heroes of Greek and Roman antiquity, or with native English or Danish heroes. But a considerable number lie outside this scheme, such as *Floris and Blancheflur*, a theme probably imported out of the Orient, or a group on the theme of the patient wife; and there are the charming shorter tales called lays.

The romances of Arthur far outnumber the others in England. That shadowy Welsh leader, who in the fifth century, if ever he lived at all, hurled back the Saxons for a time, rapidly became a Welsh hero. From Wales he traveled in song to Brittany, with Welsh fugitives from the Saxons, and later, Bretons mingling with Normans doubtless shared generously with them the legends of Arthur. Back again on the Welsh border it remained for Geoffrey of Monmouth to give the heroic legend the semblance of history, unite it with all the use of chivalry, and hand it with this increment over to the French poets, from whom the great story, now heavy-laden with accretion of legendary and chivalric matter, is drawn by English romancers. A figure like Arthur by force of gravity always draws to himself stories originally independent. Such are the legend of the Grail and the story of Tristram; even a late thirteenth-century version of the Tristram story in the North, which the author claims to have heard from Thomas the Rhymer of Erceldoune, does not mention Arthur.

Of the twenty and odd Middle English Arthurian romances the best, aside from the great *Gawain and the Green Knight*, are an alliterative *Morte Arthure* after 1350; another, *Le Morte Arthur*, in eight-line stanzas of four-stress lines, which treats of Lancelot and Elaine; and *Ywain and Gawain* in couplets, a unique translation, much reduced, from Chrétien de Troyes's masterpiece, *Yvain*. All three are out of the north, and the last, though earliest, shows high proficiency in narrative and metre, with the native English homeliness ever and again making itself felt.

Among Arthur's knights, his nephew Gawain is the English favorite. In more than half the Middle English romances of Arthur he is the principal figure, valorous, courteous, charming, as in many French accounts; and he is the hero of the greatest of them, *Gawain and the Green Knight*. The mean and treacherous Gawain, as portrayed by Tennyson, was born of another French tradition, and was not much entertained by Englishmen until Malory's time in the fifteenth century.

Story-tellers always like to localize strange tales in familiar places. The romance entitled *The Adventures of Arthur* is a case in point. It makes Carlisle and the neighborhood the scene of a spirited and spectacular account of Gawain, of strange apparitions, hunt, feast, and fight, where all is valor, fine clothes, good counsel, generosity, and ladies' tenderness.

The tale is set forth in elaborate thirteen-line stanzas, of nine long, rhymed alliterative lines, ending a short "wheel" of four, and each stanza bound to the one before by repeating in its first line a word caught from the last line of its predecessor. The device, known technically as *concatenatio,* comes to Middle English poetry from French, though it is not limited to these languages.

Good as this poem is, its preoccupation with accessories and ingenious metre are unmistakable signs of the decadence of the romance in Chaucer's time.

The "matter of France," the legend of Charlemagne, somehow found English soil less congenial. This hero was historical; vigorous and luxuriant French poetry grew out of his name; first epic and heroic as in the *Song of Roland,* sung as William conquered England at Hastings; then later, romantic and feudal, increasing like the Arthurian story by centripetal power of such a name over extraneous legends. Yet the English adaptations were late and few, favoring such of the famous peers as Ogier, Firumbras, Otnel (Otinel), Roland, and, in late prose accounts, Renaud of Montauban and Huon of Bordeaux.

More popular was the "matter" of classical antiquity, especially concerning Alexander and Troy. Alexander, ever after his time a popular hero, became a medieval favorite all over Europe, but so swathed in accumulated fable, exploit, and moral, that he could never have recognized himself. In the fourteenth century three or four vigorous English poems were made out of French or Latin legends of Alexander.

However, the Troy story was of more weight because of the belief that Brutus, sprung from Aeneas, founded Britain. Through Geoffrey of Monmouth, Wace, Layamon, and many a chronicle and poem the belief was confirmed down to the time of Spenser and Elizabeth. The English Troy romances are distinguished at least by their length; Lydgate's ran beyond 30,000 lines.

But the importance of the Troy story in Middle English owes most to Chaucer's use of it in his greatest poem, *Troilus and Criseyde.* The like is the case with the story of Thebes, which, though distinguished in France by a long *roman,* and in Italy by no less a master than Boccaccio, is worthily represented in English only by the greatest of the *Canterbury Tales*, the one told by the Knight.

Local English and Danish matter, first to enter English in romance form, is most conspicuous in *King Horn* and *Havelok*. It includes also the stories of the cherished Sir Guy and Sir Bevis, already elaborated by French poets, and of a brutal, but finally submissive, King Athelstan. More significant is the tale of Gamelyn, perhaps meditated by Chaucer for his cook. It is an ancestor of Shakespeare's *As You Like It*, and a collateral relative of Robin Hood lore. Like *Havelok* it is full of villainy, brawn, big hearts, and rough justice; all about an abused, exiled, but husky young hero, who in the end returns from the woods, manhandles and hangs his enemies, sets up his friends, and marries.

In this group also belongs the highly diverting romance of *William of Palerne*, a curious blend of the werewolf tale with adventures of Greek romance. It is distinguished as one of the first attempts to revive the old alliterative line.

There remain the lays—those exquisite miniature romances, like highly wrought illuminations in late manuscripts.

> Some tell of weal, and some of woe,
> Some of joy and mirth,
> Some of treachery, some of guile,
> Of happenings every little while.
> Some of gibes and ribaldry—
> And some there be of faery.
> Of everything a man might meet,
> • But most of love it is they treat.

Out of Brittany first came these lays, sung by harpers. So at any rate says the poet just quoted, at the opening of the lay of *Sir Orfeo*. But as usual, the popular folk-form becomes polished and sophisticated by the urban artist. Such an artist was Marie de France, who lived in England in Henry II's time, and became the supreme specialist in composing French *lais* which she professes to have got out of old Breton songs.

Not till 1300 was the first lay made English—*Sir Orfeo*, just quoted. Orfeo, it seems, was once king at Winchester, and a marvellous harper as well. He was descended from King Pluto, and on the distaff side from King Juno(!). One day his queen Herodis, out a-maying, was charmed away by a mysterious lover. Orfeo, barefoot, unkempt, with only his harp, sought her winter and summer, until he won to faeryland and a great castle of crystal and gold. Admission was easy for a minstrel, and there he found his wife. By the spell of his music he at last got the faery king's consent to take her away. Back in Winchester the poor beggar was not recognized, though any harper is welcome for dear King Orfeo's sake. But in a dramatic finale his music breaks through all disguise, and his devoted steward and lords send the furniture spinning in their plunge forward to embrace his adored feet.

One has no difficulty here in making out the old myth of Orpheus and Eurydice, quaintly overgrown with chivalry and Celtic fairy lore. But the peculiar quality of this and other lays is a certain tenderness, certain unuttered implications of elemental perennial human truths beneath the tale that especially charm our modern minds.

Similar are the *Lai le Freine, Sir Launfal, Sir Degare, Emare,* of various dates in Chaucer's century; and more famous, the tale told by Chaucer's Franklin and the other tale by the Wife of Bath.

Of course the favorite themes and devices of the "romance" are few—but so they are of the modern novel. "Fierce wars and faithful loves" are indispensable. The quest to strange lands, the exile, the return in disguise, the test of courage and fidelity, long separation of lovers, recognition, magic, triumph at last over villainy and treachery—these repeat themselves from one romance to another. Yet one cannot fail to see the narrator's skill in capturing a wandering ear. Whether a professional roaming over the land, or an amateur with a reputation at the local hostelry, he was on his mettle as an artist, localizing his tale, yet featuring new wonders; interspersing homely, racy bits of low life with impossibly gorgeous costuming and setting; or with refreshing interludes of meadow or sea or bird song; leading up with skilful suspense to a highly dramatic situation and dialogue; pointing the fabric at the right time with wise or witty comment of his own, shifting the action when it is time.

But degeneracy set in. Though romances had always been recited or chanted, yet by 1300 they began to be more and more read by such as could read. Story gave way to overloading accessories, and in the fifteenth and sixteenth centuries the romances diluted and diffused themselves on the lower level of prose.

MIDDLE ENGLISH SONG

The English people have always sung. From the party at which poor Cædmon made so sorry a figure on through the centuries, any intimate glimpse of English life finds song an indispensable part of it.

Lyric as is the English spirit, the relics of it in the way of recorded songs are comparatively scanty. The reason is clear. Folk-songs are not learned by note; they flit from ear to ear, anonymously, for a good song belongs not to the composer but to the people. Who ever learned *Suwanee River* by note? How many can name the composer? Thus there may be plenty of songs without a written record.

Doubtless the English people kept singing all through the turbulent seven centuries from Cædmon to Chaucer. Rare snatches in Old English are overheard, Cædmon's hymn, bits of *Beowulf, Deor's Lament,* riddles, charms, *Brunanburh.* We hear of a twelfth-century priest who was kept awake all night while the roystering villagers were singing and dancing in the churchyard. Next morning at service he would have begun, "Dominus vobiscum," as usual, but to the scandal of the whole diocese out slipped a snatch of "Sweety mine, take pity."

After the Conquest we catch nothing but brief fragments till the thirteenth century is well under way. Everyone knows, and some can sing, the old popular round,

> Sumer is icumen in,
> Lhudè sing cuccù. . . .[1]

---

[1] Summer now is come again:
Loudly sing "cuckoo."

It dates from 1230 to 1240, and is one of a few scant relics of its time. But while English songsters could never have been wholly mute, the language did not reach that clear vibrant stage of inherent and natural tunefulness where the tune is not forced upon the words, but already singing in them, till after 1250. And then, as English was still the plebeian language, English song, whatever it lacked, at least kept in its cadence a measure of homely English vigor. All forms of high sophisticated art, building, sculpture, music, as well as poetry, have sprung from primitive popular forms. And they keep alive only by resuming from time to time their connection with the primitive soil of their origins. So with English song.

The Middle English song is of highly complex foreign origin. On French soil, in Provence, and by consequence in Anglo-Norman circles, had accumulated a vast store of popular song. This grew chiefly in the course of the great twelfth century. There were carols and rounds that sprang from folk-dances; there were work-songs, especially of women spinning or sewing; there were *aubes*, the parting dialogue-songs of lovers interrupted by the watchman's cry at dawn (surviving most famously in *Romeo and Juliet*[1]); there were songs of the ill-married, still questing wife; songs of spring; *chansons d'aventure*, of the general formula, "I went walking tother day, And saw a fair maid by the way. . . ."

While all this popular song continued to flourish, the polite love-poetry of the castle, the love-songs of Provençal *troubadour* and French *trouvère*, springing from the folk-song, took on exquisite refinement of music and sentiment, and developed much of the familiar romantic thought and phrase which has come echoing down through sonnet and conventional lyric without number, even to our own time. Through the court of Henry III (1216-1272) and Eleanor of Provence passed and repassed many a Provençal, French, and Anglo-Norman singer, many a wandering cleric with his trading stock of song, courtly and otherwise.

There were besides in great number Latin hymns and devotional poems of the time, which by no means remained de-

[1] Act 3 sc. 5

voutly apart. The same wandering worldly clerks and friars—
Chaucer's tuneful friar is a case in point—kept up a constant
give and take of tune, image, phrase, and device between sacred
and secular song.

Now as most English songsters were bi-lingual or even tri-
lingual, Middle English songs could hardly be more in their
inception than a reflection of French and Latin song of the
time. Yet the English language of 1250 and later, especially
in the south, has its own native sweetness, and from the south
and west come most of the surviving songs. And while the
language has neither the compass nor range which it will command in Elizabeth's day, it has the limited delicacy of small
viol or lute, such as it never caught before nor after the height
of Middle English song.

One thirteenth-century love song begins:

> Bytuene Mersh and Averil
> when spray biginneth to springè,
> the lutel foul hath hirè wyl
> on hyrè lud to syngè.
> Ich libbe in louèlongingè
> for semlokest of allè thingè;
> He may me blissè bringè,
> icham in hire baundoun.
> An hendy hap ichabbe yhent,
> ichot, from heuene it is me sent,
> from allè wymmen mi loue is lent,
> and lyht on Alysoun . . .[1]

This exquisite song, with a tune lurking in the words, bears

[1] Now March is turning to April,
    And tender buds are springing;
The little birds with all their will
    Their merry notes are singing.
    My heart like them with love is winging,
    My ear with her sweet name is ringing;
    That lovely thing my life is bringing
      Beneath her durance boon.
    Happy the lot for me so meant;
    I wot, it is from heaven sent.
For other women my love is spent
    To light on Alysoun.

trace of the languishing courtly lover, and yet is resonant of folk-song, with its homespun phrase and its shapely Alysoun of the black eye, brown brow, and "lossom chere." Such is to be expected while English is still the plebeian language, even though the song first sang itself in the ear of clerk or gentleman. The early English love lyric is essentially popular, yet with polite features.

The like is true of the well-known

> Lenten ys come with love to tounè,
> With blosmen and with briddes rounè,[1] . . .

or of,

> Blow, northerne wynd,
> Sent thou me my suetyng! . . .

or of,

> When the nyhtegalè singes, the wodes waxen grenè,
> Lef and gras and blosme springes, in Averyl, Y wenè;
> Ant love is to myn hertè gon with onè spere so kenè,
> Nyht and day my blod hit drynkes, myn hertè deth to tenè.[2]

Far more numerous are the recorded religious songs, but only because all surviving collections of the songs were made in religious houses. Naturally these follow very closely in all respects Latin hymns and French religious and secular songs. Sometimes they are even interlarded in macaronic fashion with Latin or French lines. Sometimes the religious song is almost parallel with a very secular song, as if religious words had been set to a popular tune. Now and then an old *reverdie* or *chanson d'aventure* is thinly and quaintly disguised in the religious habit. "The devil," it would seem, "was not to have all the good tunes." Richard Rolle, the mystic, touches the common point between sacred and secular when he cites "I languish for love" from the Song of Solomon, and remarks: "He that mykel lufes, hym lyst[3] oft syng of his luf, for ioy that he or scho hase

[1] song
[2] grief
[3] he likes

whan thai thynk on that that thai lufe, namely if their lover be
trew and lufand."[1] The favorite theme is penitential, and Old
English melancholy strongly pervades these lyrics. Sometimes
the old theme of Boethius and of *The Wanderer*—"Ubi sunt
. . . ?"—recurs, as in the Love Rune of Thomas of Hales.
written at a young nun's request:

> Hwer is Paris and Heleyne,
>> That weren so bryht and feyre on bleo?[2]
> Amadas and Ideyne,
>> Tristram, Yseude, and all theo?

In most exquisite unison are the language and the tune in
many songs of adoration to the Virgin and to the Child, as in
this from Shropshire:

> This flour is faire and fresche of heuè,
> Hit fades never, bot ever is new;
> The blissful branche this flour on grew
>> A flour of grace,
>> ayains all sorow hit is solás!

Harsh in tone and cadence are the tunes called forth by
political events. Seldom do they wax exultant or laudatory;
rather they snarl in bitter but vigorous discord at public and
political abuses. Many of these are in the rougher northern
dialects, and often the harsher melody of the old alliterative
verse intrudes again. A handful of the best are by one Laurence
Minot, otherwise unknown.

Into his song on Edward III's invasion of France has entered
the popular energy which backed the Hundred Years' War. It
rings with a sound premonitory of Drayton:

> Edward, ourè cumly king,
> In Braband has his woning,[3]
>> With many cumly knight;
> And in that land, trewly to tell,
> Ordanis he still for to dwell
>> To time he think to fight. . . .

[1] loving
[2] face
[3] is abiding

> Ourè king and his men held the feldè
> Stalworthy, with spere and scheldè,
>   And thoght to win his right,
> With lordes, and with knightes kenè,
> And other doghty men bydenè,[1]
>   That war ful frek[2] to fight.

After 1300 it would seem that with increase of technical skill the number of songs greatly multiplied. Yet more and more they became weaned from musical setting, and turned into the lyric poem without music, sometimes called the literary lyric. English song had to await new revival from popular carols and the impulse of Italian music before it rose to its greatest height in the sixteenth century.

Yet through all the changes of English song the soft cadence of lyric Middle English may be caught however faintly rising and falling; and no one can capture the full pleasure of later lyric whose ear is not attuned to the peculiar music of the language in song of the thirteenth and fourteenth centuries.

[1] together
[2] bold

CHAPTER 4

Renaissance of the Fourteenth Century

THE English literary Renaissance of the fourteenth century, the time of Chaucer, was like all other high revivals, a time of rich inheritance, sharp issues, and great personalities.

English wealth was mounting, and with special rapidity after 1350. Much of it came from the raw wool trade with the weavers of Flanders at Ghent, Bruges, and Arras. Then Edward III brought Flemish weavers to England by way of increasing the profits. In 1337 began the Hundred Years' War with France. It was a popular venture because it was at first successful, and hardly a man, high or low, came back without his goodly share of plunder.

But the heritage was deeper than mere wealth. The common English stock, fortified by breeding with Norman virtues, had slowly grown to be an element of great importance in society. English political institutions had gradually been taking form. Historians love to dwell on the victories won at Crécy, Poitiers and Agincourt through the skill of English yeomen at the long bow—a skill developed by practice since childhood back on the village green. Here the arrows of common footmen overcame the feudal chevaliers, as if in token of a new age routing an old. This English success against France quickened in Englishmen a new sense of England as a nation, of her safe independence and her power. Such awakening of national consciousness was perhaps as necessary to the making of Chaucer, as to the making of Shakespeare two centuries after.

Literature inherited also the language at last ready for grander literary creations; and it received from foreign hands the moulds for them too, in many a form and device, well-

77

wrought and adapted to its purpose—romance, song, allegory, vision, debate, tale, metres—a rich equipment indeed.

But with this rich inheritance came sharp issues and rapid change. In 1349-50 the Black Death destroyed a third to a half of the people, and reappeared with all its horrors and uncertainties in 1360 and in 1379. Laborers became few, and the demand increased accordingly. Villeins were rapidly passing from a state of serfdom to a state of paid labor. Disputes and disorders over wages and abuses rose to the unsuccessful Peasants' Revolt in 1381; but, if the revolt failed in the moment, it left the tiller of soil a more regarded and conscious person than ever hitherto. With a place in the world, he finds also his place in literature.

The rising villein, the yeomen with long bows at Crécy and Poitiers, a bit later the first cannon knocking holes in castle walls—all these, if one could have read them, were signs that feudalism was passing. This issue between the old feudal order and a new humanism lies deep in literature of Chaucer's time; but still unfaded externally are all the pomp and circumstance, the color and picturesque usage, the social ideals of feudal chivalry.

At any time such changing conditions as these tend to lawlessness, extravagance, corruption, and graft. The time of Chaucer was no exception. Deep and wide ran venal peculation, through public life, through courts of justice, through the Church, and no other defect of the times calls forth such frequent and scathing reproof as this.

In Chaucer's day the Church was everybody's concern. It affected in some manner high and low, near and remote. The scholastic disputes in theology during the twelfth and thirteenth centuries had settled and put in order all details of belief, with the usual consequence that they tended in actual practice to harden into mere canting formula. Such formalism, joined as it was, and usually is, with corrupt practice, provoked criticism, attack, and reform.

Against it, however, a force had developed, working quietly but powerfully within the Church itself. This was an intense revival of religious mysticism, a burning desire to rise past all formulas and through all ritual to immediate ecstatic and personal sense of God. Such names as St. Bernard, St. Francis, St. Bonaventura, Dante, mark the tradition on the Continent. In England it had already been manifest in works like the *Ancren Riwle*, and the best of the religious songs. Nor did it end in mystic contemplation only, but bore its fruit in thousands of noble lives spent obscurely in good works, like that of Chaucer's Parson. Within the Church this tradition of mysticism was the chief antiseptic influence. It reminds us of the Methodist revival in the Church of England four hundred years later.

Furthermore the monopoly of learning by the clergy for above two hundred years had been declining. As the level of enlightenment rose among intelligent laymen their judgment of a corrupt clergy became mordant and devastating. Chaucer, Langland, Gower, the Gawain poet, though regular enough churchmen, are as outspoken against abuses as the heretic Wyclif himself.

With this same increase of layman's intelligence great literary personalities emerge. Hitherto, much of English Literature has been anonymous, or only in rare instances has it been the peculiar radiation of a single great mind. Henceforth it becomes more personal, reflecting on its various sides the individuality of a single poet.

MANNING OF BOURNE (BRUNNE)

No man of the times is more engaging than Robert Manning of Bourne, Lincolnshire. He is not a great genius, but in part he makes up the lack by his amiable and gentle humanity. What we know of him we owe to his own artless remarks. Born on the edge of the fens, he sojourned at Cambridge, where he knew Robert the Bruce and his brothers. One of them astonished good-natured Manning with his skill as a sculptor. For the rest his days were spent in the religious life in the priories at Sempringham and at Sixhills, whence he could see the great towers of Lincoln Cathedral looming across the levels,

> where Lincoln bell
> Flings o'er the fen that ponderous knell.

His treatise called *Handlyng Synne* is an adaptation of the Anglo-French *Manuel des Péchés* by William of Wadington, and runs to more than 12,000 four-stress lines. It treats in order the ten commandments, the seven deadly sins, twelve points of confession, twelve graces—a discouraging program on the face of it. Not so in Robert's hands. He writes as he says, not for clerks, but for "lewd" (uneducated) men, who know only English and who delight in tales and rhymes at games, feasts, and "at the ale." And while all Christians are his audience, he bears in mind especially the men of Bourne and of his own fellowship, in which he has been living now these fifteen years; there was the prior, good Don John of Camelton, "that now ys gone," whose "maneres" he well remembers. So his work, like his original, contains bits of sermonizing, profusely illustrated with many a diverting tale and anecdote, but so reconstructed by Robert as to suit his humble purpose. Vigorously but with sympathetic understanding he rebukes the village and rural misbehavior—witchcraft, swearing, drinking and gambling, profaning of Sunday with carols, dancing, maying, wrestling, or "summer games." Lords should not rob tenants; laborers should not shirk on the job; rich men should be up betimes and not come yawning and stretching to mass, nor should men gabble together during service, nor drink at the tavern before noon; no scandalous gossip either, to which the English are prone. Attend only the plays on the Resurrection and the Nativity in the church, not those of secular tendency in street or grove. His exhortation is always brief, practical, to the point; and then

> A lytel tale y shal you tellè
> That y herde onys[1] a frerè[2] spellè.[3]

Swearing, the special sin of the rich, he makes odious with a story of one who dreamed of a fair Mother holding before him her Baby Boy all torn, broken, bloodstained, and profaned with the dreamer's terrible oaths. He woke to swear no more.

[1] once
[2] friar
[3] relate

Robert tells a pleasant anecdote of the noble Bishop Grosse-tête of Lincoln, who loved minstrelsy and kept harpers in the next room—a doubtful practice perhaps; yet the good bishop defended it, for the harp's sweet notes defeat the devil's wiles, and when men hear gleemen sing, let them thank God, for the joys of music foreshadow the joys of heaven. Robert tells the tale with gusto. Clearly he loved innocent convivialities himself, for he grows reminiscent at times of *Havelok* and other old romances, but especially of *Tristrem*, the best of them; though singers sometimes ruin the simple old tale by silly embellishment.

He began the *Handlyng Synne* in 1303, when close to forty. In 1338, as an old man he finished another enormous task, *The Story of England,* chiefly from Bede, Wace, Pierre de Langtoft, and others, but with goodly bits of the same genial Robert, still writing for his "lewd" friends, since he had not wit nor taste for fine writing, that they may have solace and entertainment (not to say edification), when they sit together.

On the whole through Robert's work we find ourselves in a medieval English village, its dull humdrum relieved only by picturesque if sometimes brutal amusements. But, better than that, we stroll through its lanes at the side of a very good, human, practical, lovable man.

ROLLE OF HAMPOLE (ABOUT 1300-1349)

A greater than Manning is the hermit Richard Rolle of Hampole. He sprang of plain origin in northeastern Yorkshire about 1300. A precocious youngster, he was maintained at Oxford by a younger son of the Neville family, a worldly young priest who doubtless had in mind worldly uses for Richard. The boy learned a good deal at Oxford, and perhaps even sojourned for a time in Paris, but patrons and pedantry and pride of scholars revolted him, and he went home in some disgust. It was at the Feast of the Assumption in August, as he knelt in prayer in a chapel, that he experienced a strange and happy passion towards God, which grew in a few months to an exalted ecstasy, as it were in a region of heavenly song and music. Thenceforth his soul rose on flames of love for

Christ to the highest stage of human contemplation. This exaltation he maintained throughout life.

He made an odd start, however. Taking his father's rainhood and borrowing a white and gray dress from his sister, he made such a figure of himself that the poor girl fled for fear her brother had gone mad. At mass the wife of John de Dalton, keeper of Pickering forest, found this queer body kneeling in her place. Presently, however, he donned vestments, and preached a sermon that moved his listeners to tears. The lady's sons recognized him as an Oxford acquaintance, and she invited him to dinner. He behaved oddly, hung aloof, ate little, and tried to run away; but Dalton, a grasping upstart, saw how he might be turned to account, and gave him a place for a cell somewhere about his manor. After four years the plan proved not a success. For one thing, the squire's lady used to entertain crowds of curious dinner guests by taking them out to see her hermit. His proud soul revolted, and he began his homeless wanderings over the wild Yorkshire moors. Perhaps he had other patrons. Various were his retreats till near the end of his life he settled at Hampole.

Like many an able youth he early had a talent for both piquing and eluding the curiosity of others, and his writings are always tantalizing and mystifying the reader with autobiographical allusion. He was evidently a susceptible and sensitive young man and attractive to women. One experience of temptation to worldly love he later recalls in mysterious but significant terms, and his self-reproach for youthful vanities is akin to the passionate regrets of Bunyan in *Grace Abounding*. Yet he had in him a vein of clear laughter, and his soul is upborne by the joy of his perennial vision.

The twenty-five years or so of his active life—he died at Hampole near Doncaster, perhaps of the Black Death, in 1349 —were crowded with writing and preaching and counsel. No wonder so eccentric and gifted an egoist kept free of the organized ecclesiastical interests, and was more or less persecuted by bishops and monks. His hand falls heavily upon rich, worldly, lazy, and unworthy churchmen, upon scholars and doctors, and he finds many a poor man and old wife "more expert of God's love, and less of worldly liking, than a great divine."

His life was not all ecstasy; at any rate his writings yield not a few bits of hard-headed practical advice. His earlier works in Latin run a good deal to Biblical commentary, including his natural favorite, the Song of Solomon. They show at times an abandoned indulgence in alliteration, rhyme, assonance, and other rhetorical devices, after the medieval fashion, though not looked for in one so austere as Richard. But they contain also most of his notes on himself; and the *Incendium Amoris*, charmingly turned into English in 1435 by Richard Misyn, embodies the peculiar lithe, intense, and soaring energies of Rolle's mind. His later writings are in English, ostensibly designed for everyday perusal of less learned people, especially of nuns, by whom his admonition was highly valued. Emotional, exclamatory, erotic in imagery, his manner is never vapid nor soft. His vision of the Crucified is grim even to the point of ghastly realism, and in his *Form of Living* he will allow that love for God or man is true love only when it is stalwart: "For luf es stalward als the dede, that slees al lifand thyng in erth"—"For love is stalwart as death that slays all living things in the earth; and hard as hell that spares naught to them that are dead. Therefore he that loves God perfectly, grieves him not, whatsoever shame or anguish he suffers; but he joyfully yearns that he be worthy to suffer torment and pain for Christ's love; and is glad when men reproach him and speak ill of him. . . . For he or she can love no whit who may not suffer pain and wrath for their friend's love, for they who thus love feel no pain."

This was written primarily for an anchoress named Margaret Butler of Kirkley, to whose spiritual welfare he was especially devoted, and whom he twice brought out of a mysterious epileptic seizure. Occasionally he breaks the bonds of prose, and sings; but he had neither the scope of mind nor gift of song to be a great poet.

The name and power of one so extraordinary could not be confined to the nunneries and wastes of Yorkshire. His fame overflowed England. Visitors crowded round him. His works multiplied into a host of copies. Immediately after his death, the legend of miracles sprang up, and a generation later his followers were expecting him to be canonized. Well on into the Reformation his memory flourished over northern Europe. A name so great inevitably drew to itself many a work of which he was not the author.

Of these the conspicuous instance is *The Prick of Conscience*, a long poem on the misery of life, the fear of Death, on Purgatory, the pains of Hell, the joys of Heaven. Though on occasion it employs a vivid figure—comparing man to a tree, as in Swift's *Sermon on a Broomstick*—and though it found a host of medieval readers, it lacks the vigor and movement characteristic of the Hermit of Hampole.

WYCLIF (ABOUT 1320-1384)

Like Richard, John Wyclif was bred of hardy Yorkshire stock, its fibre toughened by ages of contention with marauding Scots and bleak conditions of the moors. He was born about 1320. Out of his lowly birthplace he somehow got to Oxford, and in that small but lively centre of medieval scholasticism and intellectual energy he found a congenial medium. For nearly forty years, as student and master, he breathed the academic atmosphere as his natural element, and it gave him the profound learning and skill in argument that he needed for his task. But these only reinforced great native virtues, a love of justice and intrinsic values, a belief in the common man, chivalric enterprise in his behalf, and a compelling influence over other men. Such virtues penetrate his writings, and, as in Abraham Lincoln, make them literature.

In his twenties he already so stoutly supported English resistance to Papal tribute that King Edward rewarded him with the rectory of Lutterworth near Warwick, which became his refuge in later years when the storm broke at last. On every side he saw abuses—Popes, prelates, monks, and friars, degenerate and unworthy with wealth, ease, and intrigue. On the other hand were poverty and oppression; and everywhere spiritual starvation. In his first efforts he attacked the vested church interests, chiefly in their segregation of lands and wealth to their uses—

lands which in proper use should support the people at large. In this movement he was aided and abetted by Edward III's powerful son, John of Gaunt, by Percy of Northumberland, and others of the mighty who scented rich spoils of the clergy afar off.

But honest Wyclif saw that the trouble lay deeper than economic issues. He appealed from forms to reality, questioned the old doctrines under which insincere hypocrites in high places were masking, demanded a new realization of their meaning, and a new appeal from doctors and glozers to the teaching of the Gospels. "Lord, where is fredom of Christ whenne men ben casten in siche bondage?" "Therfore fle ypocrisye, and be scolere of treuthe; and outher [either] seme that thou art, or be that thou semes." Loud on every hand rose the yell of "Heretic." Even many of his old supporters deserted him. The free spirit at Oxford, which eagerly responded to Wyclif's appeal, was throttled and strangled by royal and church authority for a century to come. Wyclif and his immediate followers fled from Oxford; but though only three or four years of life were left to him, amid his parish duties at Lutterworth he continued to preach, write, and put into effect his simple insistence on truth. Many a young priest he inspired to go in barefoot poverty through the land, preaching and doing good.

Wyclif hated war, and sought no social overturn; in fact he upheld the English manor; nor did he preach sectarian separation from the church. Yet his teachings gave rise to a large following known by their nickname as Lollards, as were Puritans and Methodists in later times. By persecutions, burnings, silencings, and recantings Lollardry was cut off from the learned, and pretty much identified with the unlearned and socially inferior classes; and Harry Bailey's sneer at the good parson as a "Loller," while Chaucer's pilgrims journeyed to Canterbury, was probably more social than religious. Lollardry long continued, however, to smoulder under cover among the poor and the neglected countryfolk, and thus survived to spring into powerful regeneration two hundred years later. So Wyclif's tradition is resumed in the Reformation of

Elizabeth's time, and Milton calls him "that divine and admirable spirit."

Some thirty separate English works and two volumes of sermons—"plain sermons for the people" he calls them—are included in Wyclif's authentic writings. Besides there are works in Latin. Whether English or Latin, most of the treatises are brief—commentaries, admonitions, simple declaration of his views on Pope, clergy, or doctrine; but many are vigorously controversial, especially in his last years. Various and sundry writers have been called by critics "the father of English prose." Such paternity cannot be proved; there were Alfred, Ælfric, Wulfstan, three and four hundred years earlier. Wyclif, however, wields a greater language than theirs; perhaps he deserves the title as much as anyone. He wrote in the Midland dialect from which "standard" English is descended. His prose is like him—untricked, unadorned, solid in texture and in argument, vigorous, even, full of natural, unconscious music, compelling, with a certain sober sweetness that enables us to see how he charmed both high and humble.

But his most famous work is his English Bible, executed in detail chiefly by his disciples Nicholas of Hereford and John Purvey, but no doubt inspired, designed, and overseen by Wyclif himself. As the laity had grown more intelligent, and corruption of the "clerks" had increased, selfish ecclesiastical interests scented a danger to themselves in the increasing popular interest in Holy Writ. To be sure, ordinary men and women then knew far more about Bible story than they do today—for all our presses and propagations. On every hand it was narrated, rhymed, carved, painted, and acted; but there was no one text in English of the time for the common man who could read. "Yit the lewid puple crieth aftir Holi Writ, to kunne[1] it, and kepe it, with greet cost and peril of here lif." There was plenty of precedent, too, the translators argued, for the Bible in the vernacular—Jerome had made it accessible in Latin of his time, Bede and Alfred, in English of theirs, not to mention a French version of these very times.

[1] con

The translation was made not from original tongues of course, but from Jerome's "Vulgate." Two versions were made during the last two or three years at Lutterworth, and the two disciples must have worked valiantly. The first version in its zeal to be literal sacrifices English idiom to the Latin; but the second version, revised by Purvey into "trewe and open" English, became a subtle but powerful determinant in English literary prose, and an influence upon all subsequent English versions. Phrases such as "a well of water springing up into everlasting life" (John 4.14) and "the deep things of God" (1 Cor. 2.10), we owe to Wyclif.

During his last two years Wyclif was paralysed and dumb, yet seems to have labored on to the end. Forty-one years after his death, his enemies in vain rage exhumed, burned, and scattered his remains to the four winds. "And thus," says old Thomas Fuller, "the Ashes of Wycliff are the Emblem of his Doctrine, which now is dispersed all the World over."

"LANGLAND"

Wyclif's surprised indignation at the abuses of his time drove him into deeds and controversy. A far different minister of vengeance did these same abuses call forth out of the West. This was the poet usually called William Langland. Of late certain writers have refused to accept this as the poet's name, or his identity with the person so vividly revealed in the course of the poem.

Whatever the fact, William emerges from its lines a living image. Tall, gaunt, rangy, big-boned, roughclad; with the loose, free walk and movements that cling through life to the farm-bred lad; his speech deep and slow; his poet's eye burning but gentle; his look grave, with underlying generous smile that illumines his presence in rare moments—such is the figure that the reader of the *Vision of Piers Plowman* discerns through the poem.

If we may accept what he and early memoranda say of himself, he was born among the Malvern Hills. It has been guessed on slender evidence that he was the natural son of a gentleman,

Eustace de Rokayle, and a farmer's daughter. Boy and youth, he lived the careless country life, had his health,

> And lymes to labore with, and lovede wel fare,
> And no dede to do bote drynke and to slepe.[1]

Thus he grew to manhood, working hard, and mastering the manifold handy arts of farm life. His farm, some think, was the tract called Longland today, lying pleasantly in a quiet valley southwest of Malvern Hills. There, or wherever, wrapt in rough "russet," he learned to tend sheep, mow, reap, bind, pitch on to the load, harrow, care for pigs and geese, set a hedge, cook, cobble, sew, and sing in the choir,

> Other eny other kyns craft that to the comune nedeth.[2]

But by an unknown disability he became

> to waik to worche with sykel other with sythe,
> And to long, leyf me, lowe for to stoupe,
> To worchen as a workeman eny whyle to dure.[3]

Yet it was through that singing in the choir that his powers and imagination had been awakened. His soul yearned up out of the farmyard mire to the cloister and the school. There the mind could find peace and security for its proper business.

> For in cloistre cometh no man to chide ne to fihte,
> But all is buxumnesse there and bokes to rede and to lerne.[4]

His father and his friends sent him to school. Somewhere William learned a good deal, but he never, for whatever reason, perhaps his birth, became more than an acolyte in the church, one who could sing certain services, but not mass, could marry, and do small clerical chores—for a consideration.

---

[1] And limbs to labor with, and loved good fare,
  With nothing to do but drink and sleep.
[2] Or any other handiwork the community called for.
  [3] too weak to work with sickle or scythe,
And too tall, believe me, to stoop over low
Or stand work of a workman, for any long while.
[4] For in cloister cometh no man to censure or contend,
  But there all is gentleness with books to read and to learn.

How he came to London no one knows. There he is in middle life, living poorly in a cottage on Cornhill with his wife Kit. Thus like many another since,

> ich lyve in Londone and on Londone bothe.

But if his labor brought little, his eye, ear, and heart took possession of all within reach, the abounding life of common sort in the country and the city, good and bad, religious and secular. He abominates the world's evils, pities its failings, understands its ills, and knows the basic remedies.

Such, whether the poet, or only a shadowy fiction in the poem, seems to have been William Langland. Meanwhile there is the poem.

The *Vision of Piers Plowman* has come down to us in three versions commonly distinguished as A, B, and C. B and C contain the substance of A often amplified or altered; but they are also extended to more than twice the original length by supplementary matter, much of it inferior to the first dozen "passus" or cantos common to all three. Hence the suspicion, not yet generally accepted, that different hands fashioned the different versions. But whatever the truth, internal evidence would suggest for A a date about 1363, for B not long after 1377, and for C possibly as late as 1393, after the decline of the weak Richard II has set in, and he is sinking to his abdication. If the one poet wrote all three, they are the work of his young manhood, his middle life, and his old age.

The poem is a series of allegorical dreams. It opens of a May morning among the Malvern Hills, where some recognize today traces of all the details in the setting of the poem. The poet was wandering about like a shepherd. He stretched himself out on a brookside, stared at the running water till he grew drowsy at its murmur, and sank into a dream. And behold, a great castle towered above him to the east, with a deep vale and dungeon below.

> A faire felde ful of folke fonde I there bytwene,
> Of all maner of men, the mene and the riche,
> Worchyng and wandryng as the worlde asketh—

farmers, wasters, tradesmen, beggars, pilgrims, hermits, friars, pardoners, priests, clerks, bishops, lords, ladies, all kinds of craftsmen, taverners—a thronging Vanity Fair, each busy in his way mid a din of street cries and popular songs.

Suddenly a lovely lady descends from the castle, who explains to the dreamer that she is Holy Church, the castle is the Tower of Truth, that is God, and the dungeon is the abode of the Father of Falsehood. At length she turns him to a vision of a gaudy woman much adorned called Meed (Graft). Many a man wishes to marry her—lawyers, scholars, knights, officers of justice—and mid a throng of suitors she rides a sheriff to Westminster to have legalized her marriage to False and Flattery. The King, however, puts her following to flight, False takes refuge with friars and merchants. But fair Lady Meed is welcome at Westminster, and the King offers her to Conscience, who refuses indignantly to kiss, let alone marry her. To settle the broil thus started the King sends for Reason, who dramatically takes the lead, humiliates the impostors, and proclaims the law of justice, which the King accepts: "That law shall be a laborer, who carts dung afield; and love shall lead the land!"

During an *entr'acte* the poet wakens, moves on a few paces, and, reciting his Creed and "babbling his beads," dreams again. Reason is now preaching to the field of folk—preaching the Gospel of work—and so effectively that not the crowd only but the Seven Deadly Sins, flock to repent and go thronging along the road in a rout to find the Truth of God. They meet a pilgrim from the Holy Sepulchre. Does he know where Truth lives? No, and he never heard even a palmer inquire before. Thereupon a poor ploughman "put forth his head." "I know Him well, have worked His farm and been His handy man for fifty winters." "Here is something, Piers, to pay you to show us the way." "Nay,

> I nolde fange a ferthynge for seynt Thomas shryne!"[1]

So honest Piers points out to the motley crowd, jostling, joking, muttering, "crying upward to Christ and his pure Mother," the

---

[1] Nay, I wouldn't take a farthing for St. Thomas's shrine!

devious way to the moated castle of Truth, with its bridge, gate, and wicket, and seven virtues as guards at the postern. "But how can we find the way, or enter when we arrive?" "Work! Work, everyone of you—even ladies and knights—on behalf of the poor." An angry waster interrupts: "I never did work, and will not begin now." But Hunger comes, and pinches and knocks him and the rest into a better mind, observing, "If men grouch, bid them go swink, and they will sleep the sweeter." It is common sense that whether

> In dykinge or delvynge, or travailing in prayers—
> Contemplatyf lyf or actyf lyf—cryst wolde men wroughte.[1]

As for Piers, he is content with his simple vegetables, his cow and calf, and his mare to haul dung afield. The best medicine is hunger; though, with the high wages, labor has nowadays grown fastidious and fault-finding; but a time of reckoning will come. Meanwhile the rich too must not forget their duties of charity, public benefactions, and endowing schools.

All which, with our inflations, and depressions, our problems of labor and capital, sounds modern enough.

A patronizing priest asks Piers where he got so much learning.

> "Abstinence the abesse," quod Pieres, "myne a. b. c. me taughte,
> And conscience come afterward and kenned me moche more."

The Bible too he has read. Whereupon their wrangling waxes so high that the poet wakes, sees the sun setting to the south, and "meatless and moneyless," goes his way.

In all three versions the poem was variously extended beyond this point in a search for Do Well, Do Better, Do Best. The scheme, however, is less definite, and the movement slackens with interpolated preachments, till the reader is forced to the conclusion that less skilful hands have tried to carry on what had proved a most successful work; or that the poet's genius, as sometimes happens, relaxed when young manhood was past, was tempted to "improve" his earlier work, and,

---

[1] In ditching or digging, or laboring in prayer—
Contemplative life or active life—Christ would that men worked.

except for flashes of the old vigor now and then, unconsciously fell, as one has said, to inditing imitations of himself.

At any rate he knew something of literary tradition outside of sacred writings. The dream and the allegory are time-honored medieval devices; and usually in the dream appears the fair lady. They are commonly traced back to such Latin precedents as the *Dream of Scipio* by Macrobius about the year 400, to the fair lady Philosophy in Boethius's famous *Consolation of Philosophy*, soon after 500, or to Lady Nature in the much perused *Complaint of Nature* by Alain de L'Isle (twelfth century). Dreams and visions, combined with allegory, religious and secular, abound in French, and "William" may have known, among others, such models as De Guileville's *Pélérinage de Vie Humaine* and the celebrated *Roman de la Rose*.

As for allegory it was an almost universal medium of the Middle Ages. To be sure the Greeks and Romans had employed it. Even in Homer is a trace of it, and Aeschylus, Plato, Virgil, and the myth-allegories of the Stoics offer examples which will occur to many. In Biblical literature the Book of Ezekiel and the Book of Revelation bequeathed a rich symbolism. But medieval literature was often peculiarly engaged in trying to make invisible things visible or at least comprehensible. This is hard enough to do in physical matters, as any scientist will agree. In spiritual mysteries it requires for success a body of accepted symbols—such as the Cross, the Seven Sins, the Four Virtues, the Pilgrimage of Life, the Castle of the Soul—and a common heritage of fairly fixed conviction in his audience about the matters treated by the poet. Such symbolism and allegory bore daily on the mind of a medieval man or woman, through all the art that surrounded him on all sides. What wonder that he looked at all animals, plants, Bible story, and classic myth as potential allegory. But symbols are now so faded, and our beliefs so at variance, that medieval allegory often seems to us remote, meaningless, and dull. Our own allegory of political cartoons, poor as allegory, is sometimes powerful enough to sway a nation. How much more the rich, varied, suggestive, and beautiful allegory of the medieval poet singing to medieval listeners.

But the *Vision of Piers Plowman* has by no means lost its power in this age, based as it is upon some of our most cherished ideas—the dignity of humble labor, the elemental beauty of the human heart that is trained in the severe school of Nature, the supreme need of honesty, justice, industry, our passionate hope for better things. Furthermore it is the work of a great poet, full of indelible pictures such as that of Glutton and his crowd drinking all day Sunday at the tavern till he walks crooked as a gleeman's cur. Such homely and racy comparison—"dainty as a dog in a kitchen"—imparts the strong flavor of the common man's wit. Vivid men and women constantly emerge from the crowd to be at once absorbed again but never forgotten, and the whole bears heavily upon the mind with the impression always of the crowd, not of individuals as in Bunyan. Piers is at all times a living figure, and necessarily so since he is the mouthpiece of the poet himself.

The poem is satire; and while the modern reader is more engrossed with its thronging spectacle than with its satirical assault upon the evils of the day, yet its satire was doubtless a chief reason for its popularity—its satire and its elevation of the peasant. It survives in nearly fifty manuscripts written during its first hundred years.

As a work of poetic art it is far inferior to Dante's great allegory—less varied, less luminous, less sustained, less exalted. Not less serious, however. It is like a gray, rambling English church of divers alterations in divers times, its fabric permeated with the labors, humors, grievances, sins, and hopes of the generations who have lived and worshipped in its shadow.

THE GAWAIN POET

Out of the northwestern wilds, from Lancashire or western Yorkshire, emerged the unnamed figure of another great poet, one whose masterpiece, *Gawain and the Green Knight,* is the most exquisitely wrought and proportioned, in some respects the greatest, poem in Middle English. Three other poems—*Patience, Purity, The Pearl*—are ostensibly from the same hand,

and perhaps a fourth, the charming saint's legend of St. Erken-
wald. In spite of much guessing, conjecture, and research, the
poet's name and identity are still unknown; he is usually called
"the Gawain poet." His language is difficult for the modern
reader on account of his dialect, which, though it is touched
with artificial modifications, is essentially the obscure language
of fourteenth-century Yorkshire or Lancashire. Yet in his work
the poet unconsciously gives the reader a most intimate sense
of his personal quality.

What seem to be his earlier poems, *Patience* and *Purity*, are
? homiletic works. But the good medieval preacher had invariably to be a good story-teller. Hence *Patience* is chiefly occupied with a lively version of the story of Jonah (oddly enough
not Job, as one would expect) full of vivid details. In the
storm passengers in a panic throw overboard

Her [their] bagges, & her fether beddes, & her bryht wedes,

together with chests, coffers, and chains; and the whale rises
to Jonah while the folk still hold him by the feet. Into the huge
throat he slips, "like a mote in a minster door."

Purity is a longer poem of the same sort, urging not only
chastity but purity in the larger sense of general sinlessness,
on the text, "Blessed are the pure in heart." But sincere as
is the poet's suasion, the poem is really a cluster of Bible
stories—the parable of the wedding of the King's son, the
stories of the Flood, of the burning of Sodom, and of Belshaz-
zar's feast and the writing on the wall. The poet's range has
broadened, his stroke is more dexterous and effective. The
terrible storm of the flood is set forth true to English tradition from the Old English *Exodus* down; but we find also a
charming idyll of Abraham in the shade of an oak at his
"house-door," and a resplendent spectacle of the Temple and
its fittings, all in ornate Gothic style, glittering with metal and
precious stones.

More moving, and more mysterious, is *The Pearl*. The poet
possessed a rarely beautiful pearl which one day slipped down
into the grass of a fair garden and was lost. In agony day
after day he visited the flowery spot, and mourned at the

mound where she sank into the dark mold. Worn out at last with grief and self-pity, he fell into deep slumber, and his soul was borne in a dream to the fair summer country of the Earthly Paradise. As he hurried in his excitement along the turfy bank of a river, he caught sight, on the farther bank, of his lost Pearl, dearer to him "than aunt or niece," a maiden arrayed all in white and pearls. Dismay, shame, fear, joy struck him dumb, till she smilingly made as if to speak. Then his incoherent feelings burst forth in a torrent, until she gently rebuked him, and showed him the way of peace in forgetting himself and accepting God's way.

As his soul clears, she directs him up along the river till he gains a little hilltop. There the gleaming City of God bursts upon his sight, and, like the full moon rising at twilight, emerges the vast procession of the redeemed, the Pearl rejoicing among them.

> They walked with joy beyond compare
> The golden road that shone like glass;
> A hundred thousand I thought they were,
> And all alike their raiment was.
> Hard to tell the happiest there.
> In front the Lamb with stately pace
> His seven golden horns doth bear;
> And priceless pearls his garments grace.
> Thus to the throne they move apace,
> Not thronged but ranked in even plight,
> And mild as maidens seem at mass;
> So walk they forth in great delight.

Transported with the vision the poet plunges forward to cross the river but is thrust back, and wakes with his head on the very mound where he had lost his Pearl. But his life is now transformed into patient service and expectation of reunion with her in eternal joy.

Some have maintained that this poem is a mere allegorical fiction to convey certain theological ideas, or various phases of religious experience. But the very intense and impassioned quality of the poem, reflecting as it does the type of mind deeply preoccupied with its own state and experience, are more than a mere conventional literary fiction can contain.

Impassioned as the poet was, his poem is so symmetrical in form and so conventional in its elements that, without his intensity to fill it and make it real, it would seem purely artificial. The metre is a rigid twelve-line stanza, one hundred and one of them, strictly and elaborately rhymed, in groups of five, and linked together with a common phrase or cadence. The poem is a composite of medieval literary device—the dream, the debate, the allegorical disguise of the pearl, homiletic and theological exposition, insistence on chivalric virtues, and adorations in chivalric terms. Clearly the author was highly sophisticated in literature. He may indeed have known the *New Life* in which Dante mourns his lost lady, or Boccaccio's lament for his little daughter in his eclogue called *Olympias*.

But, in *Gawain and the Green Knight* he attains his full stature. Here the seasoned and sophisticated poet has taken popular matter and the common popular form of the romance as composers select folk-songs, and has transformed them into a great work of art.

The story opens with a New-Year festival at Camelot, when in rides a huge green knight, all in gorgeous green trappings, on a green horse. "Who will chop off my head with this green axe, and let me chop off his, at the green chapel. a year hence?" All are dismayed and silent.

Then young Gawain accepts the challenge, and swings a great blow. Across the floor leaps the head; the body strides after it, vaults to the saddle, and with a laughing reminder of the contract, is gone.

In their fair courses the seasons pass and the year wears on till November and All Saints. Then Gawain makes ready for his journey to keep the New Year tryst. Long, lonely, and cheerless it is, into the wild mountains of north Wales along the Menai Straits, and into the desolation of Wirral. Homesick he is plodding through the driving sleet on Christmas Eve when he comes upon a fair castle.

Here he finds a hearty welcome and luxurious comfort;[1] and the bluff and brawny Lord of the Castle, rejoicing to have so distinguished a guest, makes a playful contract with Gawain. Each day he goes hunting, while Gawain rests in bed. At night each is to give the other his day's quarry. On successive days the man brings home a deer, a boar, a fox. On successive days, in his absence, his Lady comes to Gawain's bed and tempts him. He parries her, at first timidly like the deer, next day fiercely like the boar at bay, the third day with fox-like wiles. Each day she kisses him. Each night Gawain gives his host hearty busses in exchange for the quarry. But the third day he is weak enough to accept the lady's gift of a wound-proof girdle.

The New Year is at hand, and he must now be off for his tryst with the Green Knight at the Green Chapel. On the very day he is led to a desolate snow-filled hollow among the cliffs; and deserted by all, he comes at last upon a chapel of turf. Out strides the Green Knight, axe in hand; Gawain kneels, and the blow falls, but is stayed. Poor Gawain flinches. A second time the falling axe is stayed, but this time he does not waver. The third blow wounds him slightly, and he springs, with nerves overwrought, to defence. But the Green Knight coolly explains that he was Gawain's recent host, Bercilak de Hautdesert; that Morgan the enchantress, Arthur's half-sister, had devised the whole plot; that Gawain's one error in accepting the lady's protecting girdle had cost him the little wound. Gawain, with mingled shame and happy relief, refuses to return as Bercilak's guest, and makes his long, lonely way back to Camelot.

Such in brief is the story. It employs various traditional elements of old romance, quest and adventure, courtesy, love; but two old themes of chivalry the poet has wrought into a close-fitting whole—the challenge and the temptation—and has united them by many logical bonds of character and action. These motives seem to have come to the poet through his knowledge of French romance, which in turn derived them from older Celtic legend. Some scholars go so far as to as-

[1] See above p. 48

sume a lost French original from which *Gawain and the Green Knight* was adapted. But if such an original were discovered, it would probably not impair the credit of the Gawain poet any more than Holinshed impairs that of Shakespeare.

Not only is the poem closely coherent, but it shows the same nice symmetry as *The Pearl.* The 2500 lines fall into four "fits" or acts, the first and fourth devoted to the challenge, and enclosing the two devoted to the temptation. The third act includes three skilfully varied scenes in which each day's temptation is enveloped in the story of the day's hunt. And the whole poem is neatly brought round at the end to the point of beginning.

In metre it is less rigid than *The Pearl*—in varied unrhymed long stanzas of alliterative verse, each rounded off with "bob and wheel," a short quatrain attached to the stanza by a three-syllable phrase.

Alliterative verse is usually beset with sins of prolixity and tortured artificial phrase; but this poet's energy of imagination rises above these faults, and fills his line with natural music in unison with his thought and feeling. For he delights in many things—in good cheer, fair raiment, rich furnishings, fine manners, in the change of seasons, in all details of the hunt, in the moss-green Welsh winter forest of oak and hawthorn, in lonely mountain glades muffled in snow, in the delicate parry of playful talk. He well understands certain issues of warfare in the human soul; to him sin is extraneous filth; and its opposite is steadfast, active endurance, as adorable to him as it was to Milton. These issues he has wrought into the highly dramatic and very human scenes of the romance, particularly in the closing scene between Bercilak and Gawain.

Who was this great poet? We may never know; yet his greatness will ever tease the curiosity of scholars till he may some day be found. Meanwhile conjectures are not wanting. If, as seems likely, he wrote *The Pearl,* he may, as some reason, have been a secular clerk in the service of the Earl of Pembroke, son of Edward III, and *The Pearl* may have been an elegy for the Earl's dead little daughter Margaret (a pearl).

Or he may have been John Erghome, an Augustinian friar in Yorkshire. Nothing is proved.

Unlike his contemporaries the Gawain poet is neither satirist nor reformer. Clearly he knows and loves the church; possibly he served in a lower clerical rank as some great man's chaplain, for the details of courtly life in various aspects are matters of course to him. He could not have been unaware of the time's abuses; indeed, like many sensitive folk, may have felt helpless and paralysed by them. He avoided public strife and contention, cared little for fame, and was preoccupied rather with the warfare of the individual soul. Amid the abuses about him he found his nurture in the surviving beauty of old ritual, architecture, music, literature, in Nature and the pure human heart. Nor is his a fugitive and cloistered virtue, for all his work is unmistakably charged with a certain hearty, cheerful, winning gentleness that identifies him far more than a knowledge of his name could ever do.

CHAPTER 5

Chaucer

(1340?-1400)

WELL on in the pilgrims' famous journey to Canterbury, Harry Bailey, the host of the Tabard and master of ceremonies, called on Chaucer for his story. The poet had hitherto kept in the background, though before they had set out, he had made a point of speaking with each of his fellow travellers. "What a man!" said the Host;

> "Thou lookest as thou woldest fynde an hare,
> For evere upon the ground I se thee stare."

"Come forward, man, look cheerful" (the Prioress had just finished a sad story), "What a dainty waist! Like mine" (the Host was a big fellow).

> "He semeth elvyssh by his contenauncè,
> For unto no wight dooth he daliauncè."

Chaucer protests that he is no story-teller, knows only one old rhyme; "some dainty thing," the Host infers from his looks. But it proves to be a tedious old romance, so tedious that the Host stops it, for even he is bored with its bourgeois commonplace.

How much of this is Chaucer's true portrait of himself, and how much ironical sly caricature? There is reason to think that he was not tall, but ruddy, plump, and cheerful, with pointed beard, and, one imagines, of kindling eye, quiet voice, and few words. In his *House of Fame* he has the eagle reprove

him for indifference even to his next-door neighbors; for
after office hours he runs home,

> And also domb as any stoon
> Thou sittest at another book,

like a hermit. And in the Prologue to the *Legend of Good
Women* he confesses that nothing can tear him away from
his books, but a holiday or the spring,

> Whan that I here the smalè foules syngè,
> And that the floures gynnè for to spryngè.

Many a sleepless night he takes an old romance to bed with
him. It is clear at any rate that this man loved the country,
loved an old book, loved fun even to the point of his own
joke on himself. And it will appear that, big or small, assertive or shy, nothing human escaped his ever questing eye
and ear.

Geoffrey, son of John Chaucer a wine merchant, was born
in London not earlier than 1340. He came of middle-class
stock, but through some association of his father with the Court,
became a youthful page to Elizabeth, wife of Lionel, Duke of
Clarence, younger son to Edward III, and thus began his great
career.

Like Arcite in the *Knight's Tale,* it seems

> his name is sprongè,
> Bothe of his dedes and his goodè tongè.

First "valet," then "squire" or secretary in the King's household, his duties became more and more responsible. Meantime
in 1359 he had gone campaigning in France, was taken prisoner, and ransomed. In his middle twenties he married a
lady-in-waiting, Philippa Roet, eventually the sister-in-law of
John of Gaunt. Two sons, Thomas and "litel sone Lowis,"
were born—whether other children is not known; nor whether
the marriage was happy. Certain lines of the poet about marriage have led some to think that it was not, but that does
not follow. The most happily married are sometimes the very

ones to think every other venture but theirs either a failure, or at best only a partial success.

Meanwhile Chaucer seems to have had no university education. Possibly as a lad he went to a London school. The cathedral school of St. Paul's in his day was equal to providing such equipment of literary knowledge as he had. He spoke and read French of course, and probably spoke, certainly read, Italian. He also read Latin, yet not so easily but that on occasion he found an Italian "crib" easier. With such gift of tongues he proceeded in the rigorous manner of a genius to educate himself, ranging freely through many writers, and appropriating what he required. Of these four were chief— Boethius and his *Consolation of Philosophy;* Jean de Meun, satiric co-author of the *Roman de la Rose;* Boccaccio, both in his Italian and his Latin works; and Ovid, who was Chaucer's favorite narrator of classical lore. In one place he speaks of owning sixty books "olde and newe," a large library for the times.

In 1367 Chaucer was rewarded by a life pension for services to the King, and the next year he made his first recorded official journey to the Continent. Meanwhile, as a young courtier in his twenties he turned off "balades, roundels, virelayes" in the fashionable manner of contemporary French poets, studio pieces, probably in far greater number than have survived. He may also have begun his translation of the *Roman de la Rose.* Translations are often a great poet's means of schooling himself in the technique of his art. In 1369 he wrote his first considerable poem, *The Book of the Duchess,* in memory of the lovely young Blanche, wife of John of Gaunt, just dead of the plague.

During his thirties Chaucer was much engaged in diplomatic services, and an important member of some eight commissions to Flanders, France, or Italy. Of these the Italian journeys of 1373 and 1378 were of most importance. All told he must have spent a year's time in Italy, including Florence, and such contact with the world of Dante, Petrarch, and Boccaccio had profound influence on his mind and art. Some wish to believe that he met the great Petrarch, but proof is still wanting.

The years from 1374 to 1386 were a busy time. Not only had he his diplomatic duties, but he was serving as Comptroller of Customs, in a responsible post of the bustling port. Salary was small, but there were good perquisites and associations with men of wealth and importance. Yet he somehow hoarded leisure enough to finish several great poems—his *House of Fame*, his *Parliament of Birds*, and his greatest complete work, *Troilus and Criseyde*. Besides, he translated Boethius's *Consolation* and wrote several of the stories afterwards embodied in the *Canterbury Tales*, including that of the Knight. He lived with Philippa in a rent-free house over Aldgate in the city wall to the east, which, thus removed, looked into the city on one side and across country on the other— like the poet who lived in it. As the years passed he became a man of substance and importance, receiving various royal benefits, among them a daily pitcher of the royal wine, afterwards commuted to an annuity. It has been guessed that during these years of business his average income varied, in equivalent, from $10,000 to $15,000. !

In 1386 he ceased to be Comptroller, gave up the Aldgate house, and seems to have retired to an estate of his own in Kent, not far from town, and lived as a country gentleman. He was justice of the peace, and sat briefly in Parliament as member for Kent. But business did not get the best of poetry. He began his collection of tales called *The Legend of Good Women*, interrupted in 1387 by the grander and more absorbing scheme of *The Canterbury Tales*. And among the rest he had his literary friends—the poet Gower, the scholar Ralph Strode, and the distinguished French poet, Deschamps, who sent him a highly laudatory ballade honoring the "grant translateur, noble Geoffroy Chaucier."

Thus he lived a busy practical life along with a busy poetical one, and who shall say which was more important to his art? Greater responsibilities awaited him. From 1389 to 1391 he was Clerk of the King's Works and had charge of repairs on some eleven royal abodes together with their grounds, not to mention incidental tasks of erecting temporary stands for tournaments, and the repair of banks and bridges along four miles of the Thames below London. For two years he seems to have discharged the heavy duties of this office ably and well. He was then appointed to be forester of the royal forest at North Petherton in Somerset. His last decade may have been divided between the forest and London; or possibly he never saw the forest, but farmed out his duties and enjoyed the income. Somehow during his last years he became less wealthy, though perhaps not so poor as has been supposed. His *Complaint to His Purse,* one of his last poems, is a whimsical perversion of lyric love. Various are the records of his suits, debts, payments, and collections. In 1399 he took a house close to Westminster Abbey. There he died the next year, and was the first of the famous poets to be buried in what has become the Poets' Corner.

Through all the turmoil of the times and its three kings, the decline of Edward III, the misbehavior of Richard II, the usurpation of Henry IV, in spite of vicissitudes these kings were alike in their regard for the welfare of their faithful and gentle servant Geoffrey Chaucer.

Chaucer's poetry has been divided between a French period, an Italian period, and an English period. French influences no doubt determined the quality of his early work, and he was deeply schooled in them; Italian influences followed from reading Dante, Petrarch, and Boccaccio; however, neither French nor Italian influences were ever superseded, but were subtly absorbed by the growing energies of his native English genius.

Chiefly from his early years, but also scattered through his life, issued short "complaints," to his Lady, to Pity, of Mars, of Venus; envoys, like his jokes on his friends Scogan and Bukton; ballades, like the noble one on Truth, on Gentilesse, and on Lack of Steadfastness.

From early youth Chaucer had doubtless been a reader of the famous love allegory called the *Roman de la Rose.* At any rate either in his youth, or perhaps not until his forties, he translated at least a part of this vast poem. The first 4068 lines were the work of Guillaume de Lorris, born about 1200. Forty years after Guillaume laid down his pen, it was continued to 22,000 lines by Jean Clopinel de Meun.

Guillaume, the idealist of chivalric love, when not yet twenty, dreamed, so he says, a May morning dream of bright fields and birds, of a garden enclosed in frescoed walls and filled with fair ladies dancing. By a Narcissus fountain a lovely rosebud was bursting into bloom. An arrow from the love-god's bow pierced his heart, and he would forthwith have seized the rosebud, for it was his lady-love. But affairs of the heart are not so easy. Between hosts of allegorical friends, such as Generosity, Fair-Welcome, and Courtesy, and hosts of allegorical enemies, such as Jealousy, Danger (Woman's Disdain), and Wicked Tongue, the poet's love is put to trial, the plot is complicated, vicissitudes arise, and various nice points are debated at length. Doubtless Guillaume, like any kind novelist, would have brought his lover eventually into happy possession, but at the moment of the lover's deepest despair his work broke off.

When resumed by Jean, the fair dream light has faded, and the action slackens under the cold literal daylight of Jean's cynical satire. Yet he keeps the scheme and the characters; if only to deliver long speeches which strip the medieval cult of courtly love naked of all its idealism.

This extraordinary work had enormous influence, direct or indirect, not on Chaucer only, but on much of the poetry of the next three centuries. It is another instance of the quickening influences from the South that breathed warm life into English Literature. It is an epitome of medieval literary devices, conventions, and ideas about love. In its day it was enormously popular in France and England, and is still an amusing, often charming, handbook of the code of love in the medieval world. The allegory, the dream, the May morning, the meadow, the garden, the frescoes of famous love affairs, the fountain, the trial of the lover, the porter Idleness, the personifications, the arrows of Cupid, the debate, the contrast of carnal and ideal love in Venus and Cupid, the siege—

these and other devices appear and reappear in various combinations of various poetic merit.

Fragments survive of a Middle English translation of several thousand lines, but with the doubtful exception of the first 1200 lines they are not Chaucer's. Yet translate the poem he did, at least in part, thus schooling himself in all its allegorical devices, and what is far more important, attuning the English language to the exquisite refinements of French love poetry, in accents of which it was hitherto incapable. Thus he built the great instrument for his mature performance yet to come.

The dream loveliness of Guillaume captivated Chaucer; but so also did the cynicism of Jean. This we infer from the frequent reminiscence of the *Roman* in his various works. Chaucer was great enough to embrace both and realize the usefulness of each. In one he valued the rich heritage of the chivalric age, now passing away; in the other he recognized the weakness of that age through the depreciating eye of Jean and the new spirit of the dawning Renaissance.

In his exquisite and youthful *Book of the Duchess* Chaucer employed several of the court-of-love devices—an old love story of Ceys and Alcyone from Ovid and Machaut, the May-dream, the birds singing matins, the meadow, the cruelty of Fortune, and the "complaint," this time not of the lover, but of the widower. For John of Gaunt disguised as a "man in black," laments in a "debate" the loss of his beloved "White," the Duchess Blanche. She had died in 1369.

Within the next ten years Chaucer again uses the court-of-love devices in a grander project—*The House of Fame*. Again the dream, the temple, the frescoes, the allegory; again Venus and the rehearsal of old love-stories. But it is now December, not May, and the landscape a desert from which the austere eagle of Jove carries Chaucer, as he had carried Dante, up to a "sudden view of all this world at once," past clouds and brewing storms to the palace of the goddess Fame. There amid reverberations of all the world's music, and babel of the world's rumor, crowds of men press forward to the goddess's throne for fame. It is a picturesque, but disillusioned review of the perennial human instinct of self-advertisement. The poem has come down to us not quite complete, but its two thousand lines reveal a Chaucer emerging from his French school. His stroke is more vigorous with new Italian energies, especially those of Dante—for he had already sojourned many months in Italy. Virgil, Ovid, Macrobius, and others have reinforced his growing powers. Old romance now serves a grander, more austere use. Through the allegorical veil we discern a Chaucer amid the world of men, interested but coolly observing how most things are at sixes or at sevens, yet heartily detesting pretence and dishonesty.

Once again, probably in the early eighties, Chaucer fingers the old devices in his *Parliament of Birds*. He falls adreaming over the popular *Somnium Scipionis,* and in a lovely garden on St. Valentine's Day hears the birds "debate" a love affair. Some have associated the poem in one way or another with the betrothal of young King Richard to Anne of Bohemia, or with a wedding in John of Gaunt's family, but nothing is proved. The allegory of birds of prey (peers), water-birds (merchants), seed-birds (farmers), and worm-birds (lower class) suggests something in the poet's mind of larger social import than a mere love affair, even a king's.

Somewhere in the 1380's his greatest complete work engaged his energies—the *Troilus and Criseyde*. Grand in its very proportions—it is cast into five books of seven-line stanzas, totalling more than eight thousand lines—it is grander still in its simplicity and its searchings of the human heart. For his story Chaucer went to Boccaccio, who in his poem *Filostrato* had developed a mere love episode in the *Roman de Troie* of Benoit de Sainte-Maure, written about 1160, and in a Latin prose version of the *Roman* by Guido delle Colonne of 1287. Chaucer also consulted Benoit and Guido, besides Joseph of Exeter's twelfth-century Latin poem. Ostensibly then the *Troilus* of Chaucer is one of those romances of chivalry dealing with the "matter of Troy" which go back for their story, not to Homer, but, by link after link, to late Latin versions of the famous tale. But Chaucer has built something far exceeding the limits of a mere literary species.

The events are simple enough. Criseyde is a fair young widow of Troy, whose father has deserted and gone over to the Greeks. Troilus, boasting himself love-proof, falls desperately in love with her. His friend Pandarus, also Criseyde's uncle, manipulates a series of communications and meetings by which Criseyde's heart is won, and the two lovers are for two or three years consummately and secretly happy. But an exchange of prisoners tears them apart; and, though she promises in ten days to return to her courtly lover, the Greek Diomede, a common, masterful man of action, irresistibly usurps Troilus's place in her heart. Poor Troilus in despair, rushes to his death in battle.

Such is the bare story told by Boccaccio and Chaucer. But Chaucer has modified and expanded the material, and, like a good playwright, has detached himself from the narrative. He has cast it into five books, as it were into five acts, and each book is but a succession of scenes in dialogue with briefest description, rapid stage direction, and occasional lyric intervals. In the first book the hopeless Troilus is transformed by Pandarus's promise of help; in the second the lovers meet for the first time; in the third the affair is consummated; in the fourth they part; in the fifth Troilus despairs at last. The poet shows all a dramatist's skill in crises, transitions, interludes, and suspense.

But in a profounder sense he is a dramatist. He has humanized his characters and set them in highly dramatic contrast with each other. Troilus is the central figure—young, engaging, active, the perfect courtly lover, an idealist, loyal and enduring, to whom lack of faith and disloyalty are simply incomprehensible. On the other hand Criseyde—sweet, helpless, lovely, without much mind, easily subject to the will of others, yet ever practically aware of her situation, to whom the present necessity is far more pressing than past or future; who thus, like many another, proves untrue in the end, breaks a man's heart without really meaning to, yet seems hardly to deserve the harsh condemnation which both Troilus and Pandarus hurl after her. Then Pandarus, a warm, loyal friend, practical, intriguing and resourceful, conventional, correct, sensible, but incapable of idealism, laughing down matters of serious concern, genial and likable without charm— he is a perfect foil to the principals.

Great power the poet shows in his invention or elaboration of scenes—the first meeting of the two after Deiphobus's dinner-party, where the suspense and secrecy are heightened by the hurried manipulations of Pandarus; or the meeting of consummation at Pandarus's house; or the scene where Troilus seeks comfort but finds only desolation in gazing at the shuttered and deserted house of his lady. Not less is the vigor and sophistication of Chaucer's dialogue. Wit, finesse, badinage, quick interplay, strong emotion, laughter, tears, trembling, all enter into the wonderful scene wherein Pandarus first tells Criseyde of Troilus's passion. With equal delicacy Chaucer traces the course by which "Troilus and Troietown," when once Criseyde has gone over to the Greeks, slid "knotteles thorughout hire herte."

With all the fears and hopes of a lonely lover, Troilus on the tenth day climbs the walls to catch the first glimpse of Criseyde returning as she had promised. All day he watches. Once in the gloaming he thinks he sees her. Then in deep night he goes home still hoping. At the very moment she is listening with interest to Diomede's first compelling plea. The irony of the situation is in tune with the irony of the whole poem. The perfect lover finds his perfect mate. With the skilful help of a friend and happy accident they possess one another in bliss. All is as it should be. Yet the end is betrayal and death. Troilus can only moan: "I have it not deserved." Pandarus had done his best. In his dismay he can only curse the woman. Yet such is the world, says Chaucer:

> In ech estat is litel hertes reste;
> God leve us for to take it for the beste!

This world seems all a matter of blind Fortune or destiny. Meanwhile what remedy? Beneath the poem runs a stream of laughter, which breaks forth at times in the various voices— hearty, or bubbling, or cynical, or bitterly mirthless. And the soul of Troilus at last looking down from Heaven's felicity laughs at the pettiness and confusion he has left behind.

To such conclusions averring the destiny or mutability of mundane things, Chaucer may have been encouraged by reading his favorite Boethius *On the Consolation of Philosophy*. But the *Troilus* ends with an epilogue and prayer. And though this is a literary convention, yet in the present instance these closing lines are vibrant with tension which is anything but specious, as he commends young, fresh lovers who would love aright to consider "that sothfast Crist"

> For he nyl falsen no wight, dar I seye.

The *Troilus and Criseyde* is a medieval poem. Its Troy is medieval, its costumes, its social manners. It embodies the ideals of courtly love—the enduring lover, his acute distress, the lady slow yielding, the consummation without marriage, the secrecy; yet an ideal love by courtly standards, which is far above mere carnal desire, for it brings the man to noblest realization of himself, and condemns utterly the unfaithful one.

But Chaucer has touched the old conventions with the greatness that undates them, charging them with thought, feeling, and behavior that are still and at all times human. The fine young man of ordinary mind, physically active and courageous, passively luxuriating in his emotions; the woman, sweet, of good intention, equal only to the immediate moment, far more actual than Irene Forsyte; the disillusioned man of the world, unprincipled but devoted, with no ideals other than those of his "set"; the selfish, irresistible, always successful, woman-questing, unloved man of affairs: the reader of *Troilus* has not merely read about these, he has met them in the flesh.

In 1385, by the appointment of a deputy controller, Chaucer gained more leisure for his beloved books, and soon after he was at work upon his *Legend of Good Women*. It turned out to be a rehearsal for his grand masterpiece, consisting of a long Prologue and nine tales completed, with ten more projected.

The tales are sweetly, briefly, and gracefully told—about

Thisbe, Dido, Ariadne, Philomela, and other such love-lorn
ladies of antiquity. Ovid, in his *Heroides,* and Boccaccio had
successfully compiled such groups. But vary them as he could,
Chaucer seems to have been bored with their sweet monotony,
and to have forsaken them for perhaps the same reason that
their lovers did. /

His Prologue pleased him more, for he revised it after he
had abandoned the legends. We must agree with his preference. It opens with a confession of faith:

> A thousand sythes have I herd men telle
> That there is joye in hevene, and peyne in helle.

Perhaps. No living man has been in either. We can only believe old books. As for Chaucer,

> these olde aproved storyes
> Of holynesse, of regnes, of victoryes,
> Of love, of hate, of othere sondry thynges—

it is between them and a meadow in May that his heart is
divided. At all events he once slept and dreamed in such a
meadow—and of course found himself again in the complete
setting of the court of love, fair ladies and all. This time he
adores not the rose, but the daisy, as in French margarite
poems—Love's queen, Alceste, possibly at moments an allegorical disguise for Queen Anne, to whom he dedicated the
poem. The god of love scolds him for his slander of women,
for example, of Criseyde. Alceste "debates" the case, and im-
poses the gentle penance of composing the legends of good
women. The old conventions still, but so subdued to the
poet's power that he can play with them as he pleases, and
make them serve the mature vigor of his artistic purpose.

The *Legend* may have been crowded from Chaucer's mind
by the lustier idea of the *Canterbury Tales.* Such groups of
"frame-stories" had been devised long before—*Arabian
Nights, The Seven Sages,* Boccaccio's *Decameron*—but the
one most like Chaucer's scheme of a pilgrimage is the *Novelle*
of Sercambi of Lucca, written after 1374. Whatever its source,
the new project sprang up into stout and original growth in

the English poet's mind. Everyone has read of the thirty or so pilgrims at the Tabard Inn of an evening, cheered by a good supper, and all agog with travellers' anticipation of the exciting journey to Canterbury and the shrine of St. Thomas the Martyr. It is springtime;

> Thanne longen folk to goon on pilgrimages.

Which is Chaucer's grave way of saying, with a twinkle, that when spring gets into his bones, one feels like breaking bounds, and cutting a caper.

And what an array of rank and calling—high, humble, bad, good, lively, dull—no wonder some have thought it was the poet's object to have all classes represented. More likely his poet's eye had singled out of his wide world certain picturesque originals to begin with. There was, it seems, an actual Tabard Inn in Southwark, and an actual, well-known innkeeper named Henry Bailey. These figures, real or imaginary, he developed with due regard to artistic and dramatic juxtaposition. It was a happy idea of Chaucer's to assemble this odd assortment away from home and social hindrance, in that genial humor of the road that melts the barriers and lets the mind flow free.

By the Host's proposal each of the pilgrims was to tell two stories on the journey out, and two on the way back, making about one hundred and twenty altogether. Only a quarter of these were finished, together with the great *Prologue*, single prologues to various tales, and "links" or passages of transition between certain of the tales. In its unfinished state the work consists of ten fragments, but the exact order in which Chaucer would have arranged them, whether all were tales for the outward journey, or some for the return, whether the sixty miles to Canterbury were to be covered in two, three, or four days, are still questions of debate. Some are literal enough to object that one mount could not easily tell a tale to thirty other mounts strung along the road. Chaucer's comment on such a comment would be worth having. He has created genial conditions perfect for story-telling, and that is enough.

Clearly the Knight was to begin, followed in order by the

Miller, the Reeve, the Cook. Then the succession is broken;
and the final order, even if it was settled in Chaucer's mind,
cannot be determined.

1387 is the usually accepted date at which Chaucer entered
upon his grand undertaking, though several of the tales, certainly the Knight's and the Second Nun's, had already been
composed. We may think of the poet during those last thirteen
years finding, as he had leisure, his happiest solace in work
on his masterpiece.

The great *Prologue* is doubtless the most original part of
the *Canterbury Tales*. There is precedent in plenty for the tales
themselves, but nothing before in literature like this astonishing series of portraits. One knows not whether to wonder most
at their variety, their grouping, or the easy vigor of execution.

The reader passes as it were through chamber after chamber
of a portrait gallery. There are finished full-lengths, half-
lengths, sketches, miniatures. The Knight is flanked by Squire
and Yeoman. Three superb full-length portraits of Prioress,
Monk, and Friar, fill another wall. The grave Clerk stands in
fine contrast between the Merchant and the Man of Law. A
brilliant sketch in white, blue, orange-red, and black, pure as
an old illumination, drawn as by magic, is the Miller; the
Yeoman is a smaller one in green. Variously does Chaucer combine features, manners, history, costume, and accoutrements.
Where the mind of the subject is shallow he leans on externals
for effect. But in such as the Knight, the Friar, or the Parson, color and objects are subdued, and the deeper, graver
quality of heart and mind preoccupy us. With the strict economy of the great artist he chooses the all-significant detail:

> Of fustian he wered a gypon,
> Al bismotered with his habergeon.

Which is not only picturesque, but expresses more than pages
could the seasoned, hard-riding, unromantic knight in the real
world—no plumed young carpet-dandy of old romance.

The supreme reality of Chaucer's portraits convinces one
that he had originals for at least some of them. There was
Harry Bailey; and perhaps Henry of Lancaster suggested the

Knight. In any case the Prologue carries us into the living, actual English world of the fourteenth century. Yet it has an even deeper reality, reminding us of people and types we know. The Knight and the modern explorer, the Prioress and the lady-principal, the Merchant and the commercial traveller, the punctilious lawyer—these are obvious modern counterparts; and not modern only, for they will be familiar in every age.

Chaucer's portraits embody a triple reality. They are individuals sharply defined; yet they are also typical—a typical monk; a typical seaman; beneath all is the base of common unchanging humanity which alone makes the greatest art and poetry.

One of Chaucer's favorite words is "old," and in his *Canterbury Tales,* as elsewhere, he has chosen only stories told before. In this he is but like the others of his class—Shakespeare, Spenser, Milton. Besides, like his Pardoner, he prefers

> oldè stories longè tyme agoon,
> For lewed[1] peple loven tales oldè.

But his interest was not merely antiquarian. Stories oft-told have improved by the telling, and have absorbed something human from every skilful hand that touched them; a new-minted tale is barren.

> For out of olde feldes, as men seith,
> Cometh al this newe corn fro yeer to yere;
> And out of olde bokes, in good feith,
> Cometh al this newe science that men lere.

Varied as were his sources, he therefore dared to select well-worn "favorites," which took new life from his magic touch. The Knight repeats a high romance of two men and a girl from the "matter" of Thebes, as told by Boccaccio in his *Teseide.* The Miller and the Reeve tell racy *fabliaux* of common life, often written down, oftener told in a corner, and cleverly localized, after the habit of those who purvey them. The Wife of Bath, vulgar and blowsy, was naturally put down

[1] uneducated

for a *fabliau*, but Chaucer, with exquisite art, gives her a "lay,"
a charming old fairy-tale known in all lands, of the disenchant-
ing kiss. Less appropriately the Man of Law repeats the ever-
moving story of Constance, long-suffering from one mother-
in-law after another, not to mention others; more than twenty
versions of the tale were current at the time. Out of old Christian tradition came the Prioress's high and tender story of the
little school-boy martyr. Everywhere, in Orient and Occident,
was known a story like the edifying *exemplum* of the Pardoner.
The Franklin recalls an old Breton lay. The jolly "sweete
preest" draws from the animal cycle of Reynard, famous over
all Europe, but especially in France and Germany, a rousing
tale of the Cock and the Fox.

Not more varied are the origins of these tales than their
quality and manner of telling. *The Knight's Tale* is a most skilful condensation of Boccaccio, which Chaucer has made wholly
his own, warm with old romance, dignified with courtly love,
splendidly picturesque in setting and spectacle. It unfolds itself
essentially in act and scene as did *Troilus*. And yet sympathetic
as he is with all this beauty, Chaucer is never wholly nor sol-
emnly committed to it. There is Theseus, magnanimous, dignified, likable; yet sententious, long-winded, without sense of
humor, soft towards the ladies, and greedy of the "public eye"
—in short, one perennial kind of politician. Other touches of
amusing realism, of Chaucer's sly humor, often too sly to be
caught at once, or his sudden droll reversals of mood, as at
the moving death of Arcite—all these elements serve as foils
to the romance, and tend not to wreck its delicate beauty, but
to refine it.

But not all is delicacy. With broad and unerring stroke
Chaucer presents the rough, coarse, sometimes brutal farce
that delights the ordinary man, yet always with the verve of
the great artist. At the opposite extreme are the stories of
the Man of Law, the Prioress, the Clerk, the Second Nun, all
in the same seven-line stanza of lyric quality, setting forth examples of high and devoted patience of women and children
under affliction. On this plane the poet holds in check his instinct to make fun, and reverently clothes these exalted figures

in the tender and delicate beauty characteristic of the ripest medieval art.

The Priest's story of the cock and the fox, and the Pardoner's story of the rioters and their ruinous folly, are a comic and a serious example of the same method. After a strikingly picturesque beginning, to get attention, the tale begins to move, though at a pace purposely so slow that the reader grows impatient—the modern reader is often exasperated. But gradually it gathers momentum, and at last rushes headlong to an overwhelming conclusion.

Both stories are charged with Chaucer's usual vivid, distinct animation. His animals, for all their humanity, never for a moment cease to be animals. Chaunticler is a Theseus, yet never ceases to be a cock; Dame Pertelote combines the virtues of the Wife of Bath and the Prioress, yet is all hen.

The *Pardoner's Tale,* which is only an *exemplum* in the clever but shameless sermon of that precious rascal, deals with events rather than characters—events in which moral cause and effect and destiny agree. And the dominating figure of that strange, meek, old man! Chaucer clothes him in uncanny mystery—is he Death? or the Evil One? or some moral force? or just a wise old man? Nothing can surpass Chaucer's subtlety in this bit of art.

Chaucer's greatness is based on his power of portraiture. He has the clarity of Holbein, a wider range than Velasquez, and more pictorial power than Sargent. His representation of Nature ignores the grand, the sublime—later times were to discover these—but it is full of the creative energy which permeated Nature, as his times saw it.

> Emelye, that fairer was to sene
> Than is the lylie upon his stalke grene.

Not primarily a resemblance of color, or delicacy, or stateliness, or what not, but of the fresh life that fills the whole plant, and flowers in all the other graces.

With such powers Chaucer generally used, and needed, little poetic embellishment. True, his earlier work is often "aureate" with all the flowers and "colors" of medieval rhetoric, and he can for the occasion recall these fineries later. But his imagery is usually simple and natural. He loved a racy proverbial simile, caught from the wit of common men. It is no wonder that his wide range between coarse and fine, between high and low, and his relish for everything human, made him, and make him, a popular poet for all times that can read him.

Yet what conclusions did he draw from this amusing, sad, gross, noble, lively, good, bad world that surged about him, but did not overwhelm him? Fortune or Destiny seems to have some part in it, he agrees with Boethius; a man must face the situation like a man. He favors the man capable of dreams and ideals and mysticism over the merely practical man of affairs. The world is full of gross abuses and wrongs and impostures. What can one do about it? Chaucer is no reformer like Wyclif or Langland. He views the rascals with amused contempt, or sometimes transfixes them with terrible power. At times he questions old beliefs about Heaven and Hell, and what becomes of the soul, but with no bitter scepticism; and the faith of the old Church, without its fine points of doctrine, is still a comfort to him.

In fine his view of life is sympathetic though aloof. He keeps out of the tragic depths, and views his wide world with the detachment of the comedian, transcribing it for us vigorously, but with delicate and profound subtlety.

CHAPTER 6

Decline

GOWER (1330?-1408)

ONE of Chaucer's literary associates was "moral Gower," to whom he inscribed the *Troilus*. John Gower was the elder by several years, though he survived his greater friend. He was a Kentish gentleman of good substance, generous to the church, a lover of peace, and keenly interested in public affairs. He had great expectations of young King Richard, but as both king and times went to the bad, his waning hopes turned to Henry Bolingbroke, soon to make himself Henry IV.

Gower took his literary talents seriously, lightening the account of his stewardship to God, as he put it, with three enormous works, the *Miroir de l'Omme* of 30,000 lines in French, the *Vox Clamantis* of some 10,000 lines in Latin, and the *Confessio Amantis* of almost 34,000 lines in English. He added for good measure various minor works in all three tongues. The *Miroir* is a deliberate, tedious, but well-rounded allegory of the human soul and its usual war with sin. The Latin work hopefully addresses the young king, and at the same time points out the almost hopeless conditions in England—the Peasants' Revolt, the panic of the "classes," the spread of Lollardry.

Perhaps Richard was edified, for one day when Gower met the royal barge on the Thames, he was summoned aboard to receive the order for a new book, something entertaining—on Love. Poor Gower was then sick and old. Was this a cruel joke of the King's, or a mad whim? He sets manfully to work, and after a review of good old times and the bad case of this

shoddy present, when men "feigne chalk for chese," he di-
agnoses the malady as a complication of division and greed.
With everything so gone to wrack, what can poor Gower do
alone? What, but

> lete it overpasse
> And treten upon othre thinges.

So he rears the old framework of the court-of-love, with himself a lover confessing to the priest Genius, like penitent Nature in the *Roman de la Rose*. There follow eight books, strung
on the line of the Seven Deadly Sins, a library of short stories
from Ovid, the Bible, and wherever, ranging from brief anecdote to the grand finale of Apollonius of Tyre, the story of
Shakespeare's *Pericles*. They are *exempla* of much interpolated
moral admonition and love-talk, ingredients not always happily blended. The stories of Chaucer's Man of Law and Wife
of Bath are included. The exact relation of this collection to
Chaucer's *Legend of Good Women* and the *Canterbury Tales*
cannot be ascertained. At any rate it was not eclipsed by them,
for it succeeded enormously, and was read for two centuries.
Let us not wonder; the perennial human hunger for fiction,
somewhat overfed nowadays, met, after all, with slenderer,
and generally more delicate fare, at Gower's and Chaucer's
hands.

At the end of the *Confessio* famous lovers, including Solomon, his wives and concubines, come crowding and leering
about the poor old amorous man. In a mirror handed him by
Venus he catches a glimpse of his eyes, sad and faded, and
his sallow, thin, and wrinkled cheeks. Reason returns, Genius
absolves him, and Venus gently rouses him from his dream.
He smiles as he thinks of the beads she pressed into his hand
at the last, and goes home to pray for the regeneration of
clergy, knight, merchant, and king. This touching close is the
most moving part of the whole poem.

Gower was a good workman; his lines are faultless, moving
at even pace, so much a day; he will not hurry, he will not be
hurried. He abounds in the "gentleness of old romance."
Rarely comes a flush of excitement as in the tale of Medea.

Yet every part is coolly finished and well-rounded, and in this respect he could instruct Chaucer. His knowledge seems encyclopedic. Yet in learning he is a mere dilettante compared with his great contemporary, and in art a journeyman.

THE FIFTEENTH CENTURY

After the death of Chaucer in 1400, England produced no literature of quality as great as his till the time of Elizabeth.

For the century that followed him English culture stagnated and fell away. Doubtless the chief reason for this arrested growth was almost continuous war. The Hundred Years' War, which opened so prosperously under Edward III, in spite of the much-sung victory of Agincourt, wore on to a dreary and ignominious close as the last English soldiers stole out of France in 1453. Only two years later began the civil Wars of the Roses, to drag on for another generation, till the old medieval world had at last bled itself to death, and the strong Tudor hand of Henry VII in 1485 established a new order in the land.

What with misrule and mismanagement, the cultural and social level sank far below the level of Chaucer's day. It was, as one of the times says, "a right wild" England, hard, violent, unjust, dreary. Long afterward Shakespeare unerringly perceived and reflected it in the first act of *Richard III*. Perhaps no single bit of writing can impart with equal concentration the hard quality of fifteenth century English life, at least among the upper classes. But the best contemporary witness is the great collection of letters known as *The Paston Letters*. The Pastons were a substantial Norfolk family. Incidentally the letters are full of intimate and amusing details, but they are chiefly occupied with constant strife to maintain the family's property and position by fair means or foul against the corruption, violence, and anarchy all about them, in high places and low.

LYDGATE (1370?-1451?)

In such conditions polite literature could only mark time if it survived at all. The old forms and devices reappear again

and again in enfeebled instances, and Chaucer is followed by
a school of imitators. But "no man ever became great by imitation." Of these imitators the chief was John Lydgate, who
was already a young poet when Chaucer died. He was born
at Lydgate, near Newmarket, about 1370. He had been a
fractious youngster, untruthful and impudent; but one day
when he was fifteen, as he walked along a cloister, his eye fell
casually upon a crucifix painted on the wall, with the word
"vide." Deep into his soul the figure burned its way. His hour
struck, he entered the religious life, and became a monk of
St. Edmundsbury. But years of struggle and insubordination
were to follow before he found peace. Monk though he was,
he visited many cities and lands, in his "thred-bare coule,"
including Paris and perhaps Italy, and had some narrow escapes. He enjoyed also the acquaintance and patronage of the
great, including the illustrious Duke Humphrey of Gloucester,
Henry V's brother. In his last years he sought the peace of his
old monastery again.

His talent was prolific to the extent of more than 120,000
lines, in poems long and less long, numbering at least one
hundred and sixty. He must have known his Chaucer by heart.
Servile reminiscence of phrase and cadence is continual. Personal acquaintance with Chaucer in his youth is not unlikely,
and over twenty times he pauses in his verse either to mention
him or praise him and his works at length. He always uses
Chaucerian metres—four-stress and five-stress couplets, the
eight-line, and particularly the seven-line stanza. His *Siege of
Thebes,* an old romance from the French, he alleged in a clever
prologue to have been a tale told by himself to Chaucer's pilgrims on their return journey.

He also made from Guido delle Colonne's prose account
his *Troy Book* in 30,000 lines of heroic couplet. But it is over-
topped at 36,000 lines by the *Fall of Princes,* done at Duke
Humphrey's order, and based on a French version of Boccaccio's Latin work on the falls of famous men, *De Casibus Illus-
trium Virorum.* ❦

Gynnyth at Adam & endith at kyng John [of France].

It belongs to the same morose family of ill fortune as Chaucer's *Monk's Tale,* and the *Mirror for Magistrates* of Elizabeth's time.

We can no longer endure these debauches of gloom; we only wonder at the host of readers who loved them in late medieval and Tudor times, and were perfectly happy to luxuriate in the woe of innumerable "falls" and "complaints." Was it by reason of the misery and discomfort of the times? Or was it a survival of the Anglo-Saxon elegiac strain? Or an insecure sense of the old world slipping and dissolving into a new age? Whatever its cause, this passion for woe is significant, and had its eventual part in the creation of great English tragedy.

Another colossus was Lydgate's *Pilgrimage of the Life of Man* from the French allegorical pilgrimage by Deguileville. It belongs to the poetic strain of which in time sprang Bunyan's masterpiece. For the rest, Lydgate's inventory includes a court-of-love poem—*The Temple of Glass*—moral allegories called *The Assembly of Gods,* and *The Court of Sapience,* saints' lives, especially a fine one of St. Margaret, "mummings," animal and bird poems, satires on fashions, devotional poems, and his autobiographical *Testament.*

Whatever else Lydgate learned from his adored Chaucer, he failed to learn brevity. Everything he undertakes must be carried to lengths. "Longe stories *a* woord may not expresse." His workmanship is uniformly good, but then it *is* uniform. Perhaps he comes nearest the vibrant poetry of his own heart in passages of adoration to the Virgin or to Christ, especially in his *Testament* and his *Life of Our Lady.*

OCCLEVE (1370?-1450?)

Less prolix than Lydgate was Thomas Occleve, but not less devoted to his dear master and his father Chaucer, who

> fayn wolde han me taght,
> But I was dul, and lerned lite or naght.

His poetry gives no hint of country breeding, and he lived a cockney life, mostly in the Strand. He had been trained for the priesthood, but somehow missed out, and for many years earned his slender living as a copyist in the office of the Privy Seal, with occasional patronage of the great. By his own account, till he was about forty he ran a frisky course among the taverns; but he talks of it like the unconsidered old fellow whose reminiscence is a much deeper purple than the fact.

At middle age he married—for love. But evil days came upon him: he was ill, for a time mad, poor, deserted by his old friends. Through it all his wife, it would appear, took faithful care of him.

His _Regiment of Princes,_ his greatest work, in almost 800 seven-line stanzas, he designed as instruction to young Prince Henry, soon to reign as sixth of the name. It is based on Aegidius's _De Regimine Principum,_ illustrated with anecdote, and embodies a wide range of reading. But if the royal scion read it, his edification had to wait for 2,000 lines, while Occleve recounts his rambling wayside discourse with an old beggar. He talks on volubly about himself, about women, about the bad times, and how hard it is to get along, and how much harder than you would think it is to copy, copy, all these years; he feels it terribly in his eyes, his back, his stomach; and so on. In other poems also, _La Male Regle,_ his _Complaint,_ his _Dialogue_ with a friend, his ballades, whatever the nominal subject, it is Occleve, his life and opinions, which are uppermost and recurrent. He is a timid, unassuming egoist, this fifteenth-century Pepys, amusing and amiable in his verse, though in the flesh, one suspects, he might now and then have been a bore.

Henry VI was insane, anyhow.

He is talented, usually lively; sometimes rising to the pitch of simple glowing devotion so characteristic of Middle English. And if he is less an artist than Lydgate, his intimacy often makes him more readable.

OTHER CHAUCERIANS

Chaucerian styles in literature, more or less artificial and "aureate," continued in many anonymous poems. A conspicuous specimen is the _Court of Love,_ lively enough, but memorable as furnishing the most complete exhibit of the conventions of that convention. Far more lovely is _The Flower_

and the Leaf, by the first unmistakable poetess in English Literature. It is an exquisite and most tuneful pageant of knights
and ladies, set in the trim, green, medieval garden landscape.
With true feminine subtlety in scheme of color and costume,
it presents the issue between the green laurel of enduring
fame and the transient beauty of the daisy. Later, when the
Chaucerian music had died out of the language, the poetess
wrote a less successful *Assembly of Ladies,* in which the costuming sounds like a glorified society report. The eternal feminine is sweetly discernible in

> Thus as I stood musing ful busily,
> I thought to take good hede of her aray:
> Her gown was blew, this wot I verely,
> Of good fasoun, and furred wel with gray.

JAMES I OF SCOTLAND (1394-1437)

Soon after Chaucer's death a young Scottish prince was
brought captive to London. For nearly twenty years he was
held in exile, yet with all cultural and social privileges. One
day from his cell-window he spied the fair Jane Beaufort
walking in the garden, and fell in love with her. At least so
he tells it in his *King's Quair,* though the cell-and-garden setting may be borrowed from the *Knight's Tale* of his admired
Chaucer. But he married the lady and returned to Scotland to
rule ably as James I. His violent death at forty-two is told in
Rossetti's fine poem *The King's Tragedy. The King's Quair*
[Book] is one of the finest products of the Chaucerian school.
To be sure it employs again the worn old love allegory, but
makes it new and young by the warm, genuine, high-hearted
temper of the poet; and his seven-line stanzas sing with a
new music which has justly earned for this metre the name of
"rhyme royal."

DUNBAR (1465?-1530?)

The art and school of Chaucer did not confine itself to English bounds, but captivated other poets of Scotland than King
James, such as Henryson, Lyndsay, Douglas, and best known

of them all, William Dunbar. To "reverend Chaucere, rose
of rethoris all," to Gower and Lydgate, Dunbar confesses their
debt:

> Your angel mouthis most mellifluate
> Our rude langage has clere illumynate, . . .
> This ile before was bare and desolate
> Of rethorike or lusty fresch endyte.

His two Chaucerian May-dream poems are perhaps his best
known—*The Thrissil and the Rois,* in which thistle and rose
are crowned king and queen of flowers to celebrate the wedding of James IV to Margaret Tudor; and *The Goldyn Targe,*
wherein the poet at an allegorical archery contest is wounded
and made prisoner to Lady Beauty. The first is in rhyme roya',
the second in a difficult nine-line stanza admitting only two
rhymes. The rough Scots burr imitating the "sugurit lippis and
tongis aureate" of the Chaucerians in these artificial measures
is indeed a mingling of thistle and rose, with a resultant beauty
and vigor of its own quite foreign to southern poetry.

Little is known about Dunbar. He seems once in young manhood to have knocked about the world as a friar, but, revolted
by the prevalent practice of that calling, became a pensioner
and laureate of the King. Yet his frank and hearty soul uttered
itself freely in vigorous comment on the vicious brutality he
saw in and about the Scottish court, while the quality of his
singing voice is modified and softened now and then with his
tender reverence for the Queen. In his *Dance of the Sevin Deidly
Synnis* lively and picturesque allegory is mingled with reality,
much as in the opening of Burns's *Holy Fair;* and the two
men are akin in their humor, as one may see who will read
The Petition of the Gray Horse, Auld Dunbar.

MALORY

The most distinguished English writer of the fifteenth century was Sir Thomas Malory, of the estate of Newbold Revel
near Rugby. He came of Norman line, and as a young man was
in the following of Richard Beauchamp, Earl of Warwick,
"the fadre of courtesie." There is fair reason to think that in

his impressionable teens he accompanied the Earl on his extensive two-year tour of Europe, in which the usage and chivalry of the high world were to be seen at their best. He doubtless served valiantly in the French wars. What may have been the stirrings of his chivalrous soul if, as seems likely, he looked upon the dreadful death of Joan of Arc at Rouen?

On his return he served in Parliament. Then after 1442 follow nearly twenty turbulent, mysterious years. We have only the court records to go on, but according to these Sir Thomas was continually under arrest for such crimes as cattle-lifting, forcible entry, larceny, rape, jail-breaking, and conspiracy. His trials were repeatedly postponed or inconclusive. The mere records would make him appear a desperate outlaw.

But there is his book, with an unmistakable gentleman behind it. Let us remember that it was a day of gross injustice. Sir Thomas lived in Wyclif's old region, and the air was full of Lollard hatred of rapacious lords and abbots. Accusations and proceedings were dictated by the vested interests, and Sir Thomas for whatever reason took his stand against them. He would seem to have been associated with humbler men in vain and frantic resistance to oppressions of the time. Without other recourse he took to violence. He may have been ill-advised, troublesome, obdurate, but a gallant soul for all that.

He led raids on two religious houses hated by their neighbors for their hard dealings. Once he broke jail by swimming the moat. From 1451 to 1460 the story is a tangle of imprisonment, durance, bail, and French leave. After 1460 the years are wellnigh blank, except that he lay confined in Newgate. He seems to have been more a political prisoner than a felon. He was twice passed over by a general pardon, once in 1468 perhaps for taking sides with the Lancastrians. In 1469 or 1470, the year before his death, he closed his great work, asking "all gentlemen and gentlewomen that read this book of Arthur" to pray for his deliverance.

Over the way from Newgate was the library of the Grey Friars, chiefly founded by Lord Mayor Richard Whittington, and during his not uncomfortable confinement Sir Thomas may well have had the range of it, gathering the matter for his

"Dick" and his famous cat of legend.

Morte d'Arthur. He often speaks of his original as "the frensshe book," but no such single book has appeared. It may have existed, or he may have used the term as a symbol for his own compiling. The *Morte d'Arthur* at any rate derives from various late French prose romances on Tristram, Lancelot, Percival, and Merlin, and from English originals, including the alliterative romance *Le Morte Arthur*. It is, first of all, a vast repository in twenty-one books of medieval chivalric legend accumulated about the name of King Arthur. It was made late in the fifteenth century, when the days of active chivalry were over and the natural growth of the legends had ceased. The book is a sort of Arthurian museum to which English poets, artists, and readers generally have gone for their Arthurian matter, from that day to this. Spenser, Tennyson, Morris, Abbey are among its heavy debtors, and the *Morte d'Arthur* has done more than any other book to keep alive the glorious memory of Arthur.

But it is also the greatest prose masterpiece English Literature had yet produced, and one of the greatest altogether. Historians of fiction sometimes call it the first English novel. Read on end it seems at first incoherent and fragmentary. Many legends are picked up, handled, and dropped; but later the main strands, the Grail story, the Tristram story, the love of Lancelot and Guinevere, the Round Table, begin to emerge, and to converge upon the passing of the great principals and all their noble world.

Much has been made of Sir Thomas's prose style. It looks simple, unconscious, like the direct statement of a bright boy. Sentences are elementary and brief, verbs and other words of action prevail, all words are concrete. But appearances deceive; in fact Sir Thomas devised this beautiful but artificial style as a quaint, expressive, vigorous medium, the best in which to set forth the fading and lamented glories of the good old days. The characteristic sweetness of Middle English melody is gone, but the old vigors are there, and with the rapidly disappearing inflections, the movement is freer and more direct.

So it befell on a night, at midnight he arrived afore a castle, on the back side, which was rich and fair And there was a postern opened towards the sea, and was open without any keeping, save two lions kept the entry; and the moon shone clear. Anon Sir Launcelot heard a voice that said, Launcelot, go out of this ship, and enter into the castle, where thou shalt see a great part of thy desire. Then he ran to his arms, and so armed him, and so he went to the gate, and saw the lions. Then set he hand to his sword, and drew it. Then there came a dwarf suddenly, and smote him on the arm so sore that the sword fell out of his hand. Then heard he a voice say, Oh man of evil faith and poor belief, wherefore trowest thou more on thy harness than in thy Maker? for He might more avail thee than thine armour, in whose service thou art set. Then said Launcelot, Fair Father Jesu Christ, I thank thee of thy great mercy, that thou re- provest me of my misdeed.

Events quickly follow events, speeches and dialogue are brief, scenes are set not by description but incidentally and vividly, and the even, strong forward stride keeps up. Colors, forms, actions are clear and simple. There is no sentimentality, no vague symbolism or subtlety, no shadowy Celtic fairy-lore, no exquisite shades of character. The whole is spread broad, plain, and even, like a fine picture-book; it has the clear definition of wall painting and stained glass in which moderns have loved to reproduce it. It is the old story, dear to the author, carefully enshrined in his loving emblazonry.

Its charm is the charm of Sir Thomas himself, and his pas- sions and experience underlie it. He loved horses, hunting, action in the open air. In the grown man survived the boy, and thus he wrote a book for both boy and man. He had been beaten in a hard struggle with the brutality and disorder of his times. In the old days, he says, gentlemen and gentlewomen were constant and high-minded. Now their love is but a hasty heat, "soon hot, soon cold: this is no stability." What must his stout soul have suffered during the long years of confinement! What wonder that he, "a gentleman of the old school," cre- ated a spacious world out of the old materials, in which he was free to live, range, act, and dream, and into which he poured his old adventures, his loves, his sufferings, and pos- sibly his hopes.

When Caxton printed the book in 1485, he did so "that noble men may see and learn the noble acts of chivalry"; and he besought lords and ladies that they "take the good and honest acts in their remembrance, and to follow the same." Perhaps Sir Thomas, as he wrote, also looked forward out of his troubles more than he looked back, but even his highest expectations could not foresee the subtle and transforming influence of his work, direct or indirect, upon the modern mind, both adolescent and mature.

PART THREE

COURTIER AND BURGHER

CHAPTER 7

The Renaissance

"The Renaissance." It is a name long in use for the general revival of European culture from, say, 1450 on, which was nourished on the rediscovered civilization of Greece and Rome, and through a new science and new political and educational theories led to the modern emancipation of the human mind.

But with better knowledge of the facts it has become clear that this revival began long before 1450, indeed was making interrupted starts back as far as Chaucer's time, nay, even in the days of *Beowulf* and the Irish missionaries.

But whether this last revival is really a new Renaissance, the latest of several in succession through seven centuries, or whether it is only a late phase of one continuous but fluctuating movement, is not here to determine. It remains the most complex, perhaps the deepest change with which we have to reckon.

This Renaissance; this new birth; this revolution in the mind of Europe—what was it? So confusing were its many features and actions, that one can hardly do better than remember that it was primarily bred and reared by a new and ever clearer realization of Greek and Roman ideas, and the Greek and Roman world. From this revival spring practically all the multiform changes of life, art, and ideals included in the term Renaissance.

Without the revival of the ancient world some change would doubtless have come to pass. Yet to the ancients and their ideas more than to any other influence except native tradition, we owe not only our modern literature, art, architecture, but our conceptions of science, our modern sense of beauty in Nature and the human body, of truth in the physical world, of government, of education, of philosophy, of the importance and the absorbing interest of the individual man.

All these new ideas and conceptions reborn out of the ancient world did not, as often averred, destroy and sweep away the faith, the chivalric ideal, and the social organization of the Middle Ages. But they did modify and transform them, reshaping them at first rapidly, then more slowly, into the Christian civilization of our own time. Our democracy, our courtesy, our freedom of faith and speech, are the offspring of this union of Greek and Roman culture with medieval.

After Rome fell in 496, the culture of classical antiquity died down to its roots, but the roots were always alive, deep in European soil, and ready at any favorable moment to spring up again. So they did more than once—in the English monasteries of Bede's time, at the court of Charlemagne, and again in France in the great twelfth century. These revivals never got well under way. Disorders stopped the first two, and the all-absorbing scholastic theology, though based on Aristotle, dwarfed the third, yet not before it had produced many copies of classical manuscripts and such a humanist as John of Salisbury.

But in Italy, amid Roman ruins and remains, as society became more stable in the thirteenth and fourteenth centuries, the great revival again set in. Dante, in his *Divine Comedy* and his other works, gave his readers a new sense of the human reality of Latin poets, especially Virgil. Petrarch and Boccaccio spent most of their great genius collecting manuscripts, interpreting the ancients and bringing them back to life. Wandering

Greek scholars came out of the East, were entertained by these
two great Italians, and the modern study of Greek began.

Very limited at first, the study of Greek was then, as at other
times, a high index of cultivation. Other revivals had come
chiefly through Latin. Now men's minds found immediate contact in Greek with Homer, Plato, and Aristotle—men who had
long been famous through Latin writers, but whom these moderns had never yet seen face to face.

Petrarch, Boccaccio, and their successors in the study of the
ancients were called "humanists." They viewed the ancient
world as a group of great personalities—Socrates, Virgil,
Cicero, Homer, the philosophers—which naturally made them
think of themselves in the same terms; hence the name "humanism" for the study of Greek and Latin, and for the view
of life which such study commands. The humanists talked
about Homer, Cicero, and Plato as if they were friends in the
flesh, and wrote letters to them.

When Petrarch and Boccaccio died Chaucer was still young.
Yet he had seen Italy, and his poetry is full of strong impulses
of the revival. He knew no Greek, but he made abundant and
admiring use of Latin poets and classic myth, and his humanism is manifest in his subtle understanding of human nature,
and in his living portraiture of many human varieties.

In Italy and France the Renaissance developed in due course
during the fourteenth and fifteenth centuries. But in England
after Chaucer it subsided and paused for one hundred years.
Wars and misrule gave it no chance. Only in 1485, at the close
of the petty battle of Bosworth Field, where the first great
Tudor, Henry VII, overthrew Richard III, a new order began.

While the Tudors ruled, from 1485 to the death of Elizabeth in 1603, England was passing the prolific youth of her
Renaissance. In its first half her energies were spent in readjustments and the rejuvenation of old traditions which reached
to the depths of her being. Such readjustments and transformations postponed the magnificent literary harvest for which
they were preparing until the reign of Elizabeth.

Various old frameworks, social, political, religious, dissolved or slowly assumed new forms. Henry VII made an end

of the enfeebled old feudal barons, and with them passed
the feudal world. In its place gradually rose the new nationalism. But first the strong hand was necessary, and the Tudor
theory was one of absolute rule. The ideals of the Italian
tyrant princes—d'Estes, Sforzas, Medici—such as were later
embodied in Machiavelli's book, *The Prince,* served as a model
for the Court of Henry VIII. So the Court became the dominant centre of national culture for the sixteenth century and
more. Old Chivalry was changed to new Courtesy.

> Of Court, it seemes, men Courtesie doe call,
> For that it there most useth to abound;
> And well beseemeth that in Princes hall
> That vertue should be plentifully found.

So observes Edmund Spenser, who was in a position to know.
He and others comment too on the crude new aristocracy which
the monarch had created to take the place of the feudal barons.

But against such absolutism was slowly rising from beneath
that indispensable, fertilizing element in the making of England, the common people.

For one thing, after the long fifteenth-century wars they were
again getting rich, rapidly and sensationally. Wool-raising,
weaving, speculation in the vast holdings of the Church which
were being seized and distributed to favorites by Henry VIII,
privateering among rich Spanish and Portuguese treasure-ships
—these were common means of piling up private sudden wealth
for energetic commoner as well as aristocrat. Tudor society exhibits all the familiar crudities and social shift which attend
quick affluence, and such crudities, with the slow cultural rise
of the "new" citizenry, will, if kept in mind, account for many
things to be met with in Elizabethan life and literature.

Common men, as their lives found more room, were learning, observing, thinking for themselves. The authorities in matters of religious faith as they grew more worldly forfeited their
power. Men must see for themselves. The Bible, for example,
what did it actually say, and what did it mean? The old crav-
ings of Lollardry, still alive in humble and obscure hearts,

sprang into new life, and one English translation of the Bible succeeded another.

Laymen in the Middle Ages were well versed in Bible stories, but by almost every other means than reading for themselves. The Protestant Reformation reasserted the supremacy of the Bible, as the only safe guide for faith and practice of the individual man, and tried to strip it of the traditional glosses and interpretations. Tindale's words are famous: "If God spare me life, ere many years I will cause the boy that driveth the plow to know more of the Scriptures" than the theologians.

William Tindale (d. 1536) was of obscure origin, an Oxford and Cambridge scholar, laboring in exile, and at last suffering martyrdom near Brussels. He had caught undying inspiration from the great humanist Erasmus (1466-1536), and made his English Bible with all the powers of a devoted scholar and a devout man. Though not complete, yet it has served as the determining basis of English versions to this day. Biblical translation is by its nature conservative, and the supreme language and style of our English Bible, which more than any other single generating force has entered into the bone and fibre of English prose and poetry, even of Shelley and Swinburne, Whitman and Hardy, owes more to Tindale than to any other one man.

Miles Coverdale (1488-1568), gentle soul, completed Tindale's work, smoothing certain of the rougher rhythms, and introducing such familiar terms as "lovingkindness" and "tender mercy." His version of 1537 was the first Bible printed in England. The Matthew Bible (1537), and the Great, or Cranmer's Bible (1539-40), were essentially versions of Tindale and Coverdale. The Rheims and Douay version was Catholic.

But the Geneva Bible (1560), of Calvinist origin, became the familiar household version, the Bible of such as Spenser and Shakespeare, and was not superseded in the popular ear till the Authorized Version of King James in 1611. Tindale, and in greater measure the Geneva, had gone back to Hebrew and Greek originals, though the Latin versions, especially the so-called Vulgate of St. Jerome, were always in the translator's eye.

The English Bible, then, is a work of broad composite authorship, embodied in language purified and simplified by many refinings, and charged with spiritual energies of many great souls, bringing the best of ancient Hebrew history and ideals to reinforce those of modern England. It has been the library of humble and great, a treasury of the best literature, vigorous, exalted, easy to understand, and universal in its human range. Its noble cadences and rhythms heard almost daily have charmed the English ear from childhood, and attuned it to the finest music of poetry.

CAXTON (1422?-1491)

Before Henry VIII became king there had already been devised on the continent the most powerful instrument of all for common enlightenment—the printing-press. It was to make cheap and accessible the means of nurture by which the world was to grow.

The art of printing was late in reaching England. William Caxton, a well-educated Kentish man, went abroad in his youth and became well off in the cloth business, so that in his forties he could afford to abandon himself to literature. A printing-press at Cologne in 1471 fascinated his practical mind, and three or four years later he printed his first book at Bruges, his own English translation from French called *The Recuyell of the Histories of Troy*. This was the first book printed in English. In 1476 he returned, press and all, to England. Nearly eighty other items, great and small, he issued before his death in 1491. They include Chaucer, Lydgate, Gower, old romance, the *Golden Legend* of saints' lives, and liturgies; but for his edition of Malory's *Morte d'Arthur* that work might hitherto have been unknown. Caxton's books and those of his apprentice and follower, Wynkyn de Worde, show the survival of medieval taste, but about 1510 the press responded to the stimulus of Erasmus and the New Learning, and humanistic and religious works multiplied apace.

Caxton was not a mere printer, but a literary man. He made

his own translations from the French, and his little prefaces and conclusions are rare blendings of good critical sense, humor, and mellow quality of mind and style. He is a fine specimen of the mingling of old and new—the old language, whose rapid change he laments, the old chivalry and romance, the new enterprise and individualism meet in this self-reliant, rising young layman, holding in his hand the instrument which has moulded the modern mind.

REJUVENATION

Looking backward, one may see that after 1400 the momentum of medieval literature was spent. The school of Chaucer, with all its modes and matter—the Court of Love, Chivalry, lyric forms, rhetoric and devices, grew feebler and feebler. What new enthusiasms were there to take their place?

There was the matter newly recovered out of ancient authors—history, biography, poetry, speculations on philosophy, politics, and Nature. There was—as always—love, in this case the old courtly love made young by the infusion of Plato's philosophy; and there was medieval mysticism likewise renewed by mingling with Plato's mystical ideas. There were the problems and themes of the Reformed Religion. There were besides the fascinating forms of ancient literature to copy and emulate. All these interests and enthusiasms stirred Italy and France before England was ready for them. Wherefore English literature of the Renaissance was often created under the influence of Italian and French successes in imitation of the ancients, even though the ancient classics were at the same time directly in the English eye. Yet through all modifications medieval ideas persist. The medieval notion of tragedy as a fall of the mighty from prosperity to adversity becomes transmuted eventually by the new cultural forces into such masterpieces as *Macbeth* and *Othello*.

With the feudal decay and the accession of new knowledge, new ideas, and new nationalism, life became suddenly fluid and plastic. New men emerged, and gained wealth, enlightenment, importance. The whole world was expanding. New lands late found beyond the seas contained infinite wealth, infinite possibilities. Men's minds were dilated with hopes and swam with heady dreams. It seemed there was no bound to their imaginings or powers. As Tamburlaine says in Marlowe's play:

> Nature that fram'd us of foure Elements,
> Warring within our breasts for regiment,
> Doth teach us all to have aspyring minds:
> Our soules, whose faculties can comprehend
> The wondrous Architecture of the world:
> And measure every wandring plannets course,
> Still climing after knowledge infinite,
> And alwaies mooving as the restles Spheares,
> Wils us to weare our selves and never rest,
> Untill we reach the ripest fruit of all. . . .

We have already observed that great literature, however refined or learned or polite, must draw its essential vigor through the tap-root reaching deep into the common life of its people. Throughout the course of English Literature this is true, and examples abound. Folk-song at intervals revives the politer lyric. The popular ballads, though somewhat patronized by polite literature till late in the eighteenth century, were none the less imparting vital strength to it. Especially in the Tudor Renaissance was literature fertilized by the interfusion of the new learning and common English energies. What more convincing example than the rise of Elizabethan drama?

SKELTON (1460?-1529)

An early instance, however, of the two elements not wholly fused is John Skelton. A university man, tutor to Prince Henry, the Eighth to be, much at Court, bred in the "aureate" Chaucerian tradition, capable of high elegance, yet he launched his fun and his boisterous satire in homely phrase and vigorous doggerel. He made bold to revive the wilting stock of poetry by bringing in rich, new soil from the low places. With a hint from the exquisite dead-sparrow poem of Catullus, and with spadefuls of learning and church ritual shoveled roughly in, he makes a broad-grinning, racy lament for little Jane Scrope's

Philip Sparrow which the cat ate. Through the mouth of rag-tag Colin Clout he rakes the priesthood. His *Tunning* (brewing) *of Elinor Rumming* is *genre* painting in bold strokes, of life in the tavern, rougher far than Burns:

> For though my rime be ragged,
> Tattered and jagged,
> Rudely rain-beaten
> Rusty and moth-eaten,
> . If ye take well therwith,
> It hath in it some pith.

In his *Bowge* (rations) *of Court* he belabored the vices of the great, and in later poems bombarded the magnificent Cardinal Wolsey with his rough satire, till prison, we are told, was a last resort to keep him quiet.

In Skelton were met the two new energies which in time united to produce the literature of Elizabeth's England. But his homely vigor and his classical learning never blended, never merged one in the other. Indeed, his learning was superficial, and his sympathies more medieval than humanistic. The merging of polite learning with national vigors necessary to great literature required more time. Two generations of political and religious disturbance, of social and economic revolution, of educational decline and revival, must intervene before the day of Spenser, Sidney, and Shakespeare.

PLATONISM

Somewhere behind all great revivals lurks a philosopher. The philosopher of the Renaissance was Plato. Certain Platonic ideas, often much colored or extended into "Neoplatonism" by intervening minds, serve almost like a formula to explain thought and poetry of the Renaissance or later. As Aristotle, systematic, logical, scientific, had supported the scholastic theological thought of the Middle Ages, so the daring, ranging, speculative, exploring mind of the Revival turned to Plato. His reputation had been high in all earlier times, but chiefly at second-hand. In Petrarch's day Greek copies of his works began to reach Italy, and humanistic study of Plato culminated.

late in the fifteenth century, in the famous Platonic "Academy" at Florence, composed of the Medici, Ficino, Pico della Mirandola, and well-known painters and sculptors. Thence the Platonic enthusiasm spread to England.

Designs of ideal commonwealths, conceptions of good manners, of good behavior, and of the gentleman, notions of romantic love, the view of this world as but an imperfect copy of a perfect one, realization of God through love rather than through formal knowledge—these familiar ideas are part of the inheritance, direct or indirect, from Plato. Old chivalry was rejuvenated by contact with his speculation on love, especially as contained in the dialogues of the *Symposium* and the *Phaedrus.* There may be found the germinating seed of ideas grown commonplace in modern love poetry—of ideal love distinguished from lust; of love as an ennobling and regenerating experience; of affinity and "the marriage of true minds"; of love and poetic inspiration as a kind of divine madness, a super-sanity. Plays, sonnets, odes, fiction, never tire of variations on these themes. Nor did the striking resemblance between the teaching of Plato's Socrates, that through love a man may rise to immortal perfection, and the fundamental teaching of Christianity escape notice; and Plato became a sturdier pagan prop of Christian faith than Aristotle.

CHAPTER 8

Under Four Tudors

THROUGH the disordered fifteenth century, Greek humanism could make small headway in England. A half dozen men got to Italy for a few years, caught what they could of the new classical learning, and came home with their packs full of books. Among these was the enlightened Duke Humphrey of Gloucester, patron of Lydgate and others, and benefactor of Oxford with 235 books. "Good" Duke Humphrey they called him, winking at his private life. There was also John Tiptoft, Earl of Worcester, a princely collector, and John Free who learned Greek and was the best scholar of the lot.

But these cases were sporadic, and the time was not ripe. With the accession (1509) of Henry VIII men's hopes for better things rose, and were partly justified. Under young Henry's intelligent protection gathered a group of extraordinary humanists. They are usually labeled the "Oxford Reformers." All but one saw Italy; all of them knew Greek, and through them the vitality of the Greek mind streamed into that enterprising Tudor world. William Grocyn taught Greek at Oxford; Thomas Linacre humanized the theory and practice of medicine; John Colet, as Dean of St. Paul's, electrified the throng, and scandalized his old fogy bishop, by his new-style sermons in the cathedral, wherein he painted a new humanized portrait of St. Paul. He gave his fortune to found St. Paul's School, where 153 boys "of all lands and nations," were to be "instructed in the fear of God, and then in Latin and Greek literature." Erasmus, the Dutch humanist, but a wandering citizen of the world, came and went, teaching Greek, overwhelming with ridicule the corruption and ignorance of the clergy, his scholar's pen ever busy, even on horseback, with humanistic works. His *Letters* and his *Praise of Folly*, originally in Latin, contain the most living and human picture of the times.

These so-called "Oxford Reformers" carried their scholarship into the world, and preferred the active life of London to the retirement of Oxford; which is all the evidence we need of their humanism.

MORE (1478-1535)

The finest figure among them was Sir Thomas More. He was a man of irresistible charm, of great intellect and playful wit, who rose on his practical merits to be Chancellor. Though on terms of intimate familiarity with the King, he was never deceived by it. In the end he suffered martyrdom for his convictions at the very hand which had once lain familiarly on his shoulder, as the two walked together in More's garden at Chelsea, but which had now grown heavy and cruel with the years. With all his learned distinction in his private life, More was simple, genial, devout, and adored by his children. He read consumingly such ancient authors as Plato, the witty Lucian, the Latin comedians, Horace, and Seneca; and moulded himself with the ancients ever in his eye, till he became almost a reincarnation of the best Greek qualities.

Strange it is that out of all this early revival of literary energy came only one great masterpiece, More's *Utopia*, and that in Latin prose. It first appeared in 1516, but the English version by Ralph Robinson in 1551 makes of it an English classic.

With such as Plato's *Republic*, Augustine's *City of God*, the schemes of Plutarch, Cicero, and Tacitus as models, More sketched an ideal commonwealth. Men dreamed of ideal commonwealths all through Tudor times and later, as Shakespeare's *Tempest* bears witness. Spenser's *Faery Queen* and Bacon's *New Atlantis* are conspicuous examples. Whether the dream was a symptom of human desire to escape from the tightening absolutism of Renaissance rulers, or a sign that men were stirred by the flood-tide of change running deep and

strong beneath them, or by the discovery of new lands overseas, one cannot say. Probably all three.

We now read the famous second book of *Utopia* with admiration of its good sense, with amusement at its masked fun,
its satire and extravagance, with astonishment at its uncanny pre-
monition of present needs. The elective monarchy; two years
on the farm for every man; the six-hour day; iron as the precious
metal because it is useful; liberal and vocational training, especially in Greek, open to all but with some choice; hatred of
war; non-sectarian Christianity—all these sound very modern.
Curiously enough another great political idealist named William Penn took the plan of Utopia's capital for his Philadel-
phia, whence it has reproduced itself in many a smaller town
of Pennsylvania.

The charm of More asserts itself in his opening scene. Coming out of Antwerp Cathedral after mass, he sees his friend
Peter Giles talking with a bronzed and bearded old sailor, who
proves to be one of Vespucci's fellow-voyagers to South
America, yet a scholar, especially in Greek philosophy. He is
Raphael Hythlodaye, of Portugal. They retire to a green corner
in More's garden, listen to Raphael's tales of hair-breadth escapes, and discuss evils of the times. Then after a good dinner
indoors, they come out again to hear Raphael talk through the
afternoon about his five years' sojourn in Utopia. Altogether
Sir Thomas More is the best-proportioned example of incarnate
English humanism.

What with the New Learning and comparative order under
the strong hand of young Henry VIII, one wonders that the
literary revival still had to wait another fifty years, till the latter
end of the century. But the King's growing selfishness and
egotism, the weakness of young Edward VI (1547-1553), the
bigotry and infatuation of Catholic Mary (1553-1558), and
the nation's long ordeal of making up its mind in the matter of
religion, were conditions most demoralizing to culture or literary effort. Had Henry VIII used at least a fair part of the
church wealth to establish schools, colleges, and libraries, and
had Elizabeth immediately succeeded him, the glories of the

great period might have been earlier and even brighter than they were. Who shall say?

.Though education declined at the middle of the century, it was one subject of which the times never tired. Many of the great masterpieces of the Elizabethan century were chiefly concerned with breeding and education—of princes, of gentlemen, of everyone.

ELYOT, CHEKE, ASCHAM

Utopia is an example. Another is the vast *Boke named the Governour* which More's friend, Sir Thomas Elyot (1499?-1546), courtier, diplomat, humanist, "devised" in 1531. It comprises not only a theory of state, but a compendium of the classical learning and sports which went to the making of an Italian gentleman, along with ideals of virtue that were more English. It went through edition after edition on into Elizabeth's reign, popular no doubt as a useful short-cut for "new" men to the fashionable humanistic culture.

Sir Thomas was educated privately. These were dark days for the universities and schools; yet a few brave souls carried on.

One was Sir John Cheke (1514-1557), "who taught Cambridge and King Edward Greek." He was a great interpreter of Greek literature, but indiscreetly meddled with the dangerous politics of the time, was threatened with the heretic's stake, and died young in broken-hearted humiliation, on the very eve of Elizabeth's accession. His pupil Roger Ascham (1515-1568), though less learned, was more prudent. With his passion for Greek culture he oddly combined a passion for archery and cock-fighting, and his works are the works of a sporting scholar. His *Toxophilus*, on archery, embodies Greek theories of physical training, and he planned, but never wrote, a treatise on the cock-main. Though tutor to Elizabeth and the unhappy Lady Jane Grey, he kept safely within his "Cockpit of Learning," and produced in 1563, early in the new reign, his famous *Schoolmaster*. It was suggested by his friend Elyot's *The Governour*, but is less ponderous and more readable. No book on education was ever so fascinating. The man was a clever and

skilful teacher, an example to teachers in any age, and far
beyond his times; but he was more—a genial, upright, lively
humanist. His reminiscence of Lady Jane Grey in the first book
has never been surpassed by any biographical portrait in English. His friend, Dr. Nicholas Wotton, "a man milde of nature, with soft voice, and fewe wordes," spoke the mind of
wise Roger himself, when he said: "In mine opinion the
Scholehouse should be in deede, as it is called by name, the
house of playe and pleasure, and not of feare and bondage: and
as I do remember, so saith Socrates."

CHAPTER 9

Elizabeth

AT LAST the great Queen came. Whatever she lacked, she had an uncanny sense of the heart and mind of her people. Men instinctively discovered it, their wilted courage revived, and they worshipped and served her with all their powers and talents. She was a queen, not a king. All the inherited promptings of the old chivalry rose within her people. She became an incarnation of their new, vigorous, young England, saving them from haughty Spain and their other papal enemies. Allowing all one will for the customary Renaissance flattery, it is not enough to account for the ringing accents of a hundred acclamations such as Spenser's dedication of his *Faery Queen*: "To the most high, mightie, and magnificent Empresse, renowmed for Pietie, Vertue, and all Gratious Government. . . ." Extravagant as their praise now sounds, their hearts were enough in it to save most of it from emptiness of hollow adulation.

But Elizabethan society was crude and unstable. The medieval aristocracy was gone; parvenus rose by sudden wealth, politics, and bold strokes of adventure; speculation and vulgar extravagance prevailed; sudden ruin was common. Hence perhaps the literary fashion of "complaints," the popularity of "Fortune" and "Mutability" as themes of Elizabethan song and story. Hence also the profounder instinct of the times for great tragedy.

Young English aristocrats, no doubt aware of their defects in manners and culture, made it fashionable to take the Italian tour, ostensibly for their culture's sake. Whatever refinement

they got, their morals were none the better for immediate contact with the ways of the Italian Renaissance. Ascham scolds
them roundly for it, and quotes the Italian proverb,

> An Englishman Italianate
> Is but a devil incarnate.[1]

In social conditions so relaxed men's passions ran high and
loose. Men and values were black or white, bad or good, without subtle blendings—all which is reflected in the grossness,
extravagance, or excess that sometimes offend us in Elizabethan
literature.

But crudity of manners and morals evoked their own antidote, and books dealing with courtesy, education, and behavior, were, as we have seen, always in lively demand. Such
was Elyot's *Governour*, Ascham's *Schoolmaster*, Lyly's *Euphues*,
and such was essentially Spenser's great *Faery Queen*. Such too
were Richard Mulcaster's (1530?-1611) astonishing *Positions*
and *Elementary*, though devised more for the crude new bourgeoisie than the crude aristocracy.

But no single book exerted such power, directly or indirectly,
in shaping the ideal of the Elizabethan man of breeding as did
Sir Thomas Hoby's (1530-1566) translation of the Italian
Castiglione's *The Courtier*. Hoby's version is an English classic.
Sir Philip Sidney, "the glass of fashion and the mould of
form," most admired gentleman of his time, always had a copy
in his pocket, and through courtier and poet it entered into
the fibre of all attempts to portray the gentleman, even
Shakespeare's.

The chief elements of the ideal are those of old chivalry—
courage, constancy, generous behavior to fellows, protection of
women, skill in horsemanship, sports, and other polite accomplishments. But these are much deepened by new humanistic
ideals, especially Plato's noble conception of love as a spiritual
regenerator, and the moderation of the passions from Aristotle.
Hoby's *Courtier* more than any other book puts the reader in
possession of the higher social ideals of Renaissance times.

---

[1] Inglese italianato è un diavolo incarnato.

TOTTEL'S MISCELLANY (1557); WYATT (1503?-1542)
SURREY (1517?-1547)

In the darkest hour before the Elizabethan dawn, the last year of Mary, appeared a little book called *Songs and Sonnets*, commonly known as *Tottel's Miscellany* (1557). Into this small compass was distilled the best English song of nearly forty years, and in turn it proved the chief propagator of English love poetry for a generation more. It comprised over three hundred short poems, went through ten editions in the next thirty years, and was the forerunner of many anthologies during the reign of Elizabeth.

Its chief distinction lay in the poems it included from the hands of Sir Thomas Wyatt and Henry Howard, Earl of Surrey. Wyatt had composed nearly a third of the collection, Surrey only about forty songs. Among the poets were Grimald, Vaux, Norton, and Heywood. Most of them were Cambridge men.

Both Wyatt and Surrey were highly cultivated courtiers under Henry VIII, but Wyatt, born about 1503, was some fourteen years the elder. In poetry Surrey was his devoted follower. Such Renaissance gentlemen practised poetry as an elegant accomplishment, without thought of publication. Both men were dead long before the *Miscellany* appeared.

Wyatt had an active public career at home and in diplomatic service abroad. He experienced the downs as well as the ups of that shuttlecock time, and was once close to the block in the Tower for treason. He died at thirty-nine. Surrey was more exalted, a proud member of the proud Howard family, boasting royal blood and distinctions. He was a man of strong affections and quick temper, now basking in royal favor, now confined in the Fleet or the Tower. He served his king well, especially as a soldier in Scotland and France. But he was not yet thirty when he was entrapped in a court intrigue, falsely accused of treason, and executed.

Romancers have made much of his supposed attachment to a sweet Irish child of nine, Elizabeth Fitzgerald.

Bright is her hewe, and Geraldine she hight,

as the innocent sonnet says from which the tale first sprang.

The *Miscellany* contains a highly assorted stock—in a wide variety of metres—of sonnets, epigrams, satires, moralizings, eulogy, elegy, and one pastoral. Nearly all of Wyatt's poems are on love, some on the illusions of court life. Both his and Surrey's clearly served their authors as an artistic means of escape from the hard and strenuous world to which their lot condemned them. Wyatt's verse is vigorous, sometimes rough, from his struggle with that stubborn medium, the new English. But Surrey, by Wyatt's example, has carried the struggle from Wyatt's partial triumph to his own complete victory, and his poems are the highest achievement of the book.

The book, as it turned out, taught English Literature a new art of poetry. Much of it, especially Wyatt's work, was translated from Petrarch's love poetry, and that of other Italians. Much was drawn from Latin poets, Horace, Martial, and Ovid. It was full of imported conceits, and of a new "poetic" phrase and diction that circulated long and wide. Its metres became standard; the Elizabethan sonnet ending always with a couplet is said to have been invented by Surrey, though it is approached by Wyatt. At any rate metrical fashions were set by this precedent—blank verse, alternate rhyming of five-stress lines, and the strange sing-song "poulter's measure" of six and seven:

> And when I felt the aire so pleasant round about,
> Lorde, to myself how glad I was that I had gotten out.

The love poetry in the *Miscellany*—and love is the prevailing theme—is artificial and empty of thought. Its sincerity lies in its music. Since Chaucer the language had suffered swift and, as a poetic instrument, disastrous change. In 1483 Caxton remarked that even in his lifetime the alteration had been so rapid that "bytwene playn, rude, and curious I stande abasshed." Yet he finds it a speech easier to understand. It had lost its medieval music. Was it capable of developing a new music? The *Miscellany* is the answer. Under Wyatt's fingers the music began to stir, and rose to fuller melody in Surrey's lines. Alliteration, correctness of metre, identity of natural and metrical accent of words were all a part of it.

But these poets achieved something subtler and deeper. In

both, especially in Surrey, is heard for the first time the new
music and cadence of the English lyric that found its counterpart in the airs and madrigals of the great Elizabethan
composers:

> As oft as I behold and see
> The sovereign beauty that me bound,
> The nigher my comfort is to me,
> Alas the fresher is my wound.

Though intended for the refined ear, some of the songs
found a broad and vulgar vogue, and we come on the grave-
digger in *Hamlet* raucously bawling a corrupt snatch of Vaux's

> I loathe that I did love,
> In youth that I thought sweet.

The *Miscellany*, not intrinsically great, is a safe index of
Elizabethan taste.

MIRROR FOR MAGISTRATES; ANTIQUARIES

Another such index is the *Mirror for Magistrates*, a work
bred out of Lydgate's *Falls of Princes*. It is a collection of dole-
ful tales in verse of how men conspicuous at various points in
England's history fell from their high estate. Beginning with
nineteen tales in 1559, it had gone through eight enlargements
by 1610, when it had swollen to a hundred. No eminent poets
contributed except Drayton and Sackville. But the *Mirror* reflects in its success both the Elizabethan appetite for "tragedy,"
and the new patriotism.

To a new edition of the *Mirror* in 1563 Sackville, then
about twenty-seven, contributed his noble *Induction*. The poet
as he walked abroad of a starry winter's night met a forlorn
woman, Sorrow, "Forewither'd and forespent." She conducted
him to the lower world where he interviewed princes of renown who had been "whirled down" to low estate by Fortune's wheel. Grim figures lurk about Hellgate—Remorse, Revenge, Care, Malady, and Old Age—

> His wither'd fist still knocking at Death's door,
> Fumbling and drivelling, as he draws his breath.

Visions of old unhappy far-off things and battles long ago are vividly "depainted" and "portrayed" on the wall. Though reminiscent of Chaucer and others, the poem lives with an austere energy in both its music and its imagination. It surely took an important part in the poetic schooling of Spenser, of whom at times it seems almost a primitive version. Its cadence, vocabulary, syntax, the structure of its line and stanza, its archaisms, its allegorical figures suggest that it must have been such a favorite with the poet's poet that he had it by heart.

From the first Tudor, Henry VII, England had been waxing in national strength. As she grew she became more aware of it, and thrilled with such patriotism as finds tongue in old Gaunt's famous speech in *Richard II*.[1] A new sense of her past and her antiquities awoke within her.

Many were the "chronicles," in metre and in prose, that were supplied through the century to satisfy patriotic curiosity. John Stow's *Summary of English Chronicles* was standard and reached ten editions. But Raphael Holinshed, compiler of the book which he called *Chronicles*, is more famous as purveyor of historical matter to the two greatest poets of the age, Shakespeare and Spenser. Whoever would amuse himself does well to read the *Description of England* by William Harrison, prefaced to Holinshed. It is to visit Elizabeth's England as the familiar guest of a lively and genial man who knows that you will enjoy it.

William Camden, more learned than Holinshed, issued his Latin *Britannia* in 1586, of which the erudite consumed several editions before it became an English classic at the hand of Philemon Holland in 1610. It is really a huge historical guide to all parts of England, a museum which readers like Spenser ransacked for history, local sights, antiquities, verse, legend and oddity, of which they could make proper use.

VOYAGES

At the opening of the Second Book of the *Faery Queen* Spenser reproaches the man who scoffs at his tale as mere "painted forgery."

[1] Quoted below on pages 188-9

> But let that man with better sence advize,
> That of the world least part to us is red:
> And dayly how through hardy enterprize,
> Many great Regions are discovered,
> Which to late age were never mentioned.
> Who ever heard of th'Indian Peru?
> Or who in venturous vessell measured
> The Amazons huge river now found trew?
> Or fruitfullest Virginia who did ever vew?
>
> Yet all these were, when no man did them know;
> Yet have from wisest ages hidden beene:
> And later times things more unknowne shall show.

The pulse of excitement and romance which throbs in the rhythm of these lines often stirs in the literature of Elizabeth's reign. We have felt it already in Marlowe, whose fiery genius was especially subject to it. It was roused and quickened by the wonderful tales of adventure and discovery brought back by such voyagers as Frobisher, Hawkins, Gilbert, and Drake, in the sixties, seventies, and eighties. In the eighties too Raleigh had made his three attempts to found a colony in Virginia, and was doubtless full of the subject when he and Spenser talked together.

In 1582 Richard Hakluyt published his *Divers Voyages touching the discoverie of America,* and in 1589 the first volume of his famous *Principal Navigations.* In these works may be read accounts of great Elizabethan voyages and their predecessors. It must be said, that after all the romantic poetizing and dreaming the world has done over these gallant adventures, Hakluyt's accounts seem prosaic and disappointing. But one must realize a deal of excited talk rising about these bold explorers and their followers after their return, wherever they found themselves, in tavern, street, hall, cottage, or theatre. And a traveller's tale notoriously loses nothing by the telling. So by the ear more than by printed words this ferment spread.

Gorgeous dreams of both Orient and Occident shimmered and swam in the imagination of poet and dramatist. Marlowe's

Tamburlaine and *Faustus* and *Jew of Malta* ferment with visions of far lands, and of the wealth and power which they promised. The spell mingled with the patriotism of the time and awoke the idea of the great empire to be realized only through hundreds of years. Such thoughts ring out in Chapman's *De Guiana* and Drayton's ode *To the Virginian Voyage*. The very music of poetry and romance clung about the strange names of far-off lands, those vast shores "washed with the furthest sea,"[1] and sings in hundreds of lines down to its grandest volume in Milton's geographical interludes:

> . . . from the destind Walls
> Of *Cambalu*, seat of *Cathaian Can*
> And *Samarchand* by *Oxus, Temirs* Throne,
> To *Paquin* of *Sinaean* Kings, and thence
> To *Agra* and *Lahor* of great *Mogul*
> Down to the golden *Chersonese*. . . .
> Rich *Mexico* the seat of *Motezume*,
> And *Cusco* in *Peru*, the richer seat
> Of *Atabalipa*, and yet unspoil'd
> *Guiana*. . . .[2]

In Shakespeare's *Othello* the lure of the sea and the far splendors of the Orient lend a certain grandeur to the characters and action. In *The Tempest,* beneath all its romantic fancy and charm, the poet is realistically engaged with actual problems of contacts between civilization and savagery, not to say savagery in civilization. He associates with far, unknown lands, especially the Western World, that perennial vision of the ideal commonwealth prevalent in his time, and recurrent with the English longing westward overseas, from More's *Utopia* and Daniel's *Musophilus* (1601) to Coleridge and Shelley, even to Samuel Butler and D. H. Lawrence. Its hopes of a better order of life and better men seem to mingle with a tinge of homesickness in such names as *New* England, *New* York, *New* Hampshire.

[1] *Romeo and Juliet*, 2.2.83
[2] *Paradise Lost*, 11.388-410

TRANSLATORS

As the language revealed new resources, and the popular mind and curiosity expanded, the art of translation attained its greatest height. Through many an English version the culture of the ancients, of Italy, of France, entered abundantly into the growth of English Literature. The list is long, but Hoby's *Courtier*, North's *Plutarch*, Florio's *Montaigne*, the tragedies of Seneca by various hands, Holland's *Pliny*, *Livy*, and *Suetonius*, Golding's *Ovid*, Harington's *Ariosto*, Chapman's *Homer*, and above all the King James or Authorized translation of the Bible, not only became classics in our tongue, but in turn creators through the minds of Spenser, Sidney, Shakespeare, Keats, and a host of lesser poets and dramatists.

The sixteenth century was almost gone before English poetry recovered from an unhappy sense of its provincial inferiority. Writing in 1583 Sir Philip Sidney is in despair; he can recall nothing of distinction besides Chaucer's *Troilus*, the *Mirror*, Surrey, and his friend Spenser's debut in the *Shepherd's Calendar*. Tottel hoped to show by his *Miscellany* that English poetry could vie with "the workes of divers Latines, Italians, and others," but in his hope seems to lurk a misgiving. It is natural, then, that English poetry in its first Renaissance endeavors affected many foreign artificialities of imagery, phrase, and diction, ashamed of its coarser native vigors and native traditions. The perfect blend of cultured refinements with English common stock was not even yet accomplished.

GASCOIGNE (1525?-1577)

George Gascoigne was a man of enough talent, but not enough genius, to achieve this blend. Sidney does not mention him, yet he breaks in upon all the artificialities with refreshing sincerity. He was of knightly family, a clever young rapscallion both at Trinity, Cambridge, and as law-student at the Middle Temple. Till he was forty and more he was dissipated and so extravagant that his father cast him off. Then he married an endowed widow with a country estate, but lived on in chronic debt. He travelled at home and in France, served in

Parliament, and had two or three years of wild adventure in Holland, helping the Dutch drive out the Spaniards.

His pen was prolific in verse and prose of all sorts; it sounds like the overflow of an exuberant mind, producing readily and casually, even on horseback, by the way. He loves the old English words more than such "as smell of the Inkhorne"; and would rather "make our native language commendable in it selfe, than gay with the feathers of straunge birdes." This racy element of native proverb and idiom comes naturally in his verse and gives it hearty relish. He scorns "mealy-mouthed" poets, and would "stande in stoute and sturdie speech." But he has awakened also a new music in the tongue, more baritone, less exquisite than Surrey's, yet destined long to survive in later poets when the rare lute-like music of Elizabethan song had died away. Besides his famous songs, "Sing lullaby, as women do," "And if I did, what then?" he left many a diverting piece, on love, the Court, Fortune, and other topics of the times, whose wit, verve, and autobiographic frankness keep them from decay. At times, as in the opening of *Dan Bartholomew of Bathe*, and in *Dulce Bellum Inexpertis*, an account of his adventures in Holland, one feels the irrepressible daring energy of Byron, especially of *Don Juan*; and in many ways the men were alike. Gascoigne wrote easily and much. *Jocasta*, a tragedy adapted from Euripides in blank verse, and a comedy in prose called *Supposes* (*Mistaken Identities*) from Ariosto, both for performance at Gray's Inn, and both pioneers in the drama, show the man's fertility. In his *Steel Glass*, a vigorous but diffuse satire in blank verse, he holds up a mirror of trusty, polished steel to the iniquities of his day, and indicts all classes, Monarch (Elizabeth excepted), Knight, Priest, Burgher, Peasant, for their inconstancy, their unreliability, their greed and vulgar ostentation, their duplicity. This satire also was a very early specimen of its kind. Gascoigne had not the imagination of a great poet, but he had music, enterprise, eloquence, and a basis of elemental humanity.

LYLY (1554?-1606)

John Lyly, a generation younger than Gascoigne, is one of those tragic persons whose great talents far overtop the petty objective of their ambitions. The man was a poet and play-wright of high order, yet through the active years of his life his heart was set on being Master of Court Revels, and he died in his early fifties embittered with disappointment.

He was of rural Kentish plebeian origin, a little man, we hear, and by all symptoms a ladies' man. He had rather have his *Euphues* "shut in a lady's cabinet, than open in a scholar's study." This is just the sort of man that, however great his talents, might set his heart narrowly and perversely on social success.

He won his B.A. at Oxford, and at Cambridge his M.A.; but, like many a gifted young person, he dodged the more severe academic discipline, and cultivated poetry. Then he sought the only field open to high talent—the Court. In the first year, 1579, he launched his most brilliant success, *Euphues: the Anatomy of Wit,* and woke to find himself famous. With speedy elation he next year produced its sequel, *Euphues and his England.*

Euphues, a young Athenian, visits Naples, picks up a bosom friend, Philautus, and falls in and out of love; in the sequel the two visit England, which of course gives Lyly many op-portunities. The slight plot makes the book a novel of a sort. It is really a book of manners, of ostentatious elegance, which was just what a crudish aristocracy, and a cruder but aspiring bourgeoisie wanted. Hence its popularity.

It imported Italian and classical polite learning, and espe-cially polite conversation on polite topics. The Italian high-society game of "Questions," or witty debate on subjects of social interest, is adapted and exploited by Lyly. "There is scarce three words uttered but the third is 'love.'" There is also much pondering of friendship, discreet behavior, and re-ligion, with a generous flavoring of solid English sense.

The book is most famous for its style, to which it gave wide advertisement and a name, Euphuism. Here is a specimen:

For as the finest ruby staineth the color of the rest that be in place, or as the sun dimmeth the moon that she cannot be discerned, so this gallant girl, more fair than fortunate, and yet more fortunate than faithful, eclipsed the beauty of them all and changed their colors.

The pairing of clause and phrase in equal length, word balancing word, and sound balancing sound, the similes from nature, the underlying rhythm—these are the symptoms of Euphuism. It derives from the rhetoric of medieval sermons and ceremonials, though not without some classical modification. Lyly did not introduce Euphuism, but his book made it the fashion, and got people to writing it, talking it, and imitating *Euphues* in many a novel. Of course it was a fad, and quickly bred its antidote of ridicule; fat Sir John Falstaff getting Euphuistic in his burlesque curtain lecture to Prince Hal, is a fine instance: "For though the camomile, the more it is trodden on the faster it grows, yet youth, the more it is wasted the sooner it wears."[1]

Euphuism had by that time been the mode for twenty years or so, and still continued to be an influence; but Lyly was not spared the mortification of outliving the fashion which he created, and which gave him sudden fame.

Yet he was far more than a mere literary caterer to a modish world. He taught English prose a great lesson in measured music and balance, a lesson which it never wholly forgot.

For a dozen years after *Euphues* Lyly labored to entertain the Court with his plays, and here too he was creative and original. Eight comedies proved him an ingenious and resourceful playwright, and tried out many a dramaturgic device which Shakespeare was soon to find ready to his hand. Most of his plays are based on Greek myth or history turned to Elizabethan use. Three of them are idyllic pastoral comedy, after the Italian manner; one, *Campaspe,* is drawn from the story of Alexander, and is one of the first English "historical" plays. Its modern fame is probably owing to its familiar incidental lyric, "Cupid and my Campaspe played at cards for kisses," a clever imitation of Latin and Greek epigram in the Anacreontic manner of the Greek Anthology.

His greatest play is *Endymion,* one of three in which he uses a classic myth as a safe allegorical disguise for comment on more or less dangerous situations in Court. He is the first of his time to attempt this delicate business, the more delicate

[1] *Henry IV,* Part I.2.4

when satirical personal comment in public had to be covert to
be safe, and had not the broad license which it has since won
and now enjoys. The play is based on Lucian's dialogue between the Moon and Venus. Diana, in *Endymion*, is, of course,
the chaste Elizabeth, but what pointed inferences courtiers
whispered to their neighbors as they saw enacted the goddess's
love for the shepherd lad we shall never know. They buzzed
no doubt; meanwhile Lyly failed to get the petty preferments
he coveted.

Among the ancient and foreign models, he chose his own—
romantic Ovid, vivacious Lucian, florid Apuleius, Italian pastorals, and others, especially Boccaccio's *Filocolo*. He was unwittingly a rich purveyor of Renaissance culture to both the
polite and the popular Elizabethan mind.

SIDNEY (1554-1586)

The finest incarnation of humanistic virtues in his times was
Sir Philip Sidney. He was born in 1554. On both sides he was
an aristocrat. His mother came of the exalted house of Lisle
and Dudley. Robert Dudley, Earl of Leicester, was her brother.
Philip's father, Sir Henry Sidney, was utterly uncorrupted by
the vices of the time, and the Queen had no servant more wise,
energetic, faithful, honest, and unrewarded than he.

Philip was destined to be spoiled if any boy ever was, by
rank, looks, and easy success. As Spenser says, doubtless with
him in mind,

> Some so goodly gratious are by kind,
> That every action doth them much commend,
> And in the eyes of men great liking find.[1]

To this irresistible grace was added mind, aspiration, and a
measure of genius. He had, however, to struggle with strait-
ened means, ill health, and, like many of his time, an unruly
temper.

At Shrewsbury School he was a comrade of Fulke Greville,
who in aftertimes wrote a fine *Life* of Sidney. At Oxford for
three years he was at Christ Church, where he found illus-

---

[1] *Faery Queen*, 6.2.2

trious friends—Camden the antiquary, and Richard Hakluyt editor of the famous *Voyages*.

He was groomed for the Court under Leicester and the favoring eye of the great Cecil, and sent, like all young bloods, to travel for three years among the courts and humanistic *élite* of Paris, Vienna, Venice, Padua, Poland, and Germany. In Paris he saw the horrors of the St. Bartholomew massacre, the memory of which surely entered into his passionate devotion to the Protestant cause. He made his closest friend of the scholar-diplomatist, Languet, thirty-five years his elder; but Sidney's precocity overcame these differences of age. The letters between them show whence Sidney's chief humanistic and spiritual inspiration came, and make one of the most fascinating books of the Renaissance. Languet must have seen in Sidney's ardent temper reasons to be worried about his moral dangers while in Italy. But he, or the boy's natural high seriousness, steered him safely through them, and at twenty-one he reached home and the world of the Court again.

The remaining eleven years of his life were crowded full. Young as he was, he was almost overwhelmed with popularity, responsibilities, and honors. Men looked to him wistfully as the hoped-for leader of the Protestant cause in Europe. He was the Queen's messenger to the Low Countries, and joined his uncle Leicester in urging Elizabeth to help them in their struggle with Catholic Spain.

He may have been twenty-three when he met the eccentric Cambridge pundit, Gabriel Harvey, and through him Edmund Spenser. Spenser was two years older, of far humbler social rank, raw from the university, and not yet known for a poet. Sidney was ever aware of his own rank. Yet some intimacy seems to have developed, if not a close friendship, and for two years a lively traffic in literary ideas went on in their coterie, which included Dyer, Harvey, and perhaps Greville. Some one in joke called it an Areopagus, but it never assumed the significance of the French Pléiade, though it sympathized no doubt with the doctrines of that group.

In their enthusiasm for the classics and their youthful passion for reform in English poetry, these young sophisticates experimented in English quantitative verse on the principles of Latin metre, in preference to native stresses and rhyme; but Spenser's truer instinct readily discerned the absurdity of it. "Why, a God's name," he asked, "may we not have the kingdom of our language?" The permanent fruits of their thought are probably embodied in Sidney's *Defence of Poesy*, written down later and not published till nine years after he died.

In despair at the low condition of English poetry, having himself "slipped into the title of a poet," he would defend poetry in general against its enemies. There is no proof that he here had especially in mind Gosson's *School of Abuse*, an attack on the stage which had been inscribed to him. In effect poetry is not a matter of metre and rhyme, but of inventive imagination, idealizing and transforming this world of ours, thereby subtly and profoundly making us all better men without our conscious knowledge. His ideas derive mainly from Plato, Aristotle's *Poetics*, and Horace's *Art of Poetry*, but also include a large heritage of medieval theory and thought transmitted through Boccaccio. The great merit of Sidney's essay lies partly in the high enthusiasm and charm of the man, partly in its authority as the honest utterance of a practising poet.

At the age of sixteen his beautiful sister Mary had by marriage become Countess of Pembroke. Between the two there was the warmest devotion and literary sympathy, and "Sidney's sister, Pembroke's mother," became the admired patroness of various poets in after years. In the retirement of her stately country seat at Wilton near Salisbury he began for her his romance of *Arcadia,* which he afterwards continued in casual sheets but never finished. It is a long and episodic account of the loves and other adventures of Musidorus and Pyrochles, two mutually devoted young princes, in a mapless, remote world where wilderness mingles with idyllic pastoral or courtly setting. Such pastoral romances Sidney could have read in Italian, notably in the *Arcadia* of Sannazaro. They are an outgrowth of old pastoral poetry, medieval romance, and such a Greek novel as the famous *Daphnis and Chloe*. In times of artificial and courtly restraint, finer souls turn to the pastoral escape, and Sidney, already tiring of the Court in spite of his success, seeks relief with his sister at Wilton and in Arcadia.

Though not easily read nowadays, Sidney's "novel" met with enormous popularity, was circulated in manuscript, and during the century after the author's death went through many editions. It is full of events, and its high-flown style, in spite of Sidney's protest against Euphuism, its sentiment, its wit, and the scarcity of fiction generally are enough to account for its fame. To English poetry and drama it furnished material, including no less than Shakespeare's story of the Duke of Gloucester in *King Lear*, and suggestions for the *Faery Queen*. It contains nearly forty interpolated lyric poems from Sidney's hand, and glows in every part with his generous and chivalric temper.

Before he was twenty Sidney may have begun to write sonnets merely as a literary exercise. But his cycle of 108 sonnets known as *Astrophel and Stella*, the first in English, seems for the most part to have uttered a genuine passion, and every reader naturally inquires for the lady. A number of the sonnets were unquestionably addressed to Penelope Devereux, daughter of his older friend the Earl of Essex, considered by their elders as a possible wife for Sidney. Hence the still persistent view that when she subsequently married Lord Rich, Sidney, thus balked, took sudden fire and poured out his passion in the sonnets. The facts are not clear. After Sidney's death in 1586 certain friends including Spenser seem to have been worried by the scandal, and apparently wished the world to believe that Stella was Frances Walsingham, whom Sidney married in 1583. But embarrassing difficulties confront any fixed opinion.

The sonnet was born in Provence and matured in Italy in the thirteenth century. Dante and Petrarch were its early masters, and the Petrarchan form of fourteen lines rhyming abba, abba, cde, cde, with variations in the last six lines, became standard. In English, where rhymes are less easy, the "Shakespearian" form of three quatrains rhyming alternately plus a couplet had developed through Wyatt and Surrey. Sidney's sonnets are in all stages of modulation between the two.

So strict and conventional is the form of the sonnet that many have been prone to suspect its sincerity, whoever the author, and to postulate for the sonneteer of the Renaissance at most an imaginary ideal as the object of his ardors. Stella they find but a sublimated figment. And though Sidney protests that he is "no pick-purse of another's wit," yet there is no denying that his, like most Elizabethan sonnets, are full of traditional devices of the species, and many of them are mere adaptations of sonnets by Petrarch to his Laura, and of other Italian and French sonnets. The measure of their sincerity each reader must take for himself. Nevertheless ardent young men in an ardent age and atmosphere will hardly be playing with the high explosive contained in sonnets without suffering serious and very real accidents to heart and mind, however casually they began.

Of Sidney himself his sonnets contain much—his love of books, of horses, of jousts, his intensity, his tight rein upon his passions, like the pupil of Aristotle that he confesses himself. But he is also the pupil of Plato, and would in the end turn his earthly passion to spiritual result. The last and favorite sonnet of the series,

> Leave me, O Love, which reachest but to dust,

is a glorious embodiment of this idea.

Sidney boasted that "what I speak doth flow in verse." Yet for all its spontaneity, wit, and substance, his verse often halts and grinds, which is the more surprising in his time when verse and music were in the closest alliance. If he spoke slightingly of his own performance, and left orders to have *Arcadia* burned, it was perhaps but the fashionable aristocratic disparagement of literature as the mere by-product of an avocation. Yet in his heart he took poetry not as the elegant pastime of polite wits, but as a regenerator of men; and in his reference to the old ballads he implies his sense of their elemental vigors.

The story of his death after the field of Zutphen, told by his friend Greville, where he declined the cup of water in favor of a common soldier, and laid down his gallant life for the cause of human freedom, is too well known to rehearse. In his last hours of suffering he was supremely happy, possibly at the release of his idealistic spirit from his turbulent body and a rough if admiring world.

CHAPTER 10

Spenser c.1552 – 1599

ANOTHER in whom idealism was ever at war with worldliness was Edmund Spenser. As a poet he gathered unto himself the highest and most vital qualities of Elizabethan poetry, and has been imparting them to English poets in every generation since, even to Masefield.

He was sensitive about his middle-class origin, as we infer from his claim of connection with "an house of auncient fame," and from his life-long "idle hopes" for high position. Born in London probably in 1552, he came under that extraordinary teacher, Mulcaster, at Merchant Tailors' School, who was educating "not a mind, not a body, but a man." The classics, English, acting, and above all music, went to the making of his poetry. To Puritan Cambridge, breeder of poets, he proceeded, and in Pembroke College was probably a pupil, certainly a warm friend, of Gabriel Harvey, who later gave him his introduction to Sidney's group and the Court. Plato, Aristotle, Italian and French poetry, political and religious questions possessed his mind.

Then opened the career at Court. For three years or more he was in the whirl of its excitements, the intrigues of the antipapal party with which he was thrown, literature, love, and high hopes of preferment. Probably about this time he was first married. His wife may have been a girl of nineteen named Maccabeus Child, of whom almost nothing is known. But one whom he calls Rosalind, an unidentified lady of mystery, perhaps at Court, roused in him a hopeless passion, which he cherished and sang about, and even remembered tenderly long years after when married a second time.

In 1579 was published his *Shepherd's Calendar*, dedicated

163

to Sidney. The "new poet," for whom Sidney and others had been hoping almost without hope, had arrived.

Into the *Calendar* Spenser had learnedly imported the old poetic devices of the classical and Renaissance pastoral poets, especially the French, but he made them English as far as rustic English customs and names, like Colin Clout, homely idiom, archaic language and native metres could make them. The twelve eclogues, one for each month, touch most of the themes of the pastoral from mere idyll in March and May, to love complaint for his Rosalind, criticism of the times under pastoral veil, eulogy, and elegy. In October he touches a higher strain, the Platonic idea of poetic inspiration, and already one catches a hint of that sweet, deep-voiced music which later he was to stir in the language at will.

The *Calendar* and most of Spenser's other early poems were studio pieces in preparation for his great work, on which he was already embarked in these days at Court. If they sound artificial to us, it is perhaps because their art, now antique, was then new, and a large part of their inspiration was the poet's youthful delight in his success with a new technique. Chiefly did he study the French poets, Marot, Ronsard, DuBellay, and their theories of poetic language. But it hardly needed their theories to encourage his natural instinct for English language and poetry of earlier times. Chaucer, whom he famously proclaimed "a well of English undefyled," he humbly acknowledged as his master, and he reinforced his native element by close familiarity with the Middle English tradition, especially such as the anonymous *Ploughman's Tale* and Sackville's *Induction*. Most of his early poems are of the medieval breed of "complaints"—Visions, Ruins, "sundrie small Poemes of the Worlds Vanitie." The *Tears of the Muses* rehearses the same despair over English Literature that Sidney felt. Even if, as some think, this poem was not written till 1589 or 1590, it is pitched in the same youthful minor key as his earlier flights.

One of these Complaints, however, made destiny for its author. *Mother Hubbard's Tale,* ostensibly an old dame's yarn about a Fox and an Ape, draws its matter from the medieval Reynard lore, and lays aside Elizabethan poetic finery for plain homespun, in imitation of Chaucer. Under such very thin cover it attacks many abuses, but especially the man of power, Cecil, Lord Burghley. Spenser, a little dizzy with success, hopes, and zeal for the Leicester party, went too far, and for his indiscretion found himself packed off to a safe distance in Ireland as the Secretary of Lord Grey, the Lord Lieutenant. It was virtually an exile.

For the ten years following 1579 this rare poet and idealist had to make his hard way amid disorder, uncertainty, barbarism, untold human misery, and the greed and animalism of frontier life; but some alleviation he found in a few friends, in the romantic, other-world loveliness of Irish stream, meadow, forest, and mountain, above all in the "delightfull land of Faery," into which he escaped from the sordid world of men, as he wrought from time to time upon his vast undertaking, the *Faery Queen*.

In 1589 he settled on the estate of Kilcolman Castle, in the fair rich country just north of Cork. It had been confiscated from an Irish "rebel," and given him as an English colonist. At the time Walter Raleigh was his neighbor; he had known him years before, and the two compared notes and poems at Kilcolman with the result that Raleigh urged Spenser to visit the Court with him and bring his work along. Spenser has left an account of the visit in one of his most intimate poems, *Colin Clout's Come Home Again*.

Once in London, he hurried through the press the completed books, I to III, of the *Faery Queen*, was well received by Elizabeth, and soon found all the world reading his poem and no doubt vying one with another in pointing out its veiled allusions to contemporary persons and events. More than a year the poet remained in London, collecting and revising many of his youthful efforts and adding new poems under the title *Complaints*, issuing his *Daphnaida*, a memorial poem for a lady of the proud Howard family. The youthful gloom of the *Complaints* is gratefully relieved by a new butterfly poem, *Muiopotmos*, a tale in the manner of Ovid, as light, gorgeous, and exquisite as the butterfly hero himself.

Daily Spenser hoped for reward in some high appointment,

but hoped in vain. A pension of fifty pounds was the utmost. His charming pastoral *Colin Clout* may have been written on the way back to Ireland, or soon after reaching home; it is full of profuse compliment to the ladies and gentlemen and poets whom he had just left. But he kept and revised the poem against publication on the eve of his next visit.

After a courtship of more than a year, in 1594 he married as his second wife Elizabeth Boyle. The next year appeared 89 sonnets called *Amoretti,* many of which may have been composed earlier in life; but most of them probably record his courtship of this wife of his forties. Translation, adaptation, convention, and conceit abound, as in all sonnet cycles, but many of the sonnets are vibrant with the deep Spenserian music, such as number 68 beginning "Most glorious Lord of life." High above the sonnets rises his hymn in honor of his own marriage, the *Epithalamion.* It far transcends its original by Catullus, and in grandeur of stanza, structure, glory of imagery, depth and magic of cadence, subtle variation from strain to strain, high spiritual values based on a robust physical exuberance, it is one of the few noblest lyrics in the language.

Meanwhile three more books of the *Faery Queen* were coming on. In 1595 he published with *Colin Clout* a belated and somewhat chilled elegy on Sidney called *Astrophel* after the Greek pastoral elegiac convention. 1596 saw Spenser again in London and Books IV to VI soon issued with a new printing of the first three. The same year appeared his *Four Hymns.* These may be taken as the best epitome of the Platonic and Neoplatonic ideas so congenial to the Elizabethan poet. The first two, on profane love and beauty, he puts forth as youthful poems revamped, but the third and fourth are exalted rhapsodies in which the doctrines of Plato's *Symposium* and *Phaedrus* are merged with the mystical tradition of Christianity. One more poem, his last, called the *Prothalamion,* he wrote late in 1596 in honor of the double betrothal ceremony of two daughters of the Earl of Worcester. If it has less grandeur than the *Epithalamion,* yet nothing from Spenser's hand is more exquisitely wrought. And its joy for the happiness of others is most delicately tempered with the poet's own weariness of the sordid career he had had to follow.

Even this second flood of poetry won no worldly reward, and he returned to Ireland to face darkening clouds of revolt and disaster. In 1598 they broke; Kilcolman was burned as he fled with his family. He rushed to England with reports, and hardly arrived before he was taken ill. Broken, disheartened, perhaps disillusioned, he the more readily succumbed, and died not yet fifty, early in 1599.

The *Faery Queen* is a book of manners, far exceeding in grandeur and beauty the many others that the times called forth. It was the poet's stated end "to fashion a gentleman or noble person in vertuous and gentle discipline."[1] He dreamed of a greater England, conscious of her past, and strong above all fear of invasion. High-bred and high-minded Englishmen were essential thereto. But around him, pervading the Court, he saw sharp practice, hot tempers, and dangerous passions ungoverned and unreined, besetting even his very friends, nay, himself. Especially notorious were lust, sudden anger, slanderous malice, greed, and the "hunger of ambitious mindes."[2] In his *Mother Hubbard's Tale* and in *Colin Clout* he has twice contrasted the black side of the Court with the white in ringing passages. What could serve as an antidote to these dangerous parvenu crudities? What but the poetry of poets such as Spenser well knew himself to be, who, as he said, "labor to better the manners of men, and through the sweet bait of their numbers, to steal into the young spirits a desire of honor and virtue?"[3] So too had Sidney said in effect. With his great poem Spenser would charm men into high behavior.

To this end the *Faery Queen* is a vast compilation of stories of all sorts, history, old romance, mythology, legend, allegory, pastoral idyll, rather loosely grouped under the love-story of King Arthur and Gloriana (Elizabeth); Arthur, the Welsh king, was chosen no doubt out of regard for Elizabeth the Welshwoman.

[1] Letter to Sir Walter Raleigh published with the *Faery Queen*
[2] *Faery Queen,* 5.12.1
[3] *View of the Present State of Ireland*

Spenser had already experimented with a wide variety of metres—lines of four, five, or six stresses, old "fourteeners," tumbling metre in mistaken imitation of Chaucer, couplets, stanzas of six, seven, and eight lines, the sonnet—nearly every traditional metre still surviving in English. But for his purpose he invented a new one, the Spenserian stanza, possibly by adding a six-stress line to the eight-line stanza used by Chaucer in the *Monk's Tale.* It fitted his voice exactly, and many voices after him.

He accepted too the medieval practice of allegory, partly because people learn better for a little guessing, where more is meant than meets the ear, partly because it was safer in ticklish times like his, partly to provoke talk. His allegory shifts and changes, without the fixed values of Dante. It is twofold, at times shadowing the glorious events of English history or personal affairs of people in Court, at times suggesting the grand ideas of conduct which men needed. Malory, Geoffrey of Monmouth and other historians; Greek and Latin poets, especially Homer, Virgil, and Ovid; Aristotle and Plato, particularly their doctrines as adapted to the making of a gentleman in the Fourth Book of the *Courtier;* Ariosto's *Orlando Furioso* and Tasso's *Jerusalem Delivered;* handbooks of mythology—these suggest only the most conspicuous books which Spenser had by him as he wrought amid Irish hardships on his *Faery Queen.*

The reader once more is transported to Faery Land, that haunt of Renaissance poetic imagination, call it Utopia, Arcadia, Forest of Arden, or whatever, where anything may happen. There scene, pageant, action, and situation unfold and dissolve in a succession which it is often difficult to follow, but perhaps on that account all the more useful to Spenser's purpose of suggesting secondary allegorical meanings and provoking our speculation. The magic of superworldliness which pervades the poem, at least after the First Book, may well be the effect of his delight in the unearthly beauty of Irish mountains, forests, vales, and streams.

The books differ widely. The First, of Holiness, is the story of the young Red Cross Knight, St. George of England, and how his love for Una, with its Platonic chivalry, carries him through trials and misunderstanding to heavenly vision and achievement in the end. Young George, though of royal blood, was brought up on the farm, and his career is made to shadow forth England's triumph over the almost overwhelming forces of Spain and the Papacy.

The Second Book, of Temperance, conducts Sir Guyon through trials which discipline him in the Aristotelian virtue of self-control, especially control of hot temper, greed, worldly ambition, and carnal desire. Guyon serves no lady of his heart. In the end he overthrows the Bower of Bliss. Based chiefly on the ethics of Aristotle and Plato, and richly imbued with classic myth and Renaissance sensuousness, this book seems more pagan than the others.

The Third Book, of Chastity, and the Fourth, of Friendship, are really a unit. Britomart, the woman-warrior of royal British line, and Artegall are dominant in both. Their love-friendship, high-minded, enduring, resolute, intelligent, transcends in every way the fifty other love affairs of the two books, which illustrate fifty variations of human love between noble and bestial. The two books are a kind of symphonic elaboration on the theme of romantic love with friendship, as the most exalting influence in human life.

The Fifth Book, of Justice, with Artegall (Lord Grey) as its hero, embodies the struggle of English Protestantism against the forces represented by Mary Queen of Scots, the struggle of the Low Countries with Spain, of the Protestant cause in France, and the troubles in Ireland. The four themes are but four aspects of the one cause, the cause which Spenser so ardently shared with Raleigh, Leicester, the Sidneys, and their party at Court.

The Sixth, of Courtesy, is in many respects the finest book of them all. At least it is at once the most tranquil and radiant, and in the end most despairing of lasting mundane happiness. In it we catch two fleeting glimpses of the ideal world, once when Colin Clout is piping to the dancing graces on Mount Acidale, and once in a lovely pastoral idyll, shattered, however, by the intrusion of animal barbarism.

A fragment of another book, on Mutability, seems to hint at

the dread consequences of some feared successor to Elizabeth, and expresses, as does the whole poem, the poet's sense of tragedy in the uncertainty of human life.

> For, all that moveth, doth in Change delight:
> But thence-forth all shall rest eternally
> With Him that is the God of Sabbaoth hight:
> O that great Sabbaoth God, graunt me that Sabaoth's sight.

The *Faery Queen* like most Elizabethan literature was seasoned to satisfy the Elizabethan relish for strong meats. Modern taste finds itself cloyed at times by the excess of sensuous beauty in the poem, and offended by its grotesque, even repulsive, extravagance. Yet its variations of exquisite music, its splendid pageantry, its prolific imaginings, its fertility in ideas, make it a poem for all the ages. Its charm, its subtle suggestion, its inexhaustible power to engender poetry in every generation since his day, wholly justify Spenser's title, the poet's poet.

CHAPTER 11

Drama and Dramatists

MIRACLE PLAYS AND MORALITIES

EVERYONE of us from tender years has had within him the dramatic instinct. Everyone can recall how in times of excitement, intense concentration, admiration, high spirits, we and our mates fell into dramatic imitation of something we had seen, read, or imagined.

These dramatic instincts, latent in a people, under favoring conditions may develop to produce a high form of art which we call drama, and the rise of English drama through some six centuries to Shakespeare follows the course of these favoring conditions, though the course is in places obscure or devious.

With minstrels on the one hand and popular folk-festivals on the other, even back in primitive times, dramatic manifestations in spectacles, mummings, and the like occurred, and their tradition may historically have survived in the masque and pageant, as well as in the court jester of Shakespeare's time.

But alongside this uncertain tradition was another, more vigorous and distinct, rising out of religion. The services of the medieval church were full of dramatic moments, especially those of Easter and the preceding week. Such, for example, were the simulated burying of the Cross and the Host and their subsequent resurrection. As early as the tenth century the mass at Easter paused long enough for one chorister enacting the angel to say, or sing, in Latin: "Whom seek ye in the sepulchre, O servants of Christ?" and three others, impersonating the three Marys, reply: "Jesus of Nazareth crucified, O servants of Heaven." The angel answers: "He is not here; He is risen as

He foretold. Go, proclaim that He hath risen from the grave."
A similar dramatic episode rose between Mary and the seeking
shepherds at a Christmas mass.

Slowly through three or four centuries this Latin religious
drama devised and acted by clerics increased in length and
variety. It extended itself to a great number of Biblical and
religious subjects, flourished wherever the Roman Church flourished in Europe, and survived, at least in traces, almost to modern times.

But by the thirteenth century a more vigorous scion was
springing from the main stock. With the rise of modern tongues
this church drama became more variously nationalized. Bits of
vernacular intruded into the Latin text; skilful laymen were
enlisted as actors; the plays became so thronged and popular
that they were moved from the church into the churchyard,
and thence out into the more secular market or guildhall. Thus
during the hundred years or so from about 1250, out of the
church drama came a presentation of the plays by laymen, and
the sacred drama long continued to be acted, on the one side
by church people, on the other by laymen. But the lay interpretation lent itself to freer development and often to license.
Witness Robert Manning's discrimination above.[1] By 1400 the
lay drama had created in England, as on the Continent, great
cycles or series of plays covering sacred history and a few lives
of saints, all in English.

From the thirteenth to the fifteenth century these "miracle-
plays" or "mysteries," as they are called, were enacted in
some 125 towns and villages. In many of the larger towns of
England these cycles had their separate local development, probably under the stimulus and ingenuity of the clever amateur
actors in the excitement of rehearsal and performance. The
new feast of Corpus Christi in May or June gave better weather
for out-door presentation than Christmas and Easter. The local
city government took charge and assigned the plays among the
various trade-guilds of the town, no doubt stirring a rivalry that
made for excellence. So on the great feast-day in late spring
stages on wheels moved forth to their stations through the city,

---

[1] Page 80

and the citizen could pass from one to another, thus witnessing as much of the cycle as his time allowed. The performances were sometimes continued for three days.

Of these cycles the texts of only four have come down to us—of Chester, with twenty-five plays; of York, with forty-eight complete plays; of "Coventry," with forty-four; and of the Towneley or Wakefield cycle of thirty-two.

Stages devices were crude to our way of thinking—a semblance of a ship for Noah, a dragon's mouth for Hell. But costuming and make-up were a matter of concern as the quaint expense accounts prove, with "2 cotes & a payre hosen for Eve, stayned," "a face & heare for ye Father," and "a new coat & a peir hoes for Gabriell."

Certain figures became traditional. Even as late as Shakespeare's time Herod was expected to roar and rant; Satan with his imp made noisy farce; Noah's shrewish wife and the shepherds abiding in the field developed plenty of slapstick. Wife, shepherds, common folk, local color, and all are English as English.

Local talent of a very high order must have developed, and no doubt there were instances of masterly skill and memorable interpretation of the famous scenes both comic and tragic. Even a marvellous "coc croyng," surely a masterpiece, was on occasion rewarded with fourpence.

It is customary to speak patronizingly of the artless crudity of these plays. But the proof of their excellence is not in the reading but in the acting. The York or Chester Noah play, the Chester *Abraham's Sacrifice,* the Chester *Shepherd's Play* and the famous *Secunda Pastorum* of the Towneley group, in the hands of intelligent actors even today prove themselves works of high? dramatic art, with their delicious comedy, their simple tenderness, their power and depth of feeling.

Out of the church play had sprung the more vigorous branch, the miracle-play, though the festival play in church by clerics kept on without much change till Tudor times. Likewise about 1400 or earlier, when the *Romance of the Rose* had much increased the allegorical habit of poetry, an offshoot from the miracle-play appears called the "morality." It deals in allegory,

always with essentially the same matter, the conflict of the personified human soul with sin amid contending vices and virtues,
and ends in one of two ways, triumph or damnation. It is an
old motive in literature, called the *psychomachia* (soul-fight),
older indeed than Prudentius of the fifth century, back to whose
allegorical *Psychomachia* it is usually traced. Being a struggle
it contains high dramatic possibilities, and on second thought
we realize that tragedies of Shakespeare and many another more
recent play or tale are essentially of this sort.

Few texts of the moralities remain. *Mankind, The Castle of
Perseverance* (fifteenth century), *Lusty Juventus,* Skelton's
Magnificence, and Sir David Lyndsay's *Satire of the Three Estates,* which is not quite true to form (sixteenth century), are
fair examples. But the greatest of them all is *Everyman,* as its
power in modern revival shows. Like the miracle-plays, these
moralities were acted by the people, and while the personifications gave some chance for invention, similarity of plot arrested the growth of the form, except as it escaped into such
masterpieces as Marlowe's *Dr. Faustus* and the First Book of
the *Faery Queen,* which in essence are moralities.

INTERLUDES

While this popular religious drama continued to flourish in
the fifteenth and sixteenth centuries, still another branch was
emerging, in the direction of plays on secular subjects, by professional actors, acted in the banqueting hall of lord, guild, or,
in time, of college. Such are the so-called "interludes," short
plays often farcical, in which that remarkable man John Heywood (1497?-1580?) specialized, with possibly the help of Sir
Thomas More. His *Pardoner and the Friar, Four P's, The
Weather* (a subject potentially dramatic at any time), were
coarse and lively farces to amuse the *élite* of Henry VIII's day.
"Interlude" is a term loosely used, but in its more original
meaning is perhaps only a "play between" two or more persons. Some wish to think that in the maker and actor of interludes we encounter again the old professional entertainer,
descendant from scop and minstrel of earliest times, as distinguished from the more amateur drama of miracle and morality.

ANCIENT MODELS

However that may be, the various strains of native dramatic energy and skill now come into contact with that powerful agency, the Renaissance of Greek and Roman literature, especially of Greek and Latin drama. From it they learned all-important lessons in structure, style, more exact conceptions of comedy and tragedy, and from it they drew on an inexhaustible store of new matter. Plautus and Terence were the models for comedy; and Seneca, rather than the greater tragic writers of the Greeks, for tragedy. Though Seneca's plays are not for the stage, his bombast and his extravagant horrors were a little more to the strong Elizabethan taste than Greek refinements. These Romans taught orderly division into five acts, which became prescriptive down to the last century. Seneca suggested the effective use of ghosts, the "chorus," and revenge, and a kind of rhetoric which at times degenerated into booming bombast about Hell and Heaven:

> Then as I look down to the damned Fiends,
> Fiends, look on me, and thou dread god of Hell,
> With ebon sceptre strike this hatefull earth,
> And make it swallow both of us at once.[1]

Which essentially we meet somewhat refined in Hamlet's

> O all you host of Heaven! O earth! What else,
> And shall I couple Hell, O fie! Hold, hold, my heart!

From Terence are descended such stock characters as the rascally servant, the smart lover, the grumpy father, and the strutting military man.

EARLY PLAYS

The middle of the sixteenth century abounded in plays most of which have disappeared. There were tragedies and comedies on the learned Latin models and adaptations from the Italian, for polite folk in college, Court, and Inns of Court; such were Gascoigne's plays, the so-called first English tragedy by Thomas

---

[1] Marlowe, *Tamburlaine,* Part I.4.2. 1470-3

Sackville and Thomas Norton named *Gorboduc or Ferrex and Porrex,* and "Mr. S's" comedy, *Gammer Gurton's Needle. Gorboduc,* stiff as it is, used blank verse and Italian dumbshow (as in *Hamlet*) by way of improvements. The comedy is better. Though devised after Terence's plan, *Gammer Gurton* is so full of racy English life and fun that it is still good matter for the stage.

Meanwhile in the inn-yards the crowd were delighting in diffuse historical plays, especially of English history, and tragicomedy like Edwards's *Damon and Pithias* and Preston's pompous *Cambises,* of which Falstaff makes such rare fun. Learned Sidney in his *Defence* disparages these crude but lively plays of the innyard. He no doubt preferred the finer and more academic *Ralph Roister Doister* (about 1553) by Nicholas Udall. It has a good Terentian plot and characters, especially the swagger military title-part; but Ralph's servant, Merygreeke, is bred from the comic Vice of the morality, and the play is essentially English. Since it is at once well-made, popular, and early, it has long but inaccurately worn the title "the First English Comedy."

Miracle-play, church play, morality, learned "classical" plays, and popular mixtures of various sorts—all going on early in Elizabeth's time. Out of this medley, in a union of native dramatic vigor with art, the drama of Shakespeare takes form.

THE THEATRE

As we sit today in the theatre waiting for the curtain, it is amusing to recognize in certain features of the house traces of their homely origin. Our theatre is of triple ancestry. Its round shape has persisted from the Elizabethan bear-garden; its roof and general arrangement of seats from the "private" enclosed theatre of the classes; but in its galleries and the floor of the house we may recognize the galleries and cobbled court of the old inn, still to be seen in many English towns, where companies of strolling players were wont to set up a temporary stage in the courtyard and play in the open air. Certain old London inns housed performances so habitually as to become essentially playhouses.

The first regular public playhouses were the Theatre and the Curtain, of about 1576, and the private Blackfriars of the same time; but the public theatres, as centres of danger, were kept out of town, first to the north, afterwards south of the Thames, where the famous Globe rose in 1599. "Private" theatres were distinguished chiefly by being roofed, charging higher prices, and having companies of boys for actors. They were evolved by converting some roomy old interior to theatrical use.

These houses seem to have been spacious. The Blackfriars stage measured 46 by 25 feet, and some of the public theatres held over 2000 people. The "apron" or proscenium of our stage is a vestigial trace of the Elizabethan stage projecting far into the yard or pit. A curtain towards the back shut off a recess, and over it was a balcony for the frequent "enter above" of old plays. Doors on either side gave access, but movable scenery was little used till the Restoration.

UNIVERSITY WITS

During the decade between 1584 and 1594 a group of playwrights usually called the University Wits were unawares preparing the way for Shakespeare. They were all, certainly all but one, of either Oxford or Cambridge, where they could find experience in "classical" drama before their plunge into London. They were John Lyly, Robert Greene, George Peele, Thomas Kyd, Thomas Lodge, Thomas Nashe, and Christopher Marlowe, and they all led a rough and tough life of it among the theatres.

Of these none is more picturesque than Greene (1560?-1592) with his "iolly long red peake [beard]" and amiable face. During his dozen years in London he lived wild and deep yet with a mind close to virtue, made warm friends and enemies, wrote much, and died repentant in the devoted care of a poor cobbler and his wife. His autobiographical *Groatsworth of Wit* written near his end is a most touching human document. He wrote very popular romances, especially *Pandosto* and *Menaphon,* both often reprinted, but notable to us as the matrices of a few exquisite songs, Greene's finest performance. Best known is "Weep not, my wanton." Besides a welter of pam-

phlets he made five comedies, of which the most deserving is
Friar Bacon and Friar Bungay, an amusing affair of magic and
hocus-pocus, with a charming romance between Lacy, Earl of
Lincoln, and the lowly but lovely Margaret, the Keeper's
daughter. The verse is stilted and stalking, but it cannot overcome the unmistakable quality of English countryside which
prevails throughout.

The same authentic quality pervades Peele's (1558?-1597?)
Old Wives Tale, wherein a fairy story is enacted against homely
rural background, yet sharpened with a tang of satire. This
compound of homeliness and airy fancy proved a fruitful source
of artistic success in Shakespeare, as also in Milton's _Comus,_
which derives in part from Peele's play.

But Kyd's (1557?-1595?) _Spanish Tragedy_ about 1589 was
perhaps the best piece of mere stagecraft hitherto produced. It
is a Senecan tragedy of revenge in high life, with a ghost as
Chorus, a play within the play, love, five murders and two sui-
cides, "strong" situations and big speeches. All of which helped
to earn it its long popular success. The avenger creates suspense
by his hesitation, which with other resemblances leaves no
doubt that Shakespeare recalled it as he composed _Hamlet_.

MARLOWE (1564-1593)

No other of the group, however, was so great a genius as
Christopher Marlowe. Born at Canterbury in 1564, he was
trained at Cambridge, and after receiving the degree of M.A.
in 1587 plunged into the world of London. In the next six
years he must have lived fiercely, bickering, brawling, writing
seven plays and various poems, and living in close if subsidiary
association with men like Raleigh and Walsingham, in whose
secret service for the protection of the Queen he was engaged.
In his consorting with great men and momentous events he
felt the heady stimulus of Renaissance ideas and speculation,
and with youthful boldness inclined like Shelley to sceptical
extremes. A May day in 1593 he spent with three rascally
secret service associates down at an inn in Deptford. In the
evening they quarreled about the reckoning. Marlowe, always
hot-tempered, struck at one Ingram Frizer with his dagger, who

in turn stabbed him to death and was acquitted in self-defence. It was a brief and sensational life, but the legend of blasphemy and license that for three centuries has hung over the man's memory is now happily dispelled, or much qualified.

His greatest plays are *Tamburlaine,* in two parts, *The Jew of Malta, Edward II,* and *Dr. Faustus.* They represent an astonishing and rapid growth in technique and understanding. *Tamburlaine* (1587?) is a gorgeous pageant in two plays of that sturdy hero's rise from the soil through triumph after triumph over effete nations. He wins by compulsion the heart of the captive Zenocrate, and dies grandiosely at the close. The pulse of the play beats strong, not with dramatic excitement, but with the rhythm of a new blank verse whose sonorous cadence must have been a joy to actor and audience alike. The play thrills with Renaissance visions of power, and with sounding rhapsodies of geographic names that sent Elizabethan imagination off in yearning dreams of remote worlds and wealth and adventure.

It has been generally supposed that within a year of *Tamburlaine* Marlowe produced *Dr. Faustus,* though its maturity of thought makes 1592 a more probable date. Taking his matter from an English version of a German account, this young poet still in his twenties wrought the first grand dramatic study of tragic destiny in human character, in one of the highest masterpieces of English Literature. It is the familiar legend of the super-talented young man who sold his soul to the Devil to gain all that the Renaissance so passionately lusted after, and was therein damned. But Marlowe presents it stark and austere, free from the sentimentality with which the romantics have colored it in the modern mind.

Briefly and without division into act and scene, Marlowe rushes through the twenty-four years with skilful condensation of the time, yet giving a strong suggestion of the development and degeneration of his hero. Young, brilliant, and inquisitive, Faustus finds himself bored with the ease of his attainment, becomes infatuate and then dizzy with his dreams of superhuman power. Once in possession of this power he scorns all spiritual values, commits shocking sacrilege, sets his heart vaguely on mere knowledge for its own sake or as a means to wealth, on political and military power, rich clothes, food, and carnal pleasure. Compunctions visit him at times in the form of a Good Angel and an Old Man, and even in the impassioned warnings of Mephistopheles himself, and there are moments of boredom and disgust which his tempter beguiles with engrossing shows. Episode after episode shows Faustus wasting his great powers in ever sillier and more trivial ways, bored, tired, disillusioned, and at times worried, until the terrible last scene of his realization and frantic vain attempt to bargain with God. The young poet handles these high issues with uncanny intelligence and sympathy, not as mere stage motives, but as elemental realities of grave moment to himself.

The play is a fine example of medieval survival suffused with the quality of the Renaissance. It is in effect a morality, the human soul in losing struggle with evil. Good and bad angels, devils and Deadly Sins, are reminiscent of old allegory, and the first half is strongly flavored with old scholastic learning. But the assertive individualism, the quick pulse of aspiration, the scepticism, the roving vision of worlds unrealized, the poet's scrutiny of the human heart—all these are qualities of Marlowe's own time.

As a piece of stage technique *Dr. Faustus* has obvious faults. The falling action of the hero's degeneration, with its trivialities, creates a difficult anticlimax. The scenes as we have them are not all well concluded and joined. The comic scenes of low life have been much disparaged, but the test is the acting, and here again resourceful actors have revealed in them a yield of fun that is at once hearty, exuberant, and often delicate, not suspected by the unimagining eye of the reading critic.

The Jew of Malta, within two years of *Tamburlaine*, shows better stage management, more flexibility and diversity. Its hero is a Machiavellian bad man, greedy, intriguing on a grand scale, treacherous even in his family, until he pleases every one by his unexpected demise in a boiling cauldron which he had set for someone else. The underplot of love is mawkish, and from a vigorous beginning the play descends to shallow melodrama. Yet it swells with Marlowe's superb verse and Renaissance aspiration, and has the added glory, together with a lost play called *The Jew,* of furnishing Shakespeare with his Shylock story almost ready made.

Marlowe's most mature play, at least in technique, is *Edward II* (1591?). Here he moves with the skilful flexibility of an expert. It is another study of a degenerating mind, like Shakespeare's *Richard II,* less generalized than *Faustus,* yet with many subtle shades of personality in the hero and others. A reader who turns from Shakespeare to *Edward II* needs no demonstration to prove that Marlowe had wrought out a dramatic technique fitted to the great master's hand. He is first to present the tragic struggle within the soul, not the soul of a king, but of a human individual, whose greatness is a greatness of Nature. He breathed intense feeling into his plays through the stirring music of a new blank verse, so musical and so spontaneous that it often sounds more fluent and easy than prose; and at moments occur interludes of poetic outburst, like the passages beginning

> If all the pens that ever poets held,[1]

and

> Was this the face that launcht a thousand ships
> And burnt the topless towers of Ilium?[2]

that delight and rest the audience with their spell.

Marlowe's power as a poet was not confined to his plays. Besides his unfinished retelling of the tale of *Hero and Leander,* his "Come live with me and be my love"[3] will never be forgotten. Its lyric sweetness is safe beyond any harm from the literal reality of so clever an answer as *The Nymph's Reply,* ascribed to Raleigh.

Marlowe died at twenty-nine. His unfulfilled renown has suffered from scandal and the eclipsing shadow of his greater successor. What he might have become who can say? At twenty-nine Shakespeare had done nothing so mature as *Edward II.*

[1] *Tamburlaine,* Part I.5.2.1942-1954
[2] *Faustus,* 1328
[3] *The Passionate Shepherd to his Love*

Yet Marlowe had never shown much comprehension of a woman's heart, nor told in drama a great love story, nor indicated the range of understanding among the varieties of human nature which is necessary to the greatest dramatist. Without him would Shakespeare have been Shakespeare? Not a profitable question perhaps—not so profitable as the great poet's regard for this unhappy, storm-tossed, and possibly beloved young genius, implied in his tender allusion:

> Dead shepherd, now I find thy saw of might:
> Who ever lov'd that lov'd not at first sight?[1]

[1] *As You Like It,* 3.5.81,2; Marlowe. *Hero and Leander,* 1.176

CHAPTER 12
Shakespeare (1564–1616)

IT HAS become customary to regard Shakespeare as the greatest of English poets, if not the greatest in modern times. Since Garrick acted and later Coleridge praised, that is, during the last century and a half, an idolatry of Shakespeare has prevailed which has hardly been fair to Shakespeare, and which he would doubtless have been the first to deprecate. Yet there is indeed an uncanny magic about a man who can do so many supremely difficult things so easily, with so high an average of just-rightness, whose wit never stales, who delights and startles us with the living and speaking reality of his copies from human life, with their range and variety, and yet clothes the whole in the charm which is poetry and makes it a joy for ever.

It seems strange to us that no one of his acquaintances who realized his greatness as they did took the trouble to set down what he could gather about the man. One portrait gives us some credible notion of his head and features. It is the bust over his tomb, viewed from beneath in profile, as in the frontispiece of the Oxford edition. Yet Shakespeare as a man in the flesh is more indistinct to us than Chaucer or Dante or Virgil. The authentic facts are few and not extraordinary; but they have been heavily overgrown with legend and conjecture which must be continually pruned back.

He was born on or about April 23, 1564, at Stratford. His father was a rising citizen, dealer in farm products, who was alderman and bailiff when this oldest son was four. Of his boyhood we have only the background—old Stratford by the river in lay-out much as today, with half-timber and stone houses, walled gardens, the sweet old church at the edge of the town, and beyond, the fields, lanes, grey churches, and villages of Warwickshire, still redolent of medieval England and all its charm. Warwick Castle is but eight miles away, Kenilworth, where the Queen was welcomed with gorgeous pageantry, only thirteen, and Coventry, where religious plays were still acted, twenty. Stratford grammar school inducted the town's youth into such ancient authors as Virgil, Ovid, Horace, Cicero, Terence, and Sallust, and made the boys better Latinists than are college men today. How much of this, if any, Shakespeare got, no one knows.

At eighteen he married Anne Hathaway, eight years his senior. The union apparently was hurried, and Susanna Shakespeare was born six months later. Betrothal in that day was, even before the law, the essential wedding bond. Hamnet and Judith, twins, were born less than two years later. So far as known there were no children after this.

From twenty-one to twenty-eight his way of life is unknown. How or why he got to London, and into the theatrical life, no one can say. Stories of his being a horse-holder and call-boy at the theatre are stories. Certain it is that once begun he made so ready a success as a playwright, and perhaps actor, as to draw the scorn of Greene in behalf of the "wits," who in his dying *Groatsworth of Wit* calls him "an upstart crow, beautified with our feathers," who "being an absolute Johannes Factotum, is in his owne conceit the only Shake-scene in a countrie."

From about twenty-six to thirty he was getting his hand in. He found excellent discipline in revamping old plays and in collaboration, as in the three parts of *Henry VI,* and the horrible *Titus Andronicus.* But the very ingenious *Comedy of Errors,* a farce doubly farced from Plautus, by giving two masters, who are doublets, servants who are also doublets; the exquisite *Love's Labor's Lost,* which plays with literary and Court affectations from France and Italy; and the dreary but powerful *Richard III,* show bold and ranging experimentation.

From thirty to thirty-seven the poet enjoyed success both in art and fortune. It is the time of *Midsummer Night's Dream, Romeo and Juliet, Richard II, Merchant of Venice,* the two plays on Henry **IV**, *Henry V, Merry Wives, Julius Caesar,* and the glorious comedies, *Much Ado about Nothing, As You Like It,* and *Twelfth Night*. He also published two narrative poems, *Venus and Adonis* and *The Rape of Lucrece,* each dedicated to the Earl of Southampton. In 1599, on second application, the poet's father gained a coat of arms, possibly by the effort of his oncoming son. At any rate, when thirty-three the poet was able to buy the largest house in Stratford and begin a rather long list of transactions in real estate both in Stratford and London.

He was associated with the Burbages at the old Theatre, and after 1599 at the Globe, and in 1608 at the Blackfriars. He may for a time have been at the Swan and the Rose. His company gave private performances before the Queen, by command, and under a succession of eminent patrons became for years the leading London company. No doubt Shakespeare's skill as a playwright had everything to do with this pre-eminence. The plays of this period have in their texture the vigorous ease, the firmness of touch and exuberant play of mind, that naturally go with assured success. In 1596, during this success, the poet's only son died in his twelfth year.

The period between the age of thirty-seven and forty-five seems by all evidence to pass through the shadow. It was prolific with eleven plays, seven of which were the tragedies *Hamlet, Lear, Othello, Macbeth, Timon, Antony and Cleopatra,* and *Coriolanus*. It includes also those bitter problem "comedies" on sex, *All's Well that Ends Well* and *Measure for Measure,* from which the light of romance had faded. Some would read a deep personal tragedy into the poet's life during these years; some find the change only the playwright's conformity to a general change in literary fashions at the time. One can only guess. The forties are a time of peculiar trial for anyone, when youth has suddenly defaulted and left but a riddle in its place; and in that day men aged faster than now. Certainly in the plays he has incarnated the elemental forces of life in high potential, and set them in conflict with each other. As in the men and the best poetry of his time, these forces are intense and extreme—ambition, greed, lust, envy and malice, wanton cruelty, contending with generous idealism, devotion, refinement, and love of order—sinners and offenders dragging down with themselves the guiltless and the unconcerned.

Then about 1610, when Shakespeare is forty-six, he begins to treat the same motives in a different way in the romances or mellower tragi-comedies, *Cymbeline, Winter's Tale,* and *Tempest.* Deep wrongs they exhibit, but they resolve themselves in forgiveness and peace—not sentimental nor forced by theatrical demand, but real, and with a suggestion of tranquil idealism.

After the Queen died in 1603 Shakespeare seems to have acted less often, though his company was now under the King's patronage and played before him on many occasions. During this last period of the romances he was withdrawing more and more to Stratford, though he lent his veteran help in the making of *Henry VIII* and *Two Noble Kinsmen.* His wife and daughters had lived all these years at Stratford, increasing in consequence with the poet's success; and it looks as if his relations with them, in spite of long absences, were contented enough. On April 23, 1616 (old style; May 4 of our calendar) he died, and in obedience to his well-known epitaph, his bones have lain undisturbed in the noble old church by the Avon, now a world shrine.

"Not of an age, but for all time." True enough of Shakespeare, of whom Jonson first said it, it is true of all greatest poets, who transcend their period and illustrate its tendencies with less precision than smaller men. Yet Shakespeare is an epitome of the forms and motives that had been hitherto upgathered into English Literature and English culture. He had not much formal education—great genius has a way of getting its own—nor such birth and position as Sidney. He was, therefore, with his humble origin, the more fit to bring the common English energies into fertile conjunction with the higher culture of the times.

His plays are permeated with medieval chivalry, sometimes obvious, sometimes implicit, in their language and conception of love, their social organization, their manners; Romeo, Hotspur, Prince Hal, Orlando, are notable descendants from chivalry or the Court of Love. The medieval notion of comedy as a story that begins ill and ends well, or of tragedy as that of a lofty personage like Lear or Macbeth fallen from his high estate, in the manner of Lydgate's *Falls* or the *Mirror for Magistrates,* had their part in determining the comedies and tragedies of Shakespeare.

But the medieval element in his work was blended with the ideas and temper of the Renaissance. He knew Ovid in Golding's translation, and Plutarch in North's classic version from the French; yet his use of translations does not prove his ignorance of the original—as able linguists as Chaucer and Spenser resorted to cribs. From Ovid he caught many a fragment of myth which he used to glorify great moments in his plays, and touch them with the magic of universal poetic beauty. From Plutarch came the matter for his Roman plays, and through Plutarch his quick, intuitive comprehension of Roman character. His debt to Seneca was the debt of all tragedians of the time.[1] From Plautus he made his most roisterous farce. From time to time in sonnet and play comes the flush of the fashionable Platonic conception of love and inspiration: true love as against lust; love the regenerator; love yearning to perpetuate transient beauty by creation; "the marriage of true minds"; beauty of woman but the shadow of eternal beauty; warm and intense friendships especially between men; love and inspiration but a kind of super-sane madness, since

> The lunatic, the lover, and the poet,
> Are of imagination all compact.

With the rest he inherits from the ancients the pastoral "escape," and makes charming traditional use of the pastoral miniature or idyll in *As You Like It* and *The Winter's Tale.*

But much of the Renaissance culture in his plays comes to him by way of Italy and France. Again and again he draws upon Italian stories from Bandello, Cinthio, Fiorentino for both comedy and tragedy. He loves a scene in Italy or France, or perhaps prefers one because his provincial English audience, looking ever southward for manners, preferred it. And those high-bred gentlemen and ladies ever stepping with stately dig-

[1] See p. 175

nity in and out of his plays, with their leisurely courtliness
and charming speech, are of the Italian courts, and may be met
in Hoby's translation of *The Courtier*. The doctrine and manners of that book enter deeply into the fashioning of figures
as great and courtly as Hamlet and Othello.

But alien culture mingled in the poet with a richer native
element. Practically all his dramatic devices had been naturalized or developed, and were waiting ready to his hand when he
came—blank verse, stage prose, the double plot, the blend of
love and comedy, of humor and tragedy; the play within the
play, the comic mischief-maker or Vice from the morality, the
interpolated song, the girl disguised as a boy, division into five
acts, and much more. These were no novelties.

But his English inheritance included the more substantial
treasure that he brought with him from his youth in the country, the folk-lore and folk-song, the suggestive symbolism and
usage of a people not long since Catholic, and much that was
hallowed and mellowed by centuries of human tradition. Of
this sort was his keen sense of England's history, much quickened in all minds by the new national consciousness and the
defeat of the Armada. And he lets old Gaunt in *Richard II*
thrill the audience when he utters the feelings of all Elizabethan
England:

> This royal throne of kings, this scepter'd isle,
> This earth of majesty, this seat of Mars,
> This other Eden, demi-paradise,
> This fortress built by Nature for herself
> Against infection and the hand of war,
> This happy breed of men, this little world,
> This precious stone set in the silver sea,
> Which serves it in the office of a wall,
> Or as a moat defensive to a house,
> Against the envy of less happier lands,
> This blessed plot, this earth, this realm, this England,
> This nurse, this teeming womb of royal kings,
> Fear'd by their breed and famous by their birth,
> Renowned by their deeds as far from home,—

For Christian service and true chivalry,—
As is the sepulchre in stubborn Jewry
Of the world's ransom, blessed Mary's Son:
This land of such dear souls, this dear, dear land,
Dear for her reputation through the world.

But no one wishes to think of Shakespeare as a mere compound of manifold cultures, capable of analysis. All these elements were fused in his super-intelligence or genius, his profound sense of humanity actually in the flesh, and his talent
for reproducing it in art. They were subject to his control, and
received new form and pressure from his hand.

With our present-day idea that originality means revolt from
tradition, we are likely to be puzzled by the natural readiness
with which so great a genius as Shakespeare accepted traditional material and traditional forms. In them he found room
enough even for powers as great and versatile as his.

His early *Venus and Adonis* and *Rape of Lucrece* are picturesque rehearsals in impassioned verse, of classic myth, like
Marlowe's *Hero and Leander* and even various of Chaucer's
tales, with a Renaissance excess, now of sensuousness, now of
moral edification.

Probably no subject in English Literature has provoked so
much gossip and infatuation as Shakespeare's sonnets. To whom
were they addressed? To what women real or fictitious? Or
what men? What were the deep tragedies in his life, the mock-
eries, the hard usage and bitter misgivings which they darkly
veil? It is vain to inquire. Yet these 154 sonnets, the work of a
man still young, ostensibly touching his most intimate personal
life, were published for all the world to see seven years before
his death, when he was a successful and distinguished citizen.

For sixty years since the days of Wyatt there had been sporadic sonneteering in England. Sidney's sequence, *Astrophel and
Stella,* printed in 1591, but chiefly composed and circulated in
manuscript at least a decade before, made the sonnet a leading
poetic fashion for the rest of the century. At least twenty-five
sequences appeared in that time, in which among others Wat-
son shed *Tears of Fancie,* Daniel wooed his Delia, Lodge his
Phillis, Barnes his Parthenophe, Giles Fletcher his Licia, Con-

stable his Diana, Drayton his Idea, and Spenser his Elizabeth
or whomever else. Shakespeare followed the fashion, except
that he made no ostensible sequence.

Though traces of Sidney's *Arcadia* and of Daniel are discernible in his sonnets, they belong to the sonnet family at large.
In the best instances the three quatrains rise in three waves of
accumulating imagery that break and spread in the final couplet as a breaker spends itself on broad beach sands. The conventions and "conceits" abound, but are not inconsistent with
sincerity. Sometimes he laughs at the worn conceits, as in number 130; sometimes he plays with his theme, or puns; sometimes he is bitter; sometimes by way of love or friendship he
touches such primal matters of life as time, affinity, decay,
death, with grandeur of music and meaning that overflow the
bounds of the sonnet, and are monumental.

While the polite world was sonneteering, all the Elizabethan
world, high and low, was singing. Never before nor since has
England produced such exquisite songs, both words and music,
nor in such number as during Shakespeare's lifetime. He is
easily the master of them all in making the words, though
others sometimes produced single songs as good as his. Nearly
one hundred songs and snatches are scattered throughout his
plays, occurring at just the moment when they will give point
to the action or yield the lyric relief which the spectator instinctively needs. Their effect is in part that which the Greeks
provided in their choruses. But aside from their dramatic setting these songs would alone have proved the poet's greatness,
ranging from homely folk-song to "Full fathom five," and
"Hark, hark! the lark at heaven's gate sings." The melody is
in the words, and where the old tunes have survived, it is clear
enough that Shakespeare, like Burns or any first-rate lyric poet,
composed songs with a tune in his ear.

Like all great poets Shakespeare preferred old stories to any
that he might have invented himself. Perhaps it is because they
came to him shaped and humanized by much handling, laden
with accumulated human feeling, their quality softened by age.
Yet mere age was not enough, and that busy and questing mind
must have scanned and rejected an enormous amount of ma-

terial to find what exactly fitted his purpose, seemed suitable for the stage, and could rouse his imagination.

He also preferred remote places—Denmark, Italy, Athens, Illyria, the seacoast and "desarts" of Bohemia. Except the English historical plays, only three, the *Merry Wives of Windsor, Cymbeline*, and *Lear* take place in England, and in the two last, it is not a familiar England, but a remote, barbaric, Celtic Britain. Was it to gratify the roving Elizabethan imagination? Or to free the action from petty comparison with literal realities? Or to gain that romantic illusion and poetic power for which distance of place or time are requisite? Yet he knew the practical value of stage reality. Chiefly by minor plots and minor characters, using prose rather than verse, he counterbalances remote scene and character with that which is pure-bred English and Elizabethan. In the Italian romance of *Romeo and Juliet,* the Nurse, Old Capulet, and the servants were produced in Shakespeare's England and nowhere else. So with his mobs, the Porter in *Macbeth,* Dogberry and Verges, old Corydon, Touchstone, Sir Toby Belch and the amusing moron, Sir Andrew Aguecheek, Kent in *Lear*, Launcelot Gobbo, Stephano, Emilia, Autolycus, Horatio, the gravediggers—these and their doings are all English.

In reading Shakespeare we are too prone to forget that he did not write as does the narrative poet, for us to read. He surely never dreamed of his plays as matter for classrooms. He was, in conceiving and executing his work, primarily an actor, a stage-manager, a playwright, thinking not of fame in ages to come, but of immediate success in the theatre. He seems to have been strangely indifferent about the preservation of his plays to posterity. Other Renaissance poets—Chaucer, Spenser, Milton—after the example of Horace and Ovid and the Italians, were deeply concerned about fame, "that last infirmity of noble mind." Quite possibly Shakespeare never once thought of his plays as "literature." It is therefore better to see them well acted than to read them, or in reading them to imagine oneself seeing them or, better still, acting in them, through every part and moment. For they are after all plays, and "poetry" is but one element in them, albeit the most important.

When Shakespeare began his apprenticeship about 1590, England was still exultant over the defeat of the Armada, and the English historical or "chronicle" play was highly popular. Accordingly he gauged the market, and produced nine such plays in as many years, beginning with his collaboration on *Henry VI*. But as they succeed one another they become less and less of the chronicle type, that is, diffuse scenes showing many striking moments in course of an active lifetime, and draw nearer to the strict form of tragedy on the one hand and of comedy on the other. The action contracts into focus upon one supreme event, such as the fight between Hotspur and Prince Hal in *Henry IV*, Part 1; and it concerns itself, not with a whole career, but with events which historically covered a little more than a year, and in the play are effectively intensified and reduced to ten days. There are in these historical plays semblances of the greater tragic figures yet to be conceived, in his dramatic handling of the bad Richard III, of the ill-adjusted introvert Richard II, of the noble but not quite sober Hotspur, even of degenerating Falstaff. In *Henry IV* comedy asserts itself as a fine artistic foil and counterbalance to the serious plot, reinforcing it and pointing it, until the overwhelming personality of Falstaff tends to eclipse any historical or tragic aspect of the play.

For Falstaff is one of the most astonishing feats of all literature. Gross, old, ugly, guilty of every sin in the calendar, selfish, treacherous, too lazy to be brave, yet at first he exhibits agility, lightness, and vivacity of mind in comic contrast with his flabby bulk, and the poet has clothed him infinitely in that most difficult of all human qualities to portray—charm; so that he disarms all criticism, and everyone from his cronies in the play to the spectator and the modern reader is helpless before him, or hotly resents any indictment of his patent and shameless vices, and springs to his defence. And when all is over with him the poet allows the old rascal still to beguile us in Dame Quickly's homely but touching account of how he died, playing with flowers and babbling o' green fields as he went away to Arthur's bosom.

Falstaff is not the only person fashioned in drama or fiction to win the world's favor by personal charm, but he is doubtless the most masterly and daring instance. Indeed Shakespeare has bestowed this rare grace upon his men and women with a bountiful hand. Prince Hal transformed as Henry V, Hamlet, Othello, Lear, all have this gift in rich measure, and the hero-ines of the comedies, however varied, are alike in their mys-terious power of attraction.

In his so-called romantic comedies it was Shakespeare's prac-tice to combine in one artistic whole various themes, plots, or groups of persons, but all united by a multitude of little links, and all related to one grand theme. In the *Merchant of Venice* the theme is wealth and worth, and the several affairs of Portia, of Antonio, of Jessica, even of Launcelot, are variously con-cerned with this interest, each reinforcing the rest by its differ-ences, yet all so harmoniously and subtly combined that at the end of the play one leaves with a sense of having seen a single but indelible action.

The same variety and unity he achieves in *As You Like It;* Rosalind, her father, Orlando and his brother, Touchstone, Phebe—each in his own affair and experience finds "the uses of adversity." They all conspire under the playwright's skill, to cast about us the spell and charm of the forest—no local forest, but one of the imagination. Yet the poet knows, whether we discover it or not, that the charm of the forest, or of any other place, is but the charm and wit of the people we meet there. Depopulate it of these, and the charm is fled.

In *Much Ado about Nothing* the romantic "major plot" has paled at the momentous affair of Beatrice and Benedick. The play sounds various notes in the scale of wit, from the slow instinctive sense of Dogberry, through the clever unfeeling smartness of the Italianate gentlemen, to the wit of the two well-matured principals, who are in intelligence head and shoulders above and ahead of the rest, and whose wit plays spontaneously over great depth of feeling. With understanding heart they recognize each other from the beginning, and fool the rest, who stupidly think they are fooling them.

A similar measure of depth as of unity in variety, underlies merry *Twelfth Night*, from underdone Sir Andrew to the gentle, resourceful Viola, who is more concerned for the troubles of others than for her own. Yet all that was called for in making this play was a gay device of fun to divert Christmas revellers, perhaps Queen and Court. The Duke, Olivia, Malvolio are grown-up spoiled children suffering from vanity; Malvolio is probably incurable, but his case helps to make the others look less serious, and indeed they are easily cured by a little sharp discipline of the heart which the sane Viola is the means of administering. Similar but rougher discipline is applied to Malvolio through the high jinks of Sir Toby Belch and company— Sir Toby in many respects a miniature of Falstaff. Their fun never fades but plays timelessly over the depths, as Carlyle says, "like sunshine on the deep sea."

Ushered in as it were by those bitter problem plays, *All's Well that Ends Well* and *Measure for Measure,* is the series of tragedies, in which Shakespeare embodied that most satisfactory form of tragic drama, long ago evolved by the Greeks. Most likely it was his artistic instinct, his intuition for dramatic effect rather than knowledge of Greek tragedy, that led him to it. His tragedies show a great personality, usually in high social position, in a losing conflict with three elemental forces in life: luck or fate, other personalities, or a mortal weakness in the man's own nature. Here are the three great determinants in any life, but in tragedy the most effective is the inherent weakness of the hero. In his youthful *Romeo and Juliet* Shakespeare had let fate far outweigh the other forces in determining the end; but in the later tragedies the hero's responsibility weighs much more heavily, though the playwright, knowing his business, takes care that the hero's fate shall seem harder to us than he deserved. Macbeth was a treacherous murderer, and surely deserved what he got. And yet the dramatist shifts the guilt in a measure to his wife, makes us watch him losing the game point by point, and at last exhibits him in so magnificent a show of courage with his back to the wall that we cannot but pity him, as we more or less pity all Shakespeare's tragic figures.

Elizabethan dramatists seldom make a tragic hero of an Englishman, and the nationality of Shakespeare's heroes is variously Italian, Roman, Dane, Moor, Gael, Greek, and Briton.

In no other way do his breadth of sympathy and power of impersonation show themselves more astonishing than in the way he endows these figures with their national characteristics. Usually he has chosen men past their youth, on the verge of one disillusionment or other; but in *Lear*, sometimes called his greatest play, he has made bold to select a warm-hearted, amiable, not very wise old man on the margin of senility, still capable of disillusionment. The war of brutal barbarism with high nobility of soul in this play is too violent, and its pathos too heartbreaking, for best stage success; yet Shakespeare has mastered these elemental energies and kept them in bounds by his highest feat of dramatic construction. One plot was not enough to set forth this terrible theme. He employs two. So the story of self-reliant Lear with two ungrateful daughters and one devoted daughter is throughout iterated in a minor key by the story of pliant Gloucester with one ungrateful and one grateful son. And the many particulars of character, incident, and treatment by which the secondary plot is at once likened to, and distinguished from, the main story, and united with it, reveal the man's almost superhuman skill as a dramatic artist.

Two plays, *Midsummer Night's Dream* and *Tempest,* one early and the other late, with their song, dance, and pageantry, may seem at first to be in lighter vein, in the manner of a festive masque. And indeed the earlier is thought of some to have been composed to adorn some noble wedding. But lightly as the poet's fancy plays, the depths still lie calm beneath. *Midsummer Night's Dream* is woven of four or five strands— the settled, conventional world of parents and those in control; the pretty, absorbed, but troubled world of young lovers; the fairy world; the world of hard-handed, clumsy workmen; and the transcendent world of Oberon, who looks down upon all of them with mingled pity, amusement, and active concern. With his exquisite art and humor Shakespeare interweaves these strands of life into a play that intimates, as the greatest poetry should, things too deep for explicit utterance.

In the *Tempest* Oberon has become Prospero, older, wearier with the burden of the world, but transcendent still, and yet more deeply concerned, through the human relationship of his lovely daughter, with the affairs of men and with Nature. Whether from reading Montaigne, from tales of returned voyagers, or talk of the hour, the poet seems to be occupied with certain questions of civilization, and the *Tempest*, against a wild natural background, exhibits specimens variously civilized from the highest in Prospero down to Stephano, who as a savage in civilization appears lower in the scale and less dignified than the primitive Caliban himself. Nor has Shakespeare left out those disruptive agents always operating on higher levels of society with their intrigue and conspiracy and cynical disparagement of all ideals. Hints of these matters the play contains, yet in the sweet, tranquil, if slightly saddened temper of all his last plays.

From one whose whole habit of life as actor and playwright it was to transform himself into a thousand other personalities we need not look for an expression of definite convictions. Yet with all their differences his great men and women have certain composite traits. Again and again they are shown groping either curiously, like Hamlet, or incautiously, like Macbeth and Lear, along that dangerous border between the visible world and the more terribly real invisible world. And the signs of mental unhealth, sometimes mounting to madness, which they experience somehow deeply interested Shakespeare. So that neurologists today recognize in Hamlet a true-to-type case of neurasthenia, which the practical playwright saw only as first-rate dramatic material.

Long ago Shakespeare was compared to Nature herself, and the comparison holds. He, like Nature, is always fresh, alive, perennial. He is not confined to a historical period. Everyone sees something in him, no two see quite alike. This wide and deep range of discovery in his plays and poems gives us the most compelling proof of his genius.

CHAPTER 13

Turn of the Century

"In 1603 the great Queen died." With the turn of the century and the change of rulers, comes a change in men's minds, and a like change in literature. The fires of Elizabethan passion and the flush of Elizabethan dreams seem suddenly to die down. The mystical Platonic doctrines of life go out of fashion, and Petrarchan sonneteering ceases like bird-songs in August. In prose the flowing periodic tradition of Cicero makes way for a new prose of short, epigrammatic sentences, more like the essays of Seneca. The prose of Ascham and Sidney turns into the prose of Bacon and Taylor.[1] In both prose and verse composition becomes more cool and methodical.

All high composition is the effect of heated instinct combined with the cool calculation of conscious art. The effect varies according to the proportionate part of each. In the literature of Elizabeth instinct seemed paramount. But the new literature reversed the scale and asserted the importance of conscious art. Calculated effects, clarity, succinct and well-ordered construction, the literary doctrine of Horace, rather than the more mystical creed of Sidney—such are symptoms of the change. Unluckily this new doctrine has long worn the faded label "classicism," a mischievous term, since the ancient literatures had as much to do with the making of Elizabethan literature and of romantic literature generally, as of this thing called "classicism."

BEN JONSON (1573-1637)

Of the new doctrine the great apostle was Ben Jonson. Burly, big-featured, out of sturdy common stock of the Scotch border,

[1] See pp. 221, 263

once a bricklayer, through solid literary achievement and force of personality he rose, still in his thirties, to be a favorite of King and Court, and made warm friends and furious enemies on every hand. Within him still burned the Renaissance passions, and he had enormous capacity for both love and hate. Twice he killed his man in single combat.

He had the mental capacity and memory of a great scholar as well as the prolific genius of a poet, but his creations reflect a twofold power. His great works are caricatures of the literal life of London, high and low, vigorous and satirical, yet he made out of old myths and legends many a masque most exquisitely wrought and finished.

He was born about 1573, nine years Shakespeare's junior, and got formal education at Westminster; he missed the University, but being a genius he doubtless owed much of his erudition to himself and to one who believed in him, William Camden, learned friend of Spenser, master in Westminster,

> Camden! most reverend head, to whom I owe
> All that I am in arts, all that I know.

King James, himself a pedant, loved a learned man, and though he could not wholly appreciate the best of Jonson, welcomed him in the Court. There he had many friends, including the lamented Prince Henry of Wales, and in the ten years or so after 1604 turned out one successful comedy after another, and was in constant demand for masques and entertainments to celebrate progresses, visits, weddings, and feasts of the great. He was England's first poet-laureate.

The last twelve years of his life, when his royal patron was dead, and Charles I reigned, for whom perhaps Jonson's product was too robust, were a pitiful season of failing health and powers, poverty, and seeing himself out of date. His great library, one of the finest collections in England, was burned, and about him like an old dog at bay came snarling younger and more prosperous enemies. Yet he had also a strong and devoted following of young literary disciples whom he called "the tribe of Ben," and when he died he may have been aware of having established a great literary tradition, which was to prevail for a century and more after him.

It was an ancient and medieval theory of physiology that man is made of four humors or liquids, and that if these are tempered in equal parts, he is of even temperament; but if one exceeds the others, it makes him peculiar; if his sanguis or blood prevails, he is sanguine; if phlegm, he is phlegmatic; if melancholé, or black bile, he is melancholy; if cholé, or bile, he is choleric. Thus "humor" came to mean eccentricity.

In the comedy of "humors" a single character stands for some eccentricity, like the grump, the big bluff, the dandy, the cheerful liar, and such; the humor still reappears on occasion to enliven a musical extravaganza. Before Jonson, in Shakespeare and Chapman, one finds traces of humors; but Jonson professed the humors as his special doctrine, and went back to Latin comedy for his originals. The name of a person indicates his humor, and in the play the character lives up, or down, to his name. Fastidious Brisk, in *Every Man Out of His Humor*, is, as one might guess, "a neat, spruce, affecting courtier." Sir Politick Would-be, in *Volpone,* Morose, in *The Silent Woman*, "a gentleman that loves no noise," Sir Epicure Mammon, in *The Alchemist,* and Zeal-of-the-Land Busy, a hypocritical Puritan in *Bartholomew Fair,* are "humorous." It is but a step from such fun to allegorical satire, and Jonson, with his belief in the moral value of poetry, made lively use of this terrible instrument to satirize the fools and knaves on every hand, especially in the Court, and to carry on his invidious war with the other poets and playwrights, Dekker, Marston, and Daniel; though both parties surely realized the advertising value of the quarrel, and were glad to keep it up in the interests of good business more than spite. *Every Man Out of His Humor, Cynthia's Revels,* and *The Poetaster* are scathing.

The scene of Jonson's comedies is never Illyria or the seacoast of Bohemia; it is London. The street-cries, the shops, the scamps, the hurlyburly, households of gentry or of solid, trading middle class, fairs and freaks, pedants—all mingle to make Jonson's teeming, restless, smelly, noisy London. No glamorous half light of romance, but brutal broad daylight floods his stage with reality.

His greatest comedies are *Volpone* (*The Fox*), in which a rich old rascal swindles his expectant flatterers, and is brought to justice; *The Alchemist,* a grand exhibit of imposture on all hands; and *Bartholomew Fair,* showing the amenities of low life, and certain curious "respectables" getting their fingers burnt thereby. They are full of noisy fools and knaves, but not handled by a hopeless cynic.

The fun of these plays is no longer appreciated, but it is there; and intelligent, resourceful acting will reveal it. The lines abound in opportunity for the actor, and are racy with the strong, pungent flavor of Jonson's Elizabethan English. Often they glow with the deep fire of his poetry. They are the work of a practical stage artist who knew his audience and his business; and though their contemporaneous satire and slang and allusion have faded with time, and they may seem dull to the reader, acting brightens their colors and sets them in motion again.

Jonson also attempted two Roman tragedies, *Sejanus* and *Catiline,* doubtless encouraged by the success of *Julius Caesar.* A certain oratorical grandeur they have, and are carefully based on ancient histories; but mere learning does not insure dramatic success.

The charm of Jonson is in his masques and entertainments, of which he devised more than thirty.

The English masque was a court entertainment of both native and foreign stock. The old Christmas "mummings" and "disguisings" at Court went back to Chaucer's time, but in the days of Henry VIII they met the Italian masque imported from France, and the French masque originally Italian. Henceforth the masque became essentially a grand entry of courtiers masked and costumed, who at the end of their little action chose partners from the audience for the dance to follow. Through Elizabeth's time, as wealth increased, the masque developed, always in mutually helpful relation to other literature— the allegory of the morality, the pageantry of Spenser's *Faery Queen,* the plays of Lyly, Peele, and Shakespeare. Its heyday was the reigns of James I and Charles I, the first forty years of the seventeenth century, and its high priest was Jonson. Architects, designers, professional dancers and singers, composers of music and words all worked together, until, in the days of Charles and the architect Inigo Jones, the masques became unwieldy with extravagance and an easy mark of Puritan disapproval. Yet no doubt the arts of stage-setting and of the opera owe much to the development of the masque.

Jonson's masques are masterly ingenious miniatures made of bits of old myth, allegory, quaint or recondite lore, highly flavored with learning for the royal palate—a bit too highly for ours.

His *Oberon* in honor of his friend Prince Henry opens in pitch darkness. A rising moon shows a wild rocky place in the woods, satyrs peep forth one by one, and with grotesque but exquisite dance, song, and dialogue search for their adored Oberon. The forest dissolves into a gorgeous palace ablaze and awhirl with dancing and singing fays, beyond and above whom are grouped the court ladies and gentlemen as maskers, and in apotheosis the Prince as Oberon. He descends in a bear-drawn chariot among the fays and satyrs, amid songs, fine speeches, and ballet, in which he and the maskers mingle in "measures, corantos, galliards, etc.," until the morning star and the dawn (probably real) break the spell, and they separate with a last song. With modern equipment what might not such a show have been!

This grotesque and burlesque element of the satyrs was a device of Jonson's own. It is known as the antimasque, and serves as foil and racy Jonsonian antidote to mere airy-fairyness, into which the masque might easily have evaporated.

But Jonson is never more the poet than in his songs. Most of them are incidental to masques and plays, and are mainly in the tradition of full-throated Elizabethan lyric.

Elizabethan poetry of any sort could never have been the glorious thing it was, had not the loveliest music of modern times been continuously ringing in the poet's and the people's ear. There were no music machines, and no highly artificialized professionals; everyone did his own singing and revelled in the

wealth of song written for parts, madrigals, canzonets, motets
—some of it most intricate, wherein words and music perfectly agreed

> In notes with many a winding bout
> Of linkéd sweetness long drawn out
> With wanton heed and giddy cunning,
> The melting voice through mazes running,
> Untwisting all the chains that tie
> The hidden soul of harmony.

No man was a gentleman who could not "sing his part sure
and at first sight withall." England was vibrant too with "airs,"
single melodies for songs. Dowland, Weelkes, Byrd, Gibbons,
Ferrabosco, were among the great composers, but much of the
melody was anonymous and traditional. So too were many of the
lyrics. It need surprise no one that, however mediocre a poet
might be in other respects, the language and music of the times
enabled him to write a first-rate song.

Thomas Campion wrote both words and music, meanwhile
practising physic, and published them in several books of
"airs." He is a major songster in all the anthologies, where
one is sure to find his "When to her lute Corinna sings" and
"The man of life upright."

But Jonson with his learning subtly modified the artless
Elizabethan lyric. Imbued as he was in the Greek and Latin
anthologies, in the epigram of Martial and the ode of Horace,
his songs, while not less singable, show art of arrangement,
sense, and order. Nothing can outdo the cleverness with which
he turned an old Latin epigram, "Semper munditias," "Still to
be neat, still to be drest," into a song for *The Silent Woman*;
or fishing up some obscure passages out of certain unfamiliar
Greek prose letters, made the immortal "Drink to me only with
thine eyes" for its inseparable tune, probably revamped by
Colonel Mellish out of an old melody. In such rare combination of learned art with native English song he unawares
taught the lyric poets of the seventeenth century to sing, and
founded "the tribe of Ben."

In comedy and in song English Literature learned from him. But his "school" went further. He set the illustrious precedent for that "art" form, the Pindaric ode, a tradition descending through no less than Cowley, Dryden, Gray, Wordsworth, and Shelley.

In his vigorous epigrams, epistles, satires, and elegies we meet the first expert use of the "heroic" couplet as the instrument of which Pope was to become the supreme master. Jonson, disciple of Horace, and satirist, knows how to fit his sententious meaning into its neat and even mould, has discovered its deep and measured music, its balance and symmetry. He may be accepted as the inventor of the metrical mouthpiece for the coming Age of Sense.

The dimensions of this burly poet are somewhat lost in the spreading shadow of Shakespeare, and in his preoccupation with matters peculiar to his times. His defects are only too easy to see. That is why so many dilate on his overweight of learning, his want of sympathy and charm, and are hardly aware of his fire, his vigor, his virile actuality, his delicate artistry, and his fertile originality as shown in his powerful shaping of literary traditions.

> Live to that point I will, for which I am man,
> And dwell as in my centre, as I can,
> Still looking to, and ever loving heaven;
> With reverence using all the gifts thence given:
> 'Mongst which, if I have any friendships sent,
> Such as are square, well-tagged, and permanent,
> Not built with canvas, paper, and false lights,
> As are the glorious scenes at the great sights: . . .
> But all so clear, and led by Reason's flame,
> As but to stumble in her sight were shame;
> These I will honour, love, embrace, and serve,
> And free it from all question to preserve. . . .
>   First give me faith, who know
> Myself a little; I will take you so,
> As you have writ yourself: now stand, and then,
> Sir, you are Sealed of the Tribe of Ben.

CHAPMAN (1559?-1634?)

Older than Shakespeare and Marlowe was George Chapman, though his work, done mostly in his forties, makes him seem of later date. He is a dim and tragic figure, more tragic than any he created, forced by poverty to uncongenial literary hackwork, soothing his powerful but feverish mind with the Christian Stoicism that quieted other turbulent minds of the Renaissance. Of obscure origin and education, he read widely if not accurately in Greek and Latin literature. His philosophic mind had many of the passions and instincts of the poet, yet staggered and stammered when it came to utterance—

> The chaos whence this stifled verse
> By violence breaks.

So he calls it in his autobiographical poem *To M. Harriots*. Vague or obscure, turgid or incoherent as he is, yet at times poetic fire and expression coincide in superb passages. Poets from Waller to Swinburne have acclaimed him, and Keats's great sonnet has made him better known at large than his own work.

Of his few plays the tragedies, *Bussy d'Ambois* (before 1607), *The Revenge of Bussy d'Ambois* (before 1614), and the comedy, *All Fools* (written 1599; revised before 1605), are best known, though his hand in *Eastward Ho!* is said to have imparted much of its excellence to that play. His work is of Jonson's shop; but the sensuous world was to him a muddle, and romantic love a closed book. If his plays are difficult to read, they must have been impossible on the stage.

His version of Homer, the first in English, was also hackwork. Whatever its defects as a translation, it has its high moments and its virtues, somewhat in common with the virtues of Homer himself, the pure serene, the wide expanse, which the English language was never lithe and energetic enough to convey except in the spacious time of Elizabeth. Bravely this ill-adjusted, stifled man bore himself, for he was remembered after his time as "a person of most reverend aspect, religious and temperate, qualities rarely meeting in a poet."

JACOBEAN DRAMA

Even while Shakespeare was producing his great tragedies and romances, and Jonson pouring out his dazzling comedies, a host of brilliant playwrights was emerging, only slightly younger than the two giants of Elizabethan and Jacobean drama. These were to build up, with their predecessors, the brilliant repertoire of plays that gave such lustre to the London theatres until they were closed by the Puritans in 1642.

It was a span of eighty years, a long lifetime, from *Gorboduc* in 1561 to the closing; yet we may imagine an intelligent well-preserved man who loved plays from his youth, full of most interesting reminiscence in his last days of the rise and fall of this magnificent pageant as he had followed it at the theatres. Nearly a thousand plays of the period are either extant or mentioned, and there must have been many forgotten, though probably not of the greatest. Thomas Heywood boasts that he wrote, or had "a maine finger" in, 220 plays of which we have but twenty-four.

These dramatists were of all sorts and conditions. Francis Beaumont and John Marston were sons of gentlemen. Both were Oxford men, as was also Philip Massinger, who came of good middle class. John Fletcher's father, of a literary line, became Bishop of London. But John Webster was a tailor's son, who himself began life as such; Middleton had some learning, but no social standing—Jonson called him a "base fellow"; Dekker seems to have been an obscure, unlicked, talented cockney, in and out of jail from time to time; and Thomas Heywood, a prolific literary hack, came out of the obscure welter of London; yet he was a Cambridge man, and none of them all could surpass him in the creation of a gentleman.

Today a successful playwright does not have to be a poet. Few are. But these men were poets in every instance, and their plays are starred with superb single passages of gorgeous or moving poetry, which did much to elevate the action and suffuse it with poetic glamor. Besides they were, with hardly an exception, great songsters, especially Fletcher, Beaumont, Heywood, and Webster, and like their predecessors could turn a haunting song for any moment in the play that required it.

But first of all they were practical stage men, with an eye single to the spectator rather than the reader. To capture an audience with immediate effect was the object, regardless of fame or posterity or mention in a brief history of literature. They must have regarded their work as a craft, not inspired creation. So they were always collaborating, two, three, or even five having parts in the composition of a single play, and wholly indifferent about the literary credit due to each. Some, like Webster, did better alone than in collaboration. Others found their genius more happy and fertile in union with another.

The famous partnership is of course that of Beaumont (1584-1616) and Fletcher (1579-1625), who, according to quaint Aubrey, had a "wonderful consimility of phansy." The best remembered fruits of this wedded "phansy" were a tragi-comedy, *Philaster,* full of Shakespearian reminiscence, wherein a doting lady disguises herself as a page to follow the man she loves; two dramas, *The Maid's Tragedy* and *A King and No King,* under the auspices of erotic and cruel oriental poten-tates; and the riotous burlesque or *revue* called *The Knight of the Burning Pestle.* Beaumont brought to the partnership skill in construction and a certain solidity of style and workmanship; Fletcher furnished liveliness, fluency, and exuberance of style. Highly sensitive to theatrical fashion, all these playwrights knew what old devices to discard, and what to repeat. The clown, fairies, historical themes, plots from Plutarch and an-cient history, all went out. So too did the pastoral idyll except for Fletcher's charming *Faithful Shepherdess* (1610), adapted from Guarini's *Pastor Fido,* and Jonson's *Sad Shepherd, a Tale of Robin Hood,* written in the sunset of his stormy life. But old Senecan horrors, ghosts, and revenge at times return, and the moral dregs of Italian Renaissance literature are sounded in quest of horrors creepy enough to stir a rapidly sophisticat-ing audience.

Webster's (1580?-1625?) *White Devil* is a case in point, wherein the notable Vittoria, seeking the "larger" life, contrives the death of her husband and the Duchess, marries the Duke, grandly faces down her accusers, is pursued, and, game to the end, bares her breast and turns upon her assassins. The play is spell-binding with gloom. In his *Duchess of Malfi* horror piles on horror. The Duchess, a sweet and noble woman, commits the indiscretion of loving and marrying her steward; whereupon her brothers ingeniously persecute her to her death. She is confined among raving maniacs, and on occasion reaching to grasp her brother's hand, clasps a dead and amputated one. At the end the toll of violent death includes five men, three women, and two children. In retrospect one may laugh at such devices, but in Webster's powerful stage representation it is a different matter. Single strokes constantly remind one of Shakespeare, yet the difference is the difference between noble tragedy and high-class melodrama.

On the other hand, with Jonson's success, the fashion of local life and familiar reality waxed strong both in comedy and serious drama. Middleton's (1570-1627) comedies, *Michaelmas Term, A Trick to Catch the Old One, A Mad World, My Masters,* and *A Chaste Maid in Cheapside,* are all about rascally nephews and grandsons, swindlers, gallants, town women, dupes from the country, disordered middle-class households, and the humors of London generally.

Abler than Middleton was Philip Massinger (1583-1640), a mysterious and obscure figure, who subdued an excellent mind to the mere demands of success in the theatrical workshop. He got his training by collaborating with Fletcher, and in his late thirties and forties wrote many plays of his own, of which a number are lost. His comedies engage with the humors and the shift and pretense of a grasping parvenu society. His serious plays, such as *The Roman Actor* and *The Duke of Milan,* are equally good stage-stuff, abounding in black wickedness and white virtue, stirring stage moments, dramatic momentum, and fine rounded speeches which must have been an actor's delight. Such plays are made to be seen, not read and pondered; to serve their purpose consistent and true-to-life character is not requisite. Yet Massinger has proved to have a certain dramatic durability, and some of his comedies at least have been acted or revamped long after his time. Such is *The City Madam,* and particularly *A New Way to Pay Old Debts,* which offers a tempting chance for character acting in the new-rich miser, Sir Giles Overreach, who in the end goes mad with thwarted greed.

The drama tended in some respects to become, along with society, more sophisticated and aristocratic, but certainly not exclusive. As the last years of Elizabeth passed into the new century and Stuart times, many a commoner had grown in wealth and consequence, and more slowly in culture. Hence the increasing sophistication of the stage, but also the increasing importance of the bourgeoisie as a stage theme, from burlesque to tragedy.

Thomas Deloney had written a book called *The Gentle Craft,* full of stories about up-and-coming shoemakers; and Dekker, thoroughbred cockney, took from it the edifying tale of Simon Eyre, who rose from apprentice to Lord Mayor, and out of the tale made his famous play, *Shoemakers' Holiday.* Eyre is a hearty, lusty, outspeaking, good-natured citizen, set up by his success, yet friend and brother of all workmen, affecting big words he hears at the play which are beyond him, and a bit hen-pecked at home. A double plot deals with the ever popular triumph of love and intrinsic worth over class distinctions, and of virtue and honesty over evil intention. The themes are no longer new to us, but under Dekker's skill no doubt thrilled his audience. Yet even today this play is revived, and reveals the vulgarian stage stuff transformed by the subtle sweetness and charm of Dekker himself, as Goldsmith was later to get much the same effect in play and novel, and in the same way.

A comedy to gratify the same hearty, popular taste and moral code was *Eastward Ho!* (1605), devised by three hands, Jonson, Chapman, and Marston. It follows the courses of a good and a naughty apprentice, with those of the good and the naughty daughter of their master, and vividly traverses the ups and downs of the London bourgeois life of the day, and the humors of Thames-side. Incidentally it got its clever creators into jail for its girds at the Scotch, which offended his lately enthroned Majesty, James I.

Back in 1587 an anonymous tragedy of English domestic adultery, avarice, and murder, entitled *Arden of Feversham*, had scored a success. And now, as citizens grew in consequence, "domestic tragedy" flourished. The *Yorkshire Tragedy*, suggested by murders perpetrated in 1605, shows in headlong fashion the crimes of a debauched gamester, who returns ruined to his family, and in mad frenzy either murders or tries to murder wife and children. In restored calm of mind he meets his doom at the end.

Thomas Heywood's masterpiece, *A Woman Killed with Kindness* (1603), is a domestic play of pathos rather than tragedy. An essentially good woman, Mrs. Frankford, during her husband's absence, is seduced by her husband's friend and *protégé*. On his return Frankford, at first incredulous, is forced to accept the facts. While the situation is still tense and unresolved, Heywood inserts a memorable scene where the three are playing cards. Most deftly he has filled the scene with mellow English domestic charm, which is curiously heightened as it is disturbed by the growing uneasiness of the husband. The erring wife is sent to a lonely house in the country apart from husband and children. On the way her husband's messenger overtakes her with her lute, which she had left, and to which she had once sung sweet old songs for him. In agony she has it crushed on the coach-wheels. Her lover meets her, is abhorred as the plague, and goes away a branded exile. She dies of a broken heart. It is still more than a hundred years to Richardson, Sterne, and sentimental comedy; yet this play of Heywood's gave the citizenry their money's worth in pathos and sentimentality.

His *Fair Maid of the West* is a lively melodrama all about buxom Besse Bridges of Plymouth, a sterling lass, true amid trials to her gallant Spencer gone fighting overseas, whom she follows in her own ship and rescues from the rascal Spaniards.

In Heywood's *Four Prentices of London* four sons of a French earl have taken refuge in London under disguise of apprentices. But blood tells; they embark on an expedition to

Jerusalem, and cover themselves with glory. Heywood flatters the tradesmen to the top of their bent, especially their passion for old romances of chivalry, now purveyed to them in lengthy prose versions.

All their weaknesses, their pride, vulgarity, and sentimentality are deliciously and riotously satirized in Beaumont and Fletcher's *Knight of the Burning Pestle*. A citizen and his wife in the audience interrupt the prologue to *The London Merchant*, demanding a knight-errantry play instead, in which their romance-struck apprentice shall act the lead. The result is a diverting hotch-potch of the original play and the callow strutting of Ralph, the apprentice, as a wandering knight, interrupted more than once by the citizen and his wife. It touches the permanent vagaries of the class, contains excellent songs, and still has power to delight an audience.

After Shakespeare the drama shows gradual decadence. Not in stage technique—its skill in capturing its audience keeps up to the end. But consistency of plot and character and depth, which are not necessary to the momentary thrill of the audience, it sacrifices to be sensational, sentimental, or amusing in its incidents. Thus some of the plots have the look of having been made up as the playwright went along, and the reader finds it impossible to remember them. Unnatural crime, horrors, obscenity, declamation serve in a high theatrical moment to score a passing stage success, let the reader on cool afterthought find what fault he will. Such sensations were not devised for him. But the poetic talent of these dramatists was often very great, so great that one at times regrets the concessions it made to the transitory uses of the stage.

DRAYTON (1563-1631)

Born the year before Shakespeare and Marlowe, the Elizabethan poet Michael Drayton practised the art of poetry assiduously all his years, until Charles I was reigning. Yet he continued essentially the Elizabethan. He produced a great deal, not all of it inspired, which he was continually revising. Much of it is English "history" in metre, and met high admiration in its patriotic day, as the many editions show. A fair unknown for whom he cherished a poetic devotion thirty or more years of his bachelor life was the object of his sonnet sequence to "Idea." Of this, three or four fine numbers are still remembered, including the superb dramatic sonnet, not published till he was fifty-six:

> Since there's no help, come let us kiss and part,—
> Nay I have done, you get no more of me;
> And I am glad, yea, glad with all my heart,
> That thus so cleanly I myself can free. . . .

Drayton was a devoted patriot, deep versed in chronicles of Holinshed, Speed, and others, and stirred by the expanding national energies of his time. His poetic powers were never greater than in his ballad on Agincourt, "Fair stood the wind for France," with its short, full-volumed trumpet blasts, echoing to a distance of two hundred and fifty years in Tennyson's *Charge of the Light Brigade*. No less was he roused by the accounts of the voyagers:

> Thy voyages attend,
> Industrious Hakluyt!
>   Whose reading shall inflame
>   Men to seek fame;
> And much commend
>   To after times thy wit.

Thus ends the ode *To the Virginian Voyage*, celebrating the glories of "Virginia, Earth's only Paradise," its game, its soil, "and useful sassafras."

Meanwhile all the rest was but incidental to the progress of his crowning work, *Poly-Olbion,* a long and detailed historical and topographic description of Great Britain. It belonged to the class of literature known as "chorographic," much admired and practised in Elizabethan times, even by Spenser in his glorifications of English and Irish rivers. Certainly it expresses the passionate devotion of Englishmen to their beloved land, in their desire to clothe every stream and nook of it, even its flowers and birds, with music and the poetry of legend and antiquity. *Poly-Olbion* is richly laden with learning, sometimes even sagging to lower levels; yet again it rises to passages of great splendor and beauty, and always has the peculiar vigor of Drayton's natural style. If one wonders how these Elizabethan poets wrote so much passable verse without waiting for the high moments of inspiration, let him again recall how near to poetry the ordinary Elizabethan language was, and how slight a touch served to transform it.

Drayton seems a genial, winsome soul. He did not love book-sellers—"they are a company of base knaves, whom I both scorn and kick at"—but he found great patrons readily, and was friend of all the great poets of the time including Spenser, whom he deeply admired and assiduously imitated.

HOOKER (1554?-1600)

During the last thirty years of Elizabeth's reign there were ominous stirrings of the strife which was in time to rise to the height of the Puritan Revolution. The questions about ritual, vestments, bishops, and theological points seem to us trivial, but were all-important in their day, and engaged laymen and clerics alike. Some participants were sincere, but some surely entertained themselves with the quarrel, making of it a neigh-borhood affair. It reached its first heat in the Marprelate war of pamphlets from 1584 to 1593, over the question whether bishops should be abolished. At the close of this episode there emerged on the scene a grave and quiet figure, of keen mind and gentle temper, who had found himself unwillingly en-gaged in defence of the established order of bishops. It was Richard Hooker, born probably in 1554, of humble origin, but a distinguished scholar at Oxford. All he asked was a quiet parish far from the din, where he could ponder the whole matter in pious leisure. This was granted to him, and the result was his great book, *Of the Laws of Ecclesiastical Polity* (1593 on), which raised the subject from petty squabbling to tran-scendent heights of eternal spiritual laws. His enormous read-ing, his organization of his vast subject, his skill and closeness of reasoning are after all but the minor virtues of the book. He resolves the questions which tortured that day, and supports the practical Anglican position against disruptive Puritanism;

but what still engages us is not his power of reason, but his warm and intuitive understanding of the spiritual needs and experience of the human heart. And this abundant humanity, the very personality of the man himself, flows through every sentence in an artless music that persuades and wins the reader far beyond the power of mere reason.

There will come a time when three words uttered with charity and meekness shall receive a far more blessed reward than three thousand volumes written with disdainful sharpness of wit.

I wish that men would more give themselves to meditate what we have by the sacrament and less to dispute of the manner how.

The love of things ancient doth argue stayedness, but levity and want of experience maketh apt unto innovations. That which wisdom did first begin, and hath been with good men long continued, challengeth allowance of them that succeed, although it plead for itself nothing. That which is new if it promise not much, doth fear condemnation before trial; till trial, no man doth acquit or trust it, what good soever it pretend and promise. So that in this kind there are few things known to be good, till such time as they grow to be ancient.

Guileless and uncircumspect in worldly things, through "modesty and dim sight" he found himself married to a woman who possessed neither beauty, wealth, nor good temper; but as Izaak Walton says in his genial *Life of Hooker*, "affliction is a divine diet." At all events nothing ruffled "the dove-like temper of this meek, this matchless man." His pupils found him one day reading the Odes of Horace while he watched his sheep in the field; and his great and enduring work never kept him from the least and lowliest duties in his little country parish of Bourne, in whose church his body lies.

PART FOUR

SCHOLAR AND PARTISAN

CHAPTER 14

The Seventeenth Century

"THE Seventeenth Century" is our only name for the interval
between the death of Elizabeth in 1603 and the Revolution of
1688, in which modern England was born. Besides the grandest
achievement of Shakespeare, it includes Jonson, Milton, Dryden, and a host of other great ones, and is altogether the
richest season of our English Literature.

With the passing of the great Queen the energies that had
made Elizabethan poetry, though changed, did not pass, but
grew from an engaging if sometimes extravagant youth to
more vigorous and controlled manhood. And with maturity
came, as usual, an increasing disillusion of Renaissance hopes,
bitterness, even cynicism, such as that foreshadowed in Shakespeare's Jaques, Hamlet, and the great tragedies generally; asserting itself in epigram and satire, and flavoring other literature, sometimes with delicate subtlety. And the output does
not decline in either quality or amount, though England was
latterly rent from end to end with a life-and-death civil conflict.

It was a slow, long quarrel, leading at length to the extremes
of bloody war and the execution of the King; partly political,

partly religious, since politics and religion were still inseparable. Generally the country was divided between the Royalists
or Cavaliers, and the Puritans or Roundheads, though there
were extremes and moderates and blends of both. It was a
quarrel between King and Commons, to determine which
should be the dominant power in English government.

Parliamentary rights, taxes, ritual, Catholic questions, status
of non-conformists, church government, were all concerned in
issue after issue; but at bottom it was a new England against
an old England. London, other seaports and thriving towns
of new trade, rising landholders, yeomen and new landlords,
were generally Puritan; the old landed and rustic aristocracy
and their tenantry, the old cathedral and market towns, were
generally Royalist. Cambridge, the mother of American universities, had long been Puritan; Oxford was a Royalist strong-
hold. Roughly it was the Puritan East against the Cavalier
West.

The Cavalier stood for the mellow old social tradition of
rank and manners, and the time-hallowed Church. In fact, as
in name, he was the child of medieval chivalry. He set his
heart upon his land, his horse, his lady, and his King.

The Puritan, at best, had burning convictions on the Eternal
Verities. So deeply convinced was he that he felt that he must
convince, or compel, everyone else. He was a pioneer in all
things, even in religion, business, mechanical invention, America; yet it was not curiosity and quest of adventure that lured
him, but the search for a home, material or spiritual; for he
was essentially domestic, as his large family and snug homestead show, and he loved good cheer within reason. The contrast between Cavalier and Puritan is akin to the contrast between the American *Old* South and *New* England.

As one might expect, far the greater number of poets and
writers came from the Cavaliers; yet he who is generally reck-
oned the greatest of English poets next to Shakespeare was a
Puritan. We think of the Puritan as austerely religious and the
Cavalier as pleasure-loving; yet Donne, Herbert, Herrick,
Crashaw, Browne, Walton, were genuinely, even deeply reli-

gious, and Milton, Marvell, Hutchinson, and Cromwell's chaplain, Sterry, were lovers of beauty and music.

One characteristic is common to nearly all the writers of the seventeenth century—their learning. It was this learning, vastly increased under the peace of Elizabeth, which matured and sophisticated these new generations, a learning inspired by the national and religious stirrings of the time, and the desire thus prompted to get down to original historical facts and causes. Hence it was not a learning for its own idle parade, nor for mere material gain, but as Lord Bacon says in his *Advancement of Learning*, "to preserve and augment whatsoever is solid and fruitful; that knowledge may not be as a courtesan, for pleasure and vanity only, or as a bondwoman, to acquire and gain to her master's use, but as a spouse, for generation, fruit, and comfort."

The learning of the seventeenth century was not specialized, but broad and inclusive. When Bacon said what so astonishes us, "I have taken all knowledge to be my province," he astonished no one of his time, to whom "learning" with its ever-widening horizon still meant the whole circle or encyclopedic extent of learning, including the poetry, ideas, and history of the Greeks, Romans, and early Church Fathers, as revived and set in order by the Renaissance.

But in seventeenth century literature this learning, however massive, seldom turns cumbersome and pedantic. With it is mingled a certain vigor or mellowness of personality in measure sufficient to transform it into a quaint, rare, or glorious artistic effect. It may be that the erudition of the times was kept sweet and saved from pedantry by the vigorous part it played in the struggle between old ideas and new. The struggle is perennial of course, but rose to a crisis in this century of Bacon, Sir Thomas Browne, Descartes, Hobbes, and the new revival of Plato at Cambridge, which enlisted rare spirits like Henry More, Ralph Cudworth, and Joseph Glanville. It involved the old authority of inherited Christian and Aristotelian traditions, tangled with popular errors as they had become, in conflict with the actuality of things newly realized through an honest re-examination, that is, the authority of Nature and of

Science. In most of the literature of the century one may discern some manifestation of this contest, according as an author is partial to the Old or the New, or attempts a reconciliation. Men of poetic genius or imagination either clung to the old learning, or, like Milton and Sir Thomas Browne, offered a compromise. But Milton expressed his misgiving that he was singing in "an age too late" for poetry; for in the triumph of Science, "Reason," and Naturalism, poetry instinctively recognized a danger to itself.

BACON (1561-1626)

Men like Drayton, Hooker, Jonson, already wear their learning with a certain accustomed and substantial grace characteristic of the new time. But the most conspicuous example in literature of this expanding learning is Francis Bacon, Lord Verulam, Viscount St. Albans.

This prodigy, born in 1561 of a family associated with the Court, was from twelve to fourteen a student at Cambridge, at fifteen a professional student of law, at twenty-three in Parliament, at twenty-four gravely giving Queen and statesmen advice far beyond their times, lord chancellor at fifty-seven, for thirty years the wisest statesman of his time, and most enlightened adviser to Elizabeth and James, only to die in aged disgrace, the victim of less able enemies, in 1626. A major prophet in politics, he was also knowingly the seer for science and modern philosophy, who planned and partly wrote out a program for a new and more reliable search for truth, not only of science, but truth throughout the province of the human mind. Back in his student days he had been disgusted with the calm traditional acceptance of "principles" from Aristotle and other ancientry, without putting them to the test of the facts of life and Nature. Let us therefore, he said, appeal to the facts, searching them anew, organizing them by a new sensible method, freed from the old prejudices and errors of procedure, so that they will lead inductively to new principles and facts hitherto unknown and undreamed of. The laying down of this inductive method has won for Bacon the fre-

quent title of "the father of modern experimental science."
Surely he is its greatest prophet.

Bacon planned to embody his program in a vast work called
The Great Instauration in six parts. His *Advancement of
Learning* written in English, and the *Novum Organum* in
Latin, make up Parts 1 and 2, the only parts completed. But
they contain all of Bacon's essential quality. He disposes of
the old habits of error of the human mind, divides the vast
province of human knowledge, suggests the inductive method.
But let the modern reader turn these pages casually for their
pungent common sense, the electric energy which leaps again
and again from the aphorisms charged with that mighty mind,
the wealth of pat comparisons, the vigor and latent poetry of
his images.

. . . It is my intention to make the circuit of knowledge, noticing
what parts lie waste and uncultivated, and abandoned by the industry
of man, with a view to engage, by a faithful mapping out of the deserted tracks, the energies of public and private persons in their improvement. . . . My hope, however, is, that, if the extreme love of
my subject carry me too far, I may at least obtain the excuse of affection. It is not granted to man to love and be wise.[1]

With quick and final strokes he demolishes what he calls the
idols of the tribe, of the den, of the market, and of the theatre
—that is the fallacies or errors which we might call social,
personal, of common words, and of preconceived theory. At
the end of these few expert pages the ground looks pretty well
cleared for the new and more durable building.

This prodigy of mind was sincerely devoted to his country's
best interests, and indeed the best interests of all mankind. His
ultimate services can hardly be matched. Yet all his life he was
condemned by fate to give advice so shrewd, discerning, and
wise, that no one could be induced to follow it, neither Elizabeth, nor his charming young friend, the Earl of Essex, nor
narrow-minded James, nor Charles. Had the kings listened to
his interpretations of events, his warnings, his pointing of the
way, there need have been no war between King and Parlia-

[1] *Advancement,* 2.1

ment, Cavalier and Puritan, and the liberties purchased at such cost might well have been had as soon or sooner. Yet of these liberties Bacon had no vision. He put his faith rather in wise, strong, and efficient monarchy.

But this marvel of intellect seems curiously devoid of some personal quality—charm, the personal instinct which is the medium of unspoken intimations between man and man; and it may be this defect which makes so great and disinterested a man seem strangely immoral, or unmoral. The technique of his world included simulation, flattery, risk of disloyalty, subtle dishonesties, and he conformed to this technique in a manner which a man of his distinction could not afford, whatever we may expect of grosser men. The acts of venality for which he was deposed from the chancellorship and disgraced were not acts of corrupt motive, but they were certainly careless—for one so eminent as Bacon.

Bacon was a busy man of affairs, and one wonders where he got all the time necessary for his scientific and literary work. Among his many-sided works is his historical biography of Henry VII, the basis of most subsequent conceptions of that king and his times. A more imaginative work is the *New Atlantis*, probably written, as it happens, early in the migrations to New England. It is an incomplete sketch, in the manner of *Utopia* and many another ideal commonwealth. Plato's lost Atlantis, Bacon avers, is America, and the New Atlantis a wonderful island in the Pacific where the people were all wise and good. The "Lanthorne of this Kingdome," and the noblest foundation on earth, was a college or society, called Solomon's House, and "dedicated to the Study of the Works and Creatures of God." It is thought to have prompted the "college of philosophy" in 1645, which grew after 1660 into the Royal Society; and it is known to have inspired scientific societies on the Continent.

But of all his works the one which has come nearest to winning men's hearts is the little book of fifty-eight brief essays on a wide variety of topics—marriage, love, high position or great place, friendship, gardens, reading, honor, and "The Vicissitude of Things." They are as it were the easy overflow of that abundant and prolific mind. We have the great man of the world to ourselves in a comfortable corner by the fire, and he is talking casually of his observation of men. He speaks no longer in the swelling and ornate rhetoric of the Elizabethans, but in the new prose of short sentences, which looks impromptu, and which has been called "baroque."[1] Each sentence falls softly but distinctly upon the ear, in Bacon's natural grave subdued tone, charged with wit and wisdom; and each sentence seems like a precious new find which one must keep safely somewhere within reach at a moment's practical need. The essays make a book to read a bit at a time, lay down and take up again, pondering its weight, delighting in the man's rich collection of wisdom and anecdote from others, the brilliance of his own remark, the grave and measured music of the cadences, which grow the sweeter the more familiar they become. Speaking of conversation,

The honorablest part of talk is to give the occasion; and again to moderate and pass to somewhat else; for then a man leads the dance.

Speech of a man's self ought to be seldom, and well chosen. I knew one was wont to say in scorn: "He must needs be a wise man, he speaks so much of himself."

Or of Riches:

I cannot call Riches better than the baggage of virtue. The Roman word is better, *impedimenta*. For as baggage is to an army, so is Riches to virtue. It cannot be spared, nor left behind, but it hindreth the march; yea, and the care of it, sometimes, loseth or disturbeth the victory. Of great Riches there is no real use, except it be in the distribution; the rest is but conceit [imagination].

DONNE (1572-1631)

What Bacon lacked, Nature gave with a full and generous hand to John Donne, D.D., Dean of St. Paul's. His warm humanity was irresistible, and still is. Yet in some ways he is inscrutable, and doubtless was so to most of his many friends. He is consistent, but full of paradox. His physical passions and

[1] See pages 256-7

vitality were strong; his intellect and spiritual passions were ultimately stronger. With all his pulsing vitality, his mind and poetry are haunted with a sense of death and mortuary things, which is saved from being morbid by the abounding healthy vigor of the man's mind. Through all the trenchant wit, the rough, tortured phrase and discord of his verse, breathes somehow a healthy, natural sweetness of soul, which gives it gravity and authority. This man who united charm, physical vigor, great intellect, spiritual insight, has drawn to himself a host of idolaters, many of whom have worshipped him without fully understanding why. One of these was his friend Izaak Walton, whose brief *Life of Donne* is a masterpiece as a biographical portrait, not for the facts so much as the fascination—whether Donne's or his own—which he imparts to his account.

A dependent courtier and at last a churchman by profession, he was casually and only in his earlier years a poet; and yet, like Jonson, he turned out to be a chief determinant of the peculiarities of the "new" poetry of his century.

Donne was a Welshman, which may account for certain qualities of his verse—his verve and his love of esoteric imagery. He came of a fine old Catholic line that included Sir Thomas More, and made a precocious start by way of Oxford, and perhaps Cambridge, foreign travel, and the study of law, which he began at eighteen. During the next nine years wits, courtiers, poets gravitated to him under the spell of his brilliance and singular attraction, and he poured out most of his verse—personal epistles, elegies, satires in the manner of Roman poets, and the quantity of lyric verse upon which his fame especially is founded. Into the gay and dangerous life of London in the 1590's he plunged not with abandon, but with his whole soul, and was always master of the moment. He sailed with Essex on his daring expedition to Portugal.

At twenty-seven he fell in love with Anne More, sixteen, a niece of Sir Thomas Egerton, whose secretary and friend he had been. They were secretly married. Loss of his post, hostility of his elders, even imprisonment, were to pay for this indiscretion—as the course of true love ran in those days. The storm subsided, but for years Donne had only his charm and wits with which to defend himself and his fast-growing family against poverty and ill health. Patrons, and particularly patronesses, were kind. One was Lady Danvers, George Herbert's mother. Another whom he honored with verse was Lucy, Countess of Bedford, who often welcomed Donne at Twickenham with Jonson, Drayton, Daniel, and Chapman, and many of his personal epistles and elegies sprang from these various associations. Twice he served in Parliament.

King James himself felt the man's enchantment, and pressed him to take holy orders. Long had the young man been wrestling with such matters. Though Catholic-born, the contesting claims of the two communions were for him not a matter of counterweighed tenets, but deep, personal, and learned. As for holy orders, there was, alas, the memory of those lively young days in London, and of some pretty carnal verse composed at the time, as yet unprinted, but popular and widespread in manuscript beyond recall. Whatever its crises, the decision was not a matter of one intense agony, but a long slow uncertainty, which perhaps is harder. At last in 1615, at forty-two, he took orders, and became at once the most brilliant preacher in London.

The tide of his affairs had turned just in time for his young wife to know. Two years later she died at thirty-two, in giving birth to her twelfth child. She had been the one by whom he brought his life into a steady course, and in his loss he devoted all his superb energies to preaching. After six years as preacher to Lincoln's Inn, the King made him Dean of St. Paul's Cathedral. It was, and is, a post of highest distinction, not only for the prestige of the great cathedral and the dignity of its residence, but for its association with literature through men like John Colet, Donne, and in our day, Dean Inge. Here through his last years of ill health, with increasing wit and brilliance, he continued until his last sermon on the Ash Wednesday before his death. It was a powerful discourse which he called Death's Duel. His old mortuary interest had caused him to have his portrait painted wrapped in his shroud; the picture was engraved for a posthumous edition of this sermon, and may often be seen in reproduction.

The sermons, the best of which are still honored by luxurious editions, though probably more captivating in Donne's oral delivery, still exercise the same fascination as his verse. Their wit, their fertility of image, their fresh authentication in such a life as he spent make them live.

The first impression of his verse is that of the muscular mind behind it. It is the mind of an honest sceptic, who enjoys coming to intellectual grips with every experience, even the most sensual. With all his warm humanity he is interested in himself. His verse, even his most intense love poetry, proceeds in short jets of ingenious reasoning, turning this way and that in sheer exuberance of mind and feeling, sometimes in mere fun, sometimes in deepest gravity.

> I am two fools, I know,
>   For loving, and for saying so
>   In whining poetry;
> But where's that wiseman, that would not be I,
>   If she would not deny?
> Then as th' earth's inward narrow crooked lanes
> Do purge sea water's fretful salt away,
>   I thought, if I could draw my pains
> Through rhyme's vexation, I should them allay.
> Grief brought to numbers cannot be so fierce,
> For, he tames it, that fetters it in verse.

Donne's exuberance is most obvious in his invention of strange similes and metaphors. The simile just quoted, of sea water sweetened in earth's veins on its way to the springs, is so striking that it overshadows the thought. Yet this tendency to striking imagery was so merged in his strong feeling and intellectual vigor that it seldom errs. No more beautiful instance is there than the famous one of the compasses in his *Valediction Forbidding Mourning*, to his wife on his departure for the Continent:

> Our two souls therefore, which are one,
>   Though I must go, endure not yet
> A breach, but an expansion,
>   Like gold to airy thinness beat.

> If they be two, they are two so
>   As stiff twin compasses are two;
> Thy soul, the fix'd foot, makes no show
> To move, but doth, if th' other do.
>
> And though it in the centre sit,
>   Yet when the other far doth roam,
> It leans, and hearkens after it,
>   And grows erect, as that comes home.

At their best, similes and metaphors spring spontaneously from stress of feeling and conviction. But a fertile wit may serve as substitute for feeling, and deliberately hunt out a good figure. Indeed "wit" as used in the century and more between Jonson and Johnson was often understood to be, as Dr. Samuel defines it, "a combination of dissimilar images, or discovery of occult resemblances in things apparently unlike." Such selected figures or "conceits" run great risk of being too ingenious, farfetched, distracting. But from Donne's brilliant example the practice became general among the poets of the seventeenth century, such as Crashaw, Herbert, and Cowley, and appears at times in them all. As Carew says in his *Elegy on Donne*, he "Of rich and pregnant fancy, open'd us a mine." But without the safeguard of Donne's strong judgment, the mine often yielded mere fool's gold, and the freaks of fancy sometimes only amuse, sometimes disgust.

This poetical practice has caught from Dryden and Johnson the name of "metaphysical." But "metaphysical" poetry, at least in Donne, implies more. He was profoundly learned in the lore of metaphysics, theology, and "science" as the Renaissance had inherited it from medieval times, and many of his images are glittering fragments of this rich heritage caught up into his glowing fabric. His *Second Anniversary* in *An Anatomy of the World* is a conspicuous case.

Intense as are his love poems, no less so are his *Divine Songs*, especially two which were composed in times of illness —the *Litany*, and the moving *Hymn to God the Father*. "I have the rather mentioned this Hymn," says Walton, "for that he caused it to be set to a most grave and solemn tune, and to be often sung to the organ by the Choristers of St. Paul's Church, in his own hearing, especially at the Evening Service." And Donne told a friend, perhaps Walton himself, that "I always return from paying this public duty of prayer and praise to God, with an unexpressible tranquillity of mind; and a willingness to leave the world."

· HERBERT (1593-1633)

Donne had a young friend and admiring disciple in George Herbert. He was an aristocrat. His brother, Lord Herbert of Cherbury, was a duelling courtier and man of the world, who has won a permanent place in literature by his diverting *Autobiography*, and by his outspoken deistic scepticism, long in advance of the fashion. It was the charming mother of these two men who was the chief determinant of their intellectual start; she was also a friend and patroness to whose "warm redeeming hand" Donne was deeply grateful.

With his Cambridge training, his breeding, his connections, and his grace of person and spirit, the way to high preferment lay open and easy before George Herbert. After finishing his studies in 1616 he remained on at the University, attaining in three years to the post of public orator, "the finest place in the University," he said. It was the high road to favor at Court, and Herbert's talents readily recommended him, so that glittering distinctions were no doubt already dancing in his vision. His mother, and his own tastes, had early pointed him towards holy orders. In that direction too was distinction, probably a bishopric, and a life of graceful dignity amid the comfortable regimen and beautiful ritual of the Church, a life of secure goodness and decency. In this course he continued till he was well along in his thirties, but with growing misgivings. To Herbert this polite luxury, this virtuous respectability, which carried one so comfortably along, suddenly turned dangerous and deadly. The iron entered his soul. His health broke, his mother and old friends died, and he took the humble little parish of Bemerton, a mile from Salisbury, where hard parochial work and tuberculosis wore him out in less than three years.

In his verse one may follow the course of his spiritual life from those easy Cambridge days to the end, through social amenities, misgivings, depressions, exaltations, and tranquil calm. Even at Bemerton it varied. In *The Collar* his committed spirit plunges and tugs at the bonds:

> But as I rav'd and grew more fierce and wild
>   At every word,
> Me thoughts I heard one calling, *Child*:
>   And I reply'd, *My Lord*.

Then twice a week he walked along the Wiley to Salisbury, catching glimpses, reflected in the stream, of the great cathedral spire, where his spirit would soon be refreshed with the echoing cadences of choir and organ; or where he would take his happy "consort" in a band of fellow musicians.

Herbert made no ascetic or Puritan renunciation. In his poetry all the beauty of life—manners, sights, sounds, scents, clothes, architecture, even common objects—he brings into intense focus of his new experience, and thus gives them beauty. It is an experience stripped of all theological or traditional refinements, a direct intimacy with God, human, natural, all-absorbing, which glorifies trifles:

> Who sweeps a room, as for thy laws,
>   Makes that and th' action fine.

Herbert's poetic endeavor, like that of his life, is all towards simplicity. In *Jordan* he confesses to having first sought out "quaint words and trim invention,"

> Curling with metaphors a plain intention,
>   Decking the sense as if it were to sell.

But a "friend" whispers,

> "There is in love a sweetness ready penn'd;
>   Copy out only that, and save expense."

Thus his imagery, more "metaphysical" than even Donne's,

grows less and less fantastic as it becomes merged in the depths of his mature feeling:

> Sweet day, so cool, so calm, so bright,
> The bridal of the earth and sky,
> The dew shall weep thy fall tonight;
> For thou must die.

Donne died in 1631, and his young friend Herbert in 1633. Charles I was King. His struggle with Parliament had not yet reached its most acute stage, and these men, though abhorring the Puritan's harsh dislike of the established order, escaped the bitter civil strife that overtook other poets.

CHAPTER 15

Cavaliers

A GROUP called the "cavalier" or "courtly" poets kept alive the tradition of Elizabethan song and music. Taken together, they were twofold in their art; they generally practised the "metaphysical" use of conceits in imagery; but they also followed after the "tribe of Ben," and learned from Jonson and his models in the Greek and Latin poets how to order the ingenious argument of a song in clear sequence and simple words.

Take Carew's *Persuasions to Enjoy*:

> If the quick spirits in your eye
>   Now languish, and anon must die;
> If every sweet and every grace
> Must fly from that forsaken face;
>   Then, Celia, let us reap our joys
>   Ere time such goodly fruit destroys.
>
> Or, if that golden fleece must grow
> For ever free from aged snow;
> If those bright suns must know no shade,
> Nor your fresh beauties ever fade;
> Then, fear not, Celia, to bestow
> What, still being gather'd, still must grow.
>   Thus, either Time his sickle brings
>   In vain, or else in vain his wings.

Here is the obvious simplicity of an old singable song, the old question of fleeting youth. But there is also a bit of ingenious, "witty" imagery. And there is balanced well-ordered pro-and-con of argument.

They are, or affect to be, in love, these cavaliers, with Celia, Althea, or Julia—now casually, now desperately, now sensually, now ideally; for all that, some of them break at times into the loveliest utterance of religious emotion in our literature. A peculiar quality of the time pervades the fabric of their verse, and indeed is spread through most of the prose as well as verse of the seventeenth century. It has no name, yet is unmistakable. It is a certain mellow sweetness, sometimes droll and whimsical, sometimes touching, sometimes quaint, which has never since been recaptured by the language or its poetry. It may be the last antique remnant and flavor of medieval England, lingering in the solid substance of the Renaissance, which the language was still capable of retaining before being toughened by the Age of Reason and Democracy.

Yet these poets vary widely, and critics so differ that each reader is safe to choose and champion his favorite among them. And they are of the very sort to engage, one or other of them, a reader's jealous personal attachment.

CAREW; SUCKLING; LOVELACE

Thomas Carew (1598?-1639?) is true to form. Of old Cornish gentle family, he ran the usual course—some time at the University (Oxford in this case), law, travel, Court. Easy, idle, witty, engaging, he was much liked by the King and his fellow wits. His masque *Coelum Britannicum* dazzled the Court. His songs and poems are exquisitely finished, after Jonson's example, like a rare bit of old furniture or china; and once, in his *Elegy on Donne*, he has taken a subject great enough to deepen his feelings and intonations.

Carew died just before the Civil War. The fates of the others were more tragic. Swaggering Sir John Suckling (1609-1642), a knight's son, brought his talents to Court by way of Cambridge and the law, and there made a lively spot of color, gaming, courting an heiress, dress-parading through the 1639 campaign in Scotland. Of himself in his *Session of Poets* he says:

> He loved not the Muses so well as his sport;
> And prized black eyes, or a lucky hit
> At bowls, above all the trophies of wit.

The entire poem is worth the reading as a spirited review of this tuneful band. Suckling writes a play now and then, and turns a saucy love-song, like his "Why so pale and wan?" and

> Out upon it, I have lov'd
> Three whole days together.

His *Ballad on a Wedding* for a courtly friend is cast in the hearty voice and bluff manner of a substantial yeoman.

At the outbreak of the war Suckling was caught in a conspiracy against Parliament, fled to Paris, and in the face of ruin and a lost cause took his own life.

As true to type is Richard Lovelace (1618-1658), whose very name is a cavalier label. He was bred of old landed Kentish line, came through Oxford to Court, and went to the wars in Scotland. He was, says Wood, "of innate modesty, virtue, and courtly deportment which made him . . . much admired and adored by the female sex."

In the war he fought for his King and was twice imprisoned. At length, with his King beheaded, and his good fortune spent in the cause, he slowly sank deeper in beggary and squalor, and died neglected and well-nigh forgotten in a mean corner of London. Nearly all his verse is second or third rate, except *The Grasshopper*; but two or three times he touched the universal human heart with songs whose popularity would wear them out if they did not contain the greatness that is proof against popularity. *To Althea from Prison,* with its

> Stone walls do not a prison make
> Nor iron bars a cage;

and *To Lucasta on Going to the Wars,* with its

> I could not love thee, dear, so much,
> Lov'd I not honor more;

transcend their troubled times with a soft gleam of old—or universal—chivalry.

HERRICK (1591-1674)

The greatest of this group is the inscrutable but irresistible Robert Herrick. Apparently not precocious, he spent most of his twenties at Cambridge, and most of his thirties in London. What he did, except write verses and with Jonson and the "tribe of Ben"

> Meet at those lyric feasts
>   Made at the Sun,
> The Dog, the Triple Tun,
>   Where we such clusters had
> As made us nobly wild, not mad,

is not known. Then for eighteen years till he was fifty-six, he was settled as rector at the retired little hamlet of Dean Prior tucked away in a corner of Devon. It was not London, and he did not like it.

> More discontents I never had
>   Since I was born than here,
> Where I have been, and still am sad,
>   In this dull Devonshire;
> Yet, justly, too, I must confess,
>   I ne'er invented such
> Ennobled numbers for the press,
>   Than where I loathed so much.

During the Puritan régime he lost his living, but it was no hardship for Herrick. It meant London again, and he had plenty of friends to live on. Yet at the Restoration, now past seventy, he was sent back to the country gentry and farmers of Dean Prior, and died among them at eighty-three.

He may grumble at the dullness of his parish and its life, but it was, as he admits, the substance of his poetry:

> I sing of brooks, of blossoms, birds and bowers,
> Of April, May, of June and July-flowers;

I sing of May-poles, hock-carts, wassails, wakes,
I write of hell; I sing (and ever shall)
Of heaven, and hope to have it after all.

And a comfortable life he must have led in his snug rectory,
with his maid, Prue Baldwin, his hen, his spaniel, his goose,
his cat, his cow, and his lamb. Evidently he read from day to
day a bit of Horace, or Martial, or Catullus, or Anacreon, or
the Greek Anthology, and on such models turned a song, on
Julia, Anthea, or one of a dozen other girls, real or fancied;
a wedding song, an epitaph, or a "pious piece." No wonder
he was "much beloved by the gentry in those parts." More than
eleven hundred of these amusing or lovely miniatures make up
his *Hesperides*. A good liver he may have been but no pagan;
for he made also nearly three hundred Noble Numbers, not
so intense in their religious passion as Donne's or Herbert's,
but lovelier. A grace for a child, *Thanksgiving for His House,*
or his *Litany to the Holy Spirit*, are the ostensibly artless expression of a natural, healthy, unconscious piety, not troubled by
soul-searching agony.

Perhaps the effect of artlessness is a large part of Herrick's
witchery. His simplicity is sometimes droll, sometimes exquisite,
sometimes moving. His work is unclouded with the "metaphysical," and his four-stress iambic lines of simple words
beguile with the art which conceals art. At times he even whim-
sically affects an almost childlike sing-song.

A little stream best fits a little boat,
A little lead best fits a little float,
As my small pipe best fits my little note.

Yet the great shadow falls across his bright spirit, as in

Fair daffodils, we weep to see
You haste away so soon:
As yet the early-rising sun
Has not attained his noon.

Or in "Gather ye rosebuds while ye may," from Ausonius. He

often touched this old theme, but never so exquisitely as in his glorious idyll, *Corinna's Going a-Maying*, which ends:

> So when or you or I are made
> A fable, song, or fleeting shade,
> All love, all liking, all delight
> Lies drowned with us in endless night.
> Then while time serves, and we are but decaying,
> Come, my Corinna, come, let's go a-Maying.

CRASHAW

Royalist though he was, Herrick's inspiration was not of the Court. Another, even more segregate than he, was Richard Crashaw (1612?-1649). At Cambridge he was a prodigy in languages, music, drawing, the sort of whom his masters usually anticipate more distinction than he ever attains. Crashaw was passionately devout, and inclined by every instinct to the mystic ardors of Catholicism. Herbert's verse and example, the life of the newly canonized St. Teresa, and Ferrar's small devotional community at Little Gidding, all cast their spell over him. He read deeply in Spanish and Italian mystics. When in 1643 he was expelled by the Puritans, he fled to Paris, became a Roman Catholic, and was sent to Rome to serve a Cardinal. But the life of his underling associates revolted him, and he took refuge at Loreto, where he died, homesick and alone. Back in his best Protestant days he had made two great poems, *The Flaming Heart* and a hymn, both in honor of St. Teresa, in which grandeur of idea, power of phrase, and vibrant music all coincide under the heat of his strong ecstasy. But this happy coincidence is rare, for he is often commonplace, and sometimes sinks to depths of "conceit" which are ludicrous or disgusting.

VAUGHAN (1622-1695)

A more genial and intimate poet is Henry Vaughan, the Welshman. He called himself "Silurist" from the ancient name of his region in Wales. After Oxford he returned to practise medicine among his lovely native valleys around Brecon, and

+hus was undistressed by the agonies of war. In his late twenties he experienced some religious transformation and a cor·responding transformation as a poet. For fifty years he went his rounds as a doctor among the tranquil Welsh hills and villages, and out of that life came much verse and some great poems. His Welsh heart was warm, and his Welsh soul, as his youth passed, grew into a keen sense of unseen realities—those realities just the other side of physical life, death, and Nature, which were immediate to him as a physician on the road at all hours of the day or night. On his worst poetical side he fingers over strange old medical and hermetic lore, and is metaphysical to his heart's content—not always to ours. At his best he lifts us out of materialistic maunderings into clear and natural certainty of the unseen. His *Retreat*, the precedent of Wordsworth's famous *Ode on the Intimations of Immortality*, recalls those days

> When yet I had not walkt above
> A mile or two from my first love,
> And looking back (at that short space)
> Could see a glimpse of his bright face;
> When on some gilded cloud, or flower
> My gazing soul would dwell an hour,
> And in those weaker glories spy
> Some shadows of eternity.

In clarity, directness, simplicity, and music it makes the difficult thought easy, which is sufficient proof of great poetry, and well sustains Vaughan's poem in comparison with Wordsworth's more elaborate *Ode*.

When Vaughan sings

> I saw eternity the other night,
> Like a great ring of pure and endless light,
> All calm as it was bright;

he compels us to the same vision. He points unwaveringly

> The way which from this dead and dark abode
> Leads up to God,

not as a pious exhorter, but as one to whom it is plainer than a

sunlit road in the Usk valley. Far beyond the Welsh cottages
have his ministrations of comfort reached forth in his lines,

> They are all gone into the world of light!
>   And I alone sit lingering here;
> Their very memory is fair and bright,
>   And my sad thoughts doth clear.

> He that hath found some fledg'd bird's nest may know
>   At first sight, if the bird be flown;
> But what fair well or grove he sings in now,
>   That is to him unknown.

> And yet, as angels in some brighter dreams
>   Call to the soul, when man doth sleep:
> So some strange thoughts transcend our wonted themes,
>   And into glory peep.

WITHER (1588-1667)

One poet troublesome to the classifiers is George Wither.
He became a Puritan, yet could turn a love poem and delighted in good cheer. He loved the country, yet went to
Court and scandalized everybody by his outraged satire of its
license, and was jailed for his pains. He imitates Spenser's
pastorals, yet his favorite metre is the octosyllabic of Jonson.
Most of his work is of second, often third rate, but we are not
likely to forget one song,

> Shall I wasting in despair
> Die because a woman's fair? . . .

In the even and clear progress of its argument by stanzas, with
the retracing in the last, its heart-free regard for the lady, the
artful artlessness of becoming at times almost childishly sing-
song, as

> Be she meeker, kinder than
> Turtle-dove or pelican!
>   If she be not so to me,
>   What care I how kind she be?—

in all these points it is a true-to-type Jonsonian lyric. It is also
a very clever and captivating poem.

CHAPTER 16

Milton (1608-1674)

ABOVE all these men of moderate eminence towers, like a lone and inaccessible peak, the giant figure of John Milton. The greatness of the man and his poetry appears in the diverse opinion about him. No two ages, no two men, agree; and no one, as Goldsmith might say, has travelled over his mind. To some he has seemed the transcendent poet and seer; to others he is a monster fanatic.

Yet no other poet lived more self-consciously or has told us more about himself.

He was London-born, son of a well-to-do small banker-lawyer called a scrivener, who had been disinherited for turning Protestant, and who had a goodly talent in music. When Shakespeare died, Milton was a boy of eight, winning and serious, but no mollycoddle, as his picture proves. At forty-five he portrayed himself full-length: "My stature certainly is not tall; but it rather approaches the middle than the diminutive. . . . Nor though very thin, was I ever deficient in courage or strength: as I was wont constantly to exercise myself in the use of the broadsword, as long as it comported with my years. . . . At this moment I have the same courage, the same strength, though not the same eyes; yet so little do they betray any external appearance of injury, that they are as unclouded and bright as the eyes of those who most distinctly see. . . . My face, which is said to indicate a total privation of blood, is of a complexion entirely opposite to the pale and cadaverous; so that, though I am more than forty years old, there is scarcely anyone to whom I do not appear ten years younger than I am; and the smoothness of my skin is not in the least affected by the wrinkles of age."

He was a precocious youngster, feeding ravenously on poetry, ancient and modern, and his proud father, business man though he was, gladly saw him heading for a literary life, and let him sit up till midnight with his books, deputing a maid to trim the candles.

School at St. Paul's, John Colet's foundation, was happy; but at the University genius is seldom content; neither was Milton. At Christ's College, Cambridge, he was a bit scornful of most fellow-students and masters, and on one occasion was suspended and subject to discipline that galled his proud and sensitive soul. They called him "the lady of Christ's," yet most of them were really proud of him. How he was educating himself the verse of his university days makes clear. Much of it is in Latin according to long established academic practice. But Milton's Latin elegies are far more than exercises; they show not only his assimilation of ancient Latin poetry, especially Ovid and Propertius, but are themselves poetry, sometimes great poetry. This Latin verse was of immeasurable effect in producing the grand sonority and style of his mature English poetry. Since his paraphrase of two psalms at the age of fifteen he had been writing English verse along with the Latin. Ovid is gradually supplanted by Virgil as his model, and at nineteen, under the spell of the *Georgics*, he breaks into a brief passage of premonitory grandeur, addressed to his native language, in a *Vacation Exercise*, beginning,

> Yet I had rather if I were to choose,
> Thy service in some graver subject use,
> Such as may make thee search thy coffers round,
> Before thou clothe my fancy in fit sound. . . .

At Christmas two years and a half later he sends a Latin elegy to his dearest friend Diodati, absent on a house-party in Wales, telling how ere dawn he had begun his *Ode on Christ's Nativity*. It is an astonishing poem, especially for a man of twenty-one, not only in its learning, but in the ease with which Milton handles his materials. It is a composite of rich ingatherings from the ancients, the Church Fathers, from Italian,

French, and English poetry. Yet above all it is Milton. Here
and there he unluckily affects the new metaphysical fashion;
but he is saved from its vices by his classic taste and his devotion to Spenser.

In spite of the change of poetical fashion about 1600, the
tradition of Spenser had been strongly maintained by certain
poets. One of these was Drayton. Another was William
Browne, who in his *Britannia's Pastorals* celebrated the homely
beauties of life in Devonshire. But Giles Fletcher in his *Christ's
Victory and Triumph*, and his older brother Phineas in his
Purple Island and the English part of his *Locustae*, which
would have dismayed Spenser, went to an excess in their affectation of Spenserian allegory and style. Throughout his
life Milton found them, like Sylvester's translation of the
French Du Bartas, useful at least as baser material which his
alchemy could turn into gold. Yet he admitted that "sage and
serious" Spenser himself, as he called him, was his great
teacher. In metre, phrase, and perhaps in the first suggestion of
the subject, the *Nativity Ode* is in deep debt to Spenser. Like
Spenser in his *Hymns*, Milton varies his strict form through a
wide range of orchestration, from the exquisite

> See how from far upon the eastern road
> The star-led wizards haste with odors sweet,

to his peculiar deep organ tones,

> When at the world's last session
> The dreadful Judge in middle air shall spread his throne.

The Nativity was a common poetic subject. But Milton's
treatment is strikingly original. He celebrated the event by a
twilight pageant of the pagan gods, slowly fading into the
dawn, now grotesque, now lovely, now wistful.

Hitherto poetry had been the avocation of a man otherwise
occupied. It was so even with Chaucer and Spenser. But Milton
dedicated his life to poetry while yet at the university. He
aspired, like most great minds of the Renaissance, to encyclopedic learning and to fame, "that last infirmity of noble mind."

He was a susceptible youth, and temptations of the flesh were strong. But a temptation of the mind was stronger, the temptation to glory in learning for its own sake, without turning it to use or action. A letter prefaced to his sonnet on reaching twenty-three points to it; and near the end, in *Paradise Regained*, he allows Satan to tempt Christ with the idle glory of all the learning of the Renaissance. It was the danger of those learned times and his own besetting danger.

At twenty-four he retired for six years to his father's country-place at the snug little hamlet of Horton up the Thames, amid meadows, streams, and "tufted trees." In this retreat he read Latin and Greek on end, as another would read English; now and then he broke the monotony with a run into town to see friends or get more books on music or mathematics. Milton was at the time subjecting himself to the strictest self-discipline in composition, as the exquisite finish and slender amount of his verse show. Nothing is more instructive of a poet's self-discipline than to examine the erasures, changes, and filings in the Trinity College autograph manuscript of Milton's early poems.

But learning, love of fame, technique all together will not make a poet, without life itself lived wisely. "He who would not be frustrate of his hope to write well hereafter in laudable things, ought himself to be a true poem; that is a composition and pattern of the best and honorablest things; not presuming to sing the praises of heroic men, or famous cities, unless he have in himself the experience and practice of all that which is praiseworthy." So he later wrote of these formative years.

The results were not experiments but perfectly finished poems. The well-known pair, *L'Allegro* and *Il Penseroso*, have been too often contrasted as expressions of opposite moods, or even different personalities. There is, however, the same person and mind behind both; each is corollary of the other, like morning and afternoon. Each is a string of most delicately wrought miniatures strung upon artfully varied octosyllabics of Jonson's kind, but wrought in that greatest of all schools of poetic jewel work, the idylls of Theocritus. Various English

poems Milton may have had in mind, but the art is that of the
best Greek idyllism.

Through his musical friend Henry Lawes, he was brought
to produce the "books" for two entertainments or masques in
the Egerton family. The first, a fragment called *Arcades*, did
tuneful honor to the venerable Countess Dowager of Derby, of
an evening under the old elms at Harefield. It was forty years
since Spenser, who claimed this lady as a relative, had dedicated to her his *Tears of the Muses*.

The other was *Comus*, a masque. It employs all the features
of the masque—songs, ballets, spectacle, machinery, grotesque
antimasque, allegorical myth, mingling of the cast with the
audience. But being Milton's, it is more. Again he shows many
masters, particularly Jonson, and above all Spenser, whose
guidance is felt in phrase, temper, idea, and in most of the
plot furnished from the *Faery Queen*. But the spell of *Comus*
permeating every detail is that of the high-spirited, fine-tem-
pered, cultivated young Milton, in love with everything lovely
—sky, stars, woods at night, sea-depths, country-folk, fairy-
lore, bright color, human faces and forms, moral ideas which
convince him through his very young man's love of them. And
the Elder Brother, rightly understood, is the embodiment of
this engaging young Puritan poet himself.

Comus was performed at Ludlow Castle in September, 1634.
Early, but of uncertain date is the irregular lyric *At a Solemn
Music*, less familiar than it should be. It expresses that close
kinship between music and poetry which, as we have seen, is
the secret of the inimitable success of English poets in the
Renaissance. Milton with his special talent and skill in music is
a supreme instance. *At a Solemn Music* is a recurrence of that
peculiar Miltonic musical upsoaring felt in the *Vacation Exercise* and the *Nativity Ode*. Such lines as

> Where the bright Seraphim in burning row
> Their loud uplifted Angel trumpets blow;

and the last line,

> To live with Him and sing in endless morn of light,

sound unlabored if any ever were. One is amazed to find that they were not produced by sudden inspiration, but were the result of long and toilsome correction.

The circumstances of the production of _Lycidas_ everyone knows. Three years after _Comus_ it comes, and between twenty-five and twenty-eight Milton's youthful charm has given place to another. If one would realize the beauty of _Lycidas_, let him lay it beside the first idyll of Theocritus, Bion's _Lament for Adonis_, Virgil's fifth and tenth eclogues, and Milton's own _Epitaphium Damonis_—each a matchless poem—and discover the magic with which Milton has transmuted the old devices into a new glory. Let him also learn _Lycidas_ by heart, until its enchanting cadences enter into his own language, and its structure grows familiar part by part. He will then not care whether it is "pure" pastoral, whether the "dread voice" that lashed the clergy is inept, or whether Milton really grieved for Edward King or not. The feeling is deep enough to dictate incomparable music—feeling for Nature from most delicate details of floral design to Deva's "wizard stream" and "the shaggy top of Mona high," pity for dead youth, hatred of selfish fools, a sense of the eternal world that lies about this ephemeral one; but above all intense preoccupation with his own case, his fear of early death, his dedication to poetry, his rejection of the clerical life, and especially his besetting temptation to selfish unproductive glorification in the pride and delights of mere erudition.

Italy at first hand seemed essential to such a poet; he might even see Greece! It is again the case of northern genius warming itself under the actual skies of southern culture. For fifteen months he was abroad, chiefly in Florence and Rome, but also at Venice and Naples. It seems a powerful proof of this young man's charm that everywhere he was received by cultivated and distinguished men with genuine personal warmth and even affection; and that, too, in spite of his not very polite eagerness as a young Protestant zealot to air his views in "the very metropolis of popery," as he says. He had otherwise, besides his gifts and parts, only a few Latin poems, and a letter or two to recommend him. Nothing in his journey

impressed him more, or more stirred his patriotism by contrast, than his visit near Florence to "the famous Galileo, a
prisoner of the Inquisition, for thinking in astronomy otherwise than as the Franciscan and Dominican licensers
thought."

Civil troubles hurried him home without seeing Greece; and
domestic troubles, of his own making, supervened. He suddenly married the lively Mary Powell, of good country
Royalist family, and as suddenly repented. He was thirty-
three, she seventeen. It may have been in part a matter of
the clean, young, unworldly idealist, who has been known
to mismanage himself in such cases, but it was surely in part
the mischief of in-laws. Mary left him for two years, but returned and spent the seven last years of her life with him,
during which she bore three daughters and one son. He
was twice again married, to Katharine Woodcock, who lived
but fifteen months, and is commemorated in a lovely sonnet,
and to Elizabeth Minshull, who survived him.

For more than seven years, from 1640 to 1647, during
his thirties, Milton was a teacher, receiving in his house first
his nephews, then other boys, as pupils; one of them, Edward Phillips, recalls "his excellent judgment and way of
teaching, far above the pedantry of common public schools."
After 1637, between the age of twenty-eight and fifty, he
produced little poetry, but hurled forth pamphlet after pamphlet in the cause of "real liberty"—four against the bishops,
four in defence of divorce, and two, more precious to modern times, a little tract *Of Education* and his grand and ringing defence of the freedom of the press called *Areopagitica*.
The essay on education urges the most progressive ideas of
the times, and though its encyclopedic scope of study is now
impracticable, it is a living document based upon the invariable fact in teaching, that words are but the servants of
things, and speech the servant of action. A "complete and
generous [noble] education," he writes, "fits a man to perform justly, skilfully, and magnanimously, all the offices, both
private and public, of peace and war."

As he entered upon his thirties and his active life, a new

dominant passion possessed the poet—patriotism; but it was a glorification of England not so much for her past or her present as for her future potential. "Methinks I see in my mind a noble and puissant nation rousing herself like a strong man after sleep, and shaking her invincible locks." England is to be a Samson, breaking the bonds of oppression for herself and for the deliverance of all nations. The sentence is from the *Areopagitica*, but liberty was to him not a matter primarily of freedom from bishops, kings, censors, pedants, and star chambers. Even the Presbyterian Long Parliament must be warned against tyranny, in a scathing sonnet *On the New Forcers of Conscience*, containing one of the most learnedly witty lines in English Literature,

New Presbyter is but Old Priest writ large.

Milton's basic conviction was Plato's, that political liberty depends altogether upon the personal freedom of its citizens in heart and mind from the domination of their passions. The paradise of political freedom is lost when

> true Liberty
> Is lost, which always with right reason dwells
> Twinn'd, and from her hath no dividual being:
> Reason in man obscur'd, or not obey'd
> Immediately inordinate desires
> And upstart passions catch the government
> From Reason, and to servitude reduce
> Man till then free. Therefore since he permits
> Within himself unworthy powers to reign
> Over free Reason, God in judgment just
> Subjects him from without to violent lords;
> Who oft as undeservedly enthrall
> His outward freedom.[1]

This basic idea, first apparent in *Comus*, may be taken as the key of all Milton's later work in prose and verse.

As Latin Secretary of the Parliament from 1649, the year of Charles I's execution, to 1660, that of the Restoration of

[1] *Par. Lost*, 12.83-95

Charles II, Milton was thundering out his great pamphlets, Latin and English, to all astounded Europe in defence of the execution of the King, and of the new English ideals. Most notable are his *Defence of the English People,* 1651, and his *Second Defence,* 1654. Warned that the writing of the *Second Defence* would destroy his overtaxed eyes, he fearlessly bent himself to the labor, and rose from it blind. He was but forty-five, in the full vigor of his great mind, and his poetic masterpiece, to which he had long since dedicated himself, hardly begun. The famous sonnet on his blindness utters his patient despair at the moment; but in time he discovers that, for light denied to the sensuous eye, he has gained a compensating poetic power:

> So much the rather thou, Celestial Light,
> Shine inward, and the mind through all her powers
> Irradiate, there plant eyes, all mist from thence
> Purge, and disperse, that I may see and tell
> Of things invisible to mortal sight.[1]

In 1660 Milton issued his *Ready and Easy Way to Establish a Commonwealth.* It is a pathetic document, for, as he wrote, he knew that the high Puritan adventure in freedom had failed, and a new king with the old abuses was all but returned. Though at first pursued into hiding by the King's agents, Milton was safe from utter despair. A Christianized Stoicism, "the patience of heroic martyrdom," as he calls it, had fortified many a noble, tried spirit of the Renaissance, and it stood him in good stead, "now fallen on evil days." Did he ever suspect that the real liberties for which the Puritans had suffered were denied to England for only a generation, and would soon return to stay?

Though Milton at the Restoration lost most of his fortune, he otherwise got off easily. And then, there was his poetry.

Towards *Paradise Lost* he had been moving since he was twenty, as he says, "long choosing, and beginning late." In that premonitory passage in *Vacation Exercise* at nineteen he

[1] *Par. Lost,* 3.51-5

is foreshadowing a great epic.[1] Ten years later, in his new access of patriotism, he is reviewing British history and setting down a long list of possible subjects; and for a time the Arthurian story possesses him to the point of making a beginning of an Arthurian epic. But there are jottings of Biblical subjects also, and for a time he considered allegorical drama in Greek form as a possibility. By 1642 the theme of the Fall of Man was uppermost, and he sketched schemes and lists of characters for a drama, even drafting a few lines afterwards used in a speech of Satan in the poem.[2] Steady composition began by 1658. Though briefly interrupted in 1660, and though the productive periods were limited to late night or early morning, and that during but half the year, the poem was finished apparently in five years. It was not printed till 1667.

Paradise Lost is the greatest single poetic achievement in the language. One may wander through it as through a vast cathedral, lost in its music, its shifting beauties of color, its vista and perspective, light and shade, and rich reminiscence of ancient lore. But as one's mind becomes adjusted to its huge range and proportions, its values and qualities define themselves, and the multifarious details fall into their right places.

The ground plan is as simple as that of any other great epic. Satan resents the elevation of the Son of God above himself, and conspires against God. He suffers defeat, and with his followers is thrown into Hell newly prepared to receive him. God, to replace the rebels, creates the World and Man in a state of innocence. But Satan, in revenge, contrives the fall of Man from innocence through the eating of a forbidden apple, and his loss of Paradise therefor, and is in turn cursed of God.

This simple framework Milton has adorned and elaborated with every sort of poetic splendor—dramatic action, character, tragic consequence, lyric interlude, idyll, episode, philosophic and moral truth, myth and legend, Greek rhetoric,

[1] See p. 238
[2] *Par. Lost*, 4.32-41

oratory, fragment and phrase by the hundreds transmuted
from other writings, Hebrew, Greek, Latin, Italian, French,
and English; and at admirably chosen points he has set his
similes, singly or in glittering clusters, with a technical skill
and power of expression unexcelled even by Homer. Throughout the whole structure rises and falls continually the grandest metrical music in the language. The traditional English
blank verse, the verse of Marlowe and the other dramatists,
Milton has transformed into a new music, by wide variation,
by his use under Virgil's influence of long quantities, and by
running over his lines until the unit of his metre is no longer
a single line, but prolonged groups of lines, musical phrases,
rising and falling like the broad ground swell of open ocean.

Milton is the most learned of the English poets. He still
emulated the encyclopedic learning of his times. He was fifty
and more when he composed *Paradise Lost,* and the huge mass
of his accumulations was to him only building material for
his poem. But it was to be a grand poem. He had discarded
themes of mere national history and old romance, and chosen
an action in which the persons were God, Satan, all Mankind, and all Creation; of which the scene was all space
and the time all time. All available poetry, lore, and knowledge
of mankind must yield tribute to this theme. With all else
Milton evidently sought out every other poetic attempt to
treat the theme he could find, including Latin, Italian, French,
Dutch. He perhaps even discovered the Old English tenth-
century *Genesis B,* through his acquaintance with the Dutch
scholar Junius. If he did not know this poem, the resemblances
of his own to it are almost a miracle of coincidence. From
it, or from Spenser's *Hymn of Heavenly Love*, or both, he
may have got ideas for his ground plan.

Of course he ran the risk of failure that attends too great
artistic ambition; but to his task he brought genius, power of
mind and style, more than equal to it. However great the
mass, it is permeated with the living energy of the poet.

Learning for learning's sake he abhorred. He could not
have expected the reader to follow him in his erudition, nor
embarrass himself with commentaries painfully exploring the

poem's many allusions. Milton sought, and gained another effect—the rich texture and lustre of his fabric that comes from remote geographical and proper names, obscure myth and legend, all set to music of verse that enhances their mystery.

He also forged a style of his own, a hybrid of plain English and Virgilian Latin, full of new organ quality and volume, yet capable of most delicate modulation. It is called the "grand" style; grand as it is, it is extraordinarily clear and essentially simple, especially to the ear—more uniformly so than that of Shakespeare or most other poets.

The story of *Paradise Lost* is a double or even triple tragedy. First is the tragedy of Satan, who wrecked the noble self with which he began by admitting mean envy which grew to pride and vaulting ambition. This involved the tragedies of Adam and Eve—first Eve from her feminine ambition to be a goddess and "universal Dame"; then Adam from his masculine unreasoning and selfish passion. The old Hebrew story in Genesis is elementally simple. Milton has refined it with much that is universally and subtly human, run it in the vast mould of a Greek epic, and embellished it with every suitable poetic splendor he could lay his hands on.

People usually read only the first two books of the poem, and say that Milton has by mistake made Satan an admirable hero. They would be as competent to settle the case of Othello or Macbeth after reading only the first act. But Milton at fifty had looked evil in the eye with an expert appraisal. He therefore portrays Consummate Evil as fascinating, irresistible, seeming virtuous in his proud courage; then sinking by hardly perceptible degrees to meaner and meaner subterfuge, stormed by his passions, tortured as he recalls the peace of which his calloused heart is no longer capable, still susceptible to a trace of pity for his helpless victims; the fruits of his tragic efforts turned to dull ashes, until in *Paradise Regained* he is incurably tired and bored, like Faustus, and enters upon his temptation of the Son of God disillusioned and hopeless.

With equal subtlety Milton follows the tragedies of the

man and the woman, though in grandeur they are necessarily overshadowed by Satan's. But he makes up in some
measure for this by the power and delicacy of the temptation
scene between Satan and Eve, the subsequent scenes between
Adam and Eve, and the moving and simple dignity of the
last twenty-five lines of the poem.

There are passages in the poem no doubt where Milton
overlooked, and stepped on, the hairline between the sublime
and the ridiculous; where he did not wait for enough inspiration, but depended too much on the grand style, as in
parts of the angel narratives; yet these light up at any moment with a dance of the stars, an intimate glimpse of Nature, a lively animal grotesque, a hymn of praise, a lyric
revelation of the poet's mind. Epic though it be in its points
of form, dramatic energy animates the whole poem from the
first exchange between Satan and Beelzebub, through the superb scenes between Satan, Zephon, and Gabriel, to the scene
of reconciliation between Adam and Eve, in which, be it observed, he makes the woman the nobler figure of the two.

Paradise Regained finds fewer readers than it deserves. Of
course it suffers eclipse from its companion poem, which is
more than five times as long. Besides it is stripped of most
of the ornament which embellished the other, though no splendor in *Paradise Lost* surpasses the "broad prospect" of the
earth's expanse from the Mount of Temptation in Book III,
or the review of the ancient world and its culture in Book
IV, or the rolling organ music of proper names under which
these vast visions unfold.[1] Wordsworth called *Paradise Regained* "the most perfect in execution of anything written by
Milton"; he probably had in mind its more biblical simplicity.
Milton himself, we hear, did not like to have it suffer by
comparison. Yet it is not popular.

It is a short "epic" in the manner of the Book of Job.
One may wonder that Milton should choose the temptation
rather than the crucifixion of Christ as the act by which Man
was redeemed and Paradise regained. But throughout his life,
from the age of twenty-three to the end, his favorite poetic

[1] See p. 153

theme is the moral choice and patient endurance of trial. It underlies every poem, because it involves the case of Milton himself. This is how he comes to add to the gospel account of the temptation his own temptation—and perhaps that of his age—to idle erudition. *agon = contest — in a struggle*

With far more tragic intensity he has partly impersonated himself in the old Hebrew hero in *Samson Agonistes*. Blind, despondent, the sport and prisoner of riotous fools, his giant powers only asleep within him, "patient but undaunted," Samson rises to the supreme act by which he liberates his people at the price of his life, and "heroicly hath finish'd a life heroic." Such was Milton, or such he wished to be.

The *Samson* is another case of Hebrew story in Greek form. For years Milton had meditated such a work. His mind was saturate with the Greek drama, and the energies of that drama had entered deeply into *Paradise Lost*. Easily the most congenial because the nearest to his own case were the *Prometheus Bound* of Aeschylus, the *Oedipus at Colonus* of Sophocles, and the *Mad Heracles* of Euripides. Samson follows the *Prometheus* episode for episode, in an ingenious parallel. In character Samson is more like the aged Oedipus. In the rhetoric of the play and the use of the Chorus Milton shows a poet's usual fondness for Euripides. But the choruses are the most disappointing part of the play. The lyric gift, never great in Milton, often declines with age, and the result in *Samson,* inevitably measured by the flashing Greek choruses, is at least inadequate.

One will not discover the glory of *Samson Agonistes* by comparing it with stage drama, or looking in it for exciting event. It belongs to the class of such Greek prototypes as the *Prometheus,* the *Ajax* and the second Oedipus play of Sophocles, which rise to their grandeur by showing how a heroic person endures the disproportionate suffering that has come upon him from a weakness of his own. Energized as the case of Samson is with the egoism of Milton, it may speak for itself. Let the play be expressively read aloud entire at one sitting, and it will need no defence and little explanation.

Recent attempts to "humanize" Milton have gone about it by way of his petty personal faults, his private affairs, the cause and nature of his blindness, and even false scandal urged in the ostensible interests of truth. The man was human, but none the less great. One last sees him sitting in the sun at the door of his little house in Artillery Walk, clad in coarse gray cloth, pale, cheerful, with a satiric flavor, not too pleased with the visits of curious lion-hunters from foreign parts; breaking into song to beguile the twinges of arthritic pain, as his solicitous wife steals quietly in and out. What visions of England's future are moving behind the sightless eyes of this seer and poet, as he sits there "in calm of mind, all passion spent"?

CHAPTER 17

Odd and Even

MARVELL (1621-1678)

IN THE last years of his Latin Secretaryship the blind Milton had an assistant thirteen years younger, who became his devoted friend. This was Andrew Marvell, "of middling stature, pretty strong-set, roundish-faced, cherry-cheeked, hazel eye, brown hair." He was a quiet, practical man, admirable and likable, though quick of temper, and his poetry is as engaging as the man. He loved gardens and little girls—a childless man himself—fresh grass, mowers, and a lush English meadow. He bore a brave man's part in Parliament against the corruption and intolerance of Restoration times, and swung a deadly weapon of satire:

> This isle was well reformed, and gained renown,
> Whilst the brave Tudors wore the imperial crown:
> But since the royal race of Stuarts came,
> It has recoiled to Popery and shame;
> Misguided monarchs, rarely wise or just,
> Tainted with pride, and with impetuous lust.

His satires, circulated only in manuscript, made themselves felt. Yet he was of a sort to find few personal enemies; even Charles II, for all he was a Stuart, liked this brave, incorruptible Puritan. During the bitter years of the war he had friends on both sides.

Marvell was the country-bred son of an Anglican divine. After Cambridge and four years' travel, he lived for two or three years at a country house of the great Puritan general

Lord Fairfax, Nun Appleton in southern Yorkshire, as tutor to his daughter of twelve. Here it was that Marvell is said to have composed his poems on gardens and mowers. The formal Italian garden of his times he disapproves:

> 'Tis all enforced, the fountain and the grot,
> While the sweet fields do lie forgot,
> Where willing Nature does to all dispense
> A wild and fragrant innocence.

In this preference he is two generations ahead of the fashion, and in his poetic appreciation of children almost a century and a half. Some verses to a baby girl begin

> Come, little infant, love me now,
> While thine unsuspected years
> Clear thine aged father's brow
> From cold jealousy and fears.

Nothing more beguiling can be found than his *Picture of Little T. C. in a Prospect of Flowers.*

He loves a conceit, however, and can make excellent use of it, as in his *Drop of Dew,* and his fine devotional poem, *The Coronet.* And his octosyllabics, *Bermudas,* the song of Puritan refugees rowing from their ship to land in those delectable islands, rise above all fashions in their poetic spell.

Four years he spent at Eton as tutor to a member of Cromwell's family, and knew that learned and lovable old man John Hales, the "ever memorable," who was then dispossessed by the Puritans, and soon died deploring as he always had the whole wretched quarrel. At the same time Marvell had begun his friendship with Milton, and was writing his grand poems in honor of Cromwell and the Commonwealth. In 1660 it is said to have been Marvell's active efforts that saved Milton from harm. The rest of his life he was an honest and efficient member of Parliament for Hull, his boyhood home. Dismayed at the corruption and licence all around, he kept up his resourceful fight with the vested interests in behalf of toleration till his sudden and early end in 1678. As he says of Ben Jonson, he was

> Sworn enemy to all that do pretend.

COWLEY (1618-1667)

Abraham Cowley seems to have been a child prodigy, London born. His earliest printed poem on Pyramus and Thisbe he wrote at the age of ten. But the sober world does not find prodigies engaging, and has learned not to expect ultimate greatness from them. So it has been with Cowley, who had extraordinary talent, but not the capacity for deep passion necessary to make his poetry infectious. He was a facile youngster, confessing that he "in one morn three hundred rhimes let fall"—a dangerous symptom in any one. He felt a "secret bent of aversion" from the world. "When I was a very young boy at school, instead of running about on holidays, and playing with my fellows, I was wont to steal from them, and walk into the fields, either alone with a book, or with some one companion, if I could find any of the same temper." To the end he prayed,

> May I a small house and large garden have!
> And a few friends, and many books, both true,
> Both wise, and both delightful too!

It was the tragedy of this retiring spirit to get caught and scorched in the flame of the civil quarrel. He was a devoted royalist and hated Cromwell. In 1644 he was ejected by the Puritans from his old university Cambridge, took refuge at Oxford, and afterwards joined the royal family in France. Fate chose this sensitive man to be dangerously employed as a secret agent of the Stuarts in England, where he suffered arrest, and dreamed of seeking idyllic refuge in some "obscure retreat" in America! At the Restoration he took part in the beginning of the Royal Society, and at last had his wish for a house and garden fulfilled, up the Thames at Chertsey.

"Who now reads Cowley?" asked Pope, seventy years after his death. The answer has been the same in all times except the poet's own, when he was surprisingly ranked at the top by other poets regardless of party. A collector of old literary furniture will enjoy wandering through his rather extensive display. He will skip the stretches of Latin verse; he will not linger over the unreadable epic *Davideis,* which some think helped Milton; he will sample the lyrics that in great number compose *The Mistress,* which show Cowley in love with language, not with love, certainly not with a woman; he will find better going among the "Pindaric" odes, which owe little to Pindar but their first suggestion, their irregular stanza, and a certain elevation of style and he may discover Cowley's best among his odic and elegiac poems. Here and there is a touch of old philosophy and the ingenuity of conceit, for which Dr. Johnson in his *Life of Cowley* has given him more notoriety than he deserves. But the reader is constantly reminded of later men, especially Pope and Gray, not only by a phrase, but by the manner—the smart antithesis, the easy smooth cadence which they would have called "numbers," the preference of generalities to interesting details, the select epithet paired with every noun, the abstract nouns personified by wearing a capital, the poems on abstract subjects, Solitude, Greatness, Obscurity, etc. The real and enduring Cowley deals not with Nature or love, but with the new subject that was to engross men for a century, personalities and manners of men. It is this personal quality which ennobles his laments for Mr. William Hervey and the poet Crashaw; and his odes to Hobbes and the Royal Society should be read as superb poetical reviews of the cultural tendencies of the times.

WRITERS IN PROSE

That mellow nameless charm which is a peculiar glory of seventeenth-century literature is as potent in the writers of prose as in the poets. It comes in part from their rich learning made warm and living by their personal geniality. It is like the glory of a sweet old mansion in the warm slant afternoon sun. Sometimes these men are antiquarian with antiquarian quaintness and oddity, and their works are like the spacious attic of the same mansion with its dry spicy smell, in which we can rummage to heart's content among old forgotten cast-off things all set in order, while the clock stops, and there is no time of day. It was surely his pleasure in such rummaging that stirred the dilatory mind of Dr. Johnson, and made him distinguish

Burton's *Anatomy of Melancholy* as the only book which ever got him out of bed two hours sooner than he wished to rise.

But the combination of charm and learning with a subtle art lends to the writing of such as Jeremy Taylor and Sir Thomas Browne a higher splendor—much the same splendor as in the learned poetry of Milton, with like depth of lustre and texture in shadowy rich allusion and figure, and with correspondent music moving through many-voiced harmonies and happy modulations.

The felicity of this life is but a shadow of true happiness; for the shadow is not a body, but a resemblance of a body: and seeming to be something, is nothing; the inconstancy and speedy change of human things deserves this name, because the shadow is always altering, and ends on a sudden: and as the shadow, when it is at length, and can increase no farther, is nearest to the end; so temporal goods, and human fortunes, when they are mounted up as high as the stars, are then nearest to vanish, and disappear suddenly.[1]

Now since these dead bones have already outlasted the living ones of Methuselah, and in a yard under ground, and thin walls of clay, outworn all the strong and specious buildings above it; and quietly rested under the drums and tramplings of three conquests; what Prince can promise such diuturnity unto his Reliques, or might not gladly say,

Sic ego componi versus in ossa velim?

Time, which antiquates Antiquities, and hath an art to make dust of all things, hath yet spared these minor monuments.[2]

In such passages as these, only the difference between the rhythms of prose and the rhythms of verse seem to keep Taylor or Browne from being poets.

Among all these seventeenth-century writers of prose the manner of expression varies of course according to the person; and yet it is essentially the same, a succession of short or longer sentences, reiterating, with illustration, addition, variation, the key thought of the whole group, which is often contained in the first sentence, as in the passage just quoted from

[1] Jeremy Taylor, *Contemplations,* chap. 2
[2] Browne, *Urn Burial,* chap. 5

Taylor. It is the style of Bacon, advancing by irregular jets of the mind, as if it were thinking while it wrote, not beforehand. It has been called "baroque" from that style in all the art and building of the period which loves to depart from exact symmetry and order, and gets its effect from restless movement rather than from finished repose. It is also called "anti-Ciceronian" because it repudiates Cicero, who had been the model for finished prose until about 1600. Its loose movement, opening out like a telescope, is ideal for the expression of intimate counsel or confession, of odd whim or vagary, or genial warmth. Its sentences of uneven length admit both a variation and a harmony of tone that are necessary to its intimate music.

All of these men were naturally inclined to the royalist side. Some of them were drawn into the contention in spite of themselves; some, like Taylor and Fuller, stood in vain for tolerant conciliation; some like Walton, Burton, and Browne, withdrew as they could into retirement or avocation to write and wait for better times.

Out of just such writing is born the intimate personal essay, the confessional, which has increased and multiplied with slight interruption from Sir William Temple through Addison and Steele, Sterne, Lamb, to our own day, wherein it still flourishes in our periodicals. Its grand ancestor is Montaigne, whose *Essais,* used by Shakespeare, were much liked by certain of these seventeenth-century writers. Their apparently artless self-revelation was a stimulus and encouragement to Burton and Browne to reveal themselves as beguilingly and artlessly as the fascinating Frenchman had done.

BURTON (1577-1640)

The Anatomy of Melancholy is better known than its author; probably because this strange, curious, whimsical person is intimately present in his work to the perennial delight of all men. Robert Burton haunted Oxford all his adult life. Vicar of St. Thomas's in the town, he kept his study in Christ Church College, and his body rests in its chapel. He seems to have been an odd character, but amiable, such as only old colleges beget, cherish, and sustain.

An "anatomy" was a dissection or analysis, and "melancholy" a habit or disease of mind in most respects the same as the ills attendant upon what we are nowadays pleased to call "suppressed desires." Its antidote is creative action. We have already noticed Milton's fear of mere idle learning. The fear of this disease, and the theory of its causes and treatment, preoccupied men's minds in the Renaissance, and underlie much of their literature. Anyone who is aware of this can better understand the works of these men from Shakespeare and Milton down. "I writ of melancholy," says Burton, "by being busy to avoid melancholy. There is no greater cause of melancholy than idleness, no better cure than business."

Burton spent his life writing and revising his book. He did little else except dispel occasional dumps by stepping to the river hard by and laughing to hear the boatmen swear at each other. He wrote, or professed to write, "at first, once for all, in an extemporanean style, whatever came uppermost, as I do commonly all other exercises, standing on one leg." Just so his *Anatomy* is to be read, and has been read of many. Milton may have caught from it a suggestion for *Il Penseroso*. Dr. Johnson saw himself reflected in it, and relished many an odd bit of its lore. The whimsicality and egoism of Sterne and Lamb revelled in it, and grew more whimsical and beguiling by feeding upon it. Among the many cheerful children of this expert in melancholy the youngest is Mr. Holbrook Jackson, whose *Anatomy of Bibliomania* inherits much of the ancestral magic. "As I rove I confess," says Burton, rummaging in the dusty old collections at Oxford; so the reader now rummages with him, diverted at every moment by the humors of the men at his elbow. Sometimes his voice rises into that deep, incomparable music heard only in the writers of his times. Sometimes he means to joke; more often one cannot be sure; but underneath all runs this likable old bookmonger's antiquarian amusement at the perennial queerness of the human mind, especially his own.

Methinks sometime or other, amongst so many rich Bachelors, a benefactor should be found to build a monastical College for old, decayed, deformed, or discontented maids to live together in, that have lost their first loves, or otherwise miscarried, or else are willing howsoever to lead a single life.

Is he serious? Yet he says in another place:

To play the fool now and then is not amiss, there is a time for all things. Grave Socrates would be merry by fits, sing, dance, and take his liquor too, or else Theodoret belies him. . . . Xenophon, in his Symposium brings in Socrates as a principal Actor, no man merrier than himself, and sometimes he would ride a cock-horse with his children.

Surely Burton was, as he calls another, "a good, personate old man."

BROWNE (1605-1682)

Burton escaped the rancors of the time by staying quietly at Oxford where he belonged, and dying in 1640. Sir Thomas Browne found his refuge in practising medicine most of his life at Norwich. Withal he produced four curious works: *Pseudodoxia Epidemica,* the most elaborate, written to explode many common errors and superstitions; *Hydriotaphia,* or *Urn Burial,* an essay on burial customs; *The Garden of Cyrus,* a sort of fantasia on the quincunx; and his most famous *Religio Medici,* the religion of a doctor—always an interesting matter. The three last are brief. His titles reflect the composite man he was, and the reader encounters now the scientific doctor, who once even touches the modern curative use of milk and open air in tuberculosis; now the religious mystic who prayed in secret seven times each day wherever he happened to be; now the sceptical foe of superstition and authority; now the antiquarian believer in witches, ghosts, and the Ptolemaic system, and one who revels in everything old. The *Religio Medici* is Browne's modest, and to all appearances artless, portrait of his gentle self, a compound of opposites which do not war within him, but are blended in the warmth and beauty of his genial soul.

"Now for my life, it is a miracle of thirty years, which to
relate were not a History, but a piece of Poetry, and would
sound to common ears like a Fable." So it was to Browne,
albeit uneventful. After Oxford and four years of medicine in
France, Italy, and Holland, he settled at thirty-two in Norwich. Many years later when he was sixty-six and famous,
Charles II came to town, and would have knighted the mayor,
who gracefully declined the honor in favor of Dr. Thomas
Browne. Norwich was exactly the place for him, ancient, mellow, clean, with its fine cathedral and multitude of old churches,
its gardens—"much addicted to the flowery part," as John Evelyn said—its lovely views often painted by later masters. There
he lived comfortably in his mansion and garden, both stuffed
like a boy's pocket with curios, birds' eggs, coins, pottery, and
what not.

Town and house alike are the counterpart of Browne's mind.
He is a collector of queer old ideas and queer words—indigi-
tate, piaculous, glandulosities, ubiquitary, tabid, transpeciate.
He is pleasant and gentle, for ever beginning, "I confess . . ."
"I cannot but wonder . . ." "I am content to . . ." "I am
afraid that . . ."

There is but one first cause. . . . This is the cause I grope after in
the works of Nature; on this hangs the Providence of God. To raise
so beauteous a structure as the World and the Creatures thereof, was
but his Art, but their sundry and divided operations, with their pre-
destinated ends, are from the Treasure of His Wisdom. In the causes,
nature, and affections of the Eclipses of the Sun and Moon, there is
most excellent speculation; but to profound farther, and to contem-
plate a reason why His Providence hath so disposed and ordered their
motions in that vast circle as to conjoin and obscure each other, is a
sweeter piece of Reason, and a diviner point of Philosophy. . . .

I love to lose myself in a mystery, to pursue my Reason to an
O altitudo! . . .

I could never hear the Ave-Mary Bell without an elevation.

This was no man of controversy. Yet Protestants called him
a Catholic, Catholics proscribed him; and Quakers had hopes
of winning him to their gentle faith. He is not a thinker. His

mind reaches out for mysteries, for worn old ideas and images of Nature, Doubt, and Death, and for new mysteries of science, then clings to them and rambles over them like a beautiful vine, gracefully winding every way, and breaking into luxuriant foliage of word, phrase, and cadence.

TAYLOR (1613-1667)

None appeals more strongly to our sympathy than the gentle Dr. Jeremy Taylor. He was a respectable barber's son who sprang into brilliant and immediate success as a preacher under the unlucky Archbishop Laud. Then the Puritans triumphed, and this fine soul, gentle and conciliatory in his writings and manner of living, was destined to suffer most of his life from unwelcome controversy, or poverty, or imprisonment, or turmoil. Yet Milton of the other party counts him of the

> Men whose Life, learning, faith, and pure intent
> Would have been held in high esteem with Paul.

For two or three years during the war he found retirement at Golden Grove in Wales as a chaplain and teacher, and out of this security produced many of his great sermons, and his noble books on *Holy Living* and *Holy Dying*. But in quiet or tumult his pen was always busy, and produced much. The last nine years of his life this unoffending man lived in Ireland, whither he, of all men, was sent to breast the church troubles, then at their worst. He died there worn out at fifty-four.

Taylor's peculiar office is that most difficult one of spiritual ministration to the comfortable and cultivated classes. His *Holy Living, Holy Dying,* and *Great Exemplar,* an interpretation of Christ's life and passion, exhale his characteristic sweetness. They first captivate one with their literary cultivation, their rich imagery and glorious music. Learned as they are, they hold one's affection because they are full of the warm humanity of Taylor himself, his solid sense, his cognizance of the facts.

He hath scattered the firmament with stars, as a man sows corn in his fields, in a multitude bigger than the capacities of human order; . . . . Yet in the distribution of our time, God seems to be straight-handed, and gives it to us, not as nature gives us rivers, enough to drown us, but drop by drop, minute after minute, so that we never can have two minutes together, but He takes away one when He gives us another.[1]

To Jeremy Taylor life and death are every man's realities, full of perplexities which cannot be blinked, and which can be solved only by being spiritualized through one transcendent Pattern.

FULLER (1608-1661)

Thomas Fuller, divine, author of *The Holy State and the Profane State* and *The Worthies of England*, is one of the most diverting men of the times. Tall, careless in dress, absent of mind, with a memory that could repeat all the signs he had read in a walk through London, he reminds one outwardly of a greater doctor who tramped those streets a century later. He was antiquarian by instinct. When rambling about England with the King's army, he improved time by collecting all the information he could from churches and monuments of dead celebrities, cultivating the acquaintance and friendship of learned persons, and not refusing "to light his candle, in investigating truth, from the meanest person's discovery." The result is his *Worthies*. England, he says, is a house, "not very great, but convenient." The shires are rooms. "Now as learned Master Camden and painful Master Speed, with others, have described the rooms themselves; so is it our intention, God willing, to describe the *furniture* of those rooms, such eminent commodities which every County doth produce, with the Persons of Quality bred therein, and some other observables." And one reads on through good stories, puns, proverbs, odd scriptural instance, drolleries, unable to tell when Fuller knew he was funny, and when not. He complains that religious prejudice has caused depression in the fish trade: "Some suspect as if there were a Pope in the belly of every Fish, and some bones of Superstition in them, which would choak a conscientious person, . . . But know, that such customes grew from a treble root, of Popery, Piety, and Policy."

[1] *Holy Dying*, 2.1.2

Fuller's *Holy and Profane State* (1641) is of the same sort. It describes many types, such as the good Widow, the good Sea-Captain, the Court-Lady, and to this "character" often appends a short, illustrative biography, with a result both amusing and edifying. No wonder it has so long been popular. For it is the elusive Fuller himself that the reader pursues—he is always exuberant but gentle, and amusing but a little mystifying.

WALTON (1593-1683)

Of all these pleasant men none has been and is so beloved as Izaak Walton. His life of ninety years covered the span from Elizabeth, through Commonwealth and Restoration, almost to the Revolution of 1688, late enough to feel the cool dawn of the new century. A royalist in sympathy, he kept clear of the troubles by minding his business and going fishing.

He looks very modern. Yeoman born, he came to London, worked up to solid prosperity in the iron trade, educated himself, and irresistibly attracted the finest friends in London, such as Jonson, Donne, Drayton, John Hales, Henry Wotton, and Sir George Hastings, "an excellent angler, and now with God." "I would rather prove myself a gentleman," he says, "by being learned and humble, valiant and inoffensive, virtuous and communicable, than by any fond ostentation of riches, or, wanting those virtues myself, boast that these were in my ancestors." He was such a man as loves the words honest, wholesome, pleasant, good, quiet, stately, sweet; and they flavor his discourse like the fine savories he recommends in the proper cooking and serving of a trout.

With him literature was accidental. His first work, the little *Life of Donne,* was written in his late forties. Other biographies of Wotton, Hooker, Herbert, and Sanderson, came at intervals till he was past eighty. Had he not produced a more famous work, he might be known as the greatest master of English biographical portraiture. Fact, anecdote, the speaking person, he presents in a way hitherto beyond the reach of English biography. But in every instance the personality of Walton is so merged with the original that we delight in the beauty of the composite, rather than satisfy ourselves that here we have the actual John Donne, or Henry Wotton.

At sixty Walton brought forth his masterpiece, *The Complete Angler*. It opens of a "fine, fresh, cool morning" in May, and follows the mild adventures of the angler up and down the Lea valley for five days. Even the technical part about flies and the finesse of angling beguiles the inexpert reader with its small-boy gravity and earnestness. An amiable dispute between a hunter, a falconer, and the angler gives occasion for a delicious parody of the pedants and their cumbersome display of learned authorities. All the way there is a shifting succession of idyllic miniatures: the "meadow checquered with waterlilies and lady-smocks"; the evening spent, in tired comfort at the ale-house, with its cleanly room and lavender stuck in the windows; a pause for a song under a honeysuckle hedge, "whilst this shower falls so gently upon the teeming earth, and gives yet a sweeter smell to the lovely flowers that adorn these verdant meadows." By the way we fall into pleasant converse with country folk and other anglers, and now and then a merry song, made either by a friend, or by one of other days, Kit Marlowe or Raleigh. "They were old-fashioned poetry, but choicely good; I think much better than the strong lines that are now in fashion in this critical age."

So alluringly runs this artless account that one is moved to slip the little book into his pocket and go hunt its felicities in "honest" Izaak's footsteps, along the River Lea. But the felicities are not there, for their evasive lure is that of all idyllic miniatures, the lure of the one who made them. Walton knew this. "The whole Discourse is, or rather was, a picture of my own disposition, especially in such days and times as I have laid aside business, and gone a-fishing with honest Nat. and R. Roe; but they are gone. . . ."

PEPYS (1633-1703)

Doubtless no one would be more surprised at his literary reputation than Samuel Pepys, and surely his diary is hardly a work of literary art. But it embodies a person—very much of one—more vividly than most art could have done. Pepys's portrait by Kneller and his diary laid side by side confirm each other. In either or both he is "mighty fine," in flowing wig and lace, self-sufficient, able, genial, sensual, shrewd, of solid worth, instinctively honest. He had been a young Puritan, not too square-toed, and after the Restoration worked his way up in the Navy office to be a man of importance, eventually to be Secretary; and his culture and curiosity were signalized in his being chosen President of the Royal Society. Though a high and sometimes careless liver himself, he was disgusted at the excesses, graft, and inefficiencies of the Stuart government.

His diary he wrote in cipher, but left a key, with what expectation no one knows. It lay in code and unknown till 1825. Then one John Smith was at great expense of time and pains to decipher it. When he had finished it he found Pepys's key. Still he had his fun. The diary began in 1660, when Pepys was twenty-seven, and ran for nine years through his struggle from poverty to competence and position, when eye trouble intervened, "which is almost as much as to see myself go into my grave." Clearly this ingenuous man of the world was fascinated with the unsparing portrait of himself that grew daily under his fingers. There he is for all the world to see, busy "very betimes" in his office, but sociable, with a hearty gust for good food and drink and singing of madrigals in pleasant company; losing his temper with his pretty young wife, philandering, repenting, gossiping, ranging up and down London, his keen eye missing nothing that interests an ordinary man; downright in judging everything—whether a play, a sermon, a picture, a new book, a poem, a relative, a man, a woman; laying bare his little vanities, meannesses, vulgarities, pieties, and scruples. And one wonders why the thousands of petty details —weather, clothes, food, accounts, servants, ailments, goings and comings—are interesting. But in some way the extraordinary vitality of the man has imbued every last one of them with life, making them droll, picturesque, real, or alluring, as this strange personality touches them.

In this most honest and unconscious of books, one does not merely visit Restoration London, he lives in it; he does not merely meet Samuel Pepys, he knows him better than he knows himself; and comes to know himself better for his acquaintance with this extraordinary ordinary man.

BUNYAN (1628-1688)

Donne, Herbert, Taylor, Milton were all men of highly cultivated piety, whose utterances on matters spiritual had the graces of art to recommend them to cultivated people. John Bunyan was a poor tinker, and a tinker's son, with but schooling enough to read and write. He wished only "to be plain and simple, and lay the thing down as it was."

One who knew him describes him as a large but not corpulent man, with ruddy color and a bright eye, "wearing his hair on his upper lip, after the old British fashion; his hair reddish, but in his latter days time had sprinkled it with grey"; he had a generous mouth, a well-formed nose, and a high forehead. He was a keen observer and an excellent judge of men. His portrait shows a genial well-conditioned person, not at all the spare, flaming preacher of judgment and repentance that some have imagined him.

No book in the language is more human than his account of himself for the first thirty years or so of his life, written during his long imprisonment, and named *Grace Abounding to the Chief of Sinners*. He was a boy at Elstow, a quaint village close to Bedford, and by his own account a very bad boy. To be sure his worst offences as the chief of sinners were dancing and Sunday games, delight in the English rural sport of bell-ringing, and swearing—"the ungodliest fellow for swearing that ever she heard in all her life," said a neighbor. But he attended the Established Church regularly, and observed its forms as a matter of course. At twenty he married a good woman, both of them "as poor as poor might be," and she turned his mind to more serious things. One day in Bedford he overheard "three or four poor women sitting at a door in the sun, and talking about the things of God." Forthwith began a period of spiritual agony such as sometimes befalls a man of genius—in this instance a struggle to establish his true relationship with God. Relieved by blessed intervals of respite, it recurred over a period of years, with wide and rapid fluctuations between assurance and despair; "for my peace would be in and out, sometimes twenty times a day." At last he won through to a deep and authentic faith, out of which for nearly three centuries has flowed an abundance of comfort and assurance to the whole world.

Bunyan, though he sympathized with the Puritan party, "never cared to meddle with things that were controverted and in dispute amongst the Saints." His singular powers as a preacher soon asserted themselves, and he instinctively sought the most obscure and neglected folk for an audience. They crowded around him in barns, houses, and fields. At the Restoration such excellent preaching was found an illegal disturbance of the existing order, and Bunyan was imprisoned in Bedford for twelve years. The separation from his family was, as he says, "the pulling the flesh from my bones; . . . especially my poor blind Child, who lay nearer my heart than all I had besides. O the thoughts of the hardship I thought my Blind-one might go under would break my heart to pieces."

Much of the time his imprisonment was not close or strict, and he had opportunity to write and sometimes to preach. His pen was prolific; the list of his writings runs to sixty books and pamphlets. The two greatest, *Grace Abounding* and *Pilgrim's Progress,* were both composed in prison, the second probably during a later brief term. Famous also are the *Holy War* and the *Life and Death of Mr. Badman.* It was a tireless and devoted life to the end. In his sixtieth year he rode through the rain the long day's journey from Reading, whither he had gone to make peace in a silly family quarrel, and fell into a last brief illness.

Of *Pilgrim's Progress* Dr. Johnson said: "This is the great merit of the book, that the most cultivated men cannot find anything to praise more highly, and the child knows nothing more amusing." One hundred thousand copies are thought to have been sold while Bunyan was alive, and Part I went through nearly one hundred editions in as many years. It has been translated into more than a hundred languages and dialects. In a grand sense it has, next the Bible, been the enduring book of the people.

As the great Protestant allegory it has often been set over against Dante's *Divine Comedy*. Their opening words are almost identical; behind both is the intense spiritual agony of the author. But Bunyan is Protestant in his immediate and sole reliance upon the Bible, without gloze of theological subtlety or traditional symbol. It cannot be proved that Bunyan even knew other instances of the literary voyage of life, such as the *Faery Queen*.

In place of these the spiritual world was so immediate to him, and the spiritual life so intense and vigorous, that it made constant impact upon the homeliest things of his homely life. This had been so from early boyhood, even before "conversion." One day in a game of "cat," as he raised his bat to strike, he caught a vision of the Christ. "Have you forgot," he asks his hearers, "the close, the milk-house, the stable, the barn, and the like, where God did visit your souls?" The homely actualities of Elstow and Bedford are enough for him. Through him the spiritual realities pass into them, and they are transfigured into eternal symbols. And in turn they give reality to spiritual things. A lowly cottage, back streets, muddy roads, a fair with rows of booths, hubbub, shoddy everywhere, and rascals, gossip by the way, light-minded men and women; and when the road by the river is rough, we mount a stile and follow the softer path inside the fence. Such is the symbolic equipment of the book, supplemented by a little from the Bible and such lore of castles, dragons, giants, and enchantment as haunted every lowly hearth. Is it any wonder that the City of Destruction, the Slough of Despond, Worldly Wiseman, the House Beautiful, Vanity Fair, and the Delectable Mountains, have become a part of our daily language? Or that children at whatever age delight in being carried along by the vigorous, rapid, easy movement and variety of the action?

Language can hardly be at once simpler and more vigorous than Bunyan's, being as it is a combination of Biblical English with the racy common idiom spoken in his time. Like all great prose it has the living quality of speech, and reveals its highest power not to the eye but to the ear; which is perhaps not strange in the writing of one for whom public speech to simple people was an every-day practice.

Pilgrim's Progress is a religious allegory. So are the *Faery Queen,* the *Divine Comedy,* and parts of *Paradise Lost.* But Bunyan is not driven to speculate in far-off regions of Faeryland, the empyrean, or the abyss of Hell. Within the limits of a not very large town he finds all the human setting and materials he needs. The people moving in and out of his story are the people everyone knows in his own community—Mr. Legality; Judge Hate-good; the tall fellow Talkative; poor Little-Faith, Sincere, who was held up by three gangsters in Dead Man's Lane; that very brisk youngster, Ignorance; Mrs. Diffidence, who rules her ogreish husband Despair; good, timid, troublesome Mr. Fearing, and his plaintive invalid nephew, Feeblemind; that nature's gentleman, Mr. Greatheart. The names may remind one of the morality play, or the humors of Ben Jonson, but the persons themselves are alive in the flesh. The book is as charged with human nature in its varieties as any novel in the language. Everywhere Bunyan's shrewd discernment and hard-headed common sense are awake and dictating this picture, in which any man may recognize himself and his own world. But even thus it could not go so far towards universal acceptance, were it not for the strong warm heart pulsing through every fibre of it—the heart of one who had been in Hell and knew how his fellow-men could suffer.

CHAPTER 18

Restoration

RESTORATION DRAMA

WHEN Charles II came home "from his travels" in 1660, the theatres, practically closed since 1642, resumed in full swing. Late in Cromwell's time dramatic "entertainments" had been permitted, including a play of Davenant's called the *Siege of Rhodes*. But movable scenery, actresses, and the roofed theatre were now the order of the day, and the traffic of the stage consisted partly of old plays from Shakespeare, Beaumont and Fletcher, and Jonson, adapted to suit the newer fashion, and as fast as new playwrights could write them, of new plays. Tastes had changed. Romance of the old sort had lost its savor. Pepys saw *Midsummer Night's Dream* with disgust—"the most insipid ridiculous play that ever I saw in my life." In the new plays the humors, after Jonson, had a lively part, and they were all busy extolling monarchy, and giving the Puritans their worst, which was pretty bad.

This chapter in English drama is usually called Restoration Drama, though its course of development ran on into the next century, and traverses several changes of fashion. It is almost entirely preoccupied with sex, and usually in a literal way without romance or sentiment, especially during the licentious days of the Stuarts. Partly for this reason, and partly through changes in stage conventions, it is unsuitable for our stage except in a few instances, and some of those subject to drastic alteration. Otway's *Venice Preserved,* Wycherley's *Country Wife* thoroughly purged for modern presentation, Congreve's *Way of the World,* and Farquhar's *Beaux' Stratagem,* have been revived.

Though English and even Jonsonian in its essence, two foreign influences, Spanish and French, were of high importance in making Restoration drama. Spanish literature, rich in play and story, had done something for English drama since Marlowe's day, but never so much as at this time. Sword-and-cloak intrigue, two gallants and two ladies, interfering relatives, servants, honor, mistakes, lucky or unlucky—all this it furnished in plenty. But French influence was stronger, naturally, when one considers where the Court had spent its exile.

English tragedy of the Restoration was of the kind called "heroic," a stilted, spectacular presentation of loves, wars, loyalties, and sentiments of emperors and great folk in far-off Granada, Mexico, India, Venice, Peru, Babylon, or wherever. It wore grand titles—*The Indian Emperour, The Royal Martyr, Aureng-Zebe*. It derived partly from earlier English tragi-comedy, but its object was to be grand, and to that end grand sentiment and grand language were necessary. These it learned in part from the vast French romances like *Le Grand Cyrus,* partly from the nobler model of French tragedy, especially Corneille, partly from the prevailing interest in epic poetry and style. And there was a good deal of talk about the "unities" of place, time, and action, so rigorously observed in France. But English drama in practice retained much of its old liberty.

Though Dryden was the most conspicuous playwright of the time, Thomas Otway is to be remembered for having produced the best stage play, *Venice Preserved,* in 1682. He had been an actor and author of less worthy plays. This tragedy presents a lively story of conflict between love and friendship precipitated by conspiracy against the corrupt and vested interests. Its flexible and vigorous blank verse, its effective situations, its rather higher tone and sentiment take one back to Elizabethan times, and we wonder to come upon this solitary survival.

In comedy Molière exerted the strongest French influence. Such masters as Dryden, Wycherley, and Vanbrugh were constantly going to him for plots, situations, character, and even dialogue. But the comedy of the time, far more than the tragedy, kept its native character, and enjoyed an actual development.

It is a comedy of manners, reflecting, or refracting, the social life of the Court and near-Court levels, licentious as that was licentious, gross as that was gross, malicious, carnal, heartless, witty, idle, clever, cynical, like those who laughed at it from the boxes. *The Man of Mode, or Sir Fopling Flutter,* a plotless play by Sir George Etherege, serves as a lively example of irresponsible Restoration comedy, yet with artistic vigor that perpetuated its kind in the brilliant artificial comedy of Congreve, and a century later in Sheridan.

In Wycherley's last and best piece, *The Plain Dealer,* acted 1674, the depravity of the times is faithfully rendered, but with a certain savage attack that amounts to satire. It is an omen that a sense of decency is not altogether dead, even if asleep. The slumber was to last for a time longer. Strangely enough, though manners improved after Charles II died, comedy lingered on in the world of heartless gallantry. This it preserved as a sort of traditional artificial stage world, which made a suitable background for the wit and cynicism of Congreve and Sheridan.

CONGREVE (1670-1729)

William Congreve, the greatest English writer of pure comedy, is a fascinating figure. Born in 1670 of good old stock near Leeds, he was educated in Ireland, began law in London, and sprang into fame with his first comedy, *The Old Bachelor,* at twenty-three. The same year saw a greater triumph in his *Double Dealer.* Two years later he excelled himself in *Love for Love.* Then five years and a poor tragedy, *The Mourning Bride,* intervened, and in 1700 came his masterpiece *The Way of the World.* Alas, it failed, and Congreve in a huff quit the theatre for good, at the age of thirty, when his genius had just reached the moment of highest promise.

His plays in order exhibit not only the interesting and rapid growth of his art and technical skill, but the rise from "Restoration" comedy to something far better. In the calibre and quality of his work, as in his dates, he far outstrips the Restoration and partakes of the later age. At first he employs old "humors," old devices, old stage talk, and a touch of low life. But from the beginning the genuine Congreve emerges more brilliant and vigorous at each venture. His plots, skilfully handled, are trifles. They are artificially contrived, in an artificial world, and set forth by artificial persons, more and more exquisitely designed and drawn in successive plays and fitted into the situation. Yet the whole effect is real from the very vigor and vivacity of the brain that produced it—that flashing, tireless wit of Congreve, well-bred, refined, never fumbling or missing the mark. It is often Congreve who is speaking, not his persons.

But he created one masterpiece of character—Millamant in *The Way of the World*. She can beat them all at the game of wit, though she uses but her little finger to do it; her real worth of heart and intellect are hidden from that trifling world; and though she is well able to take care of herself amid its worldly dangers, there is, reserved from all but her lover, and at first not too apparent to him, a sweetness and playfulness that are almost like a child's. She is a rare instance of success in the portrayal of subtle charm.

As with all great playwrights, so with Congreve, the test of his work is not reading it, but seeing it acted. His plays in the reading often are hard to follow, and seem not to deserve all that is said of them. On the stage, with competent acting, they are clear and convincing.

Congreve's genius was of that rare sort that defies successful imitation. The architect, Sir John Vanbrugh, and the Irishman, Farquhar, were of lower order and their plays move in the coarse and hearty real world of Queen Anne and just before. *The Relapse* and *The Provoked Wife* by Vanbrugh, and *The Recruiting Officer* and *The Beaux' Stratagem* by Farquhar are lively, skilful, ingenious, hearty, practical stage plays, a bit shocking even to modern taste.

BUTLER (1612-1680)

The "Restoration," that is, the period from 1660 to the Revolution of 1688, developed no marked characteristics in literature except in the drama. The poet of the time now sang in the traditional manner of Jonson, or in octosyllabics, or else tuned his voice to the rhymed couplet and the new devices that were to express the new mind and appreciations of the next century. Sir Charles Sedley sings the old songs to Celia and Phyllis. Milton and Marvell rise above classification. Wilmot, Earl of Rochester, Denham, Waller, Cowley, look both ways.

Perhaps no poet better represents the Restoration itself than Samuel Butler. He was forty-eight when Charles II returned. During the Commonwealth he had moved hither and yon as clerk or secretary to people of more or less importance, and his satirical eye had gathered in a rich collection of Puritan freaks. These encountered in his mind a knowledge of Latin satirists, of *Don Quixote* and Scarron, and his famous *Hudibras* was the result. He did not publish it till 1663, when the Puritans had reached the nadir of their unpopularity, and its wit and absurdity set Charles II, the Court, and most of the world off in gales of laughter. For all that, the poor poet-jester was suffered to die in beggary at the last.

Butler makes a witty and whimsical kind of fun. Not Puritans only but strange vagaries of scientists in the new Royal Society diverted him. *The Elephant in the Moon* touches the sensational discovery implied in the title—but the elephant proved to be a mouse in the telescope!

His odd rhymes, his instinct for the eternal rather than merely contemporary foolhood of men, make *Hudibras* most readable in limited passages.

CHAPTER 19

Dryden (1631–1700)

In 1688, when England was at last rid of the Stuarts, John Dryden was fifty-seven years old. He is therefore most often regarded as a poet of the Restoration. But he transcended and overpassed his time. He lived from 1631 to 1700. Thus in mature manhood he saw the Commonwealth, the Restoration, the Revolution of 1688, and the dawn of the new century. No poet has been more abused for having produced uneven work, or for having honestly changed his mind; but of late Dryden has begun to come into the appreciation which is due him.

In some respects he reminds one of Ben Jonson—versatile, prolific, self-reliant, writing with a theory in mind; and even more than Jonson he became the literary dictator of his time. He continues the old fashion in his dependence upon the Stuart Court as poet laureate and object of its bounties.

But Dryden is half-consciously the prophet of modern literature, the father of the race that earns its living with its pen. He is the new man of letters, supporting himself by expressing in prose or song the best prevailing intelligence of his times in a way most comprehensible to those times. He is a literary journalist.

In the twenty years of his prime, between the age of thirty and fifty, he was toiling for the theatre and his livelihood; he gave the public twenty-eight plays such as it wanted, except one. His plays are starred with well-turned songs, and his best known poem is the superb lyric, *Alexander's Feast*. A public event, the death of Cromwell, the Restoration, a battle with the Dutch, the Great Fire and other events of 1666, the exploits of the Earl of Shaftesbury, the King's death, the debated doctrines of the time—all were subjects for grand metrical anthems or satires from Dryden's pen. Single-handed, under French influence, he invented modern English prose, easy, transparent, moving evenly with the development of thought, unaffected and artless, embodying all the essential modern virtues. He more than any other was its founder. With all else he was a master of criticism, of translation and adaptation.

His journalistic mind has exposed him to gross misunderstanding. Reflecting as he did the color of his times, he changed with them. Born of aristocratic Puritan country family, he honored Cromwell in verse, sang later as a royalist and an Anglican, and in 1685, the year of the accession of Catholic James, at fifty-four, became a Catholic. Whoever blames him should consider that to his great material disadvantage he later remained true to his last profession of faith; and it seems as if he had finally found his natural position toward which he had his whole life been moving. He was a readily impressionable man, interested in the new science and in sceptical philosophy, a member of the Royal Society, yet a believer in astrology.

Above all he was a great poet, not so much in imagination and invention, as in perfecting certain models of poetic art, in awakening a deep new poetic music in the language, lending it new vigor, and refining in it a new poetic medium which he handed down to other poets for a century. His congenial subjects were manners of men, ideas, literature, the proper subjects for a man and time that set high value on reason, judgment, and common sense.

There is nothing of the picturesque innovator or fiery radical about Dryden. Though he had to work hard, he seems to have been easy-going, gentle, affectionate, likable with physique to match—short, plump, florid, and sleepy-eyed. He loved fishing and bowling. He was born of good county gentry at Aldwinkle, a hamlet about twenty miles south of Peterborough. At Puritan Cambridge he seems to have been restless, and with his "roving and active" mind fetched up in London without a master's degree. Except that he made a not wholly successful marriage in 1663 with Lady Elizabeth Howard, who bore him three sons, his life was henceforth uneventful. The scandals attached to his name, and kept alive by Macaulay and others, come from those in his time who were small enough to make themselves his literary enemies, and are today discredited. In spite of his loss of court favor and gratuities at the Revolution, he maintained himself in dignity, and to the end was admired and deferred to as literary dictator. Dr. Johnson managed to rescue a reminiscence of him as a "decent old man," umpire of literary disputes at Will's Coffee-house, where, surrounded by young wits, he sat by the fire in winter in his special arm-chair, which he pleasantly called his winter seat, and which, moved to the balcony in summer, became his summer seat.

None but specialists now read most of Dryden's plays, and they not for mere pleasure. The dozen comedies are sunk in the gross animalism that preoccupied the mind of the times. And the tragedies, however "heroic," and resplendent with epic grandeur and eloquence, have a substratum of the same sort. Though warmly approved on occasion by Pepys, and glorified on the stage by the charms of Nell Gwyn, yet in general Dryden's heart was not in them. Most of them are rhymed. As long as the public wanted rhyme, he furnished it, and wrote prefaces and his famous *Essay of Dramatic Poesy* to defend the practice; but he seems to have tired of rhymed plays before the town did. His masterpiece, *All for Love,* he tells us, he wrote for himself. He was forty-seven, at the height of his dramatic and critical power, and resorted to blank verse. Being a frank adaptation of Shakespeare's glorious *Antony and Cleopatra*, the play is liable to suffer in contrast. But fair comparison of the two throws a flood of light on the literary virtues and faults of the two ages that produced them. Dryden has reduced Shakespeare's time from ten years to one day, discarded two thirds of Shakespeare's characters, reduced thirty-seven scenes in almost as many places from Rome to Alexandria, to five single acts. He has renounced the gorgeous, shifting Elizabethan pageantry, but gained in concentration, and has shown the best that the French ideals of the unities and declamation, qualified by English practical common sense, could do for English drama.

The stage had at least trained Dryden in vocal eloquence, in framing superb metrical speeches by which the great actors of the day thrilled their audiences, an art now pretty much lost. It was thus that he raised the deep strong current of his verse, till it overran the limits of the couplet, and flowed in uninterrupted stretches for the length of a good stage speech.

Dryden taught himself by persistent self-discipline. His elegy on Lord Hastings written at eighteen, a shocking crime of the metaphysical school, shows the nadir from which he rose. At first he had a strong liking for the alternate-rhyming quatrain "as more noble and of greater dignity both for the sound and number, than any other verse in use amongst us."[1] It is an opinion worth remembering because Gray, who acknowledged Dryden his metrical master, afterwards chose it for the most popular poem in the English language. Certainly in his *Cromwell* and his *Annus Mirabilis* Dryden has awakened its deepest echoes. In the first naval battle of 1666 with the Dutch, Prince Rupert arrives with reinforcements:

> His presence soon blows up the kindling fight,
> And his loud guns speak thick like angry men:
> It seem'd as slaughter had been breathed all night,
> And death new pointed his dull dart again.

Before reading *Annus Mirabilis* one should run over Pepys's eye-witness account of events in 1666.

But the rhymed or heroic couplet was more natural to the mastery of Dryden. He developed in it capacities that it had never known, and made it the ideal medium for conveying his vigorous mind. In his panegyrics, like *Astraea Redux*, it moves with the grandeur of organ and orchestra combined; in his clever prologues and epilogues it complies with all the ingenuity and verve of his wit; in *Religio Laici* and *The Hind and the Panther* it lends point and movement to argument in verse in which Dryden exhibited a new skill.

But his most powerful use of the couplet Dryden revealed in satire, and in satire he proved his highest poetic reach. His satires all were written in two years, 1681-2, at the end of

[1] Mason's *Gray*, 2.215

his active play-making. Like the rest, these poems were called
forth by occasion.

Charles II's illegitimate son, the Duke of Monmouth, was
put forward as an anti-Catholic claimant to the throne under
the energetic support of the able Shaftesbury. The attempt
amounted to a conspiracy, and Dryden met the situation with
Absalom and Achitophel. He took the Bible story of David
(Charles), Absalom (Monmouth), and Achitophel (Shaftesbury), and by a clever parallel of story and characters set
forth the whole bad business, its iniquity, its mischief, its dangers, its stupidities, for all the world to see. It proved a topical
hit of enormous success. The events have faded, but the satire
has lived on by its permanent greatness to enduring fame. In
the following passage the Jews are the English, Saul is Cromwell, Ishbosheth his son, and David is Charles II:

> The Jews, a headstrong, moody, murmuring race,
> As ever tried the extent and stretch of grace:
> God's pamper'd people, whom, debauch'd with ease,
> No king could govern, nor no God could please;
> (Gods they had tried, of every shape and size
> That God-smiths could produce, or priests devise:)
> These Adam-wits, too fortunately free,
> Began to dream they wanted liberty:
> And when no rule, no precedent was found,
> Of men by laws less circumscrib'd and bound;
> They led their wild desires to woods and caves,
> And thought that all but savages were slaves.
> They who, when Saul was dead, without a blow,
> Made foolish Ishbosheth the crown forego;
> Who banish'd David did from Hebron bring,
> And with a general shout proclaim'd him King:
> Those very Jews, who, at their very best,
> Their humor more than loyalty express'd,
> Now wondered why so long they had obey'd
> An idol monarch, which their hands had made;
> Thought they might ruin him they could create,
> Or melt him to that golden calf, a state.

These lines deal adequately with national absurdities as revealed in the events of the time; but they must stir any thought-
ful man at any time by their irresistible wit that exposes to
ridicule the everlasting nonsense and chicanery of a captious,
spoiled, and venal democracy. Such is the best satire, pungent
with particulars, personal or otherwise, but equally typical and
perennially true. Such is Dryden's.

   The poem contains some extraordinary satirical portraits—
Zimri (Buckingham) and Corah (Oates)—which were to
serve as models to Pope and other satirists. Such portraits or
"characters" form a distinct literary unit or species which it is
important for any one to recognize who would understand the
literature of the eighteenth century and after. The "character"
is well-nigh universal in literature, but it caught new life from
the revival of an old Greek writer, Theophrastus, and his little
collection of thumb-nail portraits of types—the Flatterer, the
Complacent Man, etc. In the seventeenth century it flourished
in Bishop Hall's *Characters of the Vices and Virtues* (1608),
Sir Thomas Overbury's *Characters* (1614), and Earle's *Micro-
cosmography* (1628), all of them clever, witty, and readable
concentrated sketches of typical persons, freaks, occupations, or
times of life. But the satirical "character" had long been familiar to poets from its masters Horace and Juvenal, and from
them Dryden learned the art.

> In the first rank of these did Zimri stand;
> A man so various that he seem'd to be
> Not one, but all mankind's epitome:
> Stiff in opinions, always in the wrong;
> Was everything by starts, and nothing long:
> But in the course of one revolving moon,
> Was chymist, fiddler, statesman, and buffoon. . . .

Here again is the even balance between the individual and the
universal. Dryden's satire never turns sour, never is spoiled by
his own personal resentments or grudges like Pope's; nor is it
impotent with frantic, uncontrolled indignation like Swift's or
Juvenal's. It carries the weight of a mind whose judgment,
deeply moved, but always controlled, is above the thing it is

satirizing, and larger and wiser than the judgment of the ordinary man. Hence the grandeur of Dryden's satire.

This grandeur of mind has passed into the music of the verse. It has given it body, depth, resonance, and genuine dignity, and has stamped certain phrases into standard coin of the literary realm.

In *The Medal* Dryden has drawn a full-length satirical portrait of Shaftesbury. To this a little poet, Thomas Shadwell, replied, and for his pains got impaled for ever in *Mac Flecknoe*, as heir-apparent to the throne of Dullness. He appears again as Og in Dryden's part of a second installment of *Absalom*, and Doeg represents the undistinguished Elkanah Settle:

> Doeg, though without knowing how or why,
> Made still a blundering kind of melody;
> Spurred boldly on, and dashed through thick and thin,
> Through sense and nonsense, never out nor in;
> Free from all meaning whether good or bad,
> And in one word, heroically mad.

It is clear that without spleen or meanness Dryden can have a good deal of fun with fools.

What a great poet has to say on poetry is more interesting and important than ordinary criticism. Dryden has left hundreds of pages of such comment. They usually constitute prefaces to his plays or poems and are ostensible defences of his own practice. But of greater length are the *Essay of Dramatic Poesy*, the essay on Satire, the dedication of the *Aeneid*, and the *Preface to the Fables*. While these essays may be taken as records of the taste of the times, and of imported French literary fashions, or may be occupied with even technical details, yet the artist behind them is ever striking out great general principles, and in a memorable way. His printed talk about literature still lives with the spirit and sense that explain how he became literary dictator in his time.

The last decade of his life was chiefly busy with translation and adaptation. The satirists, Juvenal, Persius, the works of Virgil, and the *Fables*, which include passages from Homer,

Ovid, Chaucer, and Boccaccio, make up the list. It was work for the trade; parvenus were increasing in the land and needed the antidotes to vulgarity and ready aids to culture commensurate with their wealth. But it was a congenial task to Dryden's hand, especially translating Virgil, whose art and music had a profound affinity with his own. On this translation he worked for three years. If, as Dr. Johnson said, we must try the effect of a translation as an English poem, we have in this version Dryden rather than Virgil, but often Dryden at his best, especially in certain parts of the *Georgics*. "'Tis only for a poet to translate a poem," he says. As a poetic translation Dryden's *Virgil* is a classic.

It was natural that one who had such control of melody and cadence in the language should have produced great lyrics. He may be regarded as a late instance of the abounding lyric utterance continuous since the day of Henry VIII. But with the old spontaneous English tunefulness is mingled a certain calculation, partly the result of Pindaric artificialities, partly the effect of the French lyric models, partly the quality of the new poetry more consciously subject to rules and studied effects. It is for this reason that Dryden's wonderful *Alexander's Feast*, describing a *tour de force*, is itself a masterly *tour de force*. Yet in it burns Dryden's own fire, the same vigor and substance and vibrant sonority at sixty-eight as always proved him a great poet.

PART FIVE

LONDON AND THE MAN OF LETTERS

CHAPTER 20

The Eighteenth Century

By 1688 a new age had dawned in England, with new ideas, new appreciations, new aspirations, new politics, new poetry, and a new manner of life. It is variously called the Eighteenth Century, the Neo-classical Age, the Augustan Age, the Age of Satire, the Age of Reason, the Sceptical Age, the Age of Pope and Johnson, the Age of Sense.

Men demanded a new appraisal of old and accepted ideas, taking into account the new science and mathematics, and appealing to "common sense." The philosophers of this age were, as philosophers always are, an index of its new ways and manners. The scepticism of Hobbes, Berkeley, and Hume in search of reality, and the "common sense" of John Locke, marked the shift of appreciation from matters remote, speculative, uncertain, to the manners of men, especially civilized men, which, in England, meant the life of London. The authority of "Nature" and science had triumphed over tradition.

Something has happened since the days of Charles I. The polite world is no longer so confined to the Court as in the Tudor and Stuart days. The Puritan cause failed, yet really triumphed in 1688, when the importance of Parliament was established; and therewith came into being two political parties, the Whigs and the Tories. For nearly two centuries they continued to represent in England much the same difference of sentiment and interests as had that between the Puritans and the Royalists. The Whigs were generally the dissenters from the Anglican church, the rising mercantile citizenry, and the city middle class led by certain of the aristocracy. The Tories were generally the landowners, the Anglican clergy, and the personal adherents of both.

Back in Elizabethan days Spenser had held that the "roote of civill conversation," that is, civilization, was courtesy.

> Of Court it seemes, men Courtesie doe call.

In 1732 Pope, speaking for the new time said,

> The proper study of mankind is Man.

Not the Court, but London, party-politics, a new and more elegant domestic life, trade, self-supporting literature, in short the English people determined the aspect and quality of eighteenth century culture. First the sophisticated town, then, as the century progressed, the country and the lower levels became the ever extending fields in which literature was to spring and flourish. As society grows democratic, so does literature; and in turn it becomes a most powerful agency in the growth of democracy.

Many new and large fortunes were piling up in new hands from the rapidly growing trade with the East, especially India. The parvenu class in the new London so increased and multiplied that it became the chief influence in fashioning the status of literature during the century.

With the growth of wealth men aspire to luxury and elegance of life. At first they are often ridiculous and clumsy, but in a generation or two attain to more intrinsic culture. Such is the course of the "Eighteenth Century" in England. Its new wealth brought into being a new domestic architecture and a new art of domestic life. It created the Georgian house, which combined good taste, hospitality, and comfort in a measure to make it the natural architecture in colonial and early American times, as well as nowadays. It transformed domestic furniture and decoration under the designing genius of Chippendale, Hepplewhite, Sheraton, and the brothers Adam. English printing and bookmaking left their old botchy habits, and attained to standards of design which they have never surpassed, and are always trying to recall. In all this improvement of fashion the skill of Italy, and particularly of France, had determinant parts, but the result was always an embodiment of the best English qualities and the ideals of the new time.

The new appreciation of manners and men, united with the new spirit of critical scepticism, observed not merely the facts, but was keenly sensitive to the faults of mankind. So it comes about that much of the literature of the century is either out-and-out satire, or is likely at any turn to take on satirical cast and quality. No period of English Literature has produced such racy, pungent, healthy, and cleansing satire as this.

A time thus preoccupied with the town, with manners, with a new material elegance of private life, with criticism of men's foibles and absurdities, found another time like its own in the Roman days of Augustus, and a poet after its own heart in that master of the art of elegant living, Horace. Because, as Pope says,

> Horace still charms with graceful negligence,
> And without method talks us into sense,
> Will, like a friend, familiarly convey
> The truest notions in the easiest way.
> He, who supreme in judgment, as in wit,
> Might boldly censure, as he boldly writ,
> Yet judged with coolness, though he sung with fire;
> His precepts teach but what his works inspire.

This passage lists most of the desired literary virtues of the times, grace, sense, human intimacy, judgment, the fire of genius tempered with rules of art and with wit.

What is this wit, "much talked of, not to be defined," as Otway says? Pope's "what oft was thought, but ne'er so well exprest" is not a definition. Sometimes "wit" seems to mean the skill with which a poet chooses an image or figure; sometimes his skill in smart contrast and antithesis; sometimes his originality of invention; and Dr. Johnson, an acknowledged specialist in wit, suggests that wit may be "that, which he that never found it, wonders how he missed"; and he remarks: "Wit is wit, . . . and, if good, will appear so at all times." When writing of metaphysical poetry, he even ventured to formulate a traditional idea of wit.[1] Vary as its definitions may, the eighteenth century was agreed that wit is most necessary to poets who study man, teach him, and satirize his fooleries. Wit was the antidote to dullness, and to be dull, or obscure, were then capital literary crimes.

Interest in men and manners is always leading one to general conclusions. Such generalizations, moral or otherwise, abound in eighteenth century literature. The tendency goes further than an occasional general or didactic statement. It determines the subject and argumentative quality of many of the best poems of the time, such as Dryden's *The Hind and the Panther* and Pope's *Essay on Man*. It rules their descriptions of Nature, from Denham's *Cooper's Hill* in 1642 to Wordsworth's *Evening Walk* in 1793. Says the old poet in *Rasselas*: "The business of a poet is to examine, not the individual, but the species; to remark general properties and large appearances. He does not number the streaks of the tulip, or describe the different shades in the verdure of the forest: he is to exhibit in his portraits of nature such prominent and striking features, as recall the original to every mind; and must neglect the minuter discriminations, which one may have remarked, and another neglected, for those characteristics which are alike obvious to vigilance and carelessness." This generalization is the very opposite of our present-day interest in picturesque and individualizing details. It explains perhaps the eighteenth-century love for abstract nouns, for personifying them, for a good, musical epithet that would express as much as an epithet can of the universal and essential character of the object. It entered into the new poetic style, splendid in the hands of Dryden and Pope, but

[1] See p. 225

tending in time to dull patter of "crystal streams," "bellowing roar," "proud Ambition," and such.

The metrical instrument best suited to the expression of these new ideas and appreciations was the rhymed or "heroic" couplet. It had been slowly fashioning itself since the days of Elizabeth. Even Spenser and Drayton sometimes struck out a couplet which might have been made in Pope's day. But Ben Jonson especially, in his occasional poems, came much nearer to the practice of later times. Two royalist poets, Sir John Denham, author of *Cooper's Hill*, and Edmund Waller, brought the couplet still closer to its finished form. Waller particularly was regarded by the masters, Dryden and Pope, as the one who had done the most for it. It was chiefly under the influence of French poetry, as Pope says in his *Epistle to Augustus*, that this correction and refinement of English metre went on:

> Wit grew polite, and numbers learn'd to flow.
> Waller was smooth; but Dryden taught to join
> The varying verse, the full-resounding line,
> The long majestic march, and energy divine.

In brief, the "correct" couplet should contain a complete unit of sense, which it fits exactly, like a perfect garment, without padding of unnecessary words, *do's* and *did's* and such. The order of words must be the natural order of prose, without resorting to inversions for mere metre's sake. A pause occurs at the end of the first line, and a greater pause at the end of the second, and the internal pause within the line keeps near the middle. The rhyme should be on a vigorous accented syllable. All which makes it seem more like prescription than poetry.

But the glory of the rhymed couplet is its "numbers," that is, the exquisite variation within these strict bounds, of its cadence, delicate or sonorous, always through its music subtly insinuating and reinforcing the meaning of the words. People who find it monotonous or sing-song have not listened to it with an ear delicately adjusted to its finer music. It must be read slowly and smoothly, and with measured dignity and proper care for the variation of cadence and movement. Whatever the poets of the rhymed couplet were not, they were singers, and knew as well as the greatest of poets the art of music in words. They seem to have rejoiced in this instrument of limited scale, because it challenged their utmost to produce exquisite melody and harmony within its bounds.

It was an instrument perfected by the poetic demands of its time. There could be no good poetry, they believed, without reason, good sense, and clarity to begin with. On these foundations and these only can good poetry be reared; to which any intelligent critic will agree. But they were equally insistent upon the fire and intensity of true genius, without which poetry was, and is, impossible.

When Dryden died in 1700 an extraordinary group of young men in London lost a revered leader. The critic Dennis was forty-three, Daniel Defoe was forty, Matt Prior was thirty-six, Swift and Arbuthnot thirty-three, Congreve thirty, Steele, twenty-nine, Addison twenty-eight, Bolingbroke twenty-two, Gay fifteen, and Pope a precocious lad of twelve. Some of these men haunted Will's Coffee-house, enthralled by Dryden's talk. All of them were to shine in the high literary splendor that sheds its glory upon the "Age of Anne."

In his *Essay on Satire* Dryden remarks: "Great contemporaries whet and cultivate each other." He was thinking possibly of the Royal Society or the group at Will's. Such sociability of literature appears in all great times; around Sir Thomas More in Tudor days, or Ben Jonson at the Mermaid; but the eighteenth century especially fostered it in the form of clubs—the Brothers and the Scriblerus, and later the Literary Club under the sway of Dr. Johnson. It may be taken as a sign of the new literary democracy.

The coffee-house now flourished in the land as a social centre for the circulation of news and ideas. Each trade or group of men had its own—clergy, brokers, Whigs, Tories, and wits, to whom Will's belonged by the sacred tradition of Dryden.

But a more important institution had arisen. With the triumph of Parliament, party government, increase of middle-class wealth, and the descent of literature from the heights to spread on the lower social levels, was born the newspaper and modern journalism. All through the days of Puritan controversy the air was filled on every side with the din of pamphlets, the first mouthpiece for the new voice of the people. And we may recall that the greatest of these was Milton's impassioned plea for the freedom of the press. Then came the more or less regular *Mercuries* of late Commonwealth and Restoration days. The first daily was ventured in 1702, and by 1738 a writer observed: "The people of Great Britain are governed by a power that was never heard of as a supreme authority in any age or country before. . . . It is the government of the Press."

Besides the newspapers the magazines came into being—the *Gentleman's Magazine* (1731), the *London Magazine*, and the reviews, the *Literary Magazine*, the *Critical*, and the *Monthly*, all by 1752—with all of which the destiny of men of letters was henceforth deeply involved.

For better or worse, this journalism of the new democracy was to modify the status, kinds, and quality of literature more and more. Even the great men of Queen Anne's time were, as compared with their predecessors, literary journalists. They wrote for a living, were sensitive and responsive to the demands of the people, not the Court, and prose rather than verse became more and more their medium.

CHAPTER 21

The Days of Pope

SWIFT (1667-1745)

AMONG all these men of Anne's generation the greatest genius
and the most tragic figure is Jonathan Swift. Everyone remembers being enthralled as a child with the sturdy figure of
Gulliver helpless among the Lilliputians, and in constant fear
from the stupid clumsiness of the huge Brobdingnagians.
Whether Swift realized it or not, such was his own plight in
a cruelly misfit world. He either moved as a proud giant
among helpless, pitiful, silly pigmies, or his sensitive and tender
heart was bruised and trampled down by the stupid great of
the world.

Swift came of ancient English family on both sides. He and
Dryden had a great-grandfather in common. He was a posthumous child, born into poverty in Hoey's Court, Dublin. A
devoted old nurse took him to England for three years, by
the end of which time he could read any part of the Bible. In
school at Kilkenny he may have ignored young Congreve. At
Trinity College, Dublin, he worked well in the classics, but
at nothing else, and got his degree by "special grace." Poor,
proud, unloved by the uncle who supported him, he took refuge with his good mother at her old home in Leicester, England, and was soon, at the age of twenty-two, taken on as
secretary or amanuensis by Sir William Temple at Moor Park
near Farnham. Here he lived, except for two interruptions,
during the next ten years. Temple was good to him, and recognized his growing powers; but to Swift's proud spirit it was a
servile and irksome business. Yet he produced at the time two

of his greatest pieces, *A Tale of a Tub* and *The Battle of the Books*, and tried to be a poet. "Cousin Swift," said Dryden, "you will never be a poet." Perhaps because Swift had gradually to admit the truth of this expert opinion, he never had a good word to say about Dryden. Verses he produced by the hundred, octosyllabics chiefly, which sometimes rise above the level of clever doggerel, as in the lines written many years later *On Stella's Birthday* and *On the Death of Dr. Swift.* The years at Moor Park gave leisure for fierce and enormous reading in the classics and foreign literature. Then, in 1699 with the death of Temple, he emerged into the world. He became vicar of Laracor, a small parish twenty-five miles northwest of Dublin. Here, in spite of long absences in London, he was scrupulous in his care of his people and parish affairs. Every day he read the service, and when only his man-servant was the congregation, he waggishly began the Confession: "Dearly beloved Roger, the Scripture moveth you and me. . . ."

In London this "mad parson" first startled and amused people in the coffee-houses, then charmed and electrified them by his wit; so much so that Addison was soon addressing him as "the most agreeable companion, the truest friend, and the greatest genius of the age," which is pretty near the fact. From associations with Temple and others he found himself arrayed with the Whigs, lent them his able pen in pamphlets, and had his head filled with promises and dancing hopes of preferment—perhaps a bishopric—all to come to bitter nothing.

Swift's soul was all his life a battle-ground of baffling and tragic paradox. Like Spenser, with all his greatness of nature and genius he coveted position and worldly consequence. The pain and suffering of others made him wince and recoil, yet he could be unsparing of word and deed even towards those he loved most. Then, his love of fun and ingenious drollery are irrepressible, and break out like the pranks of a kitten. Yet he is said to have laughed only twice, and no man's heart ever suffered more excruciating torture.

At least two of his practical jokes are classic. He had, as secretary to Lord Berkeley, to read Boyle's tiresome *Meditations* to Her Ladyship. One day he slipped in a parody *Meditation upon a Broomstick,* highly edifying and solemn on the surface, electric with fun and wit for him who knew.

But all the world was party to the other jest. John Partridge in his almanacs had got himself high reputation as a prophet of events. One day in February, 1708, appeared a pamphlet by "Isaac Bickerstaff" as from a real astrologer, prophesying the death of Partridge on the 29th of the next month. On the 30th came another describing the last illness and death on the day before of John Partridge. Partridge, poor witless block, denied the story in his next almanac, and thanked God that he was still well and hearty. Bickerstaff replied that he must be dead, for he had admitted it; nor could Isaac be answerable for an uninformed carcass that went about calling itself Partridge. The town was agog with delight. Partridge was indeed dead in reputation, and Swift famous.

In 1710 he lost his mother, "the barrier between me and death," her whom he used to walk the hundred and odd miles to see when he lived at Moor Park. In London the Whigs, who had not treated him well, were losing their hold. Swift's true sympathies had never been with them. As a clergyman and a warm champion of the English Church, his natural place was with the Tories, who welcomed him with open arms; and during the next three years his brains, counsel, and power as a writer made him the really significant man in public affairs. Through him went all matters of patronage. He had the ear of the important men, and was closely intimate with the ministers Harley and St. John. No wonder he strutted a bit, but tireless was his devotion to the government, and countless the acts of help and relief for authors, clergy, and others who came to him in need.

When Swift arrived in England from Trinity College, a young man of twenty, he first saw Esther Johnson. She was an exquisite child of six, a ward of Sir William Temple, and to Swift's lot fell the happy duty of instructing her. At Moor Park he saw her grow from a delicate child to a spirited, but gentle, intelligent woman, "beautiful, graceful, and agreeable, . . . only a little too fat." This was Swift's Stella, "the truest, most virtuous, and valuable friend, that I, or perhaps any other person ever was blessed with." She was a woman of courage too, and on occasion shot and killed a burglar. When Swift went to Laracor, he induced Stella with a friend to settle there too. Hardly has an affair in literary history bred more gossip than this of Swift and Stella. Were they married? The weight of evidence is against it. They lived apart and never met alone. Swift outlived her seventeen years. After his death a lock of her hair was found in his desk labeled, "Only a woman's hair."

During his great three years of importance among the Tories he kept a sort of letter-journal, which he periodically sent to Stella in Ireland, and which is now current as the *Journal to Stella*. It is a strange, intimate thing in which grave politics, playful scolding, trifles, and sheer nonsense are oddly mingled. But nothing else so well enables us to live day after day under the same roof with him. He recounts also the meetings of the Brothers' Club, in which men of letters, aristocrats, and commoners met at last on even footing. There were the adored Dr. Arbuthnot and Prior and St. John; and in the Scriblerus Club, which grew out of it, were added Congreve, the rising youngster Pope, and the amiable John Gay.

For three years Swift's mind and pen had been tireless in behalf of the ministry, saving it more than once from disaster, swaying the country's mind, discrediting the Whigs. All this he did gratuitously, but with hopes. Queen Anne did not like him, and he was rewarded with nothing better than the deanery of St. Patrick's, Dublin. The next year, 1714, with the death of Anne, the Tories were out for nearly fifty years, and Swift had nothing to do but resign himself to exile the rest of his life. It was not wholly unexpected; of the politicians he had written to Stella: "I use them like dogs, because I expect they will use me so."

Stella joined him in Dublin. To their embarrassment arrived in Dublin also a Miss Vanhomrigh, who had fallen madly in love with Swift in London, and whose case he had not wisely handled. She was a persistent woman, not wholly circumspect. "Vanessa," as he called her, hung about for nearly ten years, in a hopeless passion, with some risk of scandal. Swift with unwise kindness of intent kept up the acquaintance until a crisis in 1723, soon after which she died.

As Dean of St. Patrick's Swift was received by the Irish with suspicion and threats. But their miseries smote his sensitive heart, and he set about righting old wrongs and resisting new. By his pen he gave the Irish new courage, reduced crime in Dublin, saved Irish trade, raised the condition of the clergy, and with his magnificent *Drapier's Letters* fought off an English attempt to debase Irish currency, and ruin all that was left. He lived scantily himself, but was always giving to the poor, and saving for a charitable foundation at his death. From first abusing, the Irish idolized him, kept his birthday, and on occasion when an advertised eclipse did not come off as announced were content to hear that it had been postponed by order of the Dean.

But he did not love Ireland, and was afraid he might "die here in a rage, like a poisoned rat in a hole." In 1726-7 he made two visits to London, hailed with delight by the now famous Pope and survivors of the old Scriblerus. He saw a new king take the throne, the Hanoverian George II, who confessed that he did not "love boetry and bainting." At this time burst upon an enchanted world the immortal *Gulliver's Travels*, which he had devised in conclave with the Scriblerus years before.

The seventeen years remaining after Stella's death were a long and slowly deepening twilight of mental malady, melancholy, and violent despair. His old friends were dying, Ireland was hopeless, yet he still went about doing untold good. Deafness came on, with giddiness, loss of memory, pain, and three last years of vacant aphasia. To friends he said: "God bless you, good night, . . . I hope I shall never see you again."

One day he picked up a copy of *A Tale of a Tub*, glanced into it, and exclaimed: "Good God, what a genius I had when I wrote that book!" Perhaps it startled him with the peculiar electric shock that leaps from all of Swift's multitudinous writings, charged as they are with his agile wit, vigor, fun, irony, and thrust. His many volumes are an assortment of satire, letters, memoirs, sermons, tracts, "column-stuff," verse, editorials;

but touch him where you will, it is the same electrifying, energizing mind.

Much of it is mere journalism, but three of his works at
least will endure: *A Tale of a Tub, The Battle of the Books,*
and *Gulliver.* The first two were probably done in his twenties.
The *Tale* is mainly an allegory of Catholics, Lutherans, and
Calvinists, represented by the brothers Peter, Martin, and
Jack. Each inherits a stout coat, which he trims most elaborately. But when Peter grows arrogant the others rip off the
trimming, Jack violently, but Martin with care. In the story are
interpolated digressions of demolishing satire against all
bigotry, hocus-pocus, pedantry, critics, sciolists, such as the
Aeolists or Wind-philosophers. None is more diverting than
the tailor-religion, which held the universe to be a large suit
of clothes. "What is that which some call land, but a fine coat
faced with green? or the sea, but a waistcoat of water-tabby?
. . . Observe how sparkish a periwig adorns the head of a
beech, and what a fine doublet of white satin is worn by the
birch." It is a brief passage, but like others it is charged with
high potential for any reader, and indeed in this instance proved
it by firing the genius of Carlyle in his most original work,
Sartor Resartus.

Swift's fun is exuberant, spontaneous, seeming to issue from
a boundless store. It often is a lubricant to his satire, making
it more effective in the ease of its movement; but when the
fun ceases to flow, the satire grinds and shrieks: "Last week I
saw a woman flayed, and you will hardly believe how much it
altered her person for the worse."

The Battle of the Books makes merry over an old, old feud
among the learned, newly revived in France, as to whether
the Ancients were after all so great as the Moderns in science
and literature. The books in the King's library were disputing
the question when a bee blundered through the window into a
spider's web. A hot quarrel arose. The books took it up, and
Swift reports it in mock-heroic style. Unluckily he chose Bentley for one of his burlesque champions, who was not a pedant,
but has proved the greatest scholar of the times. As in the
Tale of a Tub, so here amid the riot one lights on a sudden

poetic passage, where Aesop, speaking for the Ancients, maintains that, like the bee, "we have rather chosen to fill our hives with honey and wax, thus furnishing mankind with the two noblest of things, which are sweetness and light." Whence the famous phrase of Matthew Arnold.

It is another paradox in Swift that he scorned the petty bickerings of men in which he had so often taken part. And still another that this hurt and embittered man should unwittingly have written one of the most successful books for children ever devised. Unlucky the child who has never been caught and thrilled in the illusion of Lilliput. It survives for grown-ups also, as witness the man who in vain scanned the atlases for Lilliput, and the Irish bishop who said the book was full of improbable lies, and he hardly believed a word of it. Swift had in him something of Peter Pan.

But to re-read Gulliver in manhood is to suffer the disillusion of Swift himself. He seems to pose us and upset us with another paradox—to see the world as it is, you must see it through both ends of a telescope, both tiny and in gross caricature. You must see it upsidedown, detached and flying through space, like Laputa, or change places with a horse and view your disgusting kind as Houyhnhnms look upon Yahoos. As the real world crashes down about one in more and more appalling ruin with each succeeding part of the tale, one struggles to keep one's balance, and save oneself; and herein lies perhaps such salutary effect as Swift's satire may induce. It is of course good to see the littleness of men—party politics, religious squabbles, emulations and pretence—as little; and human grossness and sensuality as gross; and human vaporings as up in the air. But it is vain to writhe and agonize under the natural limitations, physical and otherwise, of being human.

"I hate and detest that animal called man, although I heartily love John, Peter, Thomas, and so forth." So Swift wrote, in paradox, to Pope. Amid the perverse and topsy-turvy worlds in *Gulliver* rise certain fixed points of human stability, utterly unaffected by alteration of scale or physical dimension—Gulliver's high-minded friend, the counsellor Reldresal, the devoted little maid Glumdalclitch, forty feet high, and above all the sturdy, intelligent, resourceful, inquisitive, affectionate Gulliver.

The whole book embodies what is perhaps the central paradox of Swift himself—a fierce, impassioned protest against passion, and a plea for Reason and Moderation as the only means of safe living.

Swift was buried at midnight by Stella's side in St. Patrick's, safe at last, as he had hoped in his epitaph, "Ubi saeva indignatio cor ulterius lacerare nequit"—"Where savage indignation can tear the heart no more."

PRIOR (1664-1721)

Matthew Prior described himself as one "who had commonly business enough on his hands, and was only a poet by accident." He was a poor country boy, who found himself in London keeping accounts in his uncle's bar. There Lord Dorset caught him reading Horace, which led eventually to his education at Cambridge, his wide social relations among the great, and a rather conspicuous career in diplomacy under King William and Queen. Anne. People spoke of the famous Peace of Utrecht (1713) familiarly as "Matt's Peace." His literary performance had begun at twenty-two, back in 1687, when he had dared reply to Dryden's *Hind and Panther*. All along poetry was an avocation, and he found friends among the literary Tories gathered about Swift. In 1719, when he was fifty-five, poor, and out of office, Gay, Arbuthnot, and a few old friends left in London, collected and published his poems, and he was able to settle down for his last two years in ease at Down Hall in Essex.

He was most amiable, fussy about his health, and surely had a way with children. His long poems, *Alma, or the Progress of the Mind,* and *Solomon on the Vanity of the World* are well forgotten; but his lines to a five-year-old "child of quality," written at forty, and his "My noble, lovely little Peggy" to another little lady, explain well enough why he was hailed with delight by every member of a great household, young and old, from master to stable dog. His best poetry was incident to his social life, an early instance of *vers de société*; and as he began with Horace, so he ended, a lesser embodiment of the great, genial Roman's social and literary virtues.

ADDISON (1672-1719) AND STEELE (1672-1729)

At the old Charterhouse School in London, the school of Lovelace, Crashaw, John Wesley, and Thackeray, there were, about 1686, two lads of fourteen named Joseph Addison and Richard Steele. Steele was two or three years behind Addison and made of him a hero, and in time a friend almost for life. The friendship proved to be as fruitful a partnership of genius as "Beaumont and Fletcher," or "Gilbert and Sullivan," giving parentage to works far greater than either member could produce alone.

But no one could have foreseen this alliance. Addison, a dean's son and a bishop's nephew, was bred to be a "regular." Regularly distinguished for his scholarship, author of elegant Latin verses on trifles, winning his degrees and a fellowship in regular order at Magdalen, Oxford, voted a pension of £300 at twenty-seven, absent for four years on the regular Grand Tour in France and Italy, publishing accounts of his travels full of elegant reminiscences of the Roman poets, stepping into literary and social prestige with old Dryden, Congreve, and the coffee-house wits, he is at thirty regularly marked for public service as one who will reflect social and intellectual lustre on the Whig party. He is the incarnation of the social ideals of the time. Lord Chesterfield, the expert in manners, recalls that "I used to think myself in company as much above me, when I was with Mr. Addison and Mr. Pope, as if I had been with all the princes in Europe." Pope found something more charming in his conversation than he ever knew in any other man. Nor was his charm impaired by his natural diffidence and modesty.

Dick Steele was of other sort—harum-scarum, unpredictable, thriftless, affectionate and lovable, fond of a fight, Irish all through, especially in his compelling amiability and his instinct for politics. He followed Addison to Oxford, but bolted

into the army without his degree after three years, fought a
duel, and committed a sort of literary bull by writing *The
Christian Hero*, "a standing testimony against himself," to
keep himself straight, and was writing successful comedies
when Addison returned to London. His second wife, the lovely
Mary Scurlock, he adored, and he has left us a sheaf of cap-
tivating letters and notes which he sent as lover and husband:
"Dear Prue I can't come home to dinner. I languish for y^r
Welfare and will never be a moment carelesse more. Y^r Faithfull
Husband R: Steele."

What mutually attracted Steele and Addison it is hard to say.
They both had convivial tastes. Perhaps each saw in the other
the qualities he hopelessly coveted, and there were notable
gatherings including Swift, Pope, and Congreve, at Button's,
a coffee-house kept by an old servant of Addison's.

Then in 1709 out of Steele's busy mind leaped a great idea.
It was of a little periodical essay called the *Tatler* "in honor of
the fair sex," devoted to whatever is of human interest, and
published at a penny on Tuesday, Thursday, and Saturday.
"All accounts of gallantry, pleasure, and entertainment, shall
be under the article of White's Chocolate-house; poetry unde₁
that of Will's Coffee-house; Learning, under the title of Gre.
cian; foreign and domestic news you will have from St. James's
Coffee-house; and what else I have to offer on any other subject shall be dated from my own Apartment." He cleverly
borrowed the pen-name Isaac Bickerstaff, which Swift had
made famous in the Partridge joke the year before.

The *Tatler* was a skilful piece of journalism. It ran nearly two
years, and stopped in full career, probably because Steele could
not let politics alone. But he had fashioned an instrument for
an even more skilful hand. Two months later he and Addison,
who had latterly written for the *Tatler*, issued the first *Spectator*. "Like a distressed prince," he said, he called in Addison,
"and was undone by his auxiliary." Thus pleasantly does he
acknowledge the alliance which was the making of both.

The *Spectator* ran to 555 numbers, rose at its peak to a circulation of 14,000 copies, and quite outdid the *Tatler*. The

ever memorable Sir Roger de Coverley and his friends, a fiction of Steele's perfected by Addison, were figures in a mirror wherein the readers of the periodical recognized themselves as they were, or would like to be. Important among them is Sir Andrew Freeport, the bourgeois, the rich "new man," who, with Will Wimble the new connoisseur, needed exactly what the periodicals supplied—expert instruction in manners and taste, culture by the easiest and quickest means.

The *Tatler* and *Spectator* were excellent literary shopkeeping. With what sweet and hopeful satisfaction must the parvenu have read these words in the *Tatler*: "The courtier, the trader, the scholar, should all have an equal pretension to the denomination of a gentleman. That tradesman who deals with me in a commodity which I do not understand with uprightness, has much more right to that character than the courtier that gives me false hopes, or the Scholar who laughs at my ignorance. The appellation of gentleman is never to be affixed to a man's circumstances but to his behavior in them." Gently, humorously, and insinuatingly, with many an "I confess . . . ," "I cannot forbear . . . ," "I could not but observe . . . ," they exhibit little vulgarities, eccentricities, ill-breeding, fads, and affectations in a way to make the reader healthfully conscious of them; prompting him secretly to fortify himself against them with good sense. What is not done, in clubs, at coffee-houses, in the theatre, at home, on the street, on a journey, in shops, in society; cheap wit, poor conversation, party narrowness, snobbery, bad taste, silly fashions—all these are delicately made recognizable. Now and again one catches glimpses into the life of the gentry in town and country. The little mottoes each day, from Latin poets, chiefly Horace, and conveniently translated, furnished small change of classical culture. Easy criticism of the drama and literature, particularly of Milton now so fashionable, told people what it was proper to think and to say if the subject came up. Many a letter gave them models of epistolary good form. And at times the hand of Addison raised the tone to great dignity with a meditation in the Abbey, or his fine moral allegory, *The Vision of Mirza*,

or his Virgilian hymn, one of the great lyrics of its century,
beginning:

> The spacious firmament on high,
> With all the blue etherial sky,
> And spangled heavens, a shining frame,
> Their great original proclaim.

The subtle effect of this good-natured satire and instruction
upon Queen Anne's London, and indeed her whole realm, cannot be computed. Throughout the century the *Spectator* was
read and reread and imitated, until it became a part of the
very fibre of the richer and more sophisticated social life of
Dr. Johnson's time.

These essays still capture us, and will do so imperishably if
taken at intervals as they were first offered. They transport
one into the Queen-Anne world of beaux and belles, solid
tradesmen, poetasters, actors, coffee-house chat, and good conversation. And their style or manner, particularly Addison's,
can still purify and invigorate the language of the reader with
its refinement and ease. Said Dr. Johnson: "Whoever wishes
to attain an English style familiar but not coarse, and elegant
but not ostentatious must give his days and nights to the volumes of Addison."

When the *Spectator* came to an end Addison produced his
tragedy *Cato*, which succeeded more by his reputation and the
play's supposed reference to political events than by its own
merit. Though not a good play, it abounds in stately speeches
and quotable sentiments, such as

> Sweet are the slumbers of a virtuous man,

which have done heavy duty on thousands of sententious
occasions.

Both Addison and Steele mark a new refinement in the
drama. In 1698 Jeremy Collier (1650-1726) had published *A
Short View of the Immorality and Profaneness of the English
Stage*, a fierce, fanatical diatribe; but it brought to a head a
debate of long standing, and the old license of the Restoration,
stage went markedly out of fashion. Addison's tragedy and

Steele's comedies are cases in point. Steele's *The Conscious Lovers* is an early example of what is called "sentimental" comedy, which was now to rule the boards for fifty years till it was laughed off by Goldsmith. The leading rôles are of ladies and gentlemen, who all talk alike a high-flown, artificial language, full of pompous sentiments, and are actuated by generous and noble motives and delicate scruples, and the action avoids anything that is "low." The grand passion has been refined to respectful sentiment, and wit is pretty well laid asleep. Steele wrote *The Conscious Lovers* to show the folly and sin of hasty quarrels and duelling.

For all that, the friendship of over thirty years between him and his greater ally was broken by an ugly political quarrel at last, and before it could be made up, Addison was dead at the age of forty-seven.

POPE (1688-1744)

This happened in 1719. Alexander Pope was then but thirty-one, yet he was already established in his supremacy as the greatest poet of the times and their literary arbiter.

From his birth to this present moment Pope has suffered from the violent conflict between his abilities and his disabilities. Gifted with genius rare among the ablest, he was disqualified by nature and birth from living as a man among men. He was born a delicate child of elderly folk, and suffered "thro' this long disease my life" from headaches and curvature and being under size. When he was twelve, shortly before Dryden's death, he was taken, doubtless in high excitement, to see the veteran primate of verse at Will's. If the old man could but have known that in this child with the softly modulated voice and flashing eye he beheld the successor to his throne! Pope had no natural relish for rough English sport, no hearty convivial instinct, no talent for women, and shrank sensitively from the cruelties of the hunt. At Binfield near Windsor where he lived through his impressionable years till he was twenty-seven, he must often have smarted and writhed under thoughtless reminders of his physical defects.

His father was a retired linendraper, a Catholic, and as

Catholics the family were not only disqualified from social, political, or academic distinction, but were continually more or less suspect.

Nevertheless from the first the precocious lad was aware of his great talent. He "lisp'd in numbers, for the numbers came." At home he was sheltered, encouraged, perhaps spoiled. His education in private schools was desultory, but he read voraciously in English poets and the classics. Admiring elders told him he was a wonder. As he grew, he found his natural friends, after the manner of such lads, among men of talent much older than himself, such as "great Dryden's friends before," and Wycherley, now a rather doddering relic of rakish Restoration days. Young Pope soon discovered his superiority to them all.

No English poet has suffered such harsh and hasty judgment as Pope. He has been portrayed as spiteful, vindictive, suspicious, intriguing, disloyal, and delighting in falsehood for its own sake. Since shortly after his death to the present, critics have debated whether he is really a poet after all. But his poetry has always found mighty champions. Byron, of all unlikely voices, proclaimed him the most perfect English poet. And nowadays many are arising to defend not only the poetry of Pope, but his character; and it is high time.

Painfully sensitive to his physical inferiority, it is no wonder that, when Pope discovered his godlike power over others in one respect, he should have wielded that power with seeming arrogance; such at bottom was but the rebound of his instinctive resentment at the hateful disabilities of his fate, and his natural attempt to compensate for them. Hate he did—most things hatable—dullness, and bores, and fools, and pretense, and injustice, and hypocrisy. He was afraid of no one, not even the King, as witness his superb satire on the Philistine George II in his *Epistle to Augustus*. He was adored by those of his household, his servants were devoted, and his epitaph to his old nurse on the wall of Twickenham church is one of many proofs of a heart essentially kind. But his active kindness reached much further than his family and friends, to aspiring poetasters who presumed upon him, made nuisances of themselves, and were sometimes meanly ungrateful afterwards. His eminence and generosity carried a penalty, as may be seen in the opening of the *Epistle to Arbuthnot.* Let us also remember that to a real genius Pope was invariably generous, unenvious, even deferential. He was never guilty of the professional jealousy which he chastises in the *Arbuthnot.*

Pope did not begin as a satirist. His *Pastorals*, 1709, and his *Windsor Forest*, 1713, are essentially poems on Nature, though heavily weighted with literary tradition, epithets, and the generalized description then approved. It is no new insight into Nature, no new ingenuity of image, but a new and exquisite musical grace that animates these lines from the Third Pastoral, *Summer:*

> Where'er you walk cool gales shall fan the glade,
> Trees, where you sit, shall crowd into a shade;
> Where'er you tread the blushing flowers shall rise,
> And all things flourish where you turn your eyes.

To these earlier poems Pope's champions usually appeal to prove that he is a poet.

All will agree that Pope had a keen sense of the public demand, just as had Dryden, Addison, and Steele. In 1711 he devised his *Essay on Criticism*—just what aspirants to literary culture, and amateur critics wanted, something to show them how to talk about poetry, and even how to try their hand therein. Good sense, correctness, rules are necessary—in effect the virtues in art and life promulgated by the *Spectator.* But without "Nature" says Pope, again and again, there can be no poetry; and by Nature he here means the creative instinct of genius, the inborn poetic fire, the only source of life, force, and beauty in art. No one valued it more, or was more keenly aware of it in himself, than Pope. Without it, says the *Essay,* in effect, rules will avail nothing.

In 1712 he took advantage of a petty scandal in Catholic society to launch his *Rape of the Lock.* A young scamp, Lord Petre, had clipped and conveyed a ringlet of Miss Arabella Fermor's back hair, and there arose a pretty stew and stir. Pope dressed the little event up in big clothes borrowed from epic poets—Milton, Spenser, Ovid, Virgil, Homer, Catul-lus—with a charming mock-heroic effect which set everybody laughing till their ill-will evaporated, and resentment was no longer becoming. It is a dainty bit of poetic artistry in minia-ture, and as revised in 1714, with the addition of the sylphs and the epic game of cards, it became an imperishable treasure of fun and wit that never stale, and of beauty that never fades.

For the first time the native spirit of satire in Pope makes itself distinctly felt. Lightly, but with infallible aim, it touches the silly foibles and vulgarities of coxcombs and coquettes with good sense and just enough force to brush them away. But they are foibles and vulgarities, not merely of that day, but of all time, and the poet's satire already shows the durable univer-sality that made it great.

These years of the *Rape*, from 1711 to 1714, the time of the Brothers' and the Scriblerus Club, of Swift's splendor in politics, before death and evil days broke into the group, marked the high tide of happy association of talents in this brilliant age. After the Queen's death it fell, and when a decade later Swift returns as Pope's guest at Twickenham, and they try to call back the old times, it is a failure; neither is well, and Swift is getting deaf:

> The Dean sits plodding o'er a book,
> Pope walks and courts the muse.

In 1715 Pope began his five years' labor on his translation of the *Iliad*. None of his other works gives surer proof of his sense of the literary market. Dryden's *Virgil* had been a boon to the new middle class, who lacked the leisure and the Latin necessary to the culture that no gentleman could do without. By the same token they needed an English *Homer*, and Pope would make it. The result is a great English poem, but as Bentley, the super-scholar, told Pope at the time—"not Homer." Pope was hurt, and lost no chance to satirize Bentley, espe-cially in the *Dunciad*. But like Swift before him, he made the mistake this time of taking an invulnerable man, and the final score is heavily in Bentley's favor. It is a long and interesting story. Bentley knew his own strength. "I criticised his Homer," he calmly said, "and the portentous cub never forgives."

The success of the *Iliad* led naturally to the *Odyssey*, half of which was done by assistants. It is inferior; Pope was tired of translating, and much of the time merely imitated himself, which hundreds of clever versifiers had learned to do. Yet the *Homer* made his fortune, for he cleared the equivalent of $250,000 or $300,000 altogether.

Meanwhile, in 1716 he had taken the villa on the Thames at Twickenham which his name has made famous, and there he lived his remaining twenty-five years, just near enough to partake of the life of London, without being involved too much for an invalid. He amused himself developing his five acres according to the newer theories of more natural, less formal landscaping; lawn opened beyond lawn, all flanked with wild woods, and stretched down to the Thames, where he, in his barge, took the air, or made visits. The London highway crossed his grounds, and beneath it he built his artificially wild grotto, which he has sung into fame.

In the meantime, while the *Iliad* was in progress, he issued his *Elegy to the Memory of an Unfortunate Lady* and his *Eloisa to Abelard*. Both poems are usually cited to prove Pope's intensity of feeling. The elegy at least deals with a case of cruel treatment, despair, and suicide far from home, in behalf of which the poet's tender heart had been actively engaged. In the *Eloisa*, he has taken the old love story as it comes originally from Abelard's account, and set it forth in terms somewhat generalized; but its warmth comes rather from Pope's glowing rhetoric, his vibrant music, and his ever responsive pity for the sufferings of others, than from any intense vicarious realization of consuming passion. They are indeed "well-sung woes," as he says, but his last line, "He best can paint 'em who shall feel 'em most," is pathetic in a way Pope did not intend.

Today we cannot hope to understand or judge the state of things when literature first became widely popular and self-supporting. The world of letters was demoralized. Almost anyone hoped to shine, and custom and good manners had not yet enforced the unwritten laws of honor and candor among poets and scholars. Even the great ones, from Dryden to Pope, did things which simply are not done now. Such demoralization cannot excuse, but may explain, the subterfuges to which they resorted, Pope most of all. Whoever would gain a sense of this inflamed state of literature, of Pope's reasonable exasperations, of his literary ideals, of his private virtues, of the need for a literary dictator, let him read and reread, until it sings in his ears, the *Epistle to Dr. Arbuthnot*. To this add the *To Augustus*. He will at least see why Pope wrote the first of his regular satires, the *Dunciad*.

The *Dunciad* first appeared in 1728, after the *Homer* was finished. It is a mock-epic extravaganza in four books, suggested by Dryden's *Mac Flecknoe*, reminiscent of epic devices like Milton's vision on the mount in *Paradise Lost*, and the funeral games in *Aeneid* V. The goddess Dullness selects Theobald, Pope's rival editor of Shakespeare, as the new king of her realm, and through various epic episodes the poet deploys an enormous caste of dunces—literary, antiquarian, academic, noble patrons, publishers—calling by name everybody who hopelessly aspired to eminence. Most of them are now forgotten, and these shafts of wit, electrifying to those concerned, are now spent and dead. But dunces are not extinct, and, as long as the species survives, many a flash of Pope's best wit will live. The close of the poem, which always moved Pope deeply, is taken by some to be the finest passage he ever composed.

The *Dunciad* in its first year was wrapped in a network of those bluffs, intrigues, and mystifications which Pope loved. As one might expect, a blaze of rage rose on every hand which would have alarmed a less courageous man, but seemed a source of profound satisfaction to the satirist.

He was always revising, polishing, and correcting his work. Some of his pages were black with alterations. The *Dunciad* was no exception. It went through edition after edition. In 1743 Pope dethroned Theobald and put the actor Colley Cibber in his place. In this edition first appeared the fourth and greatest book.

This excellent literary man of business now did in philosophy what he had done in criticism years before. In his *Essay on Man* he embodied the popular deistic philosophy of the hour, in easy terms never before so well expressed. No work of his is so famous, and none has furnished the language with so many phrases. In this mark of a great poet he vies on even terms with Shakespeare and Gray. The philosophy for the poem was furnished him by his friend Bolingbroke (St. John), and by Shaftesbury's *Characteristics*. It is now commonplace theory that the idea of God is natural to every human mind, even lo! the poor Indian; and that as science newly reveals the extent and wonders of the universe, man's exaggerated sense of his own importance needs revision downwards. But these ideas were then new enough at large, and as Pope knew, were saleable.

The body of his work into which Pope's highest poetic energy flows is the satires—that is, his five *Moral Essays*, his six *Imitations of Horace*, his *Epistle to Arbuthnot* or *Prologue to the Satires*, and his *Epilogue to the Satires*. In these he is racy, clever, amusing, familiar, annihilating, and on occasion rises to grandeur. His piercing and burning eye glances fearlessly in all directions, and his lightning thrust drives nonsense and sentimentality beyond the horizon.

It was not a chivalric time, and Pope had not in him the instinct to idealize women. His feeling for them was one of contempt or furious rage, as with the talented Lady Mary Wortley Montagu (Sappho), or of a more or less stable social friendship, such as that with the two charming sisters in his neighborhood, Teresa and Martha Blount. With Teresa he quarrelled; with Martha some would make out that he was in love. Martha, it seems, once let fall the remark, which Pope applauded,

Most women have no characters at all.

He went on record that women have but two ruling passions, the love of pleasure and the love of sway, and that every woman is at heart a rake. In such a mind there is no room for romance.

Pope's satire, like Dryden's, is largely made up of characters or portraits, and these vary widely in quality. Some, like Sporus in the *Arbuthnot,* are so spiteful and personal that as satire they are invalidated, and have only their fierce energy of wit to commend them. Pope never attained in satire the grand and tranquil detachment of Dryden. Yet he usually rose to the level of universality. Timon with his villa in the fourth *Moral Essay, may* be the Duke of Chandos, but certainly *is* the vulgar parvenu for all time. The superb portrait of Addison, which is the climax of the *Arbuthnot,* sets forth once and for all the professional jealousy that is an infirmity of even noble minds. And Pope was in a sense quite sincere in disclaiming mere personal intention in such cases.

Literal and accurate he was when he said,

> Fools rush into my head, and so I write.

He was inspired, as others have been, by the gulf that yawns between human folly and human intelligence, and his inspiration makes itself felt in the vibrant energy, the cadence and live movement of his verse, a matter above all mere rules and contrivance. The rhymed couplet in his hands proves an instrument of ample range.

All poetry is a kind of vicarious experience. It enables us to suffer, enjoy, and realize what is beyond the limitations of our own lives. It is a safety valve for our inhibited emotions. Satire, when it is poetry, serves this end as much as tragedy. It releases and purges our shut-up and unuttered resentments, and our disgusts at what we are powerless to remedy.

> Out with it, Dunciad! let the secret pass,
> That secret to each fool, that he's an Ass:
> The truth once told (and wherefore should we lie?)
> The Queen of Midas slept, and so may I.

In finding this release for himself, Pope found it for all English-reading mankind; but with the intelligence, the truth, the feeling, and the music that make it great poetry.

GAY (1685-1732)

It is pleasant, amid these great figures, subject all of them in some measure to tragedy and bitterness, to meet with the amiable John Gay. He is distinguished at least in being beloved by all his literary contemporaries, and never having quarrelled with any. He was a man of real genius, but curiously dependent upon his friends; and Pope, Swift, and Arbuthnot all advised him in his poetic undertakings, a relation in itself not altogether safe. Though he had been a country lad, and had begun his life in London as apprentice behind a mercer's counter, he became a self-respecting favorite of dukes and duchesses, and was for ever being petted at one great house or other in town and country.

He had been in London ten years before he got to know Pope. To Pope, now famous though three years his junior, Gay, in 1713, inscribed his poem *Rural Sports*. Not a great work, yet it shows significantly an early case of poetic talent returning for its matter to homely and immediate things. His next work, suggested to him by Pope, and for an invidious purpose, turned out to be greater than was expected. It was the *Shepherd's Week*, conceived with Spenser's *Shepherd's Calendar* in mind, but was intended to ridicule the conventional pastoral by substituting genuine and less savory country life for the artificialities of that species. But his "Thursday," for example, on the model of Theocritus's famous second idyll of incantation, is made of old English country superstitions as quaint and racy as those in Burns's *Hallowe'en*.

Two years later came his *Trivia, or the Art of Walking the Streets of London*. Though not of high order, yet it poetized the familiar, and may today be taken as an express conveyance to the heart of Queen Anne's London.

By 1720 Gay got the beginning of a little fortune from a "collected" edition. Against good advice he put his returns into the famous South Sea bubble, which quickly swelled to fabulous size, then burst before his astonished gaze, and every penny vanished. But his good friends, the Duke and Duchess of

Queensberry, luckily had just fallen in love with him in time to pick him up out of despondency, destitution, and illness.

His next venture was the charming *Fables* in octosyllabics, done for the youthful Prince William, but attuned to the juvenile ear universal. And last in 1728 appeared the *Beggar's Opera*. It had developed under advice from Pope and Swift, was looked upon doubtfully by Congreve and Queensberry, and, at last produced by Rich. Manager, author, and author's illustrious friends were overwhelmed with the unprecedented and unforeseen success of the piece. Some wag said it made Gay rich, and Rich gay. It also made Rich rich. "It would do more public service," said Swift, "than all the ministers of state from Adam to Walpole." Again Gay had taken "low" material, the romance of a highwayman, and touched it with the magic of his own amiable soul so that all the world fell in love with it, and it was played from end to end of the realm and even to remote corners of Europe. Everyone was humming the airs, and its scenes decorated fans and screens. This time the Duke of Queensberry took charge of Gay's fortune, and he lived on in comfortable idleness for four years, producing nothing of moment but a second series of fables. He was buried in the Abbey "as if he had been a peer of the realm," and on his stone was cut his own careless epitaph:

> Life is a jest, and all things show it.
> I thought so once, and now I know it.

DEFOE (1660?-1731)

All of these men, with their approved education, their notions of literary finish, French in origin, were essentially aristocrats of literature. Their services in refining and edifying the thrifty new middle class, as they well knew, were in truth condescending, even though they covered the fact with consummate art. But that middle class produced its own genius, who of course could never hope to become one of the literary *élite*, but who, like Bunyan of the age before, brought forth what after all has survived as the most popular book of his century.

In 1725-7, near the end of the first George's reign, appeared in two volumes *The Complete English Tradesman*. It is full of hard-headed advice and exhortation to honest and prudent dealing, worthy of Benjamin Franklin. London, through trade, it says, has become the heart of the world. Charles II's jest that the tradesmen were the only gentry in England bade fair to be a fact; at any rate, "trade in England," says the author, "makes Gentlemen, and has peopled this nation with Gentlemen." Four years later the same hand penned *The Complete Gentleman*, who is described as "a Person of Merit and Worth; a Man of Honour, Virtue, Sense, Integrity, Honesty, and Religion, without which he is Nothing at all." Both books are from the plebeian hand of Daniel Defoe.

Defoe's span (the name had been Foe, until Daniel, in prosperity, set it up on its "De") extended over the seventy years from about 1661 to 1731, from Charles II to George II. He was a cockney Presbyterian butcher's son, a man of the masses, with powers and instincts of the modern journalist in a measure that amounted to extraordinary genius. He was enormously prolific—some 250 works have been latterly accepted as his, out of a welter of anonymous material. His brain fermented with schemes, reforms, and politics; his curiosity was irrepressible, his interest in public affairs intense, and his energy over and above providing for his family was tireless. Wiry he was in mind and body—spare, dark, with "a hooked nose, a sharp chin, gray eyes, and a large mole near his mouth."

He had obscure but good education for the ministry, and his absorbent mind picked up foreign languages and literatures as such a mind will. Swift did not know his man when he sneered at Defoe as a stupid, illiterate scribbler. Defoe chose business instead of the ministry, and variously succeeded in hosiery and roof-tiles. But journalism was his calling. His life is a series of obscure movements and passages, now Whig in its hue, now Tory, and again Whig; now in royal favor, now out, now in; in short with the same journalistic shift of protective coloring that we have observed in Dryden and Swift. After all he had a wife and six children.

Now and then the focus clears, and the light falls strong on this elusive figure. In 1701 he wrote some vigorous tortured verses called *The True-born Englishman*, and rebuked the English anti-foreign prejudice by showing that the English are in reality only thoroughbred mongrels. It had enormous success, and he was presented to King William. Again in 1702, when the question of toleration was vexed, he sprang a trap, *The Shortest Way with the Dissenters,* which was in brief to exterminate them, French fashion. Certain of the Tories, off their guard, broke into wild applause only to find that they had given their whole case away. Defoe, for his saucy cleverness, was condemned to prison after exposure on the pillory. Aloft in that place of shame for three July days in 1703 stood this gristly man of forty, overwhelmed with flowers and the pledges and plaudits of an adoring multitude. Once again he appears in his sixties, living in comfortable leisure with his "three lovely daughters," at a house with a garden and four acres in the suburbs. His body lies in Bunhill Fields, amid the roar of his London, near the graves of Bunyan, Isaac Watts the writer of hymns, William Blake, and, not far off, George Fox, the first Quaker.

While tossing off a swarm of pamphlets with his left hand, his right was engaged twice and thrice a week from 1704 to 1713 writing the *Review*. It was doubtless the precedent for the *Tatler*. Yet Defoe is usually cited as a writer of fiction rather than a journalist. Fiction and fact in such a life cannot be distinguished, and such is the man's art that his "fiction" is fact-like enough to deceive anybody. He was almost sixty when his *Robinson Crusoe* appeared. Alexander Selkirk, an able and roving Scot, had been left a castaway for some five years on the island of Juan Fernandez off Chile, and his adventures had been published. Defoe, taking them as a point of departure, transformed and developed them with his magic and his invention, so that they not merely stirred the romantic imagination of everyone in his time, but to this day the wonderful tale has never lost its power of doing so against thousands of derivative competitors. Even *Gulliver's Travels* stands in its unacknowledged debt.

In four months came another instalment of *Robinson Crusoe*, and, with incredible yield, book followed after book, and tale after tale, from this youth in his sixties, to the number of some twenty in the next six years. Among these were *The King of the Pirates, Adventures of Duncan Campbell, Captain Singleton, Moll Flanders* (of which the scene is partly in Virginia), *Journal of the Plague Year, The Highland Rogue* [Rob Roy], *Roxana,* and tales of the crooks, Jack Sheppard and Jonathan Wild. The list sounds like a boy's library of dreadfuls. But all of them, especially *Captain Singleton,* live with the baffling daylight reality that makes them true whether they ever happened or not. The literary resort to low life for material has been intermittent ever since Chaucer; but Defoe, with his Moll, his Roxana, and his highwaymen, made a specialty of it, as far as he ever had a specialty.

Yet his darting mind flies at any opening. He will edify with his *Family Instructor,* and his *Religious Courtship!* He will exploit superstition with his *Apparition of Mrs. Veal,* 1706, and his *Political History of the Devil,* 1726.

This prolific man of the people found the very style to suit his needs, so seemingly artless that it appears to be no style at all. He says in his *English Tradesman* that the perfect style is easy, plain, and familiar, "that in which a man speaking to five hundred people, of all common and various capacities, Ideots and Lunaticks excepted, should be understood by them all." It is the ideal of him who would be heard on all hands today, and Defoe was the first to attain it.

CHESTERFIELD (1694-1773)

Few English writers have the honor of surviving in an adjective. One is Philip Stanhope, Earl of Chesterfield. All the world talks of Chesterfieldian manners. Fathers there still are who put his *Letters to his Son* into their sons' hands. No one can calculate the subtle refinement of manners they have effected in men through the years.

All his life Chesterfield was an aristocratic Whig. Except for a year and more at Cambridge his education was private, in French and the classics, with a tour in Flanders, and some months among the salons of Paris. After a little experience in the House of Commons and at Court, he succeeded at thirty-one to the earldom and entered that "hospital for incurables," as he called it, the House of Lords.

From thirty-three to thirty-seven he was a very successful ambassador at the Hague. The Dutch were charmed by his good manners and his hospitality. So too was the beautiful Mlle. de Bouchet, who bore him the son made famous by the *Letters*. He was an important man under the first two Georges, held high office for brief times, and was heartily respected, but never quite "in" with Sir Robert Walpole and the Whig ring, whose corruption and intrigue he could not endure. He was a leader in the opposition which at long last ended in the downfall of the able "premier." For Chesterfield was honest, courageous, hated pretense, and scorned mere titles. In one year as Lord Lieutenant he did great service to Ireland, and he carried through the reform of the calendar from "Old Style" to "New." The last twenty years of his life he spent in retirement, writing, building, gardening, gambling, collecting, going to Bath —ways befitting a polite, affluent, and very deaf semi-invalid. At thirty-seven he had married a rich natural daughter of George I a year older than he, whom he treated with invariable kindness and respect, but who did not in any way interfere with his affairs. "Tyrawley and I have been dead these two years," said the old man, "but we don't choose to have it known." An old friend entered the room as he lay dying. "Give Dayrolles a chair," said Chesterfield. They were his last words.

Chesterfield is a fine embodiment of the admired qualities of his age, good sense, reason, moderation, all the virtues of Horace, touched with a certain French grace. "A Frenchman, who, with a fund of virtue, learning, and good sense, has the manners and good breeding of his country, is the perfection of human nature." There was no trace of mysticism or sentimentality about him. In general he entertained a low opinion of his fellow-men. The ruling passion, he thought, was any man's weakest point; and yet he had his own. It was a desire to excel in oratory, diplomacy, and as a man amongst men. If ever a man succeeded against odds, he did, for he was at the outset gawky, diffident, undersized, and without looks. But he "sacrificed all to the Graces," as he would say, and believed that any other could do as much as he.

The letters to his natural son began in 1737 when the boy was five, and ran till young Philip died thirty years thence. They are but a handful of all the letters that Chesterfield wrote, the only famous part. His heart and hopes went out to the lad, who was destined to fail in Parliament and diplomacy; his lack of talents and his birth were against him, and of course everyone was sure to be disappointed in the manners of Chesterfield's son. The old man was never finer than when, after his son's death, he learned that Philip had been secretly married for some time to a rather ordinary woman, and had two sons. The widow he treated most kindly, and began the education of the boys. But when he was dead, she sold the famous letters to a publisher in the face of violent family protest, and thus the world has them.

Encouraged perhaps by Dr. Johnson's unfair witticism about Chesterfield's morals and manners, men have often condemned the *Letters* for counselling immorality and duplicity. They forget the author's invariable honesty and integrity. They overlook his constant iteration of the belief that "learning, honour, and virtue are absolutely necessary to gain you the esteem and admiration of mankind; politeness and good breeding are equally necessary to make you welcome and agreeable in conversation and common life." He is ever urging self-control, decency, self-respect. But as he never dreamed of publication, and believed that his son's awkwardness, like his own, could be overcome with practice, it is on that side of the matter that he dwells most.

And invaluable is the coaching of this expert man of the world on many matters—how to talk and converse, how to be agreeable, how to overcome self-consciousness and put others at their ease, how to meet the social responsibility that falls on everyone in these democratic days. He abounds with memorable sentences—"Be wiser than other people, if you can; but do not tell them so"; "Wear your learning, like your watch, in a private pocket"; "Do as you would be done by is the surest method that I know of pleasing"; "Banish egotism out of your conversation, and never think of entertaining people with your own personal concerns or private affairs." "A man of the world must, like the Chameleon, be able to take every different hue; which is by no means a criminal or abject, but a necessary complaisance, for it relates only to Manners, and not to Morals." His "dissimulation," often misunderstood, is not deceit, but keeping one's mind to oneself.

Worldly Chesterfield surely was, and worldly are his *Letters*. But at least three agents raise them above the low level of mere worldliness. One is their wit. Chesterfield had in his time high reputation for his wit. The instances recorded are usually disappointing; they sound a bit conscious of living up to his reputation.[1] But he is at his best in the *Letters*, without expectant listeners. Then, his models such as Cicero's letters to his friend Atticus, and Mme. de Sévigné, have drawn him into a style that is always genial, relaxed, and easy without being cheap. Above all is what perhaps Chesterfield would least have valued, a certain intensity and passionate warmth that suffuse every letter and rise from his warm wholehearted devotion to the Graces and their gifts, and even more from his devoted yearning over this beloved natural son. These were still his ruling passions. "My greatest joy is to consider the fair prospect you have before you, and to hope and believe you will enjoy it."

[1] But see p. 335

CHAPTER 22

New Poets

THOMSON (1700-1748)

JAMES THOMSON was a hearty Scot, lazy, likable, fond of his comforts, inclined to be fat, in short the last person one at first glance would take for a vigorous pedestrian, a hard worker, least of all a poet. Yet he instinctively saw Nature and life as a poet sees them, and, says Johnson, "could not have viewed those two candles burning but with a poetical eye." Furthermore without intention or flaming zeal, he was a harbinger of the profound emotional awakening of men which was not far off—the so-called "Romantic Movement."

He was born amid those lovely hills and vales near Melrose that two generations later produced another genius, as great, as beloved as he, and now even more famous. Till he was fifteen his sensitive mind nurtured itself on the haunting charms of the Jed valley and the Cheviots, already half poetized to his hand with legend and tradition. Then came ten dour years of education at Edinburgh. Bitterly homesick at first, he latterly found himself drifting by gravity of the family wishes into his father's career as "meenister of the kirk." But poet he was and no parson, and poet he knew himself to be. In 1725 he embarked for London and the great uncertain world. He never saw Scotland again. In his pocket he had the beginnings of his greatest poem.

Scotch friends received him in London, and with their peculiar national loyalty to one another in a strange land, soon had him "acquent" with the men of importance in letters and politics. Such were of course Arbuthnot and Gay and Pope.

who became a warm friend, and with his invariable generosity welcomed a genuine poet wherever he could find one. According to the old custom Thomson dedicated, and he was a clever and discreet dedicator; his confirmed Scotch idiom and burr, his taciturnity, his indifferent clothes and manner, were quite offset by his talents, his amiability, and his convivial temper. He was liked and helped along by no less than that patroness of letters, the Countess of Hertford, by Bubb Dodington, Lord Lyttelton, and the Prince of Wales himself.

The year after he arrived in London appeared the first "Season," *Winter*. In ten months it saw four editions. The others followed in the order—*Summer*, 1727; *Spring*, 1728; and *Autumn* in a complete *Seasons*, 1730. It was new poetry, and unlike most new poetry recommended itself to both *élite* and popular taste.

The plan or "recipe" of such poems may be illustrated from Thomson's "argument" of *Winter*:

The subject proposed. Address to the Earl of Wilmington. First approach of Winter. According to the natural course of the season, various storms described. Rain. Wind. Snow. The driving of the snows: a man perishing among them, whence reflections on the wants and miseries of human life. The wolves descending from the Alps and Apennines. A winter evening described: as spent by philosophers; by the country people; in the city. Frost. A view of Winter within the polar circle. A thaw. The whole concluding with moral reflections on a future state.

Here are about a thousand lines on various and sundry matters brought together under the subject "Winter," proceeding in what seems a natural, but is really an artificial order, moving with deft transition from point to point. Such a poem is made like Virgil's *Georgics*, Spenser's *Colin Clout*, Denham's *Cooper's Hill*. Its artificial construction is not unlike that of the satires of Horace and Pope. But Thomson's *Seasons* set this desultory style for a century, a vogue sustained in even more casual forms by Young, Cowper, Wordsworth, and Byron.

Thomson abandoned the rhymed couplet of the hour for blank verse which moves with easy progress; yet he keeps much of the delicacy and force which the couplet had evoked, and many of his lines are essentially couplets unrhymed. He had devised also a style of his own, partly out of Miltonic mannerisms, partly from the "poetic" style now made traditional by Pope's *Iliad*. It is a bit swollen with artificialities, to us more amusing than poetical; but his readers, instead of plain "bird" or "fish," preferred to hear of "the tuneful race," "the plumy people," "the finny tribe," and the like. He made good use of the compound epithet, so poetic in the hands of the Greeks, of Spenser, and of Keats and Tennyson; and his accurate observation and intense feeling, with his almost invariable tunefulness, defeat all his artificialities and leave us in no doubt that, changed as our poetic fashions may be, he is a great and genuine poet.

The popularity of the *Seasons* continued for more than one hundred years; and the "argument" just cited explains it at least in part. A transcription of Nature, done with the eye on the object, showed readers familiar things freshly reproduced, and reproduced not mechanically, but with idyllic lure and deep feeling. They were delighted as anyone must be with his pictures of a shower, of a spring morning, a summer evening, of English landscape, a garden, sheep-shearing, harvesting, a hunt supper, a winter evening indoors. The poet turned their attention to simple, unsophisticated country people, and he moralized to their hearts' content; then he swept them away to strange imagined scenes—winter in the Arctic; the luxuriance and terrors of the tropics; the happy or unhappy loves of maids and swains. The program was artfully varied so that it held even the most wayward attention. Every now and then he releases a line or phrase to become literary small change in the parlance of the generations since:

> Delightful task! to rear the tender thought,
> To teach the young idea how to shoot—

or "hold high converse with the mighty dead."

But the whole fabric is tinged in shades now light, now deep, with what Thomson calls "the power of philosophic melancholy," that power which calls forth

the sudden-starting tear,
The glowing cheek, the mild dejected air,
The softened feature, and the beating heart. . . .
As fast the correspondent passions rise,
As varied, and as high: devotion raised
To rapture, and divine astonishment;
The love of nature unconfined, and, chief,
Of human race; the large ambitious wish
To make them blest; the sigh for suffering worth
Lost in obscurity; the noble scorn
Of tyrant pride; the fearless great resolve;
The wonder which the dying patriot draws,
Inspiring glory through remotest time;
The awakened throb for virtue and for fame;
The sympathies of love, and friendship dear;
With all the social offspring of the heart.

A moment's thought tells us that these "passions," the "wish," the "sigh," the "resolve," are stirred only for the pleasure one has in feeling them; they will never come to action, they are sterile, and indeed selfish. In short we are dealing with sentimentality, with sterilized emotion, pleasurable in its thrill, common because it is within everybody's range, selfish because it is usually enjoyed at the expense of another's suffering, and not altogether healthy because it is not sincere enough to act, for then the pleasure would end. Sentimentality we have come to regard as rather plebeian and childish, though we are ever liable to it. It is always rising with a rising new middle class, through cruder stages at first, but eventually refining itself and passing into far nobler appreciations. Sometimes it appears pleasurably in "feeling sorry" for situations which we do not or cannot relieve. Even common-sense Pope in *Windsor Forest* wishes us to pity with him the poor stricken game-birds, that "leave their little lives in air." The sensitive Thomson contagiously felt everything he saw; his feelings were the genuine, elemental feelings of a poet, but they easily awakened a less genuine, more sentimental response in his audience.

Sentimentality was merely incidental to his full power as a

poet. His transcriptions are alive and animate with the energies of a great genius. They rise before the reader with the same variety, vigor, and strange, restless, teeming beauty that one finds in Nature and the world. In his *Hymn* appended to the *Seasons* he utters his sense of

> the mighty hand,
> That, ever busy, wheels the silent spheres;
> Works in the secret deep; shoots, steaming, thence
> The fair profusion that o'erspreads the Spring;
> Flings from the sun direct the flaming day;
> Feeds every creature; hurls the tempest forth,
> And, as on earth this grateful change resolves,
> With transport touches all the springs of life.

This sense of a divine energy permeating Nature has tempted some to make of Thomson a poetic parent of Wordsworth; but this sense in some form is common to all poets of Nature from the Greeks down.

Thomson enjoyed some dramatic success in his day. Between thirty and forty-five he produced five tragedies and a masque. Only one has survived in common memory, and that by a bad line. *Sophonisba,* 1730, rose to a tragic crisis with the line,

> O Sophonisba! Sophonisba O!

On which a critic commented,

> O Jemmy Thomson! Jemmy Thomson O!

And Fielding ran it out in his *Tom Thumb* with

> O Huncamunca! Huncamunca O!

From his now unread *Masque of Alfred* emerged the famous *Rule Britannia*, which exhibits all the virtues, and remarkably few of the vices, of a true-to-form national anthem.

Crowned with success in 1730 Thomson took the Grand Tour in company with his pupil, the Lord Chancellor's son, and turned the fruits of travel into his favorite poem *Liberty*. It is an exaltation of British liberty in contrast with the thralldom he has observed in other nations—the sentiment afterwards condensed in *Rule Britannia*—and it doubtless suggested to Goldsmith his scheme for the *Traveller,* if indeed it was not in Byron's mind in devising *Childe Harold.* The poem is prophetic also in expressing appreciations of ancient sculpture and architecture which were well ahead of the time.

Thomson's last work was, next to the *Seasons,* his most significant—*The Castle of Indolence,* a "Spenserian" allegory in Spenserian stanza. The influence of Spenser had never ceased since the poet's day, but Thomson revived it, especially in language and metre. The stanza, which he handled with great skill, is forthwith employed by Shenstone, Beattie, and the high romantics, Burns, Byron, Shelley, Keats, and Tennyson. *The Castle* is a diverting poem, with units of Thomson's best idyllism, and amusing portraits of his friends, including Murdoch, "A little, round, fat, oily man of God," and himself, "more fat than bard beseems."

At thirty-six he took a small house and garden at Richmond, whence he often walked the ten miles to London, or the two across the river to see his friend Pope at Twickenham. Here he lived out his remaining days. About the time of his coming to Richmond, this outwardly unromantic, easy-going Epicurean fell in love with an Elizabeth Young, to whom he sings ever and anon as his Amanda. He hoped for eight years, and when she finally married another, his hold on life relaxed.

When, about 1850, Tennyson and Longfellow came to dislodge Thomson from the people's heart, they found him enthroned in splendor of gilt edges and steel engravings on the marble top of the Victorian walnut table. This was the sentimental Thomson. But the real Thomson was a breeder of new poets, a pioneer of new poetic interests and devices—such as a new sense of Nature and of common man, discursively and casually set forth, sentimentally attuned to his time, mingled with hints of far-off ages and far-off places that stir the dreams of romance. Yet in this pioneer were qualities that raised him to the even higher level of the artist who transcends all dates.

YOUNG (1683-1765)

Every one is familiar with the line,

> Tir'd Nature's sweet restorer, balmy sleep!

It is the opening line of Edward Young's once famous *Night Thoughts*, but few now read further. Yet in its day the poem was read and quoted on every hand, went through many editions, and fifty years after it appeared was glorified by William Blake with 537 of his most beautiful and daring designs. As the tide of its popularity subsided it left in the language many a shred of quotation current to this day. Who realizes that he owes to Young

> Procrastination is the thief of time?

The general theme is implied in the verses

> All, all on earth is shadow, all beyond
> Is substance; the reverse is folly's creed.

The singer of this gloomy strain was in fact a rather worldly man till well into his forties though not ill-behaved. He was a son of the Dean of Salisbury Cathedral, became a fellow of All Souls, Oxford, hobnobbed with Addison and his little "senate" at Button's, was a friend and admirer of Pope and Chesterfield, was tireless if not very successful in his hunt for a patron and in "soliciting preferment." He wrote two or three successful declamatory tragedies like Addison's *Cato*, took orders and married an earl's daughter when he was near fifty. As rector of Welwyn, a sleepy village about twenty miles north of London, he lived on comfortably till the ripe age of eighty-three, still hoping for preferment but in vain. Meanwhile he had written a good deal of verse, which he dedicated right and left to persons of consequence. Most of it was mordant satire on fools of the time, or of any time, yet without the energy of wit and music to make it live.

But late in his fifties he lost his beloved wife, and shortly before a step-daughter and son-in-law, both dear to him. Within the next four years appeared the *Night Thoughts*, a "night" at a time, until there were nine. The "nights" unluckily tended to become longer with the growing unrestraint of the successful poet, and the ninth luxuriated to nearly 2,500 lines, a little too much even for his warmest admirers.

Wit, courtier, friend and disciple of Pope, Young had been. But Pope was dying, and Young abandoned rhyme, "of which," he says, "the moderns are too fond." Like Thomson a few years earlier, he cast his great poem in blank verse. The work, though not to modern taste, is by no means prosy. It is an eighteenth-century *In Memoriam* by a stricken man, one who knew the worldly world and what he was singing about; and it has ministered comfort to many a crushed soul.

But its high popularity was chiefly due, one fears, to the rising tide of sentimentality, the common fondness for luxuriating in woe at another's expense. It is a pleasure that is always closely associated with moralising, and in the *Night Thoughts* it had full scope and opportunity for indulgence.

In his later life Young seems to have been rather a favorite with the ladies. The Duchess of Portland, the same who as a child had been Matt Prior's "noble, lovely Peggy," was for years a devoted and genuine friend. At Tunbridge Wells, whither he went annually for the waters, he was the centre of a fluttering bevy of women, chiefly blue-stockings, who delighted in his edifying, witty, and genial conversation. No wonder such a man was a warm friend also of the sentimental novelist Richardson, and even went so far in his friendship as a hearty admiration of the novel *Sir Charles Grandison*.

COLLINS (1721-1759)

William Collins—"poor, dear Collins," as his stout-hearted friend, Dr. Johnson, called him—is one of the most pathetic figures in our literature. He came out of the mellow, drowsy old cathedral town of Chichester. After a somewhat wilful academic career at Winchester and Oxford, this lovable, gifted, but dependent lad was thrust into the buffeting turmoil of London to make his living with poetry! There Johnson, sturdily fighting his own way, met Collins, loved, and befriended him. "I knew him," he says, "full of hopes, and full of projects,

versed in many languages, high in fancy, and strong in reten-
tion." Of friends he had a plenty without trying—Thomson, the
veteran actor Quin, the new sensation Garrick, Thomas Warton, and particularly Collins's old school friend Joseph Warton, whose critical ideas, departing from those of Pope, were
congenial to Collins, and found an embodiment in his poetry.
Never capable of sustained effort, he began after three or four
years to fail in body and brain, returned to Chichester when
about thirty, and died there at thirty-eight, prematurely old,
in utter collapse of mind.

Mental disturbance or abnormality of one sort or another
is so common among poets from Swift to Cowper, that historians and biographers have been prone to discover some maladjustment between the times and the poetic imagination to explain it. Thomson finds that "amid these iron times—these
dregs of life," the poet's mind is off its poise;

> the passions all
> Have burst their bounds; and reason half extinct,
> Or impotent, or else approving, sees
> The foul disorder.

And he interrupts for a page the tranquil beauty of his *Spring*,
to set forth the symptoms of this strange poetic disease. Some
wish to see it as a survival of the melancholy that so interested
old Burton. Some discern in it prophetic symptoms of awakening "romantic" wonder and imagination. Whatever the cause
and the significance, the fact remains, and Collins was a pitiful victim.

His verse, of slender amount, is so exquisite that it has waited
long for appreciation. It surely departs from the common ways
and manners of men which so fascinated the preceding generations. It first ventured no farther than the gorgeous East, with
Persian Eclogues, composed in his late teens. Of these one re-
frain persists in the ear:

> Sad was the hour, and luckless was the day,
> When first from Schiraz' walls I bent my way!

But the Orient was already a popular poetic resort, what with the growing eastern trade, and the new vogue of the *Arabian Nights.*

Then Collins left the Orient behind for "Fancy's land," and in his odes and songs—*To Fear, To Simplicity, On the Poetical Character, To Evening, The Passions, On the Death of Thomson, On the Popular Superstitions of the Highlands,* the lovely *Dirge from Cymbeline,* and his brief but touching song in memory of the English dead of the year 1746—in all these, if we can rise with the poet, we enter a transcendent world of Collins's own among "the viewless forms of air," the half disembodied personifications of abstract things, into which he has breathed reality, movement, energy. It is a world of subdued colors, subdued sounds, of twilights and loneliness, of wind and rain; and yet with the magic chiefly of his music, he has released a spell that charms and pleasantly detains us there. Gray said, unluckily over his own signature, that Collins had a "bad ear"! Perhaps the music of Collins was too tenuous, delicate, too much that of the spinet, of muted strings and harps, for the sensual ear attuned to louder and more sonorous cadence. However that may be, it is music that was never heard in English before Collins's time, nor has it since been imitated or reproduced, because it cannot be.

> Thro' glades and glooms the mingled measure stole,
> Or o'er some haunted stream with fond delay,
>   Round an holy calm diffusing,
>   Love of peace, and lonely musing,
> In hollow murmurs died away.

GRAY (1716-1771)

Collins and Gray are so persistently and habitually paired by critics and historians of literature that people often imagine them in literary partnership. As a matter of fact, we do not know that they ever saw each other. Collins's work was finished soon after Gray's had begun; when the *Elegy* appeared his mind was already failing; and Gray was not only deaf to Collins's verse, but sneered at it. In temper they were at opposite poles. They were alike in having produced a slender volume of highly concentrated verse; in writing odes to abstract subjects like Fear, Liberty, Solitude; in being esoteric "new" poets. Hence their accidental association.

Thomas Gray, by testimony of his intimate friends, was proud, fastidious, shy, of small stature, with a manner slightly effeminate, which he purposely exaggerated towards people he did not like. Johnson called him "a dull fellow," but he did not know him. Gray to his few friends was devoted and tender.

He was born in London. His father was a brute. His mother he adored. She had borne twelve children of whom only Thomas grew up, and she kept a milliner's shop, by which she saw him through Eton and Cambridge. At Eton he made a few choice friends for life, notably Richard West and Horace Walpole; at Cambridge he took his studies sullenly, says Johnson. Then came five months of the Grand Tour to Italy by invitation of Walpole. The Alps and the glories of Italy thrilled him. But fellow-travelling is an acid test of friendship, and in Italy some assumed superiority of Walpole's sent the proud Gray home on his own.

The thirty and odd remaining years of his life he spent almost entirely in Cambridge, living as a fellow-commoner at Peterhouse and Pembroke, and later as Professor of History and Modern Languages. He did no teaching, was not well, and was subject to fits of depression or the "romantic" malady. But he read and studied profoundly as his strong curiosity directed him—in classics, especially Greek, in Italian, Old Norse, botany, architecture, painting, and music, until he became without pedantry probably the most learned of the English poets, excepting perhaps Milton. Meanwhile there were periods of sojourn in London near the Museum, excursions to Scotland and elsewhere, forty-mile walks on summer days to be with his adored mother at Stoke Poges. For luckily his heavy-fisted father was dead. She lived to see her son famous, and on her tomb he commemorated her as "the careful tender mother of many children, one of whom had the misfortune to survive her." Not least of his consolations was his poetry.

First are the "odes" on *Spring, Eton College, Adversity,* the *Favorite Cat,* all much in the accepted style, generalized, personified, full of epithets, and moralized, but resounding with genuine music. The *Eton College* is sentimentalized with pity for the lusty young Etonians, "little victims" at their play without sense of ills to come. But the *Favorite Cat*, done for Walpole, with whom the old breach had been healed, shows, as do his letters, that Gray had in him a vein of exquisite fun and wit.

Of all men this sensitive, bookish recluse was appointed by fate to shape the most popular poem in the English language. The *Elegy in a Country Churchyard*, we are told, took eight years in the making; that is, Gray wrote the epitaph perhaps as early as 1742, and had the poem by him for occasional revisions till it appeared by an enforced publication in 1751. To his utter disgust and amazement, instant fame invaded his retirement.

The *Elegy* for one thing happened to be the perfect consummation and flower of a popular sentimentality which had been increasingly active for a century or more. It was a funereal emotion, nourished by the cruder Puritanism, and had flowered in an increasing profusion of plebeian mortuary verse. It had been cultivated more recently by what was called "the graveyard school," whose best known specimen is Blair's *The Grave*. The *Elegy*, it must be said, is a sentimental poem, albeit the finest of its kind. It views the poor country folk at a social distance, feels deliciously sorry for them as it thinks of their obscure life and death, though it scorns the boast of heraldry, the pomp of power, assumes for a fact that there *are* mute, inglorious Miltons, and once at least makes very doubtful sense.

Yet the fact remains that for nearly two centuries no other poem has been so read, learned by heart, recited, quoted, admired, and parodied as the *Elegy*. No poem of equal length has yielded so many familiar phrases. And the secret is not in the sentiment alone, but in the matchless music and cadence of the lines. Gray wisely chose the quatrain of ten-syllable lines, with alternate rhymes, so elevated by Dryden; but Dryden alone could not have taught him the deep sonority and melody of the *Elegy*. It is essentially the music evolved by the rhymed couplet in master hands, and under immediate modulation of the solemn hexameters of Virgil. The music of Latin and Greek verse has in these days well-nigh ceased to refine the ear, but such poetry as the *Elegy,* got by heart, may be commended as a fair substitute to one who would write, or speak, English of the quality once superinduced through the study of the classics.

In the face of his new fame the world was a bit disappointed with Gray's later poems. Two Pindaric odes, *The Progress of Poesy,* and *The Bard,* superb poetical rhapsodies, were thought by conservatives like Johnson to be difficult, obscure, and dull. But the progressives were enthusiastic. Then followed poems more novel still—the *Triumphs of Owen,* out of Welsh lore, and the *Descent of Odin* and the *Fatal Sisters.* This last draws its title from Spenser, but its matter was from an entirely new mine, the Scandinavian mythology. Such pushing out of poetic energies into remote and unexplored regions, regions to be conquered and plundered by the generations of poets to follow, was perhaps the most distinct mark of Gray's originality.

CHAPTER 23

Novels

FIELDING, at the opening of *Tom Jones,* pleasantly avers that the author of a novel is but an inn-keeper, serving an "ordinary" or public dinner to whoever will pay for what he eats: the author is cook as well as proprietor, the menu is human nature in all its varieties, and the cook can succeed only by seasoning it to all tastes. But he observes that his hungriest guests are humble folk, and most relish plain food.

The novel, or "prose fiction," is no doubt "the people's" own absorbing literary form today, and Fielding had already discerned its popular character.

In the history of any literature, prose fiction arrives late, as the arts of writing and reading become more widely common. It subsists on a reading, not a listening public, a public which has after centuries attained a measure of wealth, leisure, and diffused culture. Late in Roman times came the *Satyricon* of Petronius with its episode of Trimalchio's dinner, said to be progenitor of the modern realistic novel. Later came Apuleius's *Metamorphoses,* with the romance of Cupid and Psyche. Not less important were the Greek romances of the fourth century—Longus's *Daphnis and Chloe,* Heliodorus's *Theagenes and Chariclea,* and others.

Conditions in the Renaissance again favored prose fiction. In Elizabeth's England, Greene, Lodge, Lyly, and Sidney, following their Greek, Italian, and Spanish predecessors, indited long romances for the *élite,* while the rising middle class fed fat on Nashe, on Deloney, and on late prose versions of the old romances of chivalry, especially *Guy of Warwick* and *Bevis of Hampton.* The traditional and time-honored plot presented two young lovers cruelly separated by accident or otherwise, and struggling through infinite adventures to final felicity in each other's arms.

With the growing consequence of trade in Commonwealth and Restoration days, the distinction between the appeal of fiction to cultivated and to popular tastes fades out, and prose fiction begins to assume the vitality with which it has grown up, along with democracy, to its present supreme importance.

But though novels multiplied apace after the Restoration, no really eminent figure in England precedes Defoe, whose tales of adventure suddenly attain to a reality generations ahead of their time. It is customary to speak of Bunyan's Christian, of Crusoe and Gulliver and Sir Roger de Coverley, as heroes of fiction. But the first thoroughbred "novelist" is Samuel Richardson.

RICHARDSON (1689-1761)

The middle class demanded him, and fitly enough it produced him. He well deserves his fame even if he did blunder into it. With obscure and informal education he came to London, and rose by merit and thrift to be a substantial, honest printer. A discerning eye, if it had observed the young lad Samuel telling tales to entranced schoolmates, reading them to sewing girls, writing love letters for illiterate sighing maidens, would perhaps not have been so surprised as was Richardson himself when at fifty he set the world agog, and himself on a perch of fame, with his first book.

It was started as a group of model letters for the increasing throng who coveted the graces of polite correspondence; but it turned out to be the story of *Pamela, or Virtue Rewarded*. Pamela, the first servant-maid heroine, is beloved and dishonorably pursued by her employer, Mr. B. But first thwarted, and at last overcome by her virtue, he marries her, and she somewhat unaccountably finds in him the greatest and best of men. Thus Richardson set most British readers frantic with suspense, and dissolved them in lacrimose floods of sensibility, while a few sly ones were laughing in their sleeves. And one loud guffaw, Fielding's parody in *Joseph Andrews*, naturally enraged the blooming novelist of fifty-three, of late only a printer.

In 1747-8 Richardson outdid himself in *Clarissa Harlowe,* eight volumes. Hitherto novels in England were, in a more exact sense, plotless. But *Clarissa* had a plot, and a ghastly tale it is. A young girl, desperate with the threat of marriage to a hateful family-picked husband, appeals to her dissolute lover, Lovelace (Richardson has made the name proverbial). After laying long and vain siege to her virtue, he gains his end by drugging his victim. Clarissa dies in broken-hearted shame, and Lovelace, at least remorseful, is killed by her kinsman in a duel. This from a little, roly-poly, solemn, shy, aging person of sudden consequence. He was idolized by the ladies who deluged him with letters and tears—even such as the case-hardened Lady Mary Wortley Montagu—imploring him to spare the beautiful Clarissa, yet confessing themselves in love with that wicked Lovelace. The novel stretches out in endless epistles between the characters, who are at pains to record every minute shade of their feelings, every tear, every gesture. Nothing is more expressive of the vast stretches of ennui at the time, waiting to be filled with this grand accumulation of sentiment and sentimentality.

To read Richardson through is a feat of endurance which distinguishes few in these days, even of those who write about him. It is enough for most readers to sample his novels, and laugh or wonder at the manners and excessive sentiments which they record—behavior as absurd as perhaps ours will look a century or so hence. But what "shocker" can exceed in boldness the story of *Clarissa?* And, sentimentality granted, few novelists have equalled Richardson in his instinctive sense of the behavior of the human heart, particularly a woman's heart, under stress of strong feeling. He is sometimes labeled the first analytic novelist. Yet his very minuteness in *Clarissa* creates not only tragic suspense, but somehow raises the story by cumulative effect from a mere far-off tale of horror to a universal grandeur not unlike that of great tragedy in any age. If one seeks indirect proof of the novel's power, it is to be found in its influence abroad, in Germany, and in the minds of such age-makers as Diderot and Rousseau.

Richardson's final performance was *Sir Charles Grandison,* embodying the bourgeois idea of the perfect gentleman. The hero enters as a graceful youth of seventeen, "with fine curling auburn locks waving upon his shoulders; delicate in complexion, intelligence sparkling in fine free eyes, and good humor sweetening his lively features." This paragon rescues a pursued heroine from her abductor, and against many competitors wins at last to the foregone conclusion, much delayed by delicacy and sensibility on both sides. At times the author still shows his old power of portraiture and strong emotion, but clearly with this book his work is done.

FIELDING (1707-1754)

It would have been amusing to see Richardson and Henry Fielding side by side. Two men could not have offered a sharper foil each to the other: the one a plump, stodgy, sober, vain, middle-aged little man of business and novelist of sentiment; the other a burly youth of over six feet, strong and heavy, handsome, smiling, friendly, with patrician features, a glancing, humorous eye, and charm irresistible to man and woman alike. It is odd that one so prosy as Richardson should have been appointed to produce literature of sentiment; and that so romantic a figure as Fielding should have made his novels of the actualities of life.

Fielding's blood mingled those of an Irish and a Welsh earl not far back. Lady Mary Wortley Montagu was a second cousin. Yet this aristocrat of genius rejoiced in many of the instincts of the rank and file, toiled and rioted in Grub Street, and out of the wreck fashioned a substantial career in the law, and perennial fame in literature, before he was dead at forty-seven. In this short span he had lived the equivalent of several highly concentrated lives.

He came out of the Somerset country that forms the background of *Tom Jones.* His career began at twelve, when the motherless lad was plunged into the rough life at Eton. At eighteen he had a desperate love-affair with Sarah Andrew, and then came nearly ten years of feast-or-famine existence in London. He had to choose, he said, between the career of a hackney coachman and a hackney writer. So he became "Scriblerus Secundus," and out tumbled burlesques, *revues,* farces, to the number of twenty and odd, loaded with political satire, and roily with the sediment of Grub Street. When they succeeded he spent his money like a drunken gentleman-sailor; when they failed, . . . Once he went over to study at Leyden. At twenty-seven he married the adorable Charlotte Craddock, whom he dearly loved. Ten years of life with this robust, improvident genius, however devoted he was to her, brought her to her end. He twice enshrined her memory—as the heroine of *Tom Jones* and of *Amelia.* At her death he almost lost his reason.

His playwriting was stopped by Sir Robert Walpole's licensing act in 1737. Lord Chesterfield had fought the act in vain. Said he: "Wit, my Lords, is a sort of property; it is the property of those who have it, and too often the only property they have to depend on. . . . Thank God! we, my Lords, have a dependence of another kind." No wonder Fielding idolized him.

Then, at thirty-five, after he had settled to the law, some two years before his wife died, came unforeseen the first novel. He was grinning over the absurdities of *Pamela* and its worshippers, when his irrepressible brain conceived a burlesque, of Pamela's brother, Joseph Andrews, whose impregnable virtue is under siege of Lady Booby. But as the joke developed it grew serious in one respect: the figure of Parson Adams rose under the author's hand to become one of the great portraits of fiction, the gentle, learned, high-minded cleric, unworldly, yet clever of retort, swift of foot, and handy of fist if occasion required.

Among minor works to follow was the account of Jonathan Wild the Great, on the cynical thesis that "a great man and a great rogue are synonymous terms," and that "a man may go to Heaven with half the pains it costs him to go to Hell."

In 1749 came the great novel of the century; some would have it the greatest English novel. Its success has from the day of publication been incalculable.

Tom Jones is on a grand scale, even in the mechanics of its plot, and Fielding controls them with a master hand. The fifty speaking characters, not to mention two hundred or more supernumeraries, innkeepers, hostlers, gypsies, thieves, and such, move in order, enter, and leave just as they should. The half-dozen subplots, which seem irrelevant at first, are picked up at exactly the right time, and drawn closer and closer into the complication with the effect of a gradual, unrelenting convergence of many strands in one knot. The momentum is purposely slow at the beginning, steadily accelerating to the breathless speed of the close, yet never allowed to outstrip the suspense which the author creates about the mystery of Tom's parentage. He manipulates and plays the reader's curiosity with all the devices known to the craft. Even about externals of fact such as time of year, month, and day, or places along the London road which he had often travelled, or notables of the time, such as Beau Nash, Garrick, Hogarth, and Whitefield, Fielding is most scrupulous. Upon every new incident he enters casually, loading it at the end with its importance to the story, and likening the world to a vast machine, "in which the great wheels are originally set in motion by those which are very minute, and almost imperceptible to any but the strongest eyes."

From of old the novel had been generally plotless, a string of incidents and adventures strung on a romance or a journey. *Clarissa* had a plot; so has *Tom Jones,* in which virtually every incident has its logical and indispensable part. To be sure it is the ancient plot of the adventures of two lovers enclosed in the parenthesis of their separation and reunion; but in this man's hand it moves not casually, but with the cause and consequence of real life itself. Indeed, the presentation is such as one might expect from a man whose practical skill had been developed by the stage.

Fielding is ever protesting that he writes history, not mere fiction, that he would exhibit people as they are. True, one encounters many old-fashioned conventions of the trade—for example, the high-flown talk even in love scenes, like the sentimental comedy of the day. Did people really talk like that?

No doubt they affected to. Conventional characters turn up, benevolent gentlemen, shrivelled, sharp-tongued wives and old maids, double-faced villains. There is a good bit too of the thumping, head-breaking slap-stick and mistakes-of-a-night farce made popular by the picaresque novel. But in fiction of every age are mingled conventions and fashions bound to look silly to posterity.

In *Tom Jones* these are mere chaff to the solid truth of setting and character. He who reads is transported to Fielding's England, its country life, villages, roads, inns, London, its people high and low, all abounding with the vitality imparted to them from their creator's strong gust for life in any form. So tireless is that vigor that it overflows into the witty comment on his work prefaced to each book, on no account to be ignored, and charges every shred of the novel's texture with racy wit. Above all it has imbued various of his men and women with the enduring humanity that is universal. Such are Squire Western, Allworthy, Partridge, Sophia, with whom the author confesses himself in love, and Tom himself, whose "life was a constant struggle between honor and inclination," and whose charm was quite as much a disability as an asset. It is this dateless truth which prompted Gibbon to record his prophecy, already half fulfilled, that "the romance of *Tom Jones*, that exquisite picture of human manners, will outlive the palace of the Escorial, and the imperial eagle of the house of Austria."

Tom Jones served to give high sensation to the publication of *Amelia* in 1751. Johnson read it through without stopping, and said that it was the only book which being printed off betimes one morning, a new edition was called for before night. Meanwhile Fielding was busy in the duties of office, serving London as a police court magistrate and commissioner. Though he needed money badly enough, he accepted none of the £500 within his reach as perquisites, but cleaned up organized crime in the city, proposed reforms of the poor law, and had part in the checking of the craze for gin that had been raging for twenty-five years and seemed likely to demoralize the nation.

The high intensity of his life wore out his stalwart frame. With his second wife, a good soul, he said good-bye to his children for the last time, and set out for Lisbon to die. On the way he jotted down his *Journal of a Voyage to Lisbon*, with his old humor, vigor, and truth to life, but with a new gentleness and serenity no doubt long familiar to those nearest him.

There is a generous element of earth and soil in this man, but it is sweet, pungent, and fertile, nurturing the things that grow up towards the light. He has a discerning sense and warm adoration of that which is noble and lovely in human nature, and presents it always in some vital relation to the gross and muddy elements of life beneath it. Critics liken him to out-of-doors, its invigorating fresh air, its daylight of reality, with the teeming earth beneath, and above the enduring sun and stars and sky.

SMOLLETT (1721-1771)

In the course of his *Sentimental Journey* Sterne met, so he says, the grumpy Smelfungus coming out of the Pantheon in Paris. "Nothing but a huge cockpit," he growled. This was none other than Tobias Smollett, M.D., who seems more like a character out of a novel than a creator of both. He was a choleric Scot, bred near Glasgow, where he got some training in physic, which he practised without distinction at various times in his life. Much of his early career he has built into his first novel *Roderick Random*. At eighteen he found himself, like many a fellow-countryman, on the high road setting his face towards London. From nineteen to twenty-six he served as a surgeon in the West Indies, particularly in the horrible campaign against Cartagena; and in Jamaica he loved a creole lady, Nancy Lascelles, whom he in time married, and whom he loved faithfully even when her dowry had faded away.

Again in London, he soon produced *Roderick Random*, a confessedly picaresque or rogue novel after the model of Le Sage's *Gil Blas*. It is a plotless but fast-moving string of wild ups and downs, mostly downs, of the not very exemplary Roderick, who at the end lands in wealth and marital joy. Smollett's texture is coarse and stout, but so were the materials with which he worked, gathered in rich store out of the rough life he had lived since boyhood on sea and land.

This first novel, arriving after Fielding's *Andrews* and just before *Tom Jones*, made Smollett famous at once. Henceforth the picaresque was to be Smollett's mode, enlivened with eccentric and even grotesque characters after the manner of the old humors.

In 1750 at twenty-nine he journeyed to Paris for new material, which he made into *The Adventures of Peregrine Pickle*, more elaborate and picaresque than its predecessor. It is best known for presenting the novelist's greatest portrait, the lovable old salt, Commodore Hawser Trunnion, the precedent of many a grizzled veteran in fiction from my Uncle Toby down. It is Smollett's men that signify—his women are usually grotesques, lymphatics, or frumps, or mere figures of fun.

From thirty-five on for the remaining fifteen years of his life Smollett toiled like a galley-slave, editing the *Critical Review*, the *British Magazine*, and the *Briton*, and organizing the first literary sweatshop of hacks, which turned out universal history, compendiums of travel and geography, translations, and abridgments, in gross. Among his slaveys was one who was soon to outstrip the taskmaster in his art, Oliver Goldsmith. As by-product Smollett produced his novels, *Ferdinand Count Fathom,* and *Sir Launcelot Greaves*, and the while still practised, with great success, the coarser arts of making enemies.

Worn out at last, like Fielding, he sought health abroad, and died in Leghorn. But his tireless pen was busy to the end. Out of these last sick and weary days came his masterpiece, *Humphry Clinker*. It is a series of letters sent home to Brambleton Hall, Wales, by the testy, but kind-hearted Matthew Bramble, his attendant sister, his nephew, his niece, and his illiterate maid, from a tour of England including Bath, London, and Edinburgh. The less conscious the correspondents, the more boisterous is the humor of these letters, and the book abounds in the author's old fertility and vigor of caricature. The "love-interest" is hackneyed and negligible. But amid all the noise and farce for which Smollett had so keen a relish, one feels now and then a certain tenderness and pathos, too artless and unconscious to be sentimental. It associates itself most with the figure of the simple, unworldly Humphry himself, and may be the counterpart of that gentleness which only Smollett's family and intimates saw in him.

Humphry Clinker is for us one of the pleasantest conveyances through the rough, hearty, picturesque, human world of eighteenth-century England. Like all of Smollett, it may be read discursively.

Yet discursive journalist that he was, Smollett was probably more fertile in suggestion to his successors than any other novelist of his time, partly because of his vigor, partly because he is more obvious and tangible. The devotee of Scott, Thackeray, or Dickens will read Smollett with the added pleasure of recognizing parents of various old friends.

STERNE (1713-1768)

Laurence Sterne defies classification; strictly speaking he is no novelist, though custom has so accepted him. It is best perhaps to meet him first in Sir Joshua Reynolds's portrait, which presents a man both inscrutably grave and humorous, looking at you with an eye at once appraising, teasing, disconcerting, whimsical, sensitive. This is one Sterne. The other, at any moment susceptible to delicate and tender, especially amorous, emotions, the painter has not shown; nor any trace of the tubercular illness which slowly progressed from his late twenties to his death at fifty-five.

Sterne found the world sentimentalizing, and fed it more sentimentality; but he also laughed at it and at himself, till it joined him, and thus wiped away its delicious tears. He administered both the sweet syrup and the solvent antidote.

Sprung of good stock, clergy and landed gentry, he loved to call himself Yorick and claim his descent from the jester in *Hamlet*. He was born in Ireland where his father, an ensign, was in service; from him Laurence came by the oddities which his genius turned to high account. From Cambridge, where his tutor wisely allowed him unusual range in his work, as one "born to travel out of the common road, and to get aside from the highway path," he soon became, by his Uncle Jaques's help, prebend of York. That proud, provincial, gossiping, racing, gay, quarreling little cathedral world was his until at forty-seven he burst out into sudden blaze of fame before the great world, to the equal amazement of all concerned. He was chronically and sentimentally in love, with others as well as his wife, who, poor soul, found life with an unpredictable, amorous, sporting parson and genius a disconcerting business. Near York he had good livings, bought land, and incidentally farmed it. "I sat down quietly in the lap of the church; and if 'twas not yet covered with a fringed cushion, 'twas not naked" Thus he amused himself with clerical quarrels, dining about, reading, shooting, racing, sketching, and trips to houseparties, without his wife, at a college friend's "Crazy Castle" on the coast. Here was a good library of Sterne's kind; and between out-door sports and junketing there were literary skits all around.

Out of all this oddly-assorted life sprang up self-sown that oddly-assorted work *Tristram Shandy*. Sterne had finished two little volumes, and was trying it on some guests at the squire's hall, when some of them unaccountably drowsed off. In a rage he threw the manuscript into the fire, whence his host rescued it to the eventual delight of all the world. But it had not only to be rescued, but refused more than once by York and London publishers, revised, toned down, and then in 1760 issued in both cities, to start an unforeseen furore so wide that a letter addressed on a wager to Tristram Shandy, Europe, readily reached the author. For three months he was dined and lionized in London by lords, bishops, painters, actors, and the smart folk generally; young Boswell, not yet known to Johnson, but already an expert in such matters, found Yorick "the best companion he had ever known." Never had such a figure of a parson astonished London. "He is harmless as a child," said Mrs. Montagu, "but often a naughty boy, and a little apt to dirty his *frock*."

The Life and Opinions of Tristram Shandy is less a novel than a sort of literary *revue*. It contains persons and incidents, but no plot. All seems topsy-turvy—the Preface at the end of the second volume just before the hero is born, the forty-fifth chapter before the thirty-eighth, dashes, asterisks, blank pages and chapters, inconsequence that is at once exasperating and fascinating. "I begin," he says, "with writing the first sentence —and trusting to Almighty God for the second." And he declares that if he thought the reader could guess what the next page contained, he would tear it out of his book. Such whimsicality, which looks easy and is so hard, has tempted many an imitator to his ruin.

The book is a richly stocked museum of queer and amusing bits of learning picked up by this collector of oddities from Swift, Burton, the antiquaries, Erasmus, Rabelais, Lucian, and curious freaks of authorship suitably lodged in the library at Crazy Castle. The devoted Shandian pleasantly gathers, as he reads, an ample pocketful of literary small change most useful on occasion.

Sometimes Sterne plays in his wonted manner on the reader's sentimentality. The celebrated tale of Le Fever, the case of wandering Maria piping sadly by the way, almost rise above the sentimental level. But farce and wit and satire prevail even in these tender parts, and the reader is diverted at every turn of the page. For the author rattles on about everything—mortgages, mules, buttonholes, noses, swearwords, critics, hobbyhorses—addressing his readers now and then like a street showman at the corner, and only by apparent accident bringing us to know such worthies as Walter Shandy and his wife, of Shandy Hall, Yorick, Corporal Trim, Widow Wadman, and, great and beloved above all others, my Uncle Toby. That stout, guileless, gentle, straightforward veteran of the wars, living in sober, ingenuous fashion on his memories, has his place among the immortals of fiction, above all the tears and jests of poor Yorick. The portrait is final and complete. As for the rest there is nothing about *Tristram* that, it seems, could not go on as long as Sterne could drive his pen and folk would read.

And during the remaining eight years of his life he did go on with *Tristram,* usually two volumes at a time, issued his *Sermons,* visited London and Paris, and was idolized everywhere. But his overtaxed strength was slowly waning; so was the fashion of "Shandyism," and with it his income. He made long journeys to the south of France and Italy in vain quest of health.

At fifty-three he fell into the most intense of his many morbid passions, for a Mrs. Draper from India, less than half his age, whom he called his Eliza, and who for a time kept sentimental step with him. "I can never see or talk to this incomparable woman without bursting into tears." The *Journal to Eliza*, recently recovered, pulses with a curious and pitiful gush of emotion; yet it doubtless brought the relief of salutary expression in a way that was natural to this supersensitive invalid. As for Eliza, she one day sailed back to her very unsentimental husband in India, never to see Sterne again.

Out of his journeys southward, and this unhealthy emotionalism, mingled with his still lively whimsicality, came the *Sentimental Journey*. It plays upon his casual adventures with any one by the way from Calais to Paris and Lyons, flirtations, amenities, delicate situations, French manners, tears for a poor mendicant monk, for an old man mourning his dead ass by the roadside, for some caged and wretched starlings which Sterne would not release because he could then no longer feel sorry for them, for poor, heartbroken, disordered Maria again—the whole ending in the middle of a sentence. "I laugh till I cry, and in the same tender moments cry till I laugh. I Shandy it more than ever." Sterne had at least discovered a successful trick, and kept up "the business of sentimental writing," as he admits it to be, if for no other reason yet to satirize it and all the weeping world. A month after the *Journey* appeared, he was dead in London, alone and poor. He had his wish of being numbered with the heroes who have died with a jest.

CHAPTER 24

The Days of Johnson

WALPOLE AND LETTER-WRITING

A CENTURY so social, so interested in men and manners as the eighteenth, was of all ages the one to bring to its highest reach the art of correspondence. Through their incomparable letters we enter into more familiar intimacy with the fascinating personalities of that golden age of personality, than by more formal literary means.

The art of familiar letter-writing flourished from Dryden on. With such ancient precedent as Cicero and Pliny, with social and cultural conditions all in its favor both in France and England, this exquisite art engaged the best talents. Swift, Addison, Steele, Pope, Chesterfield, Gray, the novelists, all thought of letters as more than mere messages, and each had his theory of what a good letter should be, and practised the art accordingly.

Indeed the art of correspondence was a matter that concerned all the rising parvenu world, as the origin of *Pamela* proves, and Number Forty of the *Tatler* also, where Steele writes: "There is no rule in the world to be made for writing letters, but that of being as near what you speak face to face as you can."

But the new generation, the generation of Johnson and his friends, with its increase in wealth, sophistication, and the amenities, was able to carry the art nearer to perfection. Johnson, Goldsmith, Garrick, Reynolds, Boswell, Mrs. Montagu, Mrs. Thrale, Miss Fanny Burney, Miss Hannah More, Cowper, attained to skill in various points of good letter-writing which has been the prize-mark or despair of all their descendants. But "the Prince of Letter Writers" is the distinction usually reserved for Horace Walpole (1717-1797).

His father was the great but corrupt minister, Sir Robert Walpole, and Horace suffered the disabilities of such illustrious descent; he was all his life proud of the paternal fame, jealous for his father's questioned reputation, conscious of his own "position," and a bit of a snob. His great delight was Strawberry Hill, his Gothic villa in forty acres overlooking the Thames, a short walk above Pope's house at Twickenham. Here he set up a private press, built Gothic all around, entertained his friends, wrote and printed his own works on painting and royal authors, in which he proved himself a most accurate historian, printed the works of many others, played with his pets, notably Selima, the tabby immortalized by Gray, collected books and such, lived the life of a happy, ailing, bachelor dilettante, and above all wrote his letters.

Of these there are over three thousand in the best edition, written to a hundred and sixty different persons, but chiefly to such old friends as Sir Horace Mann, William Mason, and Lady Ossory. His model, like Chesterfield's, was Mme. de Sévigné; her letters with their spirited lightness of touch seem ever to have possessed his mind, and when he acquired her little ebony writing-cabinet, he would have enshrined it, he says, like a saint's relic, in gold and jewels. Gossip, wit, anecdote, trifles, word-sketches, society, books, doings, comings and goings at Strawberry Hill, gardening, building, all go into the fabric of the letters, and they are never for a moment dull. They are another wide door leading into the spacious and genial interior of the times. Yet as letters they are if anything too uniform in style, too little varied according to that other personality, the man or woman at the other end of the letter; too self-conscious, too aware how good a letter Horace was writing—good enough to be printed some day.

These are not the failings of Johnson's letters, nor of Cowper's, which are probably the best that the age produced. "A letter," says Cowper, "is written as a conversation is maintained, or a journey performed; not by preconcerted or premeditated means."

Snug conservative as Walpole was, yet at sixty he sympathized with the American cause, and at seventy with the beginnings of the French Revolution. He felt the first stirrings of new "romantic" feeling for the despised Middle Ages, set a new fashion with his Gothic building, and wrote up, in a kind of romantic transport that followed a dream, the first Gothic novel and tale of horror, *The Castle of Otranto*. He was at once an exemplar of the ripest Augustan culture, and a prophet of the new enthusiasms.

JOHNSON (1709-1784)

Cowper's remark just quoted points the close kinship between letter-writing and conversation. The sociable age which made a fine art of the one exalted the art of the other. From Swift, Addison, and the *Spectator* on down they talk, think, and write about conversation. But again it remained for the days of Johnson and his Circle to achieve a skill in conversation such as has not been recorded since the time of Plato's Socrates. Most conversation is volatile and loses its savor when removed from its original place and time. Conversation which is self-conscious, aware of being brilliant or "high," is not good. Mere talk is not conversation, Johnson would say; something must be discussed. He believed in it as an interesting game, requiring equipment and technique, most lively and animated when it is a contest for superiority of wit and argument, but happiest when it is "a calm, quiet interchange of sentiments." Conversation may supplement, but cannot take the place of books.

The burly figure of Johnson, born to grapple with whole libraries, his Atlantean shoulders a little stooped as under the burden of his times, is the dominant figure of the century. His was a dynamic genius, imparting its vigor through his writings, but more through his talk. He lacked the poetic imagination necessary to great works of art. It was the talents and imaginations of others that he energized, clarified, and raised to their highest potential. Through Garrick he acted, through Reynolds he painted, through Goldsmith he was a poet, and doubt-less he had his part in animating the work of many others who came in contact with him, such as Burke, Gibbon, Miss Burney, and young Sheridan.

Johnson's conversation was the medium through which he created. Boswell says it roused him to the highest pitch, and in its full glow raised him into another state of being. It cleared the mind of cant, and as Reynolds said, brushed away the rubbish. Not Boswell alone, but nearly everybody who listened to Johnson tried to record his talk. Of this dynamic Johnson Boswell's *Life* is the grand embodiment; there he is at the height of his powers, but he had won to them only through dark and bitter struggle.

The story is familiar, though too often reviewed through Macaulay's distorting lens. Johnson was the precocious son of plain, good folk in noble old Lichfield. His father was a book-seller. Even as a child his dominant power over others as-serted itself. Proud, and poor, he went to Pembroke, Oxford, where he was not wholly submissive. He confessed at fifty-four that at eighteen he already knew pretty much all he ever learned. Poverty drove him home after two years, and there followed some six years in and about Lichfield without plan or recorded event except that he failed as a teacher, and that at twenty-six he married. His wife, a widow twenty years his senior, intelligent but perhaps sometimes a little silly, was his yoke-mate through his hardest years. Her importance to him appears from the awakening of his mind and purpose at mar-riage, and his desperate and helpless grief at her death.

With his pupil Garrick he first arrived almost penniless in London. Garrick leapt to sudden fame on the stage, but John-son toiled on at literature for nearly twenty years before his assured success. He turned out hack-work for Cave's *Gentle-man's Magazine*; *London,* a satire in imitation of Juvenal, as Pope had imitated Horace; parliamentary debates written up from others' notes, taking care "that the Whig dogs should not have the best of it"; the *Life of Savage,* of which he wrote forty-eight pages at a sitting; a tragedy, *Irene,* which later failed; *The Vanity of Human Wishes,* 1749, another satirical imitation of Juvenal, written at the rate of a hundred lines a day; the *Rambler,* a semi-weekly essay in imitation of the *Spectator,* 1750-52, of which Johnson wrote nearly two hundred essays; and nearly thirty essays for the *Adventurer,* 1753. He wrote in hot haste, not enjoying it, but for a living, sitting down doggedly to it, as he would say, since "no one but a blockhead ever wrote except for money." From 1747 on for eight years he wrote as it were with his left hand, while his right was engaged on the great *Dictionary.*

The *Dictionary,* though now absorbed in dictionaries that have superseded it, and though chiefly remembered for a few humorous definitions and the superb letter to Chesterfield, is withal Johnson's greatest work. The richness and number of illustrative quotations gathered by Johnson single-handed from his vast reading, the incredibly short time in which the work was done in the face of distractions, "in sickness and in sorrow," the pungent, racy wit and aptness of the definitions—"Pedantry, the awkward ostentation of useless learning"—the deeply moving Preface—these are among the wonders of this extraordinary work.

Literary patronage and fulsome dedication to the great had, since the time of Pope, been on the decline. It was, however, still practised at times, and the intention had been to dedicate the *Dictionary* to Lord Chesterfield as the arbiter of all refinement. Of this the noble lord had been informed in 1747 by Johnson's *Plan for a Dictionary.* But he neglected the struggling author, and when at last he came in with tardy and somewhat flippant assistance, Johnson indited the famous letter which put dedication and patronage pretty well out of fashion, and spoke for the literature of growing democracy, declaring himself "unwilling that the Public should consider me as owing that to a Patron which Providence has enabled me to do for myself."

With the *Rambler* and the *Dictionary* came reputation, and one by one the new friends who were to lend lustre to the "Circle": Reynolds, Langton, Burney, Goldsmith, and in 1763 Boswell. His pension in 1762, new friends, who soon included Burke and Mr. and Mrs. Thrale, and the founding of the Lit-

erary Club, which dined weekly at a tavern, began twenty years
of comfort and leisure for Johnson, which proved one of the
most brilliant periods in the course of literary history. The
high generating focus of its radiance was Johnson and his talk.
At table, in drawing-room, tavern, coach, nursery, shop, Oxford college, or the highway and byways of Fleet Street, this
long-suffering man of large heart and frame, proud and humble, tender and just, went his unpretentious way, the open enemy
of folly and absurdity, keeping his friendships "in constant repair," loving London as his natural element, hungry for all
that is human, radiating wisdom which was "fresh from life,
not strained through books."

Of the many attempted records of this period of his greatest magnitude, Boswell's *Life* is chief and standard. Therein
Johnson's talk still lives with much of the vigor and personal
energy by which it quickened and clarified other minds in the
moment when it fell from his lips; and thus through Boswell's
magic skill his very voice has continued to invigorate minds
both great and little, as it did in his day.

This infectious vigor of both Johnson's writing and his talk
is their grand characteristic; but it was not a merely physical
energy. It is composed partly of his enormous reading, of both
the bitter and the sweet in his heroic struggle, of his acquaintance with all sorts and conditions of men, of intense
loves and righteous hatreds, of a spiritual warfare within as
desperate as Bunyan's.

Other virtues were common to Johnson's talk and writing.
One is definition. The *Dictionary* made him an expert in definition as a fine art, and all his utterance, after this work is
in full swing in his forties, is filled, in its liveliest bits, with
open or implied definition. In that century of wits he becomes
also expert in wit—"wit that *is* wit, and so appears at all
times," never losing its point. His language too "teems with
imagery" as Boswell said, with racy, homely figure, expressive
of the common mind, not flowery nor peculiarly poetic. But his
language, spoken or written, has the poetic virtue of music. It
is vibrant like strings tuned up to exact concert pitch, and its
very sound carries the listening reader along with it. Perhaps

his own remark best illustrates and summarizes the facts when at sixty-eight he said: "I value myself upon this that there is nothing of the old man in my conversation."

In 1758-60 he turned again to the essay and wrote the hundred numbers of the *Idler,* with a somewhat lighter touch. In 1759, during the week when his mother lay dying a hundred miles away at Lichfield, he wrote off his oriental tale of *Rasselas,* who escaped from the Happy Valley in Abyssinia to seek happiness through the world, and to make his choice of life. As one might guess, he succeeded in neither; but the wise old scholar and poet, Imlac, who went with him, became the oracle of many a respectable English household for years. He is worthy of it, for his talk is made of the same stout fibre as Johnson's. "Do not suffer life to stagnate; it will grow muddy for want of motion; commit yourself again to the current of the world." "To talk in public, to think in solitude, to read and to hear, to inquire and answer inquiries, is the business of a scholar. He wanders about the world without pomp or terror, and is neither known nor valued but by men like himself."

During the twenty great years Johnson wrote less, but talked more. His political pamphlets, and his *Lives of the Poets* (1777-81) he produced in his old fierce and desultory way. The fifty-two *Lives,* short and long, full of his wit, his literary instinct, his flair for human life, show that his province was "the biographical part of literature, which is what I love most."

It is customary to contrast Johnson's talk with his writing, but the difference is superficial and the common virtues intrinsic. It is true that in his earlier manner, that of the essays and *Rasselas,* he reverted from the simplicity of Dryden and Addison to the statelier balance and Latinity of such writers as Sir Thomas Browne. But both balance and Latin diction give his style a kind of architectural dignity and strength in keeping with his vigor of mind, and it is so reinforced with wit and stout Saxon words as to save it from mere grandiloquence. Unluckily it set a fashion, and when donned by ladies, even such as Miss Burney, or by any one of less mental stature than Johnson himself, it is several ridiculous sizes too large. The formality of his manner declines as he grows older, and in the *Lives,* where there is least of it, modern readers will probably enjoy themselves most.

Johnson was not an eccentric—Macaulay has been his worst advocate—but a great human heart and mind, great enough to love, labor, and endure for mankind at large. His ideas about social rank as necessary to civilization are those of a sturdy, self-reliant toiler, who had fought his own battles and those of others, who had met the King on even ground, defied the polite world and captured it, lord and lady, yet never lost his relish for elemental human life. His dislike of America was a hatred of slavery and of exploitation of the Indian. His "hatred" of the Scotch was a prejudice with which he amused himself.

He is often looked upon as the incarnation of the eighteenth century, its wit, its instinct for men and manners, its good sense, its poetic and literary theory, its love of biography, of the town, and its corresponding indifference to "Nature" and romantic mystery. This is but half of the man. He was withal deeply moved by gloomy mountain scenery, by old castles, by the Gothic grandeur of Lincoln, York, and Durham. He loved old romances, and was ever curious about primitive man and society, a valiant enemy of social injustice, haunted by a sense of the invisible world far above mere superstition. More than all he never sank into the spiritual complacency of his time, and his beautiful *Prayers and Meditations* show a heart humble, devout, awed in the continual presence of the Divine Mystery.

BOSWELL (1740-1795)

Though the real Johnson is embodied in his writings, most readers prefer to meet this superpersonality in Boswell's famous *Life of Johnson,* probably the greatest biography the world has ever seen. Men will never agree whether this book owes more of its greatness to its subject or to its author.

James Boswell, of aristocratic Scotch birth, was but twenty-two and Johnson well past fifty, when they first met in the parlor of Tom Davies' bookshop in London. Boswell had always a good deal of the eager and volatile boy about him.

Genial, naive, vain, melancholy and convivial by turns, phi-landering, lazy, eccentric—all this he may have been, but he had high social gifts, and Johnson liked him from the start. One deep instinct ruled him, a passion for acquaintance with great men, which was perhaps but his unsuspected biographical genius asserting itself. Thus he deployed every subtle art, and some not so subtle, to know Hume, Wilkes, Rousseau, Voltaire, and above all Johnson and his Circle. Reynolds's portrait of him shows a rather sensual mouth and chin, but a burning, steady eye from which no human value or eccentricity could escape. Once close to his subject, his ingenuity in calling out all the personal aspects of the man's mind—amusing, picturesque, exalted—is uncanny. He summed up his whole practice when he wrote of his hard-won interview with Voltaire: "I touched the keys in unison with his imagination. I wish you had heard the music."

But Johnson, strong, sensible, steady, animating, high-minded, was what he most needed, and the happy combination was necessary to the making of the greatest biography.

Boswell lived and practised law in Edinburgh, but annually he gravitated to Johnson and London. There he jotted, with astonishing skill and memory, the brilliant conversations of which he was a part, discussed biography with Johnson, got notes from many who had known the younger Johnson, submitted his journal to Johnson's approval, studied his great subject from every angle, in every mood, contact, or setting that he could evoke or devise. One summer (1773), he lured him away to journey amid the primitive conditions of the Hebrides, and Boswell's *Journal of a Tour to the Hebrides*, essentially a part of the *Life*, and in many respects its quintessence, exhibits the most extraordinary manipulation of Johnson against every sort of contrasting social background.

With all his busy ingenuity Boswell had learned from Johnson to be scrupulously accurate, and the *Life* is one of the most authentic books ever written. He ran half over London to fix a date correctly. He studied Johnson till he could reproduce his very tone and idiom and manner of speech.

But his genius included more than mere variety and accuracy, rare as they are. Johnson is the focal point of the thousands of his details. Boswell is never for a moment irrelevant, however strong the temptation; nor does he ever intrude. He is essentially a dramatic artist, setting his scene fittingly, as in Dilly's dining-room, in Strahan's courtyard, at the church of St. Clement Danes, in the King's library, in Johnson's study, wherever; scene and action are merged, and talk moves forward, each person speaking in part, to a stroke of imperishable wit, a flash of personality.

Biography has been written by the English ever since Bede's *Life of Saint Cuthbert,* in the eighth century, but it has not passed through steadily progressive development during that time. Edifying saints' lives or historical lives of great men mark the main tendencies until the Renaissance. But with the new appreciation of the human individual, and the recovery of lost biographers like Plutarch and Xenophon, biography developed both its theory and its art. The seventeenth century with the growing instinct for manners and men yielded lives in nearly all the kinds and methods and purposes of biography that we know. Bacon recognized as distinct the art of biography; Fuller's *Worthies* strove to delight the reader as well as edify him. Walton produced beautiful finished portraits of living reality, yet deeply tinged with his own personal charm. Aubrey gathered in a store of amusing gossip and personal particulars. Bunyan in *Grace Abounding* laid open the inner agony of his soul. Mrs. Hutchinson commemorated her beloved and devoted husband in a way to continue his life among men. John Evelyn composed the highly poetic and emotional *Life of Mrs. Godolphin,* documented with her letters and diary. Dryden conceived biography as revealing the hero "in his undress," and making us "familiar with his most private actions and conversations." We are to be "made acquainted with his passions and his follies, and find the Demi-God a Man."

So Boswell found conceptions of biography and many fine examples ready at hand. He mentions Plutarch and Mason's *Memoirs of Gray* as precedents for his record of conversations and picturesque details, though there were abundant instances in English elsewhere. But his real master was Johnson himself, whose ideas expressed in the *Rambler*[1] and in many a conversation with Boswell are embodied in the great *Life*. Ideals and creative energy Johnson thus furnished for this life of himself; but the artistic imagination, the power of imitation, the selection, the verve, the sense of the picturesque and the dramatic, the warm geniality—these are Boswell's part in this masterpiece of biography, and distinguish it as preeminent.

GOLDSMITH (1728-1774)

The Literary Club, inaugurated by Sir Joshua Reynolds in 1764, began with nine members, including besides Johnson and Reynolds, Edmund Burke, Beauclerk, Langton, Dr. Percy, and Oliver Goldsmith. Goldsmith was then thirty-six, had just won fame with his poem, *The Traveller,* and entered upon his ten last illustrious but uneasy years.

He was born and lived almost half his life in the lovely lap of country near Athlone in the centre of Ireland. There, whether as a child, a youth, or later a lively young buckeen, among the hamlets of Lissoy, Pallas, and Kilkenny West, where his revered father was vicar, the remote, simple, genial, droll life of the region entered deeply into his sensitive and tender heart. For nearly four years he was absent at Trinity College, Dublin, picking up a sort of education as a "sizar," amid menial poverty and odd irregularities.

Then came over a year's "study" of medicine at Edinburgh, followed by obscure wanderings on the Continent, in Holland, France, Switzerland, and Italy. One wonders why somebody did not get from him, and record, the details of his mildly picaresque adventures. Many of them are certainly embodied in his writings, but cannot be detached as facts. *Perhaps* he played his flute or told old tales for lodging in a peasant's hut; perhaps he joined a troupe of barnstormers; perhaps he debated at universities for money—as Johnson said, "disputed" his way through Europe. One thing is sure—the facts cannot be ascertained, simply because a fact, once entered into Goldsmith's genial Irish mind, always became so drenched and dyed in his innocent imagination that not even he could know it for

[1] Number 60.

a fact afterwards. After all the man was a great poet. "Remote, unfriended, melancholy" he may have been at times, yet no one can doubt that his warm Irish heart found an easy if uncertain way along the road, especially among the picturesque oddities of the common life he loved.

After three or more elusive years in vagabondia he turns up in London, drudging with his pen for the slave-drivers Griffith and Smollett, and later for Newbery. What he got he spent in headlong profusion on himself or others. It was a family trait —"this romantic turn," as he calls it. "Whence this love for every place and every country but that in which we reside? for every occupation but our own? this desire of fortune and yet this eagerness to dissipate?" So in spite of fame and friends, his hackwork continued, and had to continue, to the end, writing, editing, compiling, translating, abridging. He really worked himself to death, producing among others a treatise on the Cock Lane ghost, two histories of England, a Roman history, a "Grecian" history, short biographies, of Voltaire, Bolingbroke, Parnell, and one of Beau Nash, a masterpiece, besides *Poems for Young Ladies* and *Beauties of English Poesy*; and in his last year an eight-volume *History of Animated Nature,* about which he knew nothing at first hand. Yet Goldsmith on the Ant or the Crocodile is so entertaining as to disconcert the most insistent passion for literal and scientific accuracy. But however unrelieved his drudgery, no shred of his work is without at least a tinge of his warmth and charm, and his greater works are distinguished by having more of it. "My head has no share in all I write; my heart dictates the whole." His *Enquiry into the Present State of Polite Learning* (1759) is a series of engaging essays on literary conditions of the times. It brought him Percy's friendship. He had found for a short time his special excellence in the periodical essay. Scattered specimens, the *Bee,* and the hundred and twenty and odd letters that comprise the *Citizen of the World,* are no mere imitations of his predecessors, but Goldsmith's own. Old subjects turn up amid the new, and he is humorist, gentle satirist, poet, critic, by turns. Now it is the old Irish bard Carolan that engages us, now a reminiscence of how "our old dairy-maid sang me into tears with Johnny Armstrong's Last Goodnight, or the Cruelty of Barbara Allen"; now queer bodies about town; now the new sect of Methodists; now the stagecoach of Fame in which Johnson, soon to be the author's friend, is a worthy passenger; now a visit to St. Paul's or the Abbey, Vauxhall or Ranelagh; now the oriental craze or the pretentious connoisseur; now a romantic revery on the city at night, anticipating Carlyle.

The *Citizen* purports to be letters written home by a Chinese mandarin from England, whose artless comment touches English foibles with mild satire. A very slender tale of separated lovers helps the continuity of the series, as do two characters, the sensible Man in Black, and poor faded little Beau Tibbs and his wife, who are always trying to keep up appearances. Story and characters obviously grew as Goldsmith went along, and contain the germ of a novel. The device was that of Montesquieu's *Lettres Persanes,* 1721, and Boyer's *Lettres Chinoises,* 1755, from both of which Goldsmith took many suggestions, and he knew also the four Indian kings in the *Spectator,* and Marana's *Turkish Spy* translated from the French in 1687-93. But the *Citizen* is only another specimen of oriental fashions in all directions, which had been chiefly engendered and nourished in great luxuriance by the English version of the *Arabian Nights* about 1710, and the increasing oriental trade. The title too is significant of the cosmopolitanism which was a fashion with some of those who took the Grand Tour, with others a serious philosophic ideal. Says Boswell, recalling his travels: "I am, I flatter myself, completely a citizen of the world."

Goldsmith's fame in his day was founded on his poem *The Traveller,* a cosmopolitan review, like Thomson's *Liberty,* of various countries of Europe, with a grand finale in praise—and criticism—of British freedom. The poem concludes with lines contributed by Johnson, observing

> How small, of all that human hearts endure,
> That part which laws or kings can cause or cure!

It is a true-to-form eighteenth century poem, in couplets, well-ordered, on an abstract subject, fully equipped with moral

sentiments and generalized description. Yet in the almost outworn couplet is audible a new, plaintive, and gentle music; and
the fabric is studded, jewel-wise, with delicate idylls, miniatures of folk life in different lands, done from the life no doubt,
yet shimmering in that unfading light that never was on sea
or land. For Goldsmith ranks with Theocritus and Virgil and
Milton as one of the supreme idyllists.

Even greater power in this kind he puts forth in *The Deserted Village*. Whatever point it made in its time about luxury and emigration, its lasting glory is its idyllism of the village, the dance, the evening out of doors and in, the tavern,
the schoolmaster, the old vicar. Both real and transfigured, as
the best idylls are, they lure the reader on to hunt for their
originals, in a hopeless hope of getting nearer to them. To
Lissoy and other village haunts of the poet, we hurry, only to
be disappointed; and this disappointment is but a proof of the
poet's transforming, sublimating power.

One morning probably in 1762 Johnson was summoned to
Goldsmith, who was in acute pecuniary distress, with no assets
but a manuscript "novel." This Johnson sold for sixty pounds,
and temporarily relieved the situation. What thousands that
manuscript would fetch today no one can say; it was the *Vicar
of Wakefield*.

Publication was delayed till after the author was famous
by *The Traveller*. Perhaps this was lucky, for as a mere story
the *Vicar* repeats many of the old devices of distress resolved by
absurd coincidence. But its eternal values are in its delectable
humors, now roisterous, now subtle, never cheap nor coarse;
in its idyllism, especially of the fourth and fifth chapters; in
a certain grandeur imparted to the whole by the vicar, at once
innocent and wise, unsophisticated yet with a heart close to
all sorts and conditions. Humors, poetic beauty, and grandeur
are so inseparably mingled, that the book abounds in moments that will never lose their effect. Who can cease to delight in Michaelmas Eve at neighbor Flamborough's, with hot
cockles and the amenities of Lady Carolina Wilhelmina Amelia
Skeggs? Or in the family portrait of the Vicar's matronly wife

as Venus, receiving from the Vicar a copy of his works on the Whistonian controversy about monogamy?

The same delicate humors of common life, the same warm intimacy pervade his comedies, especially *She Stoops to Conquer*. No comedy in years, said Johnson, had so fulfilled "the end of comedy—making an audience merry." It never fails to transform a theatreful of utter strangers into a genial and friendly party, everyone wishing he could find himself a guest in the old country house of Squire Hardcastle, who loves everything that's old: old friends, old times, old manners, old books, old wine; or to forgather for a song with Tony Lumpkin at the Three Pigeons and with Master Muggins, who hates anything "low", since "the genteel thing is the genteel thing any time if so be that a gentleman bees in a concatenation accordingly."

The managers, even Garrick, were afraid of Goldsmith's plays. Sentimental comedy, vapid, humorless, sententious, with its stupid elegancies and scrupulous delicacies, so genteel, so squeamish of anything "low," still held the boards. Garrick must have known how silly it was; but business was business, and the public would never accept the humors of Goldsmith's bailiffs and taverns and hobbledehoy and general rural horsiness, however softened by the poet's charm. The *Good Natured Man* had only a qualified success in 1768, and Goldsmith's sensitive nerves were frayed by the wear and tear of theatrical friction. Alone with Johnson after the first performance, he broke down in tears and threw himself upon the stout and comforting heart of his friend. Five years later, after much dickering with the theatres, *She Stoops to Conquer* not only scored brilliantly, but under its human warmth and naturalness sentimental comedy melted and collapsed for ever.

In a little over a year the author was dead. His body lies in the Temple yard, but no one knows the exact spot.

Goldsmith is at once curiously elusive and intimate. The facts of his early life, his wanderings, even his burial-place have generally slipped away or refuse to be facts when he is consulted. Elusive too is the charm of his style and his art. Yet he had vast capacity for friendship, and to no poet has the human heart so warmed in personal affection as to him. Johnson saw

something of the universality of his genius, and therefore refused to write his epitaph in any but a universal language.
And he seems to have realized Goldsmith's transforming power
in recording that, whatever literary form he chose, *nullum quod
tetigit non ornavit*—he touched none that he did not adorn. Said
the Doctor: "Let not his frailties be remembered; he was a very
great man."

BURKE (1729-1797)

Goldsmith, Reynolds, and Edmund Burke made a special
trio of friendship. Goldsmith and Burke, both Irish, were about
of an age, contemporaries at Trinity College, Dublin, and
spent their twenties in obscure uncertainty in London or elsewhere. In personal quality and mind they were poles apart.
Goldsmith's talk often flashed wit, but took little direction.
He went on without knowing how to get off, said Johnson.
Burke's talk flowed in a perpetual stream, the ebullition of a
full mind. "Take up whatever topic you please, he is ready to
meet you." "Yes, Sir; if a man were to go by chance at the
same time with Burke under a shed, to shun a shower, he
would say—'this is an extraordinary man'." Once in illness
Johnson remarked that Burke called forth all his powers:
"Were I to see Burke now it would kill me."

Johnson was a Tory and Burke a Whig. In general Johnson
hated "vile Whigs," and said that the first Whig was the devil;
yet in moral seriousness these men found a firm basis of agree-
ment and friendship. "I can live very well with Burke; I love
his knowledge, his genius, his diffusion, and affluence of
conversation."

He was of greater mental stature than mere orator, or statesman, political philosopher, or critic. So his acquaintances found
him, and so he seems in all his writing. From the page emerges
the tall rather awesome figure, speaking in a voice of wide range,
with winning Irish accent, the language rushing forth in a powerful cataract of ideas, imagery, cadence, homely wisdom, noble
indignations. His chivalric soul was ever engaged in the battle
against oppression and injustice on behalf of Ireland, the
American colonies, English constitutional freedom, exploited

India, or against the violent tyranny of the mob which he discerned in the French Revolution. In condemning the Revolution he was blamed for deserting his party; and so formally he did. But the same grand ideas and motives underlie all his work—whether the *Reflections on the Revolution in France*, or the *Thoughts on the Present Discontents*, or the school-worn speech *On Conciliation*, or the unremitting prosecution of Warren Hastings for misdemeanors in India.

One wonders that such a man missed the distinctions that belonged to him, what he called "the solemn plausibilities of the world." In theory a party man, his mind was too great to submit itself to party. Cleverer and smaller men fared better. His uprightness was a tempting mark, as always, for scandal. Popular indignations are short-lived; but Burke's indignation, based on conviction, did not die, and people were bored as he thundered on. Even politicians knew him as "an extraordinary man," but were perhaps a little afraid of him, sneered at him, and kept him out. All of which, with the failure of most of his cherished causes, embittered him and exasperated his lively temper to untimely outbreak. Yet his capacity for friendship, and his active faith in the cause of justice did not fail.

One reads Burke today for the same qualities that Johnson loved in him. He teems with solid and practical ideas, but they are warm and pulsing with an earnestness and emotion that reinforce their truth. Nothing can be more salutary than Burke for those who still cling to faith in an intelligent democracy. "Those who attempt to level never equalize." "A spirit of innovation is generally the result of a selfish temper." "People will not look forward to posterity who never look backward to their ancestors."

GIBBON (1737-1794)

In 1774 Edward Gibbon was made a member of the Club. His *Decline and Fall of the Roman Empire*, on which his fame rests, had not yet begun to appear. He did not like Johnson, but seems to have kept quiet or talked in undertones when the mighty Doctor was in action. His strut and sneers "poisoned" the Club for Boswell.

The *Decline and Fall* is so identified with Gibbon that it has overshadowed the greatest autobiography in English. The *Autobiography of Edward Gibbon* is a composite work: Gibbon left six brief versions of his memoirs, which his dear friend, Lord Sheffield, skilfully merged into one. Herein he reviews swiftly but vividly his lonely and bookish childhood; his upbringing by a pious maiden aunt; his idle year at Oxford, where the masters stagnated, gossiped, and slumbered amid their undusted tomes in "dull and deep potations," and where, for all his ready money and finery he found himself rather left out. It recounts his long sojourn abroad, his one chilly amour, his vagaries from the Church of England, in which he had formally grown up, into the Church of Rome, thence into the scoffing scepticism so highly fashionable in his day; his uncongenial interval in the militia, his sittings in Parliament, where he silently helped the North administration vote England into the loss of America. These reminiscences he set down within a year of his end.

Two great moments in his life they indelibly imprint on the reader's mind. "It was at Rome, on the 15th of October, 1764, as I sat musing amidst the ruins of the Capitol, while the barefoot fryars were singing vespers in the Temple of Jupiter, that the idea of writing the decline and fall of the city first started to my mind." He was then twenty-seven. The other scene is set at Lausanne nearly twenty-three years later. "It was on the day, or rather night, of the 27th of June, 1787, between the hours of eleven and twelve, that I wrote the last lines of the last page, in a summer-house of my garden. After laying down my pen, I took several turns in a *berceau* or covered walk of acacias, which commands a prospect of the country, the lake, and the mountains. The air was temperate, the sky serene, the silver orb of the moon was reflected from the waters, and all nature was silent. I will not dissemble the first emotions of joy on the recovery of my freedom, and, perhaps, the establishment of my fame. But my pride was soon humbled, and a sober melancholy was spread over my mind, by the idea that I had taken an everlasting leave of an old and agreeable companion."

One may well forget the little, gouty, fat, puckerfaced man-ikin, with a hole for a mouth, too elegant of raiment and manners, constantly tapping his snuff-box, nervously conscious of fame that physically he could not live up to. For clearly his *Decline and Fall* is the work of a man who was in part a poet, gifted with the imagination indispensable to the writer of great history. But he also exercised the humbler virtues of the scholar—painstaking accuracy, tireless industry and devotion, discrimination among authorities. And though his history is flavored throughout with his settled prejudice against Chris-tianity, it still continues to be standard. His style he con-sciously cultivated—"the middle tone between a dull chronicle and a rhetorical declamation." And pleasant it is to review with Gibbon the matchless fading pageant of Rome, borne smoothly and comfortably along on the soft upholstery of his Latinized diction, with the pleasant undulation of its balanced clause and its cadences subsiding easily to their habitual closing use of the genitive case.

FANNY BURNEY (1752-1840)

Early in 1778 appeared an anonymous novel called *Evelina, or a Young Lady's Entrance into the World*. It is a tale of a gentleman's daughter, who after her first season in London is happily united with Lord Orville; but it is highly enlivened with many a compromising accident, with the heroine's danger from the bold advances of the rake, Sir Clement Willoughby, and with plenty of excitement from concealed identities. It was soon in everybody's hands and on everybody's tongue. Part of its success was owing to its suspense and to the mystery of the author, and part to its portrayal of certain vulgar middle-class persons. But its permanent value lies in the portrait of the young Evelina herself, for on that point the author was high authority.

The novel was the work of Miss Frances Burney, then twenty-six, but already an incurable scribbler of tales and verse, which she prudently burned. Her father, Dr. Burney, a musi-cian, and friend of Dr. Johnson, recognized Fanny's hand in the book, but it was months before the secret was out. Mean-

while at the Thrales' fine house at Streatham, where all the
high talents of the day were wont to assemble, Fanny had to
hear her novel praised by Johnson, Reynolds, and various blue-
stockings, till she was all in a twitter of "delicious confusion."

Such triumph led of course to other novels, *Cecilia* in 1782,
and *Camilla* in 1796, but each of less merit than its predecessor, for all the noise they made in their day. Miss Burney,
like most in her times, grew increasingly addicted to the John-
sonian manner, until in her later work, her *Memoirs of Dr.
Burney*, she becomes rather that figure of fun, a Johnson in
petticoats. After Johnson and Thrale were dead and the great
days gone, she served five wretched years in the queen's ward-
robe, was happily married to General d'Arblay, and lived on
till she was eighty-seven, surviving many celebrities of a later
generation, such as Jane Austen, Keats, Shelley, Byron, Scott,
Coleridge, and Charles Lamb. Scott met her once in her seventies, an attractive old lady of blessed memories.

She "journalized" most of her life. Her *Journal*, and her
Early Journal, are not mere records of people and happenings,
but in a measure works of art. At least this is true of the years
immediately after *Evelina*, those years of the high tide of the
Circle. Boswell has given us Johnson as a man among men;
but in the *Journal* he moves among women who are witty,
charming, or at least learned, fascinating them with his wit,
genially playing with the "pretty creatures," and making a
particular pet of "little Burney." In scene after scene almost
ready for the stage the famous cast appears, speaking in person and character—the Burneys, the Thrales, the "blues"—
Mrs. Montagu, Mrs. Delany, Mrs. Vesey, Mrs. Cholmondeley
—"Daddy" Crisp, the King, the Queen, the brilliant new playwright and manager Sheridan, Sir Joshua, Burke, Boswell, and
the leading man through all the best part, her adored Doctor
Johnson.

SHERIDAN (1751-1816)

In the spring of 1777 Johnson proposed to membership in
the Club one "who had written the two best comedies of his
age." These were *The Rivals* and the first comic opera with

original tunes, the progenitor of Gilbert and Sullivan, called *The Duenna*. Perhaps by "best" Johnson meant "successful"; at any rate the author, a lad who never lost his talent for success, had produced both plays at the age of twenty-three, and his name was Richard Brinsley Sheridan. He was of Irish birth, son of an elocutionist and one-time friend of Johnson, grandson of a friend and biographer of Swift. Except for six years at Harrow and his training in law, he educated himself. At twenty he fell madly in love with the sweet and adorable Elizabeth Linley, a singer in Bath, where the Sheridans lived. Parental opposition, wild escapes, pursuits, two duels, a year's delay, all made high romance of the affair. They were at last married and for a number of years lived happily. She died almost twenty years later.

At twenty-four he succeeded Garrick, first as manager and then proprietor of Drury Lane Theatre, and so continued for many years through high and low fortune. His *Trip to Scarborough*, produced in the spring of his election to the Club, failed, though it is a good play; but the same season he brought out what has proved one of the few perennial stage favorites of the English theatre, professional or amateur, *The School for Scandal*. This comedy, and in a measure all of Sheridan's plays, are artificial comedies of manners. The social background of the *School* is not that of the time, but the artificial one of the stage and many a novel since the day of Etherege and Congreve, hard, cynical, witty, and sensual.

Sheridan's matter is made up of old devices; Sir Tunbelly Clumsy, Lydia Languish, Mrs. Malaprop, Mrs. Candour, and others suggest his use of the old humors. The country girl breaking loose in high life is reminiscent of Wycherley. The coward in a fake duel, a weakness for malapropisms, are devices as old as Shakespeare. The famous screen scene and the auction are contrived for stage effect with a mixture of sentimentality, farce, and melodrama. The wit too, brilliant as it is, is contrived, often of smart contrasts. Miss Burney gives a fair sample of Sheridan's wit. They were talking of what Johnson calls "she-poets," and Sheridan remarks, like one of his characters: "A lady should not write verses till she is past receiving them."

Yet these plays deserve all their undying success, for no one ever touched these artificialities so brilliantly before, nor with so much of the magic that wins an audience. The old devices are transformed and rejuvenated by the irresistible, dazzling but likable Irish personality that permeates them, and it is to Sheridan that an audience gives its heart all unawares as everyone did who saw him in the flesh. Two more plays, the *Critic*, a clever literary burlesque in 1779, and *Pizarro*, a tragedy adapted from Kotzebue in 1799, were both well received.

Crowned with stage success and not yet thirty, Sheridan went into politics, where his amazing oratory, his wisdom, his incorruptibility and charm put him in reach of a peerage if he had wanted it. He opposed the American War; he labored for the impeachment of Warren Hastings; he was a power in various movements for reform, such as fair representation in Parliament and the freedom of the press, and threw his last energies into the defence of the country against Napoleon. He enjoyed his popularity to the end. Yet he declined in character through his latter years, and his political hopes were disappointed. He was proudest of his career in politics; but the world thought more justly: his body lies in the Poets' Corner.

CHAPTER 25

Prophets of Romance

CRABBE (1754-1832)

ONE more figure touches the perimeter of the illustrious Circle. It is the poet George Crabbe, whom Burke introduced to Johnson, and whose poem *The Village* (1783) Johnson had applauded and amended in 1781. Crabbe was then a discouraged and almost penniless young man of twenty-seven, who had brought to London only his unproved poetic talents from the dismal little coast village of Aldeburgh in Suffolk. Yet out of that sordid, brutal, humdrum, forgotten corner of England he was to make his poetry. He was moved by his genius to

> paint the Cot,
> As Truth will paint it, and as Bards will not.

Truth and Nature he declared to be his originals, and through painful realities and every-day concerns he would engage the reader, soothe his mind, and stir his sympathy. Which looks like the old sentimental appeal, but in fact proves otherwise. For Crabbe reproduced that of which he had been a very literal part, as child, youth, and grown man. Its grand effect is that of authenticity—too authentic to admit sentimentality.

> Dabbling on shore half-naked sea-boys crowd,
> Swim round a ship, or swing upon the shroud;
> Or in a bcat purloin'd with paddles play,
> And grow familiar with the watery way.

> When tides were neap, and in the sultry day
> Through the tall bounding mud-banks made their way, . . .

There anchoring, Peter chose from man to hide,
There hang his head, and view the lazy tide
In its hot slimy channel slowly glide,
Where the small eels, that left the deeper way
For the warm shore, within the shallows play,
Where gaping mussels, left upon the mud,
Slope their slow passage to the fallen flood.
Here, dull and hopeless, he'd lie down and trace
How sidelong crabs had scrawled their crooked race,
Or sadly listen to the tuneless cry
Of fishing gull or clanging golden-eye. . . .[1]

The Village brought the poet success and patronage, and he was soon outwardly a settled parson, established in various decent livings for the rest of his life. Rough Thurlow found him "as like Parson Adams as twelve to a dozen."

All his life he wrote by natural impulse, and though from time to time he "incremated" a great deal, he has left a goodly store of characters, tales, and village life generally, transcribed in a way to capture the reader and lure him on and on. Under Crabbe's guidance the old couplet with most of its old devices and mannerisms carries one easily along. Humor sometimes mildly satiric, shrewdness, vivid bits of genre painting, genuine story of village and country characters, English every bit, yet with a universal quality—the whole together makes poetry of a high order.

The Village is another of those well-planned, composite arrangements like *The Seasons*. In *The Parish Register*, composed 1798-1806, the old vicar turns the leaves, and recalls the stories, of those whose christenings, marriages, and burials are there recorded. *The Borough*, 1810, reviews in twenty-four metrical "Letters" the folk and institutions of what in germ is Aldeburgh, but "magnified." In 1812 were published twenty-one detached *Tales* of middle or low life. Crabbe confesses that Chaucer is much in his mind. In 1819 came the *Tales of the Hall*, a frame wherein two brothers, after many years' separation, exchange after-dinner reminiscences over the wine,

[1] *The Borough*

and renew their old affections to the delightful length of twenty-two books.

Crabbe's work is in many aspects good genuine "Eighteenth-Century"; yet in quality as well as date it reaches far ahead. Admired by Johnson, Burke, Reynolds, and Fox in its beginnings, it gave keen delight to Sir Walter Scott, and to Wordsworth, who found in it that very immediate contact with elemental human life that he felt necessary to keep one's heart susceptible to moral and poetic influences.

MACPHERSON (1736-1796)

In the van of the "Romantic Movement" are certain more conspicuous figures. Two of these, curiously enough, perpetrated each a literary hoax.

In 1762 appeared in London *Fingal*, an epic in six books, an alleged translation in rhythmic, Scriptural prose from the original Gaelic of Ossian, a shadowy and primitive pagan poet. James Macpherson, a burly Highland schoolmaster, was the "translator," and so ardent had become the curiosity about primitive origins that the book made a tremendous sensation. It told of the fights of the brave Fingal, king of Morven, in defending the Celts from Scandinavian and Roman invaders, against a dark background of mist and cloud and mountain and gloomy hall, with overworked imagery of flower, and star, and fire, and water in assorted states. Romanticists, enthusiasts, Scotch patriots, hailed *Fingal* with triumph as greater than Homer. But men like Gray and Johnson were suspicious, and a controversy arose about the authenticity of *Fingal* and the honesty of Macpherson which has flared and smouldered by turns almost to this day. Macpherson never would, or could, produce the originals demanded by the sceptics. He threatened to flog the outspoken Johnson, and got in turn the famous letter—"I hope I shall never be deterred from detecting what I think a cheat, by the menaces of a ruffian." When all is said, Johnson's surmise comes near the present-day verdict: "He has found names, and stories, and phrases, nay, passages in old songs, and with them has blended his own compositions, and so made what he gives to the world as the translation of an ancient poem."

It is a pity that Macpherson, canny as he was, was not canny enough to tell the whole truth, and claim full credit as the poet. Apart from any question of authenticity, and in spite of Johnson's opinion that anyone could write such stuff "if he would abandon his mind to it," *Fingal* became a fashion and even a furore all over Europe for two generations. It was perfectly in tune with the dark thrills of "Storm and Stress," and was much admired by Napoleon and imitated by Goethe and Byron.

As for Macpherson, amid all the row, and in spite of a pretty irregular life, he made a fortune, was sent to Parliament, and in the end got himself buried in the Abbey, as it happens close to the grave of his old enemy.

OLD BALLADS

Such men as Macpherson, Percy, and the others here grouped as prophets of romance were agents through whom English poetry was to renew its youth by a fresh infusion of native energies. Of these energies none other was stronger or more purifying than those released with the revival of the old ballads. At various earlier times their invigorating touch had been felt by "polite" writers, but now for the first time they may be said to have joined the main current of English Literature.

Everyone knows what is meant by "old ballads"—those stirring, but simple anonymous pieces associated with such names as Sir Patrick Spens, Thomas the Rymer, Barbara Allen, Robin Hood, or with Chevy Chase and the Border. When social conditions favored them ballads flourished not on the Border alone, but everywhere in Europe apart from cities and sophistication; and they are still to be heard in removed regions such as Newfoundland, the backwoods of Maine, and the southern Appalachians. So it happens that the best known English survivors are in the remoter dialect of the Scotch border and the North.

How they originated and developed is still a matter of warm contention among experts. The first recorded English ballad is *Judas* of the thirteenth century, but ballads must have been common before that. The sixteenth and seventeenth centuries produced most of the finest versions that survive, perhaps because the local language was then ripest for the form, and the nameless and inglorious Miltons were not wanting. But some of our noblest specimens, at least in their surviving state, date from the eighteenth century. As the common standards of modern artificial life have reached out and overtaken the art of making ballads, it is slowly dying. Writing and printing tend to arrest its growth. A recorded ballad is after all but a dried specimen. For ballads are song, and live and grow only from mouth to ear in oral circulation.

In the sixteenth century with the growth of London trade, the old ballad of the folk gave birth to an inferior offspring, the ballad of the broadside. It was quickly made up for the trade, on some local or topical theme, and hawked about London for a pittance. And though it occasionally resorted to its parent stock for a tune or a device, it is always shallower, in narrative art, theme, and music. At times of course it rises to a higher quality than mere cleverness, yet it bears to its great original much the relation that the oriental rug manufactured for the trade, in the Orient to be sure, and dispensed by the department store, bears to the genuine Turkish or Persian antique.

A genuine old ballad is at its best great poetry, even to the eye. But no one can fully appreciate a ballad till he has heard it sung to its primitive melody with or without primitive accompaniment. This lyric nature of the ballad is the soul of it, as any reader with a little ear for music may discover by reading a good ballad aloud. As he reads a tune begins to emerge from the words and suggest itself, until he finds himself no longer reading but singing. In this fullest sense a ballad is primarily lyric or song. Its favorite metre, among a goodly number, is what we know in many a hymn and poem as the quatrain in four and three, or common metre.

But the ballad also tells a story. The usual theme is a domestic or semi-private affair in local high life, though a Bible story, a fairy legend, national events, or even a bit of old romance may serve. The moral standards are those of isolated rural society—instinctive, black and white, generous, crude. The poet tells his tale by a highly concentrated dramatic method. He lets his persons speak. He keeps himself and his opinions out of sight. He flashes forth either a series of brief, vivid scenes in dialogue, or one scene so skilfully presented that the listener cannot fail to infer the whole affair, imagining omitted details, scenes, motives; and the audience is thus lured into partnership with the singer.

The famous *Edward* is a dramatic dialogue between a son who has killed his father for the inheritance, and the mother who persuaded him to the act. With even and formal pace of seven successive questions and answers, it advances cautiously, ironically, but inflexibly to the son's wild, remorseful curse of his mother at the end. Within this narrow and regular compass is concentrated matter capable of expansion into a novel or a play. The severe art of *Edward*, with necessary variations, is the art of all the best ballads.

Defects of metre, melody, and motive are bound to appear in these products of the untutored mind. As they circulated they either deteriorated or improved or varied according to the mind and abilities of the transmitting singer. But clearly a conscious art developed, a definite and intelligent notion of what to do and how to do it, handed down by tradition, part professional, part amateur; and this art seems to have been at its obscure height during the great Tudor and Stuart periods, when the English common people were emerging into conscious life.

The old ballads represent a long isolated tradition, uncolored and unwarped by passing events in the great world and by sophisticated literary fashions. Yet long before their chief revival by Bishop Percy they served from time to time as the homely, healthy nurses of polite letters. The elegant Sir Philip Sidney confesses: "I never heard the old song of Percy and Douglas that I found not my heart moved more than with a trumpet; and yet it is sung but by some blind crowder, [fiddler] with no rougher voice than rude style." The cadence, vigor, and beauty of the ballads entered deep into the mind and art of Shakespeare, and of many another country-bred poet. Even to their degenerate offspring in the broadsides English poetry has turned for new life, as in Goldsmith's "Ballad" in the eighth chapter of the *Vicar*, and in Cowper's *John Gilpin*; and Wordsworth was perhaps more susceptible to the influence of the tune and manner of the broadside ballad than to that of the genuine folk-ballad. But names like Addison, Gray, Burns, Wordsworth, Coleridge, Scott, Keats, Tennyson, Rossetti, make a list of imitators which is enough to prove the potential of romance and art stored in these high examples of genuine folk-song.

Collecting is a sophisticated practice, and was necessary to a general sophisticated appreciation of the ballad. In their day John Selden and Samuel Pepys made large collections of broadsides; but the collecting and publication of the old ballads did not begin till the eighteenth century. The first really serious instance was the book known as *Percy's Reliques*. Of all the publications of scholars and antiquaries which were fostered by, and in turn nourished the growing interest in the Middle Ages, none wrought an effect so deep and wide as this.

PERCY (1729-1811)

Thomas Percy, an Oxford man, eventually Bishop of Dromore, in Ireland, was by nature a literary antiquarian. He was of an age with Burke and Goldsmith, and a beloved member of the Circle. In 1765 he published the *Reliques*, a curious assortment of songs and ballads, some no older or more out of the way than Lovelace and Ben Jonson. Some were broadside ballads from collections in the great libraries like that of Pepys. Many of the "reliques," however, were Scotch and Border ballads set down from oral recital, but chiefly taken from a battered and neglected folio manuscript of about 1650, now famous as "Percy's Folio," which he stumbled upon and rescued from a maid who was using the precious leaves to kindle the fire.

Among his illustrious helpers were Goldsmith, Garrick, Thomas Warton, and the poet Shenstone, author of *The Schoolmistress*. And though old ballads had not been wholly forgotten, and were sometimes imitated, yet this collection made the world at large again familiar with such classics as *Chevy Chase*,

Battle of Otterbourne, Sir Patrick Spens, Edward, Edward, Sweet William's Ghost, and *Barbara Allen's Cruelty.* Percy "improved" the ballads, yet did not impair their power to generate new poetry. The extent of that power one may guess from Sir Walter Scott's boyhood reminiscence of his first encounter with Percy's volumes. It was under an old platan-tree in the garden at Kelso, and so rapt was this lusty lad of thirteen that he forgot his dinner. He went about shouting the ballads to his schoolmates, and saved his scant shillings till he could buy "unto myself a copy of these beloved volumes, nor do I believe I ever read a book half so frequently, or with half the enthusiasm." His own greater *Minstrelsy of the Scottish Border* would hardly have been compiled, had it not been for the inspiration of this book.

But in many subtler ways its influence entered into English poetic diction, both simplifying and invigorating it, and helping to release it from some of the artificialities which after Dryden and Pope had become a habit. So Wordsworth, who knew, declared in his epoch-marking Preface to the second edition of the *Lyrical Ballads.* Pointing to the influence of the *Reliques* in Germany, he adds: "For our own country, its poetry has been absolutely redeemed by it. I do not think that there is an able writer in verse of the present day who would not be proud to acknowledge his obligations to the *Reliques.*"

CHATTERTON (1752-1770)

Almost under the vast shadow of the rich old Gothic church of St. Mary Redcliffe in Bristol lived a lad named Thomas Chatterton. For generations the man of the family had been the sexton of St. Mary's, but now, out of its poverty, the family unawares brought forth a poet. The boy was reticent, but not difficult, and early became preoccupied in his loneliness with the glories of that "wonder of mansions," the church, with the rich emblazonry and carved tombs that carried him out of his lonely life into a glorious world of romance. Some old chests in an upper chamber of the church had been broken open, and the wealth of manuscripts which they contained were scattered about. Small Thomas could not, or would not, learn to read till some gorgeously illuminated letters caught his eye. To him they were another glimpse of his dream-world, and he rushed in and was soon reading everything he could seize. He was then eight. Locked in his attic retreat he pored over the old vellums, copied them, imitated them, read Chaucer, Spenser, history, hunted out old words in old dictionaries, and thus reared about himself the unsubstantial house of fancy that was his undoing.

At eleven, probably as a joke, he fooled first a schoolmate, then a teacher, with his remarkable poem *Elinoure and Juga*, written on a piece of old yellow parchment. The game was too easy. He then hoaxed a worthy burgher, who was delighted when "ancient" proofs of his noble ancestry were shown him. This doubtless was more fun yet. At twelve or thirteen young Chatterton's imagination entertained the figure of a fifteenth-century priest, named Thomas Rowley, alleged confessor to William Canynge, an old Bristol worthy. Under this name and those of other old poets, including Lydgate, he wrote his Rowley poems. From the age of thirteen for nearly four years he slaved as a lawyer's apprentice, devoting nights and Sundays to antiquities, old histories, and the sciences, and to composition. Meanwhile he grew into a proud, reticent, but prepossessing youth, loyal to his family, with extraordinary eyes like a hawk's, that had "fire rolling at the bottom of them." At length he threw himself upon London. Horace Walpole, at first receptive, grew cold when Gray detected the Rowley disguise. Exactly four months in the summer of 1770 Chatterton slaved as a hack for the periodicals, and was in a fair way to distinguish himself. But pay was small and slow; he was too proud to accept help, and after starving three days, he made a miserable end of himself. He was not yet eighteen. Gradually the whole bitter story came to the ears of the literary great. They read his poems. Collected editions began to appear, and a warm debate over their authenticity lasted some years.

In our present knowledge a mere tyro can point out the proof of their counterfeit. Spenser and his imitators, rather than Chaucer, were Chatterton's metrical originals. Of Middle

English as a living tongue he had no conception. Odd and picturesque old words, quaintly spelled, archaic mannerisms reminiscent of Shakespeare, Spenser, or the old ballads, mingled with eighteenth-century phrasing and cadence, made up the artificial medium in which he worked. But the result is an occasional exquisite piece like the *Balade of Charitie*, or the *Mynstrelles Songe*, or the *Bristowe Tragedie*, which with their delicate music and fine but artificial texture suggest that rare imaginary world of medieval romance in which Chatterton took refuge from a world he simply could not comprehend. Quite apart from his error and his tragic fate, his genius, though its renown was unfulfilled, has been the wonder of men from Johnson down, and the object of poetic tribute from Coleridge, Keats, Shelley, Rossetti, and many others. Chatterton also is a poet's poet, for his energies passed into the making of many a subsequent poem, some of which, like *The Ancient Mariner*, are more famous than any of his own.

COWPER (1731-1800)

In the mild, lush country bordering the slow-winding Ouse above Bedford lies the quiet old village of Olney. Like enough to many another English village and countryside in most respects, Olney is distinguished by having become incarnate in a poet and immortalized in his poetry. William Cowper in his natural self was a cheerful, amiable, sensitive, fun-loving, companionable man, who disliked notoriety and loved above all things his friends and the simple comforts of home. Such in human terms was Olney, and no place and poet were ever more closely identified. His *Letters*, which some prefer to his verse, are often regarded as the finest letters in English. Warm and pleasant they are with the quality of this lovable person and place, where nothing ever happened and nobody ever came. "I love talking letters dearly," he wrote, and such were his—artless, unconscious, imparting abundant life to matters of no apparent consequence, about his chickens, hares, birds, spaniels, his garden, village folk and gossip, household incidents, walks, weather and seasons—but never dull nor humdrum in Cowper's hand. Happy the youngster that has grown up with

John Gilpin in his ears, and Caldecott's pictures in his eye, until he could appreciate the subtle as well as the more riotous humors of that poem. Perhaps he also has known the graver notes of *The Loss of the Royal George*, and the exultation of "I am monarch of all I survey." Through such approach one comes to enjoy the best of Cowper's verse, to distinguish it from much that is ordinary, and to know the real and natural Cowper.

For the deranged Cowper, periodically benighted with despair and mania, is not the real Cowper; and interesting as his case may be, it has drawn too much attention to itself. His terrible fate seems not less tragic when one considers that nowadays his mental illness and its agonies might have been averted. He was a man of naturally strong religious sense, averse to responsibility and ambition, of resolute will, yet curiously dependent upon the society of fine women, and of men coarser and more ordinary than himself.

Such a man was the Reverend John Newton, rector of Olney, one time master of a slave-ship, now touched with the new religious enthusiasm of John Wesley—narrow, masterful, well-meaning. His autobiography, *The Authentic Narrative,* is a fascinating human document, and some of his hymns are still sung. He can hardly be blamed for Cowper's madness, but he may not have been the great help to the poet that he tried to be. During the association of the two, Cowper himself wrote many of the Olney hymns, such familiar ones as "God moves in a mysterious way," and "O for a closer walk with God."

But like many another, Cowper was dependent upon women not only for inspiration, but for the very impulse to write verse. When recovering from a terrible mental attack in his early thirties, he chanced to fall in with the Unwin family, father, mother, and son. Mrs. Unwin, seven years his senior, mothered him; and after her husband died she and Cowper lived on together almost thirty years in Olney and the neighborhood. Her quiet, loving ministration not only sustained him and helped to heal his illnesses of mind, but when he was almost fifty encouraged him during a period of convalescence to write verses. At this late point began his active work as a poet, in the form of eight long satiric poems on abstract subjects, such as *Table Talk, The Progress of Error, Hope, Conversation, Retirement*—in all nearly six thousand lines; and all in couplets in spite of his declared aversion to Pope's "mere mechanic art." Dull in stretches they are, yet as he criticises the times, now and then comes a passage of the same humor, life, and warmth as in his letters.

These poems were forthwith published and attracted little notice. But the lovely, vivacious Lady Austen had meanwhile come to Olney, settled in the vicarage at the bottom of the garden, and urged Cowper to go on composing. A subject? "You can write upon any—write upon this sofa!" Which he did; and thus began *The Task*, in six books entitled *The Sofa, The Time-Piece, The Garden, The Winter Evening, The Winter Morning Walk, The Winter Walk at Noon*. It is cast not in couplets, but in easy blank verse, and follows the same casual course as other long poems of its age, turning naturally from topic to topic. Its subject is really the poet's life at Olney, and the fabric is starred with delicately wrought idylls faithfully done from life, such as a walk by the Ouse, the grounds at Weston, a thatched cottage; figures like Crazy Kate, the gipsies, the arrival of the stage-coach at nightfall, a woodsman plodding through deep snow, a cloudless winter's day, evening at home:

> Now stir the fire, and close the shutters fast,
> Let fall the curtains, wheel the sofa round,
> And while the bubbling and loud hissing urn
> Throws up a steamy column, and the cups
> That cheer but not inebriate, wait on each,
> So let us welcome peaceful evening in.

Cowper's is an art exquisitely pitched between the transcendent idyllism of Goldsmith and the literal reality of Crabbe. His diction and style swell at times, but only with an undertone of humorous ingenuity. With a trace of a smile he sings of the sofa-leg's "twisted form vermicular," and calls the compost pile a "stercoraceous heap"; and his Miltonic grandeurs are not to be taken seriously as are Thomson's. To Cowper poetic composition was not an agony, but a "pleasure in poetic pains," pursuing the fleeting images with fit terms that "pencil off a faithful likeness of forms," and tingling with the mild excitement of arranging them in right order. These

> Are occupations of the poet's mind
> So pleasing, and that steal away the thought
> With such address from themes of sad import,
> That lost in his own musings, happy man!
> He feels the anxieties of life, denied
> Their wonted entertainment, all retire.
> Such joys has he that sings.

But when *The Task* was published in 1785 Cowper was already famous. It happened as suddenly as it did to Byron. One evening, some three years before, Lady Austen had cheered him with a tale of one John Gilpin. Next morning he had ready a rough draft of the famous ballad. It was published by Mrs. Unwin's son, and all England was soon rehearsing it with roars and chuckles. In his darkened old age it was the one poem Cowper could not bear to hear.

New friends crowded to the rescue; and one old one, Lady Hesketh, sister of the woman whom Cowper would once have married, spent herself in vain attempt to save his reason. At fifty-nine some one sent him a picture of his mother, whom he had lost at the age of six. None of his verse is more moving than his lines on receiving it. Always helpless without a woman's affectionate care, her death had begun for him the acute miseries of maladjustment to the rough life of Westminster School and the rougher life of London, to unsympathetic relatives and the hopeless business of making his way.

More than thirty years had passed before his finding of Mary Unwin saved him, and what she came to mean to him found utterance in his poem, twenty years later, *To Mary*. For the rest there is a blank-verse translation of Homer, translations of Milton's Latin poems, and many short occasional pieces on his pets or such amusing incidents as fill his letters.

When his gay and gentle spirit came at last to a quiet end of his long struggle with madness, his devoted young friend,

John Johnson, who had seen him safely through the final dark days, beheld on his face a look of "calmness and composure mingled with holy surprise."

BURNS (1759-1796)

No English poet has been in greater danger of becoming a mere myth than Robert Burns. His humble birth, his sudden fame, his irresistible charm, his many affairs with many women, his conviviality, his good looks, his wit, his dignity and self-possession in any social conditions however remote from his own, the frown and neglect of the world at last, his early end, the whispered gossip that sprang up immediately after, the idealized romantic portrait in every print-shop—all these particulars variously combined or distorted have resulted in notions of almost anything but Burns as he was. The patriotic Scotch have reserved the right to an opinion in the case, but when Scots honestly differ as widely from each other and the reality as do Carlyle and Stevenson, the actual Burns is not easy to come by.

Recent research has proved and disproved much. Burns was not a besotted inebriate; he drank no more than young Sir Walter Scott, never in secret, nor in the morning, nor so as to interfere with his duties, or inconvenience his family. He grew up in a homespun society, stiff with social rank and convention, inflexible in certain standards, but more lenient in matters of whiskey and the sexes than most of his critics and biographers. Burns never deserted the women who had loved him, nor disowned or neglected the children they bore him.

It is a mystery how a country so dour, so bleak, so gray and barren as Scotland should fascinate the rest of the world as it does, and hold the hearts of its people in patriotism that is a proverb. Yet amid its austerities are places where one may come into intimate and warm contact with Nature as almost nowhere else on earth. Like country, like people—morally and religiously austere, inflexible, inscrutable, canny, yet on occasion tender and warm and understanding of heart as no other, full of sensible fun, loyal, dependable, home-loving, winsome. Such are the Scotch. This mystifying Scotch charm of contrasts underlies Burns's portrait of his father in *The Cotter's Saturday Night*, and it enters largely into the make-up of the poet himself. But in him it is modified and heightened by extraordinary genius.

The father, William Burnes, genuinely religious, not merely theological, believed in education as a means to character. So Robert, his eldest, was hungry for schooling and books, and found a way through dull text-books to literature such as Allan Ramsay's *Tea Table Miscellany*, a repository of Scotch verse, to Addison, Pope's *Homer*, Gray, Shenstone, Spenser, Shakespeare, Sterne, and the fashionable novel of the hour, Mackenzie's romantic *Man of Feeling*. Not least was a collection of letters by the best epistolary hands of Queen Anne's time, on which Burns modeled his somewhat formal prose style. His schooling was scant but Scotch, and he turned it to account as a genius does.

Born at Ayr, for his first twenty-seven years he lived the hard life of an unsuccessful farmer's son in and near the small market towns of Ayrshire. An old nurse had filled the child's mind with tales and songs of fairies, witches, warlocks, kelpies, and such, to which he ascribed the awakening of his first instinct for poetry. He was from early days on the search for anyone who could sing, especially young women; and though to his grief he could never learn to carry a tune with his voice, he seized and retained old songs accurately, words and music, in his extraordinary memory; and these rich folk-songs of Scotland were the basis of his greatest poetry. It was his habit, he tells us, to whistle an old air over and over, until his intense sentiment of the moment dictated words for the tune; and thus it is that his songs are lyric in the purest sense, and the tune lies just under the surface of the words. In fact, a song by Burns, lovely as it is in the mere reading, will not yield its full beauty till it is sung artlessly by one who is master of its proper tune and of the dialect. He is a belated instance of the rare, spontaneous lyric outburst of the ballads and Elizabethan song.

Naturally most of the songs are love songs in various moods, happy or sad, simple, obvious, vigorous, natural, but above all tuneful. Never are they morbid. Much of their sweet tenderness they owe to the Lowland dialect, and of this Burns has made most artful use. He varies it in amount from moment to moment, now more, now less, so that it comes and goes like living color, according to the passing thought or feeling. His magic skill in making a song may be realized by observing how he wove the matchless "My luve's like a red, red rose," out of shreds of three indifferent old songs.

Burns is often exalted as a poet of Nature, but not because he held any subtle or profound philosophy of Nature, or in any special sense interpreted Nature. Subtler than thought, however, is the way in which he has fused his feelings with the obvious things in the world about him—flowers, birds, trees, and especially running water—until natural objects reveal their vigor and glory, otherwise veiled:

> In gowany glens thy burnie strays,
> Where bonnie lasses bleach their claes;
> Or trots by hazelly shaws and braes,
>   Wi' hawthorns gray,
> Where blackbirds join the shepherd's lays
>   At close o' day.[1]

No poet had hitherto regarded Nature and rural life with the intimate scrutiny of Burns. He was a part of it. He was known to leave plow or scythe and lose himself in long fits of staring at some wee thing. Where others had depended upon more or less detachment to produce idyllic effect, Burns's exuberant vitality, his tender heart and humor, transfigured everything he touched.

He is famous by his songs, but he found freer personal scope in his other poems—his marvellous idylls, *The Holy Fair* and *Halloween*, and his superb satirical epistles, warm with affection, to his friends—to Lapraik, Smith, "Davie" Sillar, and others—the *Address to the Deil, Death and Doctor Hornbook.* In these is the personal Burns, his riotous fun, his racy wit, his prehensile eye, his Scotch granite morality, his whole-souled scorn of formalism, hypocrisy, and corruption, his warm hu-

[1] *On Pastoral Poetry*

manity, his deference to instinct as higher authority than cold reason, his pride, his prejudice against rank, which hardly concealed his own longing for distinction, and his weaknesses. Yet all turns to poetry, and goes dancing to the infectious rhythm of traditional Scotch tunes.

Through these poems Burns becomes again almost incarnate before us—his powerful stooping farmer's figure of five feet nine, his big hands, his innate dignity, his strong-featured Scotch face full of sunshine and shadow; not the idealized face by Nasmyth or Raeburn, but of the homelier miniature by Reid, which Burns himself preferred. Yet one's attention gravitates inevitably, as in his day, to the eye. Walter Scott, a youth of fifteen, once saw Burns in Edinburgh:

His person was strong and robust: his manners rustic, not clownish; a sort of dignified plainness and simplicity. . . . There was a strong expression of sense and shrewdness in all his lineaments; the eye alone, I think, indicated the poetical character and temperament. It was large, and of a dark cast, and . . . literally *glowed* when he spoke with feeling. . . .

Burns was by no means an untutored genius. The Scotch poets Ramsay and Fergusson were his idols, and through them and the folk-song that he so much loved the genius of northern poetry for centuries back was brought down to him. Various English poets were early accessible, and his verse abounds in reminiscence of such as Spenser, Pope, Shenstone, Goldsmith, Young, Gray, and others.

The year 1786, when he was twenty-seven, was a crisis for Burns. His offer to marry Jean Armour was refused. He came near emigrating to Jamaica in disgust. In July his first book, the now priceless "Kilmarnock Burns," appeared. In October Mary Campbell, "Highland Mary," to whom he was betrothed, died. In November he left provincial Ayrshire for the first time on a triumphal journey to Edinburgh, where for half a year he was exploited as the ploughman poet, and critics who hailed this child of Nature showed how far their sincerity went by trying to "polish" his homely verses. He made friends, saw the world, enlarged some of his ideas, but did not increase his poetic power, already at its flood. He knew well enough how much all the furor was worth, and his heart was too stout to be broken by Edinburgh. Yet it spoiled his beloved Ayrshire for him. These years, 1785 to 1788, were his most abundant in poetry, though the old fire continued to flash with diminishing frequency to the end.

Through friends he took a farm near Dumfries and a post in the excise, and there established Jean Armour, now his wife, with her fast increasing family.

Burns's strong sympathy with the French Revolution brought him into sharp clash with the rock-ribbed local society, and for all his poetic celebrity he was almost ostracised. All his adult life he had suffered increasingly from nervous depression, and latterly from "rheumatic fever." His case has recently been diagnosed as a progressive disease of the heart. In debt, with the life-long habit of failure haunting him, he wasted away and died in 1796, only thirty-seven years old. Yet, not long before, when an associate's daughter had beguiled him with an old nursery tune, there arose on its plaintive cadences one of his most moving songs:

> O, wert thou in the cauld blast,
>   On yonder lea, on yonder lea,
> My plaidie to the angry airt,
>   I'd shelter thee, I'd shelter thee. . . .

BLAKE (1757-1827)

Even more removed from the main stream of literary culture than Burns was his contemporary William Blake. Yet Blake was born and lived most of his life in London.

Of late, a century after his time, the interest in Blake has risen almost to a cult, though it is pretty much confined to esoterics and collectors. His very mystery is fascinating—this cockney hierophant, an engraver by trade, who educated himself, since formal education he held "the great Sin." Obscure, visionary, content with the few good friends who helped him and dimly understood him, he was ever cheerful and genial, with the far light of his joyous mystical vision always in those eyes that looked beyond and above the smoke of human "civilization."

Blake's vision was not the occasional, memorable ecstasy of Richard Rolle, or Vaughan, or Wordsworth, or Shelley. It was with him all the time. When a Philistine compared the setting sun to a gold guinea, Blake was in a fury, for what he actually saw was the angels of God ascending and descending through its splendors. As a child he saw angels walking among the haymakers, and the face of God through the window.

It is easy, and perhaps not quite sane, to call this insanity. Perhaps it was a transcendent sanity. To Blake the spiritual world was the real world, contradicting the stupendous falsities on which man has set his perverse heart. For, as he saw it, this world has gone entirely bad, civilly, artistically, and religiously, with its codes, creeds, conventions, laws, manners, rules, rites, and traditions. It can recover only by regaining the steady vision of spiritual realities—like Blake's—and reviving the primal instinct of love, inherent in us, but stifled by the centuries. Such love is elemental, pure, trustworthy, the only way back to Eden and goodness. In which Blake anticipates now Shelley, now Wordsworth and the host of protestants against civilization to this day.

Blake's handling of these matters underwent changes in the course of his life. Sometimes in the vast prophetic books so-called of his later years it is shadowed forth in a symbolism and mythology which he created by a stupendous feat of his own almost unaided imagination; sometimes he flounders along uninspired without knowing it; sometimes he rises into a pure serene of burning sunshine free from shadows, and his poetry possesses us for the moment in its clear, limpid, strong simplicity, like the clean morning air of high mountains, from which we will soon again descend by force of habit to "the smoke and stir of this dim spot." Blake is never doctrinal nor philosophical, but immediate.

Like Michelangelo, Rossetti, and Morris, he was a double artist—uttered himself both in picture and song; but in Blake picture and song were as one compound medium. Almost from the first he published his poems by engraving them in a setting of pictures. These pictures he colored by hand with rare water-color hues, especially reds and pinks and yellows. He also taught his good and faithful wife how to help him in the coloring. Thus there were few original copies; some of his works were never even issued. As it happens, his power with pencil and brush is less generally convincing in the embellish-ment of his own poems than in his superb illustrations of *Paradise Lost*, and particularly of the *Book of Job*. His best verse is full of vigorous draftsmanship, of his peculiar warm and flaming color, as well as of exquisite and seemingly artless melody, and his pictures often have the power of suggestion that belongs more to music and poetry than to painting.

Poetry, and for that matter all art, consists in a certain inter-fusion of material things with spiritual energies. Blake com-manded spiritual energies enough to make him one of the greatest of poets, but with him the interfusion was usually not complete; he is therefore sometimes incomprehensible, some-times even absurd. Such, in spite of laborious and enthusiastic study by certain modern mystics, is the case with the prophetic books, especially *Milton, Jerusalem, America,* and the *Book of Thel*, the *Book of Urizen*, the *Book of Ahania*. Cloudy with Ossianic or oriental imagery and splendor, often Biblical in their rhythms and language, at times they settle and clear into passages of noble power and grandeur. Blake no doubt be-lieved that they were obscure only to people stupefied by the evil human habit of tradition and convention. Yet what would Chaucer or Milton or Byron have said?

But in his earlier work, his *Poetical Sketches*, 1783, *Songs of Innocence*, 1789, and *Songs of Experience*, 1794, the interfu-sion is more successful, and it is no wonder that poems such as *The Lamb, The Tiger, Infant Joy, The Little Black Boy* are well known. Their limpid simplicity is too dignified ever to have been affected. Blake, this childless man, is not "singing down" to children; his voice is tranquil with the calm of "that im-mortal sea," in Wordsworth's *Ode*, over which we as children are brought to this prisonhouse of life, and across which Blake views in cloudless weather the eternal verities. Thus it is that the lovely and ringing simplicity of these poems is not a matter of study and the file. It is better than that. But its high state is unstable, for without full inspiration it lapses towards the inane.

But the usual Blake was the fighting Blake, fighting the evils of human oppression of mind and spirit. And he fights with the sense of triumph always about him, surrounded by the cloud of spiritual witnesses and champions. Amid the strife of the various prophetic books there are, as we said, moments of poetic tranquillity in which his vision clears so that other men may catch it with him. Such are the exalted lines in *Milton*, through which England in her troubles has found her voice again. Set to music by Sir Hubert Parry, they have been thundering with new hope through street and cathedral aisle since the Great War:

> And did those feet in ancient time
>   Walk upon England's mountains green?
> And was the holy Lamb of God
>   On England's pleasant pastures seen?
>
> And did the Countenance Divine
>   Shine forth upon our clouded hills?
> And was Jerusalem builded here
>   Among these dark Satanic mills?
>
> Bring me my bow of burning gold!
>   Bring me my arrows of desire!
> Bring me my spear! O clouds, unfold!
>   Bring me my chariot of fire!
>
> I will not cease from mental fight,
>   Nor shall my sword sleep in my hand,
> Till we have built Jerusalem
>   In England's green and pleasant land.

PART SIX

ROMANCE AND LIBERTY

CHAPTER 26

Mysteries and Visions

"ROMANTICISM." Though readily manipulated and applied by classifiers and labellers, the term hardly admits of definition. Romanticism has been said to consist in a passionate sense of mystery, "half veiled and half revealed," in a disregard of cause and effect, in partial knowledge plus intense curiosity. But there is danger of making it too definite a matter, of sharply distinguishing certain poets and periods as "romantic" from others that are not. Perhaps all poetry is in some measure romantic; perhaps without romanticism poetry cannot be poetry. *Beowulf*, the Knight's Tale, Spenser, Marlowe, Shakespeare, Milton, are all in important ways romantic. Even in Dryden, Pope, Johnson, not to mention Thomson, Gray, Goldsmith, Cowper, occur moments of deep and excited sense of mystery which are romantic. Are we not, then, wrong to distinguish between poets who are "romantic" and poets who are not? Should we not rather remark the differences in degree of their romantic quality?

Love between men and women, with its passionate quest and adventure, is always romantic. So is any passionate inquiry. We even talk of the romance of Science, of Wall Street, or matters equally of fact. Inquiry and expansion raise the romantic temperature, and all through the inquiring and expanding eighteenth century one may feel, quickening and increasing, those impulses, interests, and curiosities that culminate in what is commonly called the Romantic Movement.

The Romantic Movement is but a part of the vast emotional transport that rose and swept over Europe as the eighteenth century passed into the nineteenth, and has not yet wholly spent itself. Sometimes they call it the Return to Nature. In politics it produced the French Revolution, and democratic movements generally; in English religion it brought about the Methodist or "enthusiastic" revival, and such religious emotionalism within the Church of England and without as burned down to the "evangelical" cinders of the next century. The interest in civilized men and manners progressed to a keener sense of the mere human being, humble, or primitive, or suffering, and gave rise to vast humanitarian reforms, of prisons, of slavery, of slums—reforms still going forward in full momentum.

Strong and romantic curiosity about unexplored parts of the earth, about periods of the past not hitherto understood, about the mysteries and beauties of Nature, about man in his natural state, assert themselves from Dryden on with increasing power. The Orient, from Collins's *Persian Eclogues* and Addison's *Vision of Mirza* to Fitzgerald's version of the *Rubáiyát* of Omar Khayyám, is romantically exploited in literature. The wonders of America,

> Where wild Oswego spreads her swamps around
> And Niagára stuns with thundering sound,

where Susquehanna invites Coleridge to found his utopian Pantisocracy, where Campbell's Gertrude of Wyoming in her "deep untrodden grot" smiled or wept over Shakespeare, were still matter of romance.

Remote times even more than remote places yielded romance, and the Middle Ages, long neglected, glowed deeper and deeper with romantic gloom and splendor. Gray dealt with

Scandinavian myth, Johnson and Walpole took unaccustomed delight in Gothic architecture, and Gothic romance and the tale of horror could not do without a medieval castle. Finer cases in point are Chatterton, Coleridge's *Christabel*, Keats's *Eve of St. Agnes*, or Byron's *Manfred*. But the high priest of romantic medievalism is Sir Walter Scott, in both his novels and his poems, and the Middle Ages continue "romantic" through Tennyson to Morris, though their romance is now fading in the fierce daylight of modern research.

Poets also awoke to a new and romantic sense of ancient Greece, a sense different from that of Petrarch, Marlowe, or Milton, romantic as that was. This new Greece is a bright, picturesque land of Sappho, Plato, and the theatre, the air vibrant with the music of a perfect language, a world glorious with living sculpture that embodied the Platonic ideas of the Good, the Beautiful, and the True, a world in which every man enjoyed perfect freedom through self-knowledge, revelled in philosophy, and breathed the wine-like air of that wide expanse

> Which deep-browed Homer ruled as his demesne.

English poets from Cædmon down have always been sensitive to "Nature," and in many early instances have poetized natural objects with much beauty and insight. But they have usually dealt with Nature as in a subordinate if intimate relation to human life. Through the eighteenth century, however, poets, like painters, more and more view Nature as something apart and in herself. Pope, Thomson, Collins, Cowper, Burns, Wordsworth represent a kind of succession or development of the romantic appreciation of Nature, to its culmination in Wordsworth, through whom the poetic worship of Nature has become a kind of cult.

But Man himself, who, in his cultivated state, had especially fascinated the generations of Dryden and Pope, grew more and more romantically fascinating in his natural or primitive condition. Since the early voyages of discovery and the days of Montaigne, Spenser, and Shakespeare, literature had cherished a fond belief in the Noble Savage, unspoiled by the vices and luxury of civilization, instinctively aware of God, and instinctively behaving like a gentleman. And they fell inevitably into the romantic paradox that such a state of society was happier, freer, and essentially more civilized than ours. As Dryden says of the English,

> They led their wild desires to woods and caves,
> And thought that all but savages were slaves.

From such ideas in English writers Rousseau, on French soil, compounded the high explosive that blew up in the French Revolution.

Johnson, to be sure, was not deceived by them. "No, Sir," to Boswell, who loved to bring up the subject, "You are not to talk such paradox; let me have no more on't." But the paradox, like any paradox with an element of truth in it, continued to grow more fascinating, romantic, and ominous; and with it grew the poetic fascination of man on the humbler levels of society, especially the peasant, who naturally seemed closer to Nature, and therefore purer, freer, and more dignified than other men. Indeed as Nature and Genius were identical in many minds, men were always expecting a great "natural" genius to rise out of the masses. Such expectation joyfully hailed the advent of Stephen Duck, the thresher-poet; of Ann Yearsley, the milkmaid-poetess; of James Woodhouse, and Bloomfield, and Blackett, poetical cobblers; and Henry Jones, the poetical bricklayer; the tuneful pipemaker, Bryant, and the singing butler, John Jones—pleasantly enrolled in Southey's booklet on "Uneducated Poets." Gray crowned his great *Elegy* with an epitaph to a mute inglorious poet of Nature. Faith in the "poet of Nature" persisted through many a disappointment, until at last it triumphed in the glorious coming of the inspired peasant, Robert Burns.

He it was who sang

> Gie fools their silks, and knaves their wine,
> A man's a man for a' that.

It was only a thrilling sentiment for many, who, without thinking, have turned it into mere cant. But many others, realizing the burdensome centuries of special privilege, bigotry, and oppression behind them, exulted in the plain truth of man's intrinsic worth as an individual, his natural, inherent virtue. It was the romantic truth which was to make him free, and they wrote, reasoned, and sang it on every hand in every key: political liberty and happiness through personal and individual freedom.

All through the eighteenth century one sees signs premonitory of these liberating ideas. With the stout championship of Pope and Johnson literature declared its independence from patronage, and threw itself upon public support. The writer became free and self-dependent, and survived or perished by his intrinsic merits.

But with this new freedom the man of letters almost invariably had to endure struggle, poverty, and lonely misery of neglect, or, as Johnson said, "the hiss of the world against him." It was perhaps the stress of this readjustment that caused so much of the "romantic malady" or mental disturbance already observed by Thomson. As Burns said: "There is not among all the martyrologies that ever were penned, so rueful a narrative as Johnson's *Lives of the Poets*." The weaker men, Collins, Smart, Boyse, Savage, Cowper, Chatterton, went down under it. The stronger, Thomson, Gray, Johnson, Goldsmith, Burns, Blake, Shelley, Byron, though singed and battered, held out by sheer force of genius and character and conviction. In all cases it was a war between the individual and the conventions of organized society, political, or religious, or economic, or social, rising to highest intensity in the romantic poets. In all of their works the issue is either latent or plainly operative.

Such passion for freedom was bound to find new subjects, new forms, new metres in vast variety. The couplet was retained, *if* retained, merely as one of many possible forms, not *the* form, and most poets welcomed freedom from its restraints. The old "rules" were dead letters. Greek, medieval, Renaissance lore was ransacked for material. The sonnet, the Spenserian stanza, the ballad measures, and other early metres were revived, and these and blank verse rose to an infinite range of new music hitherto unimagined.

Behind and beneath all this romantic revival, this return to Nature, lay a philosophy. The philosophy of common sense, whose apostle was Locke, was no longer adequate. By stages of scepticism men had thought or felt their way past it to a sense of the deep and awful mysteries of man's mind, of Nature, of whatever lies just beyond both. It was the very time for a revival of the mystic doctrine of Plato, and for certain conceptions embodied in the philosophy of Kant. Shelley is full of Plato, and the others often take on Platonic hue when perhaps not wholly aware of it. This romantic movement, this revival, was after all but one of the crises in the closer and closer scrutiny of Nature which had been going on for some seven centuries. Thinking men, and, in consequence, society, had been repeatedly disturbed by the discrepancy between what they learned from tradition—Biblical, Christian, Aristotelian— and what Nature in its largest sense, on closer and closer examination, had to tell; and the rift widened periodically through persecution and the desperate endeavor to reconcile the two authorities—an endeavor which has not even yet reached fulfilment. Almost every century saw a crisis in the contest. Through the seventeenth century the struggle between the authority of the new science or Nature and the authority of religious tradition was especially acute. By the eighteenth, Nature and Science seemed to have won the upper hand, but complacence now gives way to awed and romantic sense of mystery as unsuspected depths of Nature reveal themselves.

Through remote and unfamiliar places and times ranged the passionate, dreaming curiosity of romance. It peered into mysteries of Nature hitherto unrealized, into mysteries of man's life and mind, his intrinsic qualities, his primitive and elemental worth and beauty. It declared itself intensely for the freedom of the individual spirit from all the trammels that social oppression had woven about Man through the ages. It stirred itself thenceforth to active humanitarian enterprise in a thousand different ways—and still stirs us—for the physical and moral benefit of mankind.

Such are various manifestations of the "romantic" spirit which is to pervade not only the poetry of Wordsworth, Shelley, and their generation, but indeed all later English poetry to this moment.

The excitement of the Romantic Movement has betrayed us into the habit of calling it a revolt, and sharply opposing it to an imaginary eighteenth century of "rules," complacency, special prescriptive poetic language and style. We must not forget that the movement called romantic was but an extension of eighteenth-century interests and curiosities into regions which were unforeseen, and that new discoveries, as usual, look more like revolt than they really are.

The romantic poets all begin with the poetic tradition of the eighteenth century, and in many instances carry it on with modifications, into their work. There we may at any moment find the couplet, the personifications, the epithets, the generali zations, the "poetic" diction, and innumerable phrases reminis- cent of the poets from Dryden on. The odes of Coleridge are full of Gray, Scott compiled monumental editions of Dryden and Swift, and Byron considered Pope the "most perfect" of English poets.

But new discoveries, as well as old traditions, are necessary to new poetry, and the major prophets of these discoveries, Wordsworth, Coleridge, Scott, Byron, Shelley, Keats, each made his own; and with such independence that they were often at sharper variance with each other as to what constituted good poetry than they were with their eighteenth-century pred- ecessors. No one of them wholly approved of another's poetry, and their disapproval was often devastating. A poem more scathing and more entertaining than Byron's *English Bards and Scotch Reviewers*, about contemporary writers, has never been devised.

CHAPTER 27

Older Romantics

WORDSWORTH (1770-1850)

WILLIAM WORDSWORTH, though not the most popular, is often recognized as the greatest of his group. Like all other romantics, he is strongly independent, and preoccupied with his own mind and feelings, and like Milton, has much to say about them. His longest poem, running to fourteen books and nearly 8,000 lines, is *The Prelude or Growth of a Poet's Mind; an Autobiographical Poem*. It is surely "a self-watching subtilizing mind"; but psychology was then new and fascinating even as a poetic subject, and the story of the "Growth" is punctuated with less conscious moments of higher poetic intensity, when the poet recalls times especially in boyhood of rare intimacy with Nature and penetration of the mystery of life.

Besides the *Prelude* and many shorter poems, Wordsworth's best work includes *The Excursion*, in nine books, setting forth tales and instances of country life as exchanged between three men. He planned another long poem in three parts which, together with *The Excursion* as Part Two, would have been called *The Recluse*, on "Man, Nature, and Society." *The Recluse* he compared to a great Gothic church, with *The Prelude* as an ante-chapel, and his shorter poems as "little cells, oratories, and sepulchral recesses." No one will regret the unfinished structure. Like the *Faery Queen*, or Beauvais Cathedral, it embodies as it stands the best the builder had to give.

Wordsworth's poetic discoveries were in the region of Nature that lies immediately about us, and in the lives and characters and humble arts and objects that are in closest touch and alliance with Nature. Other poets had already dealt with these matters—Thomson, Gray, Goldsmith, Cowper, Crabbe—and Wordsworth learned from them; but his originality lay in the delicate intensity and penetration and passion with which he observed and felt and interpreted Nature in his verse.

He was born at Cockermouth on the edge of the Cumberland lake region, of an old middle-class family long established in those parts. The country is wild and beautiful, and had for generations been peopled with sturdy independent farmers and shepherds, close to the soil, and comparatively free from the feudal restraints of English life elsewhere. It was just the world to nurse the genius of Wordsworth.

He had been a rather ungovernable child, and as a boy ranged like a wild animal over the country, in that tacit understanding and close conspiracy of boyhood with Nature that mystifies one's elders, and in mature retrospect puzzles the man himself. As a child, he lost his mother, and as a boy, his father. His school days at Hawkshead, on the milder Esthwaite Water, were filled with those memorable "spots of time," moments in Nature, that haunt the memory of any sensitive child brought up in the country: once when he was skating at twilight with his mates; once when he stole a boat and the looming mountains frightened him with his guilt; once when the hooting of the owls that he had stirred up with his own hootings suddenly ceased, and the sound of a distant cataract rushed in upon him in the silence with a strange intimation; once when he waited on the misty road for the horses to take him home for the Christmas holiday—that vacation when his father died. These and many more "spots of time" recollected in after years, touched with the poet's mature imagination, flamed up into his finest poetry, to reveal unsuspected poetry in the world close at hand and rouse many a fading memory in the minds of his readers.

Not until he was separated from this intense and happy boyhood world could he begin to realize its significance. After his first year at Cambridge its meaning began to dawn upon him. One vacation, returning home over the mountain from a night of dancing, he saw the sun rise "in memorable pomp."

His heart was full; he made no vows, but vows were made
for him,

> that I should be, else sinning greatly,
> A dedicated Spirit.

But there followed years of confusion and uncertainty between seventeen and twenty-seven—two more years at Cambridge, summers at home, visits to glamorous London, a tour
of France and Switzerland just after the Revolution. Then
came at twenty-two the momentous visit of nearly a year in
Orleans, Blois, and Paris, his warm friendship with the young
French officer Michel Beaupuy at Blois, and his love affair with
Annette Vallon, whose daughter by Wordsworth appears as
the "dear child" in the sonnet, "It is a beauteous evening,"
written ten years later. With his usual intensity the poet, like
other idealists, was heart and soul in sympathy with the Revolution, and saw the new and perfect world just at hand. He
would even have taken some active part, but lack of funds sent
him home.

Three unsettled years follow, before the great period begins,
including the publication of *An Evening Walk* and *Descriptive
Sketches*, those curious blends in rhymed couplets of the old
manner and the new.

Of all these troubled years the *Prelude* tells the engrossing
story; but it should be read in its first impassioned form, written close to the events, though unpublished till 1926, not in
the version to which Wordsworth reduced it in old age when
he was no longer a great poet.

In France his experience with the Revolution had awakened
in him a new sense. His quick sympathy with Nature was extended to include human life, at least the men, women, and
children who live in unsophisticated poverty or simplicity
close to Nature herself. He had read what most progressive
men of the day were reading—Rousseau. Rousseau called for
a new society of equality reared in place of the existent one, a
simple, individualistic society based upon the natural and elemental goodness of man; and he proposed an education
through experience rather than discipline. Such proposals have

determined our modern political and educational ideals more than those of any other single man.

During his obscure years from twenty-three to twenty-five Wordsworth was in London from time to time and associated with the circle of William Godwin in lively but not very conspicuous propagation of the new French radical and revolutionary ideas. Godwin's book, *An Enquiry Concerning Political Justice,* though in some respects allied with the philosophers of yester-year, Locke and Hume, demanded a society freed from vested interests and creeds, in which each individual man should have equal and full opportunity. Wordsworth's poor tragedy *The Borderers* and his poem *Guilt and Sorrow* show traces of Godwin.

But profounder and more stable influences were at hand. After long separation he and his beloved sister Dorothy were joyfully together again. Sweet, guileless, tender, devoted, strongly emotional, alert in eye and ear, she was herself a poet in all but the gift of song, and, like many another woman, she joyfully gave herself up to be a large part of the poet in the man she adored.

> She, in the midst of all, preserved me still
> A Poet, made me seek beneath that name,
> And that alone, my office upon earth.

The rest of Wordsworth's life they lived together, even after the poet's marriage. But Dorothy was, of all the world, for his ten most productive years, the one person essential to the poet. Her journal admits us to their intimate happy life day by day, and the process by which much of his poetry came into being.

At Racedown, a farm in Dorset, brother and sister settled for nearly two years, about the time when Wordsworth first encountered that other shaping influence, Coleridge. Strong affinities and imperative needs in both men brought them into closest friendship, and the Wordsworths went to live in the mansion, Alfoxden, to be near Coleridge at Nether Stowey in the Quantock Hills of Somerset. A charming mild region it is of little round hills and wooded ravines and old villages.

quite unlike the Lakes. Here the two men endlessly walked and talked, and "wantoned in wild Poesy," until together they evolved the famous *Lyrical Ballads* (1798). To Wordsworth the lovable and communicative Coleridge gave abundantly of his enormous reading, and under the stimulus of sister and friend Wordsworth's power of song came into its season of fullness.

The two years at Alfoxden were followed by seven months in Germany, whither Coleridge went to learn the new German philosophy and criticism, while Wordsworth wrote verse which he could as well have written elsewhere. The next year, the poet's thirtieth, brother and sister took Dove Cottage, at Grasmere, among the Lakes, near the original boyhood fountains of poetry in him, and Coleridge followed to live at Keswick, twelve miles away. In 1802 Wordsworth married Dorothy's friend Mary Hutchinson and five children came in rapid succession. At Dove Cottage dwelt the Wordsworths for some eight years. But with the increasing family larger habitations were necessary, until in 1813 Rydal Mount, a fine house overlooking the lake from the hillside, became the poet's home for the remaining thirty-seven years of his life.

The *Lyrical Ballads* in 1798 had included Coleridge's *Ancient Mariner*, and Wordsworth's *Simon Lee, We are Seven,* and *Tintern Abbey*. A new edition in 1800 included *Michael* and Wordsworth's famous preface in which he has recited his poetic creed. But let us be ever aware that his poetry was first conceived under strong emotional pressure exerted by life and Nature upon his imagination, and that his statement of what poetry should be was set down in cooler afterthought. It was not according to a theory, but under immediate sense of the poetic that he composed. Nevertheless he describes his own poetic effect better than another could. He insists on the supreme importance of intense emotion, so intense in fact that in the moment of it composition is impossible, and becomes possible only when the emotion is "recollected in tranquillity." Even so, Dorothy tells us, the great calm of *Michael* and other poems was not attained without such "vast expense of emotion" as brought on pain and suffering.

Furthermore the emotions necessary to poetry are less clouded and restrained in the incidents and situations of common life, and the language of common men contains more poetical vigor than the gaudy, empty, inflated style into which "modern writers" had fallen. Which any one conversant with the racy phrase of intelligent country-folk knows well enough. And if as Coleridge observed, Wordsworth did not in his verse actually employ the idiom of common men, yet through his long and familiar intercourse with his Cumberland folk he developed a simple style stripped of adipose eighteenth-century rhetoric and sinewy with the vigors of an ancient common speech.

By the same token the healthy human mind is perfectly capable of emotional excitement without the application of "gross and violent stimulants," and the more susceptible it is, the higher the type of mind.

But we all have a measure of contempt for emotions which we cannot feel. The anthropoid stevedore scorns the tears of the homesick emigrant; and many even devoted lovers of Wordsworth cannot quite attain to adequate emotion, let alone a straight face, over Peter Bell and his good and gentle ass, or the chills of Harry Gill, or the "drunken pleasures" of Betty Foy on recovering her lost idiot son.

> Yet, the gods approve
> The depth, and not the tumult, of the soul;

and the capacity for deep feeling in response to the elemental tragedy or joy in humble or familiar lives, and to

> a sense sublime
> Of something far more deeply interfused,
> Whose dwelling is the light of setting suns,
> And the round ocean and the living air,
> And the blue sky, and in the mind of man—

these form the basis of highest poetic pleasure, of wise and happy living, and sound character. And the fruits of such feelings in action and character redeem them from stagnating as mere sentimentality.

Hence Wordsworth's poems on humble life, such as *Michael*, show an unusual adjustment of focus. Instead of dwelling, as a sentimentalist would, upon the pathos of separation of father from son, or, like the cheap moralist, on the perils of bad companions in the big and wicked city, he touches these matters almost with careless indifference, and throws his whole poetic power into the figure of Michael, grand but broken in the tearless grief of old age.

In the *Prelude* at length, and in *Tintern Abbey* with much higher concentration, he has traced the course from boyhood of such development in his own soul.

At twenty-three, just at the end of his most turbulent years, Wordsworth had first seen Tintern Abbey on one of his many rambles afoot; five years later he again passed that way. Meanwhile, reinforced by the companionship of his sister and Coleridge, his great powers had come into harmonious play, and on the road up the lovely Wye valley he composed the great *Lines*. From the glad coarse animal pleasures which he felt as a boy in the open, through the dizzy raptures only five years back, when he raced wildly over the mountains, and waterfalls haunted him like a passion, and mountain, rock, and wood were an appetite, on to this moment he has toiled, till he can now discern through Nature the still, sad music of humanity, and realizes in it

> A motion and a spirit that impels
> All thinking things, all objects of all thought,
> And rolls through all things.

Hence in Nature thus apprehended he finds, as any sensitive soul may find after him,

> The guide, the guardian of my heart, and soul
> Of all my moral being.

From this point follow plainly enough the *Ode to Duty*, and the *Character of the Happy Warrior* in or after 1805, and the glorious *Ode on Intimations of Immortality*, which was in course of composition from 1802 to 1806. In the *Ode* he clings passionately to every remnant of those childhood flashes, when the glory of Nature startled him with shocks that afterwards seemed like reminiscences of a better world in which he had dwelt before he was born, with the assurance, if a man can hold fast to it, of his return thither after this life.

It is clear, then, what place in all this belongs to his old huntsmen, his leech gatherer, his grand figure of Michael, his Ruth, his poor Susan and his solitary reaper, his tale of poor Margaret, his children, his country weddings and funerals, his animals and homely accoutrements. The "simple" Wordsworth is a fiction sustained by Byron's satire. Truth to tell, he is one of the most subtle and difficult of poets, which may account for the sharp division of his readers into worshippers and scoffers. Like Milton he sought "fit audience though few."

From his French days the poet had taken keenest interest in public affairs, and England's wars with France awoke in him a statesman's concern for the political health and ills of his country. In 1802 the sonnets of Milton, which Dorothy read to him, inspired his first sonnets. In succeeding years he wrote some 375 altogether. Most of these are local and occasional, but the finest are the earlier patriotic ones, rebuking his countrymen for their greed and their loss of humane imagination. Such of them as "Milton, thou shouldst be living at this hour," and "The world is too much with us," sound the soul-animating strain and trumpet notes of their great Miltonic original; but the natural music of Wordsworth's sonnets is more akin to the sustained and intimate quality of the cello.

His was an independent genius, not prone like Milton or Spenser to reflect other literary influence. But the romanticists often found delight in seventeenth-century writers. The *Ode on Intimations of Immortality* had a precedent in Vaughan's *Retreat*. *The Character of the Happy Warrior* bears a not wholly accidental family resemblance to Hall's "character," *The Valiant Man*. His friendship with Coleridge had led him to books of travel and wonders in far countries. Plato too was a part of his Cambridge reading, and the Platonic cast of *Tintern Abbey* and the *Ode on Intimations,* not to say the im-

plied Platonism in much of his poetry, can hardly be so for-
tuitous as some seem to think.

After the completion of the *Excursion* in 1813 Wordsworth
continued to compose during the thirty-seven years that remained; but the divine fire flashed less and less frequently.
Disillusioned with the ways of revolution and reform, he settled
back into complacent acceptance of the best things as they
are. At seventy-three his achievement was honored by appointment as Poet Laureate.

Luckily perhaps, Wordsworth has never occasioned a furore.
He has fathered no "school" of style as did Chaucer, or Spenser,
or Milton. But his power has gone forth more subtly and profoundly into all places than if he had. Everywhere we are
more sensitively aware of Nature and of humble life than
before his day; they give us more pleasure; our eyes and
ears are trained to observe them and discern the beauty that
lies in them, and the new power is one of the most precious
gifts to our times. From Carlyle to Robert Frost the agents of
this new sense and vision have been innumerable; but their
greatest pioneer, and one to whom they owe more than they
are probably aware, is Wordsworth.

COLERIDGE (1772-1834)

Of a June day in 1797 a young man of twenty-four came
awkwardly bounding across the field at Racedown to greet
Wordsworth and his sister. His gait, as he himself said, suggested "indolence capable of great energies." His thick lips
and open mouth, since he could not breathe through his nose,
and his fat, pale jowl were anything but prepossessing. But the
high forehead, and the eye, more, as Dorothy observed, like
the poet's in a fine frenzy rolling than any she had seen, made
manifest to all beholders the exalted genius sent to dwell in
this alien body.

> O capacious Soul!
> Placed on this earth to love and understand,
> And from thy presence shed the light of love, . . .
> Thy kindred influence to my heart of hearts

Did also find its way. Thus fear relaxed
Her overweening grasp; thus thoughts and things
In the self-haunting spirit learned to take
More rational proportions.[1]

Striking was his contrast with the tall, gaunt, cliff-featured
mountaineer who met him, looking more farmer than poet.
It was a moment of high import for English poetry, since the
triple alliance thus begun was necessary to some of its noblest
verse.

From the beginning Samuel Taylor Coleridge found himself in a misfit world. Always a dreamer, though often of
splendid and noble dreams, he was, as a lad in Devonshire,
and in school at Christ's Hospital, at bay among the other
boys, and took refuge in ravenous reading, especially the *Arabian Nights*, in dreams, and in his own awareness of his exceptional powers. The terrible master Boyer, of whom he has
left an amusing reminiscence, stood for the earlier school of
sense in poetry, and made an impression upon the mind as
well as the body of this boy, whose extraordinary memory
and imagination the old pedagogue was forced to admire.

At Cambridge Coleridge made two attempts to escape from
what seemed to him an intolerable world of debts and maladjustment, but which was really himself. One was a brief
and hopeless venture among the dragoons; the other, in company with a few enthusiasts including Southey, was a wild
project to found a "Pantisocracy," or equal rule by all, somewhere on the Susquehanna. Perhaps they had heard of Asylum,
a colony of French royalist refugees, already established on
the river with that alluring name; or more likely of Dr. Priestley's sojourn in exile at Northumberland in the same fair
valley. At any rate Coleridge did hearken to the smooth suasion
of a young land agent and of a glowing advertisement disguised as "Letters from America," 1794.

This man with memory, imagination, speculation, metaphysical sense, and knowledge beyond any of his time, was strangely

[1] *Prelude,* 14.277

removed from the ordinary facts of ordinary life; in his helpless predicament he was appealingly dependent upon others.

> To be beloved is all I need,
> And whom I love, I love indeed![1]

The hearts of many went out to him, not in pity so much as
in surrender to his amiability and to the magic of his brilliant, unebbing flow of talk. He was "an archangel, somewhat damaged," said the devoted Charles Lamb. He had made
a misfit marriage with Sara Fricker, "a sad fiddle-faddler," according to Dorothy Wordsworth. Sara was not interested in
genius; she had perhaps something to say on her side—and
said it.

Coleridge was teeming with projects and schemes of books,
poems, reforms, but if he got them started, he could not carry
them on. Hence the fragmentary state of most of his work. But
from twenty-five to thirty his alliance with the Wordsworths
brought to a focus his vast unmanageable powers long enough
to produce the few great poems that rise above the body of his
second-rate work. Most of these were composed in his twenty-
sixth year.

His previous *Monody on the Death of Chatterton*, 1795, and
his *Ode to the Departing Year*, 1796, are resonant if artificial
specimens of the "Pindaric" tradition, reminiscent of Gray,
with plenty of personification, apostrophe, and reiteration. In
Frost at Midnight he recalls that he was city-bred,

> And saw nought lovely but the sky and stars.

But he had hardly met Dorothy Wordsworth twice when his
eyes were opened to the loveliness of the Quantock landscape about Nether Stowey:

> The many-steepled tract magnificent
> Of hilly fields and meadows, and the sea,
> With some fair bark, perhaps, whose sails light up
> The slip of smooth clear blue betwixt two Isles
> Of purple shadow.[2]

[1] *Pains of Sleep*
[2] *This Lime-Tree Bower*

But the strange miracles of *The Ancient Mariner*, of *Kubla Khan*, and of *Christabel* were at hand. The year before, 1796, he had written: "I have read almost everything—a library cormorant. I am deep in all out of the way books"; metaphysics, poetry, accounts of all the strange phantasms, dreamers—these, he said, were his "darling studies." Among these were many books of travel—Bartram on America, Martens, Cook, Purchas's *Pilgrimage*, Strabo, and such. From all this reading his superhuman memory had stored untold wealth of curious detail. Then by the mystery of a suddenly attuned creative imagination the right details are summoned and arrayed in the simplest of schemes modelled after the primitive old ballad, and the result is *The Ancient Mariner*. Such simplicity of form and style may have been Wordsworth's doing. It results in a tale so plain that every schoolchild is expected to understand it. But this simplicity lies over depths and wonders and intimations—in the music of the verse, in the events and phenomena of the tale—that reach beyond any reader's range of wonder, and draw him forth

Alone on a wide, wide sea

of those mysteries which are perhaps the basic, but overlooked realities of life. And this is Coleridge. Thus during this brief season of 1797-8 conditions favored the exact and clear focus of his vast powers and accumulations in this great work, as they never did again. Youth, happiness, the Wordsworths, Nature united to release the "great energies" from the bonds of indolence.

He was never well. As far back as his schooldays he had been subject to "rheumatic fever," and at times underwent deep depression, excruciating pains, and sore throat. It looks like bad tonsils. Opiates seem to have been prescribed to relieve the boy's pain. To these he resorted in recurrent attacks, and in the course of years the habit fastened upon him. Partly this, but more a confirmed toxicosis, led at long last to the disintegration of his vast powers. Such was not yet his case when he dreamed the poem *Kubla Khan*. The story is familiar, how he fell into an opiate dream over Purchas's *Pilgrimage*, and awoke to write a part of the poem he had dreamed, when "a person on business from Porlock" interrupted him, and the rest fled. The fragment is a magic bit of romantic Orientalism, as *The Ancient Mariner* is romance of medievalism and distant lands.

Medieval also is the fragment *Christabel*, a transcendent poetizing of the mysteries and glooms that ran coarse riot in the "Gothic" novels. Unfinished as it is, it embodies finer virtues than the metrical romances of Scott and Byron which it anticipates. The metre itself is original—a couplet whose lines contain four marked stresses, with unstressed syllables varying from three to eight. It may have been suggested by Spenser's attempt to produce what he thought was Chaucer's metre in his May and September eclogues of the *Shepherd's Calendar*.

The "great energies" swelled once more in 1798 to the ode, *France*, in stanzas of twenty-one lines suggested perhaps by Spenser's *Prothalamion*. It is a superb embodiment of the disillusionment of the French Revolution, with the seer's shrewd conclusion that liberty is not for society, but for the individual whose sense of God and Nature is unspoiled by the world.

In the spring of 1802, almost on the very day that Wordsworth was lamenting his loss of the "visionary gleam" in the *Ode on Intimations*, Coleridge was likewise engaged on *Dejection: an Ode*, a pitiful outcry of dismay at the waning of his "shaping spirit of Imagination." As of old, he still sees the beauties of moon, star, and cloud, but "I see, not feel, how beautiful they are."

Half his life remained, in which he was to show an eminence in criticism and metaphysics as high as he had already shown in poetry. His criticism has come down to us imperfectly recorded in notes on his many lectures, in his *Table Talk* reported by his nephew, and in his *Biographia Literaria*, which contains his masterly opinion of Wordsworth. Yet these fragments were to influence criticism for the rest of the century. This man—poet, psychologist, metaphysician, encyclopedic scholar—at his best makes both modern literary research and modern impressionism look near-sighted or fumbling. With the German criticism of Schlegel and others, and Kant's profounder idea of Reason, above all with his own experience in the heights and depths of human genius, he divines with un-canny sense the instinctive purposes and modes of workman-ship in Shakespeare and other poets.

From his works it is difficult to realize the spell that Cole-ridge cast upon those who knew him. He said that his mind was more *energic* than energetic. Like Johnson's it seems to have worked by energizing the minds of others—Wordsworth, Hazlitt, Lamb, De Quincey, John Stuart Mill, and many a lesser admirer. His talk, said Wordsworth, flowed with the abundance of a majestic river, "the sound or sight of whose course you caught at intervals, which was sometimes concealed by forests, sometimes lost in sand, then came flashing out broad and dis-tinct, then again took a turn which your eye could not follow, yet you knew and felt it was the same river."

He had, like Johnson, wit and play, and had gazed into the tragic depths; but Johnson's keen sense of the ordinary reali-ties of life has perhaps made it possible for us, with Boswell's magic, to feel his actual fascination as his friends felt it; whereas Coleridge is tragic and frustrate even in this, that his power to attract is but in small measure transmitted and pre-served through fragments of his art.

SOUTHEY (1774-1843)

Wordsworth, Coleridge, and Robert Southey have, since their day, been called the "Lake Poets," for no very good rea-son other than local. When young Coleridge and Southey were dreaming their early wild dream of Pantisocracy, they had married sisters, Sara and Edith Fricker, of Bristol; in later years the Southeys had followed Coleridge to Keswick, and there they settled in the same house, where Southey un-dertook the burdens of both families, since Coleridge was not equal to that of his own.

Southey was an excellent and prolific literary workman. Un-luckily he and some of his friends believed that he was a genius, which has not helped his reputation. At any rate he may be remembered as a successful man of letters, a tireless worker, and an entertaining and likable person. Even as a

child, he was sure of himself, and told a lady that nothing is
so easy as to write a play. At Oxford he had already written
20,000 verses, "15,000 worthless." Of these his epic, *Joan of
Arc,* in twelve books, was written in six weeks. Other "epics"
followed before he was forty, *Madoc,* on Welsh and Mexican
themes, *Thalaba,* an Arabian story, *Kehama,* on a Hindoo motive, and *Roderick* "the last of the Goths," in Spanish setting.

As a schoolboy he had picked up a book on religious ceremonies, and then and there resolved to illustrate all the poetical
mythologies in heroic poems. These just mentioned are the
astonishing result. In spite of certain "purple patches" not of
deepest dye, they are now seldom read. Yet they are solid
spoils of the romantic search for poetic riches in far-off places
and times, and helped enrich greater poets than he.

Southey is better known by his ballads in the kind of *The
Ancient Mariner,* and certain of his short poems which, if not
great, have about them that easy song and sentiment that made
them everybody's durable poetic property.

All his life he was wont to carry on three or four projects
in verse or prose simultaneously. After forty most of his work
was in prose, and its volume is immense: huge histories, com-
pilations, steady contributions on politics and literature for the
Quarterly Review, and the like. His beloved family and others
had to be provided for; he was generous to a fault, and "pen-
and-inkmanship" was his one resource. Out of the mass of his
work, his little lives of Nelson, Cowper, and Wesley, whatever their defects, are still read for their clear and easy style.

Southey is worth knowing for the man himself, if not for
most of his work. As a youngster he revelled in the luxury of
revolt. He got himself expelled from Westminster, was refused
at Christ Church, Oxford, read Rousseau and *Werther,* was all
for the French Revolution and Pantisocracy, and knocked about,
an almost penniless rebel. But like the other romantic poets
who lived long enough, he suffered disillusion in his hope for
the dawning social millennium; his ardors cooled and his poetic
powers declined; he settled back upon the comfortable traditions of English Church and State. At this point he accepted
the Laureateship, with hesitation, for he hated the "odeous"

job as he called it. But there were still the adored wife and children to be considered. However, he declined a baronetcy in 1835.

One may best find Southey in his letters, and in the strange miscellany, *The Doctor,* after the whimsical manner of Sterne— by the skip-and-dip method. He had a boy's heart, was "invincibly cheerful," relished good nonsense, and, like Squire Hardcastle, loved old friends, old books, and old wine—if it was to be had. His spare pennies he spent book-hunting, and among his 14,000 volumes were many rare items. With stout limb and normal health, with his fun, his clear conscience, his hard work and snug family life, he was, it would seem, a more companionable man than most of his greater contemporaries.

LANDOR (1775-1864)

Both men were past thirty when, in 1808, Southey met Walter Savage Landor, whose friendship, in spite of Landor's highly explosive temper, Southey was to keep for life. Southey had, since its appearance ten years before, much admired Landor's poem *Gebir,* a long Egyptian romance in highly chastened style.

Landor was a burly figure, who in all his eighty-nine years, like Southey, never wholly lost his boyhood. His chief disability was a temper that was for ever blazing up to defend his "rights," personal or political, real or imaginary. He was usually impractical, always generous to the point of indiscretion, most humanly tender towards children or animals or flowers; and it is such personal qualities as these that everywhere warm what might otherwise be ungenial or cold in the fabric of his work. He was born and lived free from the slavery of poverty or drudging for his living. In school and at Oxford he showed extraordinary affinity for the Greek, and particularly the Latin, poets, so that their quality passed into him in abundant measure. Half of his long life after forty he spent in Italy, chiefly at Florence, where, under warmer and more cheerful auspices, he composed the *Imaginary Conversations,* mostly in prose. By these he is best known.

Some find difficulty in classifying Landor as a romantic. He is deeply imbued with classical antiquity, and his creative fire, unlike his temper, is always under strong control. But all the past, as he shows in his *Conversations* again and again, is to him matter for poetic and romantic dreaming, touched with loveliness and mystery, whether the speakers are Greek, Roman, mythical, medieval, Italian, or eighteenth-century English. Such they appear beside the equally exquisite, but riotous and satiric dialogues of Lucian, and though they contain dramatic moments, the drama is not intense. Nor does the style of the speakers vary greatly, from Dr. Johnson to Helen of Troy, from Washington to Boccaccio's Fiammetta. Yet all of the dialogues, especially the medieval and Greek conversations, are finely wrought cameos, animated by the artist's very delight in his work; and the Greek to whom he is nearest is Theocritus. His best works are delicate idylls, and no finer specimen of its kind can be found in English verse than *The Hamadryad*, a little epic or idyll as finished and sweet as any by the Greek master.

It is perhaps the combination of his large-hearted tenderness with Hellenistic delicacy which has lent unfading loveliness to the famous but tiny song, *Rose Aylmer*.

Acquainted with Wordsworth, Coleridge, Lamb, and the later romantic generation, Landor lived to be not only the friend of Dickens, but to meet young Swinburne, upon whose art he was to exert a profound influence. What stronger proof of his "romantic" power, unless it be such words as these:

Look at any old mansion-house, and let the sun shine as gloriously as it may on the golden vanes, or the arms recently quartered over the gateway, or the embayed window, and on the happy pair that haply is toying at it; nevertheless, thou mayest say that of a certainty the same fabric hath seen much sorrow within its chambers, and heard many wailings: and each time this was the heaviest stroke of all. Funerals have passed along through the stout-hearted knights upon the wainscot, and amid the laughing nymphs upon the arras. Old servants have shaken their heads, as if somebody had deceived them, when they found that beauty and nobility could perish.

LAMB (1775-1834)

Charles Lamb is one of the few whose readers are not content merely to admire or "appreciate." Their hearts go out to him. He is beloved as are Goldsmith, Walton, or Jane Austen. Those who knew him in the flesh were of the same heart and mind as his friends of today.

His portrait shows him the fine-featured, fine-bred man that he was, bravely endeavoring to hide the scars of his suffering. He was too manly to sentimentalize or feel sorry for himself, or bid for the sympathy of others, yet none more warmly loved his friends.

The most faithful image of Lamb is in his letters. No letters more entertaining were ever indited or received, and one cannot but realize how he diverted himself as he wrote them, and how joyfully they were torn open and read by his devoted friends, Coleridge, Southey, Manning, Barton, even Wordsworth. They overflow with sensible nonsense, puns, capers and cavortings, kind affection, personalities at once gentle and pungent, quaint phrases and home shots, diverting trifles of domestic news and gossip, odd likes and dislikes; they are to all appearances unstudied and spontaneous.

The same engaging person comes forward in the *Essays of Elia* and *Last Essays of Elia*, but with a difference. These are the poetic version of Lamb himself, as his letters are the prose. Born within easy earshot of Bow bells, London was as much poetry to him as the Lakes to Wordsworth. He was not "romance-bit about Nature"; London was his medium—its streets, shops, theatres, lamps, watchmen, its very noises, smells, smoke, dirt and mud, from St. Paul's to Charing Cross, its bookstalls haunted by the spirits of old playwrights and of such worthies as Fuller, Burton, and Sir Thomas Browne. It was impossible, he found, to be dull in Fleet Street, and he confesses to frequent tears "in the motley Strand from fulness of joy at so much life."

This glamor of London is a part of the romance which pervades the essays of Elia, but not all. For Lamb saw, and touched what he saw, with a rare quality of reminiscence that

makes it poetry, something akin to the idyllic power of Goldsmith, yet his own. His childhood, his schooldays at Christ's
Hospital, many a dear and odd figure along the years, the
London that was, Oxford from without, the mellow countryside of Hertfordshire, with the fragrant old house and pictures
and library, where as a child he had gone to see his mother's
kin, nights at the theatre, clerking at India House, domestic
episodes, his comradeship with his sister Mary, older by eleven
years—these and many other actual details of his life are
wrought into the essays, but so merged with his wholesome
and natural dreams as to turn them from autobiography into
poetry. His poem, *The Old Familiar Faces,* though composed
years before the essays, illustrates the same romantic process.
He dreams of the wife and children that never were, of fellowship with old authors, of old London, and lures us with him
into the rich-hued, romantic, by-gone world of courtiers and
lovely ladies, some good, some wayward, the world of Shakespeare, Beaumont and Fletcher, Ford, and the rest. He seems to
have elected the reader from all other men to share his own
personal confidence, and subtly to have honored him with ad-
mittance into his charmed and happy life, his drollery, his rare
friends, his wholesome sister, his pensive and tender reminiscence.

But the actual circumstances were brutally otherwise; only
at the price of cruellest suffering was this rare quality realized.
Lamb was but twenty when he had an unhappy love affair—
followed by a short period of mental derangement. Hardly had
he recovered (1796) when his sister Mary, in a sudden fit of
violent insanity, killed her mother with a knife as they were
about to sit down to dinner, wounded her father, and only
by Charles's interference was saved from further mischief.
Throughout the rest of their devoted life together she was
subject every year or two to these attacks, and removed to
a dismal retreat for recovery. Thus this blackest of shadows
hung constantly over them, and "marked" them, he said, as
it followed them from one habitation to another. Now and
then the genial tone of his letters is shattered by an agonized
cry to his dearest friend Coleridge.

In the circumstances marriage was hardly to be considered; yet at forty-four he proposed to the actress Fanny Kelly in a letter of consummate beauty, and took her natural refusal with the same brave and jesting front that glorified all his agonies. From the age of seventeen for more than thirty years he was a clerk at India House, drudging day in and day out to earn his own and Mary's living. From fits of depression, loneliness, and the black shadow ever hanging over, he found fleeting relief in "a cheerful glass," to which he was too readily susceptible. His grand consolation was his friends, especially Coleridge, the friend of his old Christ's Hospital days, without whom he confesses that he would have been "worthless."

Personal and familiar Lamb's essays are, the forerunner of a long line that still finds readers in our literary magazines. They are in the tradition of graceful egoism fathered by Montaigne, but interrupted by the more objective essays of the eighteenth century. Spontaneous as they seem, they are works of most nicely calculated art. Occasionally an essay reminds one of the most genial specimens in the school of Addison and Steele, but Lamb's heart's love was the seventeenth-century authors—Fuller, Wither, Burton, Browne, Taylor, Milton. His style is often in their baroque manner, his phrase is their phrase, and he loves to borrow from them a quaint mannerism, an old word or idiom of time-mellowed savor. The Bible, old plays of Shakespeare and others serve him in like manner, so that his work has the effect of fine and careful inweaving of borrowed threads, saved from being obvious or laborious by the warm feeling which his sufferings and denials had refined.

The essays, composed from time to time for the public prints, were not begun till Lamb was forty-five, and followed one another over the next ten or more years. They are the quintessence of all his other work, which was not extensive, and which was perhaps the more exquisite for not being the important means of his support. A few sonnets, after Samuel Bowles, Coleridge's early model; incidental verses; a domestic tragedy, *John Woodvil*, in the Jacobean manner; and the famous *Tales from Shakespeare*, for which Mary did the comedies, constitute the most of it. These last, with various stories or verses for children, by himself and Mary, and his retelling of stories from Chapman's *Odyssey,* "for children and *men,*" show not only his fine work in mosaic, but his feeling and tact for children, spending itself in literature for the world's children, since he had none to call him father. His *Specimens of English Dramatic Poets,* 1808, carried with it his critical comments, whose romantic and infectious enthusiasm was a powerful stimulus in the revival of such as Marlowe and his successors. But above and beyond all the grace and art of his best work is the man himself, who overcame his bitter suffering by concern for others, and veiled it in humorous play that only gave it greater dignity. To his friend Barton he wrote: "You and I are something besides being Writers, Thank God."

HAZLITT (1778-1830)

Among the brilliant talkers gathered about Lamb's table at his Thursday evening parties was the super-reporter, journalist, and man of letters, William Hazlitt. Yet he was a segregate man, not from shyness or self-depreciation so much as his disposition to set himself up a party of one member. He says in his lively essay *On Going a Journey,* "I like to go by myself"; and living to oneself he defines as living in the world, not of it. Even his friendships went stale, except perhaps the friendship of Coleridge, whose spell he could not break, and of Lamb, whose affection would not let him go.

In the course of his journalistic life he wrote much for the day that was passing over him, and forgot it forthwith; yet certain of his essays, the mature and slowly ripened fruit of his informal cultivation, survive and will survive.

His education—he would never have been happy in a university—grew by a succession of alluvial deposits, of Unitarian theology, of training to become a painter, of metaphysics, of passionate youthful interest in the French Revolution. But nothing he wrote is so memorable as his reminiscence of his meeting at nineteen with Coleridge, then twenty-three, who had come to preach in his father's Unitarian chapel at Wem near Shrewsbury. Only five and a half years separated them, yet to

the entranced boy it seemed like worlds and ages. His essay on
First Acquaintance with Poets tells the story of the meeting,
his ecstatic walk six miles with Coleridge on his way home, and
his happy visit to Nether Stowey in the spring. This, with his
later portrait of Coleridge, more reluctant in its still compulsory
admiration, give us our most convincing idea of the irresistible
witchery which the talk of Coleridge in the flesh cast over
young men.

Like other romantics Hazlitt disparaged most writing of
his time, and turned from "the dust and smoke and noise of
modern literature" back to "the pure, silent air of immortality."
He preferred Montaigne, the old poets and antique writers,
Pope and the novelists and essayists of the eighteenth century, the style of Burke, but especially the sentiment of Rousseau, and of the Germans. Yet he is ever the romantic egoist,
and "I like" and "I hate" he repeats almost with the regularity of a ritual.

But these likes, and these hates too, wilful and impression-
istic as they usually are, often launch a fertilizing idea into
the reader's mind, or impart the galvanic energies of that eccentric nature in which they were incandescent. It is the same,
whether he talks about painting and painters, poets and poetry,
books and authors, the art of writing or a prizefight, walking
or reading, youth, death, or the extraordinary round of every-
day living.

He wrote an essay *On Gusto*, especially in painting and fine
arts. By "gusto" he seems to mean the emotional energy and
enthusiasm that inform all work of masters in any art. But
he really discovered this gusto in himself, always the egoist;
and this gusto, imparted to his writing, has kept it alive.
There is a measure of it in most that he writes, even on
ephemeral occasion. It strongly pervades his portraits of other
men, in whom he touches with liveliest vigor what he knows
himself to be, or wishes to be. "Cobbett," he says, "cannot
agree to anything established, nor to set up anything else in
its stead"—a trait which Hazlitt had not to go as far as Cobbett to discover. To the end he charged Coleridge and other

fellow enthusiasts about the French Revolution with faint-hearted apostasy, for becoming disillusioned and conservative!

With all his "gusto" Hazlitt changes like the weather—now fair and sunny, or stormy, rough, tranquil, humid, overcast, according to the mood, yet always free as out-of-doors. His manner is easy and fluent, but runs over depths of culture and allusion not found in most modern journalism. Now and then he likes to dress up in old clothes, the aphoristic or the baroque style of seventeenth-century masters, the style of an old "character" writer like Earle or Overbury; or again he exhibits the luxuriance of Sir Thomas Browne, like an illuminated fountain. As he wrote, he always had good talk in mind, and his writing was based upon the soundest of all principles: "No style is good that is not fit to be spoken or read aloud with effect."

Hazlitt might find old friendships losing their savor, or recall unnumbered misadventures of the heart, or write *On the Pleasure of Hating*, but he confessed at the end to a happy life, and said: "I have loitered my life away, reading books, looking at pictures, going to plays, hearing, thinking, writing on what pleased me best. I have wanted only one thing to make me happy; but wanting that, have wanted everything!" Was it genius?

DE QUINCEY (1785-1859)

Another of the "Lake" group, younger than the rest, was Thomas De Quincey. He too was drawn into it by the centripetal attraction of Coleridge and Wordsworth. Slight, wiry, reticent, with "a talent for silence," given to revery, he was not made for intimacies. Far finer and more exquisite than Hazlitt, he lacked Hazlitt's gusto. He had in fact a kind of passion for being miserable and for conditions of misery in others, which lends a morbid hue both to him and his work at times, and at times lapses into melodrama. In his twenties he became addicted to opium—the practice began in paroxysms of pain from toothache and other ills—and he rather exploited his habit and his struggles with it. But the fact remains that thrice in later years he almost overcame the habit, and that in spite of his hardships his physical constitution and literary powers endured until he died at seventy-four.

Nor was he morbid in his tenderness of heart, in his love for children—he had eight of his own—and in his brotherly tenderness for outcasts of any sort. With uncalculating and open hand he gave to the wretched, and was beset by beggars. He had in his youth wilfully shared their misery.

De Quincey's art is, at its best, like Lamb's, reminiscent and autobiographic. But wanting Lamb's exquisite charm, it exerts a certain power through the keen and delicate response of De Quincey himself, child and youth, to agonizing conditions of life which he rather relished and enjoyed recording. For like his fellow romantics he was much preoccupied with states of mind, especially his own. His *Autobiographic Sketches*, and his famous *Confessions of an Opium Eater*, written and reworked in the latter half of his life, belong in the class of great autobiography, though no doubt he has thrown over the incidents the transforming light of imagination. The *Autobiographic Sketches* recall his baffled and blind agony at five when his sister died; how his older brother William bullied him; how he gloried "in being despised"; how they fought the factory boys day after day; how William admitted that "though a monstrous coward, you don't run away"; how little Thomas defended his tropical kingdom of Gombroon against his brother's mightier (of course) Tigrosylvania; how he ran away from Manchester Grammar School because he would not stand the stupid oppression of his guardians and other grown-ups. He recounts his extraordinary precocity in Greek; his none too modest conversation with George III; his early impressions of London, of Ireland, of English travel; his brother's adventures among pirates; his own as a young prig among bluestockings and connoisseurs. In the *Confessions* he reviews in vivid detail his rebellious escape from school and guardians, and wellnigh destitute wanderings in Wales and later among the gutters of London. There he grew weak and ill and was tenderly cared for by an outcast girl afterwards swallowed up in the vortex of London beyond all his power to trace her. Of his years at Oxford, where, like other romantic geniuses, he was ill at ease, he has almost nothing to say.

In his reminiscent portraits of Wordsworth, Coleridge, Lamb, and others he is personal to the point of indiscretion. He had a "vast capacity for veneration," and his youthful thrill at his first encounter with these men almost makes them reincarnate before us. For twelve years he was settled at Grasmere in the cottage vacated by Wordsworth. There he married the devoted Margaret Simpson, who more than twenty years nobly followed her career of wifely care for this difficult man of letters. During a few years in London, and throughout the latter half of his life in Edinburgh, he toiled for the periodicals, such as the *London Magazine, Blackwood's,* and *Tait's.* He became a genial but eccentric figure, who, when one lodging grew congested with books and papers, abandoned it for another, leaving behind him a trail of these literary jams.

His gift for revery, heightened by opium—the whole process may be followed in the *Confessions*—gave rise to his literary fantasias, once more famous than now. Such are his *Daughter of Lebanon,* his *Suspiria,* and the famous *Dream Fugue* in *The English Mailcoach.* Architectural grandeurs, Gothic and oriental, surging splendors of form and color and sound, flooding and ebbing, float on a tide of language musical almost to the point of poetry. They have, however, when not at their best a tendency to specious and empty effects, like the later work of Gustave Doré.

For De Quincey's art and style are conscious. His familiarity with Greek may have had a subtle effect upon the habitual music of his language. Except for an allusion here and there it seems to have left small trace otherwise. At its best his language runs with the constant undulating and rippling smoothness of a clear stream in the hills. It has an affinity with the luxuriant and sustained utterance of Sir Thomas Browne and Dr. Johnson. But he had not learned the Greek lesson of restraint and economy and purity, and his performing as he did for an ephemeral audience betrayed him into divarications, digressions, and sometimes falsetto tricks of style as well as art, which compel the most resolute reader to skip in spite of himself.

SCOTT (1771-1832)

Amid all the storm-racked, ill-adjusted writers of the "romantic" kind suffering from the disabilities of genius, one is glad to come upon the robust and happy figure of Sir Walter Scott. In most ways his career was that of a normal, successful, and healthy man of the world. The biography by his son-in-law, John Lockhart, next to Boswell's the noblest biography in English, paints Scott full length, a gentleman, and a genius who, like Chaucer and Shakespeare, had a keen relish for vigorous human life in all ranks and forms, moving among them, from king to outcast, always at his ease. For all his romance, there is much of the eighteenth-century humanist about him.

He represents Scotland more broadly than did Burns; for Burns, though no less patriotic, was born a peasant in Ayrshire, and sang for Scotland with local intensity. Scott, bred in Edinburgh, came to maturity in both town and country; and the rich history, legend, and ballad lore of the Border, together with the folk and the scene that produced them, he drew into his very fibre and being.

The old Scotland into which he was born in 1771 was rapidly passing. It had been loose and wild and feudal and picturesque, and the centuries of Border strife and poverty and Calvinism had made for the striking traits of character and sharp issues of which great story is composed. The old life had been lived close to the soil, which made all ranks of society, lord, farmer, and shepherd, near kin, and the scenic background correspondingly interesting and romantic. But except through local ballads and songs it had been mute, and had found no voice or pen to give it utterance to the world. Walter Scott came just as this rich old life was disintegrating, in time to catch and save it in his poetry and novels.

The energies of a new Scotland were stirring, stimulated in part by a closer contact with England, and Scott was not only developed by them, but in time greatly increased them. Formal education and early social life he had in Edinburgh, but from childhood he was half the time in the country, somewhere in the Tweed valley or its tributaries, or venturing over the Cheviot hills into the wilder valleys towards England. From his childhood discovery of Percy's *Reliques*, his passion for the ballads sent him hunting everywhere into hut, cottage, field, and country-house; and his extraordinary memory stored these songs away with legend and anecdote against the day when his shaping hand grew strong.

At eighteen months he was lamed for life by infantile paralysis, which marred an otherwise superb physique, but perhaps kept his fighting blood and venturesome spirit from making an early end of him. Nevertheless he rode, hunted, dared, and roistered with the best of them. As for his education otherwise, though he followed through the formal course of the "High School" in Edinburgh, he got most of it himself—Latin poets, French and Italian poets, German romantics, and the old English poets, especially Spenser, the early dramatists and above all Shakespeare, in whose plays he became almost letter-perfect. Then he read law and was admitted to the bar in Edinburgh. A disappointment in love left a lifelong scar; yet he happily married at twenty-six, and with an increasing family of sons and daughters, friends, wealth, and position, he seemed to become what every sane man would wish to be.

As Sheriff of Selkirk at twenty-eight, his duties as well as his liking brought him into closest intimacy with the countryside. As Clerk of Session at thirty-five in Edinburgh he had always before him that spectacle of human life which the lawyer sees, and which for range and breadth is hardly equalled by any other. Such was the making of this great romantic poet, not by agonies and contention with the world, nor by self-dedication and conscious discipline. As a poet he matured late, yet all his previous life had gone unawares into the making.

After early renderings of modern German ballads with something of the gloom and shudders of the Gothic tale of terror about them, he had made a collection of genuine old ballads, the famous *Minstrelsy of the Scottish Border*. Many were in a ruinous condition, and Scott, more poet than scholar, repaired them. But his repairs show in their skill the maturing genius; for under this stern discipline he had learned economy and severity of expression. More important, the old tunes, so burdened with all that is both hard and tender in human life, had awakened in him his own rare gift of song. He had notable helpers in his collecting, among them the extraordinary scholar Leyden, and that red-haired, burly, rude, genial, vain James Hogg, "the Ettrick Shepherd," singer of a number of excellent Scottish songs, and of a romance, *The Queen's Wake*.

With the old ballads Scott published modern imitations; one of these grew out of bounds, and turned into a hybrid between an old ballad and a medieval romance. It was the *Lay of the Last Minstrel*. On its appearance separately, when Scott was thirty-three, he leaped into sensational and unlooked-for fame through all the English-speaking world. No one was more surprised than he, for he never thought or spoke highly of his own work.

The measure of the *Lay* is an imitation of the peculiar four-stress measure of the as yet unpublished *Christabel*, which Scott had heard, with traces of the old *rime couée* of Chaucer's *Sir Thopas* and other Middle English romances,[1] and interpolations of the ballad four-and-three. The defects of this first success—as indeed of any of Scott's work, are too obvious to dwell upon. But his magician's power of clothing a scene or locality with imperishable glamor, of carrying an action forward, and the reader with it, on the vigorous rush of his verse, are enough to account for his sudden popularity, not to say a latent spell ready to be released at any time by good oral rendering. Scott shared with Homer and Virgil and Milton the epic power to link names of men and places into a melody that forthwith endows a man or a place with the distinction of poetry, and sets them apart from all others.

Three years after the *Lay* came *Marmion*, and two years later the *Lady of the Lake*. Popular success rose to a high climax with this last romance, and then declined through the romances of the next five years, *Rokeby, Bridal of Triermain,* and *Lord of the Isles*. Scott defined a romance as "a fictitious narrative framed and combined at the pleasure of the writer"; sub-

[1] See p. 66.

ject only to the rules of "good sense, good taste, and good morals," and the necessity of never being heavy or prosaic.

> I love the license all too well,
> In sounds now lowly, and now strong,
> To raise the desultory song.

Such wilfulness and independence were characteristic of the romantics, and partly explain why there was so much hit or miss about the quality of their work. But Scott had the sense never to admire nor defend what turned out to be bad.

He knew that after the *Lady of the Lake* his relish for the metrical romance was declining. But he also saw, without a touch of envy, that another had charmed the multitude of his listeners away from him—the young man of mystery and passion, Lord Byron.

The enduring virtues of the romances which are foreshadowed in the *Lay* mature in the later examples. Scott learns to tell a story in better order; explores various of "the fair fields of old romance"—medieval chivalry in *Marmion*, clan warfare of the Highlands in the *Lady of the Lake*, the civil wars of Cavalier and Roundhead in *Rokeby*, the return of Bruce in the *Lord of the Isles*. In short he had done all to prepare himself for the grander performance of the novels.

No agent of advertising is so powerful as literature, and one proof of Scott's success is the tide of tourists to the Border and the Trossachs, which rose at once on publication of the various romances, and which has never since ebbed. For, whatever their faults, Scott's novels have in them a certain engaging enthusiasm and exuberance which never failed the man. With all his genius and distinction and dignity, the boy in him never died. He was a boy about dogs and horses and daring sport, with a boy's love of stirring tale and pageantry and romance, of success and happy endings; and whoever is bored with this boy's exuberance in his romances and novels should take alarm at such a symptom of age in his own soul.

But though he gave over the writing of metrical romances, he had shown in them one supreme proof of his eminence as a poet which never declined. This is the interpolated songs.

Scott was, like the ancient minstrel that he was pleased to imagine himself, and like the Elizabethans, a maker of pure song that sings itself. All through the romances these songs are strewn, such as *Lochinvar*, "That day of wrath" from an old Latin hymn, "Soldier, rest, thy warfare o'er," "Hail to the Chief," "O Brignall banks," and many more. But no less tuneful are those songs scattered through the novels—the wild songs of Meg Merrilies in *Guy Mannering*, the dirge for Athelstane in *Ivanhoe*, *County Guy* in *Quentin Durward*, or above all *Proud Maisie* in the *Heart of Midlothian*. Like the chorus in Greek tragedy, or the songs in Shakespeare, they are exactly timed to give restful pause to the action, to relieve the accumulated emotion of both actor and reader, and to perform the mystery that only the lyric can perform, of lifting the action toward the level of the universal, and clothing it with dignity.

Scott was beyond forty when his career as a novelist began. He had tried his hand on the first part of *Waverley*, nine years before, not with success. He may have begun other attempts that in time turned into other of his novels. Then suddenly the flood-gates of genius were opened, and he finished the last two-thirds of *Waverley* in twenty-six days. *Guy Mannering* he wrote in six weeks, and at the height of his powers produced within thirty months *Rob Roy, The Heart of Midlothian, The Bride of Lammermoor, A Legend of Montrose,* and *Ivanhoe*. Much of this time he was desperately ill. *The Bride of Lammermoor* he dictated amid such paroxysms of pain that when he afterwards saw it in print, it was as new to him as if another had written it. Half the year he had to spend five or six hours a day in court; into the other half he crammed the business of his growing house and estate at Abbotsford, with its continuous stream of guests and good times, his various literary by-products, such as his monumental editions of Dryden and Swift, his articles, and his large correspondence.

The story is famous of the man in Edinburgh who nearly went mad with the sight of an unknown scribe near the window of a neighboring house: "It fascinates my eye—it never stops—page after page is finished and thrown on that heap of MS. and still goes on unwearied—and so it will be till candles are brought in, and God knows how long after that. It is the same every night—I can't stand a sight of it. . . ." It was only Walter Scott at work. No man of letters, it would seem, ever led a more crowded and prolific life.

His first nine novels had in one way or other to do with Scottish life and history. He was ever varying his theme, period, and combination of character to keep the public which he had won, and which was so necessary to his income. Then in *Ivanhoe* he turned suddenly back with astounding success to the medieval pageantry of *Marmion*, and followed it with other "historical" romances, such as *Kenilworth, Quentin Durward,* and *The Talisman.*

The publication of *Waverley*, 1814, is often regarded as the day of advent of the modern novel. Since Smollett and Miss Burney the novel had sadly declined—not in numbers, but in quality. The presses poured out more fiction than ever, but for the most part poor stuff of sentiment and impossibility. Scott has his fun with it in his Introduction to *Waverley.* The Gothic tale of terror, a pretty crude affair with its devices of dungeons, tombs, ghosts, ruins, cruel persecution of lovers, and mysteries, had nevertheless attained some power in Mrs. Radcliffe's *Mysteries of Udolpho*, and in Lewis's *The Monk*, and became sublimated both in the verse and the prose of the great romantics. Not the least of those whom it affected was Scott himself; its lurid gleam flares at frequent points in his poems and novels, notably *The Lay of the Last Minstrel, The Bride of Lammermoor, The Betrothed.*

In the memorable fifth chapter of her *Northanger Abbey* Miss Jane Austen pauses to protest against the low reputation of the novel, and then proceeds to all manner of sport with Mrs. Radcliffe in the tale that follows. She had caught a vision of the novel's great possibilities, and had realized them in her *Pride and Prejudice* and *Sense and Sensibility*; but these novels made no stir. Jane Porter's *Thaddeus of Warsaw* and *Scottish Chiefs* were successful omens of the triumph that awaited a *good* historical novel, such as *Waverley.* Yet Scott was so ashamed of appearing as a mere novelist, after his distinction as a poet, that he would not own to the book, and labelled his others "By the Author of *Waverley*." For thirteen years he kept his secret, though by degrees the world guessed it to a certainty.

It is useless to discount the alloy in the novels, whether in characters, plot, or style. There are melodrama, high-life heroes and heroines, stage villains, and old worn plots of separated lovers, return of the exile, and false incrimination. But these are redeemed with the unfailing boy's gusto of the author. It is easy to carp at the historical errors in *Ivanhoe, Kenilworth,* or *Quentin Durward.* Scott knew them as well as anyone else, but did not care, if only he threw open a glamorous world of deeds and adventure and picturesque pageantry, and told his story with all the thrills of tense situation and sudden change and final triumph of manly virtue. And this he has done with grand and disarming success.

But over and above the profusion in which he produced them there are giant dimensions of genius in Scott's novels. So vivid is the Scotch setting that, as in Hardy, it becomes a part of the action. The variety and living actuality of his Scotch characters, their racy homeliness and the wit and humor in their dialect toughening the texture of his fabric, the inexhaustible variation of scene and situation, all show how vast was Scott's ingathering of every detail of Scotch life, how deeply he loved it, and how his great heart took it all to himself. An aristocrat by instinct, he was of the true sort that mingles with any class on even plane. A herdsman, abashed at meeting the great man, found that "he is just a chield like oursels." With highest, sometimes with tragic dignity, he clothes even the humblest of his people—Jeanie Deans, Meg Merrilies, Dandie Dinmont, Saunders Mucklebackit.

He knows too how to create a breathless situation, how to combine and offset his characters, how to erect a sustaining pillar of good sense amidst the vagaries of a crowded cast of characters, how to rise through suspense to a climax of action or decisive incident. And if he sometimes failed through pushing his work without inspiration, his faith in his powers did not wane. "If it isna weel bobbit, we'll bob it again," he used to say.

The exuberant fullness of his capacious mind lends high energy to his work. Law, history, economics, astrology, heraldry, manners, poetry, theology—there seems no end to it, and its exuberance saves it from pedantry. The quotations that head his chapters overflow from his reading, or when they don't, he cleverly forges one as from an "Old Play."

He admits the use of the "Big Bow-wow strain," and his high-life people talk and write their letters in a stiff, dried-up medium kept over too long from Johnson and Gibbon. But he devised also for his historical romances a pungent speech out of Shakespeare and other Elizabethan writers, and his Scots is pure and racy from the source. In Scots or English he rises to the simplest and grandest in high moments, such as the speech of Claverhouse on death in *Old Mortality*.

Out of the swarm of incident and people emerge always his simple ideals of courage, and truth, and greatness of heart. Not with shallow moralistic enforcement, but as a part of the man himself. For he was essentially greater than his work. He had his weakness: he loved popularity; he was sanguine and unwise in material affairs; he was extravagant at Abbotsford, and mortgaged his future with the publishers Ballantyne and Constable till he landed in bankruptcy; he clung to the old order; he loved rank; he delighted in making himself a beneficent feudal laird in his little domain of Abbotsford; the offer of the laureateship, though he declined it, and his baronetcy at forty-seven, brought him the fullest gratification. He always regarded his art as an avocation, and declared his scorn of being "the mere poet."

But these were infirmities of a noble mind. He slaved to pay his creditors, though he died with half the debt still owing. His eminence was but a trust for the happiness of even the least of the many who were adoringly dependent upon him, and his pen brought him the supreme satisfaction of knowing that he provided deep and innocent pleasure for millions.

JANE AUSTEN (1775-1817)

Late in life Sir Walter noted in his Journal that he had just read Miss Jane Austen's *Pride and Prejudice* for at least the third time. "That young lady had a talent for describing the involvements, and feelings, and characters of ordinary life, which is to me the most wonderful I ever met with. The Big Bow-wow strain I can do myself like any now going; but the exquisite touch, which renders ordinary commonplace things and characters interesting . . . is denied to me. What a pity such a gifted creature died so early!" She was but forty-one at her death in 1817, and not long before may have had the satisfaction of reading an appreciative review of her novels from Scott's hand, the first important recognition she had had. Yet her first novel had been begun nineteen years before, all but one were now finished, though only three had been published. So exquisite is her art that she could not score a grand success nor become the fashion, even had her heart been set on it. Scott's range is vast, epic, national, thronging. He feels in every one of his persons the past—the story, traditions, social moulds of the generations that have produced that character. He is never closely concerned with the issues of private and domestic life. But Miss Austen's world is limited, private, of the immediate moment, and the cast is small. Yet she is one of the great masters of the craft.

She took Miss Burney as her model. Her *Northanger Abbey* clearly reflects *Evelina*; *Cecilia* helped her in *Emma* and *Pride and Prejudice*, and *Camilla* in her first novel *Sense and Sensibility*. In characters, in situations, in theme and motive the two novelists are alike. They have in common their interest in "sensibility," which was then so fashionable in fiction and in life, and had been since Richardson's time. A true and engaging sensibility they like to distinguish from a false, and as a foil to set equally engaging good sense over against both. But Miss Austen far outstrips her forerunner in subtlety, lifelikeness, and charm, and in her sense and implication of the unchanging values of life that lie beneath the petty events she records.

Her career was externally limited. She was one of a clergyman's large and lively family at sleepy little Steventon not far from Winchester. There were four older brothers—all nice companionable fellows, it would seem. One likes to think she had precedent of her own for the childhood she gives to the charming and ingenuous Catherine Morland: "She could never learn anything before she was taught, and sometimes not even then. . . . Provided they were all story and no reflection, she had never any objection to books at all. . . . She was fond of all boy's plays, and greatly preferred cricket, not merely to dolls, but to the more heroic enjoyments of infancy, nursing a dormouse, feeding a canary-bird, or watering a rose-bush. . . . She loved nothing so well in the world as rolling down the green slope at the back of the house."

By the time she was twenty-three Jane had started to write *Sense and Sensibility, Pride and Prejudice,* and *Northanger Abbey,* not with an eye to fame, but chiefly out of the innocent amusement that she and the family got from watching the parish and county life around them, and reading the sloppy and bugaboo novels of the day. When her father aged and died, the old life ended. It was not till thirteen years later, living with her mother and beloved sister (such sisters one meets in her novels) at Chawton, another mislaid village, that she wrote, between thirty-six and forty, *Mansfield Park, Emma,* and *Persuasion.* In her late twenties she lived at Bath, but never in London. She had no chance to hobnob with the great or the conspicuous. Her first novel, *Sense and Sensibility,* was not published till thirteen years after it was finished. *Pride and Prejudice* was declined by the publisher, except at her own risk, and *Northanger Abbey* she sold for but ten pounds to one who then refused to print it! Yet *Pride and Prejudice* has turned out the most popular and diverting of her works, and *Northanger Abbey* is for many the favorite, though the later ones, *Emma* and *Persuasion* are subtler, more exquisitely wrought, and finer in quality.

She wisely confined her work to her own little world, and these limitations were to her advantage. Country gentlemen and ladies, the village, the "Park," the Rectory, the amenities of Bath, with most of her people comfortably endowed, and those who worked never conspicuously busy—it is a removed world in which the chief preoccupations are all the trifles and devices in the art of getting happily and suitably married.

Its snobs, bores, boors, vulgarians, climbers, geese, and incompetents are more amusing than repulsive. Yet she makes certain of these, like Mr. Woodhouse and Miss Bates, subtly amiable—one knows not how. She even allows some of her very nice people to be silly, or to forget themselves for a moment, as nice people have been known to do. But they are true ladies and gentlemen, and she presents them in large variety.

In this corner of life where there is nothing to do and nothing ever happens arise the conflicts which might even make for tragedy, and in Miss Austen's hand do make for serious business—the sharp clash of intrinsic merit with a tight and closely circumscribed social convention or a wayward fashion. And she loves to reveal a fine young person's gradual realization of herself—preferably *herself*—through a course of successive disillusions.

Hasty impression has sometimes found her matchmaking too much engaged with considerations of fortune and rank; but in every instance her burden proves to be, for her worthier young folk, the marriage of true minds, and for the rest an equal justice of affinities.

So real was her little world that one has the sense of having known certain of her people, not of having read about them. They are still living—one meets them, and in fact always will, whatever one's date. This life-like vitality no doubt owes something to the verve and the care which she mingled in writing her novels. They are never really dull, however dull she sometimes purposely makes her people. Her wit, her humor, her shrewdness, her direct and unlabored way of uttering the just word, her almost perfect art of ordering and telling the tale, her own very keen delight in the business, fill her novels with the power of giving delight that only the finest art can yield. As she sat sewing by the fire, she would of a sudden "burst out laughing, jump up and run across the room to her desk, write something down, and then come back to the fire and go on quietly working." Her casual note was perhaps to set unnumbered thousands laughing not unkindly at the perennial human comedy.

Sir Walter, and no doubt her contemporaries, seem to have

admired Jane Austen's novels chiefly for their lifelikeness or "naturalness." But other and higher values they also contain, or they could not have raised up an idolatrous cult of readers who exalt them above all other fiction. They have caught and preserved a charming world in miniature, whose charm only increases, the farther that world fades into the past—a charm of costume, of manners, of furniture, of country houses and village street, of a settled, contented society, of good breeding and leisure and genuine human excellence, often indeed thrown into relief by instances of the contrary, but instances which sink as by gravitation to their true and natural cheapness.

It is not distance but the quality of Miss Austen herself that makes her world alluring. She loved the dull round into which she was born—not dull to her—wherein men and women could be observed at leisure and close range. Her steady eye dwelt upon them with quiet delight, with unerring admiration of the best, taking also undisturbed account of the worst. She was in many ways like Portia, and in her novels has embodied decrees of her sweet justice that cannot be impugned.

CHAPTER 28

Younger Romantics

BYRON (1788-1824)

THE *Lady of the Lake* was published in 1810. It marked the crisis of Scott's popularity as a poet. At the moment a young poet in his early twenties, and some seventeen years younger than Scott, was throwing off a work that was to capture the world's imagination as Scott had never done. He was George Gordon, Lord Byron, and his poem was the first two cantos of *Childe Harold*.

He still has power to captivate young men, as he captivated the whole generation of our young great or great-great grandfathers. In Byron they found, and find, a heroic example of their real or imaginary selves, one whose passions and longings are at war with a constricted world that does not, and simply cannot, understand.

Byron was generous, warm-hearted, headlong, sometimes vulgar and ostentatious, adventurous, clothed in mystery of his own creating, and gifted with a terrible power of cynical satire, with which he took just revenge upon a world that first adored and petted, then disowned him.

Perhaps more young readers have first discovered the fascination of poetry in reading Byron than through any other poet. His genius was not labored, but impromptu and fiery like that of Marlowe. Its swift and prolific abundance is astounding. At eighteen he published his first poems as *Fugitive Pieces*. At nineteen came his *Hours of Idleness*, full of immature promise, which called down the thunder of the old-school *Edinburgh Review*, edited by Jeffrey—that literary bully who in turn drew for his pains the scathing fire of this youngster's *English Bards and Scotch Reviewers.* The four cantos of *Childe Harold* were composed in one to two months each. His romances, *The Giaour, The Bride of Abydos, The Corsair, Lara, The Siege of Corinth, Parisina,* he wrote in two or three weeks each, and his *Prisoner of Chillon* in two rainy days. The cantos of *Don Juan* took usually a month apiece, and in less than two years, after he was thirty-three, he produced five dramas. Nearly all of the vast body of his verse he composed between twenty and thirty-five.

So spontaneous is even his best verse that it seems strangely like natural speech—close to one's ordinary emotional language. It makes the reader feel as if common speech must be charged just under the surface with the electrical energies of poetry, awaiting a touch—almost anyone's—to release it into flaming song.

The mystery with which Byron surrounded himself and surcharged his verse heightened the romance of his naturally romantic figure. But it has also stirred up more talk, much of it irrelevant to his poetry, than perhaps has obscured any other author.

Byron inherited stormy passions from both sides. His father and his grandfather, "the wicked lord," were lawless and dissipated. His mother alternately spoiled him and raved at him. He was lame from birth, a misfortune from which his physical vanity suffered most. At ten he succeeded to his title. In school at Harrow he made warm friends, was athletic in spite of his lameness—sparred, swam, played cricket—yet was unhappy, and at times disorderly notwithstanding his deep admiration for the master, Dr. Drury. At Trinity College, Cambridge, he spent, all told, two wild years. Yet from childhood he was educating himself by voracious reading—history and novels "by the thousand"; and he had got an intimate knowledge of the Bible, particularly the Old Testament, always peculiarly congenial to his mind.

Before he was ten he had devoured all the books on the East that he could find, and his dreams of oriental romance came partly true when at twenty-one he journeyed by way of Portugal, Spain, and Malta, then through Albania, to Constantinople and Greece, where he spent many months. His travels he recorded in the first two cantos of *Childe Harold*. They were published on his return, and he "woke one morning and found himself famous." His oriental enthusiasm poured itself into a number of specious metrical romances, and caught with its infection the public mind, which delighted in his beautiful dark-eyed Leilas and Zuleikas, his bold, passionate men of mystery, and the local color of capotes, suliotes, chibouques, and tchocadars.

> The scene was savage, but the scene was new.

The Corsair sold 14,000 copies in one day. But, popular fancy aside, omens of the enduring glory of Byron are already at hand—the swift, easy, and tuneful interpolated lyrics, his outbursts of generous feeling, his passion for freedom, his romantic lament for the departed glories of Greece, as in the opening of *The Giaour*, his direct sense of the obvious beauty in rock and river and forest and mountain, or of a tranquil, moonlit night, as in the first canto of *Lara*, or the third of *Childe Harold*, his infectious vigor of physical action, his moving dramatic moments like the parting of Conrad and Medora in *The Corsair*.

The five years from 1811 to 1816, which he spent in England, were filled with high lights and deep shadows. He was idolized, and yet kept himself in a splendid isolation. Old friends died, including his mother, whom, for all her weaknesses, he really loved. But he attracted new friends, including the Irish poet, Tom Moore; Thomas Campbell, author of *Gertrude of Wyoming*; and Samuel Rogers, whose *Italy*, a descriptive travel poem, was soon to follow *Childe Harold*, but at a considerable distance. One affair of the heart succeeded another. His financial distresses grew more acute. His library was sold, and he was forced at length to part with the picturesque family seat at Newstead Abbey in Nottinghamshire. In 1815 he married Anne Milbanke, but their union was soon a wreck in circumstances that no end of gossip, scandal, and research have ever been able to make clear.

Society indignantly disowned Byron, and he with equal scorn disowned England. In 1816 he left his native soil for ever, a voluntary exile, to spend the last eight years of his life abroad, almost entirely in Italy.

Those last years in England had, however, seen the maturing of his genius. Besides his romances, they had yielded his stirring *Ode to Napoleon*, the *Monody on the Death of Sheridan*, and, grandest of all, his *Prometheus*, in whose god-like suffering, like many another tortured spirit, he saw his counterpart. And the *Hebrew Melodies* composed for music represent indeed the finest balance of anything he ever wrote. In them his fevered turbulence is quieted by its alliance with the sweet and noble equanimity of the Old Testament, and the result is a loveliness of song which he never quite captured elsewhere.

His wanderings on the way to Italy quickly were embodied in cantos three and four of *Childe Harold*. Mountain scenery, by day or night, cities, buildings, statues, all received at his bountiful hand the baptism of poetry which has distinguished and sanctified them to travellers in every decade ever since. The Rhine, Switzerland, and Italy became "Byronized" to English-speaking people—and in fact to nations of other tongues—for a century. He turned statuary into poetry with the new and fashionable appreciation from Germany; for painting he seemed not to care.

Through all of Byron's poetry from beginning to end keeps reappearing, with little variation, a figure which, in the face of Byron's half-hearted denial, the world insisted upon taking for Byron himself—

> That man of loneliness and mystery,
> Scarce seen to smile, and seldom heard to sigh.

Byron it may not be, but he was not unwilling to have it follow him like his shadow—strongwilled, disillusioned, friendless, always at war with the conventional world, tortured with remorse mixed with a sad and tender memory. It reaches its grand apotheosis in *Manfred*, where it is powerfully blended with such accessories of romance as mountain scenery and medieval monasticism, and reinforced with the energies of Milton's Satan and of Marlowe's *Faustus*. In spite of its gravitation at times towards melodrama, and mere "storm and stress," this "Satanism," as it has been called, was an important agent in Byron's protest, and the romantic protest generally, against outworn social and political standards.

In Italy Byron's satiric power reasserted itself, first in *Beppo*, then more brilliantly in the successive cantos of *Don Juan*, composed at intervals from 1818 to 1823. *Don Juan* is the most dazzling of his works. It embodies the full compass of his genius. Its swift and inexhaustible play of many effects—its shrewd waggery, its pathos, cynicism, tenderness, humor, horrors, lovely idylls, songs, fertility of rhyme, devastating satire, moods and egoism, all deployed with easiest impromptu—astound the reader with this man's overwhelming poetic power.

In *Don Juan*, as in any of his sustained works, there are lapses and sinkings. This is to be expected in so uncalculating a genius. Yet Byron's lack of discipline is counterbalanced by solid elements in his training and tastes—his early if tedious experience with Latin and Greek classics; his affinity for the Old Testament; and his faith in Pope as the "most *perfect*" of English poets. All these had their effect. Moreover he welcomed metrical discipline. "The good old and now neglected heroic couplet" he found "the best adapted measure to our language," and he used it with all the energy, if not with the finish and economy and intensity, of Pope. The Spenserian stanza was "the measure most after my own heart," and he shows uncanny skill in the use of it, especially through the last cantos of *Childe Harold*. The four-stress couplet, revived and newly attuned by Coleridge and Scott, was another measure adapted to Byron's hand; and through the period of his romances, he handled it with easy mastery, particularly in *Mazeppa* and *The Prisoner of Chillon*.

Byron's poetic genius, so vigorous and prolific, was such as most people would choose to have for their own. It does not

often soar, and it sometimes stumbles and falls amid its swift-
est and easiest career. Yet its exuberance and vigor make it a
strong stimulant to the reader or listener, especially in *Childe
Harold, Mazeppa,* or *Manfred*; and it has moments, if only
moments, of music as sweet or tuneful as English verse has
ever known. Such are the *Hebrew Melodies,* "When we two
parted," and "She walks in beauty," or "The castled Crag of
Drachenfels" in *Childe Harold* III; or "The Isles of Greece"
from *Don Juan* III. No spirit of the times was so potent and
far-reaching as Byron's. Nearly every English poet for two
generations felt the Byronic thrill at one time or another.
Through all its latitude and longitude literary Europe stirred
to sympathetic vibration with his life and his poetry, his scepticism, his liberalism, his honest hardihood of mind, as well as
his cheaper effects, his mystifying pose and claptrap. Admirers,
imitators, and literary offspring included, besides shoals of
minor poets, such grand figures as Goethe, Heine, the Brownings, Lamartine, Hugo, de Musset, Sand, Arnold, and Pushkin.

The last eight years of his life—the years of exile—Byron
lived chiefly at Geneva, Venice, Pisa, and Genoa. They were
years, it must be said, of a good deal of idle philandering. But
they were prolific in poetry. Italy, like the near East, fertilized
his genius—those "countries of chivalry, history, and fable," as
he called them. From time to time he fell in with Shelley,
whose ethereal spirit is felt at moments in Byron's later poetry,
when he touches transcendent realities and catches music from

> The overpowering mysteries of space—
> The innumerable worlds that were and are.

At thirty-five, though worn out with malaria and his desultory manner of life, his generous and liberty-loving soul was
roused by the struggle of the Greeks for freedom from the
Turks. He gave himself to the enterprise, and was accepted as
a leader. Eight months before he died he sailed for Greece.
There were exasperating delays, amid which he bore himself
with his finest patience and courage. Death, probably from
meningitis, overtook him at Missolonghi while he was wearily
waiting for action. Three months earlier, on the morning of his

thirty-sixth birthday, he had brought forth his last poem, with
its premonitory ending:

> If thou regret'st thy youth, why live?
> The land of honourable death
> Is here:—up to the Field, and give
> Away thy breath:

> Seek out—less often sought than found—
> A soldier's grave, for thee the best;
> Then look around, and choose thy ground,
> And take thy Rest.

MOORE (1779-1852)

Elder than Byron and the rest of the group, more popular
in his day than most of them, yet far below them in final esti-
mation, was Thomas Moore, Irish born, at school with Sheridan, trained at Trinity College, Dublin. After five years'
knocking about in the United States and Canada he came to
study law in London, and soon captured the world of its
drawing-rooms with his talented singing of Irish songs. In
1807 he began the publication of his *Irish Melodies*, full of
plaintive and popular sentiment, which went on with high
profit to himself for nearly thirty years. No better exemplar of
the perennially popular song can be found than his lyrics.
Springing from a tuneful Irish mind, and composed to Irish
tunes already familiar, songs like "Oft in the stilly night" and
"The Last Rose of Summer" seem likely to defy ups and downs
of literary fashion indefinitely. Though he does not embody the
nobler and finer virtues of ancient Irish song, Tom Moore has,
for the time, been accepted as a kind of Irish national poet.

His *Lalla Rookh*, trading on the special order of romantic
orientalism made popular by Byron, but bookish, unauthentic,
and sentimental, had withal such vogue that it is almost invariably to be found even yet on the shelves of long settled
households, however scant their lettered outfit.

Lovers of biographical literature will most value Moore for
his *Life of Lord Byron*, still the best, and for his letters and

journals. They contain Moore himself, darting about among celebrities and friends, from anecdote to anecdote, tuneful, honest, and artless.

SHELLEY (1792-1822)

In 1812 Southey, disillusioned by the "failure" of the French Revolution, wrote to a friend: "Here is a man at Keswick, who acts upon me as my own ghost would do. He is just what I was in 1794. His name is Shelley, son of the member for Shoreham; with £6000 a year entailed upon him, and as much more in his father's power to cut off. Beginning with romances of ghosts and murder, and with poetry at Eton, he passed at Oxford into metaphysics; printed half-a-dozen pages, which he entitled 'The Necessity of Atheism'; . . . was expelled in consequence; married a girl of seventeen, after being turned out of doors by his father; and here they both are, in lodgings, living upon £200 a year, which her father allows them. . . . I tell him all the difference between us is that he is nineteen, and I am thirty-seven."

The girl was Harriet Westbrook, daughter of an innkeeper. Shelley married her out of chivalric pity. After three restless years—in Edinburgh, the Lake Country, Ireland, Wales, and London—he gave her up and eloped to Italy with Mary, gifted daughter of William Godwin and Mary Wollstonecraft. For four years he had endured most of the humiliations of poverty. At twenty-three he came into his own fortune. A restless soul, like Petrarch and Byron, he found no fixed abode, but every few months was up and away, to Ireland, to Wales, to England again, to Switzerland, to Italy and back, from town to country, country to town. His last three years he lived here and there in that "Paradise of exiles, Italy." The story of his drowning while sailing his own boat home from Leghorn to Lerici, of the burning of his body on the shore, and of the snatching of his heart from the pyre, is a tale on every tongue. He was not quite thirty years old.

At least two false conceptions of Shelley have survived him. According to one, now happily outlived, he was a dangerous, Satanic enemy of all religion, order, morals; according to the

other he was, in Matthew Arnold's specious phrase, a "beautiful and ineffectual angel, beating in the void his luminous
wings in vain." Surviving portraits are sickly and effeminate,
except the picture by West. In this he looks more the man he
was—of tender and open heart, generous, winning, quick and
vigorous in action, incorruptible, inflexible, exasperated with
the greed and stupidity of mankind. Byron knew him as "the
most gentle, the most amiable, least worldly-minded person I
ever met."

At school from ten to eighteen, chiefly at Eton, he suffered
what a sensitive high-strung lad of genius suffers; but he made
a few warm friends, did some extravagant writing, revelled in
"necromancy," dangerous chemical experiments, and the
trumpery of tales of terror, and won the nickname, "Mad
Shelley."

But at some time during these years, at seventeen or eight
een, he met the strange experience, a sudden blinding intima
tion of ideal beauty, of "Nature's naked loveliness," which he
describes in the preludes to the *Revolt of Islam* and *Alastor*,
and in the *Hymn to Intellectual Beauty*. Thus he became a
poet.

His acquaintance at Oxford with Godwin's *Enquiry Concerning Political Justice*, his expulsion, his break with his father,
served to settle his nonsense, clear his mind, and release his
gift of song.

The family, bred for generations in propertied conservatism,
and rejoicing in a baronetcy, was the last from which such a
poet was to be expected. To be sure, Sir Philip Sidney, two
hundred and fifty years before, was a kinsman, and the two had
many striking points in common—in their gallant chivalry,
their theory and practice of poetry. But this youngster Shelley
was a radical, would not renounce his atheistic views, apologize
to Oxford, toady for a political career, nor humiliate himself
to the tyranny of convention, for his father or anyone else. Into
his first marriage he was in some measure lured by his own
chivalry, and it owed its tragic ruin as much to the constant
intermeddling of his wife's older unmarried sister as to any
other cause.

Shelley's affairs, like those of Byron and Burns, have led to no end of talk, condemnation, and excuse. But genius of high order, especially in a time so full of revolutionary impulse as theirs, is unsubmissive to conditions that fit ordinary society. Mary Godwin was perhaps a better mate for Shelley than any other woman he ever knew. Though their elopement was quite in accord with Godwin's theories of free love, the "philosopher" was in a fury over it; yet his rage did not keep him from accepting Shelley's financial aid for some time after.

For not only did the burden of mankind's misery at large weigh heavily on Shelley's mind and heart; any single instance touched him to the quick and stirred his generous hand to relief. During his last year in England, at Great Marlowe on the Thames, he worked manfully to relieve the poor in that region who were suffering from the new industrial conditions. He loved "the starlight smile of children," knew how to romp and play with them on even terms, and was a devoted father.

He saw the wretched world about him as the result of centuries of tyranny, greed, violence, selfish exploitation of men and women and children, misrepresentation, and obscuration of the truth. It was a conspiracy of king, priest, and soldier, perverting, corrupting, and destroying everything. Only the spiritual forces of Love and Joy and Truth ruling the human heart could ever prevail against it, and of such a victory the vision was ever before him. To it he committed the gallant energies of his genius. It is his one grand theme. At twenty he was in Ireland writing and working for Irish freedom. Most of his longer poems rehearse the struggle for human liberty. In *Queen Mab*, written when he was twenty-one, the Fairy Queen transports the soul of Ianthe aloft to a vision, first of the human misery from war and superstition and trade, then of man's recovery through reason, science, and purity of heart. *Alastor* (1816) traces the fatal agony of a young poet in conflict with this perverted world. In his longest poem, *The Revolt of Islam* (1818), first called *Laon and Cythna*, he sets forth in allegory the liberation of the world from tyranny through the love and martyrdom of a high-souled young man and woman. With glowing hope he turns to America, "a People mighty in its youth," whence will come release to the mother country from the inbred monsters which now oppress her. In his greatest work, *Prometheus Unbound,* he shows how Intelligence linked with Love (Asia) and Vision (Panthea), supported by popular brute strength (Demogorgon), will in the end overthrow all tyranny (Jupiter). In his Spenserian *Mask of Anarchy,* roused by the news of the "Manchester Massacre," he pictures the pageant and chariot of the skeleton Anarchy threatening to crush Hope, and exhorts the hosts of English laborers to resist such exploitation, not by violence, but by return to old English liberties, by Love and Justice and Wisdom and Science and Poetry. In *The Triumph of Life* a similar chariot and charioteer move along, dragging tyrants behind them, and crushing the mad misguided human horde beneath the wheels. His extravaganza in the manner of Aristophanes, *Swellfoot the Tyrant,* reiterates the theme; and he touches it again at the close of his gorgeous Spenserian phantasy, *The Witch of Atlas,* who in her wilful capricious rovings makes fools of kings, priests, and soldiers. It is implied in his terrible drama, *The Cenci,* with its Shakespearian atmosphere, where the lovely Beatrice suffers unjust death at the hands of the law for killing a brutal father who had done her incestuous wrong. *Hellas,* written within a year of his death, and inspired by the *Persae* of Aeschylus, is a half dramatic, half lyric representation of old Greek love of liberty rising to free modern Greece from Turkish tyranny in the face of all Europe.

> Let the tyrants rule the desert they have made;
> Let the free possess the paradise they claim.

Such regeneration of the world should be easy enough. Do we not learn from Rousseau and Godwin that all men in their natural state are not only free and equal, but good?

Progressive as were Shelley's ideas, the abounding spring of his "romanticism" was in Greek literature, especially in the plays of Aeschylus and in the thought and imagery of Plato. His little essay, *A Defence of Poetry,* sets forth a Platonic theory that all his works illustrate. He delighted too in the Homeric Hymns of which he made spirited English versions, and in the radiant and diminutive imagery of Theocritus and his kind.

The *Prometheus Unbound* is his most elaborate composition. The old Prometheus story of vicarious suffering for mankind had been shaped by Aeschylus to his hand. But this basic theme he develops with resonant echoes, not only of the old play, but of *King Lear*, Milton's *Samson*, Marlowe's *Faustus*, into a spectacle of the tragic sufferer like Goethe's Faust and Byron's Manfred. There are traces of romantic storm and stress, of the shudders of the old tale of terror in which he had once dabbled; but the whole fabric is etherealized into a glorification of human freedom through love and intelligence. Past dazzling transcriptions of sunset, deep water, dark woods, domed and statued cities, snow peaks and vast expanse of plain, a Crucifixion, an Aphrodite rising from the sea, it moves forward with the swift and free momentum of Shelley's natural music, now light, now deep, to the lyric finale of all Nature and humankind.

Like Spenser, Shelley saw about him a world in desperate need of regeneration; like Spenser he found the most convenient medium for expression of his ideas in allegory; like Spenser he found natural nourishment for his genius in Plato, especially in the ideas contained in the *Symposium*, which he translated for his wife. The Spenserian stanza, "a measure inexpressibly beautiful," as he says, he used for his most sustained work, the *Revolt of Islam*, and for his most carefully wrought, *Adonais*.

Shelley loved a boat. Wherever he lived, by the Thames, the Arno, the lake of Geneva, the lagoons of Venice, he owned or had the use of a boat. His inspiration, always sensitive to local conditions, was often strongest when he was drifting or sailing alone. It is not surprising that in poem after poem, such as *Queen Mab, Alastor, The Witch of Atlas, Adonais*, the boat, usually self-propelled or borne on swift current, past towering cliffs or dark pine forest or sunlit glades, leaps lightly forward with the rapid movement of his verse, a symbol of his own mind. For the swift movement of rapidly flowing water is the natural movement of his melody. Which is to be expected in one always so sensitively aware of the Platonic spiritual beauty manifest in all physical beauty. Hence his love of things evanescent and half disembodied, of light in all its forms, of dew, mists, clouds, sky, ice, fire, wind, falling leaves, vanishing birds, and of the dark and lonely mysteries of caverns, old ruins, deep evergreen forest, unscaled heights, and death.

Excellent examples are his short poems, which have always been the favorites, such as *Lines among the Euganean Hills, Stanzas in Dejection near Naples, The Cloud, The West Wind, Arethusa, To Night,* "Music when soft voices die," *Indian Serenade, Ozymandias,* and *To a Skylark.*

When Shelley learned of the death of John Keats in Rome, he was convinced that the scathing review of Keats's work by the vested literary interests in the *Quarterly* had caused it. He had hardly known Keats, and except for *Hyperion,* did not appreciate much of his poetry. Yet his old chivalric fire leaped into flame at the stupid cruelty of the reviewer, and he sprang to a noble revenge in his *Adonais.*

This splendid memorial is his most carefully wrought poem. It springs from three ancient pastoral elegies, as lovely as Shelley's and as exquisitely made—Theocritus's lament for Daphnis, Bion's for Adonis, and Moschus's for Bion. But the sensuous details of the originals Shelley has touched with his peculiar transforming and etherealizing power, and Aphrodite becomes his Platonic Urania, cupids and wood-gods turn to the poetic imaginings of the dead poet, and mourning deities are changed into extraordinary shadow portraits of Byron and Shelley himself. He floods with his peculiar poetic glamor the old cemetery on the edge of Rome where Keats was buried, and where now lie the remains of Shelley himself with those of his little son William. The poem rises on the long swell of the Spenserian stanza to a glorious Platonic apotheosis of the soul of Keats, and ends with the strange prophecy of his own fate a year later:

> My spirit's bark is driven
> Far from the shore, far from the trembling throng
> Whose sails were never to the tempest given. . . .

I am borne darkly, fearfully, afar;
    Whilst, burning through the inmost veil of heaven,
The soul of Adonais, like a star,
    Beacons from the abode where the Eternal are.

KEATS (1795-1821)

If the aristocratic families of Byron and Shelley seemed unlikely to produce a great poet, the origin of John Keats seems just as unaccountable. His father, foreman in a London livery-stable, married the owner's daughter, and became proprietor. Yet Keats's parents were not ordinary people. The father, but for an untimely fall from his horse, would doubtless have strained every nerve to give his three sons, John, George, and Tom, a university education. The mother was vivacious and intelligent, and her boys adored her. In school at Enfield, John was a sturdy, lively youngster, handy with his fists, "a terrier for courage," warm-hearted, often fighting with those he loved most, especially George. He could take a prize when he wished; but from his early teens he, poet-like, read himself into an education in the early English poets, especially Spenser and Shakespeare and Milton, and in handbooks of classic myth such as Lemprière's *Classical Dictionary*, which he is said to have had by heart. At fifteen his guardian apprenticed him to a surgeon at Edmonton. Here and in London he worked well for six years of his short life, in both the study and practice of medicine, but at twenty-one gave it over for the real call of poetry.

He grew to be broad of shoulder, though hardly over five feet tall, with fair auburn hair, fine features, and the poet's eye. Friends always gravitated to him—men rather than women— George Cowden Clark, Charles Mathew, Leigh Hunt, the painters Haydon and Severn, Reynolds, Brown, and the young Oxford man, Bailey. But for Keats's social sensitiveness Shelley would doubtless have been an intimate. He exhibited no poetic eccentricities except lonely depressions now and then even in boyhood, and curious preoccupations with the wind or clouds in the country. His genius gave him independence. He evaded criticism and literary advice from Hunt, and even from Shelley.

He spoke of the scathing reviews of *Endymion*, especially in the *Quarterly*, which tried to thwart his fame, as "a mere matter of the moment—I think I shall be among the English poets after my death."

Keats won his poetic technique with hard self-discipline, which may be traced in "I stood tiptoe upon a little hill," an early experiment with the theme of Endymion, and in *Calidore* composed in Spenserian stanza; but particularly in his *Epistles* in rhymed couplets, which deal intimately with his early poetic experience. One evening in October, 1816, Clarke brought home a borrowed copy of the noble 1616 folio of Chapman's translation of Homer. Most of the night they read together among the great passages, and the next morning Keats sent Clarke a copy of his famous sonnet fresh minted, *On First Looking into Chapman's Homer,* sometimes called the most nearly perfect sonnet in English.

Between April and December, 1817, Keats began and finished his longest work *Endymion.* In four thousand lines it elaborates the old theme, popular in all lands and ages, of love between a mortal and an immortal. The tale of Endymion's love for Cynthia the moon is seconded by the stories of Venus and Adonis, Glaucus and Scylla, and Alpheus and Arethusa. Keats's reading of Spenser, of Drayton's *Endimion and Phoebe* and *Man in the Moone*, and particularly of Shelley's *Alastor* was his obvious literary inspiration in creating the poem; but the deeper prompting was the tortured soul of a young poet. In *Alastor*, however, the Poet perishes; in *Endymion* his soul is redeemed through his love of Nature and of his kind. The poem is not allegory, it lacks the necessary symbolism and system. But it looks towards allegory, for Endymion's discontents, disillusion, unfulfilled longings, visions, vague quests of the soul borne on magic boat or wing or cloud, as in *Alastor*, figure forth the vague though insistent and impatient dreams of most young people, raised to their highest power in a poet. Somehow the texture of the whole work is quickened by the unconscious personal charm of Keats himself, his play, his eagerness, his enthusiasm. Once these qualities blend subtly with a certain native grandeur, often overlooked in Keats, in the great *Hymn to Pan*, in the First Book, wherein his instinctive sense of meaning in the old Greek myth enables him to utter perfectly its profound mystery. This he blends with exquisite idyllic play as rare as that of the Greek poet Theocritus, from whom he seems to have caught it; or, better, in whom he recognized a kindred spirit. Wordsworth's grudging approval of the hymn, to Keats's face, as "a pretty piece of paganism" reflects more on himself than on Keats.

The year 1818 was a year of crisis for the poet. He met in London other men of letters—Wordsworth, whom at first he greatly admired, Shelley, Godwin, Lamb, Hazlitt. He wrote *Isabella*, of which he never thought well. *Endymion* was published. In the summer he toured on foot the Lakes and Scotland—a revelation to one accustomed to the "unhealthy and o'er-darkened ways" of London. But his naturally bright and cheerful horizon began to lower. His beloved brother George emigrated to Kentucky, leaving the care of their consumptive brother Tom to the poet. In August and September came the brutal reviews from *Blackwood's* and the *Quarterly*. In the autumn he met, and almost instantly fell into his unhappy passion for, Fanny Brawne, then eighteen, the lively, independent, and not uncultivated daughter of neighbors at Hampstead. In December Tom died, and Keats himself showed warning symptoms of tuberculosis.

Yet his genius, robust and cheerful and social, was not to be daunted or downed by such accidents. Within little more than a year he produced his superb torso, *Hyperion,* his charming *Bards of Passion*, and *Fancy*, his two pieces of medieval romanticism, *The Eve of St. Agnes* and *La Belle Dame Sans Merci, Lamia,* and, most glorious of all, his Odes. As a kind of burden to his song he was at the same time writing his marvellous letters to George and other friends, full of unconscious heroic courage and spirits.

The swift accumulation of his poetic riches was gathered up into the volume of 1820, which gained him speedy recognition in the face of illiberal critics. But his strength and power to create were gone, and with them all hope of marriage with Miss Brawne. In the autumn he went to Italy with his devoted friend Severn, and amid suffering, in dejection totally alien to him, he died in Rome, February 23, 1821. His body lies in the Protestant Cemetery, not far from the grave of Shelley. He was twenty-five.

"Romantic" Keats may have been, but the basis of his poetry is in his five senses and a certain realism. While other poets are keen of eye or ear, or both, Keats feels and smells and tastes as well, delicately and incessantly responsive to the five-fold impact of loveliness on every hand. Evidently he delighted to throw himself down in a patch of grass, or bracken, or flowers, to watch little fleecy clouds shifting in deep blue over-head, or the sweep of wind over deep grain or grass, or the moon riding high, or a stretch of still water. More than once he ex-presses his liking for some view, preferably with a bit of lake or sea, which he has caught in the frame of a window-casing. With such actuality he begins.

> For what has made the sage or poet write
> But the fair paradise of Nature's light?

But he has transfigured it with poetic spell into such miracles as the famous

> magic casements, opening on the foam
> Of perilous seas in faery lands forlorn.

Such words as "cool," "moist," "cold," "green," "dark," "leaf," "ground," both alone and in rich variety of compounds, are favorites.

Another significant favorite is "little." London-bred, it is as if smaller and more familiar and comprehensible things pro-duced in him full poetic intensity without resort to sensa-tional grandeurs of Nature. Hills in the Isle of Wight be-come transformed to his poetic vision of Mount Latmos, and Canterbury Cathedral turns to the temple of Cynthia and

> The vesper hymn, far swollen, soft and full,
> Through the dark pillars of those sylvan aisles.

He loves little, intimate things, things in miniature, and reveals
their beauty by his rare poetic play with them—

> Beaded bubbles winking at the brim;

fauns and satyrs pelting

> each other on the crown
> With silvery oak apples, and fir cones brown,

the little town by river or sea shore; Cupids,

> Rubbing their sleepy eyes with lazy wrists,
> And doubling over head their little fists
> In backward yawns;

"the small gnats" mourning "in a wailful choir,"

> Among the river sallows, borne aloft
>   Or sinking as the light wind lives or dies;
> And full-grown lambs loud bleat from hilly bourne;
> Hedge-crickets sing; and now with treble soft
> The red-breast whistles from a garden croft;
>   And gathering swallows twitter in the skies.

It is this exquisite skill in miniature, this fine idyllism that
lends much of their beauty to the Odes, especially those *To a
Nightingale, On a Grecian Urn, To Psyche, To Autumn, Bards
of Passion,* and the lines, *Fancy.* It proves his kinship with the
poet of *L'Allegro,* with the Greek Theocritus, the Anacreontics,
and poets of the Greek Anthology.

Keats has been called the most Greek of English poets. He
never read Greek, though he once planned to study it with a
learned friend. His ear had somehow caught its "vowel'd un-
dersong." But he had a poet's uncanny sense of the living
beauty inherent in Greek art and poetry. He felt the grand
energies of Homer, and of those sculptures which the much-
reviled Lord Elgin had managed to bring away from the Parthe-
non, and which Keats could revel in at the British Museum.
Indeed the statuesque grouping and portrayal of Saturn, Thea,
and Hyperion in *Hyperion* is under the shaping spell of the
Elgin marbles. He delighted in many of the old myths which

he had first read in school, and divined in them a meaning as fresh as when they were first conceived.

All perfect beauty, that of a nightingale's song, an old romance, an old word, an autumn evening, of the delicate idyll on a Greek urn, of the Elgin marbles, of Homer, of a myth, is never to him "antique." It is timeless, always youthful, will not submit to a date, "is a joy for ever." He is close to notions of Plato in this and in identifying such Beauty with Truth. At any rate the playfulness and affectionate geniality of the man, mingled with the high powers of his genius, have imparted to his best work that radiance of timeless youth which he found the antidote to human ills.

In *Hyperion* some find Keats's highest reach as a poet. It is surely free from the excessive luxuriance of his earlier work, and is clothed with a grandeur and dignity which he owes in part to his study of Milton, partly to his theme, the struggle of old gods with new, partly to Greek sculpture. But it is not a wholly intrinsic grandeur, born of conviction, like that of Homer or Virgil or Milton; rather it resembles that of a late Greek in Alexandria imitating the primitive masters whom he admired, and whose energies he would try to recall.

"I think Poetry," wrote Keats to his friend Taylor, "should surprise by a fine excess and not by Singularity—it should strike the Reader as a wording of his own highest thoughts, and appear almost a Remembrance. . . . The rise, the progress, the setting of imagery should like the sun come natural to him [the reader]. . . . If Poetry comes not as naturally as the Leaves to a tree it had better not come at all."

To poets of a later day Keats has been a subtle inspiration, especially to Tennyson and to the Pre-Raphaelites, in their painting as well as in their verse. His love for the flavor of a single old word or epithet, his treatment of picture and pageant, as in *Lamia* and *The Eve of St. Agnes*, his use of real and actual Nature as a basis of his most romantic imaginings, his peculiar music—in these particulars and in others, the reader of modern verse often finds himself thinking: "That is like Keats."

HUNT (1784-1859)

Not so much for literary greatness, as for his courage and amiability, and his prolific pen, has Leigh Hunt found his place among these greater names. He was associated with the more illustrious writers of two generations. He first discovered Keats, introduced him to Shelley, Hazlitt, Godwin, and Wordsworth, and warmly befriended his earlier literary projects—perhaps too warmly for their good. It was under his roof at Hampstead that Keats and Shelley met. Before he died at seventy-four he had become a neighbor and good friend of Carlyle, a friend of Dickens; he knew Hawthorne, read Emerson, and was the encourager of the young poets, Browning, Tennyson, and Rossetti. In his sixties he wrote what will probably be his most memorable book, his *Autobiography*, which as biography Carlyle set next to Boswell's *Johnson*. It is a crowded gallery of vivid scenes and very human portraits of the great poets and men of letters whom Hunt knew, and not least among them, the playful, keen, skilful, sometimes pathetic figure of Hunt himself, "gentlest of the wise," as Shelley called him. The picture of the burning of Shelley's body is indelible.

Hunt began life as poet and journalist. Some dozen periodicals all told he started and edited, most of them unable to survive a twelvemonth. But his weekly *Examiner* ran for thirteen years, and here and in his *Indicator* he first published his best essays. His family was large; his earnings, in spite of desperate industry, were small. Yet he had high courage: he defended single-handed the new poetry against the savage reactionary reviews in *Blackwood's* and the *Quarterly*; for telling the truth in the *Examiner* about the dissolute Prince Regent, and refusing to promise future silence in the matter, Hunt and his brother were sent to prison for two years. There he went on writing, was visited and comforted by Tom Moore, Byron, and Shelley, and became the subject of a sonnet by Keats. In 1822 he went, wife, brood of seven youngsters, and all, to Italy to join Shelley and Byron in a literary venture, but had hardly arrived when Shelley was drowned. Byron lost his interest, and the Hunts, after two years of privation, at last reached England again. In 1828 Hunt published his notorious *Lord Byron and some of his Contemporaries*, a realistic and literal account of the man; but it so outraged the world, which at the moment had clothed his Lordship in glamour and idolatry, that the poor author was almost overwhelmed with attack. Literary iconoclasm finds a more responsive audience today. It was this book which Hunt afterwards tempered and elaborated into his *Autobiography*.

As a poet he was a good journeyman; his sonnet *The Grass-hopper and the Cricket*, written in competition with Keats, and his *Abou Ben Adhem*, are still favorites. Much of his energy went into purveying literary culture to middle-class contemporaries through his criticism and anthologies, his exploiting of old plays and Italian poets, his short stories and anecdotes, down to *Readings for Railways*. The most significant venture was his *Imagination and Fancy*, 1844, including poets from Marlowe to Keats, and an essay, "What is Poetry?" based upon ideas of Coleridge, a document in English criticism.

PART SEVEN

VICTORIA

CHAPTER 29

New Classes and New Empire

THE progress of England is like a river among the hills. A broad, calm reach or still-water, ominously deep, suddenly breaks into a headlong, turbulent plunge, which in turn settles into another long expanse of calm. The tranquil stretch of the eighteenth century, when aristocracy and popular rights seemed to be adjusted in happy equilibrium, when common sense, reason, domestic comfort, and fine manners all made this seem to the complacent citizen "the best possible of worlds," wherein "whatever is is right," nevertheless had welling and swirling within it new energies, a new sense of the mystery of Man and Nature, which swept on to a profound revolution of ideas and living. In its earlier phases it is sometimes called the Romantic Revolution, in its later the Industrial Revolution, but it has found no adequate name.

We must content ourselves to observe that in the twenty-five or more years between the French Revolution (1789) and the end of the wars with Napoleon (1815), England was not free from fear or danger, from ferment and utmost national exertion. Her revolution, though less violent, was as profound as that of France. From this ordeal she emerged only to be appalled by terrible misery and hardship among her laboring poor. Then by many slow and hard-wrought reforms and new prosperity, she entered upon that quieter expanse of undreamed greatness implied in the name "Victorian."

Meanwhile from 1750 to 1830 her population had more than doubled. The old forests had been exhausted, and iron and coal had become in their stead a necessity. To bring iron and coal together for manufacture required transportation. Canals, paved roads by Mr. MacAdam, the steam engine (1785), the steamboat (1812), the steam printing-press (1814), railways and the locomotive (1825) mark stages in the growth of the new industrialism. Master and apprentice disappeared, handcraft and village life decayed, and population was herded in swarming new centres of manufacture; huge cities like Manchester, Birmingham, and Liverpool grew rapidly out of obscure villages, and Lancashire, London, Clyde, and the "Black Country" engulfed old rural beauty. In 1804 Blake already discerned the evil omen of "these dark, Satanic mills"; and by 1836 Mr. Pickwick was approaching Birmingham after nightfall amid the lurid glare of the furnaces, the roar of the factories, and throngs of working people.

In the country, enclosures which had been creeping forward since the sixteenth century and had been especially flagrant in the eighteenth had gradually absorbed the land into great estates, and made an end of small holdings. Methods of agriculture improved, but the farmer sank in social dignity towards the status of a hireling, and the new issue was drawn between landlord and laborer. Bad feeling led to rick-burning, poaching, and other social disorders, which yield matter for many a Victorian novel. Out of this turmoil of dissolution rose two distinct but fluctuating new classes. The first grew and flourished with those whose enterprise, talents, and energy enabled them to take advantage of the new industrial and mercantile conditions, and to emerge into wealth and importance. It became the new middle class, the substantial, Victorian *bourgeoisie.* The other class was recruited of those who, lacking the mettle of the first, became their employees—the new laboring class.

All Victorian literature is concerned in one way or other with these two classes—their interfluctuations, their struggles with each other or with the old aristocratic régime, their battling either to win their rights, or to realize their social and cultural aspirations. The novels of the century offer a magnificent review of these struggles, though none is more vivid than a retrospective chronicle of a middle-class family, written in the next century, Galsworthy's *Forsyte Saga*. For the middle class it was at first a struggle for representation in the government. In 1828-9 Dissenters and Catholics were first admitted to a legitimate part in public affairs. In 1832 the famous Reform Bill disfranchised the "rotten boroughs," and representation passed from the old intrenched land interests to fairer distribution among the increasing and newly assorted population.

The laboring class suffered at first from miserable exploitation by their employers, but the new humanitarian spirit was astir for rapid reform through factory laws and poor laws, which did something to relieve the wretched conditions. Two early episodes in the long struggle became almost symbolic in literature: one was the Manchester Massacre or "Peterloo" (1819), when 50,000 protesting artisans, gathered peacefully at St. Peter's Field, Manchester, were set upon by the soldiery with the loss of many lives; the other, known as "Chartism," was the People's Charter (1837), petitioning the government for manhood suffrage and no property qualification for entering Parliament. Revision of the barbarous old criminal code, and the abolition of slavery added two more to the list of great reforms.

Amid all this pain and travail a new world was being born —our world of middle and industrial classes, of capital and labor, of science applied to the convenience and safety of the many, of swarming cities, of a new sort of government concerned in, and responsible for, the welfare of the governed, in short, of democracy. Such struggles and upturnings, such strenuous if peaceful progress, long had their fertilizing effect upon literature. As under Elizabeth and Anne, so under another queen rose a great literary revival. In 1837 Victoria came to the throne.

The grand Victorian period, so disparaged and misunderstood of late, was primarily the long and tranquil stretch of fat peace between the forties and the seventies, merely stirred by the Crimean War. Peaceful it may have been, but not stagnant. Manufacture, commerce, science, engineering, religion, education, especially of women, put forth unheard-of energies to the building of the New Empire.

The Victorian literary revival is another instance of the strong upthrust from beneath of new energies, of new men with new opportunity for wealth and achievement; at first often vulgar, crude, "new rich," but nevertheless essential and indispensable to the revival. Such, as we saw, was the time of Chaucer, of Shakespeare, of Defoe and Pope and Johnson, and such more than ever is the time of Victoria. No index or exponent of Victorian literature is so generally applicable, so significant, as its relation to the history and rise of the new middle class. From that very class came the most vigorous recruits to literature. Macaulay, Dickens, Thackeray, Ruskin, George Eliot, the Brownings, Trollope, Morris, Meredith, Hardy, were all of stock that was rising in position or wealth or culture.

These struggles and social fluctuations produce many a literary motive. It is just the time to breed snobs and snobbery for the use of Thackeray and Trollope. It is prolific in socially ill-matched love-affairs and tragedies which extend in long and numerous literary succession, down to the *Ordeal of Richard Feverel* and later. The wrongs of the poor, the struggles of labor, the emergence of the leader from the lower ranks variously preoccupy Carlyle, Dickens, Ruskin, George Eliot, and Morris. Such conspicuous novels as Disraeli's *Sybil*, Mrs. Gaskell's *Mary Barton* and *North and South*, Charlotte Brontë's *Shirley*, Dickens's *Hard Times*, Kingsley's *Alton Locke*, and Meredith's *Evan Harrington* show how vital were these themes and how teeming with dramatic motive and situation.

But the field of what is called "manners," the deficiencies

of culture among the rising classes, their aspiration to "respectability" and refinement, and the whole question of what good manners and refinement really are—this is a field especially fertile in literature. As in Congreve's time flourished the comedy of manners, so in this fluid but comparatively tranquil time of Victoria flourishes the novel of manners in such hands as those of Trollope, George Eliot, and a multitude of successors and lesser lights.

A "new" man may be rich and in some ways important. But his old vulgarity still clings to him, he is ashamed of it, seizes upon any quick and speedy course to a counterfeit refinement which he cannot distinguish from the real. Such is one important aspect of the rising new middle class of Victorian England. It is at first vulgar, crude, stodgy in its new respectability, in its moral code and its inherited religion, eager to spend its new money in display, infecting all society with ambitious and unscrupulous materialism, with the desire to get rich quick, as in Trollope's *Way We Live Now*. Bulwer-Lytton catered to its pretensions in his many melodramatic novels of fashionable life, in his Harley, and his Pelham, who instead of the colors then fashionable for men's evening wear chose black as being more distinguished, and by this easy stroke condemned men to formal evening sables even unto this day.

"The curse of England," said Macaulay, "is the obstinate determination of the middle classes to make their sons what they call gentlemen." Such defects of its qualities inspired directly or indirectly much of the Victorian poetry and prose. It made even Wordsworth swear—"Great God! I'd rather be a pagan. . . ." Carlyle is ever sneering at its "gigs and respectability." Ruskin spent most of his superb energies, first trying to open the dull and vulgar middle-class eye to the beauties of painting, buildings, and Nature, then to the social ugliness of factories and machines. Arnold berated the class as Philistines. Browning and Tennyson, Morris and the Pre-Raphaelites, ranged far in search of the springs of the world's beauty from which to replenish the arid Philistine world, and came back heavy-laden from Italy, Greece, and the Middle Ages.

Thus the war with vulgarity was, as it were, a civil war, in which the poets and literary artists found themselves in conflict with the very class to which they owed their best energies, and indeed in most cases their origin.

The strongest present-day objection to the Victorians points to their moral code and standards. "Mid-Victorians" appear to us priggish, hidebound, hypocritical. Naturally an emergent middle-class looked well to its proprieties and respectabilities, especially a class with the Puritan inheritance, and still on the whole "evangelical."

But the moral concerns of Victorian literature cannot be taken so lightly. They are an essential part of its greatness. They represent the nation's rise from the debauch of morals which had intervened since the last days of George III's reign. To them Victorian literature owes its solidity, its grand proportions, the broad yet sharp issues in human life which it is constantly drawing; and any appreciation of Victorian literature which disregards them must be partial. Gloomy and narrow they may sometimes seem, but genuinely human they were.

The same imposing dignity that pervaded the manners and morals of the Victorians expressed itself in their outward life —in the spacious, high, formal interiors of their houses, in their massive hair-cloth furniture, their plush and ormolu, in awesome expanse of heavy Brussels carpet. Such was the natural and proper setting of new, conscious worldly success and moral complacency.

In keeping with the rest was their religion—evangelical, often unlovely, with a strong tendency among the livelier minds to rationalism. "Evangelicalism" is the doctrine and manner of life into which the religious revival of the eighteenth century settled after two or three generations, that is in the earlier half of the nineteenth century. It tended to become formal, even stolid. It was continually laboring with religious self-consciousness; it was much preoccupied, often painfully, with salvation of souls and the prescribed course necessary thereto; it was Biblical and literal; it made much of conscience; it was strictly sabbatarian; it made sharp distinction between sacred and secular, with the effect that its worship, its architecture, even its private life were starved for beauty; but it left plenty of room for material gains six days a week. Where it was merely formal it tended to breed hypocrites; where it was sincere it produced noble but not always genial characters. It was the recrudescence of the old Puritanism. It included most Dissenters and the "low-church" element in the Church of England.

It was perhaps the ugliness and gloom of Evangelicalism that, as much as anything else, gave rise to the "Oxford Movement," led by Keble, Newman, and Pusey, and sent men to the ancient and the medieval church in quest of refreshing beauty of usage, ritual, and doctrine. Its traces are obvious in much of the literature after 1833. It inspired many novels such as Shorthouse's *John Inglesant*, and influenced by way of opposition Kingsley's *Yeast, Alton Locke,* and *Hypatia.*

But Victorian religion suffered not only from evangelical failure to glorify God and enjoy Him. Under the discoveries and speculations of science it became a highly uncomfortable matter for the more intelligent. Darwin's doctrine of evolution, published in his *Origin of Species* (1859), was but one of various scientific considerations which upset snug old formulas, and bred unhappy scepticism and agnosticism in men who could not cope with these tests of faith, nor could yet know enough to transcend them. Such was the predicament of Matthew Arnold, and, more cheerfully, of Herbert Spencer, Huxley, and Tyndall.

With science, or perhaps as a part of it, went the study of history, with its historical criticism and the growing historical sense of everything. It sought—and still seeks—by studying origins and lines of development, to account for everything from an epic poem to swallowtails. It both nourished and fed upon the new idea of progress and improvement, which has now become instinctive with us. Long before Darwin it was in the air. "In every experimental science there is a tendency toward perfection," wrote Macaulay.[1] Indeed as early as 1744

---

[1] *History of England,* chap. 3, near beginning

Akenside hints the doctrine in his poem, *Pleasures of the Imagination.*

All this change furnished plenty of materials and themes for literature, and proved most sophisticating. But it has carried with it its penalty. It runs grave risk of becoming super-sophisticate; of indifference, of weaning men from a faith in their own times to "praise every century *but* this"—a capital offence in the eye of the satirist.[1]

At length, as the energies and endeavors of this great Victorian nineteenth century are spent, this seems to be its fate— to be super-sophisticate, to decline into languor of mind and conviction, satiety, the habit of disparagement, academic dry rot. The battle with the Philistine seemed by the nineties to be won; but new energies for new battles were not yet forthcoming.

The symptoms of this decay appear early, as early as Arnold's wistful, helpless longing for the "free onward impulse" of the scholar gipsy as an antidote to his own academic disease:

> O born in days when wits were fresh and clear,
>   And life ran gaily as the sparkling Thames;
>   Before this strange disease of modern life,
>   With its sick hurry, its divided aims,
>   Its heads o'ertaxed, its palsied hearts, was rife. . . .

It is not surprising that sophisticates like Mr. Santayana should now view Browning as a crude barbarian; or that Mr. T. S. Eliot and others should endeavor to galvanize their literary energies by consorting with giants of Elizabethan and Jacobean days.

[1] Ko Ko in *The Mikado*

CHAPTER 30

Biographers and Prophets

MACAULAY (1800-1859)

In his many essays on history and literature, and in his *History of England*, Thomas Babington Macaulay served his middle class well. He supplied them in a most easy and agreeable way with the information in history, biography, and literature of which they felt the need, and which otherwise they could not readily come by. Naturally his high talents for the task won him immediate and unvarying success. Latterly he has been attacked for his partiality and prejudice, for his unreliability in details and his general superficiality. Yet he had his great if not enduring qualities.

In many ways he is close to the times of Pope and Johnson, as if no romantic movement had ever taken place. To almost all of the great literature of his own time, and to that of the romantic generation before him, he was indifferent or contemptuous. His dominant interest is the eighteenth century. His great *History* was designed to stretch from James II to Sir Robert Walpole. For all the abuse he heaps on Johnson's style, his own is a direct descendant from Johnson's with strong family resemblance. "It is remarkable that to the last he entertained a fixed contempt for all those modes of life and those studies which tend to emancipate the mind from the prejudices of a particular age or a particular nation." This is Macaulay writing of Johnson. It might as well be Johnson writing of Macaulay. The two were alike in their love of biography, of London, of intellectual battle; in their forthright utterance of opinion, their vast reading, their retentive memories, their domestic kindliness, their friendships, even in their physical bulk and clumsiness.

But Macaulay was inferior to Johnson in wit and intellect and spiritual depth. He had waged no struggle with poverty or failure or neglect. He endured no agony of soul. He never attempted any pursuit against the grain. Overwhelming success and recognition were his from the publication of his first essay, that on Milton, till, in 1857, he was made a baron. A few months later his achievements were honored with burial in the Abbey.

He was a son of Zachary Macaulay, a man who had made money in the Indies, but who became an active supporter of Wilberforce in the abolition of slavery. Young Macaulay by way of the bar entered public life, and from his first speech in Parliament at thirty, was a conspicuous figure. He threw himself whole-heartedly into the cause of the returning Whigs and their struggles for reform. From thirty-three to thirty-seven he was in India as a very useful member of the supreme council. For ten years more he continued in active politics and held various high offices in the government, but kept the last decade of his life for his *History* and latest essays. His public career was honest and shrewd, with a keen sense of the realities. But he was vehement, belligerent, and too ready to think a man who did not agree with him a fool.

When he was four or five he was taken to see Walpole's house at Strawberry Hill. A servant spilled some hot coffee on his leg. After a little, to the anxious inquiry of his hostess he replied: "Thank you, Madam, the agony is abated." At that stage it is not easy to tell a prodigy from a prig. "Yes, Mamma," said he, "industry shall be my bread and attention my butter."

At six he was reading everything he could lay hands on, and beginning to write a compendium of universal history. In Trinity College, Cambridge, he was a student of some distinction, consuming his literature both ancient and modern with a ravenous appetite. His power of acquisition and his memory were all his life phenomenal. He kept up his classics both Greek and Latin by constant re-reading—on long voyages, in

India, late at night, at any odd minute, meanwhile adding new languages, such as Portuguese while sailing from Madras to Calcutta, and the newly fashionable German. No wonder that the imaginary "schoolboy," always turning up in his essays as a disconcerting example of common knowledge, is so repulsive to the young. Anywhere, or any time, he had a book by him, as proof against boredom. Even in crowded streets he was often seen striding along, tearing the heart out of a book, a little disheveled, with one thumb in the pocket of his handsome embroidered waistcoat, for which article of finery he had a weakness. Such promenades were his only exercise.

His nephew tells us that if *Paradise Lost* and the *Pilgrim's Progress* were to perish, Macaulay could have restored them both letter-perfect from memory. He beguiled the hours of a night voyage to Dublin reciting to himself whole books of Milton's epic. He thought he could probably rewrite *Sir Charles Grandison* from memory.

It would seem that such industry, such memory, and such wide range would have made him a faithful recorder of the past. In imagination he was really nearer to being a poet or a novelist than a historian. The past was as the present to him; and London was his inspiration. Once in its streets, his mind teeming with countless details associated with every name and court and gateway he encountered, his "love of castle-building" as he called it took possession of him. "The past is, in my mind, soon constructed into a romance." As he walked through old London and Paris, he composed long conversations between the great of the past.

Thus it was that he wrote his essays and his *History*. They are essentially romance, which accounts for their defects as well as for their virtues. They cast about the reader a spell which carries him along with the author into old times. They are done with a broad easy stroke, in black and white and strong contrasting colors. Smug prejudice and hasty impression seem as persuasive and reasonable in his skilful hands as his more reliable and solid judgment. But if he deceives his readers, he has first deceived himself. His discourse moves on with a strong, pleasant, even momentum of style. The reader meets no resistance. He surrenders himself unawares to Macaulay's plausible generalities, and is made to feel that he is rapidly becoming master of the subject, just as Macaulay is sure that he himself already is.

Much the same virtues recommended his *Lays of Ancient Rome* and other verse to the multitude of his readers. Their easy vigor, their vividness, their sententiousness, their simple if noisy rhythm and cadence stir at any rate the more superficial enjoyments of poetry.

At eighteen he had written: "If my life be a life of literature, it shall certainly be one of literature directed to moral ends." Such it proved to be. Through all his work runs an element of Victorian morality, which in its narrower limitations has betrayed him into unsympathetic misjudgment of certain figures of the past—notably Bacon and Horace Walpole. In its broader scope, however, it imparts to all his works a solid ballast and equilibrium that often saves them from becoming merely specious.

CARLYLE (1795-1881)

The new industrial age had bred a new "science"—political economy—"the dismal science," according to Carlyle. Springing from the common-sense philosophy of John Locke, it took definite form under Adam Smith's theories in his *Wealth of Nations* (1776) and the imported French doctrine of *laissez-faire*, and waxed mighty in the school of the Utilitarians, of whom Jeremy Bentham was the chief, and James Mill, Paley, and Francis Place were leading lights. The benevolent Jeremy found the whole economic case a matter of pleasures and pains. These he was prepared to weigh and measure by a neat system of his own. The self-interest of the individual, if free to act, would in the aggregate result in "the greatest good to the greatest number." Of any new proposal he demanded to know: "What is the use of it?" Thus the world of men was conceived as a machine of checks and balances, making ultimately for general happiness.

The Utilitarians undoubtedly did much good; but the spectacle of hopeless misery and injustice all about, getting worse if anything, refuted their proposed solutions with grim facts, and gave some men pause. Happiness depends upon mysterious imponderables beyond the reach of well-meaning Benthams. The world is not so simple as a machine. Man is not just an "omnivorous biped that wears breeches." "Where else is the God's-Presence manifested not to our eyes only, but to our hearts, as in our fellow man?"

It is the voice of a prophet out of the wild Burns country of the north—Thomas Carlyle. He was of Scottish peasant origin, son of a rugged, God-fearing stone-mason, with a heart of smouldering fire. Carlyle was born in a wee house reared by his father's own toil-worn hand in the dour village of Ecclefechan in the lower Annandale. Most of his life he was at close grips with poverty. He was intended for the "kirk," but his liberal studies and reading at the University in Edinburgh wrecked his orthodoxy and turned his purpose to a literary life. A sardonic vein, like Swift's, got him the nicknames "Jonathan" and "Dean."

While his father and brothers were wringing a scant living from poor soil, he made his lean way tutoring, and teaching at Annan and Kircaldy. He tried and forsook the law, read widely, and witnessed the strike of 60,000 desperate workmen in the factories of Glasgow, himself at a desperate loss for a profession. Meanwhile the "dyspepsia" which tortured him most of his life laid hold upon him. Thus at twenty-five the world like "one, huge, dead, immeasurable Steam-engine" seemed on the point of crushing him. Perhaps the Utilitarians were right; it might be a machine universe after all.

At this point he met and fell in love with Jane Welsh, a doctor's daughter of Haddington. She was a spirited girl, living in dull surroundings, and she recognized Carlyle's genius and encouraged him. Gossip as people may and have about this marriage, they cannot obliterate the fact that these two were well-mated comrades. Indeed, Jane Welsh was as necessary to the full flowering of Carlyle's genius, as was Dorothy Wordsworth to her brother or Mrs. Unwin to Cowper. Carlyle's powers in literature did not assert themselves till his marriage, and during the fifteen years that he survived his wife he produced nothing of his old high quality.

Between the meeting and the wedding dragged five long, disheartening years. A rival, a snobbish disapproving mother in the way, Jane's first uncertainty, Carlyle's poverty, his spiritual agony, all were mingled in his "baphometic fire baptism" as he calls it in *Sartor*. Then came the sudden crisis, the "conversion," which he describes in the "Everlasting No" of *Sartor*, when he asks of himself: "What *art* thou afraid of? . . . There rushed like a stream of fire over my whole soul; and I shook base Fear away from me for ever. I was strong, of unknown strength; a spirit, almost a god." One thinks of similar crises and dedications—Herbert's, Bunyan's, Shelley's, Wordsworth's.

Meanwhile from his early reading of Madame de Staël's *Allemagne* he had found his way into German literature— to Goethe, Schiller, Richter, Novalis, and above all to Kant. He turned this knowledge to account in various translations and essays, introducing the British readers to the increasingly fashionable German writers. Of this bread-and-cheese work his *Life* of the congenial Schiller was perhaps the most substantial. During these dark years it is not unnatural that the *Sturm und Drang*, the Storm and Stress, of the German romanticists, should have taken a possession of him which it never wholly relinquished. When Byron died he broke into a tremor. So did Jane. A ferment of sentimentality pervades Teufelsdröck's inflated rhapsody on the night-life of Weiss-nichtwo. Such super-emotion was, or became, an involuntary habit with him, and he cannot, even in a familiar letter, mention anything so casual as stepping into the street without a perceptible rise of literary temperature. He suffers from that vice of literary self-consciousness which was engendered in the romantic movement, and afflicts the "literary" person even to this day. But from the Germans he drew things of far more value, especially from Goethe and Kant; self-reliance, reverence for the human and the godlike in all men, the authority of certain deeper intimations of moral and religious truth over the inferences of mere reason, the antidote to shallow common-sense. These demolished for him the machine universe, and freed his frantic soul.

Two years after their marriage the Carlyles retired to the lonely, upland, wind-swept farm of Craigenputtock. There amid much journalistic work on German literature Carlyle produced his great essays on Burns and on Johnson, and his most original work, *Sartor Resartus,* while his wife subdued her delicate and not always patient hand to unaccustomed housework.

When *Sartor* began to appear in *Fraser's Magazine* such was the storm of protest at this strange and monstrous stuff that the editor turned it back upon Carlyle to save his periodical. The like had never been seen. The *Tailor Newly Patched,* as the title goes, is perhaps a hint that the thought of the book is but the eternal thought of Plato restated to suit the needs of the times. It springs from a witty passage on clothes in the second section of Swift's *Tale of a Tub,*[1] and expands to show that the visible world, with all its customs and conventions, is but the outward clothing of an inner invisible spiritual reality. But on this theme Carlyle plays an amazing and fascinating series of variations, through all ranges of fancy, grotesque satire, lovely idyllism, burlesque, grim fantasies of war and human misery. He pretends to be the literary executor of one Professor Teufelsdröck, Professor of Things in General at the University of Weissnichtwo, and in the Second Book, which perhaps is best read first, sets forth the life, woes, and triumphs of the old man, in which one reads essentially Carlyle's own experience and conclusions. Too strong for the middle-class supporters of magazines, *Sartor* first appeared entire in America through the negotiations of Emerson, to succeed at home only as the English public grew a bit accustomed to the odd ways of the new prophet.

Less perhaps in its central thought than in its astonishing variety and vigor, its power to set the reader's mind working and observing things he had never thought of before, lies the life of this book. It puts forth a rough dynamic energy, in which there is at times something primitive and natural, like the forces of Nature from which this Scotch peasant drew his own.

[1] See page 295.

He is the sworn enemy of all outworn convention and formula no longer supported by the reality which it once clothed. Away with old clothes; they are but rags and imposture.

Carlyle had made two visits to London, where he met Coleridge and began his friendships with Leigh Hunt and John Stuart Mill. He and his wife now at the end of six years took farewell of Craigenputtock and the moors, and set out on the high road to London. Here Hunt found them the well-known little house in Chelsea which became their abode for the rest of their lives, and is now a literary shrine. They were poor indeed, but Carlyle bravely set about the *French Revolution*, writing desperately for bread. When the first volume was done, Mill borrowed the manuscript, and lent it to a preoccupied lady whose maid used it to kindle the morning fire until the last page was in ashes. There was nothing for Carlyle but to begin again, without a note or a recollection of what he had first written. The brave couple took it standing. At last in 1837, Carlyle now forty-one, the work was finished. He could say to the world: "You have not had for a hundred years any book that comes more direct and flamingly from the heart of man!" Surely it had never before had such a history.

The *French Revolution* is more a pictorial and musical rhapsody than a narrative, a succession of scenes at times highly dramatized, but always carefully staged, and carefully costumed by this philosopher of clothes. They open with confusion of multitude and circumstance, individuals emerge, more and more distinct, until *the* figures for whom the scene is prepared—Louis, Marie, Mirabeau, Drouet, Danton, Robespierre—draw all attention; and their gleaming distinctness is further heightened by some reiterated picturesque detail of complexion, hair, eye, or costume.

Carlyle's heart was wrung by conditions about him, and ever went out to a suffering and helpless people, but he had no confidence in their power to manage their affairs. "The History of the World," he concludes, "is but the Biography of great men." Such is the genetic idea of the rest of his work. From this text he delivered a course of lectures in 1840 on

Heroes and Hero-Worship. The gaunt figure, the artless, rustic manner, the eye burning with a kind of elemental volcanic fire from the depths of the sallow, rough-hewn face and shock of unkempt hair, the strong burr of Annandale, all delighted and fascinated his distinguished audience. But popular vogue was abhorrent to him.

In *Past and Present* he reviews the social ills of his times, the quackeries prescribed for them, in Parliament and out. He despairs of remedy except by the gift of the great leader; such for example as old Abbot Samson, sturdy, honest, capable, who in the twelfth century was raised from the ranks by the grace of God to bring order out of a hopeless mess in the monastery of St. Edmundsbury.

By the same theory it was Carlyle's work to rehabilitate Cromwell, one of the "Heroes," and a mark of obloquy ever since the Restoration. In his *Cromwell's Letters and Speeches* (1845) the world saw a different figure from the Cromwell of its almost two-century prejudice.

But his longest quest for a hero was his preoccupation with the subject of Frederick the Great of Prussia, which resulted in eight volumes. The old gifts of portraiture and pageantry had not failed, but Frederick proved, after all the long labor, not to be first-rate material for a Carlylean hero. How much aware Carlyle was of the fact does not appear, except that the *History of Frederick the Great* marked the end of his great work, and the consummation of his despair for the world. As early as 1848 he was said to have observed: "The human race has now arrived at the last stage of Jackassification." *Frederick* was finished in 1865. In that year he was honored with the Lord Rectorship of his old university. Almost in the moment of his high honor he lost his wife.

Two instincts were uppermost in Carlyle's genius—the biographical instinct and the instinct of moral reform. His history he read and wrote biographically, and biography was to him an art. Marvellous is his gift of portraiture, proved in a hundred instances—Mahomet, Dante, Voltaire, Coleridge—done always with swift, vivid, magic stroke and luminous color. They are never detached figures, but wrought with intense if sometimes mistaken sympathy or repugnance. It was his instinctive practice to warp himself into a kind of identity with the figure which preoccupied him, until the likeness became qualified with a tincture of Carlyle; but the result has the life and vigor of great art. Many regard as his masterpiece the tranquil *Life* of his friend John Sterling, in which his fine powers deploy themselves at ease, and his deep voice never breaks into falsetto from overstrain. And the same happier balance maintains in his essay on Burns and his superb essay on Johnson. At times this artistic self-possession limns a lovely miniature, such as the reminiscence of childhood in *Sartor*, or Coleridge's view southward from Highgate Hill:

Close at hand, wide sweep of flowery leafy gardens, their few houses mostly hidden, the very chimney-pots veiled under blossomy umbrage, flowed gloriously down hill; gloriously issuing in wide-tufted undulating plain-country, rich in all charms of field and town. Waving blooming country of the brightest green; dotted all over with handsome villas, handsome groves; crossed by roads and human traffic, here inaudible or heard only as a musical hum: and behind all swam, under olive-tinted haze, the illimitable limitary ocean of London, with its domes and steeples definite in the sun, big Paul's and its many memories attached to it hanging high over all.

It is easy to pick flaws in Carlyle's way of utterance; they are chiefly mannerisms and lie on the surface for all and sundry to point at. But he is not much given to rhetorical tricks and devices. The virtues of his style are personal and intrinsic—vigor and movement in imagery and in sound. So orally does he write that the reader seems to catch not infrequently a suggestion of a strong Scotch burr inherent in the very words themselves.

The man is not a deep or original thinker, though stimulating to thought in the ordinary reader's mind. But he is the preacher, believing above all in the hope for the times that resides in the great man, the man who sees the truth face to face and devotes to it all his energies, who tolerates no hocus-pocus and make-believe, who in this sense is sincere, who understands the plight of every man down to the humblest.

There is no hope for democracy in itself. Indispensable to it is the great man to lead it. Which is enough to prove Carlyle the prophet, proclaiming abroad in his own day ideas which are in the present moment coming close to the hearts of thinking men. His stature as a prophet is accordingly waxing in our times. "Two men I honor," he writes, "and no third":

First, the toilworn Craftsman that with earth-made Implement laboriously conquers the Earth, and makes her man's. Venerable to me is the hard Hand; crooked, coarse; wherein notwithstanding lies a cunning virtue, indefeasibly royal, as of the Sceptre of this Planet. Venerable too is the rugged face, all weather-tanned, besoiled, with its rude intelligence; for it is the face of a Man living manlike. . . . Hardly-entreated Brother! For us was thy back so bent, for us were thy straight limbs and fingers so deformed. . . .

A second man I honor, and still more highly: Him who is seen toiling for the spiritually indispensable; not daily bread, but the bread of Life. . . . Highest of all, when his outward and inward endeavor are one: when we can name him Artist; not earthly Craftsman only, but inspired Thinker, who with heaven-made Implement conquers Heaven for us!

Unspeakably touching is it, however, when I find both dignities united; and he that must toil outwardly for the lowest of man's wants, is also toiling inwardly for the highest. Sublimer in this world know I nothing than a Peasant Saint, could such now anywhere be met with. Such a one will take thee back to Nazareth itself.

NEWMAN (1801-1890)

In 1884, looking back over forty years, Matthew Arnold recalled the enchanting voices of his youth at Oxford. There was the voice of Newman every Sunday at the University Church, St. Mary's. "Who could resist the charm of that spiritual apparition, gliding in the dim afternoon light through the aisles of St. Mary's, rising into the pulpit, and then, in the most entrancing of voices, breaking the silence with words and thoughts which were a religious music—subtle, sweet, mournful? I seem to hear him still, saying: 'After the fever of life, after weariness and sicknesses, fightings and despondings, languor and fretfulness, struggling and succeeding; after all the changes and chances of this troubled, unhealthy state—at length comes death, at length the white throne of God, at length the beatific vision.' "

Arnold's speech is kindled in recollection of the days when the Oxford Movement was gathering momentum under the personal charm of such men as Keble, Hurrell Froude, and John Henry Newman. Known sometimes as the Tractarian, High-Church, or Anglo-Catholic Movement, it rose to restore to English religion the power and beauty, the order and unity, of which many felt the loss. The evangelical hue of ordinary English religion early in the nineteenth century, bleak and gloomy and hidebound with its formal and outworn Calvinism, spent itself chiefly in philanthropy and humanitarian projects. "Intellectual" men took to the course of "liberalism," "thinking things out for themselves," insisting only on what they considered essentials, aspiring to breadth of mind; but often the broader their minds, the shallower their convictions and the vaguer their ideas, forfeiting poetry and mysticism, and as one says, attaining rather to "dry light than divine fire."

For the needful virtues and graces thus somehow lost the Oxford Movement turned back in appeal to the seventeenth century and to the Middle Ages. The romantics, especially Sir Walter Scott, always a favorite of Newman from childhood, were still revealing the beauties of the medieval world, real or imaginary. Coleridge, Southey, and Wordsworth had stirred the deeper soil of men's meditation or quickened their torpid imaginations. To the romantics the Oxford Movement owes its immediate parentage. "It was not," says Newman, "so much a movement as a 'spirit afloat'; . . . the spiritual awakening of spiritual wants."

Keble's sermon at Oxford on July 14, 1833, pointing out the needs aforesaid, launched the Movement, and for a dozen years it waxed strong throughout the English world, not without the usual bitterness of theological and ecclesiastical controversy. After the crisis, when the University essentially repudiated it in 1845, and Newman became a Catholic, the drama was over; but its effects continued, and still continue, to permeate the Anglican Church.

In literature it was prolific in controversial novels, and it strongly colored others, such as those by Charlotte Yonge, author of the *Heir of Redclyffe*, and a disciple of Keble. It enriched English hymnology with several translations by Neale from old Latin and Greek hymns, notably "Jerusalem the golden;" it lent its impulses to the Pre-Raphaelites, especially the Rossettis. Before his famous sermon Keble had published his cyclic group of poems, *The Christian Year*, which even after a century continues to have its multitude of devotional readers.

But the preëminent literary figure of the Movement was Newman, that strange, lonely, inscrutable figure, at once winsome and irritating, courageous and dependent. Though of Dutch and Huguenot extraction, he became thoroughly and devotedly the Oxford man. His affections for men, places, institutions, customs were the most vital part of him, and his separation from his university, and afterwards from his church, cut tragically athwart them. He tells the painful but engrossing story in his *Apologia pro Vita sua*, called forth by Kingsley's unwarranted charge of dishonesty, twenty years after the sensation of Newman's conversion had died down. The book stands beside Augustine's *Confessions* and Bunyan's *Grace Abounding* as the revelation of a soul passing through travail to win peace at last. And though its gentle candor won back for him the regard of impassioned opponents, it is wellnigh impossible even today for men to speak of Newman without prejudice, for or against. Let each man read the *Apologia* for himself.

Newman speaks of "the danger of being swayed in religious inquiry by our sympathy rather than our reason," perhaps only too well aware that he was a man himself rather of the affections than of self-reliant intellect. He was almost frightened to find himself emerging by his very charm as the leader of the Movement, and deprecates his own unfitness for strategy or politics. Such a man longs for somebody or something firm, unyielding, reliable, to lean upon at last, and the *Apologia* is the story of his quest, which he tries to conduct by reason, though the more powerful impulse of sympathy keeps asserting itself.

The same implied desire for a solid intellectual basis, for a principle of unity, is embodied in his *Idea of a University*, composed during his unsuccessful rectorship of the Catholic University in Dublin. Amid these latter days of anarchy in education, and the vain and frantic cry for unity of idea, the book contains much salutary comfort. Newman's solution may not now be universally acceptable, but page after page flashes and glows with suggestions about liberal studies and the arts, and the famous definition of a gentleman at the end of the Eighth Discourse has become classic.

Speaking of Addison he commends "his delicacy and beauty of style which is very difficult to describe, but which is felt to be in exact correspondence to the ideas of which it is the expression." Is he aware how neatly his words fit the virtues of his own style? It is so utterly free from embellishment, rhetoric, tricks, mannerisms, and exhibition writing, that as style it seems not to exist at all, and his meaning is as clear as a view through plate glass. Yet it is warm with a certain music and subtle personal delicacy, the quality of the man that Arnold recalled, which persuades or rather wins approval more than strenuous argument or gorgeous color ever could. It is nearer to the quality of Greek than any other English writing.

Newman had in him the poet, thwarted perhaps by the exciting events of his early manhood. At any rate before Keble's sermon he had written devotional verse. The popular hymn, "Lead kindly light amid th' encircling gloom," he composed on a sailing vessel becalmed between Palermo and Marseilles. At sixty-five he wrote a highly imaginative dramatic monologue, *The Dream of Gerontius,* of a soul in flight from the body.

At seventy-six his beloved Trinity College, Oxford, elected him an honorary fellow, and for the first time in thirty-two years he returned to the place so crowded with memories sweet and bitter. A youth in the young manhood of Keats and Byron, he almost spanned the great Victorian century. He was created Cardinal in 1879, and died in 1890 in his ninetieth year.

CHAPTER 31

Dickens and Thackeray

DICKENS (1812-1870)

IN AN oft-quoted passage in Mrs. Gaskell's *Cranford* hearty Captain Brown, of sixty and more, asked Miss Jenkyns if she had seen any numbers of *The Pickwick Papers.* "Capital thing! Famously good!" he thought them. And he read aloud the one about Sam Weller's "swarry" at Bath. "I must say," commented Miss Jenkyns, "that they are by no means equal to Dr. Johnson. Still, perhaps the author is young. Fetch me my *Rasselas*, my dear." This was in 1836-7, and the serial advent of these sketches was a happy omen for the accession of the new Queen. The author *was* young—twenty-four in fact—when he and his Pickwick Club burst into the sudden blaze of fame.

Miss Jenkyns had, of course, not read many "novels." Otherwise *Pickwick* might have reminded her of Fielding and Smollett. But thousands besides Captain Brown rejoiced in it because a vigorous young hand had touched common mortals, things, and places all about them, and quickened them into the perennial life that only genius can bestow.

The novel was destined to be the prevailing form of literature through Victorian times, indeed to this very moment of writing. It is the natural democratic form—cheap, accessible, not dependent, like verse and drama, on oral transmission, close to journalism, diffuse, within reach of lower talent than is required to produce as good poems or plays. Passable novelists are at large in greater number than passable poets or playwrights.

When *Pickwick* appeared, many of the varieties of fiction were already in hand—the picaresque or rogue novel, the sentimental romance, the novel of "purpose," the plotless transcription of humors. Scott had cultivated the historical novel, and he with his Scotch common life, and Miss Edgeworth with her Irish tales, had opened up the resources of that much exploited commodity, local color. Miss Burney and Miss Austen, within limits, had portrayed "manners," Bulwer Lytton and Disraeli were already exhibiting in "silver fork" fiction the elegancies of high life to a wistful middle class, and Egan, and Surtees, and Hook were occupied with diversions of low life and the sporting world.

With such in hand, the great Victorians, Dickens, Thackeray, Eliot, Trollope, and the rest, were to achieve new and great things. They had a new, shifting social world to work upon, with a dissolving old régime, and old abuses to reform. New science and new politics engaged them, not to say new history and new exploration of remote lands. Above all a new and passionate interest in the subtler variations and workings of human character, stimulated by German influence, took possession of novelist and poet, sometimes to an inartistic excess. The preoccupations of the novelist are of course those of all Victorian literature. The biographical and autobiographical element in fiction increased accordingly, with a striking precedent in Carlyle's *Sartor*.

Charles Dickens was the second of eight children. His father, a navy clerk, affectionate but not thrifty, found himself and his family in almost continual difficulties. He is partly transcribed in the notable Micawber.

Charles was an unhappy little boy, humiliated by seeing his father for years in a debtor's prison, by living away from home, by long dreary labor in a blacking factory. His wretched childhood is reviewed in those painful first pages of the autobiographical *David Copperfield*. Smollett, Fielding, Sterne, *The Vicar of Wakefield, Don Quixote, The Arabian Nights,* and eighteenth-century essayists, found in his father's house, made up his reading, and indeed most of his education. His schooling, poor enough was over at fifteen. During the next nine years he raised himself by his own talents and buoyant energy from obscure poverty to fame, and found his way to affluence. He is a fine example of the very middle-class aspiration to "respectability" which in its more vulgar and selfish aspects drew some of his most scathing satire. Witness the Veneerings, the Pecksniffs, and a multitude of such. Yet he killed himself with ill-advised labor for the means of this respectability, which out of his humble origin he had never ceased to covet. A bit of vanity and vulgarity always lingered about this great man.

First as lawyer's clerk, then as a reporter, he won his training in his craft. Two instincts were dominant in him, that of the actor and that of the reporter, and these two conspired to make him the artist that he was. His novels abound in "reporting" of incident that set the pace and style of the modern newspaper "story." His sharp eye misses nothing. Every sense is alive and keen for fact, not only the usual five, but an uncommon sense of humor, pathos, and the picturesque. What such senses can seize is centripetal to his mind.

From those early days as reporter he roamed over London afoot, often a dozen or more miles a day, or preferably a night, alert in every sense and sympathy for that which by nature belonged to him—oddities of speech, incident, dress, names, the waterfront in its moods and tenses often dark enough. This habit he followed for years, even when it had got beyond his strength. Like his own Sam Weller, he was a supercockney.

Publishers of that generation used to issue novels serially or "in parts." So appeared *The Pickwick Papers*, the author feeling his way, his audience growing by leaps and bounds as his vigor and invention increased. It has no plot, but is a string of amazing incidents, with some resemblance to Addison's Sir Roger, some to Don Quixote. But while readers roared, they found themselves falling in love with the very soul of the Club and the book, glorious Mr. Pickwick himself. So they do to this day, and ever will, no doubt; which distinguishes the genius of Dickens from mere cleverness, and his fame from mere popularity.

Before *Pickwick* had finished its run, *Oliver Twist* was on the stocks, and while it was yet appearing, *Nicholas Nickleby* began its career of twenty "parts"—all within two years, as an instance of Dickens' capacity for work. They were soon followed by *Old Curiosity Shop* and *Barnaby Rudge. Oliver Twist* and its successors exhibit more plot than *Pickwick*, but it is the plot of novels of the time, written for issue in parts, casual, loose, long, often unforeseen from the beginning. And the oft-repeated Dickens themes are familiar—sweet children, nice young folk, pitiful half-wits, all imposed upon or abused by misers, crooks, and the hard of heart; meeting a pathetic end, or laboring under mysterious identity, or happily eased off by benevolent gentlemen and ladies; and restored at last to rightful wealth, rank, or each other, while the wicked perish miserably. Not in his plots is Dickens original.

At thirty he broke down from overstrain. A five months' tour in the United States, in 1842, where he was already famous, was not unmixed pleasure. The country was then at its crudest in history, and the crudities could not escape this collector of eccentricities. His *American Notes* and *Martin Chuzzlewit*, recording his impressions, were salutary but bitter medicine for the young republic, and are amusing enough today.

Before he was fifty Dickens produced in succession *Dombey and Son*, his acknowledged masterpiece *David Copperfield, Bleak House, Hard Times, Little Dorrit, The Tale of Two Cities*, and *Great Expectations*, all along with editing of periodicals, taking an active hand in philanthropies, amateur theatricals, and, by no means least, inditing the beloved *Christmas Carol* and his other Christmas Stories.

His creative energies were flagging when in 1858 he began the famous but much deplored readings from his works. Deplorable they were in their excess and their draft on his strength, but coming when they did, they subtracted little from his creative work, and satisfied the natural craving of his very human heart for immediate contact with his audience, which had been a powerful agent in all his writing. He died worn out at fifty-eight, with his last novel, *The Mystery of Edwin Drood*, unfinished, and the mystery unsolved.

Dickens's shortcomings are obvious and oft noted; he deals

in caricature, not character; his persons, some say, are "humors," exaggerated single traits, like those in old comedy; he revels in impossible coincidence, happy endings, and melodrama; he knows no subtleties, no realism; his devices are sometimes cheap and specious; worst of all, he is "moral."

To all this the true "Dickensian" is calmly and justly indifferent, knowing that the great qualities of the man are such as set at naught sophisticated critics. Let them fret; Dickens still lives, and lives not in his plots and characters, but in his persons and incidents, and in the subtle relish of "the true Dickens." With what astonishing variety, gusto, vigor he produces person and event, from the predicaments of Mr. Pickwick to honest Joe Gargery. The catalogue is long, and there is neither measure nor limit to the appreciation and thrills stirred in all generations by such immortals as Peggotty, Bumble, Quilp, Scrooge, Squeers, Swiveller, Cuttle, Gummidge, Sykes, Heep, Micawber, Gamp, Mowcher, Jellyby, Stiggins, Chadband, since they issued from the teeming brain that shaped them. To the end there is about Dickens a boy's exuberance, as if in compensation for the childhood denied him in early years.

We speak of Dickens's London and Dickens's England, as we speak of Johnson's or Shakespeare's London. The phrase measures the breadth of the man's humanism. In all his roaming of streets, his coachings, his lodging at inns, London and England became a part of him, and their romance he touched with an added romance. In certain respects his readers in other lands are better judges of him than native Englishmen. For Dickens has made the young visitor dream of a Dickens's England beforehand and, when at last he roams that land of his dreams, everywhere he finds the real thing even today, clothed with the charm that Dickens gave it—the inns, the streets, the odd folk about in town and country, the road, the village, the food, the drink, the very smells. The place is still cheerily haunted by him.

Though primarily the favorite of men and boys, he made constant use of lump-in-the-throat and heart-in-the-mouth scenes, pathetic agonies, crime, murder, and sudden death. He chuckled with laughter or shed tears in the very act of writing. Such quick and tender sympathy may not be contemned. He turned it to vast account in softening the smug, hard Victorian heart set on cruel gain. Against abuses in workhouse, school, courts, Parliament, shop, factory, church, he turned the full and blasting current of both sentiment and satire, and accomplished the profound reform of heart without which the devoted Parliamentary efforts of such as Shaftesbury and Ashley would have been vain.

Like only the greatest he belonged to everybody, bridging the Atlantic, casting current phrases adrift, and rising into proverbs, with his Pecksniff, his Turveydrop, his Heep, and his invention of that universal convenience, the "Pickwickian sense."

•THACKERAY (1811-1863)

In the late forties and fifties Dickens and Thackeray divided the supremacy in Victorian fiction. Each had his warm partisans, and men still love to point the obvious contrasts between them. In some ways they were alike—both schooled in journalism, strongly domestic by instinct, fond of children, ranging in their invention between extremes of virtue and crime through loose-plotted chronicle novels in parts. But Thackeray had the best English education obtainable, was less exuberant, more subtle, less extended, more intense, occupied with the manners of high life and pretensions of the middle class, better able to portray the English gentleman. He has always been less popular than Dickens, and worked hard and long to earn fame. Rivals though they were, and for one unhappy period enemies, Thackeray praised *David Copperfield* above his own work, and was the first to move for reconciliation.

He stood six feet four, broad, stout, rosy, a bit stooped, but firm on his feet—"a half-monstrous Cornish giant," said Carlyle. Above his blue eye peering satirically through strong spectacles his brow was arched as if in wonder at the mysterious cruelty mingled with the unearthly beauty of the world. His snub nose was a memento of a school fight with his devoted friend for life, Venables. The delicate lines of his mouth bewrayed his deep capacity for suffering and for sympathy.

William Makepeace Thackeray came of old Yorkshire yeomanry, but for three generations his forebears had followed the more learned professions. He was born in Calcutta, July 18, 1811—the family had been a good deal engaged in India, like various of his characters—and at six was sent to relatives in England to be educated. His Aunt Ritchie, worried to find that he could wear his uncle's hat, appealed to a distinguished physician, who was wise enough to say: "He has a large head, but there's a good deal in it." His school was the historic Charterhouse in London, where he was not very happy, cut some innocent capers, made friends, including John Leech of *Punch* fame, but did not shine in scholarship. At Trinity, Cambridge, it was much the same story, and the whole tale may be read, with due alterations, in the earlier parts of *Pendennis*, and in *The Newcomes*. Nevertheless at Trinity he included among his illustrious friends no less than the young Tennyson, Edward Fitzgerald, and Edward Lear. They read Shelley, and pooled their literary interests in skits and more serious experiments.

Thackeray was naturally indolent. After Cambridge he dawdled a while in Germany, met and was awed by the aged Goethe, tried and abandoned the study of law, and turned to journalism. Then began the terrible discipline of fate that qualified him to speak of human life with authority. His goodly patrimony disappeared, through failures in India, through journalistic ventures, and probably through indiscretions at play. His talent for drawing and the lure of Paris—and Bohemia—united to inspire in him the hope and the effort for two years, to make himself a painter; but clever as he was with a pencil, his genius lay elsewhere. At twenty-five he married a lovely young Irish girl, and bravely faced the world on his small earnings from magazines. His four happiest years followed. Three "little girls" as he always called them, were born, but after the third the blow fell. His wife's mind began to fail. For six years he suffered the agony of hope against hope over a loss worse than death. She proved incurable, though she lived on, thirty years after him. His home was shattered. One "little girl" died. Illusions vanished. By such vicarious suffering a great novelist was given to men. "Though my marriage was a wreck . . . I would do it again, for behold, Love is the crown and completion of all earthly good," he said. This transcendent love of his lost wife became sublimated in his adoring portrayal of such women as Lady Castlewood, Helen Pendennis, and Ethel Newcome.

Through these dark years Thackeray made his slow, hard way to reputation. Many were his contributions to *Fraser's Magazine*, and to young *Punch*, born in 1841. Among these were the comments on high society of a rascally, illiterate butler, Jeames Yellowplush, a *Paris Sketchbook,* an *Irish Sketchbook, The Great Hoggarty Diamond,* and in 1844, *Barry Lyndon,* a rogue novel, and Thackeray's greatest achievement so far. Never did he surpass the spirit, energy, and movement of this tale about the career of a brave but bad young Irish thoroughbred. In all this early work he is preoccupied with scoundrels, rogues, and thieves. "I really don't know where I get all these rascals for my books," he said. "I have certainly never lived with such people." But he *had* lived with them, at least in Fielding, whom he had read from boyhood, especially in *Jonathan Wild.*

By 1844 the rascals were giving way to snobs, and the *Book of Snobs* began appearing as sketches in *Punch.* As we have seen, the age was a high season for snobs. Thackeray studied them in all varieties and phases, so well that he incurred the ungrateful charge of being a snob himself. He was an invariable and expert marksman for pose and pretence even amongst the noblest. Which perhaps did not always make for most charitable judgment on their part. On occasion he was dining with Carlyle and two or three painters, when the talk fell upon Titian. "The great fact about Titian," said one of the artists, "is his color." "And the second great fact about him," added the next, "is his drawing." A pause. Then with strong Scotch burr Carlyle: "Here am I, a mon made in the image of God; and I know nothing about Teetian, and I care nothing about Teetian. And that's a third great fact about him." Thackeray paused as he was raising his claret to his lips, and in his gentle voice said: "Pardon me, Sir; that is not a fact about Titian. It *is* a fact, and a very lamentable fact, about Thomas Carlyle."

All through these early years of work on *Fraser's* and *Punch* Thackeray's fame was delayed by various assumed names— Yellowplush, Gahagan, Solomons, Fitz-Boodle, and his favorite, Michael Angelo Titmarsh. He was known only among literary fellowcraftsmen. Then in 1847, when he was thirty-six, began to appear in parts *Vanity Fair*. Slowly it made its way until more cultivated readers said that here was a greater than even Dickens, a new expert dealing with London "caste," its pretence, its fluctuations, its tufthunting and hardness of heart, its clash of cruelty and tenderness. *Vanity Fair* calls itself "a novel without a hero," yet it traces the career of one imperishable character, the captivating, inscrutable, pitiable Becky Sharp. Without fortune, friends, or any backing but her own wit and charm, she insinuates herself into the worldly world, disturbing its order on every hand, plotting a devious and risky course between social success and ruin, decency and sin, flaunting her little pretences, scoring her triumphs, and crashing at last to disrepute and oblivion. Yet she could not be called utterly bad—indeed had the making of a good woman in her. Over against her is the gentle Amelia Sedley, whose heart is broken by the death of her faithless husband George Osborne, and but partly patched by the good offices of Becky herself in the end. At one point the plot becomes involved with the battle of Waterloo, in which George is killed.

Not so much in the story as in the setting forth of character and situation does the book rise to the grandeur and indelible quality attained only by great genius. The moment when Rawdon Crawley discovers his wife Becky in compromising circumstances with the old rake Lord Steyne is one of the most memorable in English fiction.

Over the whole course of events plays the wit and apparently light touch of the author, his half-jesting irony serving to intensify and sharpen the tragedy the more. The upshot is, or would be, an effect of cynical satire on all life. But *Vanity*

Fair is the work of a man whose tender heart went out to all who were in trouble; who wept to hear the charity children sing at St. Paul's, and agonized over the death of his own Helen Pendennis and Colonel Newcome; who loved the English home the more for having lost his own. The alleged cynicism of Thackeray is but the suffering of a too sensitive and loving soul over tragedy all about him which he was helpless to relieve, and could only point at. "I cannot help telling the truth as I view it," he said, "and describing what I see." The Fool in *King Lear* would best have understood him. The cynic believes in little or nothing. Thackeray kept his faith and believed in the virtues of English gentlemen, which he has portrayed with a success beyond that of any other, in his Dobbin, his Warringtons, his Esmond, and above all his Colonel Newcome.

Two other novels, *Pendennis*, 1848-50, and *The Newcomes*, 1853-55, have heroes, or at least tell the tales of young men unsteadily embarking on life up to the point where they "settle down." Naturally much autobiography went to their making, particularly of *Pendennis*, which, in spite of its length, recommends itself to youthful readers with the authenticity of *Tom Jones*, to which it may be related. In his great manner Thackeray portrays the worldly old Major Pendennis and perhaps his masterpiece, Colonel Newcome, whose death with his simple "Adsum" is above all the cavillings of anti-sentimentalists.

But the genius of Thackeray was united with a strong historical instinct, or at any rate an artist's instinct for the days of Queen Anne and the Georges. Into those old times he read himself for years, not through literature alone, but in old periodicals, letters, and newspapers. The offspring of the union was perhaps the greatest historical novel in English, *Henry Esmond,* with its pendant *The Virginians*. In *Esmond* is the same power of portraiture and dramatic moments as before, together with a closely articulate and logical plot. Again it is the story of a young man struggling under handicap of supposed illegitimate birth, untoward events, and a passion for the beautiful but wilful Beatrix Esmond, his cousin, with a touch of Becky about her. In the end he marries her mother, for which many a reader has reproached the author. "*I* didn't make him do it," he protested; "they did it themselves."

Like many another teller of tales, Thackeray as he wrote found himself controlled by story and characters, not controlling them, which is only another evidence of his inspiration. The meeting of Henry and Lady Castlewood in Winchester Cathedral, the duel between Mohun and Castlewood, the suspense of the crisis at the death of Queen Anne, are passages of the author's best workmanship. Though it is a historical novel, the persons are none the less life-like. Thackeray was so in possession of the time that it was for him as the present, and persons like Swift, Addison, Steele and his Prue, move in and out, not like revivals but as living flesh and blood. This is partly an act of exquisite mimicry by the author, who was so saturated in the antique idiom that his persons actually talk as they did in their time, and so naturally and unaffectedly that at first the reader is hardly aware of it. How could one whose own style was already so exquisite, delicate, and musical, at will impersonate so faithfully people of a hundred and more years agone?

Henry Esmond and his wife settled in Virginia, and *The Virginians* continues the story of his family and of Beatrix, now a worldly old woman. Though longer and less diverting than *Esmond*, the book is enlivened with living counterfeits of Wolfe and Washington, Chesterfield and Johnson. The practice of dealing in genealogies and letting characters reappear from story to story (one of the Warringtons turns up in *Pendennis*) was carried further by Trollope, and is still not uncommon. It creates an illusion of one large and actual world, not a limited stage-set enclosing the action.

Thackeray's love of the eighteenth century expressed itself also in his lectures on *The English Humourists* and *The Four Georges*, which he used on his two visits to America in the fifties. Historians and critics have their fault to find with these estimates, yet they live as the genuine work of a great and witty impersonator.

He comes in for his share of blame these days as a Victorian preacher and sentimentalist and sponsor for sundry dull or priggish persons. But these rôles are not essential elements in the man, and what they have dictated may be skipped. In fact Thackeray disparages his own work, as if aware of such defects. But he also knew that into the best of it he had put his own great soul. In later years as he passed the little house in Young Street where he had once lived, he said to a friend, like the wag he was: "Down on your knees, you rogue, for here *Vanity Fair* was penned; and I will go down with you, for I have a high opinion of that little production myself."

In 1843 Dickens had produced the immortal *Christmas Carol*; and in 1855 Thackeray was diverting some little English exiles in Rome with his equally imperishable *The Rose and the Ring*. "It was worth while being a child in those days," says one who was, "with Dickens and Thackeray to furnish the Christmas stories." In *The Rose and the Ring* is everybody's Thackeray, genuine, intimate, spontaneous, relaxed, irresistible, laughing at the pretences and pinchbeck of high life with its basis of stodgy Victorian domesticity beneath, at outworn romance and literary devices, at pat coincidence, blank-verse prose, heavy villains, triumphant virtue, and what not. Beneath is sober actuality for the elders, and above no end of high jinks for innumerable children of all ages in all times. This tragic jester, who knew the hard world well, but was at heart a child, died on Christmas Eve, 1863, worn out at the age of fifty-two.

CHAPTER 32

Tennyson and the Brownings

TENNYSON (1809-1892)

GREAT ages are fortunate which find the one voice that can turn to music their otherwise mute beliefs and endeavors, their joy and pain. Such was Chaucer for his time; such were Shakespeare and Spenser for theirs, Pope for his, and preëminently Alfred, Lord Tennyson, for the time of Victoria. Our present disparagement of Tennyson is only our impatience with everything Victorian; for his poetry peculiarly expresses the ideas and the enthusiasms of the vast reading middle class of his day. He reasons like the middle-class liberal who keeps to the Christian faith and forms, at least in the *via media* or middle course, with a mind open to the new difficulties rising from the new science, and the prevailing evolutionary enthusiasm for progress and some good time coming.

> Behold we know not anything;
> I can but trust that good shall fall
> At last—far off—at last, to all.

His poetry sings the virtues and enthusiasms of his day, domestic and social, the patriotism, the humanitarian impulses, the utilitarian prosperity, the fascination of death, the sombre religion or scepticism, and the New Empire. At the same time he is nourishing and refining his age with the beauty which it had lost, and which he shapes for its needs out of many a corner of "the antique world." If he seems at times to be an aristocrat, he is such with the middle-class conservatism and faith in the old English order. He has as much of the body and fibre of English life in him as Dickens—perhaps more—not its lusty humors so much as its peculiar and irresistible charm mellowed by time.

Rectory and Hall bound in an immemorial intimacy,

the stout and loyal tenantry, villages, cottages, broad fields, quiet waterways, gray churches and cathedrals, the indigenous music of English bells, country-houses, gardens, lawns, Christmas cheer, old yews, cedars, and elms, waste places, birds in their kinds, seasons in their round, and flowers in their habit, sweet, gentle women, and men with

> Such fine reserve and noble reticence,
> Manners so kind yet stately, such a grace
> Of tenderest courtesy,

as only centuries of England at her best could produce—all these were his natural materials. And he comes close to homely English earth in his two monologues of the Northern Farmer, which together mark early and late phases of social change in the Victorian age.

An age, as soon as it recognizes its poet, is wont to take good care of him. Tennyson's England recognized him slowly but surely. He knew little of the lot that falls to many poets—neglect, struggle, abuse, tragic war with his times. Yet he was obscurely born, one of twelve children of a clergyman at remote Somersby, Lincolnshire. As youngsters they often played at romance. Two brothers, Frederick and Charles, became poets of distinction. At Louth grammar school, in his father's study, and at Trinity College, Cambridge, Alfred was industrious in his pursuit of the classics, history, and science, though his instruction at the University he found arid, "feeding not the heart." But he made extraordinary friends among the so-called "Apostles"—Merivale, Spedding, Trench, Thackeray, and above all, Arthur Hallam, for whom his friendship was one of the determinant passions of his life. Hallam became engaged to Tennyson's sister, and died soon after the Cambridge days. The poet's grief was overwhelming; it dictated the suicide poem, *Two Voices,* a *débat* not unlike that between the Red Cross Knight and Despair in the *Faery Queen*, and through the years sublimated itself in the hundred and more lyrics which made up *In Memoriam.*

At twenty-seven Tennyson fell in love with Emily Sellwood. The engagement dragged on till he was past forty, what with his petty income and her parents' natural disapproval. His family lost their little fortune, and he sank into alarming depression. But when he was thirty-three appeared the double volume of 1842 which founded his fame, and in 1845 he received a small pension from the government. In 1850, after ten years' enforced separation, he and Emily were married. The same year Wordsworth died, and Tennyson was made Poet Laureate.

He was an impressive figure—tall, broad and sinewy, dark, grave, quiet, with a suggestion of latent Viking ancestry and the poetic fire, but an excellent companion with intimates, breaking at times into heroic laughter. His distinctions multiplied as the nation adopted him. He twice declined a baronetcy. His old college made him honorary fellow. He acquired two stately seats, at Aldworth, Surrey, and at Farringford, in the Isle of Wight, both of them counterparts of scenes in his poetry. At seventy-four he accepted a peerage, and his death at eighty-three fell upon the English-speaking world like the end of an institution. His bones lie in the Abbey.

From his youth Tennyson seems to have known his calling. At eighteen he had collaborated with Frederick in the slender *Poems by Two Brothers;* while an undergraduate he published *Poems, chiefly Lyrical,* which contained no less an omen of his greatness than the powerful *Mariana;* at twenty-three appeared *Poems by Alfred Tennyson,* with such achievements as *The Lady of Shalott, Oenone, The Lotos-Eaters,* and *The Palace of Art.* For ten years he worked, quietly shaping some of his masterpieces against the famous issue of 1842—*Morte d'Arthur, Sir Galahad, Ulysses, Dora, Godiva, The Gardener's Daughter,* "Break, break, break," and *Locksley Hall.* He was first of all a careful, patient workman, and no man ever toiled harder or more soberly to perfect himself in his craft. He kept it up all his long life, revising and editing early poems, reading, observing, travelling, scrutinizing the work of his many masters, inventing short snatches and cadences which he saved for later use. With his minute care he joined extraordinary range and variety—of metre, subject and material, and final effect. At eighty he reviews his career under the romantic image of *Merlin and the Gleam.*

For in his very earliest work he was a son of the romantics, Byron and Moore and Scott; but in his volume of 1832 the dream-like splendors of such poems as *The Lady of Shalott, Oenone, The Palace of Art, The Lotos-Eaters* are more akin to Keats and Coleridge and Spenser. As their heir he inherits their materials, the romance of ancient Greek lore, of the Middle Ages, of remote lands and times. But more ancient and stricter masters had him in life-long discipline, such as Homer, Theocritus, Ovid, Catullus, and above all Virgil,

> Wielder of the stateliest measure
> ever moulded by the lips of man.

Like Virgil and Milton, with his rich inheritance and his art, he was an Alexandrian craftsman, especially in all his earlier verse. For example in *Ulysses*, considered by some his finest poem, he takes a situation from Canto 22 of Dante's *Inferno*, transfers it to the old age of Ulysses in Ithaca, makes of it a perfect dramatic monologue, weaving in phrases from Virgil and Homer and Horace, which he transmutes and fashions as only a poet can, sets it in a romantic and magic twilight, and suggests through it not only his own intrepid spirit, but the vision of infinite future possibility dimly apprehended by his times. So all his life again and again he "coin'd into English gold some treasure of classical song"—seizing a moment in classical myth or legend and, as in Wordsworth's *Laodamia,* turning it to dramatic monologue. His *Lucretius* shows, with high dramatic intensity, the lofty mind of the austere Latin poet breaking down under the stress of animal passion. Though it is throughout a "mosaic choicely planned" of phrases turned with uncanny skill from the noble Latin of Lucretius's poem, such minute care does not weaken a final effect as powerful as any other in Tennyson.

Like that other great Alexandrian, Theocritus, Tennyson was

essentially an idyllist, a fashioner of small and highly finished pictures. Hundreds of them are strewn from end to end of his work, from his *Lady of Shalott,* one of the most idyllic, through his classical poems, his pageants of the *Palace of Art,* and *The Dream of Fair Women,* his poems of English life, his *Princess, Maud, In Memoriam.* Of this he seems to have been aware in his very fondness for the word, "idyll"—"a small, sweet idyll," "English Idylls," and *Idylls of the King.* His work is some-times even too curiously ingenious, "laborious orient ivory sphere in sphere," resulting in many a luxuriant but not en-during phrase, and settling into a dangerous mannerism:

> Warm blue breathings of a hidden hearth.

> The tender, pink, five-beaded baby soles.

> With her milkwhite arms and shadowy hair
> She made her face a darkness from the King.

Even the greatest poets will exhibit their besetting affectations.

Tennyson was often an Alexandrian in his cultivation of archaic words and phrases, many of them Biblical. He resorts to this device at will when he desires a pastoral simplicity, as in *Dora,* or the antique epic finish in the *Idylls of the King.*

But he has far greater gifts than fine minute craftsmanship. One is the poet's supreme gift of making the language sing a new song, verse set to its own indigenous tune, the gift of Burns, or Byron, and the Elizabethans. And though it is usually peculiar to the youthful poet, it never wholly left Tennyson from "Break, break, break" to *Crossing the Bar.* At the age of five he leaned with outstretched arms upon the Lincolnshire blast and kept chanting: "I hear a voice that's speaking in the wind." Most of his songs, instead of being the ostensible over-flow of his own feeling, are partly dramatized as lyrics inter-polated in longer poems—*The Princess,* and the *Idylls; Maud* is a cycle of dramatic lyrics. *In Memoriam,* he admits, is but an accumulation of "short swallow-flights of song," and was indeed composed in moments of tense feeling during the seventeen years following the death of Hallam.

This lyric power was but part of his larger control of harmonies and melodies of speech. Always experimenting, even in his most successful work, his metrical range is astonishingly wide and varied, like the range of instrumentation in a great orchestra. For his narrative and dramatic poems he created a new blank verse, not unlike the fluent verse of Wordsworth. By frequent running over, and constant shifting of the pause within the line, together with the simplest grammatical construction, he attained to a new medium whose ease and flexibility strongly recommended itself to the popular ear. But it seldom reaches the dignity and durability of his masters, Milton and Virgil, for lack of their sustaining quantity of vowels and stoutly knit grammatical construction.

With his minute finish, his pictorial skill, his power in both melody and harmony, Tennyson combined a certain dramatic sense, the ability to seize and intensify a dramatic moment. But his dramatic sense is episodic, less adapted to the making of a play than of a dramatic monologue. And by this episodic nature of his imagination, whatever his aspirations may have been, he was destined never to achieve an epic or a great play. His longer poems are of the same episodic sort. *The Princess* is a gorgeous series of idyllic or spectacular episodes—a medley, as he says. The unity of *In Memoriam* is the loose and episodic unity of an average man's thoughts on death and immortality. But it is magnificent in its pictures and moments and single songs—the yew, "Fair ship, that from the Italian shore," storm at night, "The Danube to the Severn gave," "When on my bed the moonlight falls," Christmas Eve, "I past beside the reverend walls," night and daybreak on the lawn, "I climb the hill," "Ring out, wild bells." These remain in the mind long after the argument has faded.

By the same token the *Idylls*, though "in Twelve Books," though they follow the career of Arthur from his glorious coming to his passing and the end of the Round Table, though they coincide with the round of the year, though they contain an alleged and faint allegory of the ages of man or the struggle of the soul, yet survive rather by their picturesque and dramatic moments. In their day they were enormously successful, as the collection grew from time to time during thirty years of the poet's life. While he was making more familiar the medieval tradition, chiefly out of Malory, he was clothing it with new beauties, and presenting characters who were essentially those of a high-life Victorian novel. Indeed the *Idylls* have more than one resemblance to an episodic novel of the time, "in parts."

Maud (1854-5), though now often accepted as Tennyson's greatest performance, in its day was derided and reviled. In twenty-seven lyric episodes it reflects a tragic love-affair, not unlike that of *Locksley Hall*, wherein a solitary and rather morbid young man falls in love with his cousin Maud, is attacked by her brother, kills him, goes mad, wanders into exile, and is restored to reason after Maud's death, by going to war. The story is further complicated by Victorian social cross-currents. The public may have been offended partly by the morbid hero. His father too had gone mad and died, perhaps by his own hand, after being ruined in speculation by his brother, Maud's father, whose ill-gotten wealth had made him a lord. Moreover, the implied defence of war was no doubt distasteful. It was the year of the Crimean War; England in the brutal and oppressive struggle for gain had turned the blessings of peace to a curse. She needed the war, the poet implies, to purge the poison. Be that as it may, the poem is flooded with music from end to end in all the moods and tenses of the story, even exultant joy, which is rare in Tennyson. And it is all modulated with the most exquisite appropriateness of cadence and measure. As an old man the poet used to chant these matchless songs in a voice trembling with youthful passion.

In his sixties Tennyson, with his unflagging enterprise as an artist, began his attempt to gratify a wish, perhaps an old one, to find himself a dramatist, and produced in rapid succession six plays including *Queen Mary*, *Becket,* and *The Cup*; already past eighty he wrote *The Foresters*, a pleasant Robin Hood play. Supported by careful staging and by such actors as Irving and the Kendals, these plays enjoyed a varying success of esteem. But they are not great plays, and the poet had to content himself with the distinctions which were naturally his.

At its best, and essentially, Tennyson's genius is virile, simple, direct, and, like his adored Virgil's, sensitive to the melancholy of human life. As he once read the Second Book of the *Aeneid* he gave way to tears. With this nobler part mingled, as not uncommonly happens, a certain soft weakness, which sometimes appears in mere luxuriance of scene and phrase, or in sentimentality; or it becomes audible as an effeminate falsetto—"Call me early, mother dear." One may detect all these weaknesses in *Enoch Arden*, composed in his fifties, and not infrequently in his preceding work. And from beginning to end he had an almost morbid preoccupation with stagnant or disordered states of mind, as in *Mariana, Two Voices, St. Simeon, Locksley Hall, Maud, Lucretius, Rizpah.*

But the best Tennyson shakes off these impediments, and invigorates his song with fullness of heart and mind, with ease, and simplicity, and directness of utterance. Such is the singer of *Ulysses*, of the *Ode on the Death of Wellington*, of the charges of the two brigades, of the two *Northern Farmers*, of *The Revenge, To Virgil*, and many of his songs including the very last, *Crossing the Bar*. In these poems the finest virtues of his times unite with the hard-won expert technique of a master at moments when voice and emotion are in perfect unison.

THE BROWNINGS

ROBERT BROWNING (1812-1889); ELIZABETH BARRETT BROWNING (1806-1861)

Tennyson had no admirer more generous than Robert Browning. At the end of their lives the reputation of these fellow-poets was about equal but divergent. Tennyson was the people's poet, Browning the poet of esoterics, real or aspiring.

Little did Browning look the part. Sturdy, quick of movement, stout of hand and stubby-fingered, with round face and keen eye, he might be taken for the successful business-man, never the poet. He often passed for an American.

His mother was a devoted, open-minded evangelical. His

father, a clerk in the Bank of England, was a talented amateur
in drawing, music, and literature. Both were Non-conformists,
which at the time disqualified their son from hope of a degree
at either Oxford or Cambridge. The household in Camberwell
was characteristically middle-class and intelligent. The father
lived on till Browning's sixty-fifth year, always in friendly and
helpful sympathy with his son's career as a poet.

Browning was, he himself confesses, a "supremely passionate, unluckily precocious" youngster. His omnivorous mind
and irrepressible energy eagerly seized upon all resources at
hand—his father's excellent library, his mother's skill in music,
pictures at the Dulwich Gallery near by, Greek, Italian, and
the beauty in minutest detail of suburban Camberwell and the
later home further out at Hatcham. There were schooling,
lessons in drawing and in music. At sixteen he had a few
months at the new University of London, but he soon returned to his self-appointed and rapacious mode of education.
Pauline, his first published poem, he wrote at twenty-one, and
afterwards rejected. It recounts something of his novitiate as
a poet; for, like the greatest, he early knew himself elect to
poetry, and resolved

> to look and learn
> Mankind, its cares, hopes, fears, its woes and joys.

Late in life, in his *Parleyings with Certain People of Importance in their Day,* he recalls men whose books and ideas and
music had held a leading part in his formative years. But the
dominant influence early and late was the poetry of Shelley,
especially in its idealism and its straining for a vision of the
perfect beyond the imperfect. His feeling for Shelley dictated
Memorabilia.

Somehow young Browning suffered little of the misery of
body and soul so often the lot of young poets. He seems, his
life through, to have been as they say "adjusted." He boxed,
fenced, rode, and danced, and at fifty he learned to swim. A
certain cheerful buoyancy about him, a balance between his
abundant physical and spiritual health saved him and his
poetry, as it had saved Fielding and Scott. It lay at the base of

his life-long optimism, and was so constant that he exhibits no marked "phases" of development, but is much the same Browning to the end. His work accordingly defies sharp classification.

If any one event marked a change in his work, it was his famous marriage with Elizabeth Barrett in 1846. Everyone knows the romantic story of the dreary household in that "long, unlovely" Wimpole Street, the narrow father ruling his large household with a hand that had ruled slaves in the West Indies, slowly forcing his daughter into invalidism, part imaginary, part real; and how, like a miracle, the hearty, sanguine young Robert, first attracted by her poetry, had sought her out loved her at once, inspired her with the purpose of recovery, married her secretly, and bore her off, pet spaniel and all, in triumph to Italy. He was thirty-four, she was forty.

Till her twenties Elizabeth had lived most of her life in the charming seclusion of the Malvern Hills region. She had been a rhyming, precocious, very feminine little girl, a small bluestocking, too much idolized by her father, whom she astonished with tragedies and epics of her making, while she secretly dreamed of herself disguised as the page of her hero, Lord Byron. When she first met Browning she was the more famous poet of the two. She had made an excellent, if slightly feminine, translation of Aeschylus's heroic tragedy *Prometheus Bound*, and, among others, had composed her fine *Cowper's Grave*, and *The Cry of the Children*, one of the most powerful literary agents for reform of child-labor. But in general her earlier verse, however free and delicate its music, tends to a certain prolixity and thinness. It contains too a goodly Victorian admixture of death and tears. She had not learned economy of language from the Greek poets whom she was constantly reading and translating in verse. From the time of her meeting with Browning her poetry undergoes an obvious change.

When he first saw her she seemed, except for her great eyes and abundant dark hair, hardly corporeal. "She was such a little woman," he said; "she liked little things." Her health steadily improved. Some time after her marriage —it is uncertain how long—she first revealed to him a se-quence of forty-four sonnets inspired by her love for him

and secretly written before their marriage, which he named
Sonnets from the Portuguese. Rejoicing in her escape from
death and in the unforeseen fulfilment of her life, her song is
transmuted into a new volume and spontaneous power:

> The face of all the world is changed, I think,
> Since first I heard the footsteps of thy soul
> Move still, oh, still, beside me, as they stole
> Betwixt me and the dreadful outer brink
> Of obvious death, where I, who thought to sink,
> Was caught up into love, and taught the whole
> Of life in a new rhythm.

Her schooling under the Greeks, under Dante and Petrarch,
and Shakespeare, is all wrought into a transcendent and glorious result by her new experience. There is no finer sequence
of sonnets in English. Their lesser counterpart is to be found
in Browning's *One Word More* of nine years later. Fifteen
years of wellnigh complete happiness were to follow, till her
death in 1861. During this time she put into rather diffuse
verse her impressions in Italy and called it *Casa Guidi Windows*; and her views on various matters she expressed in some
10,000 iambics which make up *Aurora Leigh.* It is essentially
a metrical novel containing certain autobiographical passages,
and following the gloomy career of the heroine to the point of
her marriage with the not cheerful hero. But in this and in all
Mrs. Browning's poetry after her marriage one may trace the
effect of this new life—in a new intensity, concentration, vigor
of treatment, especially in descriptions, even down to the superficial mannerisms of her husband, such as congested language
and frequent use of interrogation.

When his wife died Browning was forty-nine. In profound
grief he left his beloved Italy as a home for ever. How deeply
he felt his loss, and what intimations it gave him, one may
guess from his *Prospice* and such other poems in the volume,
Dramatis Personae of 1864, as *Abt Vogler* and *Rabbi Ben
Ezra.* Ever since his suppressed *Pauline* he had been averse to
autobiographical revelations in his poetry; but the courage and
characteristic balance and faith which sustained him through

the twenty-seven years in which his wife was a memory shine cloudless in one of his last poems, the *Epilogue to Asolando*.

About a year before she died Browning one hot June day had been loitering among the market stalls by the church of San Lorenzo in Florence, when he came upon an old parchment-bound book which contained, part in print, part in manuscript, the story of a murder trial in Rome in the year 1697. It was just like him to find the suggestion for a poem in such flotsam as this, and his rapacious mind, even as he sauntered home with his treasure, was devouring the gruesome but true account. Whatever his meditations on the theme through the early part of his bereavement, it was not till three years had passed that he began composition of his grand masterpiece, *The Ring and the Book*. Four more years were necessary to complete it, and in 1868-9 it appeared in four monthly parts.

The story is simple enough: a cruel aristocrat of Arezzo persecutes his saintly but plebeian young wife; she escapes under protection of a chivalrous young monk, who helps her back to her parents in Rome. There her husband overtakes her and murders her and her parents. He is condemned and executed. But this plot is elaborated with infinite detail, into a fabric of 21,000 lines, much of it from the old book, much of it from the poet's imagination; hence the figure of the ring wrought from the pure metal of fact mingled with the alloy of the poet's mind. Besides, the facts are ten times recounted or reviewed by the whole circle of those concerned—the advocates pro and con, public opinion pro and con and neutral, Guido the husband, Caponsacchi the monk, Pompilia the wife, and the Pope, to whom the case is finally referred, together with Guido's final plea for mercy; and the narratives reflect every shade of human conduct from utterly hardened villainy through worldliness of all sorts to the saintly patience, courage, and love of Pompilia, before whom even the Pope kneels. Browning's fame had been a long time maturing, but *The Ring and the Book* was received with a general salvo from the heavy reviews, as the supreme poetical achievement of the times and the profoundest since Shakespeare.

Though not a national poet like Tennyson, Browning became the unwitting, and at heart unwilling, father of such a cult in his lifetime as never bored another English poet. Browning societies sprang up on both sides of the water, graciously accepted by the poet, while he protested that he himself was "no Browningite." This cult is not hard to explain. The poet's optimism and energy attracted many a mind weary of the forlorn struggle against defeat of spirit. His difficulty and supposed subtlety flattered the aspirations of blue-stockings, would-be esoterics, and other aspirants to "culture." It appealed to the multitude who do not value what they get too easily, but enjoy the exercise of earning it, and prize it more when won. In America Browning's energy and cheerful relish for everything made him a Victorian favorite.

But now that the cult has subsided, even his advocates find themselves slipping into the habit of noting his failings—what he is not rather than what he is: he is no stylist, they admit, he is not clear, he is not tuneful, he is no reasoner, no philosopher, to some he is hardly civilized. Yet no poet, not even Homer, was ever more nearly omnivorous in his poetic appetite. Everything stirred poetic excitement in him till his great brain was stuffed and overflowing: insects, animals, flowers, every object touched with human life—books, walls, clothes, textures, marbles, houses, pictures, musical instruments, arms, drugs, and drinking-cups;

> Scenting the world, looking it in the face, . . .
> He took such cognizance of men and things.

Not with one sense only but with all five he seized the essential quality of a thing—form, color, texture, sound, smell, taste, human use, so that he mentions it as one who knows it through and through, animating the inanimate with his own boundless energy. Far from being abstract, as some allege, his poetry suffers from superabundance of concrete things. His strong passion for things and effects sometimes overflows, like that of medieval designers, in grotesques and roisterous play. *Nationality in Drinks, The Pied Piper, Up at a Villa, Garden Fancies* are a few cases in point. This hearty abundance is ready to break out on any fit occasion—as in *Fra Lippo, Master Hugues,* or the longer poems, whether in wit, image, or rhyme —"O sieve: . . . explosive"; "fabric: dab brick." There was never such an irrepressible rhymester unless it was Byron. The same grotesque exuberance finds soberer expression in that transcendent bad dream, *Childe Roland,* which Browning was either unwilling or unable to explain.

Unnoticed things, neglected trifles, moments, bits of music, anecdotes, in touch with his imagination, fertilize into a great poem. Old pictures suggested *Andrea del Sarto* and *Fra Lippo,* a faded tapestry *Childe Roland,* a lonely walk *Pippa Passes,* and a casual old book his masterpiece.

The same abounding energy thus manifest permeates his own painting in its broad vigorous, expert stroke, with a brush full of living color. The landscape which opens *The Flight of the Duchess,* the sunrise on Pippa's holiday, the portrait of Aristophanes in *Aristophanes' Apology,* once apprehended, remain ineffaceable in the mind.

The measure of his fullness is even larger. His appreciation and technical knowledge of painting, music, sculpture, architecture; his knowledge of other times, Middle Ages, Italian Renaissance, ancient Athens, the eighteenth century, the Orient, old and new, all of which he enjoyed and treated with more accurate historical sense than romantic glamor—crowd still further the poet's mind.

Like Shelley, and many another, Browning's genius found its natural sustenance in Italy. His first visit of but a month, in 1838, he spent in Venice and Asolo; yet out of it came *Sordello* and *Pippa Passes,* whose wealth of intimate and local detail are such as would take another man years of living in the region to accumulate. And he treats these details with the matter-of-course ease that comes only with long familiarity. They have the fresh, vivid effect of John Sargent's all-seeing watercolors—which only goes further to prove how near Browning's genius was to that of a painter.

This visit, another in 1844, fourteen years of his married life, and three visits towards the end—he died in Venice—fur-

nished scene and matter for half of his work, and temper for
much more. At forty-three he sang:

> Open my heart and you will see
> Graved inside of it, "Italy."
> Such lovers old are I and she:
> So it always was, so shall ever be!

His inspiration was always responsive to location. After Mrs.
Browning's death and *The Ring and the Book*, he spent summers in Brittany; and much of his later verse takes scene and
color accordingly, including the popular *Hervé Riel*. The last
days in Italy produced *Asolando*. Yet his loyalty to England
and his keen sense of her charms and virtues, which he voices
in *Home Thoughts*, never declined.

Other times as well as other places he seized with the same
canny sense of their realities. All his life he read Homer and
Euripides, and in his sixties turned his knowledge of old Greece
to poetic account. *Balaustion's Adventure* (1871) and *Aristophanes' Apology* (1875) develop a charming story from Plutarch, and give occasion for English versions of Euripides's
Alcestis and *Mad Heracles*. But the extraordinary thing about
both poems is Browning's use of the ancient world—not romantic after the manner of Milton, or Keats, or any other
English poet, but calling that world back to life with the reality
and detailed readiness of an archeologist, or better, of one who
had lived in it. How had the poet accumulated and cherished
such store of things! At sixty-five he translated the *Agamemnon*
of Aeschylus at the request of his old friend, Carlyle, to whose
"dear and noble name" it is inscribed.

Every matter presents to him not one side, but at least two,
and often more.

> I touched a thought, I know,
>   Has tantalized me many times,
> (Like turns of thread the spiders throw
>   Mocking across our path) for rhymes
> To catch at and let go.[1]

Life looks as multiplex as a five-part fugue, or the web that

[1] *Two in the Campagna*

almost hides the gilded church vaulting in *Master Hugues.* The supreme instance is *The Ring and the Book,* with its ten versions. Most of his poetry is essentially a debate or presentation of an issue, as it were two-ply—*Porphyria's Lover* ("I debated what to do"), *Pippa Passes, The Statue and the Bust, Andrea del Sarto, Fra Lippo Lippi, Epistle of Karshish, Time's Revenges, Up at a Villa, Christmas Eve and Easter Day,* and many more. He is fond of "parley." He is always putting the question; wherefore his habit when not at his best, of exasperating the reader with a constant spray of interrogation, from *Sordello* to *Asolando.* Such incessant questioning rises out of the unending clash between transient and permanent, in love and in everything else; between perfection and imperfection, inertia and effort, renunciation and committal, sense and spirit.

Every poet is tortured with the necessity of fitting matter to form. With Browning the matter so abounds and crowds for utterance that it strains, distorts, and overflows the form. His language like his mind becomes congested, and weak but useful members—articles, conjunctions, relative pronouns, copulas—are crowded out, and sentences get crushed to mere absolute phrases. And not content with one word or phrase for one thing, his very abundance repeats it, once, twice, thrice, in synonymous words, phrases, sentences, accumulating like the kennings in Old English poetry.

This very adjustment of form to matter offers a means in Browning's case of separating his less enduring work from his greater. Such as *Sordello, Paracelsus, Christmas Eve, Hohenstiel-Schwangau, Fifine at the Fair,* and others may be superb literary curiosities, but are defeated of lasting artistic success by the very superflux of their matter. Except certain parts of the *Ring,* only his short poems keep the balance that insures their life.

Most of these appeared in groups whose titles are significant —*Dramatic Lyrics,* 1842; *Dramatic Romances,* 1845; *Men and Women,* 1855; *Dramatis Personae,* 1864; *Dramatic Idyls,* 1879. Many of them are the finest examples of dramatic monologue; and all, even those ostensibly lyric, are dramatically conceived, as of a particular person in a particular situation.

For Browning's poetic instinct was primarily dramatic. Indeed during the ten years before his marriage he wrote some eight or nine plays intended for the stage, including *Strafford, Pippa Passes, The Return of the Druses, A Blot in the 'Scutcheon*— these last two said to have been written in five days each—until he was at last compelled to forgo the cherished hope that he was a practical playwright. *Strafford* and *A Blot* had a flash of stage success, but both actor and manager saw that in spite of certain highly wrought scenes, like the Ottima-Sebald episode in *Pippa*, these were closet dramas. The difficulty is that his persons, from king to gutter-snipe, most of the time talk like Brownings.

His dramatic power is highest in the impersonation of a single character, whether in a dramatic monologue or in a narrative poem. Some of these are morally hopeless, like the bishop ordering his tomb, the duke showing the portrait of his last duchess, the Spanish monk soliloquizing, or the jealous murderer in the laboratory; sometimes they are people of parts and power, or virtue, thwarted by circumstance or their own mismanagement, like Andrea, Lippo, Karshish, Caliban, Cleon, Saul, the duke and the lady in *The Statue and the Bust*; sometimes they are intrinsic heroes either unrecognized or without relish for fame, like the grammarian, David, Hervé Riel, Pheidippides, Count Gismond, or De Lorge in *The Glove*; sometimes they are misfits like the lover in *The Last Ride*, or the poet in *Time's Revenges*; sometimes paradoxes of heroism like Ned Bratts or Ivan Ivanovitch. Clearly Browning is not fond of pomp and circumstance, of the traditional and obvious heroes of the world. Ordinary life is surcharged with poetry for him.

Seizing a critical moment usually late in a career, he turns, or allows the man or woman to turn, the intense light of the moment upon the past which has led up to it, and sometimes upon the future. Setting and circumstance accrue bit by bit as the poem proceeds, and the whole is a lifetime presented in sharpest and most intense focus. If these poems are difficult as often alleged, it is their intensity, not their obscurity, that requires rereading.

Browning's high dramatic power often obscures his extraordinary metrical adroitness and dexterity. Many of his finest monologues are in blank verse, especially those ultimately grouped under *Men and Women*, and composed in his midcareer. But in the earlier ones and the latest he adopts practically a different, and often a very difficult, measure or stanza for each poem. The dramatic energy of the poem, and the easy skill with which the poet moves in these self-imposed limitations, make us unaware of the metrical scheme, though we are none the less sensitive to its effect. No doubt the restraint of the metrical form held in check his superexuberance, and kept it in these masterpieces from upsetting the artistic balance.

Much has been made of Browning's teaching or philosophy. Far from being really subtle or esoteric, it is obvious, and, like that in Carlyle's *Sartor*, as old as Plato. Love, even in its ignoble forms, but more and more according as its forms and objects are nobler and nobler, is the supreme experience whereby we win intimations of what is perfect and infinite and immortal. All the failures and disappointments of the heart's desires here on earth are but broken arcs of the complete and invisible circle in the infinite world. Into such a conviction fit the cases of the multitude that throng Browning's poetry from first to last.

Nor is it the flimsy optimism that some allege. He was fascinated with the study of human misery, stupidity, and hardness of heart, and blinked no depth of it in holding to his faith. He knew if any did the impulses to evil and ruin that strain at a man's soul; but so balanced and normal was his mental and physical health, so all-embracing his love of things and human beings, that he could speak with certainty and authority based deeper than reason itself, "the communication," as he said, "of something more subtle than a ratiocinative process, when the convictions of 'genius' have thrilled my soul to its depths."

CHAPTER 33

Place aux Dames

THE BRONTËS

CHARLOTTE BRONTË (1816-1855);
EMILY BRONTË (1818-1848)

OF ALL Victorian literary names none has so proved its power to excite curiosity, stir romantic and dramatic imaginings, evoke chatter and personal discussion, as has the name of Brontë. The family story literally told makes a novel in itself; indeed it furnished the matter of the novels which the family produced.

Patrick Prunty, which name he himself glorified as "Brontë," came out of North Ireland, studied at Cambridge, and was led by his clerical fate to serve in the harsh moorlands of Yorkshire. He was spirited, high-tempered, tender of heart, and rather fourth-rate in his literary performance. At thirty-five he married a gentle Miss Branwell from the south. In eight years she bore him six children—Maria, Elizabeth, Charlotte, Branwell, Emily, and Anne—and in the ninth year she died. The two oldest followed her, with tuberculosis, at ten and eleven. They were all exceptional children; four at least were highly talented, and two of them, Charlotte and Emily, were geniuses.

At the head of a cheerless little Yorkshire valley full of mills, just on the edge of the wild, heaving, wind-swept moors, perches Haworth, whose rectory is the scene of most of the Brontë drama. The folk thereabouts were most of them mill-hands, pious and narrow Dissenters, bleak, hard-bitten, suspicious, the human counterpart of the lonely moors around. The Brontë children held aloof from Haworth people, but they, especially Emily, loved and consorted with the moors, until the wild spirit of the place, at once alluring and inscrutable, became a part of their nature and their art.

The motherless childhood of the four seems not to have been unhappy. Though circumscribed, and overseen by an unsympathetic aunt, the youngsters lived in a close corporation held together by lively imaginings and a heavy traffic in composition of stories, sagas, and plays, which they spun out well into their mature years, about the "Angrians" of Africa, and the "Gondals," a mountain folk of endless history in the north. Other tales on other themes—*Henry Sophona, The Spell, History of the Young Men,* and many more—suggest the good time these children made for each other. Copies survive of Charlotte's yarns written out in an exquisite microscopic hand.

With youth the omens darkened. Even as children the girls had suffered in cheerless boarding-schools; as young women Anne and Charlotte endured even more as governesses of young barbarians. Branwell, with an excellent talent for painting as well as literature, and not a little personal charm, was unstable. As a young man he found dangerous escape from the dullness of Haworth only at the Black Bull hard by. He tried various jobs elsewhere, came home in disgrace, a besotted nuisance to the household, till he died burnt out at thirty-one. Emily, mystic, stoical, and self-contained but not enterprising, roamed the moors and poured out her flaming soul in secret song, whose music is the very sound of the strong upland winds. It seems strange that such poems as *The Prisoner,* or the so-called *Last Lines* beginning "No coward soul is mine," or the poem, *The Wanderer from the Fold,* once thought to have been written in memory of Branwell in the three months between his death and hers, are not better known. Her songs are surcharged with spiritual courage and liveliest sense of things invisible, with passion unreleased.

Charlotte, small, energetic, brave, was the captain of this little band. Though she and Anne hated teaching, at twenty-six she conceived the scheme of starting a school. To equip herself with French and other languages she spent altogether a year and a half in Brussels, in the school of Paul Héger and his wife—part of the time teaching. With M. Paul, small, dark, irascible, but winning, and always kind to her, she fell in love; and crushing this secret and hopeless agony down in her heart, she came home to launch the new venture. Not a pupil appeared. She then discovered Emily's poems, and with her own and Anne's made up the famous little still-born volume, now a prize of collectors, *Poems by Currer, Ellis, and Acton Bell*. She had a horror of being known and disparaged as a female writer, and for some time maintained the male disguise.

She was now used to defeat, but not to accepting defeat. Bravely she and her sisters set to work on novels, she on *The Professor*, Anne on *Agnes Grey*, and Emily on *Wuthering Heights*. This was no longer the tale-spinning of their youth, but serious business; they were women of thirty, twenty-six, and twenty-eight. For more than a year the novels wandered about in disguise of male authorship from one indifferent publisher to another. Meanwhile, Charlotte left her drunken brother at home, to take her father to Manchester for the removal of cataracts, and momentously beguiled the hours of watching by beginning *Jane Eyre*. A year later it found an instant publisher, and instant and overwhelming success. This is not to be explained by the bare plot, which, though it ferments with a bit of sensation and what to the Victorian taste was scandal, is full of impossibilities. Yet its essential reality has made it a great classic. For the Brontë novels are a compound of the wild imaginings of the Brontë girlhood and the hard and bitter circumstance and disillusion of their lives. *Jane Eyre* and all the rest are fine mosaics of a thousand actual incidents, places, persons they knew, and Brontë devotees never tire of tracing and identifying them. Jane herself is Charlotte, little, long-suffering, shy, repressed, a smouldering volcano of passion beneath. Rochester is the tortured and pitiful soul living only in her imagination, to whom she longed to devote herself. Indeed all her work is intense with the pressure of strong feeling beneath the surface, which clothes it in a kind of fascinating mystery—not the theatrical mystery of Byron, nor the mystery of suspense, though there is a touch of both—

but the mystery at bottom of the reticent, thwarted, disillusioned, brave woman who tells the tales.

Even after *Jane Eyre* the sisters had to share the expense of publishing *Wuthering Heights*, and recognition of its worth came slowly. Charlotte herself missed its full effect. The reader cannot accept its unrelieved career of madness and misery as a copy of real life. Rather it is like a musical or poetic transcription of the strange inscrutable spirit of Emily Brontë herself, in which the untamed, disordered, overwhelming powers of the moor become incarnate, and merge themselves indistinguishably with human life; and the dark expanse is lightened at moments with the tender and unearthly light of a love affair almost heroic in depth and grandeur.

With Charlotte's fame began her visits to London, and acquaintance with the literary great. She had idolized Thackeray, but, after her habit, was inclined to disillusionment when she met him. The story of the grand dinner of celebrities he gave in her honor, and its collapse into such dullness that even the host deserted, is too well-known to repeat. She was too shy and too critical to be made a lion.

In the meantime she had begun *Shirley*, a story involved with the riots of labor against machinery, and portraying Emily in the title-rôle. Composition dragged on through what must have been the culminating trouble of her life, for in the eight months between September, 1848, and May, 1849, she lost her brother and both gifted sisters. *Shirley* was followed in three years by *Villette* (1853), containing matter from her earlier story, *The Professor*, into which is woven with her characteristic intensity her love ten years before for the Belgian teacher, M. Héger. In fact, so intense was her portrayal of Lucy Snowe's passion for Professor Paul that Trollope, with only this evidence, guessed her secret.

At twenty-three she had received two offers of marriage from clerics. Curates, by a strange feminine irony, seem to have been the special mark of her satire in life and in her books. She protests too much that they are figures of fun. At thirty-five she had another proposal from James Taylor, the sturdy agent of her publisher. Oddly enough the one to win her

heart at thirty-eight, and that in the face of her father's violent
opposition, was his curate, Arthur Nicholls. He was a fine
and gentle soul, but with a touch of Rochester's passion in his
wooing. After all the bitter and thwarted years, it seemed at
last as if her suppressed dream had come true, and her pent-up
feelings were to find happy release. Over her last letters falls
a new and sober sweetness alien to her earlier writings. Nine
months after her marriage her new life sank quite suddenly
to its close.

MRS. GASKELL (1810-1865)

Charlotte Brontë's fame brought her the friendship of Mrs.
Gaskell, now best known for her idyll of an English village,
Cranford. Cranford had its original in Knutsford, near Manchester, where, as Elizabeth Stevenson, she had spent the first
fourteen years of her life under the care of her devoted Aunt
Lumb. Her father, of whom this motherless child saw little,
was successively Unitarian minister, farmer, writer, and government clerk.

She was a beautiful girl and lively. At twenty-two she married William Gaskell, a Unitarian minister, and lived her remaining years as a pastor's wife in Manchester. Her only son
died suddenly in infancy. To raise her out of her desperate
grief her husband persuaded her to write. At thirty-seven she
finished her first book, *Mary Barton*. The plot is good melodrama: a plain but honest man is falsely accused of murder
and saved from the gallows by the heroine, who, the whiles,
has been lured almost to her ruin by the dastardly guile of a
rich manufacturer's son. In the end, of course, she marries
her true lover, the plain but honest laborer. The book
is punctuated regularly with pathetic death-beds—there must
be a dozen; Mrs. Gaskell was indeed, as Ruskin said, too "fond
of killing nice people." But it succeeded, both with experts
like Dickens, Carlyle, and Ruskin, and with people at large.
The reason is plain. It contained good solid substance to be
expected from a good solid Victorian pastor's wife with a
nimble pen in her hand—the substance of housekeeping, chil-

dren in plenty, domestic affections, accidents, distresses, and humors—all without any literary "side" or affectation.

But its chief sensation rose from the courage with which this woman handled the crying industrial issues of the "hungry forties," the low pay, squalor, strikes, indifference of employers and government. The book raised a double storm of praise and blame, which of course did more good than many "measures."

Other works from her hand included not only a goodly number of short stories, but *Ruth,* a novel bravely aimed at hidebound Victorian convention, and telling the story of a humble girl who "falls," but by her goodness at length rehabilitates herself, and of course dies at the end. *North and South* some eight years after *Mary Barton* resumes the industrial question and handles it with better understanding, though not with more spirit. Later still was *Sylvia's Lovers,* a compound of humble life and melodramatic plot, and *Wives and Daughters,* on a higher provincial social level, which many regard as her masterpiece, and which she left not quite finished.

But the permanent life in Mrs. Gaskell's art is her idyllic power within the domestic range of vision. It is obscured in her novels by "purpose" and plot, but shines with something of the unfading light of Goldsmith in *Cousin Phyllis,* one of her last, and in the immortal *Cranford.*

Mrs. Gaskell was chosen the official biographer for her friend, Charlotte Brontë. With the *Life* she took infinite pains, though at the time it raised a scandal with certain ill-considered, but, as it then seemed, authentic, information about Charlotte's father, brother, and the school at Cowan Bridge. It is, however, one of the great English biographies, both in subject and author.

The two women had at least in common their intrepid dissatisfaction with many things that were. In their day a woman needed all her courage even to publish. A "female" writer could not expect a hearing, and must therefore win it before she was known to be a woman. So Miss Brontë clung to the mask of Currer Bell till fame tore it off. Mrs. Gaskell published *Mary Barton* anonymously, and Mary Ann Evans hid so long and successfully behind George Eliot that, with all her many names to choose from, George Eliot she is now and always will be.

GEORGE ELIOT (1819-1880)

Still living in London is a man who remembers being taken as a special treat at the age of ten or so to one of George Eliot's famous Sunday afternoons at home. He was led into the presence of the worshipful gray sibyl enthroned at the end of the room, allowed to touch the tips of her fingers, favored with a gracious smile, and then taken away. This might have been in the late sixties, at the height of her reign. To all London, except some of the "new" young men, she was the oracular wise woman, possibly the greatest genius since Shakespeare, and thereby exempt from ordinary social convention. Partly because she was a woman, no novelist had ever inspired such awe. The unheard-of price of £10,000 was offered her for *Romola*, and *Middlemarch* fetched £12,000.

For a time she fitted perfectly the aspirations of advanced Victorian culture—its deep and sober scrutiny of conventions, social, moral, and religious—and her novels, preoccupied more and more with the delicate refinements of human behavior, flattered the public as it read them with a feeling that it was becoming quite esoteric. None of the great Victorians is less read now.

George Eliot was essentially two people. A lively, open-air tomboy, unconscious, affectionate, craving affection in others, laying hold upon the joys and beauties of the physical world with a lusty appetite, she was herself a solid fragment of that fertile, ancient, peacefully believing, sober and settled corner of Shakespeare's county where she was reared. This element of her soul was never wholly sophisticated out of her.

But over against it was her almost superhuman intellectuality, analysing, speculating, inquiring, which served indeed to lend vigor and toughness of fibre to her work, but which, in her latest efforts, overbore and ruined it. The conflict of these two instincts appears and reappears not only in the artistic balance, or unbalance, of her novels, but in her very characters themselves and the moral tests to which they are put.

Mary Ann Evans, born in 1819, spent most of her life till she was twenty-two in a snug old brick farmhouse at Griff near Nuneaton, Warwickshire. Her father, Robert Evans, was manager of great men's estates. He was strong as a giant, affectionate, and rather more genial than Adam Bede, of whom he is the partial original. In him the conservative English landed tradition was incarnate. Mary Ann had also an older brother whom she adored in humble subjection, like Maggie Tulliver in *The Mill on the Floss*.

At twenty-one she went with her father to live at Coventry. The girl prodigy had already, with help of private masters, stored up much knowledge of languages and literatures and music, and continued to wax more learned. Then her contact with a free-thinking manufacturer named Bray and his family, and with his intellectual friends, brought her inherited and well-ordered evangelical beliefs down with a crash, and she refused to go to church with her father. Afterthought conceded the point, and the breach between Robert Evans and his "little wench" was partly healed; but Mary Ann had passed the first crisis of conflict in her two-fold nature.

The next dozen years were years of unconscious preparation. She traveled with the Brays, met intellectuals, toiled at translation, notably Strauss's *Life of Jesus*, at thirty-two went to London, and slaved for the *Westminster Review*, came to know Herbert Spencer, and through him George Henry Lewes. He was a struggling man of letters, slight, not beautiful, warm of heart and lively, whose wife had twice deserted him and her three boys. Miss Evans and Lewes discovered between them sympathy so complete that deliberately and in the face of her bringing-up, her family, her friends, and all society, she went to live with Lewes as his wife.

For the second time her "higher" moral reasoning had won in conflict with social convention and her inherited promptings. It is the sort of clash which gives the highest dramatic potential to her greatest stories, and is especially clear in the strongly autobiographic *Mill on the Floss*. During the social isolation which followed their union Lewes discovered and roused her creative gift, and *Scenes of Clerical Life*, three short novels, appeared under the mask of "George Eliot." They commanded immediate attention and set literary folk a-guessing; but only Charles Dickens, remarking the "womanly touches" in her vigorous work, inferred that he was she.

The three stories are widely different. *Amos Barton* is pretty lacrimose. *Mr. Gilfil's Love-Story,* far the best, tells the tale of a stout young English cleric's passion for a bewildered little Italian girl, and his quiet success after long and stormy trials with odds against him. It is told with something of the sweetness of "long ago." *Janet's Repentance* sets the brutality of a drunken husband over against the quiet strength of a Methodist preacher, with a woman as the point of contention. It is a bit lurid with scenes such as the thrusting of the poor wife from a warm bed into the cold storm, and a realistic death from delirium tremens. But the great virtue of these stories rises from the rich substance of rural Warwickshire with which they are mingled, the very substance of George Eliot's childhood. With all the charm of *Mr. Gilfil's Love-Story*, this substance has not been refined and chastened to the point of becoming idyllic. Critics have suggested the influence of George Sand, but the explanation seems superfluous. For the stories are authentic, racy, lively with the life that no imitator could breathe into them, but only one of whose very self they were a part.

To greater heights the novelist arose forthwith in *Adam Bede* and *The Mill on the Floss*. The first she wrought from a story told her years before "by my Methodist Aunt Samuel" Evans, who had once comforted through her last hours a poor thing condemned to be hanged for making away with her illegitimate baby. Aunt Evans was the original of the saintly Dinah Morris. How stalwart Adam loved in vain the sweet and helpless Hetty, how she was betrayed by a "gentleman," forsook her baby, was condemned, reprieved, and transported, how the noble Dinah comforted her and in the end married Adam—such is the bare story. But George Eliot wrought it into a new masterpiece by two processes. She chose people in humble and obscure life for persons in a drama of grand passions, and attempted to enlarge these persons into heroic proportions of character. This had never been done before in a novel, nor elsewhere except by Wordsworth. But she makes her story convincing by mingling with it the rich rural substance of her early life even more generously than in her first stories. Mrs. Poyser and Bartle Massey the cobbler, with their homespun and witty choral comment on the action, the life of farm and village, of workshop and kitchen, even pigs and pups and barnyards, all conspire to the same racy and pungent effect. George Eliot's relish for these early joys of her life is often so strong as to infect her reader with the very like.

Adam Bede met with the glorious success it deserved, and the real authorship became an open secret. *The Mill on the Floss* and *Silas Marner*, made of the same general components, raised her fame to preëminence and lifted her out of poverty. The *Mill*, so strongly autobiographical, is often called her masterpiece. It contains the same stout stuff of the exuberant countryside as before, but qualified by the truth and delicacy with which Maggie Tulliver's childhood and youth are portrayed. And it rises to high tragic conflict between the passion of her heart and her earlier loyalty, and to a moral renunciation which is one of the grandest among all the Victorian treatments of that theme. *Silas Marner,* on smaller scale and in lower key, is of the same piece, with its incomparable scene at the Rainbow, its moral crisis, its moral dignity.

With her fame, and perhaps with the first slackening of Victorian strictness, people looked less askance at this extraordinary woman. She was wondered at and lionized, and she hated it; for with all her greatness, quiet intimacies were what she most loved. Lewes and she often sought refuge on the Continent. In Florence she felt the spell of the Renaissance Puritan, Savonarola, and conceived the story of *Romola*, which she wrote with more than her usual scruple for exactness, even making careful research into heraldry, costume, and the like. It is a magnificent performance, and has perhaps enthralled more readers than any other of her works. Yet a performance it is, beautifully planned and staged, rising to dramatic power, and exhibiting most subtly the progressive degeneration of a human soul. No other of her books—perhaps no other historical novel—ever cost such pains. But the matter is not her own; it is not the stuff of rural and provincial Victorian England, and no other matter could quite engage the full and natural power of her genius. She was now forty-four, and *Romola*, she said, had made her an old woman.

She was always subject to depression of spirits and body, especially during periods of composition, and for two years or more she wrote nothing. Then in a little over a decade she produced the three characteristic novels of her later period—her powerful industrial novel, *Felix Holt, Middlemarch,* and *Daniel Deronda. Middlemarch,* which she considered her finest novel, is a large, plotless block of life lifted from a provincial town of quality. In fact its full title is *Middlemarch: a Study of Provincial Life.* Her principals in all three novels are people of cultivation, with an attendant and numerous chorus of amusing individuals from all ranks. But the novels are not mere literal reproductions, for the hand of the artist has entered vigorously into the shaping, grouping, delineating, and action of both principals and subordinates. Everything is relevant to the author's design, which, she explains, "is to show the gradual action of ordinary causes rather than exceptional, and to show this in some directions which have not been from time immemorial the beaten path." She gains her almost uncanny verisimilitude not from local color, but from the natural peculiarity and humanity of every participant down to the least. The chorus is not a mob, but a group of individuals. Whereas Trollope introduces us to his world and makes us so acquainted with people that we gossip about them, George Eliot shows us people with whose counterparts we are already acquainted in our own world, revealing the amusing subtleties, the deep and tragic issues in the life immediately about us which we had taken for commonplace.

In most of her stories, especially in her late ones, she loves to occupy herself with the case of one who enters upon life with preconceived and untried notions—too high, too low, too worldly, too idealistic; who is then caught in the angry and bewildering current of real experience; whose ideas and career are either lost in the struggle, or find their right course, and emerge adjusted and authenticated by the experience. Such is the case of Adam Bede, of Gilfil, of Janet Dempster, of Maggie Tulliver, of Dorothea and of Lydgate in *Middlemarch*, of Felix Holt and Esther, of Gwendolen Harleth and Daniel Deronda. This experience is usually that of the grand passion. It bears strong resemblance to like crises in the life of the novelist herself, the wreck of her early evangelical notions, and the clash between the claims of her heart and the conventions of society.

From her muscular intellect her novels derived a stoutness of texture, which is kept flexible and pliant by the wit not only of various persons in them, but of her own comment on the action. But this intellectualism was her undoing in the end. More and more her stories are clogged with superfluous comment and interpretation, stodgy, turgid, and self-conscious; and in her last work, *The Impressions of Theophrastus Such,* the balance between her intellectuality and her old gust for human action is overset, and the play is done.

Her power of mind had driven out the old inherited beliefs of her childhood, and reduced her religion to something like the "positivism" of Comte, a religion of kindness and good works, quite devoid of anything mystical. Yet the moral austerities, and the simple mysteries of that early life of hers, as well as its simple joys, still haunted her and lent much of their vitality to her novels, from *Adam Bede* to the pure inherited Judaism of Deronda, as if confessing in them a beauty and truth which her giant reason and sophistication could not refute. Such sense of mystery seems to be reflected in her passion for music, in her love of little children, in her use of symbolism at times, such as the river Floss, and the gold in *Silas Marner*, and it found utterance in the only poem of hers which men remember, "Oh may I join the choir invisible"; in which, by the way, the old clash is audible.

In 1878 she lost George Lewes, the real partner in her genius. Eighteen months later, at the age of sixty, she married J. W. Cross, whom she had known for ten years, but died suddenly before the year was out.

CHAPTER 34

Manners, Morals, and the Arts

RUSKIN (1819-1900)

WE ARE today a generation that delights in "Arts and Crafts." We crave homespun and handwork with no cheapening trace of factory or mass production about it. We love a well bound and alluringly printed book, with a trace of the "personal" in its design. By some kindred affection we have experienced a new passion for Gothic architecture; and in our schools the study of Nature and of fine arts, both in history and practice, have sturdily and successfully jostled with older subjects for a footing. We are fired with zeal for better living conditions among the poor. We found "Settlements" and "Houses."

Such enthusiasms we inherit in general from the romantic movement, but they have come down to us by a particular tradition. Carlyle's "Gospel of Work," his protest against materialism and the exploitation of human life and labor, descended in power upon Dickens, Tennyson, the Brownings; upon Ruskin, Matthew Arnold, William Morris, Cobden-Sanderson, and a host of active disciples and allies. But especially upon John Ruskin. His part it was to associate the appreciation of beauty in Nature and in art with honest labor and personal design, as redeemers of the poor from their misery, Philistines from their stupid unloveliness, and both from Shoddy.

Ruskin was the only child of a substantial London importer of wines, "an entirely honest merchant," growing steadily richer. A grandmother had kept an inn. It was a family of tradespeople on both sides, severely evangelical. Small John

was whipped if he cried or fell downstairs. Toys were pro-
hibited. He was forced to learn long passages of the Bible—
a hardship which perhaps did him no harm as a man or writer.
His mother "devoted him to God" before birth; his father
marked him for a future bishop, or at least a "gentleman"
unsoiled by trade. At a tender age he was playing "church"
and exhorting his make-believe congregation: "People, be
good!"—an act oft encored by his mother to entertain—or
dismay—her callers. Such prophetic omens may be observed in
every suckling, but are rarely recorded because they are rarely
fulfilled. In Ruskin's case they were. He was essentially a
preacher and teacher all his life.

His mother followed him to Oxford and lived there all his
undergraduate days. She survived till he was fifty-two, ever a
devoted incubus on his life. His indulgent father was scandalized at the subversive social and economic views which his son
adopted at forty. The tragic story, tenderly and pathetically
told, may be read in Ruskin's fascinating autobiography, *Prae-
terita*.

Scott and Pope's *Homer* were Ruskin's chosen favorites from
childhood, and to them he ascribed his Tory love of things aristocratic and old. Byron was an idol. From sixteen to twenty he
loved a French girl, daughter of his father's partner, but his
mother would not hear of a Catholic daughter-in-law. At
thirty-one he married a wife prescribed by his mother; six years
later this loveless marriage was annulled. Strangely enough this
seems to have been the least unhappy interval of his life. Most
tragic of all, he was a mental invalid nearly all of his adult
years. He was cursed with the curse of Swift and Collins and
Cowper. From his Oxford days it hovered over and swooped
down with periodic threats. After he was fifty he suffered six
attacks of madness, and the last ten years before his death at
eighty were sunk in the gloom of depression or mental storm.
Rich, spoiled, bred to be a snob, parent-ridden, fighting a
losing struggle with mental disease, Ruskin seems the last
person to have become a preaching and working idealist,
moved by intense sympathy with the poor, by pity also for
the poor in mind amid their new riches, spending life and

fortune to relieve and convert his generation after his own way.

In boyhood his parents took him on various tours through Great Britain and the Continent, travelling luxuriously in their private carriage. At fourteen he caught his first view of the distant Alps, and "went down that evening . . . with my destiny fixed in all of it that was to be sacred and useful."

Ruskin himself was aware of much misspent effort. It was alas, in the nature of his insecure case. His writings fill thirty-eight volumes on painting and painters, architecture, statuary, on landscape, on geology, botany, mineralogy, books, literature, political economy, national affairs, ancient myth—and himself. Interspersed are many exquisite drawings, sometimes of rare beauty, made by his own delicate hand. Much of his work was amateur, but it was amateurism of a fine sort. He was full of schemes, of which only two or three survived birth. But out of this welter of pen, pencil, and project, rises the essential and sane Ruskin, a major prophet of the doctrine which was to save his own ruling class and times from their stupid and selfish blunders.

It is usual to point to a sharp reversal in Ruskin's interests at about the age of forty, from painting and architecture to social conditions and welfare. In point of fact the second phase is but the natural fulfilment of the first. At twenty-four came the first volume of *Modern Painters*. The fifth and last appeared when he was forty-one. Meanwhile amongst other works he wrote the *Seven Lamps of Architecture* and *Stones of Venice*. *Modern Painters* was designed ostensibly to reveal and explain the exquisite and deep truth of nature in the landscapes of the painter J. M. W. Turner. Incidentally—or predominatingly—there is much about other painters, literature, the history of culture, about Nature herself in the finest of her workmanship; and the third volume in particular teems with ideas and revelations of loveliness which possess the reader's mind less by stark reason than by their insinuating charm of utterance. The same is true of the *Seven Lamps*, and of parts of *Stones of Venice*. Happy the young man or woman who has felt their spell, whose eye has been opened and feelings sensitized by them to unsuspected forces in art, letters, and Nature, whom they have made self-supporting in his observation and judgment. "Observe" is an habitual word with Ruskin. He insists too that behind all great art there are virtues that make it great—honesty, discernment of truth, nobility, patience and courage, love of order, warm sympathies; and that these enter into great art, and make it great, as human weaknesses likewise vitiate what proves artistically poor or perverted.

Such inquiries naturally led him to demand why England, and the modern world generally, were no longer capable of great art or susceptible to its influences. So he is confronted, like the other idealists of his time, with the world's absorbing passion for money, its slavery to machines, its consequent hardness of heart, vulgarity, ugliness, materialism, and the brutal degradation of the poor—and all its riches accumulating against the day when they will be burned up in wars of suspicion between the nations. "No nation can last which has made a mob of itself, however generous at heart. . . . Above all, a nation cannot last as a money-making mob; it cannot with impunity—it cannot with existence—go on despising literature, despising science, despising art, despising nature, despising compassion and concentrating its soul on Pence."[1] In the three lectures which comprise his *Crown of Wild Olive* (1864-6), and the four essays of what he considered his best work, *Unto this Last* (1859-60), his trenchant ideas on social conditions find their most eloquent utterance. As earlier from artists and critics, so now again from political economists, his ideas provoked scorn and irritation. In fact they continue so to do in a measure which proves at least their power. It was Ruskin's contention inherited from Carlyle that wealth consists not in material things, but in the character and condition of the possessor—a contention which many professed economists have come to accept.

Though a man of working ideas rather than practical details—there was the road-making mess with his Oxford lads at Hinksey—he carried them into form in his organization of St. George's Guild and the Sheffield Museum in 1871, and

[1] *Sesame and Lilies,* Lecture I

his experiment, with the help of Octavia Hill, in improving the housing conditions of London's poor. The Guild, on paper —that is in various of the ninety-six letters under the title *Fors Clavigera* (1871-84)—is a Utopia for the reclamation of land by men and women under vows of religious faith, patriotism, and honest kindness to all creatures. It was highly organized under the "Master" (Ruskin self-appointed), and provided with certain picturesque accessories of costume, badge, and practice. Ruskin endowed the Guild with a large slice of his own fortune, and provided for its cultural needs a museum at Sheffield, for which he collected a costly array of minerals and drawings, many by his own hand. The Guild itself came to little, though it still survives past much ridicule, scorn, and discouragement. But no one can measure its vast influence in stirring the present-day enthusiasms and fashions aforesaid, or in shaping the ideals of design, workmanship, and working conditions which are daily becoming realities.

Ruskin had, and still has, a singular power of enthralling and inspiring his listeners. In spite of his scoldings, his despairs, his egoism, his flashes of unreasoning hatred for railways and other mechanical deformities of modern life, he captivated multitudes in his day. His great repute rose in his early forties, about the time he turned from criticism of art to social questions. A book of "Selections" exhibited purple patches from earlier work, and purple they were. In all his earlier works he was prone at set moments to elaborate a page or two of spectacular prose, pulsing with color, glowing with ornament, in long symmetrical balance of clauses, but borne forward on a strong current of musical cadence. Such occur in "The Mountain Glory" in the fourth volume of *Modern Painters*, and "St. Mark's" in the second volume of *Stones of Venice*. Beneath them rises and falls the regular rhythm of Old Testament English, and of the longer ground swell of Dr. Johnson's essays, which the family used to read aloud to beguile the time on their long journeys, and whose music had entered deeply into Ruskin's impressionable young mind.

English education was still in large measure oral—Ruskin's especially—and men wrote as if they were speaking, with the

sound of their words tingling or thundering in their ears. Some
of Ruskin's best writing originated as lectures. For several years
he was Professor of Fine Art at Oxford. He was a fluent talker
in public and private. All of which accounts for the irresistible
but easy momentum of his style. It reflects, too, something of
the magnetic presence often described by his hearers—the tall,
auburn-haired, well-groomed figure, rather attractive than
good-looking, with the direct, intense, but kindly blue eye, and
the invariable blue cravat.

But his personal power proves itself most in the devoted
following which rose in response to his teaching and personality. Ruskin Societies sprang up all around. Books about
him still multiply. No other literary man has been honored
with so monumental an edition of his works as that by Cook
and Wedderburn, with its thirty-eight volumes, its master index
volume, and its reproductions of his drawings.

His purple luxuriance of manner he abandoned when he
came to grips with social problems. It enraged him if anyone
praised that earlier skill, for he thought it had blinded them
to his ideas. The change was to his advantage, for he launched
forth at his best with the lithe and unimpeded energy of the
stripped athlete in *Unto this Last* and *Crown of Wild Olive*.

With his other terrible handicaps, he had perhaps too many
distracting talents, but out of the litter of his disordered career
emerges the single powerful figure of a teacher and prophet
who ranks with Carlyle and Dickens as a regenerator of the
Victorian world.

TROLLOPE (1815-1882)

Now and then an author has the power to raise up a group
of devoted and unreasoning worshippers distinguished by a
tribal or caste name; the Janeites set themselves apart in their
adoration of Jane Austen, the Dickensians through all the
earth are one in the bond of their common affection. By the
same token flourishes the numerous sect of Trollopians, who
never tire of reading, rereading, and collecting his books, and
discussing with quickening pulse the world and people of
Anthony Trollope.

In the late sixties and early seventies Trollope shared with George Eliot the summit of fame as a novelist. Thackeray was dead, and Dickens's work was done. Then with the eighties, with the new empire and the new paganism, the new seriousness with which art began to take itself for its own sake, Trollope utterly declined for two or three decades, to rise again in the next century amid an ever-increasing throng of worshippers.

Here was one who wrote altogether well over fifty novels and collections of sketches and short stories, besides ten books of travels and the like, most of them after he was forty. Naturally but a fraction of them are great. At sixty he told his own story in his engrossing *Autobiography*.

His father, with grand ideas, brought the family from affluence to indigence. His mother, never wholly aware of her heroism, went out to Cincinnati in 1827 to set up a grand "bazaar," one of her husband's last and wildest schemes. It failed. Undaunted, at fifty-one she picked up her pen and wrote a book on *Domestic Manners of the Americans*. It was an early and sprightly specimen of its numerous kind, and between the rage and the delight stirred by its brisk comment, it scored a success—which was what the Trollopes needed most. Then she took her family and fled her creditors to Belgium, where she continued to write while nursing a dying husband and son through their last days. Before she died at eighty-three this brave and lively soul had written altogether 114 volumes.

Anthony was a hulking, untidy, neglected, and everywhere unwelcome youngster. At Harrow, and for a time at Winchester School, though he craved affection, he was the butt and scorn of mates and masters, and learned nothing. At nineteen he became a clerk in the London postoffice, and led the lonely and careless life of a youth in a large city, hating his work, conscious of inferiority, and always on the point of dismissal. By his account all his early life found no relief from bitterness, though the gloom of his childhood and youth doubtless looked the deeper to him from the bright sunshine on the heights whence, after his struggle, he at last looked down.

At twenty-six he began his life in Ireland as a travelling

postal inspector. The human contacts with genial people, the open air, the foxhunting to which he heartily committed himself for the rest of his active life, his success in his work, and his marriage, all combined to correlate and set free the great powers which had been so stifled and smoldering in him that at times he had thought he was going to die. He had long beguiled his misery with castles in the air, and even thought of writing. Then suddenly at almost thirty he began. His first two Irish novels, followed by a French historical story, *La Vendée,* did not succeed. After eight years came *The Warden,* inspired during a walk about Salisbury close, but with mellow old St. Cross near Winchester for its setting. In rapid succession followed the matchless cathedral series—*Barchester Towers, Doctor Thorne, Framley Parsonage,* and the rest, interspersed with some of his greatest, *The Three Clerks,* always his favorite, wherein Trollope of the London days is Charley Tudor, and *Orley Farm.* At the height of his fame began the parliamentary series including *Phineas Finn, The Prime Minister,* and *Phineas Redux.*

With his fame in his forties Trollope finally left his beloved Ireland, to enjoy the fruits of his success as a literary clubman in London and at the hunt in the southern counties. Burly and bearded he now was, loud and deep of voice and laughter, often gruff and abrupt, with a restless black eye that missed nothing. He wore on the surface a relish of his success and consequence, and made rather a flourish of his sharp bargaining with his publishers; which was wholly natural in one whom the world had long tried to convince of his inferiority. But beneath the rough surface survived from his wretched youth a deep sympathy with human error and misfortune, and modesty wholly incommensurate with his triumph. This apparent contradiction the reader of the *Autobiography* must bear in mind.

He travelled everywhere, not only as postal inspector over Ireland and England, but on the Continent, to Egypt, South Africa, Australia and its neighborhood, and America, now on international business, now on his own, and always with an appetite for everything human. Yet his great novels are English, solid and substantial; says Hawthorne, "just as English as a beefsteak."

Critics have been prone to deny him creative imagination, that is, genius. "He only depicts." He does indeed protest that he is not inspired, and tells of scribbling his work on a pad, eight to sixteen pages a day, in trains, on boats, anywhere, counting his stint by 250 words to a page, till one novel is off the frame and another on. Which is not the ordinary way of genius. But he also confesses that in his best work his characters take complete possession of him. "I have wandered alone among the rocks and woods, crying at their grief, laughing at their absurdities, and thoroughly enjoying their joy. I have been impregnated with my own creations till it has been my only excitement to sit with the pen in my hand, and drive my team before me at as quick a pace as I could make them travel." A novelist must live, he insists, with his imagined characters "in the full reality of established intimacy. They must be with him as he lies down to sleep, and as he wakes from his dreams. He must learn to hate and to love them. He must argue with them, quarrel with them, forgive them, and even submit to them. . . . It is so that I have lived with my characters, and thence has come whatever success I have obtained. There is a gallery of them, and of all in that gallery I may say that I know the tone of the voice, and the colour of the hair, every flame of the eye, and the very clothes they wear." As the actors, so the scene. Barsetshire, "that dear county," as he calls it, became so real to him that he mapped it, "as though I had lived and wandered there." And he has made it as dear and real to others.

The strength of his work lies not in the plot, though he somehow manages to hold the interest in events, but in the reality of his persons and their manner of life. He is in short, the preëminent painter of manners which times of fluctuating society such as his call forth. "A novel," he says, "should give a picture of common life enlivened by humor and sweetened by pathos," in his case the hunt, the country-house, the Church, politics, the village and the great town—far removed all of it from the industrial agonies of the north.

So it is Trollope's world rather than single novels into which delighted readers are admitted, to stay and live; to think and talk about his people as dwellers in their neighborhood, not in books. To this end he made his style the perfect medium. Whatever its alleged defects, it is an oral style as all good style must be, lending itself better perhaps than that of any other novelist to reading aloud. He can turn it to any use—writing a perfect letter or editorial or speech; but in ordinary use it is so transparent a medium that it makes the reader unaware of print or author or language or anything but the action before him.

Real as is his world, now and then it wears, especially in Barsetshire, the transforming hue and light of poetry, as in Hiram's Hospital, or Miss Thorne's house, Ullathorne, a quality reflected also in certain of his characters. This very magic which he cast over that splendid but passing Victorian England may explain his continued following in America, even while his credit was lowest at home. Americans enjoyed themselves in that mellow, tranquil, comfortable old-world setting, so unlike their own.

All his readers play favorites among his novels, including Trollope himself, who admitted that *Doctor Thorne*, though not his preference, was his greatest success. Perhaps it contains in best balance the various qualities of a great novel. The plot is coherent and articulate, and the portraiture rises even to the grand manner. Roger Scatcherd, his wife, Dr. Thorne, Mary Thorne, and Miss Dunstable are presented with that force of conviction, and endued with that perennial life, which is proof enough of genius.

ARNOLD (1822-1888)

Like Sidney and Pope, Matthew Arnold was both poet and critic. Like theirs too was his appointed task—to soften a vulgar generation by the amenities of literature. Unlike them, however, he divided his life between the two functions. Till about forty he was the poet; thereafter his medium was almost entirely expository prose.

Sprung of the upper middle class himself, he had a patrician education compounded of a year at Winchester, four at Rugby, and three at Balliol College, Oxford. His was the Rugby of Hughes's *Tom Brown's Schooldays*, and of Arnold's great father, the Headmaster Thomas Arnold, "cheerful, and helpful, and firm," who memorably inspired in his young charges the love of integrity, purity, and learning, and made them feel the spiritual qualities of history and the classics. He kindled in them the ardors of his own refined evangelical Christianity, but what he found easy to accept the next generation found increasingly difficult, as they went slipping down to agnosticism or despair, groping for a foothold on the way. Their case is nobly expressed in Arnold's *Rugby Chapel* in memory of his father.

Arnold followed to Oxford another Rugby boy three years older named Arthur Hugh Clough, a shy, engaging youth of high promise. There amid the religious ferment rising from the Oxford Movement their deep friendship was confirmed. Honest and sensitive, Clough gave too much of his fine energies to religious questionings, and disappointed his friends' expectations. He is now known chiefly by his short agonizing poem, "Say not the struggle nought availeth," and by Arnold's fine commemoration of him in the elegy *Thyrsis*.

Arnold's nature, somewhat like George Eliot's, was twofold and divided. He began life with a strong, natural, instinctive delight in natural things.

> In my helpless cradle I
> Was breathed on by the rural Pan.[1]

This was in the region of Laleham, his birthplace, amid the mild and lovely Thames landscape such as called forth his sweetest and most spontaneous song. A deep capacity and hunger for enjoyment of his senses, for beauty, for fun and banter and social intercourse, for the full but decent exercise of his affectionate nature, for the natural and full expression of his exuberant self, for romance and mystery—this was one side of the man. Over against it the other partakes of conscious restraint, renunciation, academic regulation of **taste** "moral

[1] *Lines written in Kensington Gardens*

earnestness," unrelenting self-torture with religious doubt, insistence upon the basic value of conduct. No wonder a genius so divided and torn would be ever straining for unity, to "see life steadily and see it whole." No wonder he should have been the disciple of Goethe and Wordsworth. No wonder most of his poetry, certainly all the best, is elegiac in kind.

At some time in his early twenties Arnold was involved in an obscure romance with an unidentified French girl, probably at the Swiss town of Thun. She it was who inspired the so-called Marguerite poems, those grouped later as *Switzerland* and *Faded Leaves*, and such others as *A Memory Picture* and *A Dream*. They pulse with no imaginary passion. But some incompatibility, some restraint, is in sharp and bitter conflict with the poet's intense emotion, and this conflict reflects precisely the aforesaid division of the poet's soul.

In some form this duality, this balance, asserts itself in most of his poems, certainly in the best. World-weary old Empedocles confronts the happy young singer Callicles; in the *Strayed Reveller* Ulysses encounters the youth who already knows the ecstasy and agony of the poet's life. Similar division underlies the fervor and the disillusionment of *The New Sirens*; the humdrum village life over against the romantic mysteries of the sea-depths in the *Forsaken Merman*; the two ages in *Bacchanalia*; the contrast between Iseult of Ireland and Iseult of Brittany; the revulsion from beauty in *Dover Beach*; the blind uncertainty and the hidden self in *The Buried Life*; the desperate question of *A Summer Night*—"Madman or slave, must man be one?" It prompts the wistful farewell to the author of Obermann, who has chosen the rejuvenating influences of life amid Nature:

> Away the dreams that but deceive!
> And thou, sad guide, adieu!
> I go, fate drives me; but I leave
> Half of my life with you.

Such also his leave-taking of his early implicit faith, in *The Grande Chartreuse*. But nowhere are the two instincts held in more beautiful equilibrium than in *The Scholar-Gipsy*.

Deep-dyed in academic purple—Winchester, Rugby, Balliol, and a fellowship in Oriel—Arnold served Lord Lansdowne four years as private secretary, thereby enjoying free range on the upper levels of the world of London, then entered his thirty-five years of servitude as inspector of schools.

Patiently he plodded his often weary way about the island from school to school, interviewing teachers, catechizing youngsters, and dutifully squandering his powers in reading exercises and tests, often two or three hours at a time. His personal inspiration of teachers, his masterly reports, his study of continental education to discover what benefits it could add to that of England, the improvement of English common schools under his advice, are proof enough that this poet's soul like Milton's "the lowliest duties on herself did lay." Everywhere went with him not the shadow of his brooding heart and mind, but that genial affectionate way which so endeared him to his friends and family, like "an affable arch-angel," as an eye-witness observes. "Well, my little man, and how do you spell dog?" "Please sir, d-o-g." "Capital, very good indeed, I couldn't do it better myself. And cat?" "C-a-t." "Now this is really excellent." His marriage at twenty-eight began many years of domestic happiness, darkened at length by the loss of three sons, two of them near manhood.

From thirty-five to forty-five he held the Professorship of Poetry at Oxford, which required the periodic delivery of lectures. These were the occasion of his observations *On Trans-lating Homer*, which have opened to an unnumbered multitude the transcendent glories of the greatest epic poet. The ancient poets, especially Homer and Virgil, were ever his idols. Yet his enthusiasm for the classics as for all else was somehow embarrassed and dampened by his academic sophistication, his Oxfordism. Arnold never wholly escaped from the academic life. He was always an Oxford man. There were for him two Oxfords, as it were, one for each half of himself—the "beauti-ful city of dreaming spires," and the Oxford of sophisticated scholarship. In *The Scholar-Gipsy* he looks wistfully after one who had escaped the academic palsy, to win partnership in the simple faiths and the spontaneous and natural impulses of life. This, alas, he cannot share. It is too late. His country folk are but a part of his rural setting, as in Gray's *Elegy*, not the lusty human intimates of Goldsmith. But this wistful academic weariness with which he follows the fading figure of the gipsy, like the bright but waning other half of himself, lends its rare quality to the poem, clothing all the Oxford country-side with the unworldly elegiac light and music that only high poetry can impart. The same quality, arising from essentially the same source, pervades *Thyrsis*, sequel of *The Scholar-Gipsy*, and indeed often throughout his poetry awakens "the tremulous cadence slow," and brings "the eternal note of sadness in." His melancholy is never sentimental, but classic, genuine, out of the depths, like that of his master Virgil.

Arnold's "classicism" is more obvious but less real in his imitations—the Greek drama, *Merope,* dead from birth, the livelier Greek idylls of Callicles in *Empedocles on Etna*, the Homeric little epics, *Sohrab and Rustum* made of oriental stuff, and *Balder Dead* from the newly reviving Teutonic mythology. Into *Sohrab* Arnold has breathed much energy of narrative; but otherwise this and the other imitations are what the trade calls simulated antiques. Their Homeric simplicity is chiefly the effect of sticking to simple declarative sentences. The much commended epic similes are beautifully wrought, but are glittering jewels gratuitously inset for show, more after the manner of decadent late Latin poets than of Homer and Virgil and Milton.

In the Preface to the *Poems* of 1853 he wrote that "amid the bewildering confusion of our times . . . I seemed to myself to find the only sure guidance, the only solid footing, among the ancients." His artistic economy; his avoidance of cheap, sentimental, violent effects; a rare, fine cadence from time to time; the nobler human values which in spite of his despairs underlie his best work—these are the more genuine proof that the classics were in the very fibre of the man.

Arnold's first volume of verse appeared in 1849. Others followed in 1852, 1853, 1855, 1867; and then the music ceased. Only once more, in 1881, did it reawake with its old power in the opening and close of *Westminster Abbey* at the burial of

Dean Stanley. His poetry was never popular—elegiac poetry without sentimentality seldom is. But its dignity, its music, and its tragic contrasts bring it daily into higher appreciation.

Arnold's change from verse to prose is a mystery which each may deplore or explain in his own way. Perhaps the more sombre and renunciatory part of him at last overbalanced the other and marred the music. At any rate he became more oppressed with the weight of the vast middle class all about him, now in the sixties grown self-satisfied, stubborn, even insolent with their success, and as impervious to a new idea as the old aristocrats.

To remedy their case he was to attempt with literature what Ruskin had attempted with art. But they were now too hardened to be bombarded with the heavy artillery of Carlyle and Ruskin. He therefore employed a more insinuating method of satiric irony, the deadlier for being even-toned and good-natured. He arraigned them as Philistines, held their provincialism up to ridicule, and proposed as the cure the freer circulation of ideas through literature—civilizing ideas of the Greeks, of France and Germany, ideas unknown to middle-class England. He saw too that the old criticism of literature, the spare-or-damn ways of the old reviews, were outworn. The business of criticism, he says, is "simply to know the best that is known and thought in the world, and by making this known, to create a current of true and fresh ideas." Picking up a Philistine incident or cant phrase, such as "doing as one likes," "saying what one likes," "the Dissidence of Dissent," he plays with it till its crude fallacies all stand pitifully naked before the world. Meanwhile his own saving doctrine quietly insinuates itself by a reechoing phrase—"culture, the study of perfection," "the best that is known and thought in the world," "to make reason and the will of God prevail," "sweetness and light," borrowed from Swift's *Battle of the Books*.[1]

Thus he stung and enraged his opponents. They regarded him as an intellectual snob, and called him an elegant and spurious Jeremiah, "that very one of the Hebrew prophets whose style I admire the least." More than ever he exposed

[1] See page 296

their Philistine faith in coal, iron, machinery, numbers, and wealth to the fresh air of sweet reasonableness and enlightenment. Of such enlightenment, he held, poetry is the grand agent, especially the best poetry, since poetry is "the criticism of life," that is, it interprets life for us, sustains and consoles us. To this end the best poetry is that which deals authoritatively with the basic passions and great human actions arising from them, notably the poetry of the Greeks.

He wrote much, but his central ideas are to be found in his Preface to the Poems of 1853; his "Function of Criticism" (1864); his "Culture and Anarchy" (1869); his "Study of Poetry" (1880); and in his favorite *Discourses in America* (1883-4). These last essays beautifully present not only the essence of Arnold's critique of his times, but Arnold himself. Pendant to all these are many essays on single literary figures, English and foreign, and on Celtic literature, pointing out the "Celtic magic" and "Celtic melancholy" in English Literature, and giving strong impulse to new interest in Celtic characteristics. All these essays well served their generation, opening new vistas and stirring new ideas. For in his prose Arnold was really a charming and expert teacher, with many of the devices and even mannerisms of the profession. His thousands of disciples, finding their way to "culture" by his guidance, formed in their adoration a cult of which even yet there are traces.

Some who heard him lecture say that his delivery was dreadful. But his style, of which perhaps too much has been made— possibly because he made so much of "style" himself—is an oral style, a virtue all too rare in these latter days when the press has superseded the voice. Yet its mannerisms confine it to a plane far below Newman's style, whose Greek purity and urbanity Arnold so much admired.

The ultimate basis of Arnold's poetry and criticism is action and conduct. Literature, he maintains, springs from action, and is worthless if it does not in turn produce moral action. In this he is in tune with Sidney. But in Arnold this moral basis is more dark and austere than in Sidney; it is grounded on

Roman stoicism, the only firm footing Arnold had left, a clouded isthmus on which he wandered

> between two worlds, one dead,
> The other powerless to be born.

In his later life he engaged much in amateur Biblical criticism and theology, and pointed out to his humbler contemporaries an insecure foothold on the isthmus.

But the delicate though unstable equilibrium which was the glory of his poetry was gone; and the free natural relish for living and for the beauty of the world, in which he was closer to the Greeks than in his renunciations, has left only here and there in his later work a faint trace of itself.

CHAPTER 35

The Pre-Raphaelites

"THE elements with which the creative power works are ideas; the best ideas on every matter which literature touches, current at the time."

Such is Arnold's text for his essay on "The Function of Criticism," and in fact for most that he had to say. By current ideas he seems to mean ideas agreed upon and passionately supported by most of the thinking men of their day. He laments the passing and the dearth of such ideas in his own Victorian time.

What sort of current ideas? From time to time men have reached certain grand conclusions about their relation to the things invisible, "the eternal verities." They have formulated their view of this finite life in terms of the infinite. Such grand conclusions were the well-defined Christian ideas and convictions which sustained, supported, and vitalized the art and literature of the Middle Ages. It is not necessary that the individual artist or poet should be a fierce champion of these ideas; Chaucer was not; Dante was. But these ideas were equally requisite to each as a substantial basis and medium for his work, and a source of its essential beauty.

As medieval Christianity was necessary to the poetry of Chaucer, so was the mingling of the Christian mysticism with Plato's doctrine of love to the poetry of Spenser; the convictions of reforming Protestantism and the revival of Roman Stoicism to the poetry of Milton; the convictions that propelled the French Revolution to the romantic poets.

Each creed produces as its offspring a moral and social code, as medieval Christianity produced the code of chivalry; and when the creed grows old and dies, the code survives for a time until, like a flower cut from the plant, it also wilts and dies.

Victorian England inherited remnants of various ideas current in other times—medieval Christianity, Protestant Christianity, French Revolutionary ideas of the rights of man, even old aristocratic ideas from feudal times. But men were divided in their allegiance to these ideas, and the grasp with which they clung to them weakened from decade to decade. When the creed gave way, there remained at least for a time the support of its moral enthusiasms and views. Such among many was the case with George Eliot, whose Christian moral enthusiasms, though shorn of her early belief, survived and fashioned her novels. But even the moral and social code soon declined, and men enter upon an age like the present of general denial, of general disagreement, of "individualism," of bankruptcy in the "current ideas" necessary to greatest literature.

> All experience is an arch wherethro'
> Gleams that untravell'd world whose margin fades
> For ever and for ever when I move.[1]

So Tennyson puts the matter in his time. That fading untravelled world will soon disappear altogether and leave only the experience. Indeed, just a generation later, in 1873, Walter Pater speaks as the prophet of his hour, saying: "Not the fruit of experience, but experience itself, is the end." Such is his mature conclusion at the close of his book, *The Renaissance*.

We have left, then, as elements to work on, our experience here—events, sensations, beauty all around us, knowledge of science, history, literature, the rich and vast accumulation from the past of poetry, legend, architecture, painting, even the cloud-ruins of the picturesque old beliefs themselves. Human experience by itself and without convictions is infinite and sufficient material for poetry; and above all is the joy itself of

[1] *Ulysses*

making beautiful things like poetry—the very process for its own sake.

A straight line drawn through the quoted passage in Tennyson's *Ulysses*, through Arnold's *Dover Beach*, and Rossetti's *Sea-Limits* (which, though the earlier poem, is later in kind) will point the direction of most that is to happen in literature through late Victorian times even to the present. It marks the course through Pre-Raphaelite æstheticism, Swinburne's art for art's sake, the new paganism, the decadence of the nineties, the spirit of denial which revolts from all tradition, the restless, dissatisfied tossing from ism to ism in search of reality—symbolism, impressionism, futurism, imagism—all preoccupied with method, effect, technique rather than with grand ideas. As we look back, the direction which literature was taking appears even in the early forties: the Pre-Raphaelite Brotherhood had its obscure birth in 1848.

In its narrower sense the term Pre-Raphaelite applies to the little group of young painters including Holman Hunt, Millais, and Dante Gabriel Rossetti, who banded together to protest against the outworn ways of British art, and to dedicate themselves to new methods and ideals. English art had been great in portraiture under Reynolds and Gainsborough, and in landscape under Constable and Turner, but their days were done. These young men made a new appeal from rules to Nature herself. It may then seem strange that they should have turned to those "unnatural" primitives, the artists before Raphael, for suggestion. But there they found the fresh radiance, the integrity, the clear, bright color, the careful but not plodding finish of detail, which combined with their own youthful enthusiasm and romance, to create a new order of beauty in English painting. Human life, rather than landscape, but human life in romance, became the new matter of Pre-Raphaelite painting. The ideas of the Brotherhood fed upon literature as well as upon painting, especially upon Keats, who, in his *Eve of Saint Agnes*, was a Pre-Raphaelite before them all without knowing it, and, as Browning says, "fished the murex up" for Hobbs, Nobbs, Stokes, and Nokes to daub with. Tennyson, besides much else, was Pre-Raphaelite notably in the *Lady of Shalott.* The Brotherhood found a supporting, but not always intelligent champion in John Ruskin.

After eight years, in 1856, it gradually dissolved, but its ideals, especially incarnate in Rossetti, were now inspiring others—William Morris, and Burne-Jones, and Swinburne. "Pre-Raphaelite" became a larger term to designate in general the new painting and the new poetry which abandoned the old creeds except to treat them as lovely romantic ruins, and to find its enthusiasms in immediate experience.

ROSSETTI (1828-1882)

Dante Gabriel Rossetti, born in 1828, had three Italian grandparents. His mother's mother was English. He himself never saw Italy. His father, charming and eccentric, landed in England a political refugee after he was forty, and married. Many and wild had been his adventures, but none so signal as his fathering in four successive years of four extraordinary young Rossettis. Of these Dante was the second, Christina the youngest.

Dante proved an eager, tempestuous, winning, persuasive, tough-bitted young man, with all the generosity and selfishness of genius. He did not take to schooling, nor to any external discipline in his art or otherwise, except such as he himself imposed. In 1850 appeared—and disappeared—the Brotherhood's short-lived, but momentous organ, *The Germ.* It contained, with the rest, work of Coventry Patmore, the eventual author of *The Angel in the House,* the flawless *Dream Land* by Christina still in her teens, and Rossetti's *My Sister's Sleep* and *Blessed Damozel.* Such was the beginning.

Rossetti painted in his verse and sang in his pictures. The materials for both were the same: medieval lore both secular and religious, as in *Blessed Damozel* or *Sister Helen* (a combination of Celtic magic with the second idyll of Theocritus); old ballads, as *Stratton Water* and *The King's Tragedy*; a bit of Nature humanized; a picture already painted or planned; something close at hand like a statue at the Museum in *The Burden of Nineveh,* or *The Card Dealer*:

> Her fingers let them softly through,
>   Smooth polished silent things;
> And each one as it falls reflects
>   In swift light-shadowings,
> Blood-red and purple, green and blue,
>   The great eyes of her rings.

Above all themes for Rossetti was the matter of love. His imagination had been enlivened by translating Dante's *New Life*, and by readings in the poets of courtly love who preceded Dante. A dozen years later he published his English version of them in *Dante and his Circle*. His mind's eye had conceived the ideal image of a woman, and then suddenly she appeared in the flesh. She was a milliner's assistant, Elizabeth Siddal, and the discovery dragged her from drab obscurity into tragic fame. Tall, slender, fragile, with a wealth of copper-red hair, and clear blue-green eyes, she proved the incarnation of Pre-Raphaelite dreams, to be perpetuated in many of their pictures.

> Above the enthroning throat
> The mouth's mould testifies of voice and kiss,
> The shadowed eyes remember and foresee.
> Her face is made her shrine.[1]

Rossetti loved her and roused into practice her rather exceptional talents for painting and verse. For ten years their marriage was postponed, he always devoted, but not always loyal, she more and more sick of heart and weak in body. At last, after two brief years as his wife, she died, and he sank to the very nadir of despair. Everyone has heard how he buried his poems with her, and how after more than seven years they were by his consent exhumed and published.

In 1881, the year before his death, appeared *Ballads and Sonnets*, containing especially *The King's Tragedy* and the complete *House of Life*, a sequence, or rather collection, of sonnets most of them inspired by his love for his wife and written at different times between the age of nineteen and his

---

[1] *House of Life,* 10

death. They variously exhibit romantic imitations of the antique, of Italian and Elizabethan sonneteers, or the brilliant
color and drawing of the painter, or a strong infusion of Rossetti's intense if sometimes roily emotion. At their best they
are a marvellous blend of these elements with the sweet and
lively music peculiar to this poet.

Rossetti, at least in his early years, seems to have regarded
his painting as far more important than his poetry, and many
of his poems, such as *The Portrait* and *Sonnets for Pictures* are
really pendants for pictures, like certain old poems in the *Greek
Anthology*. Even in his more dramatic work, such as *The
King's Tragedy*, the drama is indicated by a series of tableaux
more than by action. As he worked endlessly on his pictures,
so his poems were subject to constant revision of detail. *The
Blessed Damozel,* his earliest and best poem, exists in four
versions.

As in his painting he looked to the primitives, so the very
texture of his verse, especially the earlier verse, gains both vigor
and beauty without affectation from his skilful use of archaic
words and forms. He is the progenitor of the legion of poets
and versifiers who are primarily "artists" in their work, manipu-
lating both their matter and their medium with an artist's care,
rather than being upborne on the current of great ideas.

After his wife's death Rossetti aged prematurely. The bright
qualities of his youth turned into defects. He alienated old
friends, and died at fifty-four spent in mind and body.

CHRISTINA ROSSETTI (1830-1894)

Christina Rossetti, though by circumstance inseparable from
the Pre-Raphaelites, is not to be taken for one herself. From
her dun domestic seclusion with her mother and aged father,
her teaching, her constant attendance upon Anglo-Catholic
services, her church work, her petty painting of posies on note-
paper for the trade, she looked out with some amusement on
the Brotherhood and its enthusiasms. Yet twice she met a man
out of that group who loved her, and whom she loved. Both
of them she renounced apparently because they were not of
her Anglo-Catholic faith. Her thwarted love, deep and intense,

found relief in song. Those poems called *Twice, Echo, Shut out,* and the one beginning, "When I am dead, my dearest," by their very simplicity, restraint, and symmetrical form, imply only the more the storm of fire at the centre of her being, and the strength with which she kept it in control.

Death also is a favorite theme, nor does she dwell upon it morbidly as some have thought, but with eye and voice both clear and steady, as in *Up-Hill.* And the more so perhaps because her genius can also laugh and play and delight itself like a child with gorgeous color and sound. So it does in *Goblin Market,* and for the diversion of children in the little book of verse called *Sing Song.* The gentle little girl never wholly died out of this woman with a character of refined steel.

Her passionate intensity, as often in mystics, is perhaps but deflected from earth to heaven, for it permeates also her religious verse, mingling nobly with Scriptural phrase, and never deliquescent in gush or mawkishness or morbid attenuation, or in the mere aestheticism which sometimes takes itself for religion. At times the fervor and pressure of her feeling remind one of Emily Brontë, but her flame burns more steady and clear, unswayed by the gust of passion. Some acclaim her as the greatest of English poetesses. Whether or no, in all English poetry it is hard to find so nearly perfect a fusion of feeling and image and language and music as in most of her poems. Whatever her sufferings, her mind seems to have been wholly at one with itself, never quavering or stammering or incoherent.

1859

Every point is in some way a turning-point, but the years 1858-60 are especially useful in getting our bearings. Leigh Hunt, De Quincey, and Macaulay all died in 1859. Landor had yet five years to live. Carlyle, whose opinion everyone awaited with trembling, was wrapping himself ever deeper in his "atrabiliar reflections." In 1859 Thackeray concluded the succession of his great novels with *The Virginians,* and he and Dickens were at the height of their fame. George Eliot was just entering upon hers with her *Adam Bede,* and Trollope upon his with *Doctor Thorne.* In 1859 appeared that momentous work of Darwin's, *The Origin of Species,* and alongside it *The Ordeal of Richard Feverel,* by the yet obscure Meredith. The Pre-Raphaelites had been going for over a decade, much scorned by their elders, Carlyle, Dickens, and Browning. But these elders well knew that something had happened, even if they could not tell what. In 1858 appeared *The Defence of Guenevere and Other Poems* by William Morris. Thus one age interpenetrates another.

MORRIS (1834-1896)

Said Browning of Rossetti: "You know I hate the effeminacy of his school—the men that dress up like women—that use obsolete forms too, and archaic accentuations to seem soft—fancy a man calling it a lily." He surely had not in mind one member of the school as virile as himself—William Morris.

In his prime at thirty-six Morris made a superb figure, burly and powerful, lacking perhaps a few inches of heroic height, but with a heroic head, of fine-cut features, eyes of smoldering fire, and full, broad forehead amid a tumble of dark hair and beard that brought to mind young heroes of whom he sang. His giant energy was always doing and making. From babyhood his stubby fingers twitched to be busy, or were doubled tight in habitual earnest gesture. His stormy outbursts blazed less at persons than at the wrongs of the world. In his friendships he was constant and devoted. He was of Welsh blood.

His father was a prosperous discount broker. The boy at four was deep in Scott's novels, and was soon ranging through near-by Epping Forest and among old churches and villages and favorite bits of countryside, as his love of the Middle Ages and of beauty fashioned by medieval hands grew in him apace.

At Oxford he met young Burne-Jones, the great painter to be. Both had come up to prepare for holy orders; but their chief preoccupation became poetry, Tennyson and Browning, and the thrilling ideas and music of Ruskin's prose. Morris left Oxford headed for architecture. In London he and Burne-Jones met Rossetti, four years older, who thought everybody should paint except the few who were to buy the pictures. With his irresistible persuasion he soon had the two young men at the easel. Only one painting by Morris survives.

At twenty-four he published that extraordinary book of verse, *The Defence of Guenevere,* and the next year married the beautiful Jane Burden of Oxford, who for many months had been another of the famous sitters for Pre-Raphaelite pictures of women.

Morris now built himself Red House down in his beloved Kent, close to the old pilgrim track to Canterbury. The event was momentous, for it revived the use of red brick, and made Morris a designer and maker of furniture, glass, tiles, ironwork, and various interior fittings. Only with his own hand could he deliver himself from the domestic ugliness which suffocated the human spirit on every hand. But this enforced effort led to great and unforeseen things, namely, the founding of his firm, which wrought out these new designs and began the revolution in Victorian taste which has lighted up and beautified all our domestic life.

Next his tireless hand and mind turned to the illuminating of manuscripts; then in time to the designing, dyeing, and printing of textiles; and last, in his later years, to the art of printing books. With incredible energy and skill he studied and adapted old designs and methods, revived lost processes, and left nothing untried that led to the recovery of the lost beauty, quality, and joy in the making which reflect themselves in the finished object. In all this he was the disciple of Ruskin, but with the added authority of a practical workman; not an amateur, but one whose genius quickly gave him the knowledge of many arts, any one of which other men labor years to master. All the time he was the poet.

He lived in two worlds, the actual, hideous, sordid world of a triumphant rich middle-class, tempered, however, by his happy domestic life and his friends, and the world of his imagination. That world of the imagination he began, like Blake, to rebuild in England's green and pleasant land. It was of Chaucer's time in semblance—set in rolling Kentish country, a world of small, clean towns; of stout, comfortable houses, some old, some new, but all well carved and hewn; of gardens and orchards; of fair white Gothic churches gloriously adorned; of sturdy, dark, honest genial men and strong comely women, clothed in fabrics of their own making, with fitting ornament of broidery and gem, living in fellowship made blessed by their free spirit, by song and legend, and by happy labor of hand and mind.

But to Morris these two worlds were not alien worlds. All his magnificent energies he spent in a gallant effort to redeem the sordid world by realizing the other here. All his manifold activities were united in the yearning of his great heart over the miseries to which men had brought themselves by greed and false values. In this way he seized upon what seemed to him the only concerted movement in sight, and at forty-four became an active socialist. His vision, however, transcended that of his associates, and during his last years he withdrew from participation in their efforts. He died, at sixty-two, as was said, of being the ten men that William Morris was, and was buried at Kelmscott on the upper Thames, where, for twenty-five years, in the lovely old manor which his hand had so much beautified, his restless soul had found its deepest contentment and peace.

One of the ten men was the poet, perhaps the one who will be longest remembered. If the work of his pen had been all, it would still be enormous; for besides his poetry is a large accumulation of lectures, prose romances, treatises on the relation of art to life, and on socialism, and fanciful tales like the *Dream of John Ball*, embodying his hopes for the regeneration of the world.

His glimpses of a new world set forth in simple antique English, reminding one now of Chaucer, now of Malory, now of Bunyan, but always Morris's own, make his *News from Nowhere* convincing by its very charm; and his hopes for the art and happiness of England expressed in his lectures are the more contagious because, unlike his master Ruskin, he never scolds.

His poetry was indeed the spontaneous overflow of powerful feeling. He poured it forth almost as the by-product of his other work in a stream so prolific that one might suspect its quality. But the uniform high excellence which it almost invariably maintains is amazing. The great heights it seldom if ever reaches, or those moments of intense concentration of poetic power by virtue of which certain brief passages or poems ancient or modern become "classic" and perennial. But everywhere it is lovely, like his designs, with a beguiling loveliness that is needful for dispelling the dreariness and shadows of daily living. Milton and Dante, like cathedrals, no doubt, have their indispensable exalted uses; but one needs a more intimate beauty with which to live.

Morris's first verse, *The Defence of Guenevere and Other Poems,* shows naturally the virtues and defects of his youth— dramatic energy and fiery passion and snatches of tune, not always clear or coherent. The title poem and *King Arthur's Tomb* are surprisingly rare instances of this medieval romanticist's adventures in Arthurian story; and he treats them not like others as far-off romance, but perhaps under Browning's impulse, as immediate and intense dramatic episodes. The same dramatic gift asserts itself in *Sir Peter Harpden's End,* with such flair for interplay of action and character, and such promise of success as a practical dramatist, as Browning never gave. From time to time flashes his lively delight in properties and costume and setting, in design and workmanship, in pure colors of the illuminators and of Chaucer—red, blue, green, gold, black, white—which made him at once more than craftsman and more than poet.

Nine busy years elapsed before his next flowering in *The Life and Death of Jason* (1867) and *The Earthly Paradise* (1867-70). The *Jason,* first intended as one of the tales for the cycle of the *Earthly Paradise,* outgrew those limits to a length greater than that of the *Aeneid.* In Chaucerian rhymed couplets like the *Prologue* and *The Knight's Tale,* it is episodic rather than epic. In the seventeenth and last book Morris rises to his dramatic best and shows far more psychological subtlety than some critics allow him.

The *Earthly Paradise* is a cycle, like the *Decameron* and the *Canterbury Tales,* consisting of twenty-four tales, two for each month of a year. Wanderers from the Northland have spent their lives seeking the Earthly Paradise and a way of escape from death; they land at last in a Greek city where for a year they exchange tales with old men of the town. These tales are cast into the Chaucerian four-stress and five-stress couplet and the seven-line stanza of *Troilus and Criseyde*. Chaucer was Morris's master, beautifully thrice-confessed—in the opening of the last book of *Jason*, in the Envoi of *The Earthly Paradise*, and in his last work, the superb edition of Chaucer designed and printed by Morris himself at the Kelmscott Press. Though one hears and sees Chaucer in almost every line and phrase, the imitation seems like the natural idiom of Morris, in which his own fire and play and subtle charm find expression, revealing a deep kinship between the two poets.

Like Chaucer Morris drew many of his tales from Ovid; others he found in late classical writers, the *Gesta Romanorum*, medieval romance, and Mandeville's *Travels*.

But he had also opened the rich new vein of the Norse sagas. In 1869 he had begun to study Icelandic and the sagas; later he visited Iceland more than once; and a more primitive spirit then entered into his work. Besides much editing and translating he produced in 1876 the epic poem in nearly 10,000 lines, called *Sigurd the Volsung*. It is the old tale of Sigmund, Sigurd, Brynhild, and Gudrun, and in Morris's powerful handling we have what some call "the most Homeric poem since Homer." At any rate he swings with marvellous ease and vigor the six-stress anapest couplet newly come into general use. His language no longer shows much of the pleasant archaism of his earlier work, but still keeps its simplicity of sentence and its preference for Germanic rather than Latin words. As he instinctively recognized his own qualities in Chaucer's fashioning skill and gentleness and keen insight, in Chaucer's love of love and hatred of death, so in the Norse heroes he found his counterpart in their primitive vigor, their love of fighting to overcome some fear or misery that haunts the minds of men, their vague hope of a new world to supplant this failure in which we live.

As if such yield were not enough, this restless, unsparing man filled odd hours with translations of the *Aeneid*, the *Odyssey*, and the *Beowulf*, excellent versions of course. A mere catalogue of his deeds and his writings would look incredible; it would suggest a man of inexhaustible talents, in fact of too many for the success of any single purpose. Yet here is one, by no means the "idle singer" that he called himself, albeit living in "an empty day" which was losing its old faith with none to replace it, which was sunk in greed and injustice and outward ugliness; and he, William Morris, set to work with all his talents to point the way forward to regeneration through happy fellowship and fair conditions of living and contented pride in one's work.

> For all these shall be ours and all men's
> nor shall any lack a share
> Of the toil and the gain of living
> in the days when the world grows fair.[1]

SWINBURNE (1837-1909)

Late in 1857, while Morris, Burne-Jones, and Rossetti were engaged at Oxford on their short-lived frescoes of the debating-hall, they became acquainted with an undergraduate at Balliol, small and slight of stature, with an aureole of gold-red hair and a green-blue Pre-Raphaelite eye. His name was Algernon Charles Swinburne. Though born in London, he came of an ancient aristocratic family of the northern border which had bled and suffered for old unhappy causes, and had transmitted to him a love of old ballads and a passionate devotion to the story of Mary Stuart. As a youngster at his father's house in the Isle of Wight, or at his grandfather's near Newcastle, he swam and played in the rough salt water till the sea became an intimate part of him. During an Oxford vacation he climbed the almost unscalable Culver Cliff with what was doubtless to him a delicious sense of danger. All his life exquisite pleasure and pain were strangely, even morbidly, identical to him, as his poetry shows often enough. From Eton school-days he fondly cherished two particular memories—the swimming-place and the flogging block.

Though somewhat of a prankish rebel and an odd one at

---

[1] *The Day is Coming*

both Oxford and Eton, he absorbed learning with the instinct of a genius—French, Italian, Greek, besides much reading in the English romantics and Elizabethan playwrights. From childhood the language of the Bible had grown to be almost as familiar as daily speech. From all these his poetry drew much of its richest nourishment. Among the ancients Sappho, though far more concentrated than he, was his nearest of kin. His *Sapphics*, a glorious *tour de force* in metre, whose spirit loses nothing by the imitation or strictness of his form, his *Anactoria*, and his later *On the Cliffs*, all burn with the fire he caught from the flaming fragments of the Greek poetess. In French literature, which he knew as well as English, Victor Hugo, and later Baudelaire, were his especial masters. The death of Baudelaire in 1867 inspired one of his noblest poems, *Ave atque Vale,* noble in music, passion, and melancholy to a point that ranges it with *Lycidas* and *Adonais,* and marks the summit of Swinburne's achievement.

In English Literature Landor was one of Swinburne's early idols, chiefly for his spirit of liberty and his Hellenism. Blake and Shelley, and at one time Walt Whitman and Emerson, took part in shaping his poetic mind. Like Cowper he was always susceptible to the influence of men about him who were physically his betters, but in intellect far below him.

At twenty-four he left Oxford without a degree, and the next eighteen years were his poetic prime. At forty-two, deaf and in frail health, he retired for the rest of his life to Putney under the wise and devoted care of his friend Watts-Dunton, and thus survived for thirty years more. He still wrote verse, but little that added to his early achievement; and he still poured out his excellent critical essays—on Shakespeare, Hugo, and Ben Jonson—but none to excel his essay on Blake in 1868. In this study he imported from Baudelaire and Gautier the new doctrine of "Art for Art's sake."

Swinburne's genius was not like Milton's, one that rose slowly to full power through long years of discipline; it was at its height from the beginning of his *Atalanta in Calydon* at twenty-six. This astonishing imitation of Greek tragedy de-

mands comparison with the *Samson* of Milton's maturest
years. His intimacy with Greek was such as enabled him to
compose the Greek elegiacs to Landor which precede the tragedy. In the choruses he has far more of the lyric quality and
flexible vigor of Greek choruses than Milton, especially in the
one beginning "For against all men from of old." Those who
deny Swinburne descriptive and narrative power overlook the
boar hunt in *Atalanta*, which should be set beside the boar
hunt in *Gawain and the Green Knight*. But the poet's notion
of Fate, far from being Greek, is that of a young man smarting under physical handicap and suffering his first recoil from
impact against a granite world.

   Poems and Ballads, 1866, set young England reeling with
the intoxication of its new rhythms, and staid old respectable
England aghast at its eroticism, its paganism, and its defiance
of the evangelical notion of God. Such poems as *Laus Veneris*,
Dolores, Hymn to Proserpine, Anactoria, mild enough now,
were smuggled by the young into many a household. They
represent, however, a riot of mind rather than experience,
though one of the best, *The Triumph of Time*, springs from an
experience nearest to an affair of the heart that Swinburne
seems ever to have known.

   Amid his preoccupations with love and similar Pre-Raphaelite themes was rising in Swinburne's soul the new all-engrossing
theme of liberty. The spell of Italy, at all times so powerful
in shaping English poetry, was again asserting itself through
a passionate English interest in Italy's struggle for freedom,
called the *risorgimento*. It had deeply stirred Mrs. Browning,
and now seized Swinburne, chiefly in the form of hero-worship
for Mazzini, who was of just the fiery, masterful sort to captivate him. To Mazzini he dedicates his *Songs before Sunrise*
(1871), containing his highest flights of song in such poems
as *Siena* and *The Song of the Standard*. They embody less of
actual political thought than even the poetry of Shelley, but
their music in exaltation of human liberty is glorious. The
Hymn of Man, Genesis, Hertha, and *Mater Triumphalis* are
more substantial, albeit they owe their substance to the rather

sterile Emersonian doctrine of the supreme and eternal Man-spirit.

It remains to mention, out of the abundance of Swinburne's muse, his long closet trilogy, *Chastelard, Bothwell,* and *Mary Stuart,* on which he labored many years in celebration of his favorite heroine; and his incomplete episodic treatment of the Tristram story, which surpasses in power the versions of both Arnold and Tennyson. The Prelude opens with a Lucretian praise of love which is Swinburne at his best.

Everyone observes that Swinburne's poetry is made more of music than ideas. But music is a poet's first business, and no other English poet, except perhaps Spenser, had the gift of spontaneous music in so rich a measure. It is not the lyric gift of the Elizabethans or Burns, whose words by their music suggest a tune which can be detached and separately written down. Swinburne's music is just as lyric, but is as inseparable from the words as mind from body, and carries them along with irresistible momentum.

His natural tune is anapestic, so much so that his iambic measures are always breaking into anapests. This measure he builds into all forms of line and stanza.

Along with it goes his congenital habit of duplex expression. His texture is two-ply. Everything breaks into pairs, doublets, echoes, inversions, paradox—alliterating, combining, dissolving ceaselessly like reflections in running water. Sometimes the duplication descends to a mere mannerism:

> Child yet no child of the night, and motherless mother of men.

Doubtless this double texture of his mind and language, together with his love of monosyllables, made natural his ha-bitual echo of the language and parallelisms of the Old Testa-ment. These peculiarities were easily caught and carried on by poets for a generation afterwards, notably in the work of Mr. Kipling and Mr. Noyes. But the real secret of Swinburne's music was after all his own.

In 1879, at the end of his high poetic career, Swinburne com-posed two autobiographical poems, *On the Cliffs* and *Thalas-sius.* The first confesses that the Greek Sappho is his sister, whose ruling song, like the nightingale's, down the ages has thrilled

> And breathless hearts with one bright sound fulfilled.
> The deep dark air and subtle tender sea

In *Thalassius* ("merman" as it were) from his mother the sea, he feels

> deep sea-pulses dealt
> Through nerve and jubilant vein.

This kinship with the sea underlies all his passions and enthusiasms. Throughout his poetry the sea is ever close at hand as symbol or image, and is often a dominant theme. Like the tides he is diffuse in his ebb and flow. In grand musical transcriptions of Nature such as *On the Broads* and *Hesperia* one hears and feels the rise and fall of the ground swell in his masterly imitation of Latin elegiacs. His constant duplexity of expression makes a rhythm of restless waves. Even the stream of his verse and the form of his images are fluid, and run through the mind like water through the fingers.

He has a tendency to fade into dim allegory and the abstract. With him it is always "flower" in general, not often a particular flower, and he abounds in half abstract words, like life, love, Man, light, grief, shame. The total effect is the effect of the sea, unfixed, rhythmic, surging, intoxicating, hypnotising.

By many Swinburne is regarded as the last of the six great Victorian poets. But in his denial of the old faith and theory of life, in his confinement of scope to present experience, and to art for art's sake only, in his proclaiming of a new "paganism," he was the conspicuous harbinger of what was to come.

CHAPTER 36

Late Victorians

MEREDITH (1828-1909)

LATE in 1861 for a brief time a mysterious young writer in his early thirties took lodgings with Swinburne and with Rossetti, who was just his own age, in Chelsea, that region of London sanctified by literary associations since the day of Sir Thomas More. He was sandy-haired, and sinewy, humorous, brilliant in talk, proud with an inherited Welsh and Irish pride, indulging a taste for prizefights, moving with an active stride that carried him over many miles of the woods and downs of lovely Surrey. His name was George Meredith.

His father and grandfather were "outfitters," that is, tailors, in Portsmouth. The grandfather, Melchizedec, was a man of much personal and social amenity. Meredith's mother was a fine woman, the daughter of an innkeeper. As a youngster George assumed the high manner, and got called "Gentleman Georgy"; and such essentially he is as an author. He preferred not to talk about his sartorial origin, yet he used the facts in his *Evan Harrington*, where the hero's father, a tailor known as "the great Mel," even after his death permeates the whole complication of snobberies and social strivings that make the tale. The Victorian world, with its fluctuations and its arriving middle class impinging upon the aristocracy, its consequent clash between the younger and the older generation, its endeavor to define the real gentleman, was the very world for Meredith's talents.

He never "qualified" with English public school and Oxford or Cambridge, but as a boy spent two formative years under the gentle influence of a Moravian school at Neuwied on the Rhine. He came to know Thomas Love Peacock, trenchant author of such stories as *Headlong Hall, Nightmare Abbey,* and *Crotchet Castle,* and married his daughter. But the match soon went on the rocks, and Meredith traced its tragic course with much tenderness, and found release for his feeling, in his sixteen-line sonnets, *The Tragedy of Modern Love.* Years later, at thirty-six, just as he entered upon his first success, he was again married, this time happily, and his busy but uneventful life ran its long course to a famous and honored close at eighty-one.

Meredith felt a proud disgust with his British public for its long withheld recognition. Before success arrived he had published among others, *The Shaving of Shagpat, The Ordeal of Richard Feverel, Evan Harrington,* a book of verse, *Sandra Belloni* (first called *Emilia in England*), and *Rhoda Fleming.* Various of the *élite,* such as George Eliot and Carlyle, had seen and proclaimed his merit, but to no immediate popular effect. *Sandra Belloni* (1864), with its sequel, *Vittoria* (1876), deployed the English interest of the day in the *risorgimento.*

Meredith at length arrived. *Harry Richmond* appeared in 1871, and in 1876 *Beauchamp's Career* brought him to the peak of reputation, where he maintained himself with *The Egoist, Diana of the Crossways,* and *The Amazing Marriage.* These, together with verse published in the meantime, raised a cult of the young intellectuals and established the esoteric caste of "Meredithians."

At the time of *Beauchamp's Career* he set forth the theory of his art in a lecture afterwards published as *An Essay on Comedy,* and thus became his own critic. The Comic Spirit, he finds, is not mere humor, or wit, or satire, or ridicule. It is at once more delicate, more kindly and gentle, less contemptuous and cruel. It detects the absurdity of those it loves, without loving them the less. It teaches the world to understand what ails it. It is the enemy of prosers and bores, of all unreason and pride and sentimentality and deformity of character. It was the spirit of Molière, Congreve, Fielding; of Aristophanes, Rabelais, Voltaire; of Cervantes, Chaucer, Shakespeare, Cowper at his best, Jane Austen.

Victorian society was ripe for it, a society where women were attaining social equality with men, and aspiring individuals needed the Comic Spirit to polish off their eccentricities of mind and character by way of making them gentlemen. So Meredith sets up in his novels one or more persons whose egoism of pretense or snobbery or crankery or warp of some sort makes them proper subjects for the Comic Spirit. Mingled with these—usually their victims—are some of the most engaging young men, and particularly young women, that fiction has ever produced. It is no wonder that countless young people have found in Meredith sympathy with their own tragic cases, real or imagined, of clash with obstinate eccentricities of an elder world. Such are the cases of Feverel and Harrington, Lucy Desborough, the Fleming sisters, Carinthia Kirby, Aminta Farrell. Usually the cast includes one or two persons who may not seem so interesting as the others, but who serve as points of stability in the course of events that swirl about them under propulsion of human eccentricity.

Meredith's novel is of a new sort, lacking plot, a series of events contrived or accidental, all leading up to one or more grand scenes which the reader cannot well forget. Over these plays constantly the detached spirit of the novelist himself in his witty, penetrating, figurative, not always clear comment, sometimes his own, sometimes in the mouth of one of the actors. He presents no paragons and no villains. But human perversity, selfishness, pig-headedness are so gently but steadily borne upon by his comedy that they become more odious than by a rougher agent, and put the reader on more vigilant guard against them in himself.

Meredith does not deal with humanity in the mass; he is not moved by a grand social theory or doctrine. His business is wholly with individuals. To be sure, his views on the position of women in society, on man's relation to Earth and Nature, on the equal rights of body and mind and spirit in living, are inferable from his works; yet the problem of the individual experience seems to be uppermost.

He has in him so much of the poet that his mind is teeming with imagery. The wit of his reported talk is mostly figurative; indeed some thought he talked better than he wrote. When he dips his pen, metaphor and simile jostle each other and crowd for utterance. Hence his obscurity. Images rush past the reader's mind as fast as details of landscape past the window of a train. The only way to comprehend them is to stop and walk, but most literary passengers are in too much of a hurry.

His verse, of which there is a great deal, suffers not only from plethora of imagery, but from want of music. The weight of thought and imagery, a sluggish inversion of word-order, and a certain self-conscious urging on of his muse, have fallen, as it were, upon the strings of his instrument and deadened them. But when the weight lifts, as sometimes it does, they ring with a music clear and natural like the unconscious voices of Nature herself. Such passages may be found in *The Day of the Daughter of Hades* and *Love in the Valley*, and in many of his shorter songs. In fact this natural sweetness must owe something to Meredith's intimate companionship with Nature in his long Surrey walks, to his minute and exquisite perception of details of flower, plant, tree, bird, and weather as he went along, and to his merging human life at its best with the abounding life of Earth herself. So he becomes a "new pagan," and finds old Greek myths of Nature a convenient vehicle. *Melampus, Phoebus and Admetus,* and the *Daughter of Hades* are the best of several cases in point.

Both as novelist and poet Meredith has something of the Greek god about him, viewing human life, whether erring or lovely, with a cool but sympathetic detachment. He contains a bit of Apollo and Dionysus and Hermes all three, or is like Oberon stooping to help foolish but appealing mortals as they blunder about in "a wood near Athens." And before calling him finally an aristocrat in his preferences, we must take into account the poetry of his studies in derelict humanity, his *Beggar's Soliloquy, Juggling Jerry,* and *Jump-to-Glory Jane.*

His difficulties have kept off lazy readers, but attached to him many who enjoy exercise of mind, especially when it leads to the rewards of insight and illumination to be found in his novels. At present, in the day of the concentrated and highly objective novel, wherein the novelist hides himself from view, Meredith is out of fashion. But his greater qualities are such as outlive literary fashion and endure as a permanent influence.

HARDY (1840-1928)

One day in 1869, when Meredith was reading manuscripts for a publisher, a young man named Thomas Hardy, a dozen years his junior, submitted his first novel. It was a pungent satire on aristocracy and society, on middle-class vulgarity and modern religion, and Meredith advised him to withdraw it. This he had the artistic courage to do.

Hardy was an architect out of southern Dorsetshire, where he had been born in 1840, the son of a builder, close to the ancient town of Dorchester. It is the Casterbridge of his writings, and the half-moon of country on a radius of say twenty miles round about is his Wessex—now often called "the Hardy country." For through childhood, boyhood, youth, and early manhood the region and its people grew to be a part of him, and he of them, even more intimately than Wordsworth partook of the Lakes, or Dickens of London.

In all England was no spot where the rich mould of human generations and centuries lay deeper and more fertile. Huge Druidic stones and mounds and camps, Roman roads and theatre, ruined castles and abbeys, old churches and manors, marked the strata of decayed civilizations out of which grew the folk life that nourished Hardy. To him land and life were one, a twofold land of higher heath country and low broad valleys. The heath, described once for all in *The Return of the Native*, plays its dramatic part as Egdon Heath in novel and poem. The valleys threaded by slow, brimming English rivers, abound with rich mellow old farms and villages, "haunts of ancient peace." Every bit of it was Hardy's breath and blood— roads, bridges, mills, weirs, inns, barns and steading, ballads to make the cows give down, shearing, pig-sticking, country dances, bell-ringing, folklore and ways, names, speech, stories tragic and otherwise.

For, wonning in these ancient lands,
Enchased and lettered as a tomb,
And scored with prints of perished hands,
And chronicled with dates of doom,
Though my own Being fear no bloom
I trace the lives such scenes enshrine,
Give past exemplars present room,
And their experience count as mine.[1]

In this warmer human foil to the heath lies the chief difference between Egdon Heath and the northerly moor of the Brontës.

Eton and Oxford were not for Hardy. Perhaps he was the better able to understand the wistful longing that drew Jude Fawley to the towers of Christminster. He got Latin in Dorchester school, and as he toiled on towards his profession of architect, he made his own way like Jude into the mysteries of Greek and other learning.

Hardy was thirty-one when he published his first novel, *Desperate Remedies,* a "sensation" novel somewhat in the school of Reade and Collins, but containing a favorite motive of his, that of a selfish sensualist contending for a woman with a self-sacrificing Nature's nobleman. For twenty-four years he wrote novel after novel to the number of fourteen, besides some four collections of shorter tales. His favorite unit of plot is the "triangle," which he manipulates in great variety, from his exquisite and humorous *Under the Greenwood Tree* (1872) and *The Trumpet Major* (1880), to his darkest tragedy, *Jude the Obscure* (1895).

The novels upon which his fame chiefly rests are the tragic stories, *Far from the Madding Crowd* (1874), *The Return of the Native* (1878), *The Mayor of Casterbridge* (1886), *Tess of the D'Urbervilles* (1891), and *Jude the Obscure* (1895). The protagonists are all Wessex people, close to the soil whether they are cultivated or not, and inseparable from it. For Hardy maintained that the universal and elemental values of life with which he is concerned are more operative, certainly more evident, in simple people than in those of more

[1] *On an Invitation to the United States*

artificial rank. His tragedy is ostensibly one that springs from human weakness or "tragic fault," either of several persons, as in the first two novels mentioned, or of one, as in *The Mayor* and *Jude* and essentially in *Tess*. But he seems resolved to overweight the tragic weakness of his characters against their virtues as forces in determining the outcome; though these virtues are none the less engaging for all their loss of power to shape destiny.

This arises possibly from Hardy's impression—too much, in spite of his protest, has been made of his "philosophy"—that not only the accidents of life, but human character and will, are shaped and propelled by an inscrutable and aimless Destiny or Super-Will. And his own tender heart, full of pity for all poor creatures human or lower, can only record life as thus he sees it, with its helplessness, its beauties, its tenderness, its agonies, its dooms. From early years he seems to have been haunted and baffled by the paradox of Nature's kindness and cruelty to her own.

Yet in recording this impression he is partial in at least one respect. His stories are full of accidents and coincidence, sometimes far-fetched; but he sees to it that almost without excep tion these accidents are unlucky.

His plots are almost as simple as those of Greek tragedy, and he clothes them becomingly in a style untricked with gratuitous ornament or superficial smartness. Their austerity is qualified by his warm sympathy with his persons and their helpless suffering. The story moves strongly, evenly, and rapidly to its end, wasting no time on any detail which has not its necessary part in the whole structure. Some like to trace these virtues to Hardy's knowledge and practice as an architect; more likely both spring from some native instinct as a builder.

Whether at the outcry over the frankness of his treatment of sex in *Tess* and *Jude*, or because the impulse of his genius to fiction was spent, from the age of fifty-five to his death at eighty-seven Hardy wrote no more novels, but devoted himself to poetry, to the care of verses already written, and to the composition of new poems. Seven volumes of shorter poems appeared, including *Wessex Poems, Poems of the Past and Present, Time's Laughing-stocks, Satires of Circumstance,* besides his *Famous Tragedy of the Queen of Cornwall,* a primitive British story somewhat after the manner of a Greek tragedy.

In all his poems he is most the poet when he touches "Wessex." At other times, whatever its virtues, his verse is neither at full poetic ease nor musical. But many poems like *The Dead Quire, Friends Beyond, Tess's Lament, The Oxen,* and *The Trampwoman's Tragedy,* which Hardy considered his most successful poem, shine with the rare and natural glow that rises when the great artist works with the material and the medium proper to his hand.

In 1880 appeared *The Trumpet-Major,* a novel of Wessex in Napoleonic days. About the same time Hardy began to make notes on Napoleon. The notes accumulated, with a short poem or two, and as early as 1896 he was sketching plans for a long poem and visiting Waterloo. In 1903-8 appeared the stupendous "epic-drama," *The Dynasts,* "in three Parts, nineteen Acts, and one hundred and thirty scenes." The highly varied scenes are so chosen as to give a grand impression not only of Napoleon, but of the far-flung interests and concerns, public and private, which touched his career, or were touched by it. The pageant or chronicle unfolds itself after the best method of the cinema in treating so vast a subject, by which a vivid or intense scene, skilfully chosen and timed, serves to give a deep impression of a whole too huge to be represented. The verse moves with untrammelled speed and vigor, and the prose descriptions in each scene live with Hardy's own native energy. Some of the songs and choruses are lovely.

Hovering over, and sometimes almost in, the action of the poem are groups of "phantom intelligences," choruses of the Years, of Pities, of Rumor, of Earth, and of "Spirits Sinister and Ironic." Before them the pageant moves as a spectacle upon which they keep up a running choric comment. This comment embodies the poet's impression of history and human life—the same impression that shaped the novels. He is moved with pity and dismay to behold all human will, even the indomitable will of Napoleon, advancing to its end only under full control of the hidden, aimless Super-Will.

The Dynasts, like the Pyramids or St. Peter's, overwhelms the reader by its very magnitude. Not only its size, but the poet's mastery and manipulation of infinite detail included in the vast scope of the subject astonish us. Critics therefore delight to rank the work with *Paradise Lost, Faust,* and the *Prometheus* of Aeschylus. No doubt all these works are in effect engaged with the same subject. But the matter of *The Dynasts* is different; it is new, too new to have undergone the age-long ripening and maturing process, the human handling, which went to make those earlier works, or any other great classics, great. Then, Milton and Aeschylus at least had the advantage, as Arnold might say, of grand ideas current in their time with which to work—the positive convictions of many agreeing minds; whereas Hardy is dealing only with his own impressions of human life, and impressions of its futility at that. Which cannot but "damp his intended wing" and discourage the free exercise of genius.

In two scenes, however, he returns to Wessex—one showing his beloved Wessex folk stirred with the rumor that Napoleon had landed in England, the other their excited burning of Napoleon in effigy, or in reality as one of them thought! At once Hardy is again wholly the artist, shaping with easy and powerful skill the ripe old material to which his hand had found itself so happily fitted.

STEVENSON (1850-1894)

In 1850 Scotland bestowed another rich gift upon English Literature in the genius of Robert Louis Stevenson. He was Edinburgh-born, of a family of lighthouse engineers. His father, Thomas Stevenson, was a true-to-type Scot, solid, grave, religious, set in his way, in a measure dour, with depths of warm feeling. He was not unlike his own sturdy lighthouses. Something of this character descended upon his only son, and mingled in him with the mother's buoyant and lively spirit. Besides there was "Cummy" (Alison Cunningham), the famous nurse, who brought Robert Louis through his sickly childhood, imbued him with the austere tenets of Scotch Calvinism, and filled his mind with folklore, now romantic, now hair-raising. "My parents and Cummy," he said, "brought me up on the Shorter Catechism, porridge, and the Covenanters." To Cummy he beautifully and fitly dedicated his *Child's Garden of Verses.*

Stevenson had most of the Scotch paradoxical virtues except thrift. He was doggedly persistent even while he seemed most flexible. His ill health, after driving him to all the "airts," banished him from home for the last seven of his forty-three years; yet ill or well, the spirit of the Bohemian wanderer contended in him with his deep love of Scotland.

His literary aspirations began with his success at four in a contest with his cousins for the best *History of Moses.* This he dictated as he could not yet write, and it reflects a certain grave charm which is premonitory. At school and the University of Edinburgh he was an idler—indeed professed himself as such. But this meant that he had not his heart in the study of engineering nor of the law, though he was admitted to the bar at twenty-four. He clashed with his father about his profession, about religion, about his behavior. He lost his faith, sowed a handful of wild oats, but was all the time "slogging at his trade" of writing. He "lived with words," after the French doctrine, especially of Flaubert, in quest of the *mot juste.* He played what he called the sedulous ape, constantly imitating, or rather impersonating, such writers as Sir Thomas Browne, Bunyan, and their contemporaries; Hazlitt, Lamb, Hawthorne, and Montaigne; and with such success that the delicate ear of the reader detects the changes from one of these ventriloquisms to another throughout his earlier work.

In these apprentice days technique was to him everything. "Think of technique," he advised a young writer, "when you rise and when you go to bed." No man ever worked harder in its service, and that through illness and repeated threat of death itself. He thus developed a kind of modern Stoicism which runs through such earlier essays as *Virginibus Puerisque.* But young men and maidens have never taken to these essays so much as older folk, in spite of the fine courage that permeates them. Yet the grim underlying Scotch Stoicism is much sweetened by Stevenson's charm and love of play. As he grew older he kept alive in him all of his former selves—the child, the small boy, the youth—and from the first he taught the world to play bravely in the face of shadows.

The child in Stevenson dictated the *Child's Garden of Verses*, though the relentless artist in him polished them to the last degree of finish. The boy in him dictated *Treasure Island*, and *Kidnapped*, those incomparable classics of the "crawler" kind. His greatest short stories are crawlers—*Merry Men, Thrawn Janet, Markheim*, and the longer, proverbial *Dr. Jekyll and Mr. Hyde*. But lurking even about his horrors there is a suspicion of play. One thinks inevitably of Cummy and the little chap in other days delighting themselves with a good scare over some fearsome tale of a "bogle," or an older boy frightening younger ones to the infinite thrill and glee of all concerned. "He wasn't really grown up, was he?" asked a small boy, who had been listening to *Treasure Island*.

Stevenson was nearly thirty-three when *Treasure Island* appeared. Hitherto he had wandered far in quest of health and adventure, as far as San Francisco, and Monterey, where, almost dead, he was saved by the extraordinary woman who became his wife. He had worked much for magazines, perfecting his art and waiting for fame. But he was now emerging from his stage of imitation, his chameleon habits, and becoming Stevenson himself. The change is marked in *Treasure Island*, which the great Gladstone, and doubtless thousands of others, sat up till two in the morning to finish. Its encore, *The Black Arrow*, is not so good, though at the time boys liked it better.

The years from *Treasure Island* in 1883 to *The Master of Ballantrae* in 1889 were the great harvest years of his fame and his production. Yet all the time he was ill, and not infrequently his life hung by a thread. *The Master of Ballantrae*, with all its thrills, comes from the more mature Stevenson, as appears in the solid vigor of both his portraits and his narrative.

All his life a wanderer, Stevenson turned his many adventures and observations into "copy." *Inland Voyage* and *Travels with a Donkey* show him the inveterate Bohemian that he was in Europe. *The Amateur Emigrant, Across the Plains*, and *The*

Silverado Squatters record that first painful journey of his across the Continent in 1880 and his sojourn in California. In his next journey overland, in 1888, his every condition was better, when he and his family embarked on their cruise of the South Seas, to fetch up in Samoa. Here he passed his last four years, spending too much on his estate, Vailima, mixing unhappily in local politics, but adored by the natives; and here he finished *Catriona*, the sequel to *Kidnapped*, and *The Ebb-Tide*, a crawler of the South Seas. He left unfinished *St. Ives*, a road-and-adventure story of 1814, and what he rightly regarded as his masterpiece, *Weir of Hermiston*.

We have perhaps less than half of *Weir*, with reliable indications of his plans for the whole story. Its leading theme is that of father against son, a favorite with Stevenson, mindful of such bitterness in his own past. But in the novel the father, studied from the historic Lord Braxfield, is a harsh, coarse-jesting, able, masterful, but brutal criminal judge, who was to have died in the agony of condemning his son to death. The scene is a moorland village, and the harshness of the tale finds its exquisite foil in the love story, whose unhappy course was to have been the means of bringing the lad under sentence by his father. In articulation of plot, in portraiture, in tragic clash, in setting, and in the close logical relation to each other of all four characters, *Weir of Hermiston*, even in the fragment, is the greatest of Stevenson's works. True Scot at heart, he was bitterly homesick. He had always loved a Scotch theme and setting; but in this last work his treatment of both shows tenderness and power which owe something to his far and hopeless exile.

It was Stevenson's persistent and self-conscious endeavor not to be obvious or common in his phrasing, and he saved himself by grace of saturation in Biblical language, proverb, plain Scots, or the rich antiquities of seventeenth-century English writers. These he used with just a trace of amusement that precludes affectation. But in the course of his hard years he assimilated these elements, and only near the end does he become wholly the free vigorous artist, working at last maturely with more concern for matter and effect than for manner.

PART EIGHT

WITH MANY VOICES

As THE long reach of the Victorian time nears its close, its current hurries and breaks towards a new confusion of the waters. From the beginning of its last decade, the "Nineties," the old sustaining ideas have become so disintegrated, and the clamor of voices so numerous and discordant, that a reader seeks in vain for lines of direction or groupings or schemes of things in the tendencies of literature. And his difficulty is increased by his nearness to these times and the lack of that long-withheld gift of the years, "perspective."

Since the beginning of the nineteenth century the new middle class had been coming into its own. It had grown rich, powerful, cultivated, sophisticated. The course of this growth one may follow clearly and enjoyably as it is traced by John Galsworthy (1867-1933) in his great masterpiece, *The Forsyte Saga* (begun in 1906); therein the Forsyte family through four generations may be seen rising, increasing, and multiplying under the ideal of "property first," which fashions its successful if not happy destinies. Indeed Galsworthy himself has been called a ripe Forsyte.

On the peak of sophistication are the novels of manners by Henry James (1843-1916), the American who in his thirties became essentially an Englishman. His art is self-conscious, exquisite and refined in style, in structure and portraiture, and yet by no means lacking in vigor—he much admired Turgeniev and Balzac—and his stories are ever concerned with the issue between true culture, false culture, and provincialism, from *Daisy Miller* (1878) to *The Ambassadors* (1903). Latterly his literary manner became too subtly and utterly refined for even his brother, William, the philosopher.

With the mounting increase of wealth—indeed as a part of it—had risen the vast, far-flung New Empire, on which "the sun never sets." And now with the close and fulfilment of that great Victorian time, with the Nineties, set in a certain relaxation as of weariness, a decadence clearly manifest in art and literature, in the flippant sophistication of such periodicals as *The Yellow Book* (1894) and *The Savoy* (1896), and a fagged taste which craved super-stimulants. It is manifest in such men as Le Gallienne and John Davidson, author of *Fleet Street Eclogues*, and Arthur Symons, poet of the *demi-monde*; and comes in for lively satire in Gilbert and Sullivan's operetta, *Patience,* and *The Green Carnation* (1894) by Robert Hichens. Yellow and green in fact became prevailing "literary" colors, a taste lightly touched by Gilbert's aesthete, a

> Greenery, yallery,
> Grosvenor-gallery,
> Foot-in-the-grave young man.

Oscar Wilde (1856-1900), through his own fault underrated, who paraded himself along Bond Street in velveteen knickerbockers to exemplify the new Aestheticism, who was disappointed with Niagara, and "not exactly pleased with the Atlantic," who with his wit and conversation, his clever comedies, *Lady Windermere's Fan* (1892), *A Woman of No Importance* (1893), *An Ideal Husband* (1895), and *The Importance of Being Earnest* (1895), had made himself the idol of London, who suddenly crashed down in scandal from his giddy height, who poured out his broken heart in *De Profundis* and the *Ballad of Reading Gaol,* and found cover at last in Catholicism —Oscar Wilde, usually the favorite example of the decadence of the nineties, at any rate was, as it turned out, a genius defeated by that very decadence.

Such a time calls forth its satiric jesters. They laugh and set the world laughing at the spent ideas, moribund conventions, forms, pretence, and absurdities of their times. Wilde himself was one of these jesters. A better is W. S. Gilbert (1836-1911), whose gay and topsy-turvy world almost conceals the bitterness beneath. Sweetened by the perennial music of Arthur Sullivan, the creations of this two-fold genius, from *Pinafore* (1878) to *Utopia* (1893), have in them the rare element of permanent satire, and bid fair to go on for a long time cheerfully dissolving all nonsense about social position, rank by sudden rise or ancestors, fakes, nostrums, and sentimentalities. Nor can we overlook the immortal *Alice in Wonderland* and *Through the Looking-Glass* of Lewis Carroll (Charles L. Dodgson) (1832-1898), under whose artless innocence plays many a side glance of satire. Another jester in another art, more subtle and Meredithian, more trenchant, was the caricaturist, Max Beerbohm. The spirit of jest has ever since been abroad. The sense of humor has become one of the cardinal virtues, to save the generation from taking matters, most of all themselves, too seriously. Little can nowadays succeed unaided by the spirit of humor or play or wit.

But a more searching satirist was at hand. In 1890 Bernard Shaw (1856—) was already thirty-four and hardly known. He had been slaving for a livelihood, getting an irregular education, writing socialist pamphlets and dramatic criticism. In 1892 his *Widowers' Houses* at least raised a dust with its exposure of complacent wealth exploiting the poor. Thus opens the long series of plays through forty and more years to the present moment, plays which have shaken English drama pretty well out of the coma of a century and more, which have succeeded in the face of established "rules," which have captured the audience by their vigor, wit, lively ingenuity, their unsparing and fearless ventilation of every wrong, every opinion, and every social habit of all these years of turbulent adjustment. Shaw is as it were the court jester to this whole "tragic generation," as Yeats calls it, sometimes sweet, like Touchstone, as in *Fanny's First Play* (1911) and *Pygmalion* (1912), sometimes "a bitter fool," like King Lear's, as in *Heartbreak House* (1917), hitting hard with quip and paradox that Samuel Butler in his *Way of all Flesh* had taught him to wield, withering outworn injustice with his nimble laughter, testing every current opinion with ridicule to measure its truth. "The way to get at the merits of a case is not to listen to the fool who imagines himself impartial, but to get it argued with reckless bias for and against." Which is also the theory of John Milton.

Shaw masks his own opinion behind his wit, and for his artistic success it is just as well. That it is a sound and positive opinion one cannot doubt; but when he unmasks, and expounds or prophesies, as in *Back to Methuselah*, he is no longer the artist.

The most powerful agent in clearing the close decadent air came oddly enough out of the far east. Rudyard Kipling (1865–1936), born in India, has Wesleyan preachers among his forebears, and his blood is a composite of Scotch, Irish, English, and remotely, Dutch. As a lad he got his schooling at a United Service College in England, which lends its setting to the school stories, *Stalky and Co.* From eighteen to twenty-four he worked as a newspaper man at Lahore and Allahabad. It was his time of rich ingathering as he mingled busily with wandering merchants, fakhirs, and the British soldiery. *Departmental Ditties* and *Plain Tales from the Hills* (1886, 1888) found their way to England, and Kipling himself followed the next year. He married an American lady, and for four years lived at Brattleboro, Vermont. Meanwhile the ringing, vigorous, infectious music of his verse, the energy, strangeness, humor, and elemental humanity of his stories, captured everybody high and humble—except the exquisites. They were, and still are, saying, "It's clever, but is it Art?" And Kipling retorts by giving the question to the Devil in his *Conundrum of the Workshops.*

After the turn of the century, Kipling finally settled on the coast of Sussex. But by the middle of the nineties he had reached the wide outer limits of his range. Yet so wide is his scope that the moment one tries to define it, some poem or story proves that Kipling has escaped the boundary.

He has somewhat of the exuberance and fecundity and hunger for men and things that were in Browning, whom he at first imitated. He knows, or shows us, less about women. "Sex" is with Kipling healthily a relative matter. Yet the physical man, with all the common virtues of the physical life, courage, good sportsmanship, uproarious fun, fidelity, endurance, honest self-reliance, splendid sacrifice, devotion to Queen and Empire, together with their craven opposites—black sharply projected against white—this common man is the basis of the common humanity in him which binds the superior race and the inferiors together in a mutual responsibility. As Dr. van Dyke said, he is a tribal singer, but his tribe is the British Empire. It was to mute instincts common to millions of English-speaking men that he gave clear and vigorous utterance, both in song and story. The great trio, Ortheris, Learoyd, and Mulvaney, grow sublimated almost to symbols.

It is easy to point out rough, gross, brutal things in him, but such are also in Homer and Shakespeare. Against the terrible power of *The Man who would be King,* one should set the age-old domestic English tendernesses of *An Habitation Enforced,* the perennial youth of *The Brushwood Boy,* the deep and moving mystery of *They,* the undying childhood, foreshadowed from the early *Wee Willie Winkie,* strong as ever in *Puck of Pook's Hill,* mingling by an uncanny intimacy with animals in *The Jungle Book* and the *Just So Stories,* and animating even locomotives and ships.

Whatever its defects, Kipling's genius is of the more elemental sort that is sufficient unto itself, training in with no school or tendency of art, spontaneous, making its own rules, direct, and instinctive, with a relish for things and words, and for metres that are primitive. The old "fourteener," antique even in Elizabethan days, is a favorite metrical scheme of his. Both in verse and story he is inexhaustible, but especially in his short stories, which contain his highest achievement, and number all told some 250. And while a careful examination of a dozen of the best of these reveals high technique in the species, yet their excellence is owing primarily not to artifice, but to the old human instinct to tell a story and tell it well.

The modern vogue of the "short story" may be owing to many things—the vast growth of magazine journalism, the sparing of sustained effort in writing or reading a short story, the rapid flitting of modern attention from object to object. But the short story is in fact not modern, but almost, perhaps quite,

as primitive as the song, and recurs in a highly developed
state through the course of all literatures. With the help of
French influence, especially that of Maupassant, it latterly became in English a matter of highly conscious art, and was so
fashioned by Stevenson. He recognized three germs of a good
short story—a place suggesting possibilities, a character, or an
incident.

But no single genius gave the form a stronger impulse than
Kipling, with his boundless wealth of local color, his broad
fun, his telling vigorous stroke, his horrors, his action and
sharp contrasts. In this as in other respects his influence has
been a most salutary antidote to the self-conscious formalism
and calculation and mere technique which mark the decline of
genuine creation.

The gradual disintegration of old ideas led to the discovery
of no sustaining equivalent. Various substitutes had a brief
and limited following and soon wilted under the very scepticism which had begotten them. "Art for art's sake" and aestheticism passed with the nineties. Mechanistic determinism has
gone its way. One scepticism and rejection has succeeded another. Religious and theological belief, convictions in art, grow
unstable; even faith in wealth and in science weakens, as exemplified in such novels as Conrad's *Nostromo*, or in many by
Wells, who is the extensive recorder of the scepticisms and
aspirations of his times. At length Nature herself as a model
has been rejected by certain extremists, who, well rid of her
restrictions, find "freer" expression in the mere manipulation
of words and colors and forms and musical notes.

Walter Pater (1839-1894) is perhaps as much as anyone
the prophet of the contracting faith of the age. We have already heard him limiting the artistic area to mere human experience, "gathering all we are into one desperate effort to
see and touch. . . . For art comes to you professing frankly to
give nothing but the highest quality to your moments as they
pass, and simply for those moments' sake." This is what is
called hedonism, or sometimes "the new Cyrenaicism" after the
similar old Greek school.

But such contraction of scope during the last generation or two has brought a corresponding expansion of range, and with it an enterprise of discovery, in mundane regions. Novelty of experience, novelty of setting and local color, of subjects, of human behavior and reaction, of technique and form, of theories of life and art, of antiquity, of remote corners of the earth, of social relations, of science, and sex, these have all been within easy reach, and subject to renewed and closer scrutiny than ever before. Possibly such contraction of scope and intensity of focus may account for the dramatic revival which has taken place under the genius of Pinero, Jones, Shaw, Barrie, and Galsworthy.

A revolt from tradition has always been the world's way of turning to new and better conditions. But no revolt of art and intellect has ever been so uncompromising as this of the last generation. It has even become the habit and boast of some to tolerate nothing that the world has ever done before in literature, but to make all things new, of new materials, by new laws; forgetting that heretofore all things new were made largely of old materials, and in fulfilment of the old laws.

With such disintegrations each writer or individual becomes a law unto himself, whether as to the theory and practice of literature or of life. And though Pater warns us that we have no time for speculation, yet human instinct will speculate. In our disillusioned plight therefore each has to think for himself, and each arrives at a different conclusion, without much confidence in his own or in any other's.

This is why literature of the last forty years seems hopelessly confused; criticism is in a state of anarchy; without standards, and merely a matter of individual likes or dislikes—how it seems to me, or to you, with no room for useful debate. Or at best we may ask with Mr. Croce, what the individual poet or author set out to do, what his artistic intentions were, and judge him by the success with which he has fulfilled them.

Left to his own strength and resources, and unsustained by great communal views, the individual writer, poet or novelist, has both gained and lost. Having broken utterly with the past, he is often buoyant with hope for the future. He seems also to have gained in resourcefulness and individuality. He must of course exert every talent he has to the utmost. But his very isolation and individuality have weakened him. In 1908, Meredith, in the wisdom of his eighty years, felt encouraged by the literary outlook. He said: "There may not be any first-class writers; but the second and third classes are full. There is a great elevation of the rank and file of those who are making books. Multitudes of the very same people who, a few years ago, could not write at all, are writing now with skill, if not with art."[1]

This rise of quality in the "second class" has no doubt come as a consequence of the writer's individual resourcefulness in his new self-reliance of mind. The increase in his numbers has risen with the increase in his readers, what with popular education and ever readier intercommunication the world over.

As a literary form the novel enjoys the most licensed freedom of any. It may do almost anything with itself, become almost anything, turn hybrid with other forms and still get itself called a novel. Novels will not submit to sharp classification, but the stupendous mass of them may seem a bit less amorphous if it is seen in three grand phases, though these often blend confusingly with one another.

First is the novel dealing with a cross section of life. It may have a clearly defined plot with a central character, and deal with antecedents and consequences of his fate like a good play. It may treat a mere episode or situation as an illustration of character. It may, as latterly it has done, notably in Joyce's *Ulysses*, use an excised sample of the inconsequent and continuous stream of the mind as a focal point from which the reader may gain a view of the man's past, future, and quality.

Then, the novel may be romantic; that is, it may carry us into other times and be historical, and into far places or unusual adventures or both, as do W. H. Hudson's *Green Mansions* or the delectable tales of John Buchan; or specialize in local color and dialect as in the stories of Mary Webb; or

[1] Interview with C. F. Goss in *Book News Monthly*, March, 1908

it may grow prophetic and thrill us with visions of future triumphs of science, discovery, and social blessedness. So Mr. Wells.

Or again, the novel may take biographical form and tell the "life-story" at least up to the point where the nuptial knot is tied hard and fast, and whereafter, as most novelists imply, the rest is not worth recounting. But a noble minority think otherwise, for instance Eliot in *Middlemarch*, or Wells in *Marriage*.

Into one of these three groups, or into the vast borderlands between them, virtually all novels, ancient and modern, will fall. Some may by turns belong to all three, like George Borrow's (1803-1881) autobiographical *Lavengro, Romany Rye,* and in some measure perhaps his *Bible in Spain.*

Naturally in a world so expanding as ours has been, the novel rather than poetry has been the flourishing form of literature; and with the welter of ideas and experiment it has been subject to fashion and change, for no other form is more accessible to the debate of current affairs and concerns. In 1911 H. G. Wells proposed, as if it were something new, that the novel should be the arena of discussion about every aspect of life, "until a thousand pretences and ten thousand impostures shrivel in the cold, clear air of our elucidations."

The special antecedents of our novels are such as Meredith's *Ordeal of Richard Feverel* and Samuel Butler's *Way of all Flesh,* finished after twelve years' labor in 1884, but not published till a year after the author died in 1902. *The Way of all Flesh* deals with a "risen" middle-class family, the clash between son and parents, the decay of faith and of old respectabilities, and limits its view and test of life to actual experience, pleasure, and in general the "new Cyrenaicism." Trenchant, even shocking at times, it forecasts the unabashed hardihood of much that is recent.

Another harbinger of the new fiction was George Gissing (1857-1903), whose life, made wretched by maladjustments, poverty, sickness, and solitude, dictated in his novels the perpetual duel between person and circumstance. He makes the slum his stage, but his leading persons in a measure he elevates above that level. In his *New Grub Street* (1891) one

572 WITH MANY VOICES

may learn about the under side of living by literature in the eighties.

The honored Victorian practice of publishing novels in parts or serially had tended to diffuseness and laxity in structure. But even Meredith and Hardy seem to be aware of this defect in the craft, and show the disposition to correct it. The end of the century found the art and craft of making a novel quite transformed. Long and flowery descriptions of persons or places, that flat type of character known as the "humor," comment or preachment by the author, leisurely digression, tend to disappear. If preach the author must—and Mr. Wells must—his characters are his mouthpiece. The novelist should imitate the playwright and keep out of sight; which tends to make many later novels more like plays, more concrete, more objective. Such improvements owe much to the French example, to Flaubert's *Madame Bovary*, to Maupassant. Conrad was deeply read in French. George Moore and Henry James both lived for a time in Paris, as did Arnold Bennett, amid the agitated discussions about literary art, the welter of claims between romanticism, realism, naturalism old and new, idealism, symbolism, impressionism. James, particularly, insisted upon more care for the written word, the *mot juste*, and for structure, unified by some centre of gravity, or singleness of focus—a character, an idea, a logical consummation of events.

No more astonishing example of the artist in fiction did the time bring forth than Joseph Conrad (1857-1924), the Pole, who knew no English till he was past twenty, who followed the sea the world over, rose to the rank of captain in the Mercantile Marine, and did not publish his first novel till he was close upon forty. In his preface to *The Nigger of the Narcissus* he talks of his art, his desire to stir the reader's emotions as a poet stirs them, through the senses. To that end he must mould his substance into its inevitable and proper form, and deploy his language like any other artistic medium, modelling it, coloring it, awakening its music, till the reader through emotional experience may get some glimpse even of elemental truth itself.

Such objectivity and such artistic consciousness inform the

work of the so-called Edwardian novelists, Galsworthy, Bennett, and to a less extent Wells; but in the later years, French influences have given way to Russian, form and selection to more crude and powerful effect—perhaps in part a result of the war. Current psychological theories have made themselves felt, and artistic structure has dissolved into the episodic and fantastic, and at length into the "stream of consciousness." At the moment, if Virginia Woolf is an omen, some rebound is imminent, some return to an emphasis upon spiritual values and upon the broader humanity of the great masters of English fiction in other days.

The new scrutiny of human experience, the new passion to explore the near and visible actualities of life, has led naturally to a revival of biography. In riper Victorian days biography had lost the vigor which it proved in Boswell and Lockhart, and had settled pretty much into a dull formula. Exceptions there are—one at least is Mr. J. W. Mackail's *Life of William Morris* (1899), with all conditions favorable—a great subject, and a biographer of sympathy, scholarship, learning, and high literary skill, who had known Morris well. But the day of discarded traditions and of new beginnings has included also biography, and discussion is rife concerning its theory and problems as an art. For an art it has come to be, an even more exacting art than in Boswell's day.

Two opposite tendencies are struggling for the possession of the field, and others are interfering to embroil the strife. Whereas the highest achievement in biography will not be possible till all are reconciled.

On the one hand is the imperious demand of modern historical scholarship for accuracy. And indeed the facts, literal and unadorned, would at least seem to be essential to a form of literature so dependent upon the truth as is biography. On the other hand, modern scholarship and art show an unaccountable disposition to quarrel, and in modern biography art would transcend scholarship by its intuitions and imagination, playing over the character and career of the particular person on whose portrait it is engaged.

Lytton Strachey (1880-1932) in his *Eminent Victorians* (1918) and his *Queen Victoria* (1921) set distinguished examples rather on the side of art, though in the ostensible interests of accuracy and truth he has joined heartily in the favorite occupation of his age, the demolishing of traditional illusions. This he does with detachment and a fascinating play of wit and insinuation. But the result at least has not been wholly on the side of truth. It has set smaller biographers, in the professed service of fact, hunting busily for some traditional idol to smash, or some traditional villain, or villainess, to rehabilitate; and few if any known to fame—or infamy—have escaped them.

Art as against scholarship has gone further than in Strachey, and with the French example of Maurois, and the German of Ludwig and Zweig, produced the so-called *biographie romantique*, something between a biography and a novel. But such a hybrid, essentially alien to the English genius for realities, seems unlikely to yield examples of eminence.

The problem of biography is far more complicated by what the physician and the psychologist now properly claim their right to say in the matter—and are saying. Clearly the new biographer must reconcile all these within himself—scholar, artist, realist, physician, psychologist—and be over all a true humanist and man of the world. Which, up to his date, was pretty much the sum of James Boswell.

The loss of faith in all tradition, the lonely responsibility of each individual for his own opinion and ideas, the intellectual and spiritual chaos of these latter days, have sent men groping in various directions for a foothold of reality, sometimes alone, sometimes in groups. In the earlier days poets like Meredith and Swinburne and Robert Bridges found a satisfaction in the "new paganism," a revival or realization of the truth and poetry in ancient Greek myth. Many of their poems and particularly Walter Pater's "novel," *Marius the Epicurean,* are shining examples. James Thomson in his *Proem* gives voice to their creed, beginning:

> O antique fables! beautiful and bright
> And joyous with the joyous youth of yore;
> O antique fables! for a little light
> Of that which shineth in you evermore,
> To cleanse the dimness from our weary eyes,
> And bathe our old world with a new surprise
> Of golden dawn entrancing sea and shore.

Others found inspiration and comfort more generally in antiquity: Andrew Lang in Homeric and Alexandrian poetry; Austin Dobson in the eighteenth century; Stephen Phillips in material for his dramatic poems *Ulysses* and *Paolo and Francesca*; and later Flecker, with his flair for Catullus, for the classic ideal of the French "Parnassians," for the Orient, as in his *Golden Journey to Samarkand* and other poems.

A cry of despair reverberates all through the Victorian times even to this day, despair of men who feel their anchorage slipping, or find themselves adrift and alone. Carlyle, Ruskin, Tennyson, Arnold, Swinburne, Hardy, give voice to it at times, and its echoes are heard on every hand down to Housman and T. S. Eliot's *Waste Land*.

The most pitiful and appalling instance is that of James Thomson, "B. V." (1834-1882) (B. for Bysshe to show his admiration of Shelley, V. for Vanolis, an anagram for Novalis, another literary idol). He was Scotch-born, a waif in an asylum, a pupil in a military school, then a military instructor. He loved a young girl who died, and the scar never healed. In London, Spain, Colorado, everywhere, he failed in one misfit job after another, and in spite of desperate efforts of others to befriend him, sank at last into depths of intemperance which killed him before he was fifty. Not all of his verse is gloomy, but *The City of Dreadful Night*, and his earlier *Doom of a City*, more powerful if less famous, both under the formative influence of Shelley and Dante, are the more moving because the blackness of their despair breaks now and then just enough to show a bit of tender sky and cloud, or landscape, or a fleeting glimpse of the happy wife and babes never to be his. He is too great to belong to a school, and great enough to be a poet's poet. His cadences and effects exert a certain direct energy which they seem to have conveyed to Mr. Masefield and his imitators, and he often sounds more modern than his dates.

With this new individualism of genius, now lonely, now thrown on its own resources for artistic and spiritual support, sometimes finding it, or a substitute, in this, that, or other pre-occupation, sometimes despairing, we hear in these days a good deal about the "poetic escape." No doubt poetry has at all times been some sort of escape from something, both for poet and listener; but poets have never spoken of it quite as such, not even Keats, though he comes close to it in his *Ode to a Nightingale.* Yet it has in these latter days, for what reason one can only guess, become a popular if not wholly healthy notion. The great poets might have wondered at it—might have scorned it as doctrine of cowardly retreat from the turmoil of life which was a profound source of their inspiration. But they had lived in days when there were great current ideas to sustain them.

From our modern confusion of both mind and spirit certain writers, some of them poets, have sought escape and found quiet refuge within the well-ordered security of the Church of Rome. Both Oscar Wilde and Aubrey Beardsley, worldly in their work if any ever were, at last turned to her for peace of mind. So did Ernest Dowson, who died in 1900 at thirty-three, after a life of poverty and illness and helpless dissipation, and who beautifully records his conclusion of the matter in the short poem *Benedictio Domini.* So also Lionel Johnson, almost his parallel in years and course of life, who defies "The Dark Angel" of temptation:

> Lonely, unto the Lone I go;
> Divine, to the Divinity.

So also Alfred Noyes and G. K. Chesterton.

The strangest, and at once the most splendid and most marred of these figures was Francis Thompson (1859-1907). A doctor's son, he tried to study for the priesthood and for medicine, a hopeless failure at both. He ran away from home and lost himself in the gutters of London, picking up his living along the curb, befriended by a prostitute, keeping himself up with opium, rescued at last after three years by the poetess Alice Meynell and her husband, under whose guardianship his fragile life was thenceforth maintained, with intermittent relapses to the misery of the pavements. In these intervals of restoration he composed his poems—*Poems* (1893), *Sister Songs* (1895), and *New Poems* (1896). His clear voice and exalted imagination seem utterly and strangely alien to his physical frailty and manner of life. Perversely threadbare, neglected, odd, but never besotted, lugging his books and papers in an old fishbasket, this spiritual kinsman of Shelley and Blake made his rounds of editorial offices, under the affectionate and watchful eye of more practical friends. Aeschylus, the Vulgate, and the mystics, besides Blake and Shelley, were the sublimated nourishers of his genius.

His *Anthem of Earth* gleams and flashes with the prolific splendor of his mind, a splendor which burns also in his essay on Shelley, wherein his praise of the poet is unconsciously a description of himself. At times he commands the simplicity of Wordsworth or Herrick, but his elements are air and fire.

In his *Hound of Heaven* (1893) the mute plight of many spiritual derelicts of his day and later has found expression, so that it is his most popular poem, and has been called a symbol of the spiritual unrest of the whole nineteenth century, "autobiographical of a man and an age."[1] With perhaps a hint in his title from the *Prometheus* of Aeschylus, the poet with fiery tenderness recounts his perverse and futile flight from the love of God which at last overtakes him.

The renouncing of tradition, the limiting of literature to experience and of inquiry to mundane interests, pragmatism, naturalism—such conditions of mind seem to create a sense of want, conscious or unconscious—in this tragic generation, and writers take various refuge, in aestheticism, in a jest, in antiquity, in despair, in the Church. Some of them not un-

[1] Holbrook Jackson, *The Eighteen Nineties*, p. 172

naturally resort to a new stoicism, and steel themselves to face the mystery of life with the dignity of a resolute will. Such was the spirit of Samuel Butler (1835-1902), which he embodies in his *Way of All Flesh*. The young hero after getting well bruised on hard corners of Victorian conventions and institutions, develops will and character by facing life on his own resources. This modern stoical view the reader will encounter often enough in the writing of the last forty years. However charmingly veiled, it is the Scotch granite basis of Stevenson in essay or novel. It is the steel core of Conrad's art and attraction; the strength of constitution behind the vigor of Kipling. It fortified W. E. Henley (1849-1903), the crippled but pugnacious champion of young literary candidates for fame —of Hardy, Swinburne, Stevenson, Conrad, Wells, Yeats— and dictated one of the most popular poems of the time— Henley's *Invictus*:

> I am the master of my fate:
> I am the captain of my soul.

While through Victorian times the new middle class had been coming into its own, the other class, the industrial poor, had not. All the way their unhappy case had found tongues and pens to proclaim it, to picture it, and to set forth the remedy. Carlyle, Ruskin, Kingsley, Mrs. Gaskell, George Eliot, Morris, Gissing, Hardy, Shaw, Wells, Galsworthy, Ervine, Bennett, and D. H. Lawrence and Masefield make only a sketch list of writers in one way or another concerned with the poor. Socialism, imported from the Continent and naturalized, took partial possession of the minds and writings of Morris and Shaw and Wells. But Socialism is only one manifestation of a far grander concern. If we have latterly anything approaching a great current and communal idea, it is the newly awakened "social consciousness," which enters in some measure as a shaping force into almost all the later literature.

Gissing in his *Demos* (1886), *Thyrza* (1887), *The Nether World* (1889), is full of hopeless indignation at the condition of the city's poor. It is his professed aim to set forth realistically the tedious case of the "ignobly decent." Arnold Bennett

(1867-1931), a native of the five clustered pottery towns in Staffordshire, took their dull, limited, and monotonous life for the original of his greatest works, *The Old Wives' Tale* (1908) and *Clayhanger* (1910). In 1923 and 1924 he pictured the squalor of London in *Riceyman's Steps* and *Elsie and the Child*. In the first five years of the new century H. G. Wells (1866—) discussed social matters in several books, including his *Modern Utopia* and *New Worlds for Old*, and touched them with humor in his novel *Kipps*. Masefield in his *Everlasting Mercy* and *The Widow in Bye Street* gives a terrible presentation of sin and misery and redemption in the lower stratum, and in the Prologue of *Reynard the Fox* he presents a side elevation of English life on its various levels, but without particular intention.

It is a natural part of the new social consciousness to demolish the smug ethical standards of respectability, and to prove, or try to prove, their falsity by setting up in fiction or drama a clash between them and the intrinsic goodness of the poor, or the condemned, who if in any way guilty are so through no fault of their own, but of the respectables who condemn them. There is a touch of this in Shaw; notably in *Mrs. Warren's Profession* and *Fanny's First Play*. In Galsworthy's plays, such as *The Silver Box, Justice,* and *Loyalties*, this master of stagecraft handles the theme with consummate theatrical skill. It is not new; Dickens and Mrs. Gaskell used it, but even in them it showed signs of the sentimentalism by which it may degenerate to a false conclusion—that to be rich and respectable is to be bad, and by the same token to be poor is to be essentially good and unjustly accused. To such a melodramatic misuse has the theme fallen in many a modern play and novel.

Closely related to this new social consciousness, or perhaps a part of it, is the Celtic Movement, the revived interest in Irish life and lore. Of course English Literature has ofttimes caught a refreshing breath blowing sweet out of the Irish west. Medieval romance, even such masterpieces as *Gawain and the Green Knight*, owes an unmeasured and immeasurable debt to Celtic radiance and beauty. Then there were Goldsmith and Sheridan, and Tom Moore, and Maria Edgeworth with *Castle Rackrent* (1800) and other Irish tales, and Dr. Charles Lever with *Harry Lorrequer* (1837), and William Carleton (1794-1869), who in his combination of actual Irish life with legend most nearly of all approached the quality and current of the modern Celtic movement. Arnold in his time had done something to popularize the interest in Celtic literature; but the early nineties saw the launching of a concerted "movement." On the more studious side societies sprang up for the study of Irish texts and antiquities. But in a literary way the movement had less to do with the study of ancient Gaelic or the revival of the glories of Irish culture in the sixth and seventh centuries, than with the preserving and new literary use of Irish folk-lore and life.

It enlisted the genius of the Irish-born W. B. Yeats (1865-1939), who, in his *Literary Movement in Ireland* (1901), maintains that "the common people, wherever civilization has not driven its plough too deep, keep a watch over the roots of all religion and all romance." He published folk-tales and poems which he collected from the peasantry of Connaught and elsewhere, and brought forward his associate in the movement, G. W. Russell (1867-1935), who wrote as A. E. It was their pleasure to sophisticate the old legends too much with some infusion of an alien mysticism and symbolism. But they have withal brought a fresh clear stream into the current of English Literature, and at a time when it tended to grow sluggish and roily.

Then Yeats began to write his plays of Irish life and folk-lore. So did others, A. E., and George Moore; and Lady Gregory, with whose help an Irish dramatic tradition was actually founded, of which the Abbey Theatre, Dublin, is the world-famous local habitation. But the most momentous yield of the movement is the genius of John M. Synge (1871-1909), who preferred the matter of modern peasant Ireland to old fairy-lore, and fashioned a dialect for stage use out of the sweet and racy idiom which he himself gathered fresh in the Irish country-side. His plots too he finds in the same corners, especially those of his *Shadow of the Glen* and *The*

Tinker's Wedding. The row that rose everywhere over *The Playboy of the Western World* has made this his best known work.

The Movement is by no means spent, what with the playwright O'Casey, author of *Juno and the Paycock* (1924), Lord Dunsany, and a host of tellers of tales such as Birmingham and Donn Byrne, and O'Sullivan.

Yeats's best known plays, *Land of Heart's Desire* (1894) and *Cathleen ni Houlihan* (1902), contain suggestions of a genius transcending the limitations of a mere "movement," genius which in his case has found its more natural and finer utterance in the lyric. The man's inborn Celtic instinct for the supernatural has lent itself easily to occultism and symbolism, and sought satisfaction not only in Irish lore, but in the prophetic books of Blake, in Hermetic mysteries, the Cabbala, Neoplatonism, Swedenborg, Boehme, decadent French symbolism, and the like. The shadowy symbols of the tower, natural enough to one born in the land of towers, of the spiral stair, woven textures, the tree, appear and reappear especially in his later work. Many of his poems are warm and human with his friendships, his domestic affections, his recoil from the hardened conventions, his pain at the evanescence of youth and love and beauty, and at the mystery of death. His matter variously mingles with images of the wild and mysterious Irish legend, world, and landscape. All these elements have met in his shy, sensitive, intensely visionary nature to produce a new, rare, and lovely music, wind-blown, now deep, now tenuous, like the sounds in a sea shell which he hears as he listens in revery to his own mind. It is the music of *The Lake Isle of Innisfree*, of *He Remembers Forgotten Beauty*, of *The Wild Swans at Coole*, and it comes and goes through most of his song.

Affections kindred to those of the Celtic revival are in the short-lived "Kailyard School." Henley gave this name to a small group who took as their field the rural life of Scotland. They may have been encouraged by Stevenson and his success in such tales as *Thrawn Janet*, but their chief was a Scot of no less charm, James, now Sir James, Barrie (1860-1937). The two men were in many ways intellectual brothers, with their life-long understanding of childhood, and their sense of the irreconciliation between man's hard fate and the truth of the dream world. Barrie captured the Nineties with his sketches of a Scotch village in *Auld Licht Idylls* and *A Window in Thrums,* and his novels, *The Little Minister* and *Sentimental Tommy,* and has latterly (1932) returned to the Scottish countryside in *Farewell Miss Julie Logan.* With upwards of twenty-five plays he has delighted thousands of audiences. Among the best remembered are *Quality Street, The Admirable Crichton, Peter Pan,* and *Dear Brutus.* His sentimentality before the disillusionment of the war was generally palatable, and earned a substantial success for this canny Scot. But with it goes an antidote of practical fact, of things as they are, which does not, as one might expect, destroy or refute his world of dream and fancy, but possibly makes it the more convincing by putting it beyond our clumsy, mundane reach. Barrie shares with his compatriots something of the Scottish paradox of character which we have noticed before.

Perhaps as a part of its revolt from old conventions, and partly because it has ceased to be occupied with more transcendent things, literature has of late engaged itself engrossingly with the matter of "sex." Sex, to be sure, is, and ever has been, the concern of literature, but modern insistence upon it, where the treatment is worthy of consideration, springs no doubt from the natural instinct of an age adrift to seek a basis of reality somewhere, in the natural and physical facts of life if not higher, and to strip them of the artificial inhibitions which have partly or wholly made of them a teasing mystery. The tendency is already clear in that parent of much in current fiction, Samuel Butler, and has been greatly augmented by more recent psychological theories and discovery, Freudism and the like. To name modern instances will inform no one. D. H. Lawrence, like William Blake, courageous and honest in the matter to the point of being generally misunderstood, was an upright idealist, even so much of one that like the romantic Pantisocrats, he entertained schemes of an ideal community in the New World.

Probably at no time in its history has literature been so fascinated with the questions of how it produces itself as in the last generation. It is self-conscious as it has never been before. True, in times past literature has talked freely of its inspirations, its aims, its effects, its contents, and its forms, and sometimes got itself made fun of for so doing. Nowadays both critic and creator are more concerned with tendencies, theories, and technique. We are expected to distinguish as never before between romanticism, realism, classicism, naturalism, idealistic realism, impressionism, symbolism, imagism, and assorted isms borrowed from the plastic arts. Specimens of each can be found throughout the great writers of the past, thoug'i they probably would have been much surprised and puzzled by these modern subtleties. But the rise of these distinctions, some of them grown merely academic, shows into how many fragments the single over-arching dome of literature has been shattered.

Perhaps the preëminent questions at the moment are questions of technique, of metres, of style, of imagery, of imitation of Nature, and particularly of what poetry is after all, and what it is not. Nor have the inquiries been prompted so much by the old doctrine of art for art's sake, as by a spirit of discovery for art's sake.

We have already seen the English novelists going to school to the French and to the Russians to learn their craft. We find them discussing its problems—the novelist's detachment, the problem of structure, whether or no character is to be expressed and portrayed in terms of external things or places, as it is by the Edwardians, or in terms of inner consciousness, as it is by the Georgians. Virginia Woolf joins the issue in her *Mr. Bennett and Mrs. Brown.*

In its impatient repulse of tradition literature has naturally sought escape from traditional metrical forms, and found it in some measure in "free verse." Though admiration of Walt Whitman did much to promote experiment and discovery in this medium, he by no means invented it. Distinct traces are discernible in Matthew Arnold and indeed much earlier. But the tendency of free verse to dissolve into mere prose, or to lend itself as an instrument of affected vigor or violence, or to allege effects that are apparent only to the few initiate, if to them, goes to show that art does not flourish by freedom alone. The development of free verse by mere experiment seems for the present pretty much at an end.

All the greatest poets have been inventors of new metrical measures, but innovations of latter days have, like free verse, headed for release from the stricter inherited forms. A pioneer of discovery in this way was Father Gerard Manley Hopkins (1844-1889), who in the sixties, while still at Oxford, became a Catholic, along with Coventry Patmore, and in his later life taught Greek in Dublin. His early poems he burned, and his later ones did not see the light till his friend Robert Bridges, the Laureate, published them nearly twenty years after his death. In *The Bugler's First Communion, Inversnaid,* and *The Windhover* he anticipates and achieves many modern effects —in looser syntax but higher concentration of sense, in freer distribution and grouping of stresses, in the welding of sensuous fact and emotion in the very sound and movement of his words.

Bridges (1844-1930), though of the same age, long outlived him. His career lies in the middle of the highroad—by way of Eton, Oxford, Medicine, the best friends, an honorary degree, and, near seventy, the Laureateship. His verse, most of it written after he was forty, is much of it well-ordered modern treatment of classic myth, Demeter, Psyche, Prometheus, and Homeric heroes; and many of the short poems are lovely with the loveliness of English nature made lovelier by something in tune or phrase reminiscent of earlier poets once at home and vocal amid that loveliness.

But a germ of artistic discontent lodged within the man. At eighty-five, he produced his *Testament of Beauty,* a philosophical poem in four books, showing how two dominant instincts in man, Selfhood and Breed, may prove a ladder of ascent to a sense of perfect Beauty. It is mostly Platonic of course, with an intermingling of modern science, though the order and process of the poem make one think of Lucretius and his poem *On the Nature of Things*. From time to time come flights of great beauty as the poet seeks illustration or comparison in intimate nature. And the metre, owing ultimately to association with Hopkins, is new experiment. It moves "in my loose alexandrines," as he says, with the movement of a brook in the hills running down over a bed of small stones, tossing lightly, irregularly, with short smooth intervals, now slackening, now pausing, now hurrying on.

Whatever new music latent in the English tongue waits to be awakened with new experiment, some recent poets are content to seek their music in the strict traditional forms. One of these is the lamented Rupert Brooke (1887-1915), whose lively and infectious enjoyment of everything, touched and etherealized by some happy but undefined sense in him of the unseen, took its own care of the metres regardless of new or old.

Another is A. E. Housman (1859-1936), who in his *Shropshire Lad* (1896) and *Last Poems* (1922) uses again and again the old quatrain of four-and-three and like time-honored measures. He was lately a teacher of Latin and a ripe classical scholar at Cambridge, an eminence to which he rose in spite of his undergraduate failures, and ten years as a government clerk. His materials are the Shropshire countryside, and the loveliness and tragedy of young men and girls. Perhaps he finds for his purposes more tragedy than the facts would warrant. His verse keeps the restraint and economy of Greek poetry, if not always its ease and warm radiance; but it is invariably music. His language is studiously simple and unsophisticated, but with such simplicity as carries grave meaning and implies strongest feeling; whatever incident or story his poems enfold is hinted with a concrete detail here and there, after the way of the ballads.

But his work is not cold-blooded craftsmanship. Twice in his life the vein has flowed in him hot and free, once early in 1895, when most of his first volume was composed, again in 1922, though in less measure, when he was past sixty; at other times intermittently. In his lecture *The Name and Nature of Poetry* (1933) he sets down one of the rare and precious descriptions of a poet's experience—in this case his own—in the act of poetic creation. The description is not unlike those left by Burns and Milton. In the same lecture he essays the feat so tempting to modern critics generally of seeking the nature of poetry—"pure poetry," they call it—by distilling off every accessory which is not pure poetry, such as image, matter, thought, rhetoric, form, and the like. The refined quintessence seems to be in the nature of tune, but tune so exquisite that it is like the music of the spheres, for the angels only, but to the sensual ear, as Keats says, a ditty of no tone. Tune is of course the thing indispensable to poetry, but it cannot become poetry for most ears without the alloy of words and tones.

The quest is perhaps only another instance of the time's endeavor to rid itself of all its cumbrous heritage in its search for reality. Such endeavor and such rare natural music we discover in the poetry of William Blake; not his flaming vision of the things invisible, but his gift of song at once simple and powerful in its intimations. "Blake's meaning," says Housman, "is often unimportant or virtually non-existent, so that we can listen with all our hearing to his celestial tune."[1] At all events the influence of Blake upon the last generation of poets has been both strong and indeterminate.

In his Preface of 1925 John Masefield (1874—) distinguishes two kinds of poets, to either or both of which every poet belongs, according as "they strive towards a greater elaboration of artifice or for a greater closeness to reality." And to the school of reality or life he rightly implies his allegiance. But for him its discipline has been heavy. For three years in his teens he sailed about the world in a merchant training-ship, and faced destitution or scant living by humblest labor in New York and London. All this while he was seeking his own training for literature by constant reading and rereading of the poet's poets, Chaucer, Spenser, Shakespeare, Keats, Shelley. His fine poem *Biography* traces in part the growth of his poetic mind.

In his *Salt Water Ballads* his hearty vigor and his evident

[1] *Name and Nature of Poetry*, p. 39

authority on more elemental aspects of life made him Kipling's successor in the affections of the common man. His gift of song and his hard schooling in life have enabled him to sing a tune which echoes easily in the ear and voice of the multitude; in fact he says that only poetry which is made for the ear "can be widely or lastingly popular." In longer poems which made his success, *The Everlasting Mercy, The Widow in Bye Street, The Daffodil Fields, Dauber, Right Royal*, there is a deal of physical action, some of it brutal, in rather overwhelming contrast at times with human gentleness or tenderness. So exuberant is his genius that it has not in these earlier poems learned the high lesson of artistic economy, and their effect is hurt by their excess. Chaucer has taught him much in *Reynard the Fox*, though even there he has not learned it all. Yet the portraits in Part I thrill the reader with the poet's skill in adopting the devices and technique of Chaucer, and with their precision and deft rightness of stroke; but they invite an unhappy comparison, for they are in some way lacking in the basic humanity that makes the *Prologue* of Chaucer supreme and perennial.

Mingled with most of Masefield's poetry is the warmth of gentleness, or pity, or sympathetic humor, various phases of one and the same quality in his heart. And the beauty of England which never wears out through generations of poets, is suffused in his poems with a kind of enchantment arising perhaps from his early dreams of it afar off amid inhospitable seas or lands. Or perhaps his touch is charged with the magic that comes from seeing in everything lovely—act, object, scene, or word— an intimation of the Beauty in perfection unseen. On such intimation he insists, like his friend Bridges, like Alfred Noyes, and like Plato long since. But it is singularly authentic in one whom life and discipline had forced to consider at short range the ugliest aspects of the world.

Who knows? Possibly this late quickening of the new-old idealism may be an omen that poetry and art and life itself are approaching a new comprehension of spiritual realities—comprehension indispensable to highest achievement in all three.

PART NINE

ENGLISH LITERATURE
SINCE 1910

by Thomas Riggs, Jr.

English Literature Since 1910

THE YEAR 1910 is perhaps as good as any with which to begin a brief account of that revolutionary period in English letters which, from the midpoint of the twentieth century, is still called "modern." The period can be felt as a unit before its unity can be well described. The date, of course, is merely a convenience: in 1910 King Edward VII died and King George V took the throne. For a few years before the war, Georgian literature flourished in peace; its rebellions and experiments seemed merely literary matters. But between 1910 and 1920 the landscape changed: four years of war, the Russian revolution of 1917, change in all the major conventions of English life. The war itself was not so much the cause of change as its embodiment, and thus, paradoxically, not only the mark of a dislocation from the seeming peace of the past, but the sign of a new and somber relationship to it. The year 1914 saw the eruption into actuality of those volcanic distresses of spirit which had been sensed by Blake and Wordsworth, and which Matthew Arnold had noted fifty years before the war:

> This world which seems
> To lie before us like a land of dreams,
> So various, so beautiful, so new,
> Hath really neither joy, nor love, nor light,
> Nor certitude, nor peace, nor help for pain;
> And we are here as on a darkling plain
> Swept with confused alarms of struggle and flight,
> Where ignorant armies clash by night.

With the war of 1914, Arnold's metaphor became the banality of the newspapers.

From some such historical notes as these can be fashioned a sense of a period in English letters at once isolated within its own needs and, by their very force, turned into the past with new urgencies. Within the general framework of the period can be distinguished three phases, or literary generations, marked by the sharp twists of history during a half century of shocks and changes. The first phase, roughly from 1910 to 1930, is defined at its beginning by the First World War, which sent a generation of young Englishmen to the mud of the Western Front, and at its close by the world-wide economic depression starting with the collapse of the American securities market in the fall of 1929. Writers who were coming to maturity in the atmosphere of literary excitement of prewar London either died in the war—with Rupert Brooke or Wilfred Owen; or survived the traumatic experience of trench warfare, with Robert Graves or Herbert Read or Ford Madox Ford; or continued their creative work in isolation from the war, with James Joyce or D. H. Lawrence; or maintained throughout the war a poise which enabled them in the postwar years to renew their creative effort, with Virginia Woolf and E. M. Forster. But without exception, the experience of the war, direct or indirect, marked the generation, and released the sceptical, experimental, and iconoclastic literary exuberance of the 1920's.

The second phase begins with the economic depression at the end of the twenties. The rise, during the next decade, of European fascism, with its series of macabre triumphs from the occupation of the Rhineland through the Spanish Civil War to the rape of Poland, set the stage for a literature of heightened social and political awareness. For the generation of the thirties, the Spanish Civil War, in which half a dozen talented young Englishmen of letters lost their lives, was the decisive test. The Spanish Civil War was the last hope for the liberal dream of the popular front against fascism. On the left wing of the English literary scene were the Celtic radicalism of Hugh McDiarmid, and the Oxford liberalism of W. H. Auden and his allies. The political tendency of the writings of the time was strengthened by the growing involvement of England with the European political agony, and by the example of such continental anti-Fascist writers as the great Spanish poet Garcia Lorca and the German novelist Thomas Mann. "In our time," wrote Mann, "the destiny of man presents its meaning in political terms."

The experience of the Second World War, which opens the third phase, the adoption by Britain in the postwar elections of a bold experiment in monarchic socialism, and the tense "cold war" between Soviet Russia and her former western allies are too recent to be clearly seen in relation to literary history. But certain changes suggest a returning interest in the spiritual as well as the political terms of man's destiny. Dylan Thomas and George Barker have joined the new psychology with religion in their brilliant romantic poems. Evelyn Waugh and Graham Greene write their fables on the basis of Catholic apologetics. The Protestant tradition is strong in T. S. Eliot's plays; such theologians as Kierkegaard and Heidegger are inevitable premises of literary discussion. War, political idealism, and spiritual insight are, of course, not new to the modern period, nor the monopoly of any "literary generation."

To find a name for the elusive ghost of these forty disordered and changing years is not simple, but perhaps it will do to call their literary motivation "a search for order." Only a phrase so broad can suggest a common center for the tremendous variety, the manifold directions, of the literary efforts of the half century. The idea of "search" has its most visible embodiment in the myths of the quest, which animate such divergent works as Joyce's *Ulysses,* Eliot's *The Waste Land,* and D. H. Lawrence's *Aaron's Rod,* or the many novels which follow the gropings of a young man to some kind of equation between the actual and the possible. Such a motivation is as old as human self-consciousness: one can find three aspects of it of special importance to the twentieth century. The first is that aspect of the quest which links the contemporary writer to what is primitive or prerational in his own mind and to what is primitive or prerational in the mind of his race. Here he follows the lead of the depth psychology of Freud, Jung, and their disciples, as well as the anthropological discoveries of Sir James Frazier, Malinowski, and succeeding writers on the mythological and ritual bases of the human drama. The second aspect of the quest is its demand from the writer of an unflinching honesty in relation to his own time—an honesty which has violated previous canons of beauty, previous proscriptions as to the proper subject of literature. At this point the war between the writer and social convention becomes intense. The third aspect is the necessity of releasing language to its full power as the bearer of present truths: since 1910 English literature has passed through a series of experimental and revisionist developments in the techniques of prose and verse imitation which match the experiments of the great romantics in scope and promise. The writer's task has gained an added importance by the collapse of the previously accepted formula for order: the solid categories of nineteenth-century materialism have dissolved before the researches of Planck, Heisenberg, and Einstein: the principles of uncertainty and relativity have reduced to special cases, to a mere matter of luck, the predictable and limited material universe of Huxley, Tyndall, and Spencer. Like Atlas, the writer has shouldered the burden of the world, and it is no wonder if, at times, he has staggered under that weight. What is remarkable is the heroism he has displayed. A famous passage from James Joyce's *A Portrait of the Artist as a Young Man* can serve as an epigraph for the writer's task and for the three aspects of his quest: "Welcome, O life! I go forth to encounter for the millionth time the reality of experience, and to forge in the smithy of my soul the uncreated conscience of my race."

Two traditions of nineteenth-century European writing have been important for modern English poets and novelists. The first is the tradition of naturalism, which from Flaubert in the novel and Ibsen in the drama has given later writers some of the humility, responsibility, and courage of the physical scientist before his world of quantity; the second is the tradition of symbolism, which, with the direct example of the French poets from Baudelaire to Valéry, has insisted upon form and structure in literature, and upon literature as an art of many dimensions. Through the first, modern writers have met their world; through the second, they have established contact with the medieval and classical symbolic interpretations of existence. The two traditions are to a certain extent antipathetic, but the best writing of the time has maintained and extended them as a double standard of allegiance: to life and to art.

POETRY: THE FIRST PHASE

The first generation of Georgian poets found its experience in the First World War. Rupert Brooke and Wilfred Owen did not survive it; Robert Graves, Herbert Read, and Siegfried Sassoon survived it to write about it.

The best of the war poets was Wilfred Owen (1893–1918), whose poems are marked by great sincerity and passion. In the preface for the volume of verse he did not live to see published, Owen wrote: "My subject is War, and the pity of War. The Poetry is in the pity. Yet these elegies are to this generation in no sense consolatory. They may be in the next. All a poet can do today is warn. That is why true Poets must be truthful." In such poems as *Greater Love* and *Anthem for Doomed Youth* the images of love and delight, the landscapes of the English countryside, are transformed into the images of death, the terrible landscapes of the western front. These transformations are the precise image of the experience of his generation: their shock is the power of his poetry:

> Red lips are not so red
> As the red stones kissed by the English dead. . . .

The remarkable dialogue in hell called *Strange Meeting* is perhaps the most impressive of these elegies to the "undone years." Here can be seen the technical vigor which made Owen's work so influential for the next generation of English poets: the use of assonance and off-rhyme as an instrument in imaging the discords which were his subject:

> I am the enemy you killed, my friend.
> I knew you in the dark, for so you frowned.
> Yesterday through me as you jabbed and killed.
> I parried, but my hands were loath and cold.
> Let us sleep now. . . .

Wilfred Owen was killed in action a week before the end of the war.

The early poems of Herbert Read (b. 1893) were influenced by the imagist movement, which, under the stimulus of the brilliant young philosopher T. E. Hulme and with the tireless propaganda of the American poet Ezra Pound, commanded some attention in prewar London. The imagists attacked the overpompous and overdecorated remnants of Victorian rhetoric in the name of a Spartan poetic economy. From the various manifestoes of the movement put out between 1913 and 1917, its principles can be summarized. Poetry must be compact: no word that does not advance the subject, no word that is not precise. Poetry must be concrete: the abstract judgment, and the "message" must be shunned, the image must be all. Poetry, in the words of F. S. Flint, the movement's earliest historian, must be composed "in sequence of the musical phrase, not in sequence of the metronome." Read's austere and sharp pictures of warfare in free verse are imagist poems; in his longer poems he retains the clarity and concision of imagism while going beyond its limitations. Among the most moving of Read's poems are those in which he compares the generations of the First and Second World Wars—*To a Conscript in 1940,* and *Ode written during the battle of Dunkirk, May, 1940,* as fine a poem as any on the "occasion" of the Second World War.

The anecdotal war poems of Robert Graves (b. 1895) show little of the mordant satirical and sensuous power which began to appear in his poetry toward the end of the nineteen twenties. In his later poems, written within traditional forms, Graves set up images in mockery of a dwindled and degenerate time, corrupted from its true vigor by perverse idealisms. In such memorable poems as *The Bards, The Eremites, Ogres and Pygmies,* and *Grotesques,* the menacing figures of the primitive, the archaic, the barbaric devour the feeble shapes of the present. Few English poems of the period have so sharp an edge.

Four older poets writing within the period—Hardy, Bridges, de la Mare, and Yeats—have been particularly important for the younger men. For W. H. Auden, the leading British poet of the 1930's, the poems of Thomas Hardy were his first poetic inspiration. As Auden writes, Hardy's "humility before nature, his sympathy for the suffering and the blind, and his sense of proportion are as necessary now as they ever were." The long philosophical poem of Robert Bridges, *The Testament of Beauty,* is less read than praised. It has perhaps been important, however, that the poem is there: a music of ideas, waiting until Plato is back in fashion. The poems of Walter de la Mare (b. 1879) are in different case. Since the publication of his 1906 volume de la Mare has continued to write poems of which a handful are of absolute perfection in the English lyric tradition. Delicate and sure in musical phrase, subtle and evocative of the penumbral moods of the mind, they deserve to be companioned with the poems of Campion and Landor.

Hardy, Bridges, and de la Mare remain aloof in their distinct and formed individuality from the stresses of the modern period. With William Butler Yeats (1865–1939), the modern period was the occasion for a poetic rebirth, a striking out on a new line, a rediscovery of energy in middle life.

In the year 1910 W. B. Yeats was forty-five years old; his career was visible and assured. He was the leader of the movement known as the Irish Renaissance; the astute organizer of a successful theatre; a poet and playwright of considerable distinction but not of the first rank. Few lovers of English poetry could have suspected the miraculous transformation that was then taking place. The verse that he had written since 1889, with all its graces, sounded the Pre-Raphaelite note of passivity and languor. But by the time of his death in 1939, he could look back upon twenty-five years of a productive vitality almost unmatched in the history of English poetry: the creation of a body of lyric verse which, for vigor and excitement, equals the verse of Donne and Blake. When, in 1924, he was awarded the Nobel Prize, he wrote: "My unpractised verse was full of infirmity, my Muse old as it were; and now I am old and rheumatic, and nothing to look at, but my Muse is young. I am even persuaded that she is like those angels in Swedenborg's vision and moves 'towards the day-spring of her youth.' "

The body of poetry which begins with *The Green Helmet*

(1910), reaches its peak of strength in the magnificent symbolic poems of *The Tower* (1929) and *The Winding Stair* (1931), and is recapitulated in *Last Poems and Plays* (1940), is of great variety and richness and possessed of an absolute musical mastery. As with the poems of Blake, the individual lyrics are part of a larger whole. Poem comments on poem, symbols echo and extend from one poem to another until the whole body of verse assumes a complex unity, playing upon great themes. The vision of time which animates the great poems of this period is one of discord; discord in the civilization, discord in the soul. The individual man is torn between his allegiance to the passionate sensual life, "the fury and the mire of human veins," and his aspirations toward the changeless state of being, where the soul is released from time and change. In the Byzantium of the first Christian millennium Yeats found his symbol for that state of life in which man is closest to the supernatural, and in his poems it becomes that point at which the axes of life in time and timeless life intersect: where the human is transhumanised, whether it be in moments of vision or in death itself.

As conflict is the law of the individual life in time, so for Yeats it is the law of history, and he saw the time in which he lived as the end in conflict of one great cycle of the historical process. This intuition rises to prophetic vision in one of his greatest poems, *The Second Coming,* with its striking apprehension of the present:

> Things fall apart, the center cannot hold,
> Mere anarchy is loosed upon the world,
> The blood-dimmed tide is loosed, and everywhere
> The ceremony of innocence is drowned.
> The best lack all conviction, and the worst
> Are full of passionate intensity.

But the notation of discord is not enough. "To me," Yeats wrote to Lady Dorothy Wellesley, "the supreme aim is an act of faith or reason to make one rejoice in the midst of tragedy. An impossible aim; yet I think it true that nothing can injure us." Increasingly from 1919 to his death, this note of tragic joy—or, on another level, a wild and fantastic humor—become major elements in his verse. "No man can create," Yeats wrote, "who does not believe with all his blood and nerve that man's soul is immortal." It is not that Yeats, as he grew older, loosened his grip upon "the fury and the mire," the physical passions of earth. But in his most sensual poems the passion derives authority from the sense of timeless life pressing in upon it, intensifying it, making of the individual actors in the human drama the protagonists in the history of the soul. So we see him, in such a masterly late poem as *Lapis Lazuli,* staring on "all the tragic scene" and drawing his power to rejoice from his sense of reaches of spirit that remain inviolable.

After Yeats, the most influential poet of the modern period is the American-born Thomas Stearns Eliot (b. 1888): Yeats and Eliot share the distinction of having been awarded the Nobel prize for literature.

Eliot has succeeded to the commanding place at the center of English literary life held in other times, in other ways, by such men as John Dryden and Matthew Arnold. Like his compatriot Henry James, Eliot, who became a British citizen in 1927, brought to English life the full force of the New England Puritan tradition. His grandfather was a Unitarian minister; he himself was educated in philosophy and languages at Harvard, the Sorbonne, and Cambridge. Like Henry James, Eliot has based the authority of his writing on a keen and discriminating moral insight.

Eliot's early poetry, from *Prufrock and Other Observations* (1917) to *The Waste Land* (1922), reclaimed for verse the satirical, dramatic, and descriptive latitudes that had been taken over by prose fiction. The substance of these poems is a moral revulsion against the sterilities of a materialist society. The startling images, the sudden transitions, the brilliant and unexpected flashes of wit, were something new in the contemporary poetic idiom. The poems themselves are dramatic rather than lyric, and rely heavily upon literary reminiscence. But despite their erudition, the poems bear the memorable music and the unmistakable authority of the individual poet. They are the fabric of his vision, and bring to us unforgettable images and characters of contemporary life: pathetic and futile J. Alfred

Prufrock, who has measured out his life with coffee spoons; Gerontion, stiffening in a rented house, with his "thoughts of a dry brain in a dry season"; the animal and exuberant Sweeney; or the lady of his loveliest early poem, *La Figlia che Piange* who disturbs the memory—

> Sometimes these cogitations still amaze
> The troubled midnight and the noon's repose.

Eliot's early sketches of spiritual impotence reach their complete statement in *The Waste Land* (1922), published in the same year as Joyce's *Ulysses*. The landscape, as in Browning's *Childe Roland,* is symbolic of a spiritual desolation and terror; it is generalized by the merging of images of the modern "unreal city" and by the shuffling of images of modern life with images from history. Broken images of spiritual sterility, sexual sterility, sterility of the land itself mount into a total sense of the horror of the void:

> I will show you fear in a handful of dust.

Animating this inanimate world, and embodied in the ambiguous figure who is its conscience, is the narrative of the quest for salvation, based upon a version of the Grail legend. It is the quest that embodies what there is here of hope, and adds to these despairs the aspiration of prayer, an aching upward from the area of living death.

The prayer for belief, for salvation, for rebirth, which is one aspect of *The Waste Land,* begins to take on specifically Christian terms in the lovely lyric and meditative series of poems called *Ash Wednesday* (1930). The crest of this development, and one of the high points of English religious poetry, is the magnificent series of meditations called *Four Quartets* (1945). One can note throughout the progress of Eliot's poetry from *The Waste Land* to *Four Quartets* an increasing reliance upon simplicity of statement, a dropping away of the abrupt shocks and transitions of the earlier poems, and a gradual abandonment of the dramatic and polyphonic modes for the mode of personal reflection and the clear control of the single voice. The *Four Quartets* are meditations on time and history in relation to the timelessness of spirit. They move in passages of lyric beauty to the evanescent vision of the "heart of light," the moment in the rose garden "in and out of time" where "the past and future are conquered and reconciled," where

> all shall be well
> And all manner of thing shall be well.

The early poems of T. S. Eliot's contemporary, Edith Sitwell (b. 1887), create a unique world whose relations to actuality are as tantalizing as those of the world of music. Perhaps because of their deliberate contempt for the middle-class world, with its inheritances of naturalism and of Arnold's "high seriousness," these poems appeal to a specialized taste, and have been treated with silence or wariness by most critics.

The most engaging of Miss Sitwell's early poetry is to be found in *Bucolic Comedies* (1923), *The Sleeping Beauty* (1924), and *Façade* (1926), which display her masterful evocation of the world of pastoral, legend, and baroque comedy. To a time given to a direct apprehension of the images of war and of the megalopolis, these worlds appear as worlds of escape through artifice. But all poetry is artifice, and Miss Sitwell chose to meet artifice head on, to choose unpopular artifices which are not evasions, but foils to reality.

With *Gold Coast Customs* (1929), which has been called Miss Sitwell's *Waste Land,* the world changes. The intricate harmonies become the musical accompaniment for a nightmare, in which the images of the London slum, of Lady Bamburger, and of the African savage merge into a lurid vision of evil and the rotted heart. The poem takes its place beside Conrad's *The Heart of Darkness* as an evocation of an experience of the dark forces behind the façades of civilized life.

In her later poems—brought together in *The Canticle of The Rose* (1949)—the precise ballets of the early poems and the terror of *Gold Coast Customs* are abandoned for a sibylline role. In the longer rhapsodic line, Miss Sitwell undertakes a full discursive account of a world of tragic dimensions. The force of statement is added to the brilliance of imagery. This later vision, like that of Blake or Yeats, is built of murderous opposites—the sun and the darkness, fire and ice, the heart and the hambone. The imagery is idiosyncratic but powerful; the poems reach dimensions of great dignity, and, occasionally, of tragic grandeur.

PROSE FICTION: THE FIRST PHASE

The work of half a dozen Georgian novelists—Joyce, Lawrence, Forster, Virginia Woolf, Huxley, Ford Madox Ford—is of the first rank or near it. It would be difficult to find a generation of comparable achievement in the two hundred years' history of the modern English novel, nor six writers who display such sharply divergent attitudes toward the common problems of the life of their day.

Yeats's image of the artist was a part of an aristocratic dream, and his imagination lingered among "ancestral houses," with their custom and their ceremony. His countryman, James Joyce (1882–1941), born in a middle-class Catholic household in Dublin, and knowing from childhood the bitter scrabble for money and status on the edge of destitution, maintained some of the smoldering Jacobin subversion of a class whose nightmare is of landlords. He fought with the Jacobin's hidden weapons: in the famous phrase from *A Portrait of the Artist as a Young Man,* "silence, exile and cunning." A Savonarola disguised as a Berlitz language teacher, working through years of poverty, isolation, and pain in Trieste, Zurich, and Paris, he fashioned in his fiction a frightening image of the Dublin from which he was a voluntary exile. Educated by the Jesuits, he brought to the vocation of the artist some of the single-minded and intense devotion of the Society of Jesus to its calling.

Of his first book, *Dubliners* (1914), a series of short stories, Joyce wrote: "my intention was to write a chapter in the moral history of my country and I chose Dublin because that city seemed to me to be the center of corruption." Paralysis of mind and spirit is the key to these beautifully ordered sketches of a modern purgatory. But the idea of corruption derives its force from the idea of the incorruptible, as the image of paralysis depends upon the image of the straight body; so these stories derive their pathos from the momentary glimpses of the possibilities of human life with which the more sensitive of Joyce's characters are blessed, or cursed.

All of these sensitive and damned souls are, of course, shadows of the young Joyce himself, and it is the history of this young Joyce, under the name of Stephen Dedalus, that makes up *A Portrait of the Artist as a Young Man* (1914). The supple and lucid prose of *Dubliners,* itself a high art, has here an increased color, range, and vitality, sensitive to the varied tasks put upon it; to the presentation of such memorable scenes as the Christmas dinner disrupted by the bitterness surrounding the death of Parnell; or the terrible sermon on hell which drives young Stephen from his experiments in lechery; or the lucid exposition of aesthetic in the last chapter. The action of the book is the discovery by Stephen, in defiance of the choices of self offered him by his society, of his identity as an artist.

With *Ulysses* (1933), his most triumphant creative act, Joyce transcended the almost Jansenistical severity and restraint of his earlier writing and moved into a new dimension of creative exuberance. The critical storms surrounding the linguistic boldness of this work—its extraordinary series of technical *tours de force,* its violation of the taboos of "what one doesn't mention" —have distracted attention from its substance. But it would be a shallow view of ·art to suppose that the release of technical gusto which marks the book was not also a sign of a deeper spiritual release. In *A Portrait,* Joyce had drawn the hero of intransigence, facing the stifling demands of his society with Lucifer's proud "non serviam." The same Dedalus, still Lucifer-proud, suffering now the agonies of conscience, appears as one of the three main characters in *Ulysses.* But, though one could imagine Dedalus writing *A Portrait,* one could not possibly imagine him writing *Ulysses.* To Joyce's vision has been added a new dimension of which Dedalus is incapable: the dimension of compassion, of transigent humility, of human hope, kindness, and love. Its vehicle is the hero of the book, Leopold Bloom, a middle-aged Jewish advertising solicitor, failure, and cuckold. Through the labyrinth of Dublin on June 16, 1904—"Bloomsday"—Joyce follows his hero with wit, parody, satire, gargantuan mockery, and great tenderness. The third of the central characters is Bloom's adulterous wife Molly, the feminine principle in nature, the corrupt and incorruptible Magna Mater, whose long and unrestrained soliloquy rises to lyric heights at the close of the book.

Among many devices which Joyce uses in presenting his characters, the chief is the Homeric parallel. In the title of the book Joyce asks us to compare Mr. Bloom with the prudent Greek king in the *Odyssey,* and a reader familiar with the *Odyssey* will be able to enforce the parallel in considerable detail. On the most evident level, the comparison is a vehicle of outrageous comedy, and comedy is a prime spirit of the book; but on a deeper level, Joyce is not using Ulysses merely as a point from which to mock poor Mr. Bloom; in a deeper sense, Bloom *is* Ulysses,—that at least of Ulysses which, through the banalities, vulgarities, degradations, treacheries, deceits, frustrations, and rebuffs of the city, still pursues indomitably the quest of beauty, the dream of the spirit's home.

The tendency towards pedantry in technique which gets in the reader's way in some of the later stages of *Ulysses* dominates the disintegration of language which is the mark of Joyce's last book, *Finnegan's Wake* (1949). Despite passages of great beauty arising from among multilingual puns and complex verbal mechanics, and despite the claims of those of Joyce's critics who have been able to read it with attention, it is probable that this last exercise of Joyce's genius will remain in great part unavailable even to those of his readers who have followed him willingly along the way.

The most disturbing literary personality of the modern period is displayed in the works of that erratic genius, D. H. Lawrence (1885–1930). For the twenty crowded years of his creative life he poured forth novels, short stories, poems, travel books, essays, apocalyptic tracts, and letters in profusion. In each of his Protean forms his achievement is unmistakable. His reputation has suffered from his talent for making enemies and exasperating friends; his work has suffered from what can be called a frequent collapse of art. At such points his novels cease to be novels and become a shrill scolding of the world in which he lived so intensely.

Lawrence's intensity rose out of the conflicts of his formative years, which are portrayed in his novel *Sons and Lovers*
(1913). Lawrence—the Paul Morel of the novel—was the son
of a coal-miner and of a middle-class woman of narrow but
intense moral and cultural fervor. The struggle of wills between husband and wife, ending in the destruction of the husband as a force in the family and the emotional dominance of
his wife, was, for the boy, traumatic, and burned into his mind
the shapes of conflict by which he was to see the world. In this
struggle were formed Lawrence's special intuitions: his protective tenderness for the primitive roots of personality; his revulsion against the violation of instinct at the hands of the
intellectual will. His life was a quest, of which his writings are
the reports, for a resolution of the personal conflict, for a
harmony of the spirit, for a sexual harmony between man and
woman, for a culture in which such unity of being was possible.
It was this quest that sent him to America, to Australia, to Italy,
to Mexico, and back to the Etruscan past for images to set
against those of the industrial England which he loved and
hated. Like Thoreau, he based his morality on a dialectic of life
and not-life. He attacked those false rituals which transform
man to thing; he searched for and celebrated those rituals
which release man's fullest potentialities.

The main progress in Lawrence's work over two decades is a
growing explicitness on his part, an increasing realization of the
meanings of his early attempts to image experience. For this
reason his work is curiously consistent and can be treated all of
a piece. From the beginning, his writings show the dual aspect
of criticism and celebration. As a critic of life he is close to
Joyce and Eliot. The portrait of Clifford Chatterley in his last
novel, *Lady Chatterley's Lover* (1929), sums up his critical
insights. Clifford Chatterley has returned paralyzed from the
war. His warped energy turns in two directions: to the ruthlessly
efficient management of the Tevershall pits, of which he is the
owner; and to the production of a brilliant and soulless literary
criticism, which is rewarded with the applause of the coteries.
"When I read the first version," Lawrence wrote in a defense
of that much abused book, which, because of its frankness in

description of the act of love, is still banned in England and America, "I recognized that the lameness of Clifford was symbolic of the paralysis, the deeper emotion or passional paralysis, of most men of his sort or class today." Such a paralysis is not only a warping of one man's spirit; it is the condition for the spread of the industrial blight over the English pastoral landscape—a black and soul-killing insolence to the natural rhythms of earth.

The cancerous disorder of Chatterley's personality is a result of the victory of the "mental-spiritual" part over the "blood-consciousness" of man—in more conventional terms, of intellect over instinct. As a result, the soul, which Lawrence conceived as the full harmony of personality, is destroyed. The struggle for unity of soul against the vampirism of either isolated part is the action of his novels. In *The Plumed Serpent* (1926), his extraordinary novel of Mexico, Lawrence sees North America as the civilization in which Chatterley's personality rules, in which the "mental-spiritual" consciousness has destroyed the soul. America is "the great death-continent, . . . plucking, plucking at the created soul in a man, till at last it plucked out the growing germ, and left him a creature of mechanism and automatic reaction." But the Mexican Indian is equally "half-created," with a mindless blood-consciousness. It is not in the name of a reversion to mindlessness that Lawrence writes.

Where Lawrence's hymns to unity of being are not destroyed by humorless Messianic delusions, his writing moves into a quality of beauty and mystery. Of his novels, *The Rainbow* (1915) most abounds with a sense of the possible harmony between men and nature, particularly in the earlier sections, where the Brangwens maintain their allegiance to the old pastoral landscape of England. The moonlit scene where the young lovers become conscious of their love as they move back and forth at their work among the wheatsheaves is one of these passages of pure fulfillment: the trappings of life drop away, and the actors become anonymous, ceremonial, moving with formal rhythms through an encounter determined by forces of earth larger than their isolated egos. Here we get a sense of what Lawrence meant in his essay on *The Novel* (1925) when he said, "In the great novel, the felt but unknown flame stands behind all the characters, and in their words and gestures there is a flicker of the presence."

It is in his description of the relations between men and their landscape that Lawrence's writing is perhaps most fully satisfactory, with that sureness which is the mark of true individuality. It distinguishes his finest poems—those contained in the volume *Birds, Beasts and Flowers*—or the magnificent unfinished poem *The Ship of Death,* which stands with Whitman's *Lilacs* as a poem of acceptance. Lawrence's superlative travel books—*The Sea and Sardinia* (1921) and *Mornings in Mexico* (1927)—are the record of his sensitivity to what he called the "spirit of place." He ranks with the greatest English writers on nature—Wordsworth, Thoreau, Hardy—and with such contemporary naturalists and travelers as W. H. Hudson and T. E. Lawrence.

Mention must be made of his fine prose tales,—for example, *The Prussian Officer, The Fox,* and *The Rocking-Horse Winner.* In their brief compass Lawrence attained a perfection unmarred by the collapse that too often takes place in his novels. And the record is incomplete without citing those visionary, pseudoscientific, and entirely personal tracts, *The Fantasia of the Unconscious* (1922) and *Apocalypse* (1939), in which he tried, like Yeats in *A Vision,* to formalize the insights to which his art had led him.

The disarming urbanity of the novels and stories of E. M. Forster (b. 1879), the felicity and tact of their prose, would suggest that he has little in common with the intense and apocalyptic figure of Lawrence. Forster's novels are conservative in idiom and in form. Their kinship is with the central tradition of the English novel of manners, as exemplified by Thackeray and Jane Austen, whom Forster, in his *Aspects of the Novel* (1927), places at the center of his admirations.

And yet the motivations of Forster's work suggest a relationship—in substance if not in intensity or direction—with Lawrence's work. Where Lawrence conducts a brilliant frontal assault on the conventional English gentleman—Clifford Chatterley, for example—in the names of Nature and of Eros,

Forster permits the English gentleman to glimpse—out of the corner of the eye, as it were, occasionally with the shock of recognition—the evanescent and disturbing forms of Nature and of Eros, and then to go about his business, if he can. The confrontations which Forster arranges in *Where Angels Fear to Tread* (1905) or such of his stories as *The Story of a Panic* or *The Road to Colonos* provide him with a range from high ironic comedy to pathos or to the pure terror of the unknown, the terror of the "civilized" person in the face of the atavistic shapes which sometimes rise up to appall him. Such confrontations provide the form of these fictions. The Englishman is sent on a journey to Italy or to India or to Greece, and there, among the reminiscences of older gods than his, he faces the spectres of his limitations. This catching of the Englishman off guard in a country not his own—the method whereby Henry James trapped his equally elusive American quarry—is carried to its greatest complexity and brilliance in *A Passage to India* (1924).

There is an air of fantasy throughout Forster's work—a delicate counterpoint of mythology and symbol—with which he protects his most serious values. In *A Passage to India,* for all the solidity and skill wherewith he investigates Anglo-Indian manners, the air of fantasy pervades the landscape against which the tragi-comedy is played out. It echoes in the sinister and mysterious Malabar Caves, within which Miss Quested has her ambiguous duel with the spirit of place, and shimmers at the edge of the Englishman's limited comprehension of a land of ancient mysteries. This air embodies—or disembodies—all Mr. Forster's sense of those undefined and primitive forces which, he suggests, it would be well for the Englishman to learn to recognize and to propitiate.

Of all the fine novels of the Georgian period, those of Virginia Woolf (1882-1941) are perhaps the most fully balanced and harmonious. In the best of them—*Mrs. Dalloway* (1925), *To the Lighthouse* (1927), and *The Waves* (1931)—technical means, opinions, and insight are fused. In her essay on modern fiction in *The Common Reader* (1925), she speaks of the nature of her insight and suggests her means. "Life is not a series of gig-lamps symmetrically arranged, but a luminous halo, a semi-transparent envelope surrounding us from the beginning of consciousness to the end. Is it not the task of the novelist to convey this varying, this unknown and uncircumscribed spirit, whatever aberration or complexity it may display, with as little mixture of the alien and external as possible?"

The vehicle for her perception of life is character—not character perceived, catalogued, categorized, forced into place from the outside, but character unfolding from within. Her characters exist not by virtue of "character"—though they achieve full existence—but by virtue of a certain kind of consciousness which is capable of perceiving the luminous halo. Her novels are the poems of that consciousness; their structures are analogues of its structures; the beautiful rhythms of her prose suggest its rhythms. Plot, in the conventional sense, becomes—as it did for Joyce and Proust—the delights, hesitations, and distresses of this consciousness in its unfoldings. The adventures of this consciousness, as embodied in Mrs. Dalloway, or in Mrs. Ramsay in *To the Lighthouse,* or in the six characters who form a spectrum of consciousness in *The Waves,* are the substance of her novels. When the halo is at its most luminous, life pulses and gleams like a Renoir canvas, and her characters reach the intuition of a moment like a blessing. But a novel is not a painting, and the moment cannot be arrested. The moment of luminosity is subject to peril: Mrs. Dalloway "always had the feeling that it was very, very dangerous to live even one day." The dangers have many names. There is the danger of the over-extension of consciousness itself, which, as with poor shell-shocked Septimus Smith in *Mrs. Dalloway,* becomes "macerated, until only the nerve fibres are left, . . . spread like a veil upon a rock." Or there is the direct assault of brutality on the part of hard tyrannical intelligence—usually men—capable of some "indescribable outrage—forcing your soul." Or finally, there is the danger of time, the horror of death, with which Mrs. Woolf's novels, like the plays of Webster or the poems of Donne, are filled.

The novels of Virginia Woolf might be called, in John Peale Bishop's phrase, "a criticism of ideas by life." For Aldous Huxley (b. 1894), in the years following the First World War, the novel was a means of attacking life for its difference from ideas; of assaulting life, stripping from it its pieties and protections, exposing it to the ruthlessness and mockery of a brilliant, erudite, and self-tormenting intellect. Huxley's family history involved him in the chief categories of nineteenth-century ideas. His grandfather was Thomas Huxley, the great Darwinian; his mother was related to Matthew Arnold. His novels are intimate with the arts and sciences; information about and metaphors from biology, architecture, and music crowd their pages. The shocks and crises of his novels are twentieth-century versions of the shocks and crises of the Victorians; the inability to reconcile the account of man as protoplasm with the account of man as made in the image and likeness of God.

In his first novel, *Crome Yellow* (1921), Huxley's gayety and wit are at their most diverting, and the light touch of comedy is maintained. In *Antic Hay* (1923), *Those Barren Leaves* (1925), and *Point Counter Point* (1928), the gayety becomes more desperate, the parody more murderous, the wit increasingly the instrument of self-laceration. Huxley's mimetic genius, which lies in the imitation not of life but of talk about life, produces, passes in review, and mocks the whole parade of intellectual attitudes of the nineteen twenties; those of the hedonist, the *précieux,* the scientist, the cultist, the aesthete, the sexual mystic. To each he assigns a human name; each is permitted to define himself, and—though some are treated more courteously than others—to damn himself in his own words. Precisely nothing is left: "Nil, world-soul, spiritual informer of all matter."

But Nil is a sickness of the spirit, and as the bitterness and life-loathing of the novels increase, and the brilliance becomes more livid, one can see Huxley's increasingly serious attempts to discover a figure (and an idea for which the figure stands) who will withstand the pull toward the void, who will replace thought with belief. Such a figure in *Point Counter Point* is Rampion, who was modeled on D. H. Lawrence. But Rampion, though treated kindly, is approached from without: Lawrence's intuitions of the primitive become ideas of those intuitions. The end of Lawrence's influence is seen in the terrible—and shockingly funny—projection of Utopia *à rebours, Brave New World* (1932). Here the Savage who opposes the scientific and hygienic world of the future with something approaching Lawrence's "blood-consciousness" ends in suicide.

More important than Lawrence's "blood-consciousness" in Huxley's quest for belief is his discovery of Hindu Mysticism, from which he derived an idea of self-abnegation and self-annihilation. This Indianism first became evident in *Those Barren Leaves,* and took over the controls from satire in the last half of *Eyeless in Gaza* (1936). It provides the "message" of Lawrence's novels of the forties, in which the comic inspiration labors under an increasingly heavy burden. Since life led to Nil, perhaps the denial of life might lead to Nirvana. Somewhere between Nil and Nirvana Huxley lost touch with the area in which human life is lived.

Huxley's early novels belong to a tradition of intellectual comedy which, since the days of the Restoration, has committed secular sacrilege against middle-class standards of English manners in the name of what in English life is alien, hostile, and unreconciled. On professions of virtue it looks with a feline eye. To sincerity it opposes elegance; to thrift and hard work, the baroque and frivolous; to Puritan virtue, Catholic decadence; to sentiment, wit; to realism, fantasy, parody, and caricature. Its heroes are the dandy, the cat, and the terrible child. It is, perhaps, the last and most infuriating weapon of the aristocratic idea against the middle class.

The tradition is established by Congreve, glints in the eyes of Peacock and Disraeli, and reaches a high point in the stories and plays of Oscar Wilde. In the twentieth century it has produced a series of minor masterpieces. The title of Max Beerbohm's amusing *Zuleika Dobson* (1911) suggests the interesting planes of fantasy and actuality from which the humor of the work springs. A more cruel chill invades the high comedy in the short stories of H. H. Munro (1870–1916), who wrote under the name of "Saki." Into Saki's witty notations of English manners are introduced shapes of the inhuman and the macabre: the cat, the hyena, the stoat comment upon the human scene. The standard of good form is set by the carnivore. Saki's particular sympathy with a childhood which must fight with its own non-moral weapons against a league of giants is shared by Richard Hughes (b. 1900). Hughes's novel *A High Wind in Jamaica* (1929) is a symbolical victory for childhood in its war: the pirates prove no match for the savage little cherubs. Somewhat apart from these, but sharing in their dislike for conventional standards, Norman Douglas's *South Wind* (1917) combines sophistication and a beautifully burlesqued antiquarianism in an account of a collection of eccentrics on the island of Capri.

Like Edith Sitwell's early poems, the comic novels of Ronald Firbank (1886–1929) present a special case of the modern baroque. Firbank himself is in the tradition of the English eccentrics: his evanescent, shy, nerve-wracked figure flits through the memoirs of the period like, in Osbert Sitwell's phrase, "a witty and decadent Red Indian." The strangely persuasive world of his novels is brightly colored, glittering, decadent, artificial, more closely related to the *commedia dell'arte* than to anything in the history of the novel. It is a world without "morals" but not without values. Like Blake in "The Little Black Boy," Firbank, in his beautiful Negro pastoral *Prancing Nigger* (1924), is capable of the vision of innocence. Tragedy turns to poignance of innocence and love betrayed in *The Flower Beneath the Foot* (1923), whose title is its theme. Firbank presents the actors in his strange world without the harsh prerogative of judgment. Judgment or forgiveness are not his, in charity, to allot, and even the most corrupt of his epicene churchmen or shameless great ladies is capable of sanctity. In his last novel, *Concerning the Eccentricities of Cardinal Pirelli* (1926), the worldly ecclesiast dies in most compromising circumstances, but his death is somewhat of a transfiguration. "Now that the ache of life, with its fevers, passions, doubts, its routine, vulgarity and boredom, was over, his serene, unclouded face was a marvelment to behold. Very great distinction and sweetness was visible there, together with much nobility, and love, all magnified and commingled."

The voice that speaks from the center of the English experience of the war generation is that of Ford Madox Ford (1873–1939). In *Some Do Not* (1924), *No More Parades* (1925), *A Man Could Stand Up* (1926), and *The Last Post* (1928) Ford presented the experience of his central character, Christopher Tietjens, from the prewar years through the fighting and into the aftermath of peace. In these four linked novels, which were published in one volume as *Parade's End* (1950), Ford was moved to speak for the tragedy of his time. His hero, a Yorkshireman of the ruling class, maintained an eighteenth-century passion for truth in speech and integrity in conduct, through private and public hells, in a time when hysteria—the destructive element—mounted like a fever in the individual spirit and in the spirit of the mass of men. In *It Was the Nightingale* (1933), a memoir, Ford described his return to England after his service as a line officer. "It had been revealed," he wrote, "that beneath ordered life itself was stretched the merest film with, beneath it, the abysses of Chaos. One had come from the frail shelter of the line to a world more frail than any canvas hut." There were many men who recounted the actualities of war, but Ford's luck of perception was to see the war as an image of the world from which it had developed. War was a revelation of the abysses of Chaos, and it was the heroism of Tietjens—and of Ford—to struggle to retain the vision of order within a chaotic world.

Ford's talents were great—as editor, poet, critic, fighter for the health of letters and the civilizing spirit—but his talents were prodigal of themselves, and only in *Parade's End* did they come to grips with the great tragic themes: order and chaos, permanence and change, love and hate. A master of the techniques of the novel, he produced in the Tietjens series a work of magnitude and of intensity—a work that speaks for a tragic time and a changing nation.

POETRY: LATER PHASES

In 1929—the prelude to a decade of economic and political crises concluding in the convulsions of world war—appeared the first of a series of volumes of poetry which returned the subject matter of politics to a poetry of moral ideas. The volume was *Transitional Poem,* by Cecil Day-Lewis (b. 1904). In the next year it was followed by the first volume of poetry by Wystan Hugh Auden (b. 1907) and, in 1933, by the *Poems* of Stephen Spender (b. 1909). Until the destruction of liberal hopes resulting from the Spanish Civil War and the alliance of Nazi Germany and Soviet Russia, these poets and others of their generation found common cause with the left wing of British politics, and, in various degrees of uneasiness, with the Communist party. These poets, who brought to the vision of despair a revolutionary hope, had a strong impact upon their generation.

The most significant of these poets defies categorizing. W. H. Auden is an intellectual poet of extraordinary versatility, with a far range of learning in all departments of contemporary thought and a wide catholicity of mind. At the worst, his luminous and acquisitive intelligence, like that of Aldous Huxley, is his enemy: through it, he can be betrayed into mannerisms and evasions. His verse, like Clough's, suffers at its affective sources from an indiscriminate irony which cannot resist the temptation to qualify. At his most uncertain, his strong talent mocks his Muse. The introductory poem of his latest volume, *Nones* (1951), is his apology for his own style:

> pawed-at and gossiped over
> By the promiscuous crowd,
> Concocted by editors
> Into spells that befuddle the crowd,
> All words like peace and love,
> All sane affirmative speech,
> Had been soiled, profaned, debased,
> To a horrid mechanical screech:
> No civil style survived
> That pandemonium
> But the wry, the sotto-voce,
> Ironic and monochrome:
> And where should we find shelter
> For joy or mere content
> When little was left standing
> But the suburb of dissent.

Auden's style is an uneven progress towards "a sane affirmative speech." It is often mannered and always interesting. The battery of devices which together make up "Audenism" is fully displayed in *Poems* (1930): the use, following Wilfred Owen, of off-rhymes—in themselves an ironic commentary on the differences of similars; the sprung and alliterative meters derived from Hopkins and the medieval English poets; the mixture of idioms from science and the newspapers with idioms derived from the poetic tradition. The imagery generalizes into a complex and frightening landscape of ideas, cluttered with the debris of industry and the suburbs; the landscape is the allegory under which Auden figures forth his vision of the divided society and the divided spirit. Freud and Marx are the guides to the inner and the outer limbo.

Between 1932 and 1939, Auden was increasingly occupied with verse plays. In 1939, he moved to America, where he has remained. Increasingly since the end of the thirties and the collapse of the revolutionary alignment, Auden has been centering his moral drama upon the problems of individual choice. *September 1, 1939,* that moving poem written as the world once more moved heavily into the darkness of war, is a modern parallel to *Dover Beach:*

> Defenceless under the night
> Our world in stupor lies;
> Yet, dotted everywhere,
> Ironic points of light
> Flash out wherever the Just
> Exchange their messages:
> May I, composed like them
> Of Eros and of dust,
> Beleaguered by the same
> Negation and despair,
> Show an affirming flame.

In the longer poems of the succeeding decade—*The Quest* (1941), *For the Time Being: A Christmas Oratorio* (1946), and *The Age of Anxiety* (1947)—Auden moves from Marxist to Christian terms in which to answer—and to ask—the question "What shall we do to be saved?" *For the Time Being,* despite a structural restlessness, places Auden with Eliot in the front rank of contemporary religious poets. Auden's conversion, like Eliot's, is a development rather than an abrupt about-face. He has arrived at fresh perspectives from which to portray the troubled landscape of the contemporary spirit.

Auden, Cecil Day-Lewis, Stephen Spender, the Irish poet Louis MacNeice, and the playwright and novelist Christopher Isherwood formed in the thirties a group held together by personal friendship and similar social beliefs. Spender's autobiography, *World within World* (1951), is the best account of their experience. These writers shared certain convictions about their craft and the world they lived in, but their work has less in common than is often supposed, and at the end of the decade they went their separate ways.

Spender is the distinctive lyric voice of the group; when he is following his own course, he produces a poetry of personal experience in the romantic tradition—a poetry which is the image of the journey of the individual sensibility through the shapes of its time. "The wry, the sotto-voce, ironic and monochrome" have no place in the full emotional lucidity of his best poems. Since the breakup of the anti-Fascist alignment of the thirties, Spender's poetry has become increasingly absorbed in the great personal themes of love and death, the quest for self-knowledge through the practice of his art. As he says in the preface to *Ruins and Visions* (1942), "I have deliberately turned back to a kind of writing which is more personal, and I have included within my subjects weakness and fantasy and illusion."

Day-Lewis sounded the leftist note in *Transitional Poem* (1929) and developed it in *From Feathers to Iron* (1931) and *The Magnetic Mountain* (1933). Like Auden's, his theme is the predicament of the divided man in the metallic landscape. The fourth poet of the Auden circle, Louis MacNeice (b. 1907) is more facile than Day-Lewis, more personal than Auden. His *Collected Poems* (1948) is a most readable summary of the emotions and attitudes of the day; the fear of coming catastrophe, the hovering at the nightmare's edge; the kind of historical self-pity and nostalgia which none of these poets wholly escapes; the self-conscious confusion of values. He is at his best in such catchy exercises of the wit of catastrophe as the well-known *Bagpipe Music* or when the poignance of his predicament is sharpest, as in the lovely *The Sunlight on the Garden*. His poetry since the thirties has celebrated "the Kingdom of the Individual" and the moving *Prayer before Birth* is perhaps his finest statement of human hopes and fears.

"Hugh McDiarmid" is the trade name for the astonishing and explosive literary energies possessed by the man Christopher Murray Grieve (b. 1892). Since the publication of his first volume of Scots lyrics, *Sangschaw*, in 1925, McDiarmid has been the whip of the very active Scottish literary movement, and has lashed his compatriots—and his enemies south of the border—into smarting knowledge of the native vigor of the Scots tongue and cultural heritage. In his efforts to arouse his countrymen and to confound the English, McDiarmid has laid hold of every available weapon. He has been attacked by the nationalists for subscribing to the heresy of international communism, at the same time as the communists were attacking him for nationalist deviation. The common denominator for all his energetic forays, which he maintains with an extraordinary and indiscriminate learning, is a twofold cultural program: to release Scotland from its subservience to England, and to establish Scottish culture as a living part of the Pan-Celtic and European traditions. The only weapon which seems to be not at his command is the editor's blue pencil.

Like Burns, when he tries to rescue from haggis sentiment and southern patronizing, McDiarmid writes both in an eclectic Scots of his own contriving and in the language of his enemies. The lyrics from his first two volumes, *Sangschaw* and *Penny-wheep* (1926), are the finest poems in Scots since the death of Burns. Their subjects—love, death, the stars—are handled with Burns's earthy vigor but without his sentimentalism. McDiarmid is a rarity, a naturalist by temperament, one whose world, sharply present and held, is without transcendental dimension. The world of men is hard and substantive in these poems, strangely beautiful; their language is the physics of emotion. In the short poems from these and later collections, McDiarmid achieves a disciplined perfection. In his long discursive poems, which convey the electric vigor of his mind, he becomes increasingly impatient of controls. The exuberant materialism of the *First Hymn to Lenin* (1931) has certainly no counterpart in English, perhaps no counterpart outside of the Russian poet Mayakovsky.

"Since 1939," writes John L. Sweeney in his excellent introduction to *Selected Writings of Dylan Thomas* (1946), English poetry has undergone "a shift of emphasis from social-consciousness to self-consciousness." At the end of the "Thirties" the revolutionary alliance of Auden, Spender, Day-Lewis, and MacNeice split into individual particles searching for themselves. Marx, the prophet of mass man, yielded to Freud, the prophet of individual man in his most deeply intuited privacies, and to Kierkegaard, the prophet of the drama of the individual moral choice.

18 Poems, the first book of the wild Welsh poet Dylan Thomas, appeared in 1934, when the poetry of politics was at its height, but the quality of consciousness the poems displayed lies outside of political categories. As Thomas wrote in his autobiographical *Portrait of the Artist as a Young Dog* (1940), "I was aware of me myself in the exact middle of a living story, and my body was my adventure and my name." If the poetry of Dylan Thomas has a politics, it is the politics of a world "under the eye-lids, where the inward night [drives] backwards, through the skull's base, into the wide first world." The phrase, from *The Orchards,* one of Thomas's dream stories, suggests the two worlds of his writing: the inward world, where the strange luminous shapes of dream are the keys to being: the mythal world beyond that world, where the shapes of dream merge into the universal experience of all men confronting their own mystery. In Sigmund Freud's aphorism, "Myth is the dream of a people; dream is the myth of the individual." Freud, Welsh myth, and the Bible supply the clues to the dense strong imagery of Thomas's poems, the music of whose lines call to mystery in the mind before the intellect can master them. The substance of his early poems is the body's knowledge of its journey from birth to death; their motivation, as Thomas wrote in 1934, "my individual struggle from darkness towards some measure of light."

Thomas's first volume, published when he was twenty years old, appeared with no sign of tentativeness, a fully formed individual voice, with the authority of its own dream. In this and the succeeding volumes of the thirties Thomas continued to develop the magical story of his adventure and his name. The language of such poems as "The force that through the green fuse drives the flower" or his magnificent elegy *In Memory of Ann Jones* is irresistible, and the green Welsh landscape, in its communion with the elemental forces, is a shock of pleasure after the weary landscapes of Auden. In his later development, the living story begins to be told in increasingly religious terms, marked by the influence of his seventeenth-century countryman, the mystical poet Henry Vaughan. With the middle of the century, Thomas, in the middle of the journey of his life, can look back on a poetic beginning for which the history of English literature has few parallels.

The other considerable poetic talent to emerge in the 1930's is that of George Barker (b. 1913). Barker's first book of poems (1933) shows some of the influence of Auden. He was slow to develop the personal, powerful, and involuted rhetoric of emotion which reaches its peak in *Calamiterror* (1937) and *Eros in Dogma* (1944). Of younger poets, it is too early to speak with any degree of conviction, for they are not yet supported by a sufficiently large body of work. But David Gascoyne, at one time the leader of the English surrealists; Alex Comfort; W. R. Rodgers; and such of the "apocalyptic" group as Henry Treece and the Scot J. F. Hendry have all produced original and interesting work. Thomas, Barker, the surrealists, the members of the brief "apocalyptic" movement have been spoken of as "the new romantics"; Freud, the logic of dreams, themes of religion and of sex are evident in their work.

PROSE FICTION: LATER PHASES

The novelists active during the thirties and forties have written much that is excellent, a few works of individual brilliance, but as yet there is no single figure comparable to the major Georgian novelists. Time, of course, is on the side of the earlier generation: their work is done. By the end of 1941, Lawrence, Ford, Joyce, and Virginia Woolf were dead; Forster was inactive; Huxley was increasingly obscured in eastern mysticism.

The tradition of comedy in the novel is most wittily realized in the early novels of Evelyn Waugh (b. 1903), of which at least three—*Decline and Fall* (1928), *Vile Bodies* (1930), and *A Handful of Dust* (1934)—approach perfection. With comment quite as trenchant as Samuel Butler's, but more nimble, Waugh raises to peaks of absurdity types and scenes of traditional England: the dreadful school, the corrupt aristocrat, the younger set, the county families "baying for broken glass." With *Brideshead Revisited* (1945), Waugh turned from high comedy to seriousness, and the result—as with Huxley—is a lessening of interest: although passages of the novel are moving, Waugh runs aground trying seriously to make the alliance between decadence and Catholic sanctity which Ronald Firbank, whom Waugh admires, had kept within the comic conventions. The best of the Roman Catholic novels is the work of Waugh's contemporary Graham Greene (b. 1904). Greene's "entertainments,"—*The Confidential Agent* (1939), and *The Ministry of Fear* (1943)—like the brilliant modifications of the *roman policier* written by the French novelist André Simenon— use the form of the thriller for the modern equivalent of the Gothic novel: sinister and desolate figures move through a shadow world. *Brighton Rock* (1938), a ghastly *danse macabre* in a holiday resort, uses the techniques of the thriller for the theme of guilt and mercy. This theme receives Greene's finest treatment in *The Power and the Glory* (1940), a novel of Mexico. In the figure of the corrupt priest, who yet keeps his allegiance to his priestly office, and in the action whereby he is run down and destroyed, Greene reaches a point of high achievement. *The Heart of the Matter* (1948) continues Greene's mystery story of the conscience.

The novels of Robert Graves (b. 1895) and Naomi Mitchison (b. 1897) are allied with the studies in anthropology and ancient history begun by Sir James Frazier and the Cambridge school of classical scholarship. Graves—poet, critic, essayist—is the best of contemporary historical novelists. *I, Claudius* (1935), *Claudius the God* (1938), and *Hercules, My Shipmate* (1945) are solidly specified and imaginatively striking reconstructions of the pagan times in which Graves finds his images of strong and passionate life. Miss Mitchison's *The Corn King and the Spring Queen* (1931) is another example of the modern nostalgia for the primitive situation. In this tale of the ancient Mediterranean world, the cycles of the seasons set the rhythms of human life, and man celebrates his harmony with nature in the rituals of spring. Miss Mitchison's later stories join the political interests of the English left to historical research, and in ancient Sparta she found her models for contemporary social conflicts.

Like his friends Auden and Spender, Christopher Isherwood (b. 1904) is concerned with the life of English and European intellectuals in an increasingly tyrannical society. His fiction—*Good-bye to Berlin* (1939) and *Prater Violet* (1945)—has some of the natural grace and lucidity of view which mark Spender's poems at their best. The most effective—and certainly the most popular—novel of social consciousness was written by George Orwell (1905–1950). Orwell, an honest and serious liberal journalist, whose previous works were courageous records of difficult times, found in the attack of the police state upon individual life the theme for a novel of great force. *1984,* published in 1949, throws into bleak relief the situation of individual love, of truth, and of decency in a dictatorship of the future. The novel is in the "Utopian" tradition of E. M. Forster's story *The Machine Stops* and of Huxley's *Brave New World*. It ends without hope. The hero, who has struggled for individual love against an all-embracing system in which any motive but power is subversive, is crushed in body and in spirit by the brutal mechanics of the state. *1984* is the liberal dream of individual freedom turned nightmare.

Of other novelists, Elizabeth Bowen (b. 1899) continues the tradition of the novel of sensibility, in such perceptive psychological studies of innocence and betrayal as *The Death of the Heart* (1939). The novels of Henry Green (b. 1905) are fables of manners, pastoral comedies of modern life. In the brightly-colored world of *Party-Going* (1939), *Loving* (1945), and *Nothing* (1950), all endings are happy, clouds are gathered to be dispelled. The world is an actual world, but Green plays Prospero to his characters, and with a sure art leads them from "once upon a day" to "happily ever after."

A NOTE ON POETIC DRAMA

After half a century during which his genius was the greatest living force in the English theatre, Shaw died in 1950, and with him died an era: he was the last of the great Victorians. Except for Shaw, the "realistic" English stage in the first half of the twentieth century had little of exceptional merit. Though there were many honest, or workmanlike, or moving plays, there were not many talents that could survive and thrive in the conditions of the commercial theatre. Money was made, but dramatic literature was not written—except by Irishmen and poets. And the Irish playwrights were hissed on the stage of the Abbey for their greatest accomplishments—Yeats for *The Countess Cathleen,* Synge for *The Playboy of the Western World,* O'Casey for *The Plough and the Stars.*

If poetry in the theatre is a matter of emotional effectiveness, Shaw—for such scenes as the trial of St. Joan—is a great theatrical poet. But Shaw wrote within the conventions established by Ibsen, and it is perhaps dissatisfaction with the limits of post-Ibsen naturalism that is at the bottom of the modern resurgence of poetic drama, plays in verse. The greatest of modern poetic dramatists, W. B. Yeats, had little affection for the realists and their "kitchen gabble." The plays which he wrote after he retired from active participation in the management of the Abbey Theatre in 1910 are the antithesis of the naturalist convention. They go hand in hand with the complex, passionate, symbolic poems of his middle period, and with the passionate recklessness of his old age.

The plays of Yeats's Abbey period, for all their Celtic mythology and beauties of metrical language, maintained a connection with current stage convention: they could share a bill with Shaw, and be played by the same actors. Through the influence of that indefatigable American educator Ezra Pound, Yeats discovered a convention by which he could purge himself entirely of the remnants of naturalism: this was the elaborate, ceremonial, symbolic convention of the Japanese Court theatre—the Noh play, which Ezra Pound picked up from the Oriental scholar Ernest Fenellosa, and examples of which, in Pound's English version, were printed in 1916 by the Yeats family press. Yeats's *Four Plays for Dancers,* written between 1916 and 1921, adapt the conventions of the Noh play to the material of Christian or Celtic legend. Nothing more unlike Ibsen could be imagined—nothing more remote from the absorbing topical interests of a world at war. Realistic dialogue gives way to a concise, austere, symbolic poetic speech; realistic characters are replaced by actors wearing changeless and painted masks; realist gesture and exclamation are replaced by choric commentary and by the movements of the dance. Yeats's stagecraft, sharpened by years in theatre business, combined these elements into works of great and strange beauty. In 1928, Yeats published his version in English verse of Sophocles's *King Oedipus,* and the plays of his last years show the impact of the tragic nemesis of the Greeks. *Purgatory,* his last and greatest play, was produced in 1938, and marks out a new direction: music, mask, dance, all those deliberate elements whereby he had held off the topical world are discarded for a colloquial speech of harsh sinew and terrible power, a new ease in rhythmic solutions. There are two characters only, but they are held in a cold and blinding light of relation between the living and the dead. The play is brief, but in it is packed all his power and all his passion.

In *On the Boiler,* the miscellany in which *Purgatory* was first published, printed a few brief months before his death, Yeats looked back over his experience in the theatre. "I have had greater luck than any other modern English-speaking dramatist," he wrote. "I have aimed at tragic ecstasy and here and there in my own work and the work of my friends I have seen it greatly played. What does it matter that it belongs to a dead art and to a time when a man spoke out of an experience and a culture that were not of his own time alone, but held his time, as it were, at arm's length, that he might be a spectator of the ages?"

The verse plays on which W. H. Auden and Christopher Isherwood collaborated during the 1930's make no attempt to hold their time at arm's length: the topics of the time, the situation of the time-bound, make up the subjects of these original and entertaining productions.

The Dog Beneath the Skin (1935) is a mad Marx Brothers version of Eliot's *The Waste Land.* The action of this witty piece of dramatic pyrotechnics is, like that of Eliot's poem, a quest for meaning through a changing symbolic landscape. Cynical journalists, Nazi fanatics, petrified generals, pompous vicars, decadent poets, lonely and sinister tycoons of the trusts, competitive hypochondriacs, and priests of the religion of health —are all parodied or satirized in a technique derived from equal parts of German expressionist drama, Gilbert and Sullivan, and the Music Hall Revue. At the end the Marx Brothers temporarily and rather feebly give way to Marx, and the recipe of "Repent, Unite, Act," made of one-part theology and two-parts revolution, is set off against Eliot's "Give, Sympathize, Control." *The Ascent of F6* (1937) is more serious. As the hero, Michael Ransom—a name suggestive of his capacity as dragon-slayer, reviver of English heroism, and sacrificial scapegoat to the nation's good—climbs that symbolic mountain, the nation tensely watches. There is excellent wit in the choric responses of the suburban Mr. and Mrs. A to the dramatic expedition, and in the hypocritical speeches of the bigwigs, and there is dramatic tension in the ascent. But the play suffers from muddled intentions. *On the Frontier* (1938) is less interesting, and ended the fruitful collaboration.

The most successful poet-dramatist of the period is T. S. Eliot. In *Poetry and Drama* (1950) Eliot discusses his three verse plays and the ways in which he has arrived at his present position—a position diametrically opposed to that of Yeats.

As Eliot's poetry, in the 1930's, began to turn more meditatively inward, to become in a sense more private, he began to seek an outlet for his dramatic talents in the public theatre. *Murder in the Cathedral* (1935) was the first poetic drama since James Elroy Flecker's *Hassan* (1923) to enjoy a long run in London. Like George Darley and Alfred Tennyson before him, Eliot took for his subject the murder of Thomas à Becket, and the play was first played in the cathedral at Canterbury. Its structure is eclectic: the figures of the tempters are reminiscent of the devils of the medieval morality; the magnificent choruses of the old women from Canterbury are based in Greek tragedy; the murderers, in the speeches in which they justify themselves, address the audience directly in modern colloquial prose. Becket's lonely spiritual trial, the glib suggestions of the tempters, the grief of the old women of Canterbury, combine into an austere and effective modern Christian mystery.

In *The Family Reunion* (1939), Eliot abandons costume and history for contemporary life, and the result is a strange Greek heightening of Ibsenesque drama. *The Family Reunion* is a modern *Oresteia*. Back to the country house of Wishwood, where a mother dominated by a dynastic passion waits to turn over his birthright to her wandering son, comes the son Harry, pursued by the furies. In scenes of great and brooding power, Harry wrestles with his guilt and arrives at his decision: the way of renunciation:

> Where does one go from a world of insanity?
> Somewhere on the other side of despair.
> To the worship in the desert, the thirst and deprivation,
> A stony sanctuary and a primitive altar. . . .

The concern with guilt and atonement, with moral rebirth and individual salvation is continued in *The Cocktail Party* (1950). The form is the drawing-room comedy, the verse carefully modulated, for the most part, at a level almost indistinguishable to the ear from prose, except at a few ceremonial moments in the second act. The play shows an advance in dramatic craftmanship over the previous attempts, and has had a greater stage success than any other modern verse play, perhaps at some sacrifice of boldness.

In *Poetry and Drama,* Eliot indicates the direction in which he is striving. "I have before my eyes," he writes, "a kind of mirage of the perfection of verse drama, which would be a design of human action and words, such as to present at once the two aspects of dramatic and musical order. . . . To go as far in this direction as it is possible to go, without losing that contact with the ordinary everyday world with which the drama must come to terms, seems to me the proper aim of dramatic poetry."

A NOTE ON LITERARY CRITICISM

In a time so crowded with cross-motives and so fertile in literary invention, it is no wonder that literary criticism should provide a continual and vociferous accompaniment to the artist's quest. It will remain here to note the major critical writings of the period, and to suggest their main tendencies.

The most influential of the critics of the period has been T. S. Eliot, whose critical writings have been supported by his great prestige as a poet, and whose first collection of essays, *The Sacred Wood* (1920), began that series of revaluations of the literary judgments of the nineteenth century which has been one of Eliot's most important efforts. His *Selected Essays,* in the revised edition (1949), contains the heart of his critical writings, which, without pretence of critical system, have served as a standard of taste and, in their *obiter dicta,* as a continual mine of ideas and insights. Eliot's critical enthusiasms have been infectious: the late Elizabethan dramatists, the French symbolist poets, the English metaphysicals, Dante and Dryden. Of his critical ideas, the most important and pervasive has been that of "tradition," a term he uses variously, but which comes to mean the sense of the whole past virtue of the language, in relation to which a writer can find his place in the continuity of experience. Allied with the idea of tradition is the idea of the impersonality of the poet. In reaction from the Romantic notion, Eliot wrote that poetry is not "the expression of a personality, but an escape from it." A third fertile notion has been the much-discussed idea of the "objective correlative"—"in other words," as he wrote in definition, "a set of objects, a situation, a chain of events which shall be the formula for [a] particular emotion." Tradition, impersonality, objectivity—with such terms Eliot attempted to order the extravagances of romantic individualism—and perhaps of his own. For many of these notions Eliot found an ally—if not a previous formulator—in the brilliant young philosopher T. E. Hulme (1883–1917), who was killed in the war. Hulme's conversation in prewar London salons led to the formulation of the doctrines of Imagism. In his posthumous *Speculations* (1924), edited by Herbert Read, he attacked "romanticism" as "spilt religion," and called for a return to a "classical" art based on a tragic sense of man's limitations rather than on the myth of infinite progress or of man's perfectability. Hulme and Eliot form the conservative right wing of contemporary British critical thought.

As influential as Eliot in establishing modern critical method is Ivor Armstrong Richards (b. 1893), whose *The Principles of Literary Criticism* (1924), *Practical Criticism* (1920), and *Coleridge on the Imagination* (1934) are the foundations for the close and subtle reading of texts which marks "the new criticism." The problem which Richards attacks is the problem of communication, the relation between the poem and the response of the reader. In *The Principles of Literary Criticism* he sets up his categories for the interpretation of poetry: the levels of sense, feeling, tone, and intention which must work together to produce a relevant and satisfactory response. *Practical Criticism* is the record of an absorbing and dismaying series of experiments which documented a widespread inability to comprehend words on the page. The book would be high comedy if it were not so disturbing in its cultural implications. In *Coleridge on the Imagination* Richards examines the central critical concepts of the English critic who first brought modern psychological insights to the study of the nature of poetry. The effect of Richards's writings has been most salutary. He has focused critical attention on the import of the poems themselves, and on the responsibility to the poem involved in the critical act. He has caused a healthy revolt in the methods of the teaching of literature. And his writings have opened the wide field of the psychology of poetry.

The most brilliant of the Ricardians, who constitute a loose "school" of criticism, is William Empson (b. 1906), himself an excellent and ingenious poet. Empson, a student of Richards, began under him the brilliant work in close reading which matured in his two books: *Seven Types of Ambiguity* (1930), in which he explores the multiple meanings of poetic language, and *Some Versions of Pastoral* (1935). Another influential Ricardian is F. R. Leavis (b. 1895), who through his own critical writings and the magazine *Scrutiny* has carried on Richards's methods and made of them a way to establish, in Eliot's sense, the main currents of English literary tradition.

In addition to Richards, Empson drew heavily, particularly in his second book, on both Marx and Freud to assist his interpretations. The most brilliant Marxist critic in England was Christopher St. John Sprigg (1907–1937), who wrote under the name of Christopher Caudwell. Caudwell was killed in action in the Spanish Civil War, at the age of 29. His major work, *Illusion and Reality, A Study of the Sources of Poetry* (1937), is, as Stanley Hyman says, "an exploration of the roots of poetry in the social life of man." The posthumous *Studies in a Dying Culture* (1938) continues his aberrant and talented criticism. Caudwell is the only contemporary critic of any stature to write as a Marxist, although the influence of Marx is widespread. The young poets of the left, who made in the 1930's their attempt to adjust literature and left-wing political action, accompanied their poetry by prose statements of their programs, which use Marx with greater or less fidelity. The most interesting and the most influential of these were Cecil Day-Lewis's *A New Hope for Poetry* (1936) and Stephen Spender's *The Destructive Element* (1935), in both of which sociological criticism is the vehicle for intelligent and sensitive commentary.

For the "new romanticism," which finds the sources of poetic power in the primitive and the prerational, the authority of two comparatively recent branches of investigation—anthropology, with its research into primitive religion, ritual magic, folklore and myth; and the depth psychology of Freud, Jung, Rank, and their followers—is paramount. The literature in these two fields is vast, and their effect upon critical thought perhaps more pervasive than that of Marx. Following the lead of Sir James G. Frazier, whose *The Golden Bough* (1890–1915) is one of the influential works of modern times, the "Cambridge school" of classical scholarship began its investigation, of which Jane Ellen Harrison's *Ancient Art and Ritual* (1933) is representative. The mythical bases of *The Waste Land* and of the later works of Joyce, as well as the historical novels of Robert Graves and Naomi Mitchison, are examples of the creative writer's interest in modern anthropology. With the introduction of Jung's concept of archetypal images, which relate the private fantasy to the total experiences of the race, the anthropology and the psychology of poetry meet on a common ground. Maud Bodkin's *Archetypal Patterns in Poetry* (1934) and Lord Raglan's *The Hero* (1937) are the most interesting examples of a field of investigation which is just beginning to expand. It is interesting to note that quite apart from these systematic investigations, W. B. Yeats, from his experience with the debased tradition of occultism and magic, announced similar doctrines.

Sigmund Freud's *A Theory of the Interpretation of Dreams* (1900) is as important in its effects upon literature as *The Golden Bough*. Freudian psychology and the anthropological study of myth and ritual are sister sciences, and the use of both is seen in the writings of the three English poet-critics who seem to be most highly regarded by the young poets of the mid-century.

D. H. Lawrence ranks highest in the tradition of modern romantic individualism. *Psychoanalysis and the Unconscious* (1921), *Fantasia of the Unconscious* (1922), and *Apocalypse* (1931) contain his own passionate brand of psychological terminology and personal vision. The application of his insight to literature is best displayed in *Studies in Classic American Literature* (1923), one of the most suggestive critical works of the century and a landmark in European awareness of the new world; and in *Phoenix* (1936), a posthumous collection of miscellaneous papers.

In *On English Poetry* (1922) and *Poetic Unreason* (1925) Robert Graves relates poetry both to dream and to primitive magic. The metaphors of poetry, following Freud, he associates with the metamorphoses of dream, and develops the notion—a modification of Aristotle's doctrine of catharsis—of poetry as a form of psychotherapy. In his latest book, *The White Goddess* (1950), a fantastic tracing of primitive remnants from Welsh legend through rogue song to their sources in the cradles of Western civilization, he returns, with a new emphasis, to his old love. Poetry is no longer a matter of therapy, but a form of worship, an act of ritual celebration of the "white goddess," the primitive Muse whose service has been obscured and perverted by the false gods of history.

The poet and critic Herbert Read, who is as excellent a critic of painting as of poetry, has been a consistent interpreter of developments in psychoanalytic research in relation to letters. His career since the Second World War has found him at various times allied with many phases of naturalist thought—Marxism, anarchism, surrealism, all construed as phases of possibility in the liberation of the human spirit. In the war between "romantic" and "classical," which, in *Form in Modern Poetry* (1932), he relates to the difference between fluid personality and fixed character, Read sides with the romantics. Personality, which is the basis of poetry, is dependent upon deep unconscious sources of being, for the investigation of which Read relies upon his wide reading in modern psychology. His essay on "Psychoanalysis and Criticism" in *Reason and Romanticism* (1926) is one of the first important attempts to establish psychoanalytic co-ordinates for critical purposes.

LIST OF BOOKS

by

Willard Thorp

[This list is devised only to suggest some of the better and more authoritative books likely to be of use to readers of English Literature. If a more extensive list is desired, many titles of books, essays, and studies will be found in the books here mentioned. But I take occasion to point out our increasing danger of reading too much *about* literature instead of looking long and well at literature itself.—C.G.O.]

The Cambridge History of English Literature, by many hands, though uneven in quality, is the standard encyclopedic history, and contains long bibliographies. Of texts inexpensive uniform collections will be found in the *Albion Series, Belles-Lettres Series, Everyman Library, Harvard Classics, Muses' Library, Oxford World Classics, Temple Classics.* Editions of single authors such as those provided by the Cambridge Press, the Oxford Press, and the Riverside Press are excellent for both private and public libraries. Anthologies now abound, from the various Oxford Books of Verse to those especially devised for academic use. Besides many excellent single biographies there are the rich collections in the *English Men of Letters* and the *Great Writers,* and admirably condensed accounts in the *Dictionary of National Biography.*

GENERAL

Sir Paul Harvey, *The Oxford Companion to English Literature,* 1932.
Oliver Elton, *The English Muse,* 1933.
R. M. Alden, *English Verse,* 1922.
R. M. Lovett and H. S. Hughes, *The History of the Novel in England,* 1932.
Allardyce Nicoll, *British Drama,* 1925.
F. E. Schelling, *The English Lyric,* 1913.
J. A. Williamson, *The Evolution of England,* 1931.

CHAPTER I

C. W. Kennedy, *The Earliest English Poetry,* 1943.
G. K. Anderson, *The Literature of the Anglo-Saxons,* 1949.
H. M. Chadwick, *The Heroic Age,* 1912.
W. M. Dixon, *English Epic and Heroic Poetry,* 1912.
F. B. Gummere, *Founders of England,* 1930.
F. Klaeber, *Beowulf,* 1936.
C. B. Tinker, *Beowulf* (translation), 1910.
J. D. Spaeth, *Old English Poetry* (translations), 1922.
W. W. Lawrence, *Beowulf and Epic Tradition,* 1928.
C. W. Kennedy, *The Cædmon Poems* (translation), 1916.

C. W. Kennedy, *The Poems of Cynewulf* (translation), 1910.
C. H. Whitman, *The Christ of Cynewulf* (translation), 1900.

CHAPTER 2

F. J. Snell, *The Age of Alfred*, 1912.
A. S. Cook and C. B. Tinker, *Select Translations from Old English Prose*, 1908.

CHAPTER 3

C. S. Baldwin, *Three Medieval Centuries of Literature in England*, 1932.
W. P. Ker, *English Literature, Medieval* (Home University Library).
A. C. Baugh, *History of the English Language*, 1935.
O. Jespersen, *Growth and Structure of the English Language*, 1919.
W. H. French and G. B. Hale, *Middle English Metrical Romances*, 1930.
Carleton Brown, *English Lyrics of the XIIIth Century*, 1932.
Carleton Brown, *Religious Lyrics of the XIVth Century*, 1924.
E. K. Chambers and F. Sidgwick, *Early English Lyrics*, 1926.
F. A. Patterson, *The Middle English Penitential Lyric*, 1911.

CHAPTER 4

J. J. Jusserand, *English Wayfaring Life in the Middle Ages*, 1925.
Dorothy Chadwick, *Social Life in the Days of Piers Plowman*, 1922.
G. M. Trevelyan, *England in the Age of Wyclif*, 1920.
W. A. Neilson and K. G. T. Webster, *Chief British Poets of the Fourteenth and Fifteenth Centuries*, 1916.
G. L. Kittredge, *Gawain and the Green Knight*, 1916.
J. R. R. Tolkien and E. V. Gordon, *Sir Gawain and the Green Knight*, 1925.
C. G. Osgood, *The Pearl* (translation), 1906.

CHAPTER 5

G. G. Coulton, *Chaucer and His England*, 1921.
J. L. Lowes, *Geoffrey Chaucer and the Development of his Genius*, 1934.
G. L. Kittredge, *Chaucer and his Poetry*, 1920.
R. K. Root, *The Poetry of Chaucer*, 1922.

CHAPTER 6

Eleanor Hammond, *English Verse between Chaucer and Surrey*, 1927.
Edward Hicks, *Sir Thomas Malory, his Turbulent Career*, 1928.

CHAPTER 7

Lewis Einstein, *The Renaissance in England*, 1927.
A. S. Cook, *The Authorized Version of the Bible and its Influence*, 1910.
H. R. Plomer, *William Caxton*, 1925.
J. S. Harrison, *Platonism in English Poetry of the Sixteenth and Seventeenth Centuries*, 1903.

CHAPTER 8

P. S. Allen, *The Age of Erasmus,* 1914.
Frederic Seebohm, *The Oxford Reformers* (Everyman's).
E. M. Routh, *Sir Thomas More and his Friends,* 1934.

CHAPTER 9

John Erskine, *The Elizabethan Lyric,* 1903.
J. M. Berdan, *Early Tudor Poetry,* 1920.
F. M. Padelford, *Early Sixteenth Century Lyrics,* 1907.
C. T. Onions, ed., *Shakespeare's England,* 2 vols., 1926.
F. E. Schelling, *English Literature during the Lifetime of Shakespeare,* 1910.
J. J. Jusserand, *The English Novel in the Lifetime of Shakespeare,* 1908.
Sir Walter Raleigh, *English Voyages in the Sixteenth Century,* 1906.
F. R. Amos, *Early Theories of Translation,* 1920.
M. W. Wallace, *Life of Sir Philip Sidney,* 1915.

CHAPTER 10

H. S. V. Jones, *A Spenser Handbook,* 1930.

CHAPTER 11

Karl Young, *The Drama of the Medieval Church,* 2 vols., 1933.
E. K. Chambers, *The Medieval Stage,* 2 vols., 1903.
E. K. Chambers, *The Elizabethan Stage,* 4 vols., 1923.
C. F. Tucker Brooke, *The Tudor Drama,* 1911.
F. E. Schelling, *Elizabethan Drama,* 1908.
F. S. Boas, *Marlowe and his Circle,* 1929.

CHAPTER 12

R. M. Alden, *Shakespeare,* 1922.
T. M. Parrott, *William Shakespeare,* a Handbook, 1934.
Joseph Q. Adams, *A Life of William Shakespeare,* 1925.

CHAPTER 13

John Palmer, *Ben Jonson,* 1934.
Enid Welsford, *The Court Masque,* 1927.
C. M. Gayley, *Beaumont the Dramatist,* 1914.
Rupert Brooke, *John Webster and the Elizabethan Drama,* 1916.
Oliver Elton, *Michael Drayton,* 1905.

CHAPTER 14

Basil Willey, *The Seventeenth Century Background,* 1934.
A. E. Taylor, *Francis Bacon,* 1926.
H. J. C. Grierson, *The Poems of John Donne,* 2 vols., 1912.
George Williamson, *The Donne Tradition,* 1930.
G. H. Palmer, *The English Works of George Herbert,* 3 vols., 1905.

CHAPTER 15

Sir Edmund Gosse, *Seventeenth-century Studies*, 1883.
Joan Bennett, *Four Metaphysical Poets*, 1934.
F. W. Moorman, *Robert Herrick*, 1910.

CHAPTER 16

J. H. Hanford, *A Milton Handbook*, 1933.
Sir Walter Raleigh, *Milton*, 1900.
M. Woodhull, *The Epic of Paradise Lost*, 1907.
R. D. Havens, *The Influence of Milton on English Poetry*, 1922.

CHAPTER 17

Augustine Birrell, *Andrew Marvell*, 1905.
A. H. Nethercot, *Abraham Cowley, the Muse's Hannibal*, 1934.
Sir Edmund Gosse, *Sir Thomas Browne*, 1905.
Sir Edmund Gosse, *Jeremy Taylor*, 1904.
Arthur Bryant, *Samuel Pepys*, 1933.

CHAPTER 18

L. N. Chase, *The English Heroic Play*, 1903.
C. V. Deane, *Dramatic Theory and the Rhymed Heroic Play*, 1931.
Bonamy Dobrée, *Restoration Comedy*, 1924.
Bonamy Dobrée, *Restoration Tragedy*, 1929.
R. G. Ham, *Otway and Lee*, 1931.
John Palmer, *The Comedy of Manners*, 1913.

CHAPTER 19

Mark Van Doren, *The Poetry of John Dryden*, 1931.
T. S. Eliot, *John Dryden*, 1932.
W. P. Ker, *Essays of John Dryden*, 2 vols., 1926.

CHAPTER 20

W. C. Sydney, *England and the English in the Eighteenth Century*, 2 vols., 1892.
Austin Dobson, *Eighteenth Century Vignettes*, 3 vols., 1923.
D. A. Stauffer, *English Biography before 1700*, 1930.
W. H. Irving, *John Gay's London*, 1928.
C. B. Tinker, *The Salon and English Letters*, 1915.

CHAPTER 21

Bonamy Dobrée, *Essays in Biography*, 1925.
Oswald Doughty, *English Lyric in the Age of Reason*, 1922.
J. W. Krutch, *Comedy and Conscience after the Restoration*, 1924.
Carl Van Doren, *Swift*, 1930.
G. W. Sherburn, *The Early Career of Alexander Pope*, 1934.

W. P. Trent, *Daniel Defoe, How to Know Him,* 1916.
Samuel Shellabarger, *Lord Chesterfield, a Man of the World,* 1935.

CHAPTER 22

J. W. Draper, *The Funeral Elegy,* 1929.
G. C. Macaulay, *James Thomson,* 1908.
Sir Edmund Gosse, *Gray,* 1887.
H. W. Garrod, *Collins,* 1928.

CHAPTER 23

B. W. Downs, *Richardson,* 1928.
Aurélien Digeon, *The Novels of Fielding,* 1925.
F. T. Blanchard, *Fielding the Novelist,* 1926.
Wilbur Cross, *The Life and Times of Laurence Sterne,* 1925.

CHAPTER 24

A. S. Turberville, ed., *Johnson's England,* 2 vols., 1933.
Austin Dobson, *Horace Walpole,* 1927.
Joseph E. Brown, *The Critical Opinions of Samuel Johnson,* 1926.
Sir Walter Raleigh, *Six Essays on Johnson,* 1910.
C. B. Tinker, *Young Boswell,* 1922.
Austin Dobson, *Life of Oliver Goldsmith,* 1888.
John Morley, *Burke,* 1879.
R. C. Rhodes, *Harlequin Sheridan,* 1933.

CHAPTER 25

Alfred Ainger, *Crabbe,* 1903.
J. S. Smart, *James Macpherson: an Episode in Literature,* 1905.
G. H. Gerould, *The Ballad of Tradition,* 1932.
F. B. Gummere, *The Popular Ballad,* 1907.
E. H. W. Meyerstein, *A Life of Thomas Chatterton,* 1930.
David Cecil, *The Stricken Deer or the Life of Cowper,* 1930.
W. A. Neilson, *Burns, How to Know Him,* 1917.
F. B. Snyder, *The Life of Robert Burns,* 1932.
Osbert Burdett, *William Blake,* 1926.

CHAPTER 26

Oliver Elton, *A Survey of English Literature,* 1780–1830, 2 vols., 1912.
Irving Babbitt, *Rousseau and Romanticism,* 1919.
E. Bernbaum, *Guide through the Romantic Movement,* 1931.
Edward Dowden, *The French Revolution and English Literature,* 1897.
C. B. Tinker, *Nature's Simple Plan,* 1922.

CHAPTER 27

E. Birkhead, *The Tale of Terror,* 1921.
G. M. Harper, *William Wordsworth,* 2 vols., 1923.

J. L. Lowes, *The Road to Xanadu*, 1927.

Edward Dowden, *Southey*, 1876.

Sidney Colvin, *Landor*, 1878.

E. V. Lucas, *The Life of Charles Lamb*, 2 vols., 1905.

Edmund Blunden, *Charles Lamb and his Contemporaries*, 1933.

Augustine Birrell, *Hazlitt*, 1902.

John Buchan, *Sir Walter Scott*, 1932.

W. and R. A. Austen-Leigh, *Life and Letters of Jane Austen*, 1913.

CHAPTER 28

S. C. Chew, *Byron in England*, 1924.

E. C. Mayne, *Byron*, 1924.

S. L. Gwynn, *Thomas Moore*, 1905.

H. N. Brailsford, *Shelley, Godwin, and their Circle* (Home University Library).

J. A. Symonds, *Shelley*, 1925.

Sidney Colvin, *John Keats*, 1925.

Edmund Blunden, *Leigh Hunt*, 1932.

CHAPTER 29

F. J. C. Hearnshaw, ed., *The Social and Political Ideas of Some Representative Thinkers of the Victorian Age*, 1923.

D. C. Somervell, *English Thought in the Nineteenth Century*, 1929.

Hugh Walker, *The Literature of the Victorian Era*, 1921.

G. M. Young, ed., *Early Victorian England*, 2 vols., 1934.

CHAPTER 30

Arthur Bryant, *Macaulay*, 1932.

L. F. Cazamian, *Carlyle*, 1932.

Emory Neff, *Carlyle*, 1932.

R. W. Church, *The Oxford Movement*, 1891.

Charles Sarolea, *Cardinal Newman and his Influence on Religious Life and Thought*, 1908.

CHAPTER 31

George Gissing, *Charles Dickens*, 1924.

Charles Whibley, *William Makepeace Thackeray*, 1913.

CHAPTER 32.

Geoffrey Faber, *Oxford Apostles*, 1933.

Harold Nicolson, *Tennyson*, 1923.

Hallam Tennyson, *Alfred Lord Tennyson, a Memoir by his Son*, 2 vols., 1897.

Osbert Burdett, *The Brownings*, 1929.

W. H. Griffin and H. C. Minchin, *The Life of Robert Browning*, 1910.

Mrs. Sutherland Orr, *A Handbook to the Works of Robert Browning*, 1923.

Percy Lubbock, *Elizabeth Barrett Browning in her Letters*, 1906.

CHAPTER 33

E. F. Benson, *Charlotte Brontë*, 1932.
Sir Leslie Stephen, *George Eliot*, 1902.

CHAPTER 34

J. H. Whitehouse, ed., *Ruskin the Prophet*, 1920.
Mrs. Annabel Williams-Ellis, *The Tragedy of John Ruskin*, 1928.
Michael Sadleir, *Anthony Trollope*, 1927.
H. F. Lowry, ed., *The Letters of Matthew Arnold to Arthur Hugh Clough*, 1932.
George Saintsbury, *Matthew Arnold*, 1899.

CHAPTER 35

B. I. Evans, *English Poetry in the Later Nineteenth Century*, 1933.
Max Beerbohm, *Rossetti and his Circle*, 1922.
Francis Bickley, *The Pre-Raphaelite Comedy*, 1932.
D. M. Stuart, *Christina Rossetti*, 1930.
Evelyn Waugh, *Rossetti, his Life and Works*, 1928.
G. H. Crow, *William Morris, Designer*, 1934.
J. W. Mackail, *The Life of William Morris*, new impression, 1922.
Harold Nicolson, *Swinburne*, 1926.

CHAPTER 36

J. B. Priestley, *George Meredith*, 1926.
Florence Hardy, *The Early Life of Thomas Hardy*, 1928. *The Later Years of Thomas Hardy*, 1930.
S. C. Chew, *Thomas Hardy, Poet and Novelist*, 1928.
Sidney Dark, *R. L. Stevenson*, 1931.

PART EIGHT

J. W. Cunliffe, *English Literature in the Twentieth Century*, 1933.
T. M. Parrott and W. Thorp, *Poetry of the Transition, 1850-1914*, 1932.
Osbert Burdett, *The Beardsley Period*, 1925.
Holbrook Jackson, *The Eighteen Nineties*, 1914.
W. B. Yeats, *Autobiographies*, 1927.
Edward Thomas, *Walter Pater*, 1913.
Van Wyck Brooks, *The Pilgrimage of Henry James*, 1925.
Cyril Falls, *Rudyard Kipling*, 1915.
Archibald Henderson, *Bernard Shaw, Playboy and Prophet*, 1932.
C. H. Grabo, *The Technique of the Novel*, 1928.
Everard Meynell, *Life of Francis Thompson*, 1926.
J. W. Cunliffe, *Modern English Playwrights*, 1927.
Charles Williams, *Poetry at Present*, 1930.
Bonamy Dobrée, *The Lamp and the Lute*, 1929.
F. R. Leavis, *New Bearings in English Poetry*, 1932.

PART NINE

W. Y. Tyndall, *Forces in Modern British Literature,* 1947.

Fred B. Millett, *Contemporary British Literature,* 1935.

Richard Ellmann, *Yeats, The Man and the Mask,* 1948.

Elizabeth Drew, *T. S. Eliot, The Design of His Poetry,* 1949.

Harry Levin, *James Joyce,* 1941.

Richard Aldington, *D. H. Lawrence; Portrait of a Genius But. . ,* 1950.

Francis Scarfe, *Auden and After,* 1942.

Kenneth Rexroth, ed., *The New British Poets,* 1949.

Stephen Spender, *Poetry since 1939,* 1946.

Henry Reed, *The Novel since 1939,* 1946.

E. R. Reynolds, *Modern English Drama,* 1949.

S. E. Hyman, *The Armed Vision; A Study in the Methods of Modern Literary Criticism,* 1948.

INDEX

639